ASPECTS
OF
LANGUAGE

Second Edition

ASPECTS OF LANGUAGE

Second Edition

DWIGHT BOLINGER

Harvard University

HARCOURT BRACE JOVANOVICH, INC.

New York / Chicago / San Francisco / Atlanta

To my son Bruce, in admiration and affection

Cover photograph by Norman Rothschild

ISBN: 0-15-503868-0

Library of Congress Catalog Card Number: 74-25091

Printed in the United States of America

FOREWORD
TO THE SECOND EDITION

Why a second edition?

Two forces, already well established a decade ago, have since swept the field. One is mentalism. It has changed the study of language in two ways. First, in the early 1960s it emancipated theory. Linguists in the first half of the century were reluctant to go beyond observation and take the next logical, scientific step: that of building theoretical models. That era of excessive positivism is past. Linguistics has become almost as cerebral as logic—in fact, the two have borrowed terms and treatments extensively from each other. Second, if mind and intuition were real enough to be used in analyzing the data, they were real enough to form part of the data. Mere linguistic behavior came to be valued less for itself and more for what it revealed about inborn capacities, or the genetic equipment for language—how it has evolved, how much of it is uniquely human, how it is manifested in the way children learn. The mentalistic reform has brought us the full-fledged subdiscipline of psycholinguistics, with applications as widely separated as experiments on artificial intelligence using computers, and the training of apes to communicate with humans.

The other force is a counterpart to mentalism. Mind, inborn capacities, latent tendencies are not enough. There has to be a power that wakens them and later guides them. That power is the social environment, with its expanding circles of family, playmates, school, and workaday associations, all shaping the child's inner drive for verbal expression. The corresponding subdiscipline of sociolinguistics has become the most active—one might even say combative—field within linguistics since the late 1960s. And it is a wide field. The moment we took up social origins we became involved with social problems: if we are concerned with how children learn, we have to be concerned with how they may best learn. The more we know about how existing styles of speech—from drawing room to ghetto—mold us as speakers, the more we are forced to judge the way society values the styles.

These two reorientations—language as an evolving capacity within the individual and language as a means and product of social interaction—account for many of the changes in the Second Edition. To keep abreast of the times (or, rather, not to lag behind them any farther than one could help), it was necessary to add the chapter on psychology and language learning, the one on origins, and the substantial new portions of the chapter on the social aspects of language.

The rest of the rewriting and reorganizing has hardly been less extensive. Morphology ("Sounds and Words"), lexicon, and syntax deserved chapters to themselves. There has been great discussion and controversy about such new ideas as underlying form, collocation, and higher sentences, which accordingly demanded their place. Writing had to be matched with reading. The tremendous expansion of linguistics and the attention it has been getting from the general public have made it necessary to give a fuller treatment to schools and theories. Language policy has taken on new dimensions with the public concern over Black English, Chicano, and other forms of minority speech, and with sexism in language. These issues now rival those of language conflict in emerging nations, and they get their stint, if not their due, in the chapters "Mind in the Grip of Language" and "Language and the Public Interest." Finally, though linguistics is relevant to daily life in a thousand ways, there had to be a chapter on the practical application that affects virtually everyone: effective expression. The chapter on style will not replace a handbook on composition, but it will show the connection between talking about language and making it work for us.

This book is eclectic. It tries to speak for an enlightened traditionalism. Its attitude toward usage is not puristic, but it sees purism as one of the inevitable forces that maintain stability. Its attitude toward theory is not transformationalist, but it recognizes transformationalism as the particular species of formalism in linguistics that has channeled discussion for almost two decades. Now that the tide seems to be ebbing somewhat, the reader looking for alternatives need not feel left out. Other viewpoints are given their place, and there is plenty of variety for the individual taste.

If the revision has achieved its purpose, credit goes to the many wise and generous persons who saw and pointed out the earlier defects and in many cases prescribed the remedies: John Algeo, Friedrich Braun, David DeCamp, Walburga von Raffler Engel, Jewell A. Friend, Sidney Greenbaum, Dell Hymes, Robert S. Kirsner, Betty Wallace Robinett, Sol Saporta. To these, and to others whose help may have been more indirect but was no less material, go the author's heartfelt thanks.

Special mention should be made of the valuable assistance given by Mansoor Alyeshmerni and Paul Taubr, who prepared the workbook and instructor's manual that accompany this book. Looking at *Aspects of Language* from a quite practical point of view, they were able to offer a series of extremely useful suggestions.

If the revision has missed any of its goals, what then? George Lakoff offers some advice to the disappointed but still willing reader:

> Finding out that very little works the way most introductory textbook writers would lead you to believe can be a frustrating experience. On the other hand, it can and should be an exhilarating one. After all, the less that is known, the more there is for you to find out. If you want to do something interesting with your life and are contemplating doing work in linguistics, it should be anything but frustrating to find out that there is a lot for you to do.[1]

Dwight Bolinger

---

[1] In Ann Borkin et al. (eds.), *Where the Rules Fail: A Student's Guide* (Bloomington: Indiana University Linguistics Club, 1972), p. v.

Adapted from the
FOREWORD TO THE FIRST EDITION

To read the typical book on the wonderful world of words is hardly to see in the spectacle any particular relevance to oneself. Yet there is no science that is closer to the humanness of humanity than linguistics, for its field is the means by which our personalities are defined to others and by which our thoughts are formed and gain continuity and acceptance. Until linguists can bring their point of view clearly and palatably before the student in the language classroom and the reader at large, they will have only themselves to blame for what one linguist has called the towering failure of the schools to inform ordinary citizens about language. Of no other scientific field is so much fervently believed that isn't so. And not only believed but taught.

We do not need to travel abroad nor back in time to discover the facts of language. They lie all about us, in our daily writings and conversations, open to interpretation and uninhibited by rules of what should or should not be written or said. Almost nothing of interest to the linguist goes on anywhere that does not go on in our communication here and now. This book invites all of us to see within ourselves and around ourselves the objects of a science and to glimpse how the scientist interprets them. It is intended to help the users of language detect the inner spark that created the most wonderful invention of all time.

CONTENTS

3

DISTINCTIVE SOUND   34

4

SOUNDS AND WORDS   76

5

LEXICON   99

8

MIND IN THE GRIP OF LANGUAGE   235

9

PSYCHOLOGY AND LANGUAGE LEARNING   273

10

THE ORIGIN OF LANGUAGE   306

14

WRITING AND READING   467

15

SCHOOLS AND THEORIES   506

16

LANGUAGE AND THE PUBLIC INTEREST   566

17

STYLE   600

ASPECTS OF LANGUAGE

Second Edition

BORN TO SPEAK 1

Thomas A. Edison is supposed to have parried the question of a skeptic who wanted to know what one of his fledgling inventions was good for by asking, "What good is a baby?" Appearances suggest that a baby is good for very little, least of all to itself. Completely helpless, absolutely dependent on the adults around it, seemingly unable to do much more than kick and crawl for the greater part of nine or ten months, it would seem better off in the womb a little longer until ready to make a respectable debut and scratch for itself.

Yet if the premature birth of human young is an accident, it is a fortunate one. No other living form has so much to learn about the external world and so little chance of preparing for it in advance. An eaglet has the pattern of its life laid out before it hatches from the egg. Its long evolution has equipped it to contend with definite foes, search for definite foods, mate, and rear its young according to a definite ritual. The environment is predictable enough to make the responses predictable too, and they are built into the genetic design. With human beings this is impossible. The main reason for its impossibility is language.

We know little about animal communication, but enough to say that nowhere does it even approach the complexity of human language. By the age of six or eight a child can watch a playmate carry out an intricate series of actions and give a running account of it afterward. The most that a bee can do is perform a dance that is related analogously to the

1

direction and distance of a find of nectar, much like what we do in pointing a direction to a stranger. The content of the message is slight and
highly stereotyped. With the child, the playmate's actions can be as
unpredictable as you please; he will verbalize them somehow. Attaining
this skill requires the mastery of a system that takes literally years to
learn. An early start is essential, and it cannot be in the womb. Practice
must go on in the open air where sounds are freely transmitted, for language is sound. And if language is to be socially effective it cannot be
acquired within a month or two of birth when the environment is limited
to parents and crib but must continue to grow as the child becomes
stronger and widens his contacts. Human evolution has ensured that this
will happen by providing for a brain of such extraordinary size that the
head, if allowed to mature any further before birth, would make birth
impossible—a brain, moreover, in which the speech areas are the last to
reach their full development.[1] So we might say to the skeptic's question
that a baby is good for learning language.

All that a child can be born with is instincts for language in general,
not for any particular language—exactly as with an instinct for walking
but not for walking in a given direction. This is another reason why an
early beginning is necessary: languages differ, and even the same language changes through time, so that an infant born with patterns already
set would be at a disadvantage. One still hears the foolish claim that a
child born to German parents ought to be able to learn German more
easily than some other language. Our experience discredits this. Ancestry
makes no difference. A child learns whatever language it hears, one about
as easily as another, and often two or more at the same time. Complete
adaptability confers the gift of survival. Children do not depend on a
particular culture but fit themselves to the one into which they are born
—one that in turn is maintaining itself in a not always friendly universe.
Whatever success that culture has is largely due to the understanding
and cooperation that language makes possible.

Another reason for an early beginning and a gradual growth is *permeation*. The running account that a child is able to give after performing a
series of actions or seeing one performed betokens an organized activity
that is not enclosed within itself but relates at all times to something else.
It would seem absurd to us to be told that every time we stood up, sat
down, reached for a chocolate, turned on a light, pushed a baby carriage,
or started the car we should, at the same time, be twitching in a particular way the big toe of our left foot. But just such an incessant accompaniment of everything else by our speech organs does not surprise us at
all. Other activities are self-contained. That of language penetrates them

---

[1] Lamendella 1975, Ch. 2, p. 2; Carmichael 1966, pp. 17–19.

and almost never stops. It must be developed not separately, like walking, but as part of whatever we do. So it must be on hand from the start.

The idea that there are instinctive predispositions for language has been revived recently by psychologists and linguists working in the field of child learning. For a long time language was thought to be a part of external culture and nothing more. Even the physiology of speech was seen as more or less accidental: our speech organs were really organs of digestion which happened to be utilized to satisfy a social need. Speech was an "overlaid function." A child in a languageless society, deprived of speech but permitted to chew and swallow, would not have the feeling of missing anything. That view has been almost reversed. Now it is felt that the organs of speech in their present form were shaped as much for sound production as for nourishment. The human tongue is far more agile than it needs to be for purposes of eating. More than that, everyone has experienced the discomfort and sometimes real danger of getting food caught in the windpipe; by adapting itself to speech the human pharynx has created a hazard that did not exist before. On the receiving end, the sensitivity of the human ear has been sharpened to the point that we can detect a movement of the eardrum that does not exceed one tenth of the diameter of a hydrogen molecule. We can conclude from all this—as one scientist does—that the notion of speech as a purely overlaid function is "unquestionably false."[2]

"Instinct" is a vague term. How much does it cover? There is a lively debate among linguists and psychologists (see Chapter 9) as to whether the human genetic design actually includes things as specific as the means to classify verbs into such opposing categories as "state" and "process"— an inborn grammatical receptacle, you might say, flexible enough to contain and be shaped by the particular verbs of the language the child learns. This is probably an exaggeration. What we inherit is more likely a set of general-purpose capacities used in language but also available for other skilled activities, such as tool using.

So acquiring a language calls for three things:

1. *predispositions*, as well as physical *capacities*, developed through countless centuries of natural selection;

2. a preexisting language *system*, any one of the many produced by the cultures of the world;

3. a *competence* that comes from applying the predispositions and capacities to the system through the relatively long period during which the child learns both to manipulate the physical elements of the system, such as sounds and words and grammatical rules, and to permeate them with meaning.

---

[2] Lamendella 1975, Ch. 2, p. 36.

The development of so finely graded a specialization of our organs of speech and hearing and of the nervous system to which they are attached is not surprising if we assume that society cannot survive without language and that individual human beings cannot survive without society. Natural selection will take care of it.[3] And natural selection unquestionably has. Language is species-specific. It is a uniquely human trait, shared by cultures so diverse and by individuals physically and mentally so unlike one another—from Watusi tribesmen to nanocephalic dwarfs—that the notion of its being purely a socially transmitted skill is not to be credited.[4]

This is not meant as a snub to the trained chimpanzees that have been so much in the news since 1968 (see pages 308–09). They have unquestionably attained a certain level of linguistic skill, approximately that of a human four-year-old. But there are no indications yet that chimpanzees can advance any further, and it has yet to be shown that they can communicate among themselves using anything resembling human language.

A predisposition for language implies that a child does more than echo what he or she hears. The older notion of mere plasticity has been abandoned. The first months are a preparation for language in which babbling, a completely self-directed exercise, is the main activity. Imitation begins to play a part, of course, but it too is experimental and hence creative. We see how this must be if we imagine a child already motivated to imitate and being told by his mother to say **Papa.** This sounds simple to us because we already know which features to heed and which to ignore, but the child must learn to tell them apart. Shall he imitate his mother's look, her gesture, the way she shapes her lips, the breathiness of the first consonant, the voice melody, the moving of the tongue? Even assuming that he can focus on certain things to the exclusion of others, he has no way of knowing which ones to select. He cannot then purely imitate. He must experiment and wait for approval. Imitation is an activity that is shaped creatively.

Also it is guided by meaning, much if not most of the time. Imitating just for the fun of imitating does not necessarily precede imitating with some connection to reality. In one case a child adopted his own babbling sound *gigl,* which he had originally produced spontaneously but his father imitated deliberately when they were together, as a sign for 'Daddy's here,' or something of the sort: he reverted to it whenever his father appeared on the scene. Only later did the child get around to producing an imitation just for the fun of it: he would say *dado,* his version of *hello,* when he heard his parent use that greeting on answering the telephone.[5]

---

[3] See Hockett and Ascher 1964.

[4] Lenneberg 1966.

[5] Engel 1970, p. 29.

PROGRESS

We do not know the extent to which children are taught and the extent to which they learn on their own. If learning is instinctive, then children will learn whether or not adults appoint themselves to be their teachers. But if there is an instinct to learn, for all we know there may be an instinct to teach. It is possible that parents unconsciously adopt special modes of speaking to very young children, to help them learn the important things first—impelled by the desire not so much to teach the child as to communicate with him, with teaching a by-product.

One psychologist noted the following ways in which she simplified her own speech when talking to her child:

1. the use of a more striking variant of a speech sound when there was a choice—for example, using the *t* of *table* when saying the word *butter* in place of the more usual flapped sound (almost like *budder*);

2. exaggerated intonation, with greater ups and downs of pitch;

3. slower rate;

4. simple sentence structure—for example, avoidance of the passive voice;

5. avoidance of substitute words like *it*—for example, *Where's your milk? Show me your milk* instead of *Where's your milk? Show it to me.*[6]

Most parents would probably add *repetition* to this list.

Whatever the technique, the child does not seem to follow any particular sequence, learning first to pronounce all the sounds perfectly, then to manage words, then sentences, then "correct expression." A child of twelve to eighteen months who speaks no sentences at all will be heard using sentence intonations on separate words in a perfectly normal way: *Doggie?* with rising pitch, meaning 'Is that a doggie?' or *Doggie,* with falling pitch, to comment on the dog's presence. The child's program seems to call for a developing complexity rather than for doing all of one thing before taking up the next.

The first stage of communication is this *doggie* stage, when parents feel that their children have really begun to speak. Individual words are being pronounced intelligibly—that is, so that parents can match them with words in their own speech—and are being related to things and events. It is called the *holophrastic* stage: utterance and thing are related

---

[6] Gleitman and Shipley 1963, p. 24.

one to one. The single word *mama* includes not just a person but a presence; it is a name and a sentence at the same time: 'Mama's here,' 'Take me, Mama,' or whatever. And if one equals two, two also equals one: the parental **all gone** is a single word, **awgone,** symbolizing the fascinating sensation of a disappearance.

Next is the *joining* stage, syntax in its simplest form. The child brings together two of his names for things or actions, perhaps wavering between them if both happen to be appropriate for a situation. This is the most mysterious and at the same time the greatest step of all: from a simple inward-outward connectedness to a connectedness within language. It was once thought to be a uniquely human accomplishment, but now we know that at least some animals are capable of it. The joining stage is fully in hand when putting words together becomes a form of play. There is much self-directed repetition; children's monologs sometimes sound like students doing pattern drills in a language lab. One study of the sleepytime monologs of a two-and-a-half-year-old revealed substitution drills, buildups, breakdowns, and variation drills with sound-play:

> What color?
> What color blanket?
> What color mop?
> What color glass?
>
> Block.
> Yellow block.
> Look at all the yellow block.
>
> Clock off.
> Clock.
> Off.
>
> Bobo's not throwing.
> Bobo can throw.
> Bobo can throw it.
> Bobo can throw.
> Oh.
> Oh.
> Go.
> Go.
> Go.[7]

But more than repetition, there is adventure. When a girl of this age runs to her parents and says **House eat baby**—the sort of expression that un-

---

[7] Weir 1962, pp. 82, 109, 120.

imaginative adults brush aside as preposterous or even punish as "untrue" —she is only exulting over the discovery that she can do the same with her words as with her building blocks: put them together in dazzling ways.

The third stage can be called the *connective* stage and is a solution to the complexity—and confusion—that would otherwise afflict most combinations of three or more words.[8] A two-word sentence has little need for connective tissue. The elements are of equal rank, and if one knows their meanings it is not even necessary to put them in any particular order—a child is as apt to say *awgone shoe* as to say *shoe awgone,* not to mention his magisterial indifference to "correct" grammatical indications of agreement and subordination. But the longer the sentence becomes, the more need there is for directing traffic, and the grammatical signs are posted one by one: verb endings, conjunctions, prepositions, articles, auxiliaries. At the same time the child is growing intellectually, and some of the connectives open up new depths of experience. Past and future tenses reach out from the moment of living and speaking—*I used to live in Denver; He's going to jump;* modes and conditions prefigure unreality as if it were real—*They won't leave me alone! He would cry if you did.*

This step-by-step increase in complexity is illustrated in the responses given by one child at various ages to the command *Ask your daddy what he did at work today.* At two years and five months it was *What he did at work today,* which shows enough understanding to separate the inner question from the command as a whole (*Ask your daddy* is not repeated), but no more. At the age of three, the response was *What you did at work today?* with the right change of intonation and with *you* for *he.* The child is now really asking a question but has "optimized" its form—that is, he has fitted a newly acquired expression into the mold of an old one that resembles it and is familiar and easy, in this case making the word order of statements serve also for questions. Finally, at three years and five months, the child made the right transformation of the verb and produced *What did you do at work today?*[9]

Optimizing occurs at all stages. Whenever a child is mentally ready to progress to a new stage, he will try for a time to use just the means that he already knows. He may learn a new word but not be equipped to handle all the sounds in it, and say *woof* for *roof.* He may want to ask a question but still lack the grammar for it, and say *What you did at work today?* Or he may produce a construction that is correct and familiar rather than one that is correct and unfamiliar. When four-year-olds are given a sentence like *I gave the dog the bone* they will repeat it and

---

[8] That is, *content* words—all those words other than grammatical indicators such as *that, and, when, he, by,* etc. See pages 119–21.

[9] Gleitman and Shipley 1963, p. 14.

understand it, but if they are asked to report the same event themselves they will say *I gave the bone to the dog.*[10] The construction without *to* is less general. For instance, it seldom occurs in the question *Who(m) did you give the money?;* the more normal form is *Who(m) did you give the money to?* And it is not like the related constructions in which prepositions are required: *I got the money from Mom, I got the present for Mom and then I gave it to her,* and so forth.

The fourth and final stage in the development of communication is the *recursive* stage. It comes with an awareness of linguistic structures as such. Until children have some notion of how a sentence is put together, they are unable to manipulate it as a grammatical unit. Indeed, the furthest advance that human language has made is in the power to fold in on itself, to treat a complex structure as if it were a simple entity—a kind of abstracting like that of algebra. Building a complicated sentence like *I hear that you don't like it* involves saying something like "Let S (sentence) equal N (noun)," where S is represented by *You don't like it,* a sentence that is being treated as if it were a noun, the object of *I hear.* The same awareness that enables children to build complex sentences also enables them to talk about language and to make stylistic choices. With two constructions such as *Give the bone to Dingo* and *Give Dingo the bone,* meaning rather than optimization will decide the choice. If there is a cat named Tillie who gets raw liver and both pets are about to be fed, *Give Dingo the bone* is the proper selection when Dingo was about to be given Tillie's ration; it puts the emphasis in the right place.

In real life there are no stages, only gradations. But to talk about gradations we have to clump them as if they were discontinuous, to pretend that there is a line instead of a shading between violet and red. The spectrum of language learning has been divided up, in this chapter, as if the lines between the linguistic structures were absolute. More will be seen of the true continuum in Chapter 9.

ATTAINMENT

A favorite generalization used to be that children have complete control of their language by the age of five or six. Without disparaging the truly phenomenal control of an enormously complex system that six-year-olds do achieve, we must realize that no limit can be set and that learning by the same old processes continues through life, though at a rate that diminishes so rapidly that well before adolescence it seems almost to have

---

[10] Fraser, Bellugi, and Brown 1963, p. 133.

FIGURE 1–1

**Rate of Language Learning Expressed as a Proportion
Of New to Old over Equal Intervals of Time**

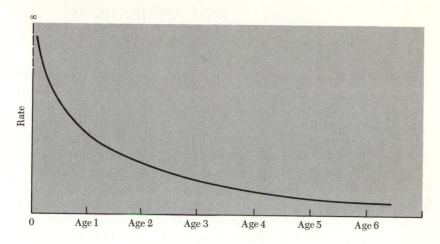

come to a stop. The rate might be described as a curve that starts by virtually touching infinity and ends by approaching zero (see Figure 1–1).

If learning never ceases, it follows that a language is never completely learned. There is always someone who knows a bit of it that we do not know.[11] In part this is because with the experimental and inventive way in which learning is done, no two people ever carry exactly the same network of shapes and patterns in their heads. A perfect command eludes us because as we catch up it moves off—"the" language exists only as imperfect copies, with original touches, in individual minds; it never stays exactly the same. All we can say is that interplay is so fast, frequent, and vital that great differences are not tolerated, networks are forced to acquire a similar weave, and all networks within cooperating distance tend to share the same grammars and vocabularies.

---

[11] Including parts of grammar as well as vocabulary. One study has shown that ninth and tenth graders get almost as many sentences wrong as they do right in their written compositions. Another has shown definite effects of education on adult speakers. See Bateman 1966, and Gleitman and Gleitman 1970.

ADDITIONAL REMARKS
AND APPLICATIONS

1. Name some examples of inter-species communication. Do you understand what a dog means when he growls? How well do animals respond to human utterances such as *No!* and *Here?* What kind of messages are these?

2. What advantages do younger children learning their first language have over older children or adults learning a second language?

3. Observe a mother speaking to her child and see what modifications she makes in her speech. Does she say *Give Mummy the shoe* rather than *Give me the shoe,* thus helping to identify *Mummy?* Does she pronounce the important words in an especially distinct way—for example, the noun *shoe* in this same sentence? Explain how the need to do this for very young children might have a stabilizing effect on language. (Do adults have a style of speech that is clear and deliberate in addition to other styles in which words are run together?)

4. Observe the vocal sounds of a very young child to see if they are communicating any kind of sense. Even though the child's speech may be unintelligible, is intonation being used appropriately? A study of one child showed that at as early as four months he was using a basic sound of *m* as a sort of carrier for intonations when pointing at objects, varying the intonation according to whether the object was desired or merely wondered about.[12] Can you think of any reason why intonation should be the first of the subsystems of language to develop?

5. Would you expect the holophrastic stage to be given up immediately once the child discovers that parts of the whole are separately meaningful, or would the two stages probably continue side by side? Consider the expression *It's good for you,* spoken by a parent every time a spoonful of medicine or a distasteful food is offered. Might the child interpret *good for you* as a unit and react negatively toward it? When you yourself say something like *I can't go out this evening*

---

[12] Engel 1964, p. 115.

—I'm tied up, do you have a mental image of yourself bound with ropes, or is *tied up* just a colorless synonym for *busy?*

6. There are dictionaries that enumerate the words in a language. What about the sentences? Is there something about the way sentences are put together that makes a sentence dictionary impossible? Is this an important difference between animal communication and human language?

7. Discuss the sentence *She went back and told the queen it* (spoken by a nine-year-old) as an example of optimizing. Compare it with *She went back and told the queen the story.* What does the comparison suggest about which of the two word forms, nouns or pronouns, is learned first?

8. A ten-year-old would be expected to have more difficulty understanding a twenty-year-old than a twenty-year-old has in understanding a ten-year-old. Is this because of the sounds, the sentence structure, or the vocabulary?

9. If you have the equipment for it, make a short recording of a two- or three-year-old's monolog while playing alone or just before going to sleep. Study it and make as many observations as you can.

References

Bateman, Donald Ray. 1966. "The Effects of a Study of a Generative Grammar upon the Structure of Written Sentences of Ninth and Tenth Graders," Ph.D. dissertation, Ohio State University, 1965, abstracted in *Linguistics* 26:21–22.

Carmichael, Leonard. 1966. "The Early Growth of Language Capacity in the Individual," in Eric H. Lenneberg (ed.), *New Directions in the Study of Language* (Cambridge, Mass.: M.I.T. Press).

Engel, Walburga von Raffler. 1964. *Il prelinguaggio infantile* (Brescia: Paideia Editrice).

———. 1970. "The Function of Repetition in Child Language," *Bollettino di Psicologia Applicata* 97–98–99:27–32.

Fraser, Colin; Ursula Bellugi; and Roger Brown. 1963. "Control of Grammar in Imitation, Comprehension, and Production," *Journal of Verbal Learning and Verbal Behavior* 2:121–35.

Gleitman, Lila R., and Henry Gleitman. 1970. *Phrase and Paraphrase* (New York: W. W. Norton).

————, and Elizabeth F. Shipley. 1963. "A Proposal for the Study of the Acquisition of English Syntax." Grant proposal submitted 1 March to National Institutes of Health.

Hockett, Charles F., and Robert Ascher. 1964. "The Human Revolution," *American Scientist* 52:71–92.

Lamendella, John T. 1975. *Introduction to the Neuropsychology of Language* (Rowley, Mass.: Newbury House). Page references are to the manuscript.

Lenneberg, Eric H. 1966. "A Biological Perspective of Language," in Eric H. Lenneberg (ed.), *New Directions in the Study of Language* (Cambridge, Mass.: M.I.T. Press).

Weir, Ruth Hirsch. 1962. *Language in the Crib* (The Hague: Mouton).

SOME TRAITS
OF LANGUAGE 2

One estimate puts the number of languages in active use in the world today somewhere between three and four thousand. Another makes it five thousand or more. The latter is probably closer to the truth, for many languages are spoken by relatively few persons—several in one small area of New Guinea have fewer than a hundred speakers each[1]— and many parts of the world are still not fully surveyed. In Colombia, almost two hundred separate languages and dialects have been identified.[2]

"Dialect" is a key word here. What constitutes "one language"? Danish and Norwegian have a high degree of mutual intelligibility; this makes them almost by definition dialects of a single language. Do we count them as two? Cantonese and Mandarin, in spite of both being "Chinese," are about as dissimilar as Portuguese and Italian. Do we count Chinese as one language? To be scientific we have to ignore politics and forget that Denmark and Norway have separate flags and China one. But even then, since differences are quantitative, we would have to know how much to allow before graduating X from "a dialect of Y" to "a language, distinct from Y."

However that may be, the number of different languages is formidable and is quite awesome if we include the tongues once spoken but now

---

[1] Dye, Townsend, and Townsend 1968.
[2] Arango Montoya 1972.

dead. Languages are like people: for all their underlying similarities, great numbers mean great variety. Variety confronts us with this question: Do we know enough about languages to be able to describe language? Can we penetrate the differences to arrive at the samenesses underneath?

The more languages we study—and previously unexplored ones give up their secrets each year by the score—the more the answer seems to be yes. Learning a new language is always in some measure repeating an old experience. Variety may be enormous, but similarities abound, and one can even attempt a definition—perhaps something like "Human language is a system of vocal-auditory communication, interacting with the experiences of its users, employing conventional signs composed of arbitrary patterned sound units and assembled according to set rules." However we word it—and obviously no one-sentence definition will ever be adequate—there is enough homogeneity to make some sort of definition possible.

LANGUAGE IS HUMAN

Languages are alike because people are alike in their capacities for communicating in a uniquely human way. Every human infant has an instinct to babble—even those deaf at birth do it, and those cut off from it by illness or surgery will resume it afterward. The incredibly complex system that constitutes every known language is mastered in most of its essentials before a child learns to divide ten by two. "Intelligence" as we generally understand it is not a requirement, yet no other animal has the same power. The most that any of the great apes has been able to manage—with intensive training—is to learn a manual sign language well enough to communicate meanings at the level of a four-year-old child (see page 309).

LANGUAGE IS BEHAVIOR

Our five-hundred-year romance with printer's ink tempts us to forget that a language can disappear without leaving a trace when its last speaker dies, and that this is still true of the majority of the world's languages, in spite of the spread of presses and tape recorders. Written records and tape recorders are embodiments of language, and writing in particular has evolved to some extent independently; but the essence of language is a way of acting. Our habit of viewing it as a *thing* is probably unavoidable, even for the linguist, but in a sense it is false.

What *is* something thing-like, in that it persists through time and from speaker to speaker, is the system that underlies the behavior. In the form in which speakers acquire it, it goes by various names—competence, knowledge, *langue*—to distinguish it from performance, or speech, or *parole,* or whatever else we may call its practical use at any given moment. Competence is to performance as a composer's skill is to an improvisation or the writing of a composition. This is what makes language so special. Breathing, grasping, and crying are also ways of acting, but we are born with them; no one gets credit for being a good breather or a good crier. With language, all we are born with is a highly specialized capacity to learn. Probably as the child acquires it the system is engraved somehow on the brain, and if we had the means to make it visible we could interpret it. For the present all we can see is the way people act, and linguists are useful only because, since we are not mind readers, we need specialists to study the behavior and infer the system.

THE MEDIUM OF LANGUAGE IS SOUND

All languages use the same channel for sending and receiving: the vibrations of the atmosphere. All set the vibrations going in the same way, by the activity of the speech organs. And all organize the vibrations in essentially the same way, into small units of sound that can be combined and recombined in distinctive ways. Except for this last point, human communication is the same as that of many other warm-blooded creatures that move on or over the earth's surface: an effective way of reaching another member of one's kind is through disturbances of the air that envelops us.

Paradoxically, what sets human speech apart also sets it above dependence on any particular medium: the capacity for intricate organization. The science of phonetics, whose domain is the sounds of speech, is to linguistics what numismatics is to finance: it makes no difference to a financial transaction what alloys are used in a coin, and it makes no difference to the brain what bits of substance are used as triggers for language —they could be pebbles graded for color or size, or, if we had a dog's olfactory sense, a scheme of discriminated smells. The choice of sound is part of our human heritage, probably for good reason. We do not have to look at or touch the signaler to catch the signal, and we do not depend on wind direction as with smell—nor, as with smell, are we unable to turn it off once it is emitted.[3] Most important, we can talk and do other things at the same time. This would be difficult if we could only make signs with our hands.

---

[3] Sebeok 1962, p. 435.

Language is sound in the same sense that a given house is wood. We can conceive of other materials, but it is as if the only tools we had were woodworking ones. If we learn a language we must learn to produce sounds. We are unable to use any other medium except as an incidental help. So part of the description of language must read as if the sound that entered into the organization of language were as indispensable as the organization itself.

LANGUAGE IS HIERARCHIC

Though glib people may seem to talk in a continuous stream, language is never truly continuous. To convey discrete meanings there have to be discrete units, and breaking the code of a new language always involves as its first task finding what the units are. At the lowest level are bits of distinctive sound meaningless in themselves—the hum of an *m* or the explosion of a *p*—which occur in clumps of one or more that we call syllables. A syllable is the smallest unit that is normally spoken by itself. It is the poet's unit, the unit of rhythm and audibility.

Above the level of meaningless sounds and syllables are the levels that are segmented both for sound and for meaning. First are words and parts of words that have some recognizable semantic makeup, such as the prefix *trans-* or the suffix *-ism.* Above the word level is the level of syntax, which is itself a complex of levels, since the unit that we call a sentence is often made up of a combination of simpler sentences, usually in some abbreviated form; and these in turn contain smaller units termed phrases, such as the prepositional phrase *to the west* and the verb phrase *ran fast.* Still higher units have to be recognized—question-and-answer, paragraph, discourse—but the larger they get, the harder it is to decide just what the structure is supposed to be. Most linguistic analysis up to very recently has stopped with the sentence.

Stratification—this organization of levels on levels—is the physical manifestation of the "infinite use of finite means," the trait that most distinguishes human communication, the basis of its tremendous resourcefulness. Dozens of distinctive sounds are organized into scores of syllables, which become the carriers of hundreds of more or less meaningful segments of words, and these in turn are built into thousands of words proper. With thousands of words we associate millions of meanings, and on top of those millions the numbers of possible sentences and discourses are astronomical. One linguist calls this scheme of things "multiple reinvestment."[4]

---

[4] Makkai 1973.

Underlying multiple reinvestment is the "structural principle," whereby instead of having unique symbols for every purpose, which would require as many completely different symbols as there are purposes, we use elementary units and recombine them. With just two units at the word level, *brick* and *red,* plus a rule of modification, we can get four different meanings in answer to the request ***Describe the house:***

It's brick.

It's red.

It's brick red.

It's red brick.

LANGUAGE CHANGES TO OUTWIT CHANGE

Every living language is in a state of dynamic equilibrium. Infinitesimal changes occur in every act of speech, and mostly make no impression—they are within the bounds of tolerance, and are not imitated nor perpetuated, because hearers simply ignore them (for example, the fumbling of someone who talks in a hurry or coughs in the middle of a word). Now and then a scintillation is captured and held. We hear a novel expression and like it. It is adaptive—fits a style or names a new object or expresses an idea succinctly. Others take it up and it "becomes part of the language." The equilibrium is temporarily upset but reestablishes itself quickly. The new expression, like an invading predator, marks out its territory, and the older inhabitants defend what is left of theirs.

The vast open-endedness of language that results from multiple reinvestment is what makes it both systematic and receptive to change. The parts are intricately interwoven, and this maintains the fabric; but they are also infinitely recombinable, and this makes for gradual, nondestructive variation. To see the value of such a system we can compare the linguistic code to the genetic code. The two are similar in many ways—so much so that geneticists themselves refer to "the syntax of the DNA chain." The hierarchical organization of meaningful units in language—from words through phrases and sentences and on up to discourses—is paralleled by ranks on ranks of genetic sequences with their inherited messages that control growth and development. Underlying both codes are meaningless subunits, called phonemes in language and nucleotide bases in genetics.[5] The changes in language and the mutations in genetics

---

[5] See Jakobson 1970, pp. 437–40.

serve a similar purpose: to outwit the random changes in society and in nature. One cannot predict an accident, but one can provide enough variety to ensure that at least one variant of a living form will be resistant enough to survive. This is no guarantee against disaster, and languages as well as species do perish. But it suffices to cope with the normal rate of random intrusions.

LANGUAGE IS EMBEDDED IN GESTURE

If language is an activity, we cannot say that it stops short at the boundary of *verbal* speech activity, for human actions are not so easily compartmentalized. We cannot even say that it stops at the boundaries of speech, for we are informed by our eyes as well as by our ears. And it is not always easy to tell one kind of message from the other. A person speaking on the telephone who contorts his mouth into a sneer may be heard as sneering, because the sound wave is distorted in characteristic ways; yet the hearer reacts as if he had seen the sneer rather than heard it. Audible gesture and visible gesture have many points in common.

Gesture is the mode of communication that human beings have in common with the higher apes. One important theory has it that articulate language—the layered system that we have been describing—developed through its earliest stages in gestural—largely visible—form and only later was transferred to speech (see pages 312–14). Even today, children acquire language "in the midst of a large amount of non-verbal communication."[6] Gesturing and talking emerge at the same time. **Bye-bye,** one of the first words learned by most infants in our culture, is almost always accompanied by a wave of the hand.

Audible and visible gesture are usually termed *paralanguage* and *kinesics,* respectively. *Body language* is another word for kinesics, but is generally reserved for movements that communicate without being part of a clearly established code—we might say that they are unconscious, if we were sure what that meant. For instance, when one is seated just crossing the legs may convey a meaning—nonchalance, perhaps. Even when nothing appears to be going on at all, *something* may be communicated—there is a language of silence.[7] Skilled verbal entertainers know exactly when and for how long to pause, to let a point sink in; spoken language demands time for decoding as well as time for speaking, and not all the work of both can be done simultaneously. And silence is effective only when one commands the field and fends off

---

[6] Engel 1973.

[7] Bruneau 1973.

would-be interrupters. To avoid being interrupted while gathering their thoughts, speakers will use a kind of audible gesture called a *hesitation sound*. This is usually a low-pitched **uh** or **unh,** but other vowel qualities may be used. Sometimes words are employed for the same purpose: **well** in English, **este** ('this') in American Spanish. If you are asked what time it is and you know, for example, you will say without hesitation, **It's ten-fifteen.** But if you have to look at your watch you may say **It's now—ten-fifteen,** inserting a drawled **now** to stall and keep command of the situation. The amount of verbalized makeweight with which a speaker packs a conversation gesturally to keep from yielding the floor is incalculable. This is one of the great stylistic differences between spoken and written language, and is why the latter has to be pruned so carefully.

Gesture may occur alone or as an accompaniment to verbal speech. If a daughter approaches her father to discuss marriage and his only answer is to pace the floor, meaning is conveyed by body movement alone.[8] If the sentence **Still, he did his best** is accompanied by a pouting lower lip and a shrug of the shoulders, visible gesture is supplying an apologetic backdrop to speech. And if **Oh, Jack's all right, but hell . . .** is spoken with a deprecatory grimace on the last two words and with the pitch on **hell** dropping to a guttural creak, the result is a trio of verbal language, visible gesture, and audible gesture.

Gestural systems that are substitutes or virtual substitutes for spoken language are a study in themselves. The visual gestures of the American Sign Language used by the deaf and the sign language of the Plains Indians are the best-known examples. Whistle language and drum language (pages 45–46) are based in their own peculiar ways on speech, and telegraphic and semaphoric signaling are based on writing—that is, on spelling. The finger-spelling used by the Japanese is similar, but accompanies speech and is used to clear up ambiguities caused by the many words in that language which sound alike but have different meanings (like the English **deign** and **Dane**).

The gestures, both audible and visible, that accompany ordinary speech are of two main types and four subtypes. The first main type is *learned* gestures. These are acquired as part of a speaker's culture, just as words are; and those of the first subclass, which can be called *lexical,* resemble words so closely that many persons regard the audible examples as "real words." In fact, a number of them have standard spellings: **uh-huh** for 'yes,' **huh?** for 'what?' **hmn** for 'I wonder,' **tsk-tsk** for the click of the tongue used to show disapproval, and so on. Visible gestures in this subclass include waving the hand for 'good-bye,' holding both hands out with palms up and shoulders raised for 'I don't know,' and putting the index finger against the lips for 'Be quiet' (often accompanied by the

---

[8] The example is from Key 1970.

audible lexical gesture *shhh*). Other cultures may use entirely different lexical gestures, or similar ones with different meanings. Our gesture for 'Come here' is holding the hand out cupped palm up with the fingers beckoning; in some other areas—for example, Mexico—it is the same except that the hand is cupped palm down—which we might mistake for a greeting rather than a summons.

The second subtype of learned gestures is *iconic:* the communicator *imitates* some aspect of the thing signified. An audible gesture for 'sound of a bee' is *bzzzz.* For 'machine gun fire' a favorite of small boys is *ah-ah-ah-ah-ah-ah,* with a glottal stop. In some cases the actual sound is used as the symbol of itself—for instance, a snore. A visible gesture for 'round' is a circle described by the fingers; one for 'wide' is an expansive movement of the hands, palms facing each other, in front of the body; one for 'so-high' is the hand held at the indicated height above the ground. And a speaker who says **I pushed him away** is apt to execute a pushing motion with the hand at the same time; most descriptions of actions are thus embellished. Iconic gestures tend to be *analog*—more of something can be shown by more of the gesture, less by less (*bzz* for a short buzz, *bzzzz* for a longer one); lexical gestures, on the other hand, are *digital*—more of them may add emphasis, but does not mean more of what they signify —*shhhh* is not quieter than *shhh* but is a more vigorous command to be quiet.

The second main type of gesture is *instinctive,* with subtypes involuntary and voluntary. No one has to learn to laugh or smile or cry or dodge a blow or blink when an object comes unexpectedly toward the eyes. These actions are controlled by the autonomic nervous system and frequently cannot be avoided even with practice. The person who blushes easily betrays embarrassment in spite of himself. But the line between involuntary and voluntary is a shifting one. In human beings the limbic system of the brain, the part that controls involuntary actions, is overlaid by higher systems, and this leads to some measure of voluntary control of reactions that in other animals are purely automatic.[9] A sign of adulthood is the "insincerity" of originally autonomous actions. A smile is no longer a betrayal of feeling but a purposive act intended to please. The hollow laugh and the crocodile tear are instinctive gestures that have become part of etiquette. In the long run all instinctive gestures acquire a social significance and take on local modifications, which is one reason why members of one culture behave awkwardly when transplanted to another.

Instinctive gestures tend to *synechdochize*—a part disappears while a part remains and stands for the whole. A catch in the throat substitutes

---

[9] Lamendella 1975, Ch. 2, pp. 23, 24, 33.

for a sob; constriction in the pharynx and the resulting sound of repressed anger symbolizes rage and the impulse to inflict injury.[10]

All gestures, but instinctive gestures especially, cooperate with language in a total communicative act. While we can usually guess a speaker's intent, we may be unsure if the gestural part is extracted. In the following utterance,

You   don't   me^an   it.

everything can remain the same, yet with one's head held slightly forward, eyes widened, and mouth left open after the last word, the result is a half-question ('You surely don't mean it, do you?'), while with head erect, eyes not widened, and mouth closed afterward, it is a confident assertion. In the first case, cooperation is a kind of competition—the words declare, but the gesture asks. When this happens the gestural meaning is usually closer to the heart of the matter than the meaning of the words and syntax—a sentence like *He's a great guy* can be reversed in meaning by a knowing look (we call such remarks ironic). Gestures of pointing are often indispensable. The sentence *He doesn't know you're on my side* immediately preceded by a sidewise toss of the head in the direction of the person referred to makes the word *he deictic* —that is, pointing—in an actual situation. Without gesture, pronouns such as *he* and *she* must take their meaning from the context, as in *Mary said she would.*

Gestures of the hands and head are used to reinforce the syllables on which an accent falls. A person too far away to hear a conversation can often tell what syllables are being emphasized by the way the speaker hammers with a fist or jabs downward with the jaw. How closely the two are related can be shown by a simple test: reversing the movement of the head—going up instead of down on each accent—in a sentence like *I will nót dó it.* It is hard to manage on the first attempt.

At the outer fringes of the system we call language is a scattering of gestural effects on speech, more curious than important. The *m* of *ho-hum* and the *p* of *yep* and *nope* come from closing the mouth as a gesture of completion. Certain gestures get tangled with sets of words and serve as a kind of semantic cohesive. The kinship of *vicious, venomous, vituperative, violent, vehement, vindictive, vitriolic, vile* (and indirectly *vital, vigorous, vim*) is helped by the suggestion of a snarl in the initial *v*. Similarly there is a suggestion of lip-smacking in the last syllable of

---

[10] Fónagy 1971, pp. 45–46.

delicious, voluptuous, salacious, luscious that results in a new slang
alteration or coinage every now and then—*scrumptious* in the early
1800s, *galuptious* about 1850, *crematious* in the 1940s, the trade name
Stillicious at about the same time, *scruptillicious* in teenage talk in the
1960s.[11]

In most accounts of language, gesture has been underrated or ignored.
Body language, along with other bodily functions, has been a partially
tabooed subject; even today one would feel embarrassed at saying to
someone, "Why did you thrust your head forward when you said that?"
though a question such as "Why did you say *absolutely* when you
weren't sure?" is commonplace. As a reflection of this, but also because
of their own traditions, linguists have concentrated on the language of
information, propositional language, which is the only kind that *writing*
can convey with a high degree of efficiency. But even this kind of language when spoken is signaled as true or false, positive or doubtful, welcome or unwelcome, by gesture; and all other forms of language—questions, commands, wishes, exclamations, denials—are heavily dependent
on it.

LANGUAGE IS BOTH ARBITRARY AND NON-ARBITRARY

If people are to cooperate they must understand one another, and understanding depends on sharing a set of values. Sometimes we agree to
agree deliberately. One person will say, "Let a_n represent the average
strength at t_n time for successive intervals of 10 seconds' duration," and
others for the sake of the argument will accept that person's values for
a, t, and *n*. In such a case the arbitrariness and conventionality of the
symbols and their relation to reality stand out boldly.

Language is similarly conventional and arbitrary. There is no need for
us to worry about our different perceptions of what a dog looks like, feels
like, or sounds like when it barks, in order to refer to one. If we are
agreed on calling it *dog* we can give socially vital warnings like **Mad
dog!** with the assurance of being understood. **Dog** has an arbitrary, conventional value in our society.

The obvious exceptions are few in number. If there were a close connection between the sound of a word and its meaning, a person who did
not know the language would be able to guess the word if he knew the
meaning and guess the meaning if he knew the word. Now and then we
can do this: **meow** in English and **miaou** in French sound the same and
mean the same. Yet even with words that imitate sounds this seldom

---

[11] *Boulder Camera* (10 June 1963).

happens (*to caw* in English is *croasser* in French; *to giggle* in English is *kichern* in German), and elsewhere it is practically never found: *square* and *box-shaped* mean the same thing but have no resemblance in sound.

Arbitrariness comes from having to code a whole universe of meanings. The main problem with such vast quantities is to find not resemblances but differences, to make a given combination of sounds sufficiently unlike every other combination so that no two will be mistaken for each other.[12] It is more important to make *wheat* and *barley* sound different than to use the names to express a family relationship as a botanist might do. Our brain can associate them if the need arises more easily than it can help us if we hear one when the other was intended.

Syntax—the grammar of arrangement—is somewhat less arbitrary than words, especially in the order of elements. We say *He came in and sat down* because that is the sequence of the actions; if we said *He sat down and came in* it would have to mean that the opposite sequence occurred —perhaps he was being supported on his feet by someone else, and decided to get back into his wheelchair to propel himself into the room. To reverse the order we need a specific grammatical instruction, say the word *after: He sat down after he came in.* But arbitrariness lingers even without such traffic signs: *ground parched corn* has *first* been parched and then ground. Often the same meanings can be conveyed by dissimilar sequences: *nonsensical,* with a prefix and a suffix, means the same as *senseless,* with just a suffix; *more handsome* and *handsomer* are usually interchangeable.

The most rigidly arbitrary level of language is that of the distinctive units of sound by which we can distinguish between *skin* and *skim* or *spare* and *scare* the moment we hear the words. It was noted earlier that the very use of sound for this purpose was, while practical, not at all necessary to the system built up from it. And once sound became the medium, the particular sounds did not matter so long as they could be told apart. What distinguishes *skin* from *skim* is the sound of [n] versus the sound of [m], but could just as well be [b] versus [g]—there is nothing in the nature of skin that decrees it shall be called *skin* and not *skib.* The only "natural" fact is that human beings are limited by their speech organs to certain dimensions of sound—we do not, for example, normally make the sound that would result from turning the tip of the tongue all the way back to the soft palate; it is too hard to reach. But given the sets of sounds we *can* make (not identical, of course, from one language to another, but highly similar), arbitrariness frees us to combine them at will. The combinations do not have to match anything in nature, and their number is therefore unlimited.

---

[12] What happens when two words come to sound the same is treated in Chapter 13.

Still, arbitrariness has its limits. Where one thing stands for another—as pictures, diagrams, and signals do—it is normal to look for resemblances. A wiring diagram for a television set represents each part and connection in detail. If someone asks directions and the person asked points to the right, the direction of travel is also to the right. Most gestures have at least an element of guessability about them; the lexical gesture for 'I don't know' described above uses empty hands to mean 'I have no information.'

Even the distinctive units of sound are not always arbitrary. There seems to be a connection, transcending individual languages, between the sounds of the vowels produced with the tongue high in the mouth and to the front, especially the vowel sound in *wee, teeny,* and the meaning of 'smallness,' while those with tongue low suggest 'largeness.' The size of the mouth cavity—this *ee* sound has the smallest opening of all—is matched with the meaning. We *chip* a small piece but *chop* a large one; a *slip* is smaller than a *slab* and a *nib* is smaller than a *knob.* Examples crop up spontaneously—"A *freep* is a baby *frope,*" said a popular entertainer in a game of Scrabble—or in modifications of existing words —for example, *least* with an exaggeratedly high tongue position for *ee,* or the following:

> "That's about the price I had in mind," said Joe Peel. "Eight to ten thousand, but of course, it would depend on the place. I might even go a *leetle* higher."[13]

Not only the vowels, but also, in some languages, certain consonants are symbolic of size. And besides size there is the related notion of distance ('small' = 'close,' 'large' = 'far').[14]

The curious thing about the balance between arbitrariness and its opposite is that, given language (or anything else) as a fact of life, much of the arbitrariness falls away. We can say that the shape of an apple is arbitrary because it "might as well" be square. But apples are a fact of life, and they are not square; and this relates them, non-arbitrarily, to the other fruits in the universe of fruit. The letter F "might as well" have the shape *ⵈ* , but it does not, and this relates it non-arbitrarily to the other shapes of the same letter: *ℱ* and f. If we accept the initial arbitrariness of the existence of almost anything, non-arbitrariness follows in most of its subsequent connections. The English language seems inexcusably arbitrary to the speaker of French, yet it is a world to itself, and within that world there are countless more or less self-evident relationships. Take the word *minuscule.* Most writers now spell it

---

[13] Frank Gruber, *The Silver Jackass* (New York: Penguin Books, 1947), p. 45.
[14] See page 275.

miniscule and pronounce it accordingly. They associate it with the prefix *mini-*. And given the words **bolt** (of lightning), (frisky) **colt,** and **jolt,** it is natural to tie a similar jarring meaning to **volt** (named for Alessandro Volta). The more volts the bigger the jolt.[15]

Almost nothing about language is arbitrary in the sense that some person sat down on some occasion and decided to invent it, the way a mathematician would invent a new symbol, picking the size and shape that is most convenient without regard for any resemblance to any other related thing. Virtually everything in language has a non-arbitrary origin. Some things evolve toward greater arbitrariness, others toward less.

LANGUAGE IS VERTICAL AS WELL AS HORIZONTAL

When we hear or look at a display of speech or writing, the dimension we are most conscious of is a horizontal one—the stream of time in speech, the span of lines in writing. Almost everything that we put in a message has to go to the right or left of something else. There is no "above" or "below," "behind" or "in front." Much that happens when a language changes is due to collisions or confusions along this course. It may be only a lapse, as when a speaker, intending to say **discussing shortly,** says **discushing,** bringing a sound that belongs on the right over to the left. Or it may be permanent, as in **horse-shoe,** in which everybody makes the *s* of the first element like the *sh* of the second. Changes in meaning may worm their way into such a change in form. For example, speakers distinguish *got to* 'had the privilege of' and *got to* 'be under obligation to' by using the unchanged form for the first meaning and a changed one for the second: **I got to get off, I gotta get off.**

If people merely parroted what they had heard before and never did any assembling of utterances on their own, it is conceivable that language might have just a single dimension. But they do assemble, and the question is, where do they go for the parts? It must be to a stockroom of some sort. And stockrooms require a scheme for storage, or we could never find what we are looking for. This is the vertical dimension of language. It is everything that our brains have hoarded since we learned our first syllable, cross-classified in a wildly complex but amazingly efficient way. Nothing less depends on it than the means to summon whatever we need the instant that we need it at the same time that we are framing our ideas for the next phrase and probably still uttering the last one. This vast

---

[15] For a discussion of the relativity of arbitrariness according to the linguist Ferdinand de Saussure, see Wittmann 1966, pp. 88–90. See below, pages 218–20, for *phonesthemes.*

storehouse of items, categories, and connections is the *competence* that we identified earlier.

The links by which we pull an item from the store are as various as links can imaginably be. There are loose ones that tie whole segments to other whole segments, such as the parental clichés that the humorist George Carlin makes the most of:

Get down from there—*you wanna break your neck?*

Be careful with that thing—*you wanna put somebody's eye out?*

Put that coat back on—*you wanna catch pneumonia?*

And there are remembered associations from outside language—our thinking apparatus will throw a line to anything to rescue a thought. Suppose you run across the term *polymath,* find that it means a person of wide learning, and want to recapture a synonym you remember having heard. The first thing that comes to mind is the word *polygraph.* Next is the mental image of a *pantograph,* but it takes a moment for the word itself to emerge. Now you have it: *pansophist.* Here we see several connections within language, in addition to the one on the outside, which is the mental picture of the instrument. It is only when an interruption occurs—when for some reason we fail to get what we want—that we see the process in slow motion. Normally the desired item presents itself with no evidence of the circuitry by which we got it.

The types of vertical association usually cited as examples are those that show highly systematic resemblances in form and meaning. The familiar ones are the lists that we learn to recite as children: numerals, days of the week, months of the year, the principal parts of a verb, the degrees of an adjective (*good, better, best*), the cases of a pronoun (*I, me, my*). Whether we ever recite them or not, our brain makes connections among related items so that they can be retrieved on demand. The number of vertical sets runs into the thousands, and the classes they represent may be small, tight, highly structured ones whose alternation follows some fairly strict grammatical rule, or loose and partially open semantic ones that may even cause speakers to hesitate at times in making a selection. An example of the former is the set of possessives that are used as nouns, which fill the slots in *I had mine, You had _____, We had _____,* and *They had _____.* An example of the latter is the set of "coins" versus the set of "values." We choose from the first when we fill the slot in a sentence like *A _____ won't go in that parking meter (penny, nickel, dime, quarter).* We choose from the second in transactions where particular coins don't matter, as in *It cost _____ (eight cents, two bits, a dollar seventy-five)*—though if we feel like it we can often pick from the first set *(It cost a dollar and a quarter = It cost a dollar and twenty-five cents),* provided the result is not too complex (**It cost a dollar and a quarter and two pennies).*[16]

The horizontal dimension of language is called *syntagmatic,* the vertical dimension, *paradigmatic.* The first is the domain of *syntax,* which is literally a "putting together," and the term *syntagm* is sometimes used to mean any unit or coherent group of units along the horizontal line, such as a word, a phrase, or a clause. A *paradigm* is any of the vertical sets that we have just discussed, but the term is used most often to refer to the sets that are tied together by some grammatical rule, such as pronouns with their cases, or verbs with their inflections for number, tense, and person.

LANGUAGES ARE SIMILARLY STRUCTURED

Languages can be related in three ways: genetically, culturally, and typologically. A genetic relationship is one between mother and daughter or between two sisters or two cousins: there is a common ancestor somewhere in the family line. A cultural relationship arises from contacts in the real world at a given time; enough speakers command a second language to adopt some of its features, most often just terms of cultural artifacts but sometimes other features as well (the borrowed words may contain unaccustomed sounds, which are then domesticated in the new language if conditions are favorable). A typological relationship is one of resemblances regardless of where they came from. English is related genetically to Dutch through the common ancestry of Germanic and Indo-European. It is related culturally to North American Indian languages, from which it has taken many place names. And it is related typologically to Chinese, which it resembles more than it resembles its own cousin Latin in the comparative lack of inflections on words. Rumanian is related genetically and typologically to the other Romance languages through the common ancestry of Vulgar Latin. It is related culturally and to some extent typologically to the other Balkan languages, especially the Slavonic ones, which have hemmed it in for centuries, cutting it off from the rest of the Latin world.

Though genetic and cultural relationships tend to spell typological ones, it often happens that languages of the same family diverge so radically in the course of time that only the most careful analysis will demonstrate their kinship. The opposite happens too: languages unrelated genetically may "converge" to a high degree of similarity. Typological

---

[16] An asterisk before a sentence indicates that the sentence is not acceptable.

resemblance is what we look to for the traits that are universal to all humankind. If we find that languages in scattered parts of the world, which could hardly be related historically, use the pitch of the voice to distinguish questions from statements, or show a predilection for certain vowel sounds over others, or manifest without exception a class of thing-words that may be called nouns, we can be fairly sure that this somehow reflects the physical and mental equipment that all speakers are born with, regardless of their linguistic heritage.

Typological similarities can be found at all levels; the degree and number of them make it possible to classify languages by types. We can match them in terms of the numbers and kinds of distinctive sounds that they have, the way they build words, and the way they arrange sentences. The second of these three methods was long the favorite; languages have been classified as *analytic* (modifications of meaning expressed by separate words: compare English *I will go* with French *j'irai*); *synthetic* (modifications built in: compare English *went* or *departed* with *did go* or *did depart*); and *polysynthetic* (extremely complex internal structure, roughly as in English *antidisestablishmentarianism* or Nahuat *čika·wka·tahto·htinemi* 'talk forcefully while walking').[17] Cutting across these categories are others depicting how modifications of meaning are handled: *isolating* (arrangement alone distinguishes relationships, as in English *Show me Tom* versus *Show Tom me*); *agglutinative* (relationships are shown by attaching elements that nevertheless retain a clear identity, as in *greenish*); *fusional* (elements are attached that virtually lose their identity in the process, as in *dearth* from *dear* + *-th*); and *modulating* (internal changes are made without the addition of anything easily seen as having an identity of its own, as in *steal, stole*). It is significant that examples of all these types of structure can be found in English. They are useful as statistical generalizations: most languages are typically more one than another—for example, Chinese is isolating and analytic, Latin fusional and synthetic—but all are mixtures to some extent.[18]

More recently, interest has shifted to sentence structure, in particular the sequence of subject, verb, and object in simple declarative sentences. Languages are classed as SVO, SOV, or VSO.[19] These arrangements are somehow basic, as it turns out that other facts of structure can be pre-

---

[17] This example is from Key 1960, p. 138. Typically the elements are deformed when they are packed together; Firth 1966, p. 83, cites English examples like *I-sht-f-thought-ikkoombidone.* Word spacing in English writing makes things appear more agglutinative (see below in text) than they are.

[18] For these classifications see especially Sapir 1921, Ch. 6.

[19] The orders VOS, OVS, and OSV do occur, but generally for special purposes, as in *The corn we ate but the beans we threw away,* where the objects have replaced the subjects as the topic.

dicted from them. For example, taking V and O as the most essential elements, it generally happens that a qualifier will use whichever one of
these two elements it qualifies as a fulcrum and will occur on the side
opposite the other element. A negative, for example, which primarily
modifies the verb will occur opposite the object, so that V is between:
NegVO or OVNeg. An adjective uses the noun (the object) as a fulcrum,
resulting in the order AdjOV or VOAdj.[20]

These are some of the large-scale generalizations that can be made
about similarities in structure. There are small-scale ones as well. For example, it is predictable that even if a language has a linking verb, young
children will not use it; they will say **Daddy here,** not **Daddy is here.**
But Latvian children are an exception. It turns out that in Latvian the
common way of saying **yes** is the verb for **is** (compare the English *"Is it
raining?"—"It is"*), and 'yes' is something that children learn very early.[21]

LANGUAGE IS HEARD AS WELL AS SPOKEN

Though every speaker is also a hearer, the psychology of one role is not
always the same as that of the other. The principle of least effort decrees
that speakers will work no harder than they have to in order to make
themselves understood. This form of laziness results in the blurring of
sounds. But the same principle decrees that listeners will work no harder
than they have to in order to understand. And this form of laziness compels speakers to use care if they expect cooperation and if they do not
want to have to repeat themselves. These are the radical and the conservative forces in language, which account for change and for resistance
to change. As they are never quite evenly balanced at any one time,
changes do occur, but then the conservative force steps in and reestablishes a norm.

The two roles are responsible for different approaches to language,
which has created no small amount of misunderstanding. Phonetics, for
example, is described almost completely in speakers' terms—the criteria
for measurement are the physiology of the speech organs and the characteristics of the sound wave—though receiving the sounds and analyzing them is as much a problem as producing them. On the other hand,
meaning is most often described from the hearer's standpoint; analysts
work hard to find out how we decode messages, even though coding them
is every bit as delicate an operation. In part the clash of approaches is
due to what we can lay hold of to study. The speech organs can be

---

[20] Lehmann 1973.
[21] Ferguson 1971, pp. 4–5.

observed; the ear and the brain cannot. We can see and hear what listeners do in putting meaning to a sentence that has already been coded
and delivered; it is almost impossible to start with meanings and observe
the process of selection and accommodation that the brain engages in to
build a sentence. As our methods improve, we may hope that this one-
sidedness will disappear.

As an example of speaker's economy versus hearer's economy, take the
expression *It was a nice day we had yesterday.* The speaker draws this
directly from storage—it is prefabricated and does not have to be built
up from word to sentence. But the hearer begins processing before everything is said. There is no way of knowing whether the words about to be
spoken will turn out to be a cliché or a freshly constructed and original
sentence. It may therefore be necessary to assume the latter and process
accordingly, until the signs that it is a cliché become unmistakable.[22]

---

[22] For T (transmitter) versus R (receiver) roles see Shubin 1969.

ADDITIONAL REMARKS
AND APPLICATIONS

1. Name three countries in which at least three mutually unintelligible languages are spoken. (The USSR is publishing in more than seventy non-Slavic languages, in addition to Slavic.)

2. Since a page of writing requires a living reader to interpret it, can a dead language be said to live on in its written records, or has the reader somehow managed to revive it in himself? Is understanding even the writings of one's own language a matter of activating its symbols, say by a form of inner speech?

3. Can the sense of touch be used for communicating in language? Consider the reading of Braille. Can the temperature sense be so used? If not, why?

4. What type of gesture is a handshake? Could one male be sure, if he held out his hand to a male member of some unknown culture, that the other male would not take it as a challenge to a wrestling match?

5. Would you say that the gesture of tilting the head slightly to one side and looking at your interlocutor out of the corner of your eye is appropriate or inappropriate to saying the following words with the intonation shown?

$$\text{Don't } _{\text{push}} \, \text{him} \, ^{\text{too}} \, ^{\text{fa}} \, _{\text{r.}}$$

6. Is the supposed "cooperation" between language and gesture sometimes contrapuntal, in that one says one thing and the other says the opposite? Think of some examples.

7. A gesture may imitate an actual event. In kissing, for example, we have the real thing; then the perfunctory kiss; then the kiss in the air, which may be "tossed." Think of another example.

8. If we think of families of words related in meaning as being less arbitrary if the relationship shows somehow in the word form, how

do the two families *inch, foot, yard, rod, mile* and *millimeter, centi-meter, meter, kilometer* compare? List two other opposing series like these (say, the popular versus the scientific names for a family of plants).

9. Does length have analog significance in English? Experiment with *long* in *It's a long road,* with *way* in *They went way out to California,* and with the syllable *de-* in *It's delicious.* Comment on *I won't, I won't, I won't!* Is some kind of "length" involved here too?

10. A story by Robert Louis Stevenson contains the sentence *As the night fell, the wind rose.* Could this be expressed *As the wind rose, the night fell?* If not, why? Does this indicate a degree of non-arbitrariness about word order?

11. Take the two sentences *The man ate the food* and *The man digested the food* and combine them in a single sentence starting with *The man who.* There are two possible answers. Are they equally plausible?

12. Consider the two headlines *Woman Running Across Street Killed* and *Woman Killed Running Across Street.* Does syntax tend to be non-arbitrary in terms of putting together things that belong together?

13. What is the member of the "value" paradigm in the British system that corresponds to *pennies* in the American "coin" paradigm?

References

Arango Montoya, Francisco. 1972. "Lenguas y dialectos indígenas," *América Indígena* 32:1169–76.
Bruneau, Thomas. 1973. "Communicative Silence," *Journal of Communication* 23:17–46.
Dye, W.; P. Townsend; and W. Townsend. 1968. "The Sepik Hill Languages," *Oceania* 39:146–58.
Engel, Walburga von Raffler. 1973. "The Correlation of Gestures and Verbalizations in First Language Acquisition." Paper read at pre–Congress Conference on Face-to-Face Interaction, Ninth International Congress of Anthropological and Ethnological Sciences, Chicago.
Ferguson, Charles A. 1971. "A Sample Research Strategy in Language Universals," *Working Papers on Language Universals,* Stanford University, 6:1–22.
Firth, J. R. 1966. *The Tongues of Men* and *Speech.* 2 bks. in 1 (London: Oxford University Press).

Fónagy, Ivan. 1971. "Synthèse de l'ironie," *Phonetica* 23:42–51.

Jakobson, Roman. 1970. "Linguistics," in *Main Trends of Research in the Social and Human Sciences*, vol. 1 (The Hague: Mouton).

Key, Harold. 1960. "Stem Construction and Affixation of Sierra Nahuat Verbs," *International Journal of American Linguistics* 26:130–45.

Key, Mary Ritchie. 1970. "Preliminary Remarks on Paralanguage and Kinesics in Human Communication," *La Linguistique*, No. 2, 17–36.

Lamendella, John T. 1975. *Introduction to the Neuropsychology of Language* (Rowley, Mass.: Newbury House). Page references are to the manuscript.

Lehmann, W. P. 1973. "A Structural Principle of Language and Its Implications," *Language* 49:47–66.

Makkai, Adam. 1973. "A Pragmo-ecological View of Linguistic Structure and Language Universals," *Language Sciences* 27:9–22.

Sapir, Edward. 1921. *Language* (New York: Harcourt Brace Jovanovich).

Sebeok, Thomas A. 1962. "Coding in the Evolution of Signaling Behavior," *Behavioral Science* 7:430–42.

Shubin, Emmanuel. 1969. "The General Principles of Semiography," *Revue Roumaine de Linguistique* 14:481–84.

Wittmann, Henri. 1966. "Two Models of the Linguistic Mechanism," *Canadian Journal of Linguistics* 11:83–93.

DISTINCTIVE SOUND 3

One of the early words a child learns is *picture.* Years later he will learn *pictorial* and *depict.* The *picture* stage is like the child who uses it, simple and direct. There are no connections yet to such relatable words as *pictorial, depict, paint, pigment* ("cognates" of *picture,* for the etymologist), or others like them which adults may or may not associate with *picture.* Each word in the child's earliest vocabulary is an entity, a unique combination of sounds, in contrast with every other combination. The sounds of the *picture* stage are the topic of this chapter. When the *picture–pictorial–depict* stage does arrive it brings with it more and more complex patterns, which are best studied in connection with the building of words out of larger elements than sounds; it is reserved for the next chapter.

How do the two stages differ? Our young learner has already acquired not only *picture* but such words as *chickie, scratch, itch, much,* and *achoo!* All these words contain a sound that helps the child to distinguish them audibly from other words: *chickie* from *Dickie, scratch* from *scrap, itch* from *it,* and *much* from *mud.* Most of the beginning words are like these: simple in structure, chiefly of native English stock—no Latinisms yet!—and starkly independent—that is, unburdened with the kinds of interconnections that develop as the child grows older: *love–lovely–loveliness–beloved,* *question–quest–request–inquest–query–inquiry–inquisitive–questionable–questionnaire.* The simple stock of beginning words, all maximally different, demands a sound system that will set *difference* above any other requirement. Sounds have but one purpose: to help tell words apart.

So it happens that as a by-product of the first words, after a fairly good control of speech has been mastered, the child begins to identify each of the distinctive sounds that make each word different from all the rest. No one knows exactly how this is done, but one by one the *ch* sound of *picture*, the *s* of *house*, the *m* of *animal*, the *t* of *toy*, and the *n* of *man* are lifted out of the limbo of surrounding sounds and take on a life of their own. *House* is distinguished from *mouse* by the simple contrast of *h* and *m*; *much* is distinguished from *chum* by reversing the positions of *m* and *ch*. The relationship among the sounds at this stage is one of straightforward *opposition*. Though some may show a greater mutual resemblance than others (*d* is more like *t* than like *ch*), in their function all are totally different: *dip* is as different from *tip* as it is from *chip*. Except when the child-as-poet is playing with sounds for fun, the fact that two sounds resemble each other is irrelevant, though it does create difficulties in hearing and speaking.

PHONETICS AND PHONOLOGY

The distinctive sounds come wrapped in an envelope of other disturbances of the air that convey such information as whether the speaker has a cold or has been eating or feels angry or is a long way off or is an adult rather than a child. Only part of the sound wave corresponds to the central organization, a narrow and precisely limited set of contrasts between various combinations of pitches, durations, loudnesses, and voice and whisper, which are the audible results of the ways we exercise our speech organs. Though no two languages are identical, these ways are similar enough to generalize about them.

We are so accustomed to looking at print with its tightly formed letter symbols and neat spaces that we like to think of "units" of sound in the same terms. And it is true that something like a succession of partially separable units does occur: we can hear a hissing segment followed by a nasal segment in the first part of the word *smell*. But things are rather badly smeared together, as we can tell if we say a word such as *arm* and try to imagine where the portion corresponding to one sound ends and the next one begins. Actually, most speakers will say *arm* with the nasal passage open during the whole word, with the result that the nasal sound, which properly belongs just to the *m*, is heard throughout. The sound of the *r* overlaps that of the vowel, and the tongue remains in the position for *r* while the *m* is being negotiated. There is no way of carving the sounds up, like beads on a string, though having the letters to follow with our eyes may fool us into thinking there is. The brain has the job of reassembling the jumble.

Of course the important thing about *arm* is to make the word as a whole recognizable, and if we miss our aim a bit on one or two of the sounds it probably will make no difference. In something like *He held me at arm's length* the listener could even miss the word *arm* entirely and still understand the sentence, for there are not many other words that could go in that position and make sense. The redundancy—surplus information—that comes in almost everything we say makes it possible to be pretty sloppy with pronunciation most of the time. Listeners will try to make sense of what they hear even if it is deliberately distorted.[1]

That being the case, and as sounds are naturally slurred in the stream of speech anyway, the result is predictable: each "distinctive sound" represents a range rather than a point. We can idealize each range and treat it as if it were a point, like the bull's-eye on a target. So long as the targets themselves are far enough apart in the universe of speech sounds, anything but a clean miss will count as a hit.

The distinctive sounds thus carve up the continuum, each with its proper zone and with unused buffer zones between. This can be seen best in the vowel sounds. Take a language that has a system of just three vowels, the *ee* of *meet,* the *a* of *father,* and the *u* of *blue,* as happens with the Tagalog language spoken in the Philippines. A speaker could "mispronounce" *meet* as *mit* and still be heard to say *meet,* because the *i* of *mit* is closer to *ee* than to *a* or to *u.* English has more than three vowels and accordingly makes a distinction between *meet* and *mit* that would not be found in the three-vowel language. This means that English speakers have learned to be a bit more discriminating in this one zone. But in any language there is still enough room within phonetic space for vowels to be kept apart without at the same time requiring that they be exactly on target every time.

The idealization that represents each area of distinctive sound is the *phoneme*. A phoneme is not a sound but an abstraction, just as a word is an abstraction: we can utter the sounds of *please,* but that single utterance is not the word *please,* for if it were, by saying it we would use it up and never be able to say it again. It goes on, as a trace in our minds, or nervous systems, or wherever. But hearing *please* over and over, used appropriately, is what put the trace there in the first place, and the same goes for the phonemes. This makes it possible to describe phonemes as if they really were sounds. There is no danger so long as we remember that

---

[1] Subjects required to react to question-and-answer pairs in which the answer does not fit the question tend to reinterpret them so that they will agree. See Fillenbaum 1971.

no two languages carve up the continuum in exactly the same way, and what is distinctive in one may not be distinctive in another. Some targets are big enough to include the range of two targets in another language; or two targets in two languages may be the same size, but overlap. From years of selective listening the speakers of a language simply do not hear what is not significant for them. This poses a problem when they try to learn another language. The Japanese confuse *r* and *l* in English because in Japanese there is a single sound where English has two. English speakers learning German sometimes substitute **k** for the sound of **ch,** as in **ach** (which can be heard in the English **pack-horse** spoken rapidly). In this case it is German that has two sounds, which contrast in **Acht** 'ban' and **Akt** 'act,' and English that has one.

The study of sounds is *acoustics;* that of speech sound is *phonetics* (which is therefore a branch of acoustics); and that of the systematic use of sound in language is *phonology.* A distinction is usually made in phonetics between *articulatory phonetics* and *acoustic phonetics;* the first looks at how speech sound is produced and the second at how it is expressed in physical terms—shape of the wave form, intensity, periodicity versus noise, presence of overtones, and so forth. Articulatory phonetics has a long history; it has always been possible to observe and describe the movements of the speech organs. Acoustic phonetics had to wait till almost the middle of this century for the tools to be created that make direct observation possible. At its deeper levels, even articulatory phonetics remains partially unexplored; instruments have only recently been developed to measure air pressure in the resonating cavities and photograph the excitation of the vocal cords. On top of this there is one whole set of links in the transmission chain that we know next to nothing about: how speech sounds are handled at the receiving end. It is easier to look into a speaker's mouth than into his ear.

ARTICULATIONS

All languages use certain articulations that interrupt the stream of voiced sound and others that let it flow freely. The first are typically the consonants, the second the vowels. The alternation between the two is essential for getting the variety of sounds that we need in order to have a large set of signaling units. The two kinds of articulations depend on each other: the consonants separate the vowels and the vowels allow the speech organs to get from one consonant position to the next. (Even in languages that reportedly have no vowels at all,[2] there is a neutral vowel-

---

[2] See pages 316–17.

like sound that separates certain consonants and makes them audible.)
Each consonant distorts the portion of a vowel that lies next to it in its
own peculiar way. Having a vowel alongside is so important to most
consonants that if a tape recording of one of them is cut so that nothing
of the vowel is left and is then played to listeners, what they report hearing is an unintelligible chirp.

In making a consonant we either shut off the air completely or narrow
the passage at some point so that it comes through noisily. The first kind
of articulation is called a *stop*, the second a *fricative*. The stopping or
narrowing can be at any point that our speech organs permit, from as far
forward as the lips to as far back and down as the vocal cords, and this
makes for a good deal of variety in the particular sounds that different
languages adopt. In English we use the following:

1. The lips. The [p] and [b] in *pane* and *bane* are stops: the lips are
   closed completely and then abruptly parted. The [f] and [v] in
   feign and *vane* are fricatives: the air keeps coming through, but
   with friction. We call [p b] *bilabials,* because both lips are involved; [f v] are *labiodentals,* involving the lower lip and the
   upper teeth. English has no bilabial fricatives (unless the exclamation variously spelled *whew!* and *phew!* is counted as a word),
   but many languages do.

2. The tongue tip on the upper front teeth. English makes no stops
   this way, but it has two fricatives—the initial sounds in *thin* and
   that—for which the symbols [θ] and [ð] are used (their names
   are *theta* and *eth,* naturally pronounced with [θ] and [ð], respectively). Since the tongue is involved in all consonants made in
   the interior of the mouth, we classify the sound by just the position that the tongue touches or approaches. Accordingly, these
   two sounds are *dentals*.

3. The tongue tip on the ridge back of the upper front teeth. The
   [t] and [d] of *to* and *do* are stops. The [s z] of *seal* and *zeal* are
   fricatives. As the ridge in question is known as the alveolar ridge,
   these sounds are *alveolars*.

4. The whole fore part of the tongue on the roof of the mouth, or
   palate. English has no simple stops made with this contact, but has
   other sounds, including the two fricatives symbolized [š ž], which
   occur at the ends of the words *ash* and *rouge.* Sounds made on the
   palate are *palatals*.

5. The rear of the tongue backed against the velum, or soft palate,
   the fleshy part of the roof of the mouth at the rear. English has
   two stops, [k g]—examples: *caw* and *go.* These sounds are *velars*.

The Scottish variety of English has a velar fricative (for example, in *loch*), and many other languages, including German, use this sound.

Of course, other positions and tongue contacts are possible. In a number of languages, typically those of India, there are sounds made on the palate not with the whole front part of the tongue, including the blade or broad central part, but only with the turned-back tip. There is also a stop sound that is used freely in many languages but is not generally counted among our distinctive sounds in English, although we use it in two peculiar ways. This is the glottal stop, symbolized [ʔ], which many people put between *the* and a following word that begins with a vowel. Most of us use it in the warning *uh-oh!* (meaning 'Look out, you're about to make a mistake') and in the negative *hunh-uh* or *unh-uh.* Some languages, of which a number in Africa are typical, produce certain of their stops by an intake of air such as one hears in the smack of a kiss or in the sound spelled *tsk! tsk!* which to us is a sign of disapproval.

The stops and fricatives are the two chief *manners* of manipulating the air at the various contact points. But there are others, one of the commonest of which is made by tapping the point of the tongue against the alveolar ridge. In American English [ɾ] sound is heard in *matter, meadow, buddy,* and many other words (and combinations like *hit 'er*) spelled with *t* or *d.* The sound is termed a *flap,* and when the tapping is repeated, as in the Italian *rosa,* it is called a *trill.* (The other organ that is loose enough to produce a tap or a trill is the uvula, and is so used in French and German.) Another manner is like a combination of a stop and a fricative. If instead of breaking the contact crisply and cleanly at the end of a [t] the tongue is withdrawn gradually, the result is the initial sound in the foreign borrowings *Tsar* and *tsetse.* Such sounds are called *affricates.* English has two palatal affricates in its native stock of words, the initial sounds in *chump* and *jump,* symbolized [č ǰ]. Still another manner consists in the direction in which the air is allowed to escape. If it is diverted through the nose before or instead of being released from the mouth, the result is a *nasal* sound, of which English has three: labial [m] in *ram,* alveolar [n] in *ran,* and velar [ŋ], called *angma,* in *rang.* If it is diverted around the sides of the tongue instead of along the median line, the result is a *lateral* sound, typified in English by [l], as in *Lee.*

Three sounds are as much like vowels as consonants: [y w r]. They have a constriction that is fairly tight but not tight enough for them to be classed as fricatives. They are termed *semivowels* and are treated here under *diphthongs.*

The most fundamental difference of all is that of voice and voicelessness. If the vocal cords are vibrating, the result is a voiced sound, as in

[v] (if we prolong a [v] and hold a finger on our Adam's apple, we can feel the vibration); if the air moves past the vocal cords without causing them to vibrate, the result is a voiceless sound, as in [f]. Voiceless and voiced consonants generally come in pairs for each position and manner: [p b], [f v], [θ ð], [t d], [s z], [š ž], [č ǰ], [k g]. Vowels are typically voiced, but English has a consonant that is like a vowel without voice: in the words *heat, hope, hail, hoot,* and so on, the [h] is made by starting the sound of the vowel without voice.

These descriptions apply to English; they do not necessarily hold for other languages. In fact, there is considerable variety even among speakers of English. For example, many speakers do not have the same [s] sound that was described above. Instead of using the tongue tip to produce the hiss, they bunch the blade or flat part of the tongue up against the alveolar ridge and get the tip out of the way by curling it down behind the lower front teeth. Even with sounds that are very much alike, one finds differences that typify one dialect or language as against another. When a voiceless-stop sound in English occurs at the beginning of a word, the voicing of the following vowel is delayed somewhat and we hear a puff of air in between, called an *aspiration.* It is enough to blow out a match held close to the lips when we say a word like *pin.* There is no such delay in French, with the result that when a Frenchman tries to say our *pin* it is apt to sound to us more like *bin*—the *voiced* stops are not aspirated in English, and we notice the lack of aspiration more than the lack of voicing. Differences in body stance, rate of speaking, typical attitudes of domination or subservience, and many other factors also influence the way sounds are produced. If speakers habitually lower their heads in deference and avoid looking at the person spoken to, the sounds do not have the same resonance as when the head is held erect and the voice is projected confidently. Our habits of being affect our habits of talking, and can involve whole societies. In some languages the beginning of an utterance is much more forceful than the end; the result is an increasing indistinctness and huddling of the final sounds.

In Table 3–1, the English consonant sounds are classified according to place and manner of articulation. Though for simplicity's sake the terms *dental, alveolar, palatal,* and *velar* are used, the more precise terms are *interdental, apicoalveolar, frontopalatal,* and *dorsovelar. Interdental* specifies that the tongue is not merely on the teeth but between them. *Apico-, fronto-,* and *dorso-* mean, respectively, that the part of the tongue making the contact is the tip, the front, and the back. On the chart, voiceless–voiced pairs are set side by side. Not all the ways of making noises with the vocal organs can be accommodated in the chart; to make it universally applicable, more categories would have to be added. A *uvular* column would be needed for French and German, to take care of the *r*-like sound produced by tapping or vibrating the uvula in contact

TABLE 3–1
The English Consonants

	Bilabial	Labiodental	Dental	Alveolar	Palatal	Velar	Glottal
STOPS	p b			t d		k g	
FRICATIVES		f v	θ ð	s z	š ž		h°
AFFRICATES					č ǰ		
NASALS	m			n		ŋ	
LATERAL				l			
SEMIVOWELS	w†			r	y		

° Classed as a fricative on the basis of acoustic effect. It sounds more or less like [f θ s], even though it is like a vowel without voice (see page 40).

† [w] is velar as well as bilabial, since the back of the tongue is raised as it is for [u].

with the raised back of the tongue. And extra rows would be needed for *ejective* and *suction* stops—the first being the type of sound that accompanies "tongue spitting" (spitting without blowing—the pressure is not from the lungs), the second the reverse, as in the lip-smacking and *tsk-tsk* sounds mentioned on page 39. But many non-English sounds that occur in other languages can be fitted into the empty slots in the English chart. The velar fricative [x] already mentioned (in Scottish *loch*, German *Achtung*, and Spanish *caja*) would go directly below [k]. The palatal nasal [ɲ], which occurs in the French *guignol* 'puppet show' and the Italian *bagno* 'bath,' would go to the right of [n]. Not all the slots could be filled in any case. Since the tongue cannot be involved in glottal sounds, that column is almost empty. The same explanation goes for there being no bilabial lateral. The almost-empty dental column reflects the fact that most sounds in that column would be indistinguishable from the ones in the alveolar column; those sounds do occur as dentals in many languages, but then the alveolar column tends to be empty.

Vowel sounds are made by *shaping* the column of air as it passes through the mouth rather than by obstructing it. Raising the jaw or lowering it has the effect of bringing the tongue close to the palate or away from it, and the tongue moves independently forward or backward. The lips may be spread or rounded. The effect of these adjustments is to change the resonating cavities, which in turn filters out certain harmonic frequencies and reinforces others, producing the characteristic qualities that differentiate the sounds. Vowels are *high, mid,* or *low,* depending on the height of the tongue (nearness to the palate); *front, central,* or *back,* according to the position of the highest part of the tongue on the horizontal axis; and most of them are *rounded* or *spread.* For English, two intermediate positions are needed for tongue height, one between high and mid, called *lower high,* and one between mid and low, called *lower mid.* Examples:

high front (spread)	[i] as in **beat**
lower high front (spread)	[ɪ] as in **bit**
mid front (spread)	[e] as in **bait**
lower mid front (spread)	[ɛ] as in **bet**
low front	[æ] as in **bat**
central	[ʌ] as in **butt**
low back	[a] as in **pot**
lower mid back (rounded)	[ɔ] as in **bought**
mid back (rounded)	[o] as in **boat**
lower high back (rounded)	[ʊ] as in **put**
high back (rounded)	[u] as in **boot**

Spread and *rounded* are listed in parentheses because as far as English is concerned they are almost automatic: except for the lowest positions [æ a], all front vowels are spread, all back are rounded. The *degree* of spreading and rounding is also automatic: it is most extreme with the highest position of the tongue (for [i] and [u]), and is absent or barely noticeable at the lowest position (for [æ] and [a]). Most languages have this same automatic relationship between front-spread and back-round, but some do not. French has a series of front-rounded vowels: the words in the pairs *fée–feu* ('fairy' and 'fire' respectively), and *père–peur* ('father' and 'fear') differ only in that with the first member the lips are spread and in the second they are rounded.

   Diphthongs are two vowel or vowel-like sounds combined in a single syllable. English makes them with one of the regular vowels plus one of the semivowels [y w r]. The tongue glides in producing a diphthong, either toward or away from the position of [y w r], and for that reason these sounds are often called glides.
   Examples:

[ay] as in **tie**	[ya] as in **yacht**
[ɔy] as in **boy**	[yɔ] as in **yawn**
[aw] as in **now**	[wa] as in **wan**
[ar] as in **car**	[ra] as in **rock**

As the final element in a diphthong, the semivowels [y] and [w] are mostly restricted to the three combinations shown, [ay ɔy aw], though some speakers use them in additional ones—for example, *lewd* [lɪwd], more generally heard as [lud]. And for most speakers of American English [r] is similarly restricted to [ɪr] as in *beer,* [ɛr] as in *bear,* [ar] as in *bar,* [ɔr] or [or] as in *bore,* and [ʊr] as in *boor.* But all three sounds may occur before any vowel. This difference in behavior is sometimes carried into the terminology: instead of the single term *semivowel,* [y w r] are called semivowels when they are the second members of a diphthong and semiconsonants when they are the first members. But the sounds are the same: a tape recording of *yacht, wan,* and *rock* played backward will yield *tie, now,* and *car.*

The vowels that have been described thus far are the *full vowels.* Diphthongs also count as full vowels. Characteristic to English and very important to the *rhythm* of the language are three other vowels, called *reduced* vowels, which are heard in the last syllables of *Willie, Willa,* and *willow,* and can be symbolized [ɨ ə ɵ]. The second of these, [ə], is called *shwa* and is the most frequent vowel in the language; for example, it occurs in all but the first syllable of *formidableness* [fɔrmədəbəlnəs] for speakers who stress the first syllable of that word. The effect on rhythm can be seen by using a string of syllables with just full vowels for comparison. This is an unusual arrangement in prose but is much used in poetry: ***Irene Carstairs' pet chimpanzee Nimrod dotes on fresh horehound drops.*** The result is a spacing out of the syllables with a fairly even beat—typical of French, Spanish, or Italian, but not of English. When syllables with reduced vowels intervene—the usual thing in English—the reduced vowels borrow time from the preceding full vowels, producing an uneven beat. Compare ***Gets out dirt plain soap can't reach,*** where all the vowels are full, with ***Takes away the dirt that common soaps can never reach,*** where every other vowel is reduced.[3] In Figure 3–1 the reduced vowels appear as a triangle within the larger frame of full vowels. Because of their interior position, reduced vowels are often referred to as *centralized.*

The vowels show more clearly than the consonants how readily one may find differences within a single language. The fact that the tongue moves smoothly backward and forward and up and down enables it to take not only all the positions shown in Figure 3–1 but also any position in between. A consonant is an easy target as a rule—the teeth, for example, occupy a discontinuous part of the mouth, and the tongue knows exactly what to aim for. But within the continuum of the mouth cavity as a whole there are no definite targets, and it is not so easy to aim true. So we find many speakers whose vowels would disagree here and there with those of the chart, in their position and even sometimes in how

---

[3] See Bolinger 1963, and Lehiste 1972.

FIGURE 3–1
The Vowels, Full and Reduced

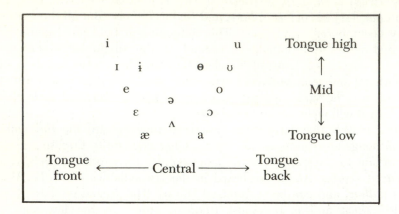

many of them there are. In some dialects of American English the reduced vowel in the last syllable of **hairy, many,** or **courtesy** (the one symbolized by [ɨ]) is as high as the full vowel [i]. Many speakers have only one vowel articulation lower than [o] in the back series: **tot** and **taught, cot** and **caught, dotter** and **daughter,** and many other such pairs are made to sound the same. This somewhat confused situation is apt to be found in a language, like English or French, that crowds a large number of vowels into the mouth-cavity continuum—they tend to interfere with one another. In a language with few vowels—say Tagalog, with its three [i a u], or Spanish, with its five [i e a o u]—this is less likely to happen.

Many languages multiply the number of their vowels by adding, part of the time, another articulation to their vowels. Here are examples of five such *secondary articulations*:

Rounding we have already noted as a feature that does not count in English because it is automatic, but it does count in French because its presence contrasts with its absence, as in **vie** 'life' and **vu** 'seen,' which differ only in rounding.

Nasalization is often found in English vowels, but it is not used for anything: **Did he go?** may be spoken with the nasal passage open or closed. In French the word pairs **beauté–bonté** ('beauty' and 'goodness' respectively) and **seau–son** ('pail' and 'sound') differ only in that the second member of each pair is nasalized.

Length is found in Classical Latin **mēto,** with its *e* lengthened, meaning 'to measure,' which contrasts with **meto,** without the extra length, meaning 'to reap.' (Consonants are sometimes lengthened too. It is often hard to decide whether a lengthened sound ought to be regarded as a single sound with extra length or as two identical sounds side by side. The latter interpretation is the usual one for such English expressions as *cattail, ripe pear,* and *sack coat.*)

Breathiness has only an emotional significance in English—something like 'concern verging on desperation.' In Gujarati, a language of India, it increases the number of vowels and may be combined with nasalization for a further increase.[4]

Tone is variation in pitch. In many languages—called *tone languages* —a higher or lower pitch on a vowel can make each one count for more than one. In Ticuna, a language of the upper Amazon, five steps of pitch are observed. The "word" *čanamu* is actually four words, depending on the combination of tones that go with it: numbering 1 for highest tone and 5 for lowest, *ča₃na₃mu₃* means 'I weave it,' *ča₃na₃mu₄* means 'I send it,' *ča₃na₃mu₅* means 'I eat it,' and *ča₃na₃mu₃₋₅* means 'I spear it.'[5] Tonal distinctions even appear in English, in dialects that have been influenced by African languages. In the West Indies the word *brother* with high-low pitch refers to one's kin, whereas with low-high it means a member of a religious or fraternal order; and similarly with *sister, mother,* and *father.* *Worker* with high-low pitch is a laborer, but with low-high it means 'seamstress.'[6] In a few tone languages, given a situation where the words and meanings apt to be appropriate are fairly familiar and predictable, it is sometimes possible to transmit just the series of tones and be understood—the hearer can guess the rest. This in stylized form is the basis of African drum signaling and also of certain forms of "whistle speech," which among speakers of tone languages sometimes substitute for normal speech. The following is George M. Cowan's description of a whistled conversation in the Mazatec dialect of Oaxaca, Mexico:

> Eusebio Martínez was observed one day standing in front of his hut, whistling to a man a considerable distance away. The man was passing on the trail below, going to market to sell a load of corn leaves which he was carrying. The man answered Eusebio's whistle with a whistle. The interchange was repeated several times with different whistles. Finally the man turned around, retraced his steps a short way and came up the footpath to Eusebio's hut. Without saying a word he dumped his load on the ground. Eusebio looked the load over, went into his hut, returned with some money, and paid the man his price. Not a word had been spoken. . . .[7]

Whistle speech is not confined to tone languages. If whispering can be made intelligible, so can whistling, even in a non-tone language, provided

---

[4] Fischer-Jørgensen 1967.

[5] Anderson 1959.

[6] Personal communication from S. R. R. Allsopp.

[7] Cowan 1948.

enough of the usual articulations of vowels and consonants are preserved. Another Mexican language, Tepehua, is whistled in this way;[8] so is Spanish, on Gomera in the Canary Islands. The intention of whistling is not necessarily playful. The Gomera whistle carries long distances (as do drum signals) and enables goatherds to converse from hilltop to hilltop.

The use of tone is extremely complex, and it is not always easy to say that it is added and subtracted just to make the vowels go farther. Often it has a kind of marking function: a negative statement, for example, may have a different tone from an affirmative one, or an active sentence from a passive.[9] The same is true of other secondary articulations. In Agbo, a language of Eastern Nigeria, an extra-strong articulation may be attached to certain verbs to indicate the progressive: *esúi* 'it is rotting,' *efíli* 'he is shredding.'[10]

As the Agbo example shows, secondary articulations may be used to multiply consonants as well as vowels. *Aspiration,* for example, which is automatic under certain conditions in English but absent in French, was added or subtracted to get extra consonants in Classical Greek, and the same is true today of North Chinese. And *voicing* of course is the secondary articulation that multiples the consonants in English, as can be seen by the pairings in the chart. (It is not usually *called* secondary, but that is because English and French and Swedish and German and the rest of the languages of Western Europe are "our" languages, in which nothing is secondary.)

PROSODY

In Chapter 2 it was stated that virtually everything in a spoken message has to go before or after something else—there is no underneath, on top of, behind, or in front of. The exception to this mostly valid generalization is a group of phenomena that is sometimes referred to as the *prosody,* sometimes as *suprasegmentals* (because they occur "on top of"—at the same time as—the before-and-after segments). They are a kind of musical accompaniment to speech, just as gesture is a kind of histrionic accompaniment. It is sometimes hard to decide where gesture stops and prosody begins.

Among the suprasegmentals, *rate of speaking* is the most gesture-like. If a speaker is in a hurry he talks fast, in spite of himself. But rate is

---

[8] Cowan 1973.

[9] Zima 1966.

[10] Bendor-Samuel and Spreda 1969.

also a device for signaling the opposite of haste. A woman may be in a hurry to have someone else get something done, yet if she wants it done with care she may say, *Take your time,* slowly and deliberately. On the other hand, even if there is no need at the very moment of speaking to race the words together, a sentence like **We've got to get out of here fast!** will move at a lively clip.

As might be expected, rate is the great distorter of articulations. Part of a speaker's competence in understanding a language consists in building a vocabulary of compacted and abbreviated words and combinations. For example, in answer to **Why didn't you bring the pliers?** a speaker may say

$$\text{[aynno]} \quad \overset{\text{ar}}{\underset{\text{e.}}{\text{where they} \searrow}}$$

in which [aynno], though it resembles **I know** more than **I don't know,** is understood as the latter; the difference is signaled by the lengthened [n]. Rate may be manipulated along with other parts of the prosody to produce patterns with particular meanings. In saying either of the following sentences,

$$\overset{It\ is\ pro}{\underset{\text{gious!}}{}}\ di \qquad\qquad \overset{I\ won't\ be\ re}{\underset{\text{sible!}}{}}\ spon$$

the speaker can achieve great emphasis by uttering the italicized syllables in a very clipped manner, yet spacing them out with pauses and then pronouncing the rest at faster than normal speed, with the drop in pitch as shown, and with the syllable just before the drop held back and then released in a loud rush.

Accent is an element of the prosody that is usually a combination of length, loudness, and pitch, with pitch the indispensable ingredient most of the time. In the two examples just cited, the accented syllables are *-di-* and *-spon-.* They stand out because they overlook a cliff—there is an abrupt drop right after them. But it is not necessary that the accent be quite so dramatic as that. In

$$\text{I'll}\ ^{\text{get}}\ \text{you an}^{\text{oth}}_{\quad\text{er one.}}$$

both *get* and *-oth-* are accented. The most prominent syllable (*-oth-* in this case) carries what is sometimes referred to as the *sentence accent* or *nuclear accent*. It usually comes close to the end of the utterance, but it may occur earlier, especially if the latter part is something repeated or already known:

                                told
Because   no body
          me I was expected to do anything like that.

The jump in pitch may be down as well as up, especially in questions. In both the following readings of the same sentence, the syllable *bro-* is accented by being pushed out of the intonational line:

          bro ther was the one who cheated him.
His

His
    bro ther was the one who cheated him?

Accent is gesture-like in that it emphasizes a word in the same way as an accompanying downward thrust of the head or a thump of the fist.[11]

Intonation is the broad undulation of the pitch curve that carries the ripples of accent on its back. The two together are often called *speech melody*, and this may well be more than a metaphor. Speech melody and musical melody may have had a common origin, and there are close ties even now between the music of a culture and its language.[12]

Three features of intonation have similar uses in all languages: range, direction, and relative height.

Range conveys emotion. When we are excited our voice extends its pitch upward. When we are depressed we speak almost in a monotone.

---

[11] Many authorities use the term *stress* instead of *accent*. In this book, *stressed* refers to the syllable that is marked in a dictionary. Thus in the next-to-last example above, the word *anything* is not accented because there is no pitch prominence on any syllable. But a dictionary marks it *'an-y-thing* or *an'-y-thing*, with a stress mark on the first syllable. What this means is that *if* the speaker decides to make the word *anything* prominent, he will put an accent on the first syllable. *Stressed* means 'accentable.'

[12] See Bolinger 1972, pp. 261–312.

As this feature is not usually under voluntary control, it is another instance of instinctive gesture.

Direction is usually connected with pause. The two together are the
punctuation marks of speech. The tendency in all languages, in making
statements, is to have a fairly high pitch toward the beginning of a sentence and then to drift down to the lowest pitch at the end; the direction
plus the following pause or silence is a kind of period. The opposite
direction is a kind of comma, occurring at a major break which is not
a final one, as in the following:

$$\text{If you're}\quad \text{read}^{\text{y}}\ \text{let's}\quad \text{g}_{\text{o}.}$$

The pitch follows a generally upward movement in **If you're ready** and
switches to a downward movement in **let's go.** In questions that are
answered by **yes** or **no,** the direction often tends to be up all the way.
Such a question, with its answer, is similar to the example just given:

$$\text{"Do you}\quad \text{like}\quad \text{them?"}\qquad \text{"Very}\quad \text{m}^{\text{u}}\text{c}_{\text{h."}}$$

In both cases what is incomplete goes up and the completion comes
down, an alternating tension and relaxation that again is basically
gestural. (Actually, as many yes–no questions in English go down in
pitch as go up. The ones that go up are those in which the speaker is
genuinely curious. Rising intonation is often cited as one grammatical
mark of a yes–no question, but it is more truly gestural, like raised
eyebrows.)

Relative height is associated with importance. If in an example like the
If you're ready one just discussed there happen to be two separations
instead of one, a higher pitch goes at the major break:

$$\text{If you're}\ \text{ready}\ \text{when I}\ \text{get}\ \text{the}^{\text{re}}\ \text{we'll}\quad \text{g}_{\text{o}.}$$

$$\text{If you're}\ \text{read}^{\text{y}}\ \text{when I}\ \text{get there}\ \text{we'll}\quad \text{g}_{\text{o}.}$$

The first says 'If you're ready when I get there': the extra-high rise in pitch puts the major break between *there* and *we'll.* The second says 'when I get there we'll go': the extra-high pitch puts the major break between *ready* and *when.* Or, when a speaker wants to show or pretend that something is of no importance, he literally "plays it down" by putting the accent at the lowest pitch:

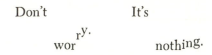

Whatever the gestural ties of intonation may be, all languages stereotype it into patterns that are more or less arbitrary. In English one can usually tell a command regardless of the syntactic form of the sentence:

On your
f
e
e
t.

makes a good command, but would be pretty abrupt as the answer to a question. (Commands, of course, are characteristically abrupt—we are assuming that we have the right to control someone's actions.) On the other hand,

fe
On your
e
t.

makes a good answer to *How am I supposed to get there?* but not a good command (though it might do for the repetition of a command). Where stereotyping is most noticeable is with instances of set verbal expressions that always or almost always occur with a particular intonation. For example, *Search me* 'I don't know' always has the shape

(The same intonation is used on *Don't look at me* when it has that meaning.) *That's the ticket* has the shape

That's
   the
     tick^{et.}

Except for stereotypes like these, intonation patterns are not confined to particular words or phrases, but cover whole utterances, whether short or long. If we wish to command someone to do something immediately, we may put the entire command intonation on the one-syllable word *Now,* or we can stretch it over **Get busy and do that right now:**

No
  \w!   Get busy and do that right no_{w.}

(Notice the jump, in both cases, on **Now,** which signals the accent.) In order to make sure that everything that belongs in the pattern gets in, we sometimes add an extra syllable if the utterance would otherwise be too short. So for the word **Christ** on a pattern that depends for its effect on having a clearly enunciated high pitch followed by an abrupt drop:

Kee-
    ^{rist} you make 'em _{strong!}

(This sentence was under a cartoon of a skull depicting someone who had just swallowed a corrosively strong drink.) **Kee-rist** is an intonational by-form of a word, such as we also find in **kerplunk, kersplash, kerboom, kerwhack.** There is a pattern of successive accents that depends for its climactic effect on having each accent higher in pitch than the preceding ones. The more there are, the greater the emphasis. So while **I'll knock the daylights out of you** says enough, if **living** is added then another accent can be produced:

                day
            liv
I'll knock the   ing
              lights out of you.

We can be pretty sure that intonation is the purpose here, since *living* with *daylights* is either nonsensical or redundant.

Just as we add words or syllables to fill out an intonation, we sometimes add them to make sure that an accent falls where we want it. This is the basis for the so-called emphatic *do* conjugation of the verb in English. In answer to **Why didn't you eat it?** one may reply either

<pre>
                         ate
            I
                      it.
</pre>

or

<pre>
                            did
             I
                         eat it.
</pre>

The latter is more usual and more effective, because *ate* includes too much—at least three things: the meaning of the verb *to eat,* the past tense, and the affirmation of the action. *Did* specializes in the latter two and gets rid of the irrelevant *eat*—one can, of course, say merely *I did.* (In the exchange *"Did you throw it away?"*—*"No, I ate it"* we could not say *I did eat it,* for the emphasis here has to be on the meaning of *eat* as against *throw away.*)

Intonation patterns are widely shared among languages, though there are considerable differences too. The Kunimaipa language of New Guinea has several patterns that resemble those in English quite closely, even including one that is like the mid-high-low curve that we use for intensification in expressions like

<pre>
       o^o ple^a so^o
          oh   se   oo
</pre>

(for example, in **So! You didn't keep your word after all!**)[13] The distinction in English between questions introduced by interrogative words *(Why did you go? Where is she? What's the difference?),* usually with a falling pitch at the end, and yes–no questions *(Is he ready? Will it work? Have you met them?),* typically with a rising pitch at the end, is shared by many languages of varied parentage.

---

[13] See Pence 1964.

ACOUSTIC PHONETICS

The organs of articulation are visible. The sound wave is not. Eye-minded scientists have to *see* things, and until that was possible not much progress was made in acoustic phonetics.

The sound spectrograph machine, unveiled shortly after the Second World War, gave phoneticians what they needed for their leap forward. It made visible exactly those components of sound that are indispensable in the coding of speech. It also opened the way to producing artificial speech of high quality, which led to a new phase in experimental phonetics: by varying each component of the signal separately, phoneticians have been able to determine what each one contributes to the intelligibility of speech. Other machines have been of similar value in more specialized ways, such as the melodic analyzer at the University of Toronto, a computer that displays intonation curves from either live or recorded speech on a television screen.

It was already known that the speech organs, like any other musical instrument, produce a fundamental pitch (the glottal tone, from the vibrations of the vocal cords) along with a series of overtones, each an even multiple of the fundamental. For example, if the fundamental tone has a frequency of 100 cycles per second, there will also be audible to a trained ear another tone at 200, another at 300, and so on. Not all sound-producing instruments produce overtones—a tuning fork is designed not to, since its utility depends on its sending out just one frequency—but overtones are what give the richness to a violin or a flute, and they are essential to speech.

The fundamental, low for males, high for females and children, is the speech melody with its ups and downs. It is the carrier wave for intonation, accent, and—in tone languages—tone. Most of the remaining information in speech is in the overtones. They are controlled by the filtering mechanism of the throat, mouth, and nose, which damp or reinforce particular frequencies in tune with the cavities that are shaped by setting the tongue in one position or another, raising or lowering the velum to involve the nasal passage, and rounding or spreading the lips.

How this mechanism works can be seen most easily in the way vowels are made. When the tongue is placed in position for the sound of [i], the resonating cavities pass and reinforce any overtones in the region of 250 cycles per second[14] and do the same with any in the region of

---

[14] Cycles are a measure of frequency. They correspond to speed of vibration. If the vibrating source completes twenty to-and-fro motions in a second, the frequency is 20 cps. This also means that the pulsations of the air—alternating compressions and decompressions—are passing a fixed point at the rate of 20 per second. One such fixed point is the ear, which apprehends the pulsations as sound. In place of cycles per second, the international term *hertz* (abbreviated *Hz*) is favored nowadays.

2500 cps, while damping the overtones at other frequencies. The bundles of overtones thus reinforced at any particular region are called *formants,* and when they are relatively steady in their pitch we hear the combination as a vowel. If they move slowly up or down, the result is a glide; if rapidly, one or another consonant. For most sounds (English [r] is an exception), two formants are enough for the sound to be identified, though the voice actually produces more. These two critical formants are the *first* (the lowest in pitch) and the *second.* So the vowel [i] consists basically of a steady first formant at about 250 cps and a steady second formant at about 2500 cps. The vowel [a] has its first at about 750 and its second at about 1200.[15] The other front vowels have intermediate values, and the back vowels all have lower second formants (see Figure 3–2).

If the two formants are made to slide just fast enough from the [a] position to the [u] position, what we hear is the diphthong [aw], as in the name **Dow.** If they slide in the opposite direction the opposite glide is produced and **Dow** becomes **wad** [wad]. If instead of this latter gradual slide there is an abrupt transition from the [w] position to the [a] position, the [wa] becomes [ba] and **wad** turns to the **bod-** of **body.** The consonants are thus essentially abrupt movements of the formants, the glides relatively slow movements, and the vowels are steady-state.

The formants do most of the work, but not quite all of it. Most consonants do have a "noise" component, which is more important for some than for others. The hissing noise is necessary for [s], especially to distinguish it from the hushing sound of [š] and the frying noise of [f]. The slight explosion that goes with [g] contributes very little; stops depend less on noise than fricatives do.

Figure 3–2 shows that female speakers (and by the same token preadolescent boys) have a slightly different range from that of adult males. Their formants tend to be higher; this corresponds to the smaller size of the female skull and the smaller resonating cavities. How is it that the sexes have no difficulty understanding each other? The answer to this question illustrates one of the most fundamental truths of language: its integral wholeness, supplying information from all levels simultaneously. It may take a moment or two to begin understanding a person whose

---

[15] Illustration: If the speaker is "singing" a fundamental pitch of 120 cps, there will be overtones at 240, 360, 480, 600, 720, 840, 960, and so on. For the vowel [a], those closest to 750, namely 600, 720, and 840 (but especially 720), will be reinforced to make the first formant, while the rest will be damped. There will also be overtones (always multiples of 120) at 1080, 1200, 1320, 1440, and so on. Those closest to 1200, namely 1080, 1200 itself, and 1320, will be reinforced as the second formant of [a], while the rest will be damped. As this shows, it makes little difference what the fundamental pitch is. One can "sing" any speech tune and there will almost always be enough overtones in the right regions to be picked up and reinforced for any vowel.

FIGURE 3–2
Average Values of First and Second Formant Frequencies
For Eight English Pure Vowels*

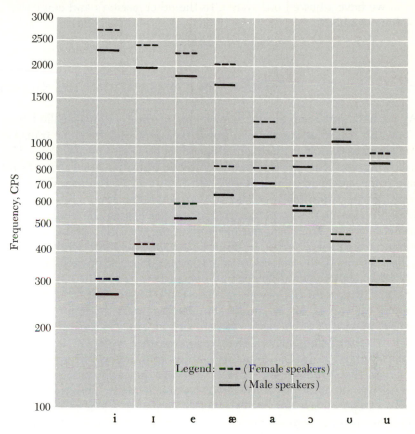

SOURCE: Adapted from Denes and Pinson 1963, p. 118. Courtesy of Bell Laboratories.
* The vowels were spoken in isolated and single-syllable words.

sounds, though in the same language, differ from ours. But we soon catch on. Suppose we are a man listening to a woman. First we subconsciously note what her highest and lowest vowel positions are. We know that those two extreme positions correspond to our own [i] and [a], even if they are somewhat higher or lower than ours. (There is very little danger that no [i] or [a] will turn up—count the number of them in any three or four lines on this page.) This gives us a kind of mental map of her vocal tract, and we can then estimate the position of her other vowels because they are almost certain to be in the same *relative* positions as ours: her [i] is to her [e] as our [i] is to our [e]. Now we confirm our hypothesis by guessing at what she is saying. Most conversations have something of the obvious about them, and if we can understand the consonants, which are more distinct than the vowels, we can usually identify a word or two. Soon we have adjusted our system to the other person's and can carry on with no trouble.[16]

SOUNDS IN COMBINATION: THE SYLLABLE

As we have just seen, abrupt movements of the formants—called *transitions*—are heard as consonants. But it turns out that different transitions are heard as the same consonant, depending on what vowel follows. If the following vowel is [i], the second-formant transition for [t] is abruptly up; if the following vowel is [u], the transition is abruptly down. And with [æ] the transition is neither up nor down, but level. Clearly it is not the direction of the transition that gives the cue to the consonant, but something else. This turns out to be what the transition points at, a fixed frequency called a *locus*. In Figure 3–3 we see how, with [t] and a following vowel, the transitions of the second formant of each vowel from [i] (2520 cps) to [u] (720 cps) all bend leftward toward a frequency of about 1800 cps. (If the vowels precede the [t] instead of following it, the figure is reversed, left to right.) Similar diagrams for other consonants would show that each has a characteristic locus. Consonants appear to have a natural frequency of their own, one that we never actually hear but is pointed to by the formants leading into or away from the vowel.

Given that a consonant cannot be heard properly unless there is a vowel next to it to provide these directional bends, perhaps the "real" units of speech are not vowels and consonants taken separately, but combinations of them—some larger unit within which events take place that phoneticians unscramble as distinctive sounds. Is there such a unit?

The obvious candidate is the syllable. Syllables have been counted for as long as there has been poetry. Children play with them, spacing them out in their jeering chants *(Fred-die-is-a-fraid-y-cat)* and emphatic warnings, like this one from a four-year-old, with each syllable separately accented: *You-bet-ter-not-say-that-to-mo-ther!* The earliest form of "sound writing" (see page 488) was syllabic, with a separate sign for each syllable, and syllabaries are still the easiest form of writing to learn.[17] Ordinary speakers seem to find the syllable the natural minimum unit of speech.

The syllable owes much of its obviousness to the role it plays in rhythm. It is the unit that comes closest to being emitted at a regular rate. Each

---

[16] See Lamendella 1975, Ch. 2, p. 38.
[17] Gelb 1963, p. 203.

FIGURE 3–3
Locus of the Consonant [t] Followed by the Vowels
From [i] (Top) to [u] (Bottom)

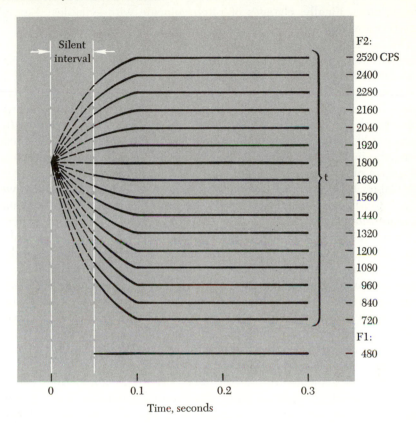

syllable is a *pulse*, or beat, timed to about one-sixth of a second,[18] and this more or less regular pulsation is tied to other rhythmic activity of the body.[19] The syllable is the unit that gathers up all the phonic events that we sense to occur "at the same time," even though instruments will show that some of them occur in sequence. Whenever we make intentional changes in our speech, the syllable is what we attach them to. If we want to make the word *beautiful* emphatic, one way is to put an accent on the first syllable:

Beau
tiful!

---

[18] Lenneberg 1967, pp. 113–15.
[19] Bullowa 1972, p. 2.

Another way is to lengthen the first syllable: *B e a u tiful!* Still another is
to add a syllable: ***Beyootiful!*** And if an insertion is to be made for humor
or emphasis, it is fitted around existing syllables: ***absoposilutely, abso-
bloodylutely.*** Finally, changes of pitch coincide with syllables: ***Funny?***
has its rise on *-ny.*

The syllable has not always received the attention it deserves.
Linguists are uncomfortable with it, partly because of its fuzzy borders.[20]
One can distinguish **Ben Tover** from *bent over* by the aspirated [tʰ] in
the first, which shows that the division is [bɛn tʰovər] rather than [bɛnt
ovər]; but often the separation is impossible to locate precisely. In ordinary speech ***one's own*** sounds like ***one zone; an ungodly*** like *a nun godly;*
palisades like *palace aides;* and so on. But despite this lack of neatness,
or maybe in part because of it, the reality of the syllable is guaranteed
by human physiology.

Syllables have a typical internal structure: a *nucleus,* which is a vowel
or a vowel-like consonant ([r] or [l], for example), with or without one
or more *satellites* in the form of consonants before or after the nucleus.
Probably the most striking thing about any language, in the impression
it makes on listeners who do not understand it and notice sounds rather
than meanings, is the way its syllables are built. The main difference is
between harmonic and inharmonic sounds, between music and noise. A
language in which the satellites are few sounds musical; one with numerous satellites, especially voiceless ones, is noisy. English stands about
midway. It has syllables consisting of a nucleus alone, as in the words
oh and ***ah,*** and syllables in which the nucleus is flanked by two or more
satellites on each side, as in ***splashed*** and ***sprints.***

Not all arrangements are possible. The permitted combinations can be
seen by building consonants one by one around a nucleus. Starting with
oh, for example, and adding successively to the left, one may get ***row,
crow,*** and ***scrow;*** with *a* (that is, the sound [e]) might come ***lay, play,***
and ***splay;*** or with ***ill,*** the words ***will*** and ***twill.*** Studying many such examples would reveal something about the possible arrangements of con-
sonants to the left of the nucleus. If there is only one it can be any
consonant in the language except [ŋ]. If there are two, [l] and [r] occur
pretty freely as the second and the stops and voiceless fricatives as the
first: ***truce, pry, plea, sly, free.*** If there are three, the first will be [s]:
splurge, stray. But there are restrictions: no [tl], no [sb], no [sfl], and
so on. A similar build-up will reveal the situation at the end of the
syllable—for example, ***oh–own–owned, bur–Bearse–burst–bursts.*** The
entire structure of English syllables can be stated in a rather complex

---

[20] One linguist has referred to the syllable as "the stepchild of linguistic analysis."
See Pike 1957, p. 38.

set of rules embodying classes of consonants and positions relative to the nucleus and to one another.

Units of sound do not stop with the syllable, but they do become progressively harder to relate to any special phonic event, so that it gets less and less profitable to try to single them out. Above the level of the syllable is the breath group—a series of syllables spoken with one expiration of breath. It generally coincides with a particular intonation shape. Still larger units can be vaguely identified with changes in timing and intonation. A person telling a story will drop to a low pitch at the end of a sentence and a still lower pitch at the end of what would be a paragraph in writing, and will slow the syllables down and drop to the lowest pitch of all at the very end.

Some linguists have thought to find special phonic events tied to the separation of words, which they have identified as *junctures.* There are such events that occur more often than not, but they are very slippery entities. The sentences **It's also easy** and **It's all so easy** can be distinguished by the greater length in **all,** but a different style of speech erases the distinction. The same is true of the following pair:

"Is it a real rock?"—"No, it's a sham rock."

"Is it a rose?"—"No, it's a shamrock."

The word **hambone,** unlike the word **trumpet,** seems to be marked by greater length of syllables in such a way that we recognize it as actually made up of two words, but then we realize that **trombone** may have the same length; the same is true of **tumbledown** (two words) and **ramshackle** (one), **bedpost** (two) and **compost** (one). If we hear the phrase **strength through joy** we know that there has to be a separation between **strength** and **through** because we can hear a double consonant [θθ], and we know that there are no double consonants within simple words in English. But we would not know that if we did not already know the structure of English.

And that is the best reason for ending the build-up of sound-units at the level of the syllable: anything higher is almost necessarily related to what speakers have learned about the meaning and structure of their language. Meaningless syllables (syllables that do not exist as words or affixes in their own right) are common. But breath groups are usually arranged by speakers to fit divisions of sense, and larger units, even more so.[21]

---

[21] Even with the syllable we sometimes resort to higher structure to make a division. This usually happens when the phonetic facts can be interpreted in more than one way, and appealing to a higher level solves the problem—and also makes it easier to fit the whole system together. How do we "hear" the word *hire?* The

SYSTEM AT THE PICTURE STAGE:
PHONEMES AND ALLOPHONES

The sounds we have been describing have mostly been the distinctive sounds of English. This was just to have a point of reference; it is easier to identify a sound as [n] and then to describe it than to start with the descriptive data and end with the identification. English has enough distinctive sounds to make this somewhat illogical procedure practical. If it had fewer, or if they were less varied, a different approach would have been necessary.[22] The important thing to remember is that we have so far been concerned with sounds as sounds—their production, transmission, and reception. Now we must look at them as points in a system, recalling what we noted earlier (page 15) about pebbles and smells.

Since a phoneme is a kind of idealization, a way has to be found to relate it to happenings in the real world—that is, to real acts of speech. This is done by setting up two entities, the *phone* and the *allophone*. The phone is a phoneme-token, a single instance of the utterance of a phoneme on a particular occasion by a particular speaker. Theoretically it differs in unimportant ways from every other phone of that phoneme that has ever been produced. No two can ever be identical, because the combination of head position, air pressure in the lungs, amount of mucus in the nose or saliva in the mouth, objects interfering between speaker and hearer, and other such disturbances at that moment in history is unique. The *allophone* is a phoneme-subtype, a particular *way* of uttering a phoneme in a particular phonological environment. For example, we have already spoken of aspirated and unaspirated [t]. Actually we should have used two separate symbols for this, [tʰ] and [t⁼], for as sounds they are different. The distinction that will be made from this point on is to put the phoneme between diagonal lines, /t/, and the allophone in brackets. So we can say that the phoneme /t/ in English has the allophones [tʰ] and [t⁼].

Each allophone must be described in relation to whatever it is that

---

[r] is sufficiently vowel-like to enable us to count an extra syllable pulse for it and say that *hire* is a two-syllable word. But we tend not to do this, even though with identical-sounding *higher* we would, to make the extra syllable match the suffix *-er*. The same is true of other pairs with final [r]: *lyre–liar, spire–spier, sire–sigher*. In some cases with [l] as well as [r] no suffixes or other higher structural elements are involved, and our only clue is spelling: *flour–flower* (the same word historically), *lisle–Lyall, vile–vial*.

[22] English has thirty-six phonemes, give or take a couple depending on whose dialect is being analyzed and who the analyst is. It has been calculated that ten phonemes is probably the smallest number to be found in any language and eighty the upper limit, with 95 percent of the world's languages having between fourteen and forty-three. See Sigurd 1963, pp. 96–97.

causes the phoneme to be pronounced that way. Comparing the words *catnip, bent, enter, stem, intake, retain,* and *team,* we find that aspiration is present in the last three but not in the first four. If we look for a common factor in the last three words we find that in all of them the /t/ is unclustered (not combined with any other consonant in the same syllable) and followed by a full vowel. In the others it is either followed by a reduced vowel (*enter*) or by none (*catnip*), or is combined in a cluster with /s/ (*stem*). Aspiration is thus characteristic of the English voiceless stops when they are unclustered and followed by full vowels, which give sufficient time for the delay in voicing that causes the aspiration. So /p/ is aspirated ([pʰ]) in *pain* and *depot* but is not aspirated ([p⁼]) in *Spain, sip,* or *apt.* And /k/ is aspirated in *decay* but not in *skill, decorate,* or *act.*

These environments can be refined still further to agree with greater or lesser degrees of aspiration. In clusters having an /l/ or an /r/ as the second member, there is a fair amount of aspiration, especially with /p/, if the other conditions remain the same. So *pry* has almost as much aspiration as *pie,* though *true* and *crew* have somewhat less than *too* and *coo.* Also, different things happen at the end of a word before a pause—the stop may or may not be "released." A release is simply a letting go of the air, a removal of the obstruction, without a vowel being added. It is like a mild aspiration. So in saying *hip* we have the choice of leaving our lips closed when we finish the word and keeping the air pent up in the mouth, or opening the lips and letting it out. The effect is most audible with /p/, least with /k/. Though there are ways of symbolizing all these variants, we have no need for such a fine-spun analysis, and will ignore them.

But this is getting ahead of the story. If all we ever hear is phones, describable in phonetic terms as allophones, how do we *know* that we have these phonemes in the first place? What right do we have to speak of allophones "of" /p/? What establishes /p/ as a phoneme?

The proof is in comparing utterances that are partly alike and finding out what it is that makes them different. Analysts working with their own language have a head start, since all speakers have a feel for the system of sounds they use, even though it may not be scientific. The person who makes a pun like *The undertaker said he was going to buy his little boy a rocking hearse* is aware—and expects the hearer to be aware—of a minimal or near-minimal contrast between *hearse* and *horse.* To speak pig Latin—*Arymay antsway ouyay otay aitway orfay erhay* for *Mary wants you to wait for her*—children have to sense the consonant-plus-vowel structure of the syllable. So this makes it fairly easy for the native speaker to hit upon *minimal pairs:* items that differ by only one element and that rather quickly reveal the phonemes when enough of them are accumulated. In English one can quickly list a riming set like *bay–day–*

Fay–gay–hay–jay–Kay–lay–may–nay–pay–ray–say–shay–way, which gives a strong hint of distinctive consonants /b d f g h ǰ k l m n p r s š w/; and it takes only a moment more to confirm them by other sets like *robe–rode–rogue–roam–roan–rope–roar.*

The analyst confronting a new language has a rougher time, for there is neither a feel nor a folklore to fall back on. Or rather there is a folklore —that of the analyst's own language—which is misleading. One who approaches English from the standpoint of a foreign language might, for instance, hear the words *vial* and *phial* and be told that they mean the same, and conclude, erroneously, that the difference between the sounds [v] and [f] is only accidental—that English has a labiodental consonant phoneme (which might be represented by some such symbol as /ꝟ/) that is indifferently voiced or voiceless. But eventually it would become clear that the feature of voice is significant in pairs like *vary–fairy, leave–leaf, shelve–shelf,* and hence that /v/ and /f/ are phonemes independent of each other.

Nor is it all smooth sailing even in one's native language. Since a phoneme consumes a certain length of time, however short, there is always the question of where the borders are and of whether a given span of time should be assigned to just one phoneme or split down the middle and assigned to two; this is the problem of *unit phoneme* versus *cluster.* In music, a combination of notes which if played simultaneously would be called a chord may be played in rapid succession and still be regarded as a kind of unit chord, termed an arpeggio. Or it may be regarded merely as a very rapid succession of independent, single notes. The same uncertainty attaches to phonemic "chords"—one can sometimes choose between regarding the combination as one unit or two.

Some clusters are fairly easy to deal with. One might hesitate briefly over words like *clay–cray–dray–flay–fray–gray–play–spay–splay–spray–stay–sway.* Are the consonant sounds preceding the vowels in these words units or clusters? If they are unit phonemes, then *sway* differs from *way* in that one starts with / ŵ / and the other with /w/; if they are clusters, then the difference is that *sway* has one more phoneme than *way,* the initial /s/. But it would soon be clear that by splitting /s/ from /w/ the total number of phonemes could be reduced—instead of three phonemes, /s/, /w/, and / ŵ /, to account for *say, way,* and *sway,* only two would be needed; and by splitting /r/ from /d/ one could account not only for *dray* in addition to *day* and *ray* but also for part of the contrast between *dry* and *yard.*

Other clusters are more troublesome. Many linguists prefer to identify the vowel portion of the word *bay* not as /e/ but as /ey/, reserving the symbol /e/ for the vowel in *bet* and not using the symbol /ε/ at all. There are good phonetic reasons for this, since *bay* does have a pronounced glide, though some of it disappears in *bait* and most of it in *baiter.*[23] Such a scheme reduces the total number of vowel phonemes and matches nicely with the other diphthongs, such as /ay/, that are needed anyway.

A similar case with the consonants is that of the initial sounds in *chump* and *jump,* which we have been treating as unit phonemes and writing as /č ǰ/. Some phonologists prefer to regard them as phoneme clusters: /tš dž/. (Notice how close *a gray chip* is to *a great ship.*) One reason for not doing so is the way the sounds fall in the consonant chart (Table 3–1) on page 41. Notice that if [č ǰ] were moved into the "stop" row, not only would that row be filled out better but the entire "affricate" row would become unnecessary. This amounts to ignoring the fricative half of the "cluster" and assuming that the "affricates" in English are merely palatal stops with automatic affrication.

There is also good psychological evidence that /č ǰ/ are sensed as units and not as combinations. When we make mistakes, switching sounds from one part of a word or phrase to another, we never split /č/ or /ǰ/ up, though we do split other clusters. *Crack some ice* can be fumbled as *Cack some rice,* splitting the cluster /kr/; but *Chuck the Ape* is never fumbled as *Tuck the Shape.*[24]

So *patterning* is the test for clusters versus simple phonemes, even though the answers it gives are not always clear. It is also the test for deciding whether phonetically different sounds are to be classed as allophones of one phoneme or as separate phonemes.

Again the problem can be understood better if we approach it backwards, assuming the existence of the phonemes and looking for phonic events in their immediate environments that may account for the manifestations being different. Phonemes are affected by the company they keep, much as letters are in ordinary handwriting. When a letter that normally ends with a stroke above the bottom of the line, like a *ƀ* or a *ʋ*, is followed by one that normally starts at the bottom, such as an *ι* or an *ʀ*, the latter starts instead where the former leaves off: *ƀι , ʋι , ƀʀ* . This is called *assimilation* of one shape to another. Assimilation of one sound to another is equally common. Between vowels an English /n/ is generally alveolar, but in the word *tenth,* if the speaker produces a following interdental /θ/, the /n/ too becomes interdental. English /r/ is normally fully voiced, but in a cluster after a voiceless /t/, as in *tree,* it is partially unvoiced.

Different positions in a word bring different influences to bear. The

---

[23] The same reasoning leads to an /ow/ rather than an /o/ in *tow* (but compare *tote* and *toter*), an /iy/ instead of an /i/ in *bee,* and an /uw/ instead of an /u/ in *boo,* with /o/ then used instead of /ɔ/, /i/ instead of /ɪ/, and /u/ instead of /ʊ/.

[24] See Fromkin 1973, pp. 112–13.

pairs *intent–indent, satin–sadden,* and *sat–sad* illustrate what happens to
/t/ and /d/ in different situations. We have no trouble hearing the difference between the two sounds. They are produced with the same position
of the tongue in all three pairs, and we seem to "hear" voicelessness as
the feature of the /t/. But it is actually manifested in three different
ways. In *intent* it appears as aspiration. In *satin* it appears as a brief
interval of silence right after the tongue makes contact. (Actually, as most
Americans pronounce the word, there is a glottal stop simultaneous with
the tongue contact and then a glottal release through the nose, with the
tongue holding its position; *sadden* does not have the glottal stop, which
eliminates the interval of silence.) In *sat* the /t/ appears as a sharp cut-
off of sound, and the burden of the difference shifts to what happens to
the vowel: it is drawled in *sad* but not in *sat.* In point of actual sound,
sad is longer. But our ear interprets both words as having about the same
length, and this means adding a little bit of nothing—silence—at the end
of *sat,* the same silence that was manifested in *satin.* All these phenomena
are read back into our minds as the voicelessness characteristic of /t/.

Of course, the mind has to be trained to read the evidence this way.
It learns to hear the similarities and ignore the differences. *Phonetic
similarity* is the key to most identifications of two or more phones as
allophones of a single phoneme. The word *Help* can be altered in a number of ways without being so disfigured that when said in an appropriate
environment it will be misunderstood. The /p/ may be released or unreleased. The /ɛ/ may be clipped or drawled. The /l/ may be a fully
articulated lateral, or it may be virtually transformed into a low-back
vowel. Since children learn words before they begin to abstract the distinctive sounds, they are prepared from the first to make allowances. So
long as the integrity of the word is kept, all is well. Minor deviations of
the distinctive sounds are tolerated if enough similarity is retained to
make for identification. (In rapid speech, as we have seen, the alterations
are sometimes anything but minor.)

The variations described for *help* are *free:* we cannot predict from
speaker to speaker, or sometimes even from occasion to occasion with the
same speaker, which ones will occur. Besides this free variation there is
also the *conditioned* variation that we have already noted—for example,
with English voiceless stops, which all speakers uniformly aspirate before
full vowels. Yet here too we have phonetic similarity. The aspirated
[pʰ] of *pill* is not so different from the unaspirated [p⁼] of *spill* as to
make it impossible for them to be "the same," psychologically. Both have
the features that are definitive for English: voicelessness and labiality.
The average speaker simply does not hear the aspiration of [pʰ] as
such; it has to be pointed out to him.

Still, we know that what for one language counts as same, for another
language counts as different, and phonetic similarity is not enough. Even

within a single language two such phonemes as /m/ and /n/ sound very much alike and yet are not heard as the same if they make a difference in meaning. Similarly with aspirated and unaspirated *p*'s, which are separate phonemes in Chinese. So in addition to phonetic similarity it is necessary to appeal to *complementary distribution*—in plain language, the recognition of two things as the same if whatever differences there are can always be correlated with something external. If a car is not moving relative to us and the horn is blowing, we hear one pitch. If it is moving toward us the pitch is automatically higher, and if away from us, automatically lower; so we learn to associate these three complementary manifestations as the "same" horn-blowing. In English the sound [pʰ] never contrasts with [p⁼] in any position—that is, never makes a difference in meaning—and accordingly we take the two as different allophones of one phoneme.

Returning to the *intent–indent, satin–sadden, sat–sad* pairs, we can list several allophones of /t/: one that is aspirated (unclustered, before full vowels), one that is combined with an interval of silence (before most consonants), and one that is *unlike* the /d/ that has a lengthened vowel before it (a /t/ in final position). The allophones of /n/ include one that is interdental (*tenth*), one that is palatal (*inch*), and one that is alveolar (*tint*). The sounds that follow /n/ force it into those positions.

A few uncertainties always remain. A radio ad for *Monk's Bread* may sound as if it were plugging *Monk Spread.* We have seen that a /p/ after an /s/ at the beginning of a syllable is not aspirated, and thus sounds so much like a /b/ that we can hardly tell them apart. So why call it a /p/ rather than a /b/? Again, the kinds of errors we make show that we sense it to be a /p/. *Don't spit the seeds* may be fumbled as *Don't pit the speeds,* not as *Don't bit the speeds;* and *Ace Bradford* may come out as *Base Radford,* but not as *Pace Radford.*

A more complex example is English /t/. In words like *butter, totter, matter, pewter, bitter, atom, sputum, motto, grotto, pity,* and *duty,* for most speakers of American English, the /t/ is reduced to a bare tap which picks up the voicing of the surrounding sounds and becomes almost if not completely indistinguishable from /d/. The result is that *bitter* sounds like *bidder, latter* like *ladder, He hit 'er* like *He hid 'er, let 'em* like *led 'em,* and so on. There are several ways of dealing with this, three of which are worth noting:

1. Continue to call it /t/. This is what most dictionaries do. The justification is that in some dialects /t/ and /d/ are still quite distinct, and it is better to assume that even among those speakers who make them sound alike, some trace of a difference may remain. After all, if we produce a clear /t/ in *atomic* we are not apt to be "thinking" of a /d/ when we say *atom,* even if we do

make it sound like **Adam**—especially if, when we slow down and say **atom** emphatically, we make a clear /t/. Following the criterion "a word is a word," we therefore transcribe **atom** with the same symbols whether in **atom** or in **atomic.**

2. Call it /d/ whenever /d/ is heard. This is what *Webster's Third New International Dictionary* does, and it is justified by phonetic realism: "a sound is a sound."

3. Call it something between the two, using a neutral symbol such as /d̶/ that implies "in this environment the distinction between /t/ and /d/ is lost." This neutral symbol is sometimes called an *archiphoneme.*

In such situations, no solution is perfectly satisfactory. These are uncertainties to be tolerated, areas of vagueness in the language itself. But the noteworthy and comforting fact is that vagueness in phonemes is the exception rather than the rule. Languages are remarkably efficient in keeping their signaling units clear and distinct.

ADDITIONAL REMARKS
AND APPLICATIONS

1. The sound [x] (see pages 39 and 41) was formerly more prevalent in European languages than it is today. (English spelling still preserves a digraph for it, representing the older pronunciation as in **enough, right, bright.**) Why do you suppose it has tended to be replaced by other sounds, such as [h] and [f], or to disappear? Why should [h] and [f] be favored as substitute sounds?

2. A number of the slots in the consonant chart (Table 3–1) are empty as far as English is concerned. In some cases the sound would be difficult if not impossible to produce (a bilabial lateral, for example). In others one could readily fit sounds from languages other than English. See if you can pronounce a syllable containing the vowel [a] and starting with each of the following:

    voiceless bilabial fricative
    voiced dental stop
    voiceless alveolar affricate
    voiced palatal lateral
    voiced velar fricative

3. Some people pronounce the word **veto** with a flapped [ɾ], others with an aspirated [tʰ]. What does this imply about the vowel sound that follows the consonant?

4. In English, as the text points out, vowels are usually nasalized automatically when in the environment of a nasal consonant. But in Bolivian Guaraní, as in French, nasalized vowels contrast with non-nasal vowels. As a result, while a word such as /ã́ɲã/ 'demon' is pronounced [ã́ɲã], one such as /á ɲa/ 'I approach,' in which the vowels are not nasalized, is pronounced [áj̆a]. Explain this as the reverse of what happens in English. (The sound [ɲ] is that of the middle consonant in English **cañon, canyon.**)

5. Tongue twisters are examples of difficult articulations: the phrase **homeland of subversives** appeared in a newspaper column; the phrase **precious brass paper fastener** was stumbled over by a speaker. Try saying them fast. What makes them difficult? (Sometimes just the repetition of a sound is bothersome. See page 393.)

6. The trilled [rr] (sometimes heard in an exaggerated pronunciation of *three: thr-r-ree*) has been a distinctive sound in a number of European languages, but has tended to give way to other *r*-like sounds. In languages where the tongue-tip trill is still required, as in Czech and Latvian, it is usually the last sound a child learns.[25] Can you think of a reason for this?

7. In the Iatmul language of New Guinea the consonants /p/ and /k/ are aspirated when they occur at the beginning of an utterance, as in English. But /t/ in the same position is pronounced interdentally, like [θ] in English. Could this Iatmul [θ] be interpreted as an aspiration too, or at least as the result of an aspiration?

8. Does English have anything resembling whistle speech? Think of the pitches used with the greeting **yoo-hoo** or the exclamation **oh, boy** (and **my gosh, good God,** and so on); are they sometimes whistled with the general meaning that they have with these words? If so, are they examples of whistled *tones* (as in Ticuna) or of whistled *intonation?*

9. The type of intonation to mark separation that is illustrated on page 49 is the most usual one in Western languages, but another type is somewhat more common in English. Say the following over to yourself and decide

   a. whether the intonation still performs the function of separating the parts of the sentence;

   b. whether you can detect a difference of some other kind (say, of mood or feeling) that distinguishes this type from the other:

---

[25] See Rūķe-Draviņa 1965.

If you had to attach the label 'matter of fact' to one of the two pairs (the pair above and the pair on page 49) and the label 'I don't care, it's up to you' to the other, where would the labels go?

10. Certain expressions are used always or almost always with one particular intonation (sometimes with minor variations). Decide whether that is the case with the following, and what the intonations are:

    a. It was Jackie, *all right.* No doubt about it.

    b. She's *all too* concerned about this. Tell her to calm down.

    c. Try this one, *for a change.*

    d. *I'll show them a thing or two!*

    e. "Is this where we get our tickets?"—"*I wouldn't know.*"

    f. *Not a single, solitary thing.*

    g. *Now you've done it!* You've gone and broken the handle!

    h. "Mary's a cad."—"*Oh, I don't know;* she's been OK with me."

    i. "Whose is this?"—"*Search me.* I've never seen it before."

    j. "I don't know, maybe it's OK, but I'm not sure I can use it."— "*Tell you what:* you take it home and try it out for a couple of days, and if you don't like it bring it back and I'll refund your money."

11. The syllable of a word to which an accent is applied when the word is accented is the *stressed syllable.* It seldom varies—knowing where the stress is, is part of knowing the word. Mark the stressed syllables in the following words: *amiableness, intentionally, conversationalist, interconversion, contravene.*

12. When written, a sentence like *Was she more or less courteous* is ambiguous. Is it ambiguous in speech? If not, why not?

13. How important is intonation in determining whether *Did you see her* is a question or not? (Can it be pronounced with a falling intonation and still be a question?) Suppose an interviewer is getting information from an interviewee and among other things says

    Your name—

    Your age—

    Your present address—

How important is intonation now in deciding whether these would be felt as questions or as commands?

14. There is a construction in English that smacks of archaism yet sur·
vives in certain forms. An example is *I don't want to go but go I
must.* Could its survival be due to its intonational effectiveness?
Explain.

15. The following sentence was spoken by someone whose family objected to his using homemade bread for toast (they thought it was
too good for that): *If I bake some frésh bread may I have some* [of
the old homemade bread] *for my toast? Fresh is* logically redundant,
because one does not bake stale bread. Why does it have to be included here?

16. Study the following pairs and see if you observe a difference in the
boldface expressions in terms of length—whether one of the expressions in each pair is pronounced more distinctly or with greater
deliberation. If you notice a difference, try to account for it as a
difference in meaning or function:

    a. The problem with that child is getting her to *grow up.*

    b. The problem with that tree is getting it to *grow up;* it has
       a tendency to spread out too much.

    c. I wonder what the temperature *is out* today.

    d. The boss *is out* today.

    e. Whose *side?*

    f. Who's *sighed?* ('Who has sighed?')

    g. "How's the temperature out today?"—*"Cool,* man."

    h. "What do you think of it?"—*"Cool,* man."

    i. Can't I have another *comforter* for this bed? It's cold in here.

    j. They say that Jesus is the *Comforter* of mankind.

If you have difficulty noting any difference in length, try another
experiment: see how fast you can speed up each expression, and
note whether one seems to lose its identity sooner than the other.

17. If you were saying the sentence *I wrote the word "cues," which is
c-u-e-s, c-u-s-e* (spelling out the letters), would you more or less consciously adjust the pauses to make sure it was understood? And in
the following sentences, would *The reason is man* be pronounced the
same way?

    We must always expect discord. The reason is man.

    "What is the reason?"—"The reason is man."

18. Pronounce the sentence **Please don't let Scarface dance that fandango too fast.** Account for anything peculiar you notice about the rhythm.

19. Compare the following two sentences:

   What do you have in the clothes line?
   What do you have on the clothesline?

   Do you hear a difference between **clothes line** and **clothesline?** If so, is it one that is likely to be heard all the time?

20. Say the sound [i] followed by the sound [o] and repeat the succession a few times. Then whistle two pitches, one high and one low, again repeating the succession. Do you note anything similar happening in the movement of your tongue? If so, does it appear that one of the pitches of a vowel (as it happens, it is the second formant) is created in much the same way as the pitch of whistling? In both cases, what is happening to the size of the cavity in front of the tongue?

21. Opera goers often complain that they cannot understand the words when a soprano hits her high notes. Suppose she is singing at a pitch of 1000 cps, which is approximately two octaves above middle C. Look at Figure 3–2 and see if you can tell what is causing the trouble.

22. The voice-operated typewriter is a machine that "listens" to a speaker and types out what the person says, using ordinary letters and spaces. Why should it be comparatively easy to build such a machine to respond to one particular voice but not to a variety of voices? What does this tell us about the superior integrative functions of the human brain?

23. Among the by-products of acoustic phonetics is one that is of controversial value in courts of law: consult the *Reader's Guide to Periodical Literature* for references to *voiceprints.*

24. Describe the allophones of /t/ in the following words: **shanties, Cervantes, mutton, pity.** Describe these allophones of /n/: **pawnshop, naughty, neat, wince, panther.** Explain the effect of the environments that cause these changes in /n/.

25. Make a chart with the English consonants on each of the two coordinates, to see how many of the cells can be filled with two-consonant final clusters in English words. Below is a partial model:

Second member of cluster

	p	b	t	d	k	g	š
p			√				
b				√			
t							
d							
k			√				
g				√			
š			√				

First member of cluster

Words used for testing: *apt, robbed, baked, tagged, flashed.* Some hints of other words to use: *lathed* (from *to lath,* not *to lathe*), *rouged, lymph, pulse, sacks, scratched.*

26. Study the following list of Guaraní words[26] and mark the syllable types, using C for consonant and V for vowel. For example, are there any CVC syllables (like those in English *tick-tock*) or CCV syllables (like English *tree*)? In marking the syllable divisions, assume (1) that when a consonant occurs between vowels it belongs in the syllable with the following vowel, and (2) that when two or three vowels occur together they belong in a single syllable.

man	/kũĩmáe/	water	/ɨ/
woman	/kúñã/	river	/ɨ/
her husband	/ĩmẽ/	house	/o/
his wife	/hẽmiréko/	roof	/opitía/
his father	/tu/	fire	/táta/
his mother	/íčɨ/	firewood	/ñepéʔa/
child	/mĩčĩáẽ/	ash	/tãnĩmu/
old man	/néči/	smoke	/tãtãtĩ/

---

[26] From Rosbottom 1968.

sky	/ára/	his head	/ĩnákã/
rain	/ãmã/	his forehead	/hesíba/
sun	/kuarái/	his hair	/íˀa/
moon	/nási/	his chin	/hãníkã/
star	/nasitáta/	his beard	/hẽnibá/
lightning	/ãmãbéra/	his neck	/inánu/
rainbow	/níˀi/	his back	/ikúpe/
day	/ára/	his shoulder	/inatíˀi/
night	/pítũ/	his arm	/iníba/
earth	/ibi/	his upper arm	/inibáipi/
tree	/ibíra/	his elbow	/hẽnibána/
its leaf	/ho/	his hand	/ípo/
its root	/hápo/	his leg	/íˀu/
fish	/píra/	his knee	/itába/
his tongue	/íkũ/	his shin	/ĩtĩmãkã/
his mouth	/inúru/	his foot	/ípi/
his lip	/héme/	his toe	/ĩpĩsã/
his tooth	/hãĩ/	his skin	/ipíre/
his nose	/ítĩ/	his bone	/ĩkãgʷẽ/
his eye	/hésa/	blood	/túgʷi/
his ear	/ĩnámi/		

27. The examples *white shoes* versus *why choose* and *nitrate* versus *night rate* are often cited in connection with syllable boundaries. What is the problem? Find a couple of additional pairs like these.

28. The most complex consonant clusters in English occur at the ends of words—for example, $/ks\theta s/$ in *sixths,* $/lkts/$ in *mulcts.* Find two or three more examples of at least three consonants together. Why does this happen only at the ends of words? (Consider how often $/s\ z\ t\ d/$ are found at the ends of words, and why.)

29. Discuss the problem of *scary* versus *'S Gary* in the following:
    "Who is it out there?"—" 'S Gary" ('It's Gary').

30. The words *azure, pleasure, measure, Asian, fusion,* and a good many more have the phoneme /ž/ in the middle of a word. Can you think of any English word in which it occurs at the beginning? The end? Look up the origin of the words *rouge* and *beige* and note how loanwords from a foreign language can extend the range of native phonemes.

31. In the Ignaciano language of Bolivia there is a fricative bilabial [ƀ] that occurs only before the vowels /e/ and /i/, and a [w] sound that occurs only before /a/. What is the phonemic situation? See if you can account for it in articulatory terms.

32. See if you have a contrast in the following: *fawned–fond, caught–cot, wrought–rot, cawed–cod.* (Speakers in some dialect areas have no contrast here.) If you do, does it carry over into *hornet–horrible, Laurie–sorry?* You almost certainly have a contrast in *mat–met, bat–bet, sad–said, shall–shell, sand–send;* see if this contrast carries over to *marry–merry, Barry–berry, arrow–error.* Do you observe anything here that suggests a blurring influence from a nearby /r/? Does something similar happen in *ferry–fairy* (compare *met–mate*)? Scots English preserves these contrasts even before /r/, but the Scots /r/ is an alveolar flap. Why should the American English variety of /r/ have the effect that it has?

33. The sentence *They can't reason with such people* can be transcribed /ðe kænt rizən wɪθ sʌč pipəl/. Identify

    a. the stop consonants
    b. the voiced consonants
    c. the voiceless fricatives
    d. the voiced fricatives
    e. the affricate
    f. the lateral
    g. the consonants that have aspirated allophones

34. Make a phonemic transcription of the following:

    a. Tell us who did.
    b. Find Chuck Connors.
    c. Get George here now.
    d. Avoid the no-passing zone.
    e. It was quite easy bicycling.

References

Anderson, Lambert. 1959. "Ticuna Vowels with Special Regard to the System of Five Tonemes," *Serie Linguística Especial*, No. 1 (Rio de Janeiro: Museu Nacional), 76–127.

Bendor-Samuel, J. T., and K. W. Spreda. 1969. "Fortis Articulation: A Feature of the Present Continuous Verb in Agbo," *Linguistics* 52:20–26.

Bolinger, Dwight. 1963. "Length, Vowel, Juncture," *Linguistics* 1:5–29.

——— (ed.). 1972. *Intonation* (Harmondsworth, England: Penguins).

Bullowa, Margaret. 1972. "From Communication to Language." Paper read at International Symposium on First Language Acquisition, Florence, Italy, manuscript p. 2.

Cowan, George M. 1948. "Mazateco Whistle Speech," *Language* 24:280–86.

———. 1973. "Segmental Features of Tepehua Whistle Speech," in *Proceedings of the VIIth Congress of Phonetic Sciences, Montreal, 1971* (The Hague: Mouton).

Denes, Peter B., and Elliot N. Pinson. 1963. *The Speech Chain*. Bell Telephone Laboratories, Inc.

Fillenbaum, Samuel. 1971. "Processing and Recall of Compatible and Incompatible Question and Answer Pairs," *Language and Speech* 14:256–65.

Fischer-Jørgensen, Eli. 1967. "Phonetic Analysis of Breathy (Murmured) Vowels in Gujarati," *Indian Linguistics* 28:71–139.

Fromkin, Victoria. 1973. "Slips of the Tongue," *Scientific American* 229:110–17.

Gelb, I. J. 1963. *A Study of Writing*, rev. ed. (Chicago: University of Chicago Press).

Lamendella, John T. 1975. *Introduction to the Neuropsychology of Language* (Rowley, Mass.: Newbury House). Page references are to the manuscript.

Lehiste, Ilse. 1972. "The Timing of Utterances and Linguistic Boundaries," *Journal of the Acoustical Society of America* 51:2018–24.

Lenneberg, Eric H. 1967. *Biological Foundations of Language* (New York: Wiley).

Pence, Alan. 1964. "Intonation in Kunimaipa (New Guinea)," *Linguistic Circle of Canberra Publications*, Series A, Occasional Papers, No. 3.

Pike, Kenneth L. 1957. "Grammemic Theory," *General Linguistics* 2:35–41.

Rosbottom, Harry. 1968. "Phonemes of the Guaraní Language," *Linguistics* 41:109–13.

Rūķe-Draviņa, Velta. 1965. "The Process of Acquisition of Apical and Uvular *r* in the Speech of Children," *Linguistics* 17:58–68.

Sigurd, Bengt. 1963. "A Note on the Number of Phonemes," *Statistical Methods in Linguistics*, No. 2.

Zima, Petr. 1966. "On the Functions of Tones in African Languages," *Travaux Linguistiques de Prague* 2:151–56.

SOUNDS AND WORDS 4

The *picture* stage—where out-and-out contrast is the only function of distinctive sounds—begins to be modified as soon as the child picks up the first rules of inflection, the plural of nouns and the past tense of verbs. This grammar lesson includes learning to attach /s/ to *cat* to make *cats,* /z/ to *dog* to make *dogs,* and /əz/ to *witch* to make *witches.* All three have the same function, so the child has no more reason to think of them as different than he has for assuming that a released /p/ in *stop* means something different from an unreleased one in the same position. The child would even find it difficult to *say* something like [kætz] or [dɔgs]; and [wɪčz] or [wɪčs], without an [ə] in between, would be almost impossible. So the contrast between /s/ and /z/, which has been making an absolute distinction between *fuss* and *fuzz* in the child's vocabulary, in this new context makes no difference at all. The same happens with the past tense: to make *worked* the rules call for adding /t/, to make *buzzed,* /d/, and to make *skidded,* /əd/. What the young speaker still needs in order to make a contrast in *bat* and *bad* is of no use in the ending of verbs. The story is repeated with possessive endings: *Jack's, John's,* and *Louise's* duplicate the /s z əz/ of the plural. The result is that for certain purposes /s/ and /z/ are felt to be automatic variants of the same underlying sound, and so are /t/ and /d/. This feeling is enhanced by the fact that the members of the pairs are very much alike anyway (so much so that some languages make no distinction between [s z] or [t d] in any position).

76

SYSTEMATIC PHONEMES AND DISTINCTIVE FEATURES

The real complications come later, as the child stops saying [pæθs] and [wayfs] and begins to say [pæðz] and [wayvz], and even more as he begins to learn the many words that English has taken from foreign languages, especially Greek and Latin. More and more the sounds that previously served only to make words as different as possible are seen to group themselves in pairs or sets that attach to words that are related. As a rule, the members of each pair are phonetically similar. The sound of *f* resembles that of *v*—position and manner are the same, only voicing is different—and though they make an absolute distinction between *half* and *have*, they are clearly related in *half* and *halve*. Though /m/ and /n/ make a total difference in *mine* and *nine*, in *grampa* and *grandfather* they are related. As more and more sophisticated words are picked up, the [č] of *picture* is entangled with the /t/ of *pictorial*, and similar connections are established between *fact* and *factual*, *rite* and *ritual*, and *rapt* and *rapture*, always guided by meaning (no such connection is made between *mute* and *mutual*). *Finish* is associated with *final*, *vineyard* with *vine*, and *linear* with *line*, creating a connection between /ɪ/ and /ay/. Schooling accelerates the process. Many people will eventually connect *strive* with *strife* and add this to *wife–wives*, *life–lives*, *knife–knives*, and other pairs in which /f/ and /v/ are associated, and some will make the same connection with *bereft–bereave* and *cleft–cleave*. Only a few will learn *revelatory* and relate it to *reveal*, strengthening the bond between /ε/ and /i/ that is also to be found in *receive–reception*, *succeed–success*, *redeem–redemption*, *supreme–supremacy*, *zeal–zealous*, and many other such pairs.

The process of interrelating sounds is never finished, for we go on learning new words all our lives, and the ones we learn later tend to have the most complex ties with one another and with the words we already know. But by early adolescence, the English-speaking child has two systems of sounds, the earlier scheme of simple oppositions and the ever-growing network of interconnected pairs and groups. The units of the first system we have been calling *phonemes* and will continue to do so, though the term *autonomous phonemes* is sometimes used, alluding to the fact that they are described independently of any particular word-forms. The units of the second system are sometimes called *morphophonemes*, because they are tightly related to the morphological, or word-forming, level of language. But the term *systematic phonemes* is favored at present and will be used here.

The list of systematic phonemes turns out to be almost identical to that of autonomous phonemes, but it is described differently. Instead of looking merely for contrasts that can be assigned to one distinctive unit or another, with the result that /m/ and /n/ are no more like each other than either is like /ǰ/ or /w/ (since *met* and *net* as words are just as different from each other as either is from *jet* or *wet*), the analyst looks for both resemblances and differences. Take for example the following pairs:

life	to live
half	to halve
grief	to grieve
staff	to stave
calf	to calve

Here one sees that there is some kind of verb-forming process involving a relationship between /f/ and /v/. With the pairs *breath–breathe, wreath–wreathe, bath–bathe,* it is apparent that a similar process involves /θ/ and /ð/. In both cases it is not a whole phoneme that changes in going from the noun to the verb, but only the feature of voice. So instead of having separate entries for these pairs in our dictionary, it is possible to enter them just once with an underlying /f/ or /θ/ respectively, and some such notation as "verb [+ voice]."

As we have already seen, processes of this kind—pluralization, verb suffixation, formation of possessives, and now verb formation—involve natural classes of sounds. The pairs /t d   s z   f v/ differ only in that the first member is voiceless and the second is voiced. The pair /t č/ that distinguished *rite–ritual, pictorial–picture, fact–factual, dental–denture, site–situate,* and so forth, differ essentially only in the addition of palatalization to the second sound. So it is natural to treat systematic phonemes not as impervious wholes but as bundles of features. The rules can then be set up to show a change of just one feature at a time. If /f/ is assigned the articulatory features of labiodental, fricative, and voiceless, and /v/ the features labiodental, fricative, and voiced, the rule for *half–halve* can be written as voiceless ⟶ voiced.

In practice, the strictly articulatory features are not the ones that are used in describing systematic phonemes. They are not quite general enough. As we saw in the last chapter, it was possible to simplify the consonant chart by moving certain items from one slot to another. For example, the [f v] pair, being labiodental, occupied a different column from that of [p b], which are bilabial. By calling both simply "labial" one can save a whole category of sounds. The same principle guides the selection of distinctive features, but it is carried to an extreme of generality that enables it to be used for many languages. (For a time it was thought that just a small set—say a dozen or so—of distinctive features

TABLE 4–1
Feature Specifications for English Systematic Consonant Phonemes

	p	b	t	d	č	j	k	g	f	v	θ	ð	s	z	š	ž	h	m	n	r	l	y	w
CONSONANTAL	+	+	+	+	+	+	+	+	+	+	+	+	+	+	+	+	+	+	+	+	+	−	−
VOCALIC	−	−	−	−	−	−	−	−	−	−	−	−	−	−	−	−	−	−	−	+	+	−	−
HIGH	−	−	−	−	+	+	+	+	−	−	−	−	−	−	+	+	−	−	−	−	−	+	+
LOW	−	−	−	−	−	−	−	−	−	−	−	−	−	−	−	−	+	−	−	−	−	−	−
BACK	−	−	−	−	−	−	+	+	−	−	−	−	−	−	−	−	−	−	−	−	−	−	+
ANTERIOR	+	+	+	+	−	−	−	−	+	+	+	+	+	+	−	−	−	+	+	−	+	−	−
CORONAL	−	−	+	+	+	+	−	−	−	−	+	+	+	+	+	+	−	−	+	+	+	−	−
CONTINUANT	−	−	−	−	−	−	−	−	+	+	+	+	+	+	+	+	+	−	−	+	+	+	+
VOICED	−	+	−	+	−	+	−	+	−	+	−	+	−	+	−	+	−	+	+	+	+	+	+
NASAL	−	−	−	−	−	−	−	−	−	−	−	−	−	−	−	−	−	+	+	−	−	−	−
STRIDENT	−	−	−	−	+	+	−	−	+	+	−	−	+	+	+	+	−	−	−	−	−	−	−
SONORANT	−	−	−	−	−	−	−	−	−	−	−	−	−	−	−	−	−	+	+	+	+	+	+

would be enough to characterize all the phonemes of all languages, but that hope has receded as our inventory of sounds from around the world has grown. Distinctive features are language-specific.)[1] In Table 4–1 we see the distinctive features of English and how they are represented in each systematic consonant phoneme. A plus signifies that the feature is present, a minus that it is absent.

To get the largest coverage possible out of the categories, they are defined somewhat more precisely and arbitrarily than the traditional sense allows. *Consonantal* and *vocalic* are used rather than *consonant* and *vowel* to suggest that the distinction between vowels and consonants is not as rigid as used to be supposed—there are sounds that share both the traits of consonants (typically, complete or partial blocking of the air stream and, acoustically, abrupt movements of the formants) and the traits of vowels (typically, free flow of air through the mouth and steady or slow-moving formants). The differences between the categories are relative. So /r/ and /l/ are viewed as being rather like both consonants and vowels and are accordingly given pluses in both the consonantal and vocalic rows, whereas /y/ and /w/ are viewed as being rather unlike

---

[1] Tae-Yong Pak 1971.

both consonants and vowels and are given minuses.[2] The features *high, low, back,* and *coronal* relate to distinct positions of the tongue during articulation. "High" means that either the front part or the back part is raised. "Low" means that the tongue is kept down, to interfere as little as possible with the flow of air (true of /h/ in English, which has no constriction). "Back" means that the part of the tongue involved in the articulation is the back part. "Coronal" means the opposite—the part of the tongue involved is the tip or blade. The sound of /r/ is coronal because it is made by curling the tip back (it is also neither high nor low, since the tongue hangs about midway in the mouth). An articulation that does not involve the tongue at all will of course get a minus on both counts—/p/, for example, is neither back nor coronal. *Anterior* refers to a general *front* position in the mouth, whether of the tongue or the lips. *Continuant* indicates whether during articulation the air stream continues to flow through the mouth without being interrupted (though not necessarily without being interfered with); it is simply the reverse of *stop* (and "stop" is what "minus-continuant" in the table means). *Nasal* has the obvious meaning, namely that the air stream passes freely through the nose, whether or not it is checked in the mouth. *Sonorant* refers to absence of any interference with the flow of glottal sound (voicedness); thus /m/ and /n/ are sonorants because the vibrating air passes unimpeded through the nose, but they are minus continuant because the air is checked in the mouth: they are "oral stops." *Strident* refers to a high degree of turbulence leading to a noisy sound. (The distinction here is rather arbitrary, because /θ ð/ are just about as noisy as /f v/.) The distinctive feature scheme has been criticized because of its arbitrariness and also because it mixes criteria from both articulation and acoustics— "high" is physiological, but "strident" refers to a quality of sound. Still, if the system works in practice, its hybrid origins should not be held against it.

Systematic phonology has been both hailed and decried as a way of showing how a language drags its past along with it. The rules that derive surface forms from underlying forms bear a more than coincidental resemblance to changes that have taken place in the past, and when we set up a rule such as /f/ ⟶ /v/ we are stating something that is both a historical fact and a present reality. It is the latter because we cannot

---

[2] Besides the fact that it simplifies the classification, there are certain justifications for this in the way the corresponding sounds are made. Thus /r l/ are more vowel-like than /y w/ because, like vowels, they can be prolonged indefinitely as steady-state sounds, whereas /y w/ cannot; this makes it possible for /r l/ to be used as the "nucleus"—the central and most prominent part—of a syllable, as in the second syllable of the words *copper* and *maple.* (Typically the syllable nucleus is a vowel.) At the same time they are more consonant-like than /y w/ because they obstruct the air passage more.

avoid associating /f/ and /v/ given all the word pairs that tie them together. Furthermore, the pairs *divide–divisible, divine–divinity, define–definitive, vice–vicious, deride–derision,* and others show a living kinship between /ay/ and /ɪ/ that reflects a change that occurred in English in the tenth century. Both sounds stem from an original /i/, and if we set up an underlying form with that vowel we get a rule that is both historical and descriptive.

An example of a historical rule showing the economy that results from this kind of notation is the one that spells out the actual phonological change that created such pairs as *breath–breathe* and *half–halve* in the language. It may be verbalized as "Continuants became voiced when they were both preceded and followed by a segment that was sonorant," and it reads as follows:

$$[+\text{continuant}] \longrightarrow [+\text{voiced}] \ / \ [+\text{sonorant}] \ \underline{\hspace{2cm}} \ [+\text{sonorant}]$$

The diagonal line / means 'in the environment of,' and the blank line is the place where the segment in question went. As all English vowels are sonorant, the formula includes vowels as well as /m n r l y w/. Besides the forms already mentioned, this takes care of *wolf–wolves, scurf–scurvy, teeth–teethe, use–use* (noun and verb), and similar pairs. (In all the examples cited except *use–use,* the modern spelling is an indication of what the pronunciation was at the critical period in the history of English. *Teethe,* for example, actually had a vowel *sound* at the end. The earlier spelling of the noun *use* was *us*—the consonant was final in the word.)

Such a rule may even be general enough to eliminate a phoneme. It is no accident that the phoneme /ŋ/, which appeared in the earlier articulatory chart, is absent from the chart of systematic phonemes. If we study the behavior of this phoneme in English we soon realize that it is something of an oddity. The other nasals, /m n/, occur freely in initial position, but /ŋ/ never does: *mine, nine,* but no */ŋayn/. When /ŋ/ occurs anywhere except before /g/ or /k/ it is almost always at a separation of some kind, either between one word and another, as in *hangman,* or just before a suffix, as in *ringing, hanger, singable.* But what makes /ŋ/ seem most suspicious is the fact that we often change an /n/ to an /ŋ/ in rapid speech when a /k/ or a /g/ follows, as in *uncooperative, incapable, ingratitude,* and *on guard,* especially in expressions that are used a great deal (it is more apt to happen with *conquest* than with *inquest,* and always with *handkerchief* but not always with *handcuff*). This makes /ŋ/ look like a mere variant of /n/. To account for it in *ring, sing,* and so forth, we posit underlying forms with /g/. In Standard English there is no [g] sound in *ringing, singing,* and the like, so an additional rule will have to delete the /g/ after the [ŋ] variant is accounted for. But the advantage is that there do exist dialects of English in which a [g] is heard—for example, urban New York; and there are also forms that in some environments actually have the /g/ even in Standard English— for example, *stronger, longer,* and *younger* based on *strong, long,* and *young.* Assuming an underlying /g/ and then deleting it accounts for the rather uncertain status of /ŋ/ as a phoneme and also describes the process that took place in the history of English: there were real /g/'s that were dropped.

Linguists who favor a systematic phonemic analysis are gratified with their windfall. To have their description of the current state of affairs backed up by history is more than they bargained for, and is seen as the same kind of recapitulation that one encounters in biology: a human fetus, for example, goes through stages in its development that resemble evolutionary stages. But some critics point out that the profoundest analysis is here being based very largely on the shallowest layer of words in our vocabulary, those added after the child already has a working phonemic system—some added quite late, and with any two persons from different levels of society having quite dissimilar accumulations of vocabulary.[3] Take a word set such as *insatiable, satiate, sate,* and *satiety.* The technique requires us to set /t/ as the underlying form and derive [š] from it. But there are many speakers who do not know either *sate* or *satiety,*[4] and for them such a derivation is psychologically unreal. They may even associate *insatiable* with such forms as *delicious, luscious, galuptious,* and *scrumptious* (see page 22), which are tied together by gesture; if they were to learn *satiety,* it would be unrelated for them. This makes it very difficult to arrive at a single set of underlying forms that will be valid for everyone, even though our phonemes and our systematic phonemes are psychological realities and are practically uni- form for all speakers.[5] It is not that we expect all speakers to have the same grammar; we know that there are some differences, but we do not expect them to be quite so idiosyncratic.

Distinctive features have other advantages besides showing relation- ships among word forms or the nature of sound changes that have taken place. One is in explaining what combinations of sounds a language permits. English allows clusters of three consonants at the beginning of a word only if the third consonant is /l/ or /r/, as in *splash, scratch, sclerose, stripe,* and so forth—no *stf-, *stm-, *sks-. This would be odd if no underlying relationship could be found between the two sounds. But when their distinctive features are compared they are seen to differ

---

[3] See Maher 1969.

[4] The frequencies of these two words are zero in Carroll, Davies, and Richman 1971.

[5] See Schane 1971.

only in the fact that /l/ is anterior and /r/ is not.[6] Similarly, if we look
at the consonants that can immediately precede /l/ and/or /r/ we find
that they are /p t k b d g s f/, of which the first six are the only English
sounds sharing the features [+consonantal −continuant −nasal −stri-
dent], while the last two share everything except the coronal feature. A
parallel case is that of initial clusters consisting of two consonants plus
/y/ or /w/. The only ones that can occur are /sky skw spy smy/ as in
skewed, squid, spurious, and *smew* (plus /sty/ and /sny/ for some speakers, as in *stupid* and *snew*). Looking again at the shared features, we find
that /y/ and /w/ have everything in common except backness. And
when /y w/ are compared with /r l/ the pairs are seen to have no
fewer than six features in common. We noted earlier that all four sounds
are somewhere between consonants and vowels.

Whatever value linguists eventually assign to underlying forms, splitting the atom of the phoneme into distinctive features was a necessary
step in the analysis of language.

WORD SHAPES

In Chapter 3, page 59, the build-up of sound-units was stopped at the
syllable, the farthest one can go without a deeper knowledge of the
structure of the language. A man from Mars, given the well-known
Martian technology, could devise a machine to tell something about the
syllabic structure of English or Inibaloi without knowing a word of either
language. But as for the words themselves, to know anything about their
structure one has to be able to discriminate them, and that can only be
done if one has some notion of their meanings, for otherwise it is usually
impossible to tell where one stops and the next one begins.

But knowing that much, as we have seen in this chapter, there is a
good deal that can be said about word structure. It is enough to know
what the units are—without necessarily being able to define each one
semantically—to be able to describe words and some of their relations
in phonological terms.

For example, knowing the way words are shaped in English, we could
predict that it might well have the words *spout, rout, tout, bout, dou(b)t,
shout, grout, knout, lout, pout, trout, scout, snout, gout, flout, kraut,
sprout,* and *clout,* which in fact it has. And we could also predict that it
might have the words *°shrout, °slout,* and *°frout,* which it does not have.

---

[6] If the tongue is positioned for [l] and drawn back gradually, the next distinguishable sound will be [r] (the tongue tip must keep contact with the roof of the
mouth).

At the same time we could exclude *tsout, *bnout, *shprout, and *vrout, not because such words are necessarily hard to pronounce, since we manage the [vr] easily enough with a foreign name such as *De Vries*, and we actually say *tsout* [tsawt] as a condensed form of *it's out.* The accuracy of our predictions merely reflects the fact that the words of any language have *canonical forms*—normal combinations of sounds—that can be described independently of their meaning.

There are, besides, the associations among words that we have been examining in this chapter. Knowing the structure of English, we can see that *one knife* and *two knives, one bath* and *two baths,* and similar correlations put words in relationships that can be described by positing underlying forms along with rules to generate the actually occurring forms. It would be unreasonable not to conclude that *knife* and *knive-* are in some sense "the same," despite their difference in sound, which is as great as that between *duff* and *dove.*

As a preliminary to relating the two, we say that *knife* and *knive-* are *morphs*—that is, they are actual spoken forms, minimal carriers of meaning. The technique of relating morphs calls for setting up another unit, the *morpheme*, which is to the morph what a phoneme is to a phone. Just as we class phones together as *allophones* of a single phoneme, so we class morphs together as *allomorphs* of a single morpheme.

If all meaning-bearing units were as big as words, the morpheme would be unnecessary as a unit; we could have log-emes (words) and allo-logs. But *knive-* is something less than a word, and the same is true of other elements, such as *trans-, contra-, pre-, de-, -dom, -ize,* and *-ing.* The smaller unit is therefore necessary, and we say that *knife* and *knive-* are allomorphs of a single underlying morpheme of the shape /nayf/,[7] which requires no change in deriving *knife* but adds voice to make *knive-.*

But how do we know that such morphemes as *trans-, contra-, de-,* and the like are not words in their own right? That one morpheme can also be one word is plain enough in forms such as *proud, fashion,* and *camera.* They cannot be broken into smaller meaningful parts. And we do say such things as *pro and con* as if *pro* and *con* were independent words.

It is usually easy for a native speaker to *sense* what a word is, but not so easy to *define* it. How can we be sure that *roadblock* is one word and *road machinery* is two? If a morpheme is 'a minimal unit of meaning,' that definition will not serve for *word* as well. Or perhaps a word is the smallest unit of language that can be used by itself. Yet there are forms that we would like to regard as words that never occur alone, such as *the*

---

[7] /nayf/ is shorthand for four columns of distinctive features, one for each systematic phoneme.

or *from* or *am.* The best definition—at least for languages like English[8]—
is probably in terms of separability. Words are the least elements between which other elements can be inserted with relative freedom. So in
the sequence *the man* we can insert *young* to get *the young man,* but
there is no way to insert something *within the* or *man.* And though we
can insert *-est* between *young* and *man* to get *the youngest man,* we cannot insert anything between *young* and *-est. Youngest* therefore is a word
but *-est* is not. And one can sense an insertion point because there is a
pause point. A speaker may be heard to say *The—uh—what do you call
it?—rappelling they do is pretty dangerous. The* is separately coded in
the brain as a sign of 'definiteness' and can be uttered separately, even
though it requires something to follow. But it would be unusual for
someone to say *The work—uh—force was late on the job that day. Work-
force* is a compound word; one will not normally start to say it until it is
possible to say all of it (unless one repeats: *The work—uh—work-force
was late on the job that day*). As with all categories in language, that of
the word has vague borders; more will be seen of them in the next
chapter.

Returning to the question of morphemes and allomorphs, something
of their variety can be seen in a sentence like *Every/one / admire/s /
Bill/'s / man/li/ness. Everyone* is a compound containing the morphemes
every and *one* (which also happen to be words when used separately);
admires is a verb containing the stem morpheme *admire-* and the suffix
morpheme *-s,* meaning 'third person singular'; *Bill's* is a possessive containing the proper noun *Bill* and the possessive morpheme *-'s;* and *manli-
ness* is a noun containing the base noun morpheme *man-* plus the adjective-forming suffix morpheme *-ly* plus the abstract-noun–forming suffix
morpheme *-ness.* As for allomorphs, *every-* normally has only one,
/ɛvrɨ/, but *-one* may appear as /wʌn/ or as /wən/, depending on speed
and emphasis. The *-s* of *admires* has the same three allomorphs as the
possessive in *Bill's* and the plural in *dogs:* /z/ in *admires,* /s/ in *takes,*
and /əz/ in *catches. Bill* has only one, but *man* has at least two: /mæn/
in the form here and when used as a independent word, and /mən/ in
many compounds, such as *workman, fireman.* The suffixes *-li-* and *-ness*
have one each, /lɨ/ and /nəs/. The only puzzle is *admire.* Is it two
morphemes or one? The *ad-* looks suspiciously like the *ad-* of *address,
adjoin,* and *adhere,* which is perhaps vaguely sensed as having something to do with the meaning 'to,' even for a person who is unaware of
the Latin source. And the meaning of the word as a whole may seem
enough like that of *miraculous* and *miracle* to suggest that *-mir-* is entitled
to be considered as a morpheme. If so, there are three allomorphs in

---

[8] The "word" problem is ably discussed for a language much unlike English in
Thomas 1962.

these three words: /mayr/, /mər/, and /mɪr/. The difficulty in deciding whether to split *admire* up or leave it intact will be looked at more closely in the next chapter. It is a difficulty that afflicts the majority of English words taken from Greek and Latin. An etymologist could even make a case for finding the *-mir-* morpheme (with a new allomorph, /mayl/) in the word *smile,* which comes from the same ultimate source; but for anybody else that would hardly make sense.

PHONOLOGICAL CONDITIONING AND MORPHOLOGICAL CONDITIONING

Two different approaches are needed to describe allomorphs. One approach relates to elements that are actually there, in the spoken chain. The other relates to elements that are not there. An example of the first is the phrase *ten percent* contrasted with *ten to six.* In *ten percent* the /n/ may accommodate itself to the following /p/, so that *ten* comes out *tem.* There are thus two allomorphs for *ten,* /tɛn/ and /tɛm/. Nothing needs to be known beyond the sounds themselves to predict that this will or may happen. Since the /n/ is "conditioned" by a neighboring sound, the type of change involved is called *phonological conditioning.*

The second approach—required for allomorphs that do not depend on actually spoken neighboring events—is exemplified in the word *dear.* There is nothing in the spoken chain to account for the difference between *dear* with its /dɪr/ allomorph and *darling* with its /dar/ allomorph. If there were, the same thing would have to happen to *year,* creating *year–yarling* rather than *year–yearling.* If we posit an underlying morpheme which generates now /dɪr/ and now /dar/, it is not to take care of what happens in the course of an utterance but of what we know about the catalog of words. The term used for this type of difference between allomorphs is *morphological conditioning.*

The allomorph /dar/ for *dear* is one of many etymological relics in English, and these, plus oddments of borrowings from foreign languages, make up most of the cases of morphological conditioning. The noun plurals in *ox–oxen, goose–geese,* and *sheep–sheep* are relics. Those in *insigne–insignia, umbo–umbones,* and *jinnee–jinn* (to pick examples as outlandish as possible) are borrowings. Together they compel us to recognize some rather peculiar allomorphs of the plural morpheme: in *geese* it is the change of an internal vowel (*foot–feet* is another example); in *sheep* it is zero (as also in *deer–deer*); and in *jinn* it is the *loss* of the final vowel. The three other words use exceptional suffixes, which is also the case with more familiar borrowings such as *stigma–stigmata* (from Greek), *datum–data* (from Latin), and *cherub–cherubim* (from Hebrew).

The changes that verbs undergo show a great variety of morphological conditioning. *Sing–sang–sung* is like *goose–geese:* both have internal changes. The form *does,* based on *do* /du/, has one internal change (/u/ ⟶ /ʌ/); *don't* has another (/u/ ⟶ /o/), even though it is the same tense as *does;* and *did* has a third (/u/ ⟶ /ɪ/), which reflects the past tense. In the forms *mean–meant, feel–felt,* and *deal–dealt* there is morphological conditioning in both the verb itself (/i/ ⟶ /ɛ/) and the past-tense morpheme. The regular allomorph of the latter would be /d/, not /t/: compare *lean–leaned, seal–sealed* and *sell–sold.*

Since all morphologically conditioned allomorphs pertain to the catalog of words, they have to be listed in the dictionary with the individual words or word sets that they belong to. It is not necessary for a dictionary to record the plural of *safe* or *birth.* A general rule covers them. But the plurals of *half* and *bath* have to be listed, or at least cross-referenced to some special rule for their formation; they are unpredictable.[9]

General rules are in the domain of phonological conditioning, not morphological conditioning. The rule for /tɛm/ in *ten percent* is an *optional* general rule. There are also *obligatory* general rules, typically involving inflections and such words as articles, pronouns, prepositions, and the like, termed *function words.* An example is the rule that covers the plural morpheme, the possessive morpheme, and the verb form *is,* as in

the bills	Bill's	Bill's here.
the roses	Rose's	Rose's here.
the pats	Pat's	Pat's here.

The allomorphs in each row are the same: /z/ in the first, /əz/ in the second, and /s/ in the third. The phonological conditioning is as follows:

1. The allomorph is /z/ after a vowel or after a consonant that is $\begin{bmatrix} +\text{voiced} \\ \left\{ \begin{array}{l} -\text{coronal} \\ -\text{strident} \end{array} \right\} \end{bmatrix}$.[10]

---

[9] This is not to say that there is no *historical* predictability. The change was brought about by phonological conditioning in the past. But now it depends on our knowledge of the word itself and of other words rather than on the environment. An example of this kind of knowledge is the noun *civilization.* Some speakers will say *The civilization of the Aztecs,* using /sɪvələzešən/ to refer to the Aztec culture, but /sɪvəlayzešən/ to refer to what the Spaniards thought they were doing when they brought Spanish culture to Mexico—'culture' versus 'act of civilizing.' It is the meaning—our knowledge of the word—that determines this, not anything predictable on the basis of the environment.

[10] This bracketing means 'a consonant that is voiced and either not coronal or not strident.'

2. The allomorph is /əz/ after a consonant $\begin{bmatrix} +\text{strident} \\ -\text{coronal} \end{bmatrix}$
that is

3. The allomorph is /s/ the rest of the time.

Another example is the indefinite article in English, which is phonologically conditioned in two ways. First, the choice between *a* and *an* is determined by whether the following word begins with a consonant or a vowel: *a pear, an apple*. Second, many speakers shift to a full vowel when the article is emphasized: *He lives in a* /ə/ *big house; Give me an* /ən/ *orange; I don't want just á* /e/ *lawyer, I want the bést lawyer; I don't want just án* /æn/ *editor, I want the bést editor.* So we have four allomorphs: /ə ən e æn/. A similar double conditioning occurs with the pronoun forms *he–him–his–her*. The first rule is "Retain the /h/ only directly after a pause (for example, *He lied*) or when accented (for example, *It's not for you, it's for him*)." The second rule allows for the reduction of the vowel when it is not accented: "How did you know he was lying?"—"*He* /hɪ/ blushed"; "Who did it?"—"*He* /hi/ did." *He* thus has three possible allomorphs:

/hi/   *I won't but he will.*

/hɪ/   *He blushed.*

/ɪ/   *I know he cheated.*

The rule for vowel reduction is fairly general among function words. The normal thing is for the vowel—whatever it is—in the accented form to become a shwa /ə/ in the unaccented form: *He works só-o-o* /so/ *hard* versus *Don't work so* /sə/ *hard; It's all right, bút . . . !* /bʌt/ versus *Nobody went but* /bət/ *me; I don't know the place he went to* /tu/[11] versus *He went to* /tə/ *Chicago; What's he asking for?* /fɔr/ versus *He's asking for* /fər/ *money; That's it!* /ɪt/ versus *Throw it* /ət/ *off.* But reduction sometimes also brings in morphological conditioning: a few function words have somewhat more drastically altered allomorphs. The negative word *not* often loses its vowel completely and becomes a consonant cluster attached to an auxiliary verb; the accented *I have nót* thus pairs with *I haven't* /nt/. Similar instances of "contraction" are *I am, I'm; she is, she's; you are, you're.* The shwa sound /ə/ is one step down from the full vowel, which is why it is called reduced; the com-

---

[11] Most function words at the end of a sentence take their full, non-shwa form whether accented or not. Thus *to* in *I don't want to* has the form /tu/ as a rule— though sometimes shwa appears, and then some writers give us the benefit of the spelling *I do' wanna.*

plete loss of the vowel is the ultimate in reduction. Even **was** can be reduced by these two steps: first to /wəz/ and then to just a prelabialized z-sound, /wz/. **Not** skips the shwa step: there is no */nət/ in such forms as **isn't** and **hadn't,** only /nt/. (Though some speakers do say /kænət/ for **cannot.**)

Returning once more to morphological conditioning, we occasionally find an extreme case in which two forms have no physical resemblance whatever. (Certain of the allomorphs of the plural morpheme are of this type; the -*a* of **data** is totally unlike the -*s* of **cats.**) The past tense of **go** is **went,** actually borrowed from a different verb, **to wend.** But since **go** and **went** pattern the same as **do–did, write–wrote, talk–talked,** and all other verbs, they have to be regarded as "different forms of the same word," and must therefore contain the same morpheme with two very different allomorphs. The same is true of **bad** and **worse.** This kind of relationship is called *suppletion.*

There is one further kind of conditioning besides phonological and morphological: *stylistic conditioning.* An informal way of saying **What's cooking?** is **What's cookin'?** with the style allomorph /ən/ standing in for the -*ing* morpheme. Similarly **I s'pose** passes for **I suppose.** Probably the majority of such variants are at least to some extent phonological. **S'pose** is the result of informally rapid speech. Even those variants that were not originally phonological may come to be felt so. Thus to answer the question **How did you know they were there?** one may say **them** with either of two degrees of apparently phonological reduction:

saw   saw

I   I

/ðəm/.   /əm/.

Both have the clearly phonological reduction to the vowel shwa, but in addition the second appears to have lost the /ð/. Actually it never had it. **Them** is from Norse, and **'em** is reduced from Old English **hem.** That of course makes no difference today: /ðɛm/, /ðəm/, and /əm/ are all allomorphs of the **them** morpheme.

Table 4–2 summarizes the different kinds of conditioning in English.

A possible fourth kind of conditioning is dialectal. If one person pronounces **schedule** as /skɛjəl/ and another as /šɛjəl/, we can say that both forms are allomorphs of the same morpheme. But it is better to use some other term, such as *diamorph,* for this kind of difference. Allomorphs should be just those differences which a single speaker might make, given the right conditions.

TABLE 4–2
Types of Conditioning

Phonological conditioning	ten cents /tɛn/
	ten percent /tɛm/
	pots /s/ *(the plural*
	mugs /z/ *morpheme)*
	só /so/
	so /sə/
Morphological conditioning	dear /dɪr/
	darling /dar/
	half /hæf/
	halves /hæv/
Suppletion	goose–geese /u/ → /i/ *(the plural*
	sheep–sheep /ø/* *morpheme)*
	datum–data /əm/ → /ə/
	go
	went
Stylistic conditioning	cooking /ɨŋ/
	cookin' /ən/

* The symbol ø stands for 'zero.'

THE COMPLEXITY OF ENGLISH MORPHOLOGY

English has an extremely complex morphology because of the vast importation of words from everywhere, particularly from the other languages of Western Europe. If only a relatively small number had been borrowed, they would have come in as indivisible units—few persons have the knowledge of Persian or Hindi to see in the word **cummerbund** a hint of English **band,** and as for **swastika,** there is no possibility of seeing through to its elements at all. But when dozens of Latin words having the negative prefix *in-* with its variants (*insufficient, illogical, irreverent, impossible*) are borrowed, not only the words themselves but the prefix too becomes part of the morphology of English—often a hazily defined part, as we saw in trying to mark the line between the *picture* stage and the *picture–pictorial–depict* stage. Borrowings from other Western languages are fitted in more or less as Latin words are, accommodating themselves to what is already there. So when Italian *imbroglio* was adopted in the eighteenth century it attached itself to *embroil,* which had come in from French more than a century earlier. *Imbroglio* now shares the semantic range of *embroil* with the more clearly related *embroilment;* the latter means the act or process of embroiling, the former the condition or result of embroiling. (With the verb *to produce,* on the other hand, the noun *production* embodies both senses.) The problem that a child faces in learning the morphological relationships between adjectives and verbs in English can be seen in the following list. The verb means 'to cause to be' whatever it is that the adjective means:

full	to fill
strong	to strengthen
open	to open
old	to age
legal	to legalize
shiny	to shine
white	to whiten
angry	to anger
liquid	to liquefy
pregnant	to impregnate
uncomfortable	to discomfort
lively	to enliven
pérfect	to perféct
wise	to wise up (in one sense)
crummy	(nothing)

In addition, the child must constantly be on guard against drawing lunatic analogies:

If outlaws are people who disobey the laws, then in-laws should be law-abiding people.

If one who is patient has patience, then one who is observant should have observance.

Linguists too have to be on their guard, and recently there has been a tendency to let the guard down. Too many Latinisms have been adopted as psychologically real elements in English and turned into underlying forms. The spelling of the English words *sign, design, resign, repugn, malign, reign,* and so forth, and the pronunciation of the related words *signature, designate, resignation, repugnant, malignant,* and *regnant* have beguiled some linguists into positing an underlying form with /g/ and a rule to delete it for the forms in which it is not pronounced. But most linguists would like their descriptions to conform to what goes on in our heads, and the behavior of speakers gives strong indications that at least some of these connections are fanciful. Do we really sense a family relationship between *design* and *designate?* If we do, then it is to be expected that the /g/ will turn up, for example, before the suffix *-able,* as it actually does in the word *inexpugnable,* which has the same *pugn* element as in *repugn* and *repugnant.* But the *-able* words are unpredictable. In one meaning of the word *designable—* 'identifiable,' which is obviously related to *designate*—the pronunciation, according to *The Oxford English Dictionary,* is /dɛzignəbəl/. But the meaning 'capable of being designed' yields /dəzáynəbəl/. This suggests that the g of *design* is no more functional than the g of *align* (also more sensibly spelled *aline*), and that *design* and *designate* are not related in our minds at all. A similar situation exists with the word *condemn.* Given the pairs *hymn–hymnal, damn–damnation, autumn–autumnal,* it looks as if there must be an underlying /n/. But if *indemnity* keeps it, why is it absent in *damage,* which is what indemnities are for? Here even with a clear semantic relationship the /n/ has disappeared (there is a perfectly good *etymological* reason for its disappearance). As for *condemnable,* if you mean 'subject to condemnation' (note that *this n* is pronounced), say /kəndɛməbəl/ (without pronouncing the *n*); but if you mean 'fit to be condemned,' say /kəndɛmnəbəl/. With the word *limn* you even have the choice of keeping or not keeping the /n/ in the present participle *limning,* which is not true of *damning, condemning,* or *hymning.*[12] And as for *contemn,* its *-able* form is not *contemnable* nor *contemnible* with an /n/, but *contemptible.*

In short, there is a point beyond which trying to dig up underlying forms is a desecration. They are tired etymological bones that have earned their rest.

---

[12] These are the pronunciations given in Kenyon and Knott 1953.

ADDITIONAL REMARKS AND APPLICATIONS

1. From the standpoint of the *"picture* stage"—that of the autonomous phonemes—is there a difference between the two nouns **links** and **lynx?** Is there a difference in systematic phonemes? Discuss. Would it affect your answer if for the noun **links** you used the expression *a golf links?*

2. What phonemic contrasts do the following minimal pairs point to?— *gristly–grisly, confusion–Confucian, spite–spied, crutch–crush, luff–love, rode–roan, mutt–much, lean–dean.* Are the two members of each pair widely different from each other? If you could measure the difference in terms of the number of distinctive features that separate one phoneme from another, how many points of difference would you say there are in /f/–/v/? In /m/–/p/?

3. Some speakers pronounce the noun **rise** as [rays] rather than [rayz]. What rule does this illustrate? Is **house** a similar case?

4. See if you can find a noun in your dictionary that has the same relationship to **scathe** that **breath** has to **breathe.** Is there an adjective that has a similar relationship to **loathe?** If you are just now learning either of these words, is it proper to regard a form with /θ/ as previously underlying the verbs? There is also a verb **to withe** and a noun **withe,** related in meaning and both pronounced /wayð/. Would the underlying form have /θ/ or /ð/?

5. If we assume that [z] is the normal sibilant before a voiced consonant in such words as **Erasmus, strabismus, cosmos, chasm,** and **dismal,** what underlying form would be needed to account for the [s] of **isthmus?**

6. The French phonemic system contains a set of nasalized vowels, as was noted in the last chapter (page 44): **beauté** /boté/ contrasts with **bonté** /bõté/. Nasal vowels do not occur before spoken /m/ or /n/—where English would indifferently nasalize the first vowel in **dynamic,** French would avoid nasalizing the one in **dynamique** in spite of the /n/ that starts the next syllable. This means that nasalized

vowels occur only when there is no following nasal consonant in the same syllable. Explain how it might be possible to posit an underlying nasal consonant directly after the vowel and in the same syllable, later to be deleted by rule, and thereby to get rid of all the nasal vowel phonemes. Is this reflected in the spelling system of French?[13]

7. Show how English numeral compounds illustrate the decimal ("base ten") system. Given the following numeral compounds in Kewa, a language of New Guinea, determine what the base is:[14]

Five:	*kode*—the thumb (or *kina kode*, the hand's thumb, with *-na* the possessive suffix, further showing its distinction from the hand)
Six:	*kode lapo*—two thumbs (or *kina kode lapo*—one hand, two thumbs)
Seven:	*kode repo*—three thumbs (*kina kode repo*—one hand, three thumbs)
Eight:	*ki lapo*—two hands
Nine:	*ki lapona kode* (*pameda*)—two hands, one thumb
Ten:	*ki lapona kode lapo*—two hands, two thumbs
Eleven:	*ki lapona kode repo*—two hands, three thumbs
Twelve:	*ki repo*—three hands
Thirteen:	*ki repona kode* (*pameda*)—three hands, one thumb
Fourteen:	*ki repona kode lapo*—three hands, two thumbs
Fifteen:	*ki repona kode repo*—three hands, three thumbs
Sixteen:	*ki mala*—four hands
Seventeen:	*ki malana kode* (*pameda*)—four hands, one thumb
Eighteen:	*ki malana kode lapo*—four hands, two thumbs
Nineteen:	*ki malana kode repo*—four hands, three thumbs
Twenty:	*ki su*—five hands

8. Does the pair *prolong–prolongation* support the idea that no systematic phoneme /ŋ/ is needed in English?

9. What is unusual about the word **gingham,** in regard to the /ŋ/?

10. Is /sf/ common as an initial cluster in English? Think of some examples. What kind of word does it occur in?

---

[13] Schane 1968, pp. 45–50.
[14] Franklin 1962, p. 4.

11. What is unusual about the following English words: *Tsar, tsetse, tsamba?* Would you judge them to be words of long standing in the language? Why?

12. A waitress in a Massachusetts restaurant explained the delay in service as the result of the fact that it was *one of the cooks' day offs.* The following appeared in a novel: *He was the toughest and hardest-bitten character I'd ever seen.*[15] Is there anything unusual about either or both of these examples? Discuss, from the standpoint of the definition of a word.

13. In making up a list of words that English might have but presumably does not have, would you be surprised to run into one or more that it actually does have and that you didn't know about? Is there such a word as *plout,* for example?

14. Describe the allomorphs of the plural morpheme in *alumnus, octopus, antenna.* In *antenna* does the form of the plural morpheme depend in any way on the meaning?

15. British English tends to favor *knelt* and *dreamt* where American English favors *kneeled* and *dreamed.* What are the differences in terms of allomorphs? The British also favor *spilt* and *smelt* (*spilled* and *smelled*) more than Americans do. Is the situation here identical with that in *knelt* and *dreamt?*

16. Discuss the allomorphs in *child–children* and *write–wrote–written.*

17. Some older pairs were *shoe–shoon, foe–fon, cow–kine.* What has happened to them? Why?

18. In Spanish the stops /b d g/ all have fricative allophones (for example, /d/ sounds like [ð] between vowels). What kind of conditioning is this?

19. The *re-* prefix has an alternate form, *red-*, in such words as *redact, redintegrate.* What kind of conditioning does this alternation represent in English? In Latin, *re-* automatically became *red-* before a vowel. (One would not have been as likely to find the same situation in Latin as in English, where both *reintegrate* and *redintegrate* exist.) What kind of conditioning did the Latin form represent? Or might it have been a mixture of two kinds?

---

[15] Alistair MacLean, *The Black Shrike* (Greenwich, Conn.: Fawcett, 1970), p. 76.

20. In your own speech do you have a glottal stop in any of the following?

    a. He works *extra hours.*

    b. This thing is *extra ugly.*

    c. She is *extra able.*

    d. She has this *extra ability.*

    e. It's *extra awful.*

    f. They need an *extra ambassador.*

    g. This is an *extra interest* of mine.

If you have, see if you can make a rule for it. Add other examples of *extra* + vowel if necessary.

21. Study the following examples and work out the allomorphs of the definite article *the* in your speech:

    a. I don't want just any woman, I want thé woman for the job.

    b. Where did you put the beer?

    c. It's on the ice.

    d. The ether was supposed to carry light waves.

    e. She's with the angels.

    f. The idioms in that language are tough to learn.

    g. All the eagles flew away.

    h. The money was no good.

Make up other examples if you need to. After you have worked out your answer, see if you get a similar one for the prefix *re-* in words such as the following: *reelect, reiterate, reopen, re-use, re-equalize.* How do *republic* and *the public* compare?

22. The two possessive forms *my* and *mine* were formerly selected according to a rule that required *my* before a consonant and *mine* the rest of the time *(Mine eyes have seen the glory, mother mine, It's mine).* Now the rule is to use *my* before any noun. What change has occurred in the type of conditioning? Has the same change occurred in *thy–thine?*

23. Identify the allomorphs in the following, and the type of conditioning, if any: *dear–dearth, worth–worthy, earth–earthy.*

24. In Spanish the verb forms *es* 'he (she, it) is' and *sería* 'he (she, it) would be' are considered to be members of the same paradigm—

that is, to be different forms of the same verb. But *es* comes from one Latin verb (*esse* 'to be') and *sería* from another (*sĕdēre* 'to sit, to be seated'). What is the term for this relationship? (Compare English *go, went.*) Is there a kind of semantic precondition for this sort of merger to take place? Are *to be* and *to sit* related in meaning? (Find a context where either one might be used with pretty much the same meaning, if you can.) If the kind of blending that yields *affrontary* through a combination of *affront* and *effrontery*[16] can be compared to the fusion of two stars that collide,[17] could *go–went, es–sería,* and other instances like them be compared to stars that are captured in a mutual gravitational field—a kind of paradigmatic double star?

25. Describe the allomorphs and the kinds of conditioning in *Whatcha doin'?*

26. Given the relationships between adjectives and their causative verbs (page 9) and other similar sets of disparities (see if you can think of some), how important does it seem to be, psychologically, for there to be actual formal similarities across categories (adjective and verb, adjective and noun, noun and verb, and so forth)?

27. Check the meaning and pronunciation of the two words *perihelion* and *aphelion.* What problem do they pose in deciding on the underlying forms of their morphemes?

28. Discuss the relationship of *flautist* and *lutanist* to *flute* and *lute.*

29. The words *agnate, cognate, pregnant, impregnate, nature, nascent, native, innate,* and many more have a common historical origin—the Latin verb *nascere,* originally *gnascere.* Conceivably in English we could have an underlying /g/, such that *nature* started out as *gnature,* or *nativity* as *gnativity.* Discuss the problems of meaning and form that this would raise. (For example, one would have to explain why the first /n/ of *in-gnate* is not pronounced [ŋ].)

30. Linguists have disputed over whether the autonomous phonemes have some direct relationship to spoken forms in our minds, as would seem to be the case if the phonemes are "real," or whether the only real units are the underlying forms along with word-forming rules. Consider whether the following evidence from misspellings suggests

---

[16] *Open Forum* (May 1964), p. 3.
[17] See pages 396–99 for more examples.

that both may have to be recognized: A writer who knows very well
how to spell *house, dealt,* and *improvise* at some time or other types
hous, delt, and *improvies.* (Is it sound or knowledge of word forms
that is most directly involved in these mistakes?) The same writer
intends to type *Raleigh* and instead types *Raleight,* and on another
occasion intends to type *soul* and instead types *sould.* (Is there anything in the sound that prompts this? If not, what does?)[18]

References

Carroll, John B.; Peter Davies; and Barry Richman. 1971. *The American
     Heritage Word Frequency Book* (New York: American Heritage).
Franklin, Karl and Joyce. 1962. "The Kewa Counting Systems," *Journal of the
     Polynesian Society* 71, No. 2.
Kenyon, John S., and Thomas A. Knott. 1953. *A Pronouncing Dictionary of
     American English* (Springfield, Mass.: Merriam).
Maher, J. P. 1969. "The Paradox of Creation and Tradition in Grammar:
     Sound Pattern of a Palimpsest," *Language Sciences* 7:15–24.
————. 1974. "English *Davit* / Old French *Daviet:* A Biblical Echo in Me-
     dieval Sailors' Speech (with Remarks on Semantic and Phonological
     Theory)," *Literary Onomastic Studies* 1:22–27.
Pak, Tae-Yong. 1971. "Convertibility Between Distinctive Features and
     Phonemes," *Linguistics* 66:97–114.
Schane, Sanford A. 1968. *French Phonology and Morphology* (Cambridge,
     Mass.: M.I.T. Press).
————. 1971. "The Phoneme Revisited," *Language* 47:503–21.
Thomas, David D. 1962. "On Defining the 'Word' in Vietnamese," *Van-hoa
     Nguyet-san* 11:519–23.

---

[18] Similar evidence is cited in Maher 1974.

LEXICON 5

When the language is supplied with subatomic particles in the form of distinctive features, atoms in the form of phonemes, and molecules in the form of syllables, what is to be done with them? One might say that the next step is to go from physics to biology, to find the cells and their assemblies that make up the living matter of language. Life needs more than form; it must have meaning. The question then is how to relate units of meaning to units of form. Everything so far has been discussed with as little commitment to meaning as possible, to the extent of defining phonemes and syllables as inherently meaningless, and word shapes as discoverable by asking only if they *have* a meaning, not what the meaning is. Now the gap has to be bridged.

COLLOCATION AND IDIOM

In the last chapter we defined words as the smallest elements that are independently coded—an abstruse way of saying that they are the pawns in the game, the common pieces that are constantly reassembled and sometimes used alone to convey a message. The one-to-one or one-to-many relationship between words and meanings is understood by every speaker. It is the one thing about the practical use of language that we know children can be effectively taught.[1] If it is not quite at the same level of awareness as the relationship between a hammer and hitting a nail, it can nevertheless be brought to that level very easily. The person struggling with an idea who says *I can't think of the right word* is never heard to say **I can't think of the right prefix* or **I can't think of the right sound* (though he may say *I can't think of the right way to put it,* which has to do with something higher up on the scale than words).

Yet words as we understand them are not the only elements that have a more or less fixed correlation with meaning. They are not even necessarily the first units that a child learns to imbue with this association. In the beginning stages a child apprehends *holistically:* the situation is not broken down, and neither is the verbal expression that accompanies it. That is why the first learning is *holophrastic:* each word is an utterance, each utterance is an undivided word, as far as the child is concerned. It is only later that words are differentiated out of larger wholes. A child asked to say the first thing that comes to mind on hearing the word *throw* will say *ball* rather than *toss,* and if asked to define *a hole* will say *a hole in the ground.*[2] The associations are "horizontal" (*syntagmatic*), and are made with external reality.

As with the phoneme, which lives on even when overlaid with the systematic relationships that were traced in the last chapter, the whole chunks that we learn also persist as coded units even after the chemical analysis into words has partially split them up. An extreme example is *How do you do?* That it is functionally a single piece is proved by its condensation to *Howdy.* Such expressions are termed *idioms,* defined as groups of words with set meanings that cannot be calculated by adding up the separate meanings of the parts. Some idioms are virtually unchangeable, like *Hold your horses,* meaning 'Don't be so impetuous'; neither subject nor verb can normally be changed to yield, say, **They hold their horses* or **He was holding his horses,* nor can the object be changed to yield, **Hold your horse.* Others allow a limited amount of manipulation; for example, *He's dead to the world,* meaning 'He's fast asleep,' can be changed for person and time: *She's dead to the world, They were dead to the world* (but not **He was dead to the universe*). Some idioms allow certain transformations but not others. *He found fault with them* can be made passive—*Fault was found with them*—but unlike *He sought help from them,* the noun cannot be turned into a pronoun. Based on *He sought help from them* we can have *He didn't seek it from me* or *What did he seek from you?;* but based on *He found fault with them* we cannot have **He didn't find it with me* or **What did he find with*

---

[1] Cazden 1972, p. 129.

[2] Ibid., p. 72.

you? There are families of idioms. One, using the expression *(to be)* *worth,* has its most compactly idiomatic form in *to be worth while,* but also appears with several other nouns accompanied by the definite article: *to be worth the bother, to be worth the trouble,* and the now quaint and literary *to be worth the candle.* Other nouns can be fitted in, of course, but the result is not sensed to the same degree as a stereotype. *It is not worth the bother* functions as a unit. It does not raise the question "What bother?"—to say *?It is not worth the bother involved*[3] would be a rather unusual expansion, whereas *It is not worth the struggle (the strain) involved* is normal, since *to be worth the struggle (strain)* is a constructed phrase, not a stereotype. *To be worth the effort* seems to lie about midway between idiom and non-idiom. The most complex member of the group is the most idiomatic one, *to be worth while.* Though *worth while* retains the stress of two words, the combination is generally written *worthwhile,* and is often put in front of a noun: *a worthwhile effort.* But it can also be separated by certain possessives, as in a radio ad: *It's worth your while to visit our showroom.* At the same time, for many if not most American speakers, the possessives that can be inserted are only those corresponding to the personal pronouns, never nouns *(*It's worth John's while)* nor indefinites *(*It isn't worth anybody's while),* and even the permitted ones tend to shade off, with *your* most acceptable and *my* probably least *(?It's worth my while).* The interrogative is impossible *(*Whose while is it worth?).* Finally, there are idioms that only a close look will detect. *I like the guy,* spoken with the intonation

$$\text{like}$$
$$\text{I}$$
$$\text{the}_{\text{guy.}}$$

implies 'There may be contrary reasons, but I like him in spite of them.' This meaning comes over if *man, fellow, girl, woman,* or *bastard* replaces *guy,* but not if the word substituted is *person, lady,* or *Judith:* the word in the *guy* slot has to be one that may have at least a tinge of deprecation. Otherwise, though the sentence continues to be normal, there is no 'in spite of.'

We might describe these differences as degrees of tightness. The three idioms *to take fright, to take courage,* and *to take heart* stand in order

---

[3] A question mark preceding an utterance indicates that the utterance is of questionable acceptability.

of increasing tightness, as can be seen when the normal word order is reversed:

> The fright that he took was indicative of his timidity.
>
> ?The courage that he took was indicative of his inner resources.
>
> *The heart that he took was indicative of his optimism.

If idioms can vary so widely in tightness, the question arises whether everything we say may be in some degree idiomatic—that is, whether there are affinities among words that continue to reflect the attachments the words had when we learned them, within larger groups. This is not a welcome view to most American linguists, who like to analyze things down to the smallest bits and then put them together again with grammatical rules, on the theory that this makes a more economical description (a small number of rules can work wonders with a not-too-large number of bits in making a tremendous variety of higher forms). Linguists working in the British tradition are not so sure. They apply the term *collocation* to those looser groupings about which something can be said over and beyond what is apparent from looking at the individual parts. Knowing the parts one can deduce the meaning, so that a collocation is not quite an idiom; but it is in some way specialized. (This would make **to be worth the bother** and **worth the trouble** collocations, but leave **to be worth while** an idiom.) The British linguist T. F. Mitchell defines a collocation as 'an abstract composite element . . . which can exhibit its own distribution qua compositum,' and illustrates as follows: "Men—specifically cement workers—work **in** cement works; others of different occupation work **on** works of art; others again, or both, **perform** good works. Not only are good works **performed** but cement works are **built** and works of art **produced**."[4] Why do builders not **produce** a building or authors not **invent** a novel, since they do invent stories and plots? No reason, as far as dictionary definitions of words are concerned. We don't say it because we don't say it. And why do we accept ***The man badly wanted them to leave*** but balk at ***The man badly wished them to leave?***[5] If *badly* is replaced with *earnestly,* both sentences are normal.

The range and variety of collocations is enormous. Some examples follow. Not all persons will agree with every judgment of acceptability that is marked here with an asterisk, question mark, or no symbol at all; but the important thing is that such judgments can be made. It is our experi-

---

[4] Mitchell 1971, p. 50.

[5] Cited in Greenbaum 1970, a study of how certain verbs and certain intensifiers tend to collocate together.

ence of expressions that are repeated over and over in given circumstances that makes for collocations (in addition to providing us with the regularities of our grammar), and it would be remarkable indeed if that experience were uniform all over the English-speaking world. The examples, then:

1. Stereotyping of the definite article

> I heard it on the radio.
> ?I heard it on radio.
>
> ?I saw it on the TV.
> I saw it on TV.

2. Set coordinations

> There was plenty of food and drink.
> There was plenty of food.
> *There was plenty of drink.

3. Linked function words

> I thought he would help me. But no, he was "busy," he said.
>
> I thought he would help me. *And yes, he was willing to.

4. Nouns stereotyped with particular adjectives

good likelihood	strong likelihood	*high likelihood
*good probability	strong probability	high probability
good possibility	strong possibility	*high possibility
good chance	*strong chance	*high chance

5. Item-to-category stereotype
(Instead of being tied to a particular word or words, the word is tied to a grammatical category. This example is of a verb that must always be used with a manner adverb.)

> I regarded them with curiosity.
> *I regarded them.
>
> He regarded me strangely.
> *He regarded me for ten minutes.

6. Adjective and noun

> She was there the livelong day.
> *She was there the livelong morning (week, year).

      They slept till broad daylight.
      *They slept till daylight was broad.

      We are common enemies.
      ?We are mutual enemies.
      We are mutual friends.
      *We are common friends.

7. Preposition and noun

      His methods are above reproach.
      *His methods are below (beneath, far from, near) reproach.

8. Miscellaneous complex phrases

      We did it against our better judgment.
      *We did it against our more mature judgment.
      ?We did it contrary to our better judgment.

      That's his lookout.
      *His lookout was to see that all the results were tallied.

      I'm accustomed to cold weather.
      I'm used to cold weather.
      Accustomed as I am to cold weather, I still prefer Florida.
      *Used as I am to cold weather, I still prefer Florida.

By the time children begin to think about matters of language, the analyzing process has gone far enough to make words the entities of which they are most aware. Words become more and more sharply defined for us as we grow older. So when we finally notice that the word *else* has a peculiar distribution, one that permits it to be used right after indefinites (*somebody else*) but not after nouns (*some person else*), and not even after all indefinites (*someplace else, where else, *sometime else*), we tend to suppose that we always had it as a free combinatory unit but some mysterious process has entangled it with a particular set of words. Actually, it has never *dis*entangled itself. We go on using it exactly as we have heard it used. *Sometime else* is impossible for the same reason that *to uncomfort* is impossible: neither *else* nor *un-* has fully emancipated itself from the maternal context. This is why in language it is so hard to be sure whether we are dealing with something freely and freshly constructed from its least elements or something assembled from rather large chunks consigned to us whole. When asked, "Did you make this cake?" we are inclined to say yes whether we used a prepared cake mix, started with the flour and eggs and sugar and baking powder, or kept the hens and ground the wheat and chopped the wood for the fire with our own two hands.

So the brain stores both the parts and the wholes, and we retrieve them when we need them. Since the lexicon purports to record all the pre-set meaning-bearing units of a language, ideally it would have to include every collocation as well as every word. In practice this is impossible—and probably in theory too. Practically, there would be no room. Theoretically, one would not know where to stop, because collocations shade off into more or less freely formed constructions and fluctuate too much from place to place and from individual to individual. Furthermore, there is no reliable way to test them, at least at the borders between collocations and constructions. *Disappearing ink* has to be the same as *vanishing ink,* yet we would say *She wrote it in disappearing ink* and probably not **She wrote it in vanishing ink. Disappearing ink* most likely is, but does not have to be, a collocation, for a particular speaker at a particular time. So commercial dictionaries never get beyond the words and some of the idioms, though many collocations are cited as if they were freely formed examples of usage. And since the analyzing process does not come to a dead halt when the words are isolated but pushes a short way into the parts of the words themselves, morphemes are singled out that are less than words. When a doctor can write a sentence like *No method has been discovered either in psycho or in any other therapy,*[6] we know that *psycho* is close to the status of a word. We can just as easily find words that are close to the status of affixes. *Ago* is an example. It follows words referring to periods of time, just as its synonym *back* does, but unlike *back, ago* is unstressed, which is characteristic of suffixes:

$$\text{It}\ ^{\text{happened}}\ _{\text{a}}\ \text{ye}_{\text{a}}\text{r}^{\text{ba}}\text{c}_{\text{k.}} \qquad \text{It}\ ^{\text{happened}}\ _{\text{a}}\ \text{year}$$
$$\text{ago.}^{7}$$

We also notice that it would be very difficult to put an *uh* between a time expression and *ago (*It happened a year—uh—ago),* so that it fails the word test described in the last chapter.

A diagram of the three elements that are kept in storage—collocations (including idioms), words, and morphemes—can be made using the phrase *indelible ink.* This phrase is chosen because it is not exactly an

---

[6] Flanders Dunbar, *Mind and Body* (New York: Random House, 1947), p. 198.

[7] If *ago* is accented, as it may be in *a long time ago,* it is for emphasis on the phrase as a whole, not on *ago.*

FIGURE 5–1
Collocations, Words, and Morphemes

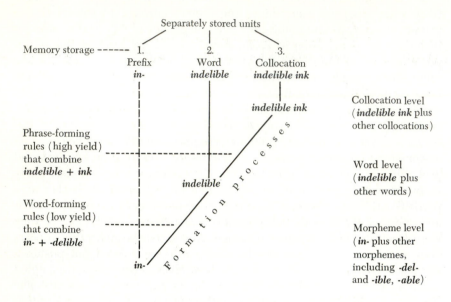

idiom—the meaning responds nicely to the separate meanings of *indelible* and *ink*—and yet an association test will quickly reveal how tight the connection is. A group of twenty-seven persons given the word *indelible* and asked to write the first word that came to mind responded as follows: eleven for *pencil,* seven for *ink,* eight for *unerasable* or a synonym, one for *tracing,* and one (the usual lunatic fringe) for *individual.* Figurative uses are virtually limited to the phrase *indelible impression* (with *indelible memory, indelible recollection,* and a few others as possible spin-offs from that); and perfectly valid uses in the literal sense—for example, *An embosser leaves an indelible mark*—would momentarily puzzle many readers or listeners. And one would refer to a magnetic recording as *unerasable,* not as *indelible.* What the primary collocations with *pencil* and *ink* have led us to expect as most appropriate for this word is a writing *material* of some kind (see Figure 5–1).

The broken vertical line in Figure 5–1 signifies that morphemes as morphemes may or may not be stored: much depends on the perceptions of individuals. Few if any speakers in a whole lifetime will be responsible for making some new combination using the negative prefix *in-* (say *inobdurate*), and some will not even give it passive recognition—hence the description "low yield" as against "high yield" in putting words together to make phrases. In learning our language we read the diagram down. Linguists tend to read it up, which has caused a great many misconceptions when they have tried to fit their descriptions to psychological reality.

LEXICON, SYNTAX, AND MORPHOLOGY

The units of lexicon—words, idioms, and collocations—are the prefabs of language. We may alter them in certain ways, as when we pluralize *raisin* to *raisins* or passivize *Put a stop to it* to *It was put a stop to,* but the parts retain certain pre-set relationships to one another. How they are *analyzed*—and now and then created—is the province of lexicon. What we *do* with them is the province of syntax. A visitor to a zoo is surprised to see two animals in adjoining cages and exclaims *A coatimundi and a polar bear!* Only the situation would be likely to bring together those two animal names. Their association is purely syntactic. The utterance may never have occurred before, and even if it has there is no connection between the present saying and any former one, as there always is between any instance of lexicon and its repetition. *Polar* plus *bear* is such an instance: the combination has been repeated again and again.

The unpredictability of syntax is often hailed as a sign of creativity. "Not to repeat" is seen as synonymous with "to invent." Perhaps the two are the same, at least sometimes. Still, the joining of the coatimundi and the polar bear in a sentence was not an invention of the speaker but a response to a situation, which also included the element of not–previously identified (hence *a* and not *the*) and the element of togetherness (hence *and* and not *or*). Whether our syntax is a response to images—directly from experience, or prompted by another speaker, or envisioned from memory, or imagined in some act of psychological creation—or is part of the creative process itself, is a question that cannot be answered with our present knowledge. The important fact is simply that in syntax we analyze the rules of communication, but in lexicon we analyze static form. This is the separation that must be made in principle, though it is sometimes hard to maintain in practice.

One part of the joint domain of syntax and lexicon that linguists treat separately is morphology, a sampling of which we have already had in connection with underlying forms. It is usually treated as part of lexicon because the elements most affected are words. So whether we are concerned with a syntactic modification, as when *friend* is equipped with a plural ending to comply with a communicative event ("we are talking about more than one") or whether we are concerned only with the make-up of some complex lexical form, as when *friend* is seen to be joined with *-ship* in *friendship,* we treat both *friends* and *friendship* as instances of morphological togetherness: *friend* + *-s* and *friend* + *-ship.* But the behavior of the two—*grammatical* morphemes such as *-s* and *lexical* morphemes such as *-ship*—is quite different and is treated separately.

Lexical morphemes: the fabrication of prefabs

Hearing the exclamation *A coatimundi and a polar bear!* no native speaker would think to himself, "There is something new here, something is changed about the language. I'll bet she made that sentence up." But hearing *I appreciate her inobduracy* a crossword-puzzle fan might well say, "Where did she get that word? I'll bet she made it up." We can analyze words, but once in a while the process is set in reverse and we create one, whether by accident or by design. The raw material generally conforms to the morphemes that can be discovered by analyzing words that already exist—practically all words that are not imported bodily from some other language are made up of old words or modifications using standard affixes like *-ness* or *un-*. The less accidental the coinage the more respect it shows toward existing formative elements. This is especially true of scientific terms: *decompression, polystyrene, perosis, cacogenesis* —old morphemes are re-used in systematic ways. But no etymological pedigree is required. The coiner may mix elements of diverse origins—as in *monolingual,* half Greek and half Latin, or in *atonement,* with its two English words *at* and *one* tagged with a Latin suffix—or even carry over a whole phrase or sentence as in *touch-me-not, what-you-may-call-it,* or *IOU.* And when something smaller than a word is needed, the speaker may ignore the official roster and patch something up with splinters, as with *bumber,* altered from *umbr-* in *umbrella,* and *-shoot,* based on the *-chute* of *parachute,* that form the word *bumbershoot.* In between are fragments of all degrees of standardized efficiency and junkyard irregularity. *Hamburger* yields *-burger,* which is reattached in *nutburger, Gainesburger,* and *cheeseburger. Cafeteria* yields *-teria,* which is reattached in *valeteria, groceteria,* and *washateria.* Trade names make easy use of almost any fragment, like the *-roni* of *macaroni* that is reattached in *Rice-a-Roni* and *Noodle-Roni,* or like *Umbroller,* a folding stroller, combining *umbrella* and *stroller.* The fabrication may re-use elements that have been re-used many times, or it may be a one-shot affair such as the punning reference to being a member of the *lowerarchy,* with *-archy* extracted from *hierarchy.* The principle is the same. Scientists and scholars may give themselves airs with high-bred affixes borrowed from classical languages, but they are linguistically no more sophisticated than the common speakers who are satisfied with leftovers from the vernacular. The only thing a morpheme is good for is to be melted down and recast in a word.

The elements that are re-used most freely are called *productive,* the others *unproductive,* though both terms are relative. The suffix *-ate* is a Latinism that can hardly be used to make new words—but then some wag thinks up *discombobulate* and people accept it. At the other extreme the suffix *-er* looks as if we ought to be able to attach it to any verb and make a noun meaning 'one who performs the action': *worker, player, murderer, digger, eater.* Yet a glance at anomalies such as the following shows that we are less free than we think:

They accused him—they were his accusers.
*They blamed him—they were his blamers.

They admire him—they are his admirers.
*They loathe him—they are his loathers.

She robs banks—she is a robber.
?She steals things—she is a stealer.[8]

These examples suggest why *-er* varies so in productivity. It is not that the language cannot *form* the noun *loather* but simply that we have no use for it. What retinue of people would it designate? A person who is widely admired has a following, and it is useful to talk of its members as *admirers.* In a more general sense we can name their opposites **haters** and have probably done so—they are the members of the club, whereas the loathers have not applied for a charter. Similarly we already have *thief* and do not need *stealer.* The absence of a word need not be due to some mysterious restriction on its formation, but to certain connections, or the lack of them, with the real world and with the stock of words already in existence. Words are not coined in order to extract the meanings of their elements and compile a new meaning from them. The new meaning is there *first,* and the coiner is looking for the best way to express it without going to too much trouble. If parts can be found whose meanings suggest the one in mind, so much the better, but that is not essential. There are other ways—context, pointing, gesture, intonation, paraphrase—to make up for the lack.

By the same token—this connection with the flux of events—the meanings of morphemes can vary as widely as their forms. When an old dress is cut down to a skirt its former function may be partly remembered, but when a remnant of it becomes a dustcloth the old function is forgotten. So while **builders** build and **talkers** talk, **undertakers** no longer undertake—the general sense that the word once had has been restricted to a narrow kind of undertaking, and *-er* is no more recognizable than the low-yield *-ian* of **mortician.** The speaker who first put together the word

---

[8] *Syntactically,* that is, in construction with a noun object, all these are possible: **Who are the blamers of the innocent, the loathers of all that is good, the stealers of sense and virtue?** But it calls for rather stilted discourse.

escapee was not bothered by the fact that the proper form was *escaper,* since *-ee* is etymologically for persons acted upon, not for persons acting. It was enough that *escapee* suggested the same 'set category of persons' idea that is carried by words like *employee* and *draftee,* and *-ee* could be twisted to fit the purpose.

The high informality of word making in English, the clutching at almost anything to nail up a new prefab, reflects the vast expansion of our culture. A supermarket that in 1966 stocked eight thousand items and by 1973 carried some fourteen thousand is one ripple in a tide of growth that carries our vocabulary along with it. We have to have names for those new items. All cultures exhibit this to some extent: the list of content-carrying words—nouns, verbs, adjectives, and most adverbs—is the one list in the catalog that has no limit. Phonemes, syllable types, rules of syntax, and certain little "function words" that will be discussed later are "closed classes"—they are almost never added to; but the major lexicon is open-ended. The relationship of morphemes to words is therefore the hardest thing in language to analyze. Asking what morphemes a word contains and what they mean is asking what the coiner of the word had in mind when he coined it and possibly what unforeseen associations it may have built up since.[9] It is less an analytical question than a question about history.

The morpheme at best continues to live a parasitic life within the word. It remains half-alive for one speaker and dies for the next; or it may be revived by education. A child who calls a tricycle a *three-wheeled bike* and later discovers other words with the prefix *bi-* may reanalyze *bicycle* into two morphemes instead of one. Hundreds of morphemes lie half-buried in the junkheaps of the etymological past. A corner of the Latin *pre-* sticks out in words like *predict, prearrange, predetermine,* and maybe *prepare*—we sense that *pre-* here has something to do with 'before'; but in the verb *present* it is almost hidden and in *preserve, pregnant,* and *prelate* it is lost from sight. No one but an etymologist remembers what the *luke-* of *lukewarm* means (it originally signified 'lukewarm' by itself—*lukewarm* = 'lukewarmly warm'). The *re-* of *reduce* and the *di-* of *digest* are only meaningless syllables to speakers of English, even though their sources are the same as the *re-* of *readjust* and the *dis-* of *distrust.*

Still, in spite of the difficulties, looking for morphemes is a necessary part of linguistic analysis. This is true partly because not all languages are quite so unsystematic (or so burdened with conflicting systems, which

---

[9] How we analyze a word into morphemes can change in the course of the word's history. A *wiseacre* is generally thought to be someone who acts wise but is not entitled to—*wise* is morphemicized by the speaker in spite of the fact that *wiseacre* originally meant 'soothsayer' and the *wise-* part is related to *witch.* More examples of such "folk etymology" will be given on pages 406–09.

comes to the same thing) as English; some of them have more regular habits of word formation. By its very irregularity English richly illustrates the variety of these habits. So, to see how words are put together, we must look backward and treat fossils as if they were still alive, and speak of "processes" that are like abandoned mines, only sporadically yielding a nugget to some determined prospector.

The make-up of words

There are two fairly well defined ways to make words. One uses words themselves as raw material for new words. It is called *compounding* or *composition*. The other attaches a lesser morpheme—an affix—to a major element—a base, frequently a word, which may already have one or more affixes incorporated in it. It is called *derivation*. **Roadblock** and **warning light** are compounds; so is **slide rule:** the separation or lack of it in writing is a fair indication of how deep the heat of fusion has penetrated, how much the individual component has kept of its own identity. There is no clear dividing line between compounds and idioms, but there are two main criteria: the productivity of the processes through which the expressions are formed and the "one-wordness" of the result. The expression **black sheep** meaning 'ne'er-do-well' could qualify as an idiom semantically; its meaning is not predictable from the combined meanings of **black** and **sheep.** But in addition it is constructed the same as **scarlet fever, short circuit, dumb show** ('pantomime'), and, with backshifted stress, *hót seat, fát lady, shárpshooter, whitefish, páleface, mádman*—that is, with *adjective plus noun.* The process is one that is repeated over and over in the creation of expressions whose parts are themselves words but which have been given (or have taken on in the course of time—see pages 417–18) an unpredictable meaning.

The "one-wordness" of compounds can be seen in the way the expressions are handled morphologically. They tend to fill a single grammatical slot in a sentence (for example, that of a verb, a noun, or an adjective) and to be inflected as single words are—on the end. *Fát lady* (in a circus) is a compound; *fátter lady* is not. The idiom **to put a stop to** is just as unitary in meaning as **to check, to stymie,** or **to inhibit.** But we do not think of it as "a word" because it is inflected internally, with **put** behaving as independently as in **to put the clock on the table:** we say **He's putting a stop to that,** not **He's put a stop to-ing that.* The occasional compound-like structure that does allow an internal inflection tends to be regularized by the ordinary speaker: the **attorneys general** type is becoming as rare as **jacks-in-the-box* or **wills-o'-the-wisp;* and we are about as apt to say **He's the hard-headedest cuss I know** as to say **He's the hardest-headed cuss I know.** Even **runners-up** tends to become **runner-ups.**

Unlike *to put a stop to,* the expression *to bad-mouth* results from two highly productive processes of formation—first a compound noun made with adjective plus noun, as in *He has a bad mouth;* then a conversion of the noun to a verb—and it shows its one-wordness in the normal inflection: *He bad-mouthed me.* So we put *to bad-mouth* down as a compound and *to put a stop to* as an idiom. *Idiom* remains a catch-all, but in time will yield to better analysis and classification. For now we need it as a cover term for expressions that are idiosyncratic not only in their meaning but also in their formation and complexity.

A feature that is often used to define noun compounds is shift of stress. Instead of *raw híde* we say *ráwhide,* and so for *hárdwood, wísecrack,* and *retáining wall.* But it is an uncertain criterion. Older generations (and Scotsmen of all generations) prefer *Salvation Ármy, paper dólls, right ángle,* and *two-by-fóur,* where many younger Americans say *Salváton Army, páper dolls, ríght angle,* and *twó-by-four.* Some speakers vacillate, preferring to stress the second element in *chocolate cáke* and the first in *spíce cake.* No one criterion will suffice to define any of the types of word grouping that one finds in English; all are gradient.

The productivity of compounding is limitless. Words are the loosest elements and combine most freely, though according to rules that linguists, with their attention focused on tighter formations, are only beginning to detect.[10] For example, the student who wrote that a textbook must have *easy-to-understand instructions* sensed that he was free to make a compound of this kind by using the words *easy* and *hard,* but not necessarily other adjectives—he would probably not have written *a nice-to-read book* or *a comfortable-to-wear jacket.* All the same, one cannot be sure of restrictions: a real estate flier reads *The at-no-cost-to-you gift is just our way of pointing out a good thing.*

Derivation is less productive. There are comparatively few affixes in English which the average speaker would feel free to attach in order to make a new word—which is another way of saying that there are few of which the average speaker is fully aware. And awareness stems from a fairly high degree of stability of meaning. As we have seen, even the agentive *-er* is rather unpredictable. But *de-*, with the sense 'remove' or 'extract,' is easily attached, as in to *de-scent* a skunk, to *de-sting* a wasp, to *de-bug* an office, to *desensitize* a nerve. A writer or speaker is free to make a word to order using it, as in this example from a popular magazine: *The vice president, manager and secretary were de-hired.*[11] But *de-* would have to be accounted a different prefix, in this respect, from the *de-* of *demand, deter, defer,* and *depend.* Other readily usable affixes are *-an* 'inhabitant or national of,' *anti-* 'against,' *astro-* 'pertaining to the stars

---

[10] Marchand 1969 and Adams 1973 are recommended.
[11] *Reader's Digest* (April 1974), p. 162.

or to astronomy,' *electro-* 'pertaining to electricity,' *-esque* 'in the style of,' *extra-* 'exceeding the usual limit,' *-ful* 'amount as measured by' (*cupful, jugful*), *inter-* 'between,' *-ish* 'approximately,' *-ism* 'doctrine,' *-itis* 'irritation of,' *-ize* 'act or make according to the norm of,' *micro-* 'very small,' *neo-* 'new,' *non-* (negation), *-ocracy* 'rule of,' *omni-* 'all,' *out-* 'surpass' (in some respect, as in *outbid, outrun*), *pan-* 'universal,' *pre-* 'before,' *post-* 'after,' *pro-* 'for,' *pseudo-* 'pretended, false,' *re-* 'again' (with the same shading off into the unrecognizable as with *de-:* for example, *to resent*), *semi-* 'half,' *super-* 'surpassingly,' *trans-* 'across,' *ultra-* 'extremely,' *-ward* 'in the direction of,' *-wise* 'as far as X is concerned.' Specialists in various fields employ technical affixes, of which those in chemistry are among the most elaborate. At times the affixed element is so much like a word that it is hard to tell a derivative from a compound. 'Teaching oneself' is called *auto-instruction* or *self-instruction;* the formations are similar but *self* exists as a separate word in the relevant sense. Other such morphemes are *-like, off-,* and *-most* (*doglike* devotion, *offset* screwdriver, *foremost* contender).

The make-up of derivatives can be highly complex. In *irrevocable* there are four morphemes, of which three are affixes—the two prefixes *ir-* and *-re-* and the suffix *-able*—and one is the base, *-voc-*. All are *bound*, which is to say that they are never used alone. The base *-voc-* appears in *vocation, provoke, vociferous,* and *vocabulary,* but not as an independent word (though *voice*, from the same historical source, is a word). In *ungetatable* there are also four morphemes, but now the *bound* morphemes *un-* and *-able* are matched by the *free* morphemes *-get-* and *-at-*.[12] From another standpoint *irrevocable* can be analyzed as *ir-revocable* and *ungetatable* as *un-getatable,* and then of course both *revocable* and *getatable* are free, since they are also words. This expresses the inner structure better than the mere chopping up into morphemes, because it shows the order in which the elements are attached. *Ungetatable* is not 'able to be not got at' but 'not able to be got at'—the elements are combined as follows:

get + at
getat + able
un + getatable

Returning to compounds, the variety is as great as the productivity. All the major categories of words are represented. There are compound prepositions, such as *alongside of* and *notwithstanding;* compound con-

---

[12] One might argue that *-able* is free too, since it is pretty close to the *able* of *It is able to be revoked.* But this comparison does not hold for some speakers, who use *able* only for animate beings: *He is able to revoke it.*

junctions, such as *whenever* and *whereas;* compound adverbs, such as *indeed* and *moreover;* compound pronouns, such as *you-all* and *myself;* compound numerals, such as *twenty-five* and *nine-tenths.* There is even a compound indefinite, *another.* As for nouns, verbs, and adjectives, the array of forms is too rich to be more than sampled. Some types with nouns:

1. Noun plus noun: *handbook, skylab, shoehorn*

2. Adjective plus noun: *greenhouse, fát lady* (at a circus), *redneck*

3. Noun plus adjective: *attorney general, notary public, cousin german* (first cousin)

4. Verb plus noun: *killjoy, breakwater, cutthroat*

5. Noun plus verb: *windbreak, toothpick, barkeep*

6. Noun plus verb plus *-er: man-eater, party-pooper, purse-snatcher*

7. Verb plus verb: *make-believe*

8. Verb plus adverb: *holdout, runoff, takeover*

9. Adverb plus verb: *downpour, outlay, afterblast*

Not all these arrangements are equally productive. Probably 1, 6, and 8 are responsible for more new nouns than any of the rest. The almost day-to-day striking of new coins with the verb-and-adverb stamp can be seen in the following, which describes some of the formations with *-in,* and incidentally lets us see the meaning veering away from 'in' toward something like 'happening related to':

> Local groups have mounted a colorful variety of demonstrations. . . . Last September nearly 1000 recipients picketed the welfare department in New York . . . ; the protest culminated in a three day *sit-in* by AFDC [Aid to Families with Dependent Children] mothers. Some 200 in Cleveland staged a *buy-in* at a local department store, carefully selecting children's books, scarves, winter coats and other items . . . , for which they instructed the store manager to bill the department of welfare. In California recipients have organized *job-ins* to demand suitable employment at regular wages for men who are able to work. . . . *Cook-ins* have been used. At a demonstration in Baltimore, a meal prepared from surplus food was served the Mayor in his office; he declined to eat it.[13]

Love-in, wade-in, and *teach-in* are other such compounds. In 1974 people were organizing *impeach-ins.*

---

[13] *The Nation* (8 May 1967), p. 583.

Compound adjectives are similarly made up. Some examples:

1. Noun plus adjective: *letter-perfect, garden-fresh, kissing-sweet*

2. Adjective plus adjective: *icy-cold, red-hot, greenish-blue*

3. Adjective or adverb plus participle: *low-slung, quick-frozen, easy-going, slow-running*

4. Adjective plus noun plus -ed: *half-witted, one-eyed, old-fashioned*

5. Adjective plus noun (related to 3 and 4 but without -ing or -ed): *white-face(d), high-class(ed), low-budget(ed), low-cost(ing), whole-grain(ed)*

6. Noun plus verb with -ing: *man-eating, truth-telling, heart-warming*

7. Noun plus past participle of verb: *store-bought, heaven-sent, company-built*

8. Noun plus noun plus -ed: *fish-faced, bull-headed, bow-legged*

Examples of compound verbs:

1. Adjective plus verb: *to hard-boil, to loose-pack, to deep-fry*

2. Adjective plus noun: *to bad-mouth, to blacklist, to cold-shoulder*

3. Noun plus verb: *to firebomb, to playact, to hand-paint*

4. Noun plus noun: *to waterlog, to spotlight, to sandpaper*

5. Adverb plus verb: *to overturn, to backpaddle, to underestimate*

6. Verb plus adverb: *to run over, to play along, to write up*

There are other ways of classifying compounds than according to the parts of speech that their elements belong to. Certain nouns, for example, can be classed together as epithets for persons: *muttonhead* (noun plus noun) and *redneck* (adjective plus noun) are functionally similar, and *clubfoot, sorehead, fishface, droopy drawers,* and *peg leg* belong to the same class. Another scheme is to classify them according to the syntactic relations of the elements. Thus *haircut, neck-shave,* and *back rub* have a nominalized verb as the second element and the object of that same verb as the first; while *cockfight, horserace,* and *rainfall* have the nominalized verb plus its subject: the cocks fight, the horses race, and the rain falls.

Compounding and derivation are not the only ways of making new words. Some, especially trade names, may be pure inventions—as pure, at least, as such creations ever are, given the fact that some analogy with what we already know invariably influences our "free" choice of sounds.

Dreft, the name of a soap powder, was coined with a hint of *soft, drift, lift, sift, deft. Kodak* was attention-getting because of its innovative use of the *k-* spelling, which has been imitated since in many other trade names. A rich source of terms relating to social and political organization is the combined pronunciation of the initial letters of composite names, sometimes pronounced letter by letter, as in *FBI, TVA, SPCA;* sometimes merged, as in *UNESCO, SEATO, NATO, SNCC.* Such words are called *acronyms.* Of late, the composite name has tended to be chosen on the basis of some already existing word that is felt to express the aim or style of the organization—for example, *PANIC* for *People Against National Identity Cards, PUSH* for *People United to Save Humanity, DOOM* for *Drugs Out Of Meat.* Naturally this leads to a drying up of acronyms as a source for anything new.[14] A third device is *reduplication.* The same morpheme is repeated, with or without modification: *hush-hush, mishmash, helter-skelter, fiddle-faddle.*

Finally, new words that are new only in a grammatical sense are made by a process called *conversion* or *zero-derivation:* a word belonging to one part of speech is extended to another part of speech, as when English turns nouns into verbs. Some of the examples of compound verbs just cited are actually converted nouns: *sandpaper, spotlight, blacklist.* The majority of one-syllable nouns in English also exist as one-syllable verbs: *hunt, to hunt; walk, to walk; sight, to sight; play, to play; crate, to crate; field, to field. Zero-derivation* is so called because it is part of a larger pattern in which something is usually added *other* than zero. *Beauty* is made into a verb by adding *-fy: beautify. Lovely* becomes a noun through the addition of *-ness: loveliness. Equate* takes *-ion* to become the noun *equation.* No matter how it is done, the essential meaning of the root word remains unchanged. Much of the business of derivation is simply getting the parts of speech to match up. We have a noun *queen* and need an adjective to mean 'like a queen'; hence *queenly.* We have an adjective *scarce* and need a noun to mean 'condition of being scarce'; hence *scarcity.* But derivation enlarges the lexicon in other ways too—for sex in *princess,* for endearment or contempt in *princeling,* for abstraction in *kingship,* and so on. Actually there is a sort of "zero-derivation" every time the meaning of a word is extended. We see this most clearly when a word moves into an area of meaning that we can label as a category of some kind (as when the mass noun *beer* becomes a count noun in *I want two beers*), but categories are merely features of meaning that happen to play some very striking role in the grammar of a language, and since "very" is a matter of degree we can never be quite sure what constitutes a category. If we want to recognize a category "causative," then when people say *healthy food* rather than *healthful food* they are "converting" *healthy* into a causative adjective.

---

[14] American Name Society *Bulletin* (December 1972), pp. 8–9.

Word-building formulas can be expressed as transformations, more commonly used in sentence building, as will be seen in the next chapter. For example, the conversion of adjectives to adverbs by adding *-ly* is regular enough to write with the rule

$$[+\text{Adj}] \longrightarrow [+\text{Adv}] / \underline{\hspace{1.5cm}} \textit{-ly}$$

—'a form that carries the feature "adjective" becomes a form that carries the feature "adverb" in the environment of an added *-ly*.' Thus from *nice* we get *nicely,* from *vain* we get *vainly,* and from *dreary* we get *drearily,* and if tomorrow the adjective *feminish* were to appear, we could expect shortly to hear *feminishly.* The usefulness of transformations is in direct proportion to the productivity of the affix.

Compounds can be described transformationally too. The familiar type represented by *rope-puller, clam digger, woodcutter, letter opener, fire extinguisher,* and so forth can be expressed as follows:

NP₁	V	NP₂	$\longrightarrow$	NP₂	V+*-er*
He (or *it*)	*opens*	*letters*		*letter*	*opener*

—'first noun phrase followed by verb followed by second noun phrase is transformed into second noun phrase followed by verb plus *-er*.' This of course skips a step. It looks beneath the compound—which means 'opener of letters'—into the derivation of *opener* from *to open.*

Table 5–1 summarizes the principal ways of forming words discussed in this section.

Grammatical morphemes: inflections and function words

Most morphemes are like the ones already described: bits of form and meaning that provide the stuff for an expanding lexicon. At the first moment one of them is pressed into service, we say that a new word has been created. As with other creative acts, we cannot be sure which way it is going to go. The person who first invented the expression *stir-crazy* might have said *jail-happy, cell-silly, pen-potty,* or anything else that came handy and was colorful. But once *stir-crazy* had made its bow, anyone wishing to compare two individuals in terms of this affliction was almost certain to do it in just one way: "Abe is *more stir-crazy* than Leo." The use of *more,* or of the suffix *-er* in *crazier,* is seen not as a way of making new words but as a way of doing something to the words we already have. It is manipulative, not creative. In the early part of the Second

TABLE 5–1
Ways of Forming Words

	Noun	*Adjective*	*Verb*	*Adverb*	*Preposition*
COMPOUNDING	short circuit face-lift shoot-out	near-black high-rise childlike	overwork waterlog playact	crosswise heavenward nevertheless	notwithstanding
DERIVATION	microorganism cupful dedication	foolish trans-Pacific eatable	bedevil glamorize outbid	neatly	despite
INVENTION	Xerox				
ACRONYMY	NATO				
REDUPLICATION	jimjams				
CONVERSION (zero-derivation)	ripoff	fun ("a fun game")	to brunch	ape ("to go ape")	adjacent ("adja- cent the build- ing")

World War, someone might have said *The news is that Hitler threatens to blitz London,* and someone else might have replied *I don't know what "blitz" means but if he ever blitzed that place he'd get blitzed right back.* The second speaker added *-ed* automatically to something he had never heard before. He did not create a "new word" but used the "same word" in a "different form."

Morphemes such as *more, -er,* and *-ed* belong to the grammar of a language and are accordingly called *grammatical morphemes.* By and large they do two things: they signal relationships within language, and they signal certain meanings that are so vital in communication that they have to be expressed over and over. An example of the first function is the morpheme *than* (which also happens to be a word), which simply relates the terms of a comparison: *John is older than Mary.* An example of the second function is the morpheme that pluralizes nouns. We can say, without committing ourselves as to how many dogs there were, *John suffered several dog bites.* But if we mention *dog* in the usual way we are forced to reveal whether there was one or more than one: *John was bitten by his neighbor's dog(s).* English speakers feel that "number" is important enough to be automatically tagged to the word. They also demand grammatical consistency: a singular must go with a singular and a plural with a plural; that is why we reject **this men, *they has,* and **she like.* Languages do not always agree on the particular kinds of meanings that are given this sort of preferential treatment but certain ones are typical: number, tense, definiteness, animateness, possession—even, in certain languages, such things as size and shape.

The two uses of grammatical morphemes just mentioned—to signal relationships within language and to signal certain favored meanings—are usually separated by linguists but are really impossible to keep apart. *Jill's book* uses the possessive morpheme *-'s* to describe ownership, a fact of the real world. *Jill's smoking* does not use it to say that *Jill* owns smoking but to show that *Jill* is the grammatical subject of the verb *smoke.* The word *that* in *That's the woman!* combined with a pointing gesture singles out an object in the real world. In *I didn't mean that* it refers to something just said, something in language.

The last example with *that* and the earlier one with *than* reveal that grammatical morphemes, like lexical morphemes, may be whole words as well as parts of words. Both the suffix *-ed* and the word *that* are grammatical morphemes. When we attach them, grammatical morphemes are called *inflections.* When we leave them by themselves they are called *function words.* The suffixes *-s, -ed, -'s,* and *-ing* are inflections. (English likes to inflect by using suffixes, but other languages may incorporate their inflections at the beginning or in the middle of words.) *That, the, my, us, he, and, when, than,* and numerous similar forms are function words.

The difference between inflections and function words is not in what they do with meanings and relationships. They are so similar in this respect that one occasionally finds an inflection and a function word both playing the same role or even alternating with each other, like *-er* and *more* in *quicker* and *more rapidly.* The difference between them lies in their behavior as physical entities. Function words share the freedom of words. Other words may be inserted between them and the items to which they belong. Thus *the man* can be split to give *the big man, the great big man, the wonderful great big man,* and so on; *more beautiful* can have additional *more's* inserted, giving *more and more beautiful* (we cannot say **prettier and -er);* and *who* can be separated fore and aft by pauses: *the man—uh—who—uh—had to leave.* Function words may be contrastively accented, which is hardly possible with inflections: we can say *Mary is happier now,* but if someone asserts that she is less happy we cannot counter with **She is happiér*—we have to say *She is móre happy.*

Though function words *may* be accented, they usually are not. All grammatical morphemes tend to be inconspicuous. Their job is to serve the main carriers of meaning, the lexical words: to relate them, refer back to them, combine them or separate them, augment them or diminish them, substitute for them, and so on. Grammatical morphemes hover about the lexical words or groups of words, attaching themselves in front or behind and sometimes in the middle; they get less attention, are less clearly articulated and less frequently accented, and their second-class citizenship leads to the changes and reductions and losses of sounds that were noted in the last chapter—the allomorphs of *a, an,* for example, or those of the past-tense inflection. Other examples: the reduction of *than* to /ən/, as in *She's better'n he is;* of *will* to /l/, as in *I'll do it;* and of *is* to /əz/ or just /s/ or /z/, as in *The first is ready, Jack's here,* and *Joanna's waiting.*

Grammatical morphemes are relatively more stable in meaning than lexical morphemes. The contrast is especially marked when we compare the two kinds of suffixes. A grammatical suffix—that is, an inflection— tends to be simply additive: we can pretty safely predict that if the plural *-s* is added to a new noun, it will mean 'more than one.' There are exceptions—*scissors, trousers, pliers*—but they cannot approach the variety of even a relatively stable lexical morpheme. Take adverbial *-ly,* for example. We expect it to add merely the meaning of 'in a certain way' to its adjective: *an enveloping affection; She is so envelopingly affectionate.* But this is not true of certain senses of *individually, constitutionally, presently,* or *perfectly.* It is true of *hopefully* in *He looked at me hopefully* but not in *Hopefully there will be no more complaints.*

Despite its usefulness, the line between grammatical and lexical morphemes is an arbitrary one. This can be seen in the behavior of the comparative suffix (inflection?) *-er.* We feel that when we say *redder* we are using a "different form of the same word *red,*" not a different word, as would be the case with *curvaceous,* based on *curve.* So *-er* seems to qualify on this score as a grammatical morpheme. It also qualifies on the score of its relationship to *more,* which is suppletive, like that of *go* and *went: -er* is used with one-syllable adjectives (*hotter, scarcer*) and two-syllable ones ending in a reduced vowel (*lovelier, narrower*), *more* with the rest (*more beautiful, more sullen*). But when we look closely at the adjectives that take one or the other form of comparison, we find things more characteristic of lexical morphemes. For one, the lower in frequency—that is, the less familiar—the adjective is, the less it is apt to be used with *-er,* even given the right phonological conditions. Sentences such as *ᵖProblems were rifer than ever,* *ᵖMary was chaster than Elizabeth,* *ᵖYou look wanner than you did last night,* and others with similar little-used one-syllable adjectives are distinctly odd, and **He is apter to go than to stay* is impossible. On the other hand, a longer adjective that is widely used more readily takes *-er.* Compare the much-used *handsome* with the little-used *winsome: Jerry is handsomer than Jim;* *ᵖOlivia is winsomer than Charlotte.* A bad-sounding combination is avoided even when the adjective is a common one: **sourer.* This does not happen with grammatical morphemes; *casts* takes its inflection *-s* despite the resulting sequence of alveolars. And there are other problems—contrasts in meaning, for example. The sentence *I've never seen a man prouder* is more likely to refer to active pride, say in the accomplishments of a daughter, whereas *I've never seen a man more proud* suggests self-pride. All in all, we are simply unable to make a neat determination of whether to call *-er* and *more* grammatical or lexical.

The same is true of many full words. We would like to distinguish between function words and "content" words, as lexical words are often called because they seem to "contain" more meaning than function words. But the distinction is hard to draw. We ordinarily think of the word *man* as a content word; certainly it is one in *Do you see that man over there?* But if in answer to *Why is he on trial?* someone says *Because he killed a man,* de-accenting *man,* then *man* is little more than 'somebody'; it is a function word filling an otherwise empty grammatical slot, and the whole idea could just as well have been expressed with *Because he did a killing.* This is the process by which the word *body* became incorporated in *everybody, somebody,* and *nobody* and by which *-man* became an unstressed suffix in *workman.*

Given the haziness of the line, we can only make certain *relative* statements about function words. They are used relatively more often than lexical words to point to elements in language or to the roles of speakers and hearers, and less often to point to things and events in the real world. They are relatively fewer than lexical words. They belong to classes that are relatively closed—new nouns are added every day, but new prepositions very rarely. And they can be *listed* with relative assurance. Grammar books recognize the following:

1. The verb *to be* when it merely links: *Flowers are pretty.*

2. The prepositions: *to, at, for, by,* etc.

3. The identifying words, or determiners, such as the articles, possessives, and demonstratives, which relate things to their environments: *the house, that man, my daughter, some idiot, another candidate, the same problem, which piece*

4. The quantifiers: *many, few, more, less, any, none,* etc., and the numerals

5. The coordinating conjunctions: *and, or, nor, but, also, so, yet*

6. The relatives, which attach adjective clauses to their antecedents: *the man who, the place where, the time when, the dog which;* also the ones that "include their antecedent"—*He gave me what* (= *that which*) *I wanted.*

7. The adverbial conjunctions, which bring adverb clauses into certain logical relationships (time, condition, concession, cause, etc.) with the sentence as a whole: *because, when, before, while, although, if, providing, unless,* etc.

8. The conjunctive adverbs, which relate a following sentence to a preceding one in certain logical ways: *besides, instead, nevertheless, still, accordingly, thereupon, hence, later,* etc.

9. The intensifiers: *too, very, quite, somewhat, a little, pretty,* etc.

10. The auxiliary verbs: *can, may, have, do, be* (in certain functions), etc.

11. The pronouns, pro-adverbs, and other pro-words, which stand in for lexical words or phrases: *it, she, he, I, them, hers, his, so* (as in *So he did*), *there, here, then,* etc.

How new function words do occasionally come into existence can be illustrated by the intensifiers. The word *very* originally meant 'truly'—even now we can say *truly good (verily good)* to intensify—and did not become a standard intensifier until the fifteenth century. Others have since been added, and some discarded. If *very* in *very good* is a function word, then so is *damned* in *damned good. Awful, real,* and *'way* are fairly recent additions (*awful good, real good, 'way better*). The turnover with intensifiers is high because the newer and more striking the intensifier the more it seems to intensify.

The English inflections can be listed more easily than the function words, though still not with complete confidence, as we have seen with the comparative *-er.* They are the following:

1. Noun, plural: *cat, cats*

2. Noun, possessive: *cat, cat's*

3. Verb, present: *to earn, earns*

4. Verb, past: *to earn, earned*

5. Verb, present participle: *to earn, earning*

6. Verb, past (or passive) participle: *to earn, earned; to fall, fallen (they have earned, they have fallen)*

7. Adjective, comparative: *sweet, sweeter*

8. Adjective, superlative: *sweet, sweetest*

The shortness of this list compared with the length of the list of function words puts English into the class of *analytic* languages (see page 28): it is one of those languages that tend to analyze out the grammatical functions and put them in separate words rather than incorporating them as affixes within lexical words. Latin is an example of the opposite type.

Table 5–2 summarizes the distinctions among the various kinds of morphemes discussed in this chapter.

TABLE 5–2
Types of English Morphemes

Kinds of Morphemes	Degrees of Independence	
	Words	Affixes
Lexical morphemes	Words incorporatable in new words by COMPOUNDING (*clam + bake → clambake*) Words incorporatable in new words by DERIVATION (*push + -y → pushy*) (mis- + *fire → misfire*)	More or less productive prefixes (*un-* in *un*denatured) Unproductive prefixes (*di-* in *di*gest) More or less productive suffixes (*-able* in orbit*able*) Unproductive suffixes (*-ose* in verb*ose*) Word fragments (*-burger* in cheese*burger*)
Grammatical morphemes	Function words (*the, of, which, my, when, and, if* . . .)	Inflectional suffixes (*-s, -ed, -ing* . . .)

ADDITIONAL REMARKS AND APPLICATIONS

1. List some idioms and decide what kinds of internal change they permit. (For example, consider the acceptability, for you, of the following: *What's the matter with her? What was the matter with him? What had been the matter with them? Which is the matter with you? That wasn't the matter with him,* and so forth.)

2. Discuss the difference between *That story seems likely* and *That's a likely story.*

3. *Of* and *about* are frequently synonymous—for example, in *They spoke of (about) you* and *It's a story of (about) adventure.* Do the following, as wholes, mean the same?

   There's no question of my doing it.
   There's no question about my doing it.

4. One of the following sentences will probably strike you as more incomplete than any of the others. Does it suggest that *not* has a peculiar affinity to another word in the sentence, and this combination requires something else to complete it?

   She was just tired.   She was not just tired.
   She was only tired.   She was not only tired.

5. Decide your preferences in the following sentences and discuss the nature of any restriction you may note:

   She paid a high price for her hat.
   She paid a heavy price for her hat.
   She paid a high price for her indiscretion.
   She paid a heavy price for her indiscretion.

6. Can you tell from the following (and any other contexts that occur to you) whether there are restrictions on the verbs that relate to their use as imperatives?

   Get there before ten o'clock!
   I'll try to get there before ten o'clock.
   Arrive before ten o'clock!

> I'll try to arrive before ten o'clock.
> Depart on time.
> Leave on time.
> I suggest that you depart on time.
> I suggest that you leave on time.

7. An adjective placed before a noun tends to characterize it, to indicate what it really is or how we want to classify it. One placed after a noun (including after a form of *to be*) tends to indicate the way the thing designated by the noun is or strikes us at the moment. Thus *the handy tools* tells us something about the nature of the tools, whereas *the tools handy* tells us where they are—'within reach.' Judge the following sentences as acceptable or unacceptable, and see if your judgments force you to recognize a special class of adjectives in the light of what happens when they are placed before or after the noun:

   a. Alice was sorry.
   b. The sorry man put on his hat.
   c. Bobbie is asleep.
   d. The asleep baby had a blissful look on its face.
   e. George was pretty personal, wasn't he? I didn't expect him to be quite so personal in his remarks.
   f. Yes, George is a personal man.
   g. Mary was positively green, she was so sick.
   h. Yes, Mary was a green woman.
   i. All of a sudden the girl was faint; she could hardly rise.
   j. The faint girl recovered and got up.

8. Discuss the following passage:

   > The indications from neurophysiology and psychology are that, instead of storing a small number of primitives [= elements] and organizing them in terms of a [relatively] large number of rules, we store a large number of complex items which we manipulate with comparatively simple operations. The central nervous system is like a special kind of computer which has rapid access to the items in a very large memory, but comparatively little ability to process these items when they have been taken out of memory. There is a great deal of evidence that muscular movements are organized in terms of complex, unalterable chunks of at least a quarter of a second in duration (and often much longer) and nothing to indicate organization in terms of short simultaneous segments which require processing with context-restricted rules.[15]

---

[15] From Ladefoged 1972, p. 282. A context-restricted rule is one that specifies what contexts a form can be used with. For instance, if the prefix **in-** for 'negation' were

9. Do individual words sometimes have idiosyncratic traits? Pronounce the following two sentences and decide whether *sharp* and *keen* differ in their sound in any marked way other than in the phonemes that make them up—for example, do you tend to accent or lengthen one of the words more than the other?

> My knife has a sharp blade.
> My knife has a keen blade.

10. Would you say that the word *bound* resembles an affix in expressions like *homeward bound, outward bound,* and *California bound?* Compare it with its synonym *headed* in as many constructions and positions as you can think of.

11. List some scientific terms and divide them into morphemes. See if you can find some words using informal morphemes, such as *bumber-, -teria, -nik* (as in *peacenik*), and so forth.

12. Discuss the following statement: "In sentence building we can predict what speakers will do; in word building we are wise after the fact."

13. What is unusual about the agentive *-er* derivatives of the verb *to execute?* Is an *executioner* the same as an *executor?* Does *executor* have some peculiarity of pronunciation that is absent in *prosecutor?*

14. *To overpower* and *to subdue* are synonyms, and have approximately the same frequency of use. Is it as easy to attach the *-er* suffix to one as to the other? If not, what is the trouble? Would there be the same trouble as a rule in attaching an inflectional suffix?

15. Is *I'll thank you to . . .* an expression of thanks?

16. List some compounds that are written with hyphens and some that are written without. Is the distinction justifiable?

17. If *postmaster general* is a compound, what about *life eternal* and *blood royal?* What is there about these expressions that is apt to make them fuse into compounds? Look up the source of the term *general* as a military rank.[16]

"context-free" it would be able to occur before any form to which its negativeness might be appropriate. But it is not context-free, since rather than *inruffled* we say **unruffled.** So *in-* is context-restricted according to some such rule as "Use before Latin-derived forms only." *Inobdurate* would be possible. According to Ladefoged, we would operate with *inobdurate* as a whole (if there were such a word), not with *in-obdurate.*

[16] Onions 1966 is a good source.

18. In the expression *He's got a good thing there,* does *good thing* qualify as a compound? If so, see whether in addition it tends to collocate only with certain verbs and in certain expressions. For example, is the meaning in question as likely to be found in the subject of a sentence as in the predicate (*A good thing would be that kind of job* versus *That kind of job would be a good thing*), and as likely after one semantically possible verb as another (*They created a good thing for him, He's looking for a good thing*)?

19. *People and events combine to jeopardize careers and their very lives,* declares an announcement for a TV program.[17] In conversational English, what other expressions can you think of in which *very* directly modifies a noun? Does *very* qualify as "collocationally restricted"?

20. In one test given to British and American college students the instructions were to complete sentences of which only the first couple of words were supplied. One such beginning was *I completely* and another was *I entirely.* How would you finish the sentences? After you have decided, check the footnote and comment on any implications there seem to be for the reality of collocations.[18]

21. Imagine that *A* is writing a letter to *B* containing one or the other of the two following sentences:

  a. I think it would be a very good idea for us to take the route that Mary suggested.

  b. I think it would be a good idea for us to take the route that Mary suggested.

See whether it would make a difference in the choice if

  c. *A* is just now making the recommendation to *B*.

  d. *B* has already made the recommendation to *A* and *A* is agreeing to it.

Match c, d to a, b. Are there collocations involved in this distinction?

22. What is the plural of *boa constrictor?* How does this compare with *attorney general?*

23. Pronounce the following sentences aloud and decide whether there

---

[17] Palo Alto *Times* (13 August 1974), p. 27.

[18] The British students overwhelmingly favored *I entirely agree;* the Americans favored it, but less so. Both the British and the Americans favored *I completely forgot.* From Greenbaum 1974.

is evidence for regarding any expressions that they contain as compounds (hyphens have been omitted):

a. She's a seven year old.

b. She's seven years old.

c. It brings a new appreciation of the high country. (a description of Yosemite National Park)

d. Do you like graham crackers?

e. I won't accept that, not by a damn sight.

f. Looking out I saw a lone shark cutting through the water.

g. Larry Livermore is a loan shark.

h. She was frightened by a grisly bear.

i. She was frightened by a grizzly bear.

j. Cut me a slice of apple pie.

k. Who invented the talking machine?

l. She's crazy about oyster stew and ice cream.

m. He never wanted to be a boy scout.

n. Who are the members of the grand jury?

o. He's a combination smart Aleck, nosey Parker, and gloomy Gus.

p. She tripped because she's near sighted.

q. She's admired because she's so far sighted.

r. You're a pain in the neck.

s. Only from Harger-Haldeman can you buy with such a small down payment.

t. He calls it a gunny sack but I call it a burlap bag.

u. Now then: What was it you were claiming?

24. Do counting words fuse into a kind of intonational unit with a following noun? Compare the following and decide your preferences:

	anx		par			anxious	
an		ious	ent	versus	an		parent

	hun		par			hundred	
a		dred	ents	versus	a		parents

		re		con			recent	
their		cent		quests	versus	their		conquests

		man		con			many	
their		y		quests	versus	their		conquests

25. Note the different stress patterns in the two columns below and see if you can attribute the difference to a difference in function. (Some of the combinations are normally written solid.)

a stone fence	a book shelf
a brick wall	an ink eraser
a screen door	a table top
a paper doll	a garbage collector
an aluminum ladder	a stone mason
a cotton dress	a paper hanger

26. What happens to the accents when compounds are further compounded? Compare the following:

   a. I gave him some leather carving tools. ('tools for carving leather')

   b. I gave him some carving tools.

   Is *leather* in sentence a more prominent than *carving* in a? Is it also more prominent than *carving* in b?

27. Single out the element in the word *tobacconist* that merely serves to connect the two meaningful morphemes. Such an element is called a *stem-forming* affix: *tobacco-* is the base but *tobaccon-* is the stem to which *-ist* is added. Think of the numerous words in English that end in *-meter* and the stems to which they are attached—for example, compare *thermometer* and *thermal, pedometer* and *pedal.* Is there a stem-forming affix in the *-meter* words? What about the word *mobocracy?*

28. The examples on pages 112–13 are culled from Marchand 1969 (pages 506–13). Consult this index yourself and decide whether for you there are additional productive affixes. Are there any in the list on pages 112–13 that you would hesitate to make a new word with?

29. Three typical noun-forming suffixes in English are *-dom* (as in *kingdom, officialdom*), *-ion* (*relation, confusion*), and *-ness* (*gladness, oneness*). List some more nouns having these suffixes. Find other noun-forming suffixes and give examples. Do the same for adjective-forming suffixes (such as *-less, -ish,* and *-ous*), and verb-forming suffixes (such as *-fy, -ize,* and *-en*). Which of these suffixes are still productive?

30. Why is it that when a person is suspected of complicity we can say *They tied him to that crime,* but when he is exonerated we cannot say **They untied him?*

31. Discuss the condition of "free" versus "bound" of the morphemes in the following words: *multiple, many-fold, manifold, multiply* (verb), *three-ply.*

32. Is there—for purposes of copyright—a kind of legal definition of "word"? Consider the relative copyrightability of **Technicolor** and **Color Movie.** (**Technicolor** is made up of standard elements: **techn-,** as in **technology;** **-i-,** as in **purify;** and **color;** compare **versicolor.**)

33. In recent years the element **-wise** has been extended from such forms as **crosswise, otherwise, slantwise** to expressions on the order of **I have all I need, money-wise; Friend-wise, she is hard up.** Originally **wise** was an independent word meaning 'manner,' which survives in **in no wise** and a few other phrases. Would you consider the new combinations to be derivatives or compounds? Discuss.

34. Would you class **half-finished** as a compound or a derivative? Does it mean the same as **semi-finished?** (Try them in these contexts: **The furniture that they have on sale is _____, needing only a bit of sanding and of stain or varnish. That job is only _____—you'll have to get back to it tomorrow.**)

35. Dekie, aged six, drove with his grandmother from California to Florida. On the way he telephoned his mother and reported that he was **car sick.** This caused a little confusion until he explained that he meant 'sick of driving in this car.' What theory of adjective compounding had he formulated in order to come up with this expression?

36. List some trade names, some acronyms, and some **-in** compounds, and discuss their formation.

37. What sort of word-making device is used in **yakety-yak?**

38. How would you describe the following forms?—**by and by, through and through, over and over, out and out, again and again, less and less.** What about **to and fro, back and forth, in and out?** Think of some more examples.

39. Give the paraphrase you would use for the following compounds: **goldsmith, locksmith, gunsmith.** Check a good dictionary for **blacksmith.**

40. Is there a semantic reason for the rarity or absence of such adverbs as

*bigly, *greenly, *dentedly (compare *pointedly*)? (Remember the *kind* of adverb that is most often formed with *-ly*.) How would the rule have to be restricted to take care of this? What about such forms as *drowsingly (compare *rousingly*), *tollingly (compare *ringingly*), *complimentingly (compare *insultingly*)? (Is *ringing,* for example, listed in dictionaries as an adjective, whereas *tolling* is not?)

41. The text gives the formula [+Adj] ⟶ [+Adv]/_____ *-ly*. Look at the following and decide which expressions sound right to you and which sound wrong. Then try to state the exceptions to the adverb-forming rule.

   a. She came in majestically.
      She came in queenlily.
      That man is surly.
      He spoke surlily.

   b. Why do they behave so oddly?
      Why do they behave so funnily?
      He spoke with ease—yes, he spoke quite easily.
      He spoke with difficulty—yes, he spoke quite difficultly.
      Secret societies try to do everything occultly.
      He pretends to be a novelist but he writes mediocrely.

   c. It's amazingly efficient.
      She's inspiringly ambitious.
      He's hoppingly (boilingly) mad.
      It's sizzlingly hot.

42. In your answer to question 25, you may have decided that the function of the left-hand column is to indicate a material of which something is made. If so, how do you account for children saying *múd pie* and *sánd castle?* (Also, did you perhaps wonder about *paper doll,* preferring yourself to stress the first element?) What can you infer about the fused status of these expressions?

43. A woman on the TV show "What's My Line?" was identified as a *dynamite blaster.* Does this mean that she blasts dynamite or that she blasts with dynamite? Or does it simply make no difference, since one probably implies the other?

44. If grammatical morphemes are not ordinarily accented, could that be one reason why children take much longer to learn them than to learn lexical content words, just because they fail to hear them or have their attention drawn to them? Or do you think that because grammatical morphemes depend on the complexities of grammar,

very young children may not yet have attained the cognitive growth to understand and use them? Could the two factors be related?

45. Schoolchildren are taught to say *worse* rather than *badder.* A *New Yorker* cartoon shows two goblins, one saying to the other *I'm badder than you.*[19] Would *worse* do here? If not, why not?

46. If *-er* and *-est* for comparative and superlative inflection were perfectly normal as grammatical morphemes, we would expect their distribution to be the same. See whether you feel that *-er* and *-est* are equally acceptable in the following, and think up more examples:

    a. She's the darlingest girl I've ever seen.

    b. She's a darlinger girl than her sister.

    c. He's the fightingest fellow I've ever met.

    d. He's fightinger than I expected him to be.

Benjamin Franklin wrote in his autobiography *The best dimensions and the properest place for the masts.*[20] Would he have been apt to use the form *properer?* If not, why not?

47. Do you find a difference in acceptability among the following? If so, can you account for it?

    a. She is much lovelier than her sister.

    b. She is much worldlier than her sister.

    c. She looked poorly yesterday and she's looking poorlier today.

48. Mention some function words that are not given in the text but belong in the categories that are listed.

49. If you accepted the following, would it compel you to add something to one of the supposedly "closed classes"?—*Would the middle class parent, absent the kinds of dependency pressures exerted on the welfare family, have even considered surgical sterilization for his children?*[21]

50. In the following pairs of *X–Y* words ("That which can be *X*-ed is *Y*-able"), indicate which have a derivative relationship between *X* and *Y* and which have a suppletive relationship:

    That which can be read is readable.

---

[19] December 1967.

[20] (New York: Rinehart, 1956), p. 171.

[21] *Poverty Law Report* (September 1973), p. 4.

> That which can be drunk is drinkable.
> That which can be known is knowable.
> That which can be discovered is discoverable.
> That which can be seen is visible.
> That which can be heard is audible.
> That which can be done is feasible.

Is the semantic relationship between *hear* and *audible* as tight as that between *know* and *knowable?* (Try saying **That which can be heard is hearable.** Is it normal?) What problem do pairs like these create for positing underlying forms? And in the following,

> That which can be read is readable.
> That which can be read is legible.

are we dealing with a single sense of *to read?*

Assuming that it seems useless to try to derive *hear* and *audible* from a single underlying form, and yet the two are paradigmatically related, does that mean that the mind has no need of formal resemblance in order to bind two things together?

References

Adams, Valerie. 1973. *An Introduction to Modern English Word Formation* (London: Longman).

Cazden, Courtney B. 1972. *Child Language and Education* (New York: Holt, Rinehart and Winston).

Greenbaum, Sidney. 1970. *Verb-Intensifier Collocations in English* (The Hague: Mouton).

———. 1974. "Some Verb-Intensifier Collocations in American and British English," *American Speech* 49. In press.

Ladefoged, Peter. 1972. "Phonetic Prerequisites for a Distinctive Feature Theory," in Albert Valdman (ed.), *Papers in Linguistics and Phonetics in Memory of Pierre Delattre* (The Hague: Mouton).

Marchand, Hans. 1969. *The Categories and Types of Present-day English Word-Formation* (Munich: C. H. Beck).

Mitchell, T. F. 1971. "Linguistic 'Goings On': Collocations and Other Lexical Matters Arising on the Syntagmatic Record," *Archivum Linguisticum*. New series 2:35–69.

Onions, C. T. 1966. *The Oxford Dictionary of English Etymology* (Oxford: Oxford University Press).

SYNTAX 6

Speakers are rather free to apply the rules of compounding. It would cause no particular surprise to hear one person ask complainingly of another *When was his most recent goof-off?* making a noun out of what already exists as a two-word verb, *to goof off.* But if he does this very often, and particularly if he creates words for which the way has not in part already been paved, the result may sound abnormal: *The royal ship-off he got was a real emotional stir-up* might be understood but the speaker would be put down as someone with strenuous mannerisms. On the other hand *Their shipping him off so royally really stirred him up emotionally* would not surprise anyone nor would—as a third possibility —*The royal send-off he got was a real emotional shake-up.*

The difference in our reactions to these sentences stems from crossing the border between morphology and syntax. In making the first sentence the speaker was behaving as if compounds could be thrown together as freely as phrases. But compounds, like other coinages, are tied to a time and a place. When they are used again they are felt to be repeated; they are additions to our vocabulary. *Send-off* and *shake-up* are now stock compounds.

Phrases, unlike words, are at the level of syntax: they can be assembled more or less at will. None of the following contain a precise term for an astronautical landing, but any one of them is suitable for referring to it:

The astronauts touched down in the vicinity of Barbados.

The astronauts came down at 6 P.M.

The astronauts let themselves down from their capsule.

The astronauts plunged down.

The astronauts got down.

The astronauts splashed down.

The fact that other things or persons have been said to touch or slip or flop down does not bar these expressions from use with astronauts. But on the morphological side there is no such freedom. The astronauts may touch down, but this is not a **touchdown,** nor is it a **comedown** nor a **letdown.** These are *terms,* preempted for other uses. To find a term for the astronauts' landing it was necessary to look elsewhere. The splash was only incidental, but **splashdown** was chosen.

The essence of syntax is freedom. How much of that precious essence our minds actually distill—how free we really are—no one can truly say; we have seen enough of collocations to be sure of that. Yet when syntax is compared with words and idioms, its freedom seems almost absolute. The speaker gives every sign of having virtually unlimited means at his disposal for building sentences, provided he builds them according to certain expectations of the hearer—expectations in the form of syntactic rules—and does not violate the restrictions that particular words impose on the kind of company they are willing to keep. The connectedness within words is established once and then repeated, but the connectedness within syntax seems to be ad-libbed.

This sounds as if it should be no trick at all for someone unfamiliar with English—or any other language—to invent good sentences once he tunes in on the pronunciation, commits to heart a respectable list of words, and learns a few rules. The pronunciation can be acquired within hours (at least to the point of intelligibility) and words can be learned by rote; but it takes years to master the intricacies of combination. Ad-libbing in language is an art, just as it is in music, the only difference being that it is an art that all are forced to acquire. The grosser rules can easily be stated—adjectives precede their nouns in English (usually), verbs must have subjects (most of the time), and interrogative words come first in a question (except when they don't); but hidden by these regulatory mountains are hundreds of mere ripples on the landscape, rules that may affect only a small set of words and that grammarians are only beginning to fill in on their relief maps. Why is it that we can say **Music's charm is that it is so soothing** but not **Italian's charm is that it is so melodious* nor **German's verbs are hard to learn?* Only because there is an insignificant rule or part of a rule that forbids us to use the possessive with the name of a language. And why can we say **They were laughing and** *carrying on and making all sorts of noise* but not **They were making all sorts of noise and carrying on and laughing?* Because of another impudent rule that requires us to put progressively farther toward the end of the sentence the expressions that cumulatively sum up the action: *carrying on* is more inclusive than *laughing* and *making all sorts of noise* is more inclusive than *carrying on.* If *generally making a nuisance of themselves* were added it would have to follow everything else.

As for the congeniality of words, their acceptance of the company of others, we can only repeat again that all words drag their past contexts with them to some extent. We may *like* something *better,* but we can only *enjoy* or *fancy* something *more.* We can say *yesterday afternoon* and *last night,* but are blocked from saying **last afternoon* and **yesterday night*—only to find that both *last evening* and *yesterday evening* are perfectly normal. All freedom is relative; originality is packaged with copious amounts of repetition.

TOGETHERNESS

The first rule of syntax, which means etymologically 'a putting together,' is that things belonging together will be together. It transcends all other rules; it is applied by very young speakers and very young deaf users of sign language alike, who will say *beautiful flowers* and *flowers beautiful, my mother* and *mother my, he came* and *came he,* indiscriminately;[1] what is important is that the words are embraced by their proximity. Togetherness may be no more than a nearness in time if a message is spoken, a nearness in space if it is written, or a grouping under a single rhythm or intonation curve.

Two kinds of examples illustrate how pervasive the principle of togetherness is in language. One is our resistance to putting something between two things that are more closely related to each other than they are to what is inserted. Teachers find it hard to enforce the rule of interior plurals in forms like *mothers-in-law* and *postmasters general*—speakers want to put the *-s* at the end. They are even more reluctant to say *hardest-working person,* inserting the *-est* between the members of the compound *hard-working;* and though some might manage it there, probably no one would say **farthest-fetched story* for *most far-fetched story.* Compare the earlier remarks on compounds (page 111).

The second kind of example shows up when two things that formerly did not belong together come to be viewed as if they did, because they

---

[1] Tervoort 1968, pp. 457–58. The speaking child at this stage will be using language more appropriate to the crib, but the principle is the same.

are side by side. Certain prepositions which at an earlier stage were felt (as is customary) to be more closely bound to the following noun, have come to acquire a closer attachment to what precedes, as our manner of spelling sometimes indicates: *lotsa* for *lots of, kinda* for *kind of, sorta* for *sort of.* And the last two have taken the further step of being used as unit adverbs: *kinda nice.* The pull from two directions—from what precedes and what follows—can be detected in mistakes that we sometimes make, like *°an idea of which he was very fond of,* where the preposition is torn between *which* and *fond.*

Given mere togetherness, and ignoring all the traffic rules of syntax, one can interpret a series like *Sick John mad me* if the words are known. It could mean 'When John is sick I'm mad,' or perhaps 'John is sick and mad at me.' But for this to be possible there has to be a second principle, that of the reasonable guess. We depend on it not only to fill in the blanks but to interpret many sentences that remain ambiguous even when the traffic signs are operating. The speaker who said *I went to check on the dry clothes* ran no risk of misunderstanding. Within the situation it could only mean 'I went to check to see whether the clothes that are drying are dry.' Getting clothes dry was the objective and *dry* and *clothes* gravitated together.

This example illustrates another kind of relatedness, which is more fundamental than anything within syntax. It is the relation between what is said and what it is said about. If one adolescent calls *Chicken!* to another adolescent, no syntax is needed to make the connection. Such connections are what language is mainly for. We call them *meaning.*

Operators

Nevertheless, without something more than mere togetherness, sentences would be intolerably ambiguous much of the time even with all the help that a situation has to offer. Often as few as three words side by side can be baffling unless they are somehow ranked and grouped, and as a rule we join more than three words, so that ranks over ranks and groups within groups become a necessity.

The traffic signals that give this information are the grammatical morphemes—function words and inflections—plus such other devices as characteristic types of emphasis or pause or pitch and characteristic arrangements. Together they can be called *operators.* They tell the hearer what goes with what, how close the connection is, what is subordinate to what, where an utterance begins and ends, and so on. They are language turned inward on itself.

As we noted earlier with the possessive *'s,* not all grammatical morphemes are pure traffic signals. Some refer to facts in the real world. The same is true of other operators. Take intonation. A level span by itself at a low pitch in the middle of an utterance is an operator that marks the accompanying words as 'not belonging'—for instance, the parenthetical *I wouldn't put it past him* in the sentence

If he does it—

and I would_n't put it ^past _him—he's ^in for ^trou ble.

But this is impure, because parentheses suggest 'unimportance' as well as grammatical 'incidentalness.' Similarly with word order: in **red brick** versus **brick red** the arrangement tells us which word is the modifier and which is the head. But in **A hundred dollars that mistake cost me!** the word order conveys an emotion; the matter-of-fact statement is **That mistake cost me a hundred dollars.**

How different operators play on different aspects of a sentence can be shown by two sets that get the same result by different means. In *I saw Mary and John together; the former was talking to the latter* the function words *former* and *latter* direct the hearer to select the first and second items just mentioned, in that order. In *I saw Mary and John together; she was talking to him* the function words *she* and *him* direct the hearer to select personal nouns with the semantic feature "female" and "male" respectively. The gross meaning of both sentences is the same.

The more complex a sentence is, the more we depend on the operators to tell us which way to go. If the operators are omitted or garbled, the connections are lost no matter how clear the content words may be. But if the operators are preserved and nonsense words substituted for the content words, one's feeling of disorientation is less acute. John Algeo illustrates both situations with the following sentences:

> Oll considerork meanork, ho mollop tharp fo concernesh bix shude largel philosophigar aspectem ith language phanse vulve increasorkrow de recent yearm engagesh sho attentuge ith scholarm.
>
> In prefarbing torming, we cannot here be pretolled with those murler dichytomical optophs of flemack which have demuggingly in arsell wems exbined the obburtion of maxans.[2]

Though in the first sentence we recognize **consider, mean, concern,** and several other familiar words, we have no idea what to do with them.

---

[2] Algeo 1972, p. 278.

We might think of a foreign language that happened to share a number of cognates with English. But with the second we are back home. Perhaps it is just from some scientific treatise in an unfamiliar field; if we met the writer on the street we could pass the time of day with him.

Constructions and constituents

Even if his statement were factually true, one might doubt the sanity of a person who said something like **George was walking down the street with Mary's elbow.** The absurdity is that it ignores the rankings of what it brings together. George has to accompany something at the same hierarchic level as himself: **George was walking down the street with Mary,** including her elbow.

The same is true with sentences and parts of sentences: togetherness has to be sorted level by level. We saw this even in the internal organization of words, with *indelible ink* (page 106). The two words **ungrace-ful** and **disgraceful** show two different patterns of hierarchic organization:

un	*grace*	*ful*

dis	*grace*	*ful*

In **ungraceful,** *-grace-* is "together with" *-ful,* and **un-** is "together with" *-graceful.* **Disgraceful** reverses these connections.

Any such self-contained stretch of speech is called a *construction,* and its parts are its *constituents.* What the diagrams show is a difference between *ultimate constituents* and *immediate constituents.* The ultimate constituents are all the morphemes, one by one. The immediate constituents are just what-goes-with-what. Thus **dis-** in **disgraceful** is an immediate constituent of *-grace-* (and vice versa), while **disgrace-** as a whole is an immediate constituent of *-ful.*

Analysis by immediate constituents is the most effective way of showing the inner layering of sentences. For example, **He said he wanted to marry her** is analyzed as follows:

He	*said*	*he*	*wanted*	*to*	*marry*	*her.*

The same relationships can be shown by tree diagrams such as the ones that follow:

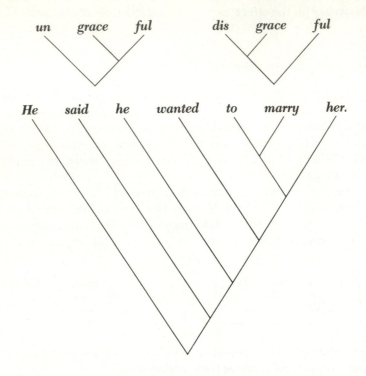

By itself, immediate-constituent analysis tells us how a stretch of speech is layered, but it tells us nothing about the nature of the elements nor the manner in which they are related. For example, **behind the house** and **only a few** have the same constituent diagram,

behind	the	house

only	a	few

but the first is actually more closely related to **in back of the old stone house on the hill,** with a diagram that looks at first glance to be quite different:

in	back	of	the	old	stone	house	on	the	hill

There is an obvious similarity between diagrams of this type and those once used for teaching grammar in the schools, and it suggests what is needed to complete the analysis: something about parts of speech, or word classes, and about subjects, predicates, modifiers, and so on, or the functions of the classes. The diagram begins to look more familiar when we label the spaces:

It	grows	in	back	of	the	old	stone	house	on	the	hill.
							Compound noun				
						Noun modified by adjective			Inner noun phrase		
					Inner noun phrase			Prepositional phrase			
			Compound preposition		Outer noun phrase, object of preposition						
	Main verb		Prepositional phrase, complement of main verb								
Subject		Predicate									
Sentence											

The labeled diagram reveals both the layering and the unlimited possibilities of embedding constructions within constructions: *in back of the old stone house on the hill* is a prepositional phrase that contains a prepositional phrase, *on the hill.* And *on the hill* could be lengthened to contain two more prepositional phrases, *on the hill up the river from here,* in which *up the river from here* modifies *hill* and *from here* modifies *up the river* as a unit, explaining how *up the river* is to be oriented:

on	the	hill	up	the	river	from	here

WORD CLASSES

Labeling a sentence diagram requires some agreement on the names used. They can be names of *classes* or names of *functions*. Those of the diagram on page 141 are not consistent. *It* is called a *subject*. That is a functional term—it does not name a class of words but the role played by a word in a sentence. ***Grows*** is called a *verb,* which is a class of words. Instead of calling *it* a subject we could have called it a *pronoun,* applying the name of its class. And instead of calling ***grows*** a verb we could have called it a *predicate,* applying the name of its function in the sentence. Classes and functions determine each other, but not in any one-to-one fashion. Since we have to start somewhere, we start with the classes, pretending that we know them independently of their functions. This is simpler because classes are exemplified by the words that are their members, and words are easy to lay hold of.

The obvious place to start is with the function words, first because the classes are small, and second because, true to their name, they have functional relationships with nouns, adjectives, and verbs that help to identify the latter, much larger, classes of words.

The classes of function words have already been enumerated (pages 121–22) and there is no need to repeat, but a closer look at one of them is necessary as an example of what most distinguishes classes of function words from classes of lexical words: the fact that function-word classes are closed rather than open. There is less difference from language to language in the open classes: nouns and verbs are universal and adjectives are nearly so, and their make-up is not so radically different that a noun cannot pretty easily be borrowed from one language into another. But the grammatical morphemes, item for item, are where differences are greatest, and function words of course share in this individuality.

Classes of function words have a marked tendency to form paradigms. This is a reflection of their tightly structured area of meaning. Taking personal pronouns as our example, we see them distributed across a matrix of features, which include *person* (first, second, third), *number* (singular and plural), *case* (subjective, objective, possessive), *modification* (adjectival, nominal), and *gender:*[3]

	Subjective	*Objective*	*Possessive*	
Singular			*Adjectival*	*Nominal*
First person	I	me	my	mine
Second person	you	you	your	yours
Third person	he (*masculine*) she (*feminine*) it (*neuter*)	him her it	his her its	his hers its
Plural				
First person	we	us	our	ours
Second person	you	you	your	yours
Third person	they	them	their	theirs

A paradigm of this sort becomes its own justification. That is, if it were not for the tight organization there would be no reason for including everything that is there. If a pronoun is defined as a substitute for some other word, then in the first three columns only the third-person forms really belong. The rest have primary uses—they are not substitutes for anything. In **I did it** the word **I** is not a substitute for a noun but a word with its own referent, 'the speaker.' Except for the paradigm the word **you** would not appear four times; but since **I-we-me-us** have to be distinguished along these parameters, so does **you.** And the paradigm is further justified by the matching paradigm of verb forms: **I am, you are, he is.**

An example of a different scheme, taken from Weri, a language of New Guinea, is shown in Table 6–1. Two sections are needed in the table because the case suffixes can only go in a certain order. Several of them may be attached to a single base, but they are always attached in the sequence shown: the agentive can only come after the first emphatic, the additive after accompaniment, and so on. Differences from the English system are striking. To begin with, there is a distinction, found in many languages of the world, between *inclusive* and *exclusive* first person: 'we' meaning 'you and I' is distinct from 'we' meaning 'he (she, they) and I.' Then the scheme of number has the peculiarity that the first person inclusive patterns as if the 'I' were not present: 'you and I' is singular, 'you two and I' is *dual,* and 'you three (or more) and I' is plural. The dual number is another difference from Modern English, though up to the thirteenth century English too had a dual: **wit** 'we two.' The case endings

---

[3] Certain forms have been left out for simplicity: the reflexives (**myself, themselves,** etc.) and the interrogatives (**who, whom, whose,** etc.).

TABLE 6–1
Weri Personal Pronouns

	Bases		
	Singular	*Non-singular*	
		dual	*plural*
First inclusive	tepir	tëarip	tëar
First exclusive	ne	tenip	ten
Second	në	arip	ar
Third	pë	pëarip	pët, pëar

Suffixes				
Order 1	*Order 2*	*Order 3*	*Order 4*	*Order 5*
emphatic -ëmint	*accompaniment* -rëng *referent* -in *benefactive* -ëmiin	*agentive* -uk	*emphatic* -iir	*additive* -ta

SOURCE: Adapted from Boxwell 1967.

differ from anything in English.[4] While the *agentive* is akin to the English subjective ("subject-like") in that it indicates the actor, the *emphatic* may mean, for instance, 'just he' as well as 'he himself.' *Accompaniment* is like English **along:** 'I you-along go-we-two' is 'I go with you.' The *benefactive* is similar to the English indirect object, which has no separate form in the English pronoun system but does turn up in the word order: **He planted us a row of sweet potatoes** indicates who benefits by the action. The *referent* includes direct objects. And so on. In addition, there is a scheme of final affixes that express 'and,' 'or,' 'question,' and 'question-location.' An example of a base combined with three suffixes is **pë-mint-ok-iir** 'he-emphatic-agent-emphatic,' as in **pë-mint-ok-iir ëër-a** 'He alone washed himself' (**-ok** is an allomorph of **-uk**).

Turning to the major classes in English, we find that nouns and verbs can be singled out rather quickly by their association with grammatical morphemes. Proper nouns take the possessive suffix (**Mary, Mary's**)

---

[4] But we might recognize a nominalizing suffix **-s** in the forms **yours, hers, ours,** and **theirs,** based on **your, her, our, their.** In **I have your copy, your** is a modifier. In **I have yours, yours** is like a noun.

and common nouns take both that[5] and one or both of the articles (*a, an; the*). Verbs can be identified as follows:

1. Verbs may carry one of four inflectional morphemes: *past (study, studied; fly, flew), perfective* (usually *-ed* or *-en,* as in *had studied, have flown*), *third-person-singular present (study, studies),* and *-ing (study, studying; fly, flying).*

2. Verbs accept *to* and the auxiliaries *can, may, will,* etc. *(to study, can study).*

3. Verbs combine with *do* and *did (He does like it; Did you like it? I don't like it).*[6]

A class-to-class relationship confirms the classes of noun and verb, which must agree with each other in number when they are together in a sentence (as subject and predicate—functions again!): *The tree grows, Trees grow.* Adjectives can only be partially identified by the inflections that they take *(pretty, prettier, prettiest,* but not *beautiful, *beautifuler, *beautifulest);* they are more easily identified by the ones they do not take *(*the beautifuls, *she beautifuled).* But their association with nouns is what determines them as a class. While there are many ifs in these tests, the scheme interlocks so tightly that most classes can be identified in a variety of ways, which leaves no doubt that they exist in the language and in the minds of speakers.

Here and there other proofs can be found of their reality. In English there is a tendency for verbs of more than one syllable to have final syllables that are more prominent than the final syllables of related nouns and adjectives. The last syllable of the adjective *intimate* has a reduced vowel, -/ət/; that of the verb *to intimate* is full, -/et/. The same change occurs in the noun-verb *prophecy* (verb spelled *-sy*) and the noun-verb *supplement.* With the noun-verb *discharge* and the noun-verb *address,* the complete shift of stress to the last syllable makes the difference all the more striking. Not all speakers agree on all items (with *graduate,* for example, some make the distinction noted here; others use -/et/ for both noun and verb), but for many of us there is a reshuffling whereby more and more nouns and verbs are distinguished in this way—a speaker who started out saying *to mánifest* may find himself saying *to*

---

[5] Not a fully reliable test, in view of the "group possessive" in such expressions as *Mac here's wife don't like it.* (Example from Gordon T. Fish, personal communication.)

[6] Does the "verb" *to be* pass this last test? There is some question as to whether *be* should be called a verb, at least in some of its uses. It was included among the function words in Chapter 5.

manifést. This tendency has become most entrenched in the *run óff* (verb) versus *rúnoff* (noun) contrast.

Sometimes a class that obviously exists in two languages may have a formal marking in one but not in the other. English distinguishes *mass nouns* from *count nouns* only through syntactic relationships, but Neapolitan marks mass nouns with double consonants after the word for 'the,' while count nouns may have single consonants: *o lupo* 'the wolf,' but **o** *llate* 'the milk.'[7]

The best evidence of all for the reality of classes is the fact that languages have ways of converting words from one class to another: *danger,* noun; **dangerous,** adjective; **dangerously,** adverb; *to endanger,* verb. English does this rather heterogeneously but not unrecognizably.

Nouns, verbs, and adjectives are three of the *parts of speech,* as the major classes of function words and lexical words have traditionally been called. There would be no reason to call them anything else except that the classical parts of speech have been limited to the most obvious ones— noun, verb, adjective, adverb, pronoun, preposition, interjection, and conjunction—and the term is apt to suggest that classification stops there, when actually it must go farther.

The adverb is a good example of the over-inclusiveness of the traditional classes. It is defined in grammar books as a word that "modifies a verb, an adjective, or another adverb." Yet one can easily find adverbs that fit one form of modification and not others. Take *very: He came in very fast, It's very good,* but not **He eats very; very* is obviously a modifier of other modifiers and not a modifier of verbs. Or consider *aside: He turned aside,* but not **an aside tasty food; aside* modifies only verbs. Many adverbs do straddle: *He worked unnecessarily, It is unnecessarily elaborate, They stayed unnecessarily long.* But this no more justifies ignoring the differences than one can justify lumping nouns and verbs together in a single class of "nerbs" on the strength of words like *run, walk, reach, play,* and *strike,* which can belong to either part of speech.

There are also cases that do not involve mere inclusion (the way individual proper nouns are included in the class of proper nouns and proper nouns are included in the class of nouns) but overlapping and intersection. If we think of number as a class, then there is a kind of number, of singularity and plurality, that crosses both nouns and verbs— not an inflectional number but an element within the meaning of the words. We see this in common nouns, subclassified into mass nouns and count nouns. As with nouns in general, we can look to the grammatical morphemes to help make the distinction. Mass nouns combine in the singular with *much, enough,* and *some* (pronounced [sm]); count nouns combine with *many,* the indefinite article *(a, an),* and the cardinal

---

[7] Iannucci 1952, p. 15.

numerals, and with **enough** and **some** only in the plural. While either class combines with **more,** conservative speakers distinguish between **less,** with mass nouns, and **fewer,** with count nouns. Examples:

Mass noun acceptable, *count noun unacceptable*	*Count noun acceptable,* *mass noun unacceptable*
enough serenity *enough letter	*many serenities many letters
too much sugar *too much bean	*one foliage one leaf
some kerosene *some [sm] dime	*two furnitures two chairs
less competition ?less concerts	*an artillery a cannon
	*fewer jewelries fewer jewels

Either acceptable

enough (some) corn (*mass*)
enough (some) beans (*count*)

Mass and *count* do more than cut the noun class in half—they do the same with verbs, in a very special way. Any verb can be either mass or count according to its form. In **too much talking,** the verb is mass. In **He talked for a moment** it is count, in the sense that there can be many such moments of talking. Grammarians refer to this distinction in verbs as *aspect*. If a noun or verb refers to one instance of something (*a flash, he jumped*), the instances are countable; if not, the sense is mass (*light, jumping*).

An intersecting pair of classes that divides nouns and verbs in still another way, and adjectives and adverbs as well, is that of *intensifiable* and *unintensifiable*. The grammatical morphemes we use to test words for this quality are the intensifiers, such as **very, somewhat, so, too, such,** etc. Thus we can say both **difficult calculus** and **differential calculus** and also **This calculus is very difficult,** but not ***This calculus is very differential.** **Difficult** is intensifiable, **differential** is unintensifiable. Other examples:

	Intensifiable	*Unintensifiable*
Verb	I wish she wouldn't gossip so.	*I wish she wouldn't preside so.
Adjective	I wish she weren't so talkative.	*I wish she weren't so presidential.

	Intensifiable	*Unintensifiable*
Adverb	I wish she wouldn't speak so freely.	*I wish she didn't speak so presidentially.
Noun	I wish she weren't such a gossip.	*I wish she weren't such a chairman (such a president).[8]

The membership of the mass–count and intensifiable–unintensifiable classes is not fixed. Just as nouns can be converted to verbs *(a joyride, to joyride),* so mass nouns can be converted to count (usually in the sense 'kind of': *gasoline, various gasolines*) and count to mass (mostly as a joke: *I didn't get much car for my money; That's a lot of house!*). Similarly with intensification, especially with large size: *I wish these star charts were not so astronomical* is unnatural with *so* because the adjective has its normal classifying sense, but in *I wish these budget figures were not so astronomical* the adjective is synonymous with *huge,* and *so* is normal.

There is a subclassification of verbs into *transitive* and *intransitive* that is recognized by all good dictionaries. It usually refers to whether or not a verb takes a direct object: we do not say merely *John needs,* but add an object: *John needs sympathy.* Nor do we say *John knelt his body— to kneel* is intransitive: *John knelt.* As with mass-count and intensification, most verbs can be shifted either way: *I flew in a plane, I flew a kite.* A somewhat different way of viewing transitivity is in terms of completeness. Does a verb in a given sense require a complement—no matter whether direct, indirect, or prepositional? From this standpoint *to depend* in its usual sense would be transitive because we have to add *on something.*[9] And *to tell* in *They told me* would be just as transitive as in *They told the story;* we do not say just *They told* (unless we mean 'They blabbed'). Though transitivity is generally thought to apply only to verbs, quite a few adjectives behave similarly. The usual sense of *fond* has to do with *liking* someone: *Jane is fond of him.* In that sense we cannot say *Jane is fond* and stop there. *Sure* is "transitive"—like the verb *know*— in *I'm sure he has it.* Even an occasional noun shows traces of transitivity. We cannot say merely *The Aztecs were inhabitants.* It means they inhabited something, and it is necessary to say what: *The Aztecs were inhabitants of Mexico.*

---

[8] Normal in a different sense: 'a chairman of that kind.' And if we create a new sense for *presidential* or *presidentially* (such as 'lofty, haughty'), we make it intensifiable and can use *so* with it. For the intensifiable-unintensifiable contrast, see Bolinger 1971.

[9] Except in the idiom *That (it) depends.*

There is also a class of verbs that take complements not of themselves but of their subjects: in *He stands convicted, convicted* modifies *he,* not *stands.* It has been termed *intensive*[10] and includes *be, seem, appear, look, grow (grow tall), become,* and so forth.

Classes are basically semantic: nouns are thing-like, verbs are event-like, adjectives are quality-like. The tie that holds each major class together goes back to some unifying experience of our childhood, which the language dramatizes by making it in some way grammatically distinctive. The child's awareness of a common bond—says the psychologist with the longest record of looking at meaning—is derived "from actual behavior toward things signified."[11] Our earliest experiences are grouped around actions and things, and the corresponding classes of verbs and nouns are found in all the languages of the world. We get a sense of detachable qualities as soon as we can see differences playing on samenesses—at least as early as our games of marking and coloring. This is a physiological peg for adjectives. Any pervasive sense experience can precipitate a class. Some languages dramatize the child's experiences with things in space through sensations of size, shape, and quantity. In the Senufo languages of Africa, nouns designating large objects are formally distinct from nouns designating small ones.[12] In Chontal, a dialect of Mayan spoken in southern Mexico, there is an elaborate categorization of things that is required whenever things are counted: separate morphemes are used to classify the world of objects into people and most animals, as distinct from other things; flat objects like leaves and sleeping mats; plants and standing trees; slender objects like snakes and sticks; unharvested fruits and nuts; drops of liquids; things rolled up; objects cut lengthwise; and so on.[13] In Tarascan, another Mexican language, things are stick-like, tortilla-like, and ball-like. The human body likewise provides some useful metaphors. Luo, a language of Africa, as well as Tarascan, has an affix signifying 'mouth-shaped.'[14]

There are lesser classes too, no one knows how many. Since meanings can cluster in infinite ways, it should not be surprising that many smaller groups of words embrace some common feature that reflects itself in a freedom, or lack of it, to combine with other items or classes. A great deal of the current work in syntax has to do with discovering and defining these classes and their syntactic effects, largely in hopes of finding which ones are widespread and perhaps universal.

---

[10] See Quirk, Greenbaum, Leech, and Svartvik 1972, pp. 38–40.

[11] Osgood 1971, p. 18.

[12] Welmers 1950, p. 131.

[13] Keller 1955.

[14] Friedrich 1972.

One such lesser class is that of sensory verbs. They are obviously related in meaning: *to see, to hear, to smell, to observe, to watch, to notice, to spy.* And they function alike, taking other verbs as complements without *to: I heard him shout, I saw her turn, I watched them go.* This is not true, for example, of the verbs *expect, want, ask, promise* and many others, which require the *to: I want you to wait, She promised to be ready,* not *I want you wait, *She promised be ready. That it is a grammatical class and not just a set of partial synonyms can be seen in the fact that the more infrequent a verb of perception is, the less likely it is ever to be used this way. We would be unlikely to say *I discerned him come or *I descried the light flash (OK flashing), though *I perceived it happen* is marginally possible.

Another minor class—cutting across all the major ones—is that of negatively biased words. These are normal whenever a negation or a question or a condition is present or implied, but not otherwise, and are often paired with some roughly synonymous affirmative word. Some of them are: *far* (adverb), *budge* (verb), *long* (a rather peculiar hybrid of adjective and adverb), *care* (verb), *faze* (verb), *mind* (verb), and *much* (adjective, adverb, or noun). Examples:

> *It is far from here. (OK *not far, too far, Is it far?* etc.) Affirmative counterpart: *It is a long way from here.*

> *Every time I poked him he budged. (OK *If he so much as budges, let him have it.*)

> *They will be long in getting here. (OK *They won't be long, Will they be long?* etc.) Affirmative counterpart: *They will be a long time getting here.*

> *He eats much, *She studies much. (OK *too much, not much,* etc.) Affirmative counterpart: *a lot.*

Again there are members that only half-belong. For some speakers *very* is less acceptable in *It's very new* (unless *very* is made quite emphatic) than in *It isn't very new, Is it very new?* and so forth; they prefer *pretty, quite,* or *awfully.* A class of this sort is interesting not only for its membership but for what it tells us about the underlying kinship between negations, questions, and conditions.

Some classes are diffuse, sharing most of their members with the opposite class but asserting exclusive claim to a few. One such class is *animate,* with the opposing class *inanimate.* The two are overtly present in *man, cow, dog* versus *tree, clock, air*—in fact, most nouns can be pretty clearly labeled one or the other. But not so with verbs. In most cases it makes no difference: *to get* can involve animate and inanimate subjects or objects equally: *The tree got new leaves, The spider got the fly.* But the verb *to damage* is less democratic. Most speakers of English would approve a sentence like *The truck collision damaged the cargo* but reject one like **The truck collision damaged the driver. Injure* is exactly the opposite, but *harm* can be used either way. Similarly with adjectives. To say after the collision that the driver was *intact* would suggest a mild attempt at humor—*intact* describes inanimate objects, not animate beings: *The television set was intact when I delivered it; *The snake was intact when I delivered it.* There are of course any number of things that only animate beings can do, with the result that a sizable number of verbs call for animate subjects: *to suffer, to dream, to be born, to dwell, to communicate,* and so forth; but the great difficulty here is our freedom to metaphorize, picturing nonliving things as if they were living, which erodes the distinction. Animateness is so important in our view of nature that it colors language in some very out-of-the-way places. Take the expression *old age.* We can say *Because of its old age the dinosaur was unable to pull itself out of the tar pit.* But we do not say **Because of its old age the house was torn down,* though we may say either *because of its age* or *because it was old.* The animate contrast is *old* (age) versus *young* (age); the inanimate one is *old* versus *new.*

Finally there are what might be termed *empty classes,* with no specific words or morphemes as members but detectible, like an invisible star, by their gravitational effect on syntax. They may actually catch our attention by the fact that other languages do embody them directly in words or grammatical morphemes. An example is the paired opposites *essence* and *accident* that are overtly manifested in certain languages—for example, Spanish, Portuguese, and Gaelic. *Essence* refers to *what* something is, its inner nature; *accident* refers to the *way* something is, the superficial appearances or positions it assumes. In Spanish the function words *ser* and *estar* make the distinction systematically. One says *Es lista* 'She is ready' in the sense 'ready-witted'—she is clever by nature. But for 'She is ready' in the sense of 'all set' to do something, the expression is *Está lista. Es bonita* means 'She is pretty' in the sense that she is a pretty girl; *Está bonita* means 'She is pretty' in her new dress, with her new hairdo, etc.—that is, she *looks* pretty. English has only indirect manifestations of the contrast. We say *I thought him (to be) clever* but not **I thought him (to be) ready.* We say *I thought her to be pretty—a really pretty girl,* but not **I thought her to be pretty in her new dress. To think X (to be) Y* is an expression of essence. On the other hand, the use of *all* as an intensifier can only be in expressions of accident: *My hands are all dirty* but not **That joke is all dirty.* A little soap and water will clean up the hands, but a dirty joke is dirty by nature.

TABLE 6–2
Major Categories and Their Intersections with Some Minor Ones

Major Category	Example	Characteristic Associated Elements	Example of Shared Form	Mass and Count Categories (respectively)
NOUN	teacher	teacher's the teacher	danger	more danger °more teacher
VERB	to study	studied did study	to endanger	jumping he jumped
ADJECTIVE	pretty	prettier	dangerous	(no exclusively mass adjectives) °numerous sugar numerous dogs
ADVERB	now intentionally	to work now to act intentionally	dangerously	

Table 6–2 summarizes the main intersections between major and minor categories that have been discussed.

Classes and functions

A noun may be "used as" a subject, a predicate nominative, an indirect object, a direct object, or a prepositional object, and a few other things besides:

> **Miss Whitmore** is a **peach** because she gave **Sally** an **A** on the **exam.**
>
>   *subject*   *predicate*   *indirect* *direct*   *prepositional*
>   *nominative*   *object*   *object*   *object*

The same class thus fulfills five functions, and other classes similarly may have more than one. A verb may function as subject, as in **To run would be cowardly.** Such is the confusion between classes and functions that we

Intensifiable and Unintensifiable Categories (respectively)	Transitive and Intransitive Categories (respectively)	Animate and Inanimate Categories (respectively)	Negative Bias Category
Such an opportunity! °Such a pebble!	°He is an inhabitant. He is a native.	The dog felt the blow. °The railing felt the blow.	°They give a damn.
to complain so °to add so	°They revealed. They lied.	The girl worried. °The girl curdled. The blow wounded the soldier. °The blow damaged the soldier.	°He will budge.
so pretty °so nitric	°She is fond. She is nice.	She is awake. °She is algebraic.	
so dangerously °so possibly	°He works very. He works hard.	°It runs joyously. It runs electrically.	°She stayed there long.

are prone to say of this last case that "the verb is used as a noun"—meaning that it shares certain of the functions that are typically fulfilled by nouns.[15] It is better to use the term *nominal* for 'used as a noun,' *adjectival* for 'used as an adjective,' and so on. Thus **to run** is a nominal, and so would be **to run fast** in **To run fast can be dangerous.** The noun **mud** is adjectival in **mud fence,** and so is the prepositional phrase in **the woman in the green dress** and the **who** clause in the phrase **the woman who is wearing the green dress.** Much of the power of language comes from our ability to bring constructions down to the level of individual words. A whole sentence, with a full array of internal functions of its own, may serve a single function in a larger sentence. The process is called *embedding* and the productivity it yields is called *recursiveness* or *recursive power.* In **I know you don't intend to use that advantage** everything from **you** on is an embedded nominal, the object of **know.**

---

[15] Certain of the functions, not all of them. This particular verb form—the infinitive—cannot be an indirect object nor the object of a preposition.

Some examples of nominals:

Noun phrase: **Your early arrival** would be no surprise to me.

Infinitive phrase: **For you to arrive early** would be no surprise to me.

-ing phrase: **Your arriving early** would be no surprise to me.

Clause: **That you should arrive early** would be no surprise to me.

—and of adjectivals:

Adjective: The only river **navigable** is to the north.

Infinitive phrase: The only river **to be trusted for navigation** is to the north.

-ing phrase: The only river **permitting navigation** is to the north.

Prepositional phrase: The only river **for navigating** is to the north.

Clause: The only river **that is navigable** is to the north.

—and of successive embeddings:

I went {yesterday}

I went {after [somebody] telephoned me}

I went {after [somebody (special)] telephoned me}

I went {after [somebody (that I really wanted to see)] telephoned me}

I went {after [somebody (that I really wanted to see/right then/)] telephoned me}

I went {after [somebody (that I really wanted to see/as soon as I could/)] telephoned me}

Grammatical, psychological, and logical functions

Subjects, objects, modifiers, and the like are not always meaningful functions; sometimes they are no more than grammatical habits. In the sentence **It's raining** the word *it* is the grammatical subject, but to claim that *is raining* "tells what 'it' is doing" is true only in a vague sense. English requires that a sentence have a subject even when there is no subject to talk about. And it is just as apt to announce a subject and then talk about something else: here we see the difference between grammatical functions and psychological ones. Separate terms are needed, and at least two are in fairly common use to refer to psychological functions: *topic* (sometimes called *psychological subject*) and *comment.* The topic is what is talked about, the comment is what is said about the topic. In *Jane is admired by all of us* and *Jane we all admire,* a comment is made about the topic *Jane,* even though *Jane* is subject in the first and object in the second. While the grammatical subject of a sentence is more often than not at the same time the topic, the roles often change. In answer to *What color is your house?* one may say *My house is red,* where the subject, *my house,* is also the topic, and the predicate, *is red,* is also the comment. But one may also answer with *I live in a réd house,* where *I* is subject but not topic. The topic is *I live in a . . . house* (which means the same as *my house* for the purpose of answering that question) and the comment is *red.* There is a tendency to put topics first in a sentence, with the result that when something other than the subject becomes the topic it is often fronted: *Every cent she had her husband squandered.* But the opposite may happen too: *Réd is the color of my house,* with everything deemphasized except *red.* (The comment normally carries the main sentence accent.)

There are also *logical* functions. In a sentence, the two inclusive *grammatical* functions are subject and predicate. But sentences are not uttered with the aim of expressing subjects and predicates but to convey something about entities and happenings in the real world or in imagination. Things exist, things happen, and things are related. The corresponding logical functions are *participants, events,* and *relations.* In the sentence *Janet brought Juliet* the two participating entities are Janet and Juliet, the event is the act of bringing, and the relationship is that of 'actor' for Janet and 'patient' for Juliet. Again, there tends to be a fairly close correspondence between the logical and the grammatical functions. *Janet* is both logical actor and grammatical subject; those two roles tend to coincide. *Juliet* is both logical patient and grammatical object. But in some grammatical constructions the functions diverge. In the passive voice, in *Juliet was brought by Janet,* for example, *Juliet* is still the patient—the "object" of the bringing—but is now the grammatical subject. Here the psychological functions have interfered; the passive voice is the best way to turn a patient into a topic by bringing it over into subject position. In the sentence *The girl felt the wind in her face* there are reasons for thinking of the wind as the actor and the girl as the patient—certainly it is doing something to her rather than she to it, in spite of the crossover of subject and object. (Here another tendency has intervened, that of "dignifying" ourselves as human beings by taking the grammatical role of subject rather than object.) But these refinements of logical relationships have a long way to go before we can be sure of their place in syntax, and most of our analysis will continue for a while to be in terms of grammatical functions and the classes that they interrelate.

Classes as features

There is another way of viewing classes besides the one adopted in this chapter. Instead of saying that the class of Canadians includes Marie Robichaud plus other individuals, and the class of French speakers includes her and others, and the class Catholic, and so on, we start with her and say that she *is* Canadian, French-speaking, and Catholic. The classes she belongs to become a way of describing her, using the "features" [+Human −Male +Adult +Canadian −English-speaking +Catholic] and so on. The minus sign is a way of economizing on terms where two classes complement each other.

So with language. The noun *furniture* is a mass noun; this means, if we take count nouns as basic, that it is [−Count]. It is also [−Animate]. Dictionaries use these labels up to a point, but only for the most obvious class memberships: *furniture* is [+Noun]. (No minus sign will serve here because there are more than two parts of speech.) The noun *cloth* is [±Count], for we can say either *She wrapped it in a cloth* (count) or *She wrapped it in cloth* (mass). The verb *to damage* is [+Verb +Transitive +Intensifiable −Animate], the last feature referring to the kind of object it can take.

SENTENCES

The sentence is the fundamental unit of syntax, but it is as hard to define as the word. Yet we feel just as secure in talking about sentences as in talking about words, so it must be that they are psychologically real and not just a linguistic construct. The traditional definition is that the sentence is the minimum part of language that expresses a complete thought, and certainly some sense of completeness is essential to it. Just as the divisions between words are "insertion points," so the divisions between sentences are "stop points." The stops may be skipped three-fourths of the time (though seldom in the didactic speech of elders to very young children), yet they happen often enough for us to build up a repertory of types of constructions and varieties of intonation that then come to be recognized as complete units in their own right. The linguist accepts as "sentences" the ones that he can use to the best advantage to predict others. For example, if someone asks *Like a slice?* and receives the reply *Yes, I would,* conversationally both the question and the answer are sentences, but together they suggest that underlying them are the complete versions *Would you like a slice?* and *Yes, I would like a slice.* Only the complete versions are suitable for describing syntactic relations—to show, for example, that *would* is an auxiliary attached to *like.* The abbreviated sentences are not ignored, but are described as "transformations" of the full forms.

There are many ways of classifying sentences. One is according to their social purpose: questions, answers, comments, commands, presentations, and the like. Grammatical functions probably started as social functions thousands of years ago. The same terms are often used for both. There are conversational, or real, questions, which are used only when the speaker seeks an answer, and grammatical questions, which have a certain form in English (inversion of the subject and auxiliary verb: *Can you wait?* rather than *You can wait*) and are most frequently used to ask real questions but often have other purposes (*Do you think I'm an idiot?* is not generally a request for information). As societies grew more complex the simpler social functions became diversified and the old forms had to be adapted to new purposes. So we have questions that do not really ask, statements that do not really assert, imperatives that do not really command, and so on. Similarly we have commands that are expressed in the regular way as imperatives *(Open the window)* or irregularly as questions or statements *(Would you like to open the window? I wish you would open the window).* The functions that concern us at this point are the grammatical ones.

Following are the major sentence types in English that do not have the added complexity of embeddings or other transformations:

1. *Mother fell.* (Nominal plus intransitive verbal.)

2. *Mother is young.* (Nominal plus copula plus complement.)

3. *Mother loves Dad.* (Nominal plus transitive verbal plus nominal.)

4. *Mother fed Dad breakfast.* (Nominal plus ditransitive verbal plus nominal plus nominal.)

5. *There is time.* (*There* plus existential plus nominal.)

The verb *to be* is a chameleon. The "complement" in the second sentence may be an adjective, a noun *(Mother is boss)*, or an adverb *(here, early)*. All that *is* does is to associate the complement with the subject. Many languages express no verb here at all, and English often omits it too: *A nice fellow, George = George is a nice fellow; George early? = Is George early?* In sentence 5 *is* expresses something akin to existence and could, in fact, be replaced with *exists.* The term *ditransitive* in 4 refers to a subclass of verbs that may take two objects, one direct and one indirect.

These simple sentences can be expanded without enlarging their basic structure. In place of 1 we could have *the woman* or *all ten trees,* which qualify as nominals as much as *mother* does; in place of merely *fell* we

could have *fell down* or *fell down abruptly.* In 2, *young* could be replaced by *like her father.* In 4, *fed* could be replaced with *taught* and
breakfast with *a lesson.* In 5, *is* could be replaced with *might be* and
time with *some other reason.* Substitutions of this kind are minor structures which are parts of sentences and cannot be defined as disguised
sentences that have worked their way into the larger structure. The distinction can be seen by comparing *the wood* and *heavy wood.* Both *the*
and *heavy* are traditionally called adjectives, since they seem to be
attached in the same way to nouns. But there is an important difference.
Heavy wood can be paraphrased as *wood that is heavy* but *the wood*
cannot be paraphrased as *°wood that is the.* Since *that is heavy* contains
all the elements of a sentence (*that,* subject; *is,* copula; *heavy,* complement), *heavy wood* can be viewed as a transformational reduction:
wood (the wood is heavy) ⟶ *heavy wood.* The accepted practice
among most American grammarians in the past decade has accordingly
been to view *the wood* as a "phrase structure" in its own right but *heavy
wood* as something else. Such phrase structures include, besides all the
simple sentences, the nominals that are made up of a noun with its determiners (*all the other people, half an apple, the same guy, my two
friends, that first time*), the verb and its auxiliaries (*might leave, would
have taken, had to be studying*), the verb and its complements (*give John
the letter, tell a story to them, go to Westlake*), and various lesser structures such as an adjective or an adverb with an intensifier (*very hot, too
near*) and a determiner with an intensifier (*almost all, fully six hundred*).

Transformations

The simple sentences listed in the last section are far from covering the
variety that one finds in English or in any other language (whose simple
sentences may or may not be like those of English). Here are some other
kinds of sentences:

1a. *Came the dawn.*

2a. I told him to be ready and *ready he was.*

3a. *Him I dislike.*

4a. *Them I gave nothing.*

5a. If there is to be war, *war there must be.*

Comparing these with the five simple sentences on page 157 we see that
each clause in heavy type represents simply an inversion. *Came the
dawn* is the same as *The dawn came* (the same structure as *Mother fell*)
except for the shift of *came* to front position, and the same happens in 5a,

with *there must be war* changed to *war there must be.* This illustrates the most rudimentary kind of transformation, the one that merely moves words around. Besides movement, transformations can be used to relate sentences through *replacement, deletion,* and *addition.* Examples of replacement:

1b. "Did the dawn come?"—"Yes, *it* did."

2b. If I have to be a failure I'll be *one* in my own way.

3b. "Does Miss Hedda Hopper play Miss Hedda Hopper in this film?"—"Yes, Miss Hedda Hopper plays *herself.*"

4b. "Did Mother feed Dad oatmeal?"—"No, *she* fed *him that* yesterday."

5b. "Will there be time tomorrow?"—"Yes, there will be time *then.*"

Replacement is a way of avoiding repetition and cutting down on excessive bulk. A short "pro" word such as a pronoun or a pro-adverb (*it* for *dawn* in 1b, *then* for *tomorrow* in 5b) takes the place of a longer segment—which may be quite long, as in *"I hope that Jack brought the stuff that I told him I wanted to have here before six o'clock so I could get to work on it."—"Yes, he brought it"* (or *"Yes, he did"*—with *did* replacing the whole predicate). In 2b, the indefinite pronoun *one* replaces the indefinite *a failure.* In 3b, the reflexive pronoun *herself* is used instead of the second repetition of the same nominal. In 4b, the demonstrative ("pointing") pronoun *that* replaces *oatmeal.*

Deletion may affect anything from a single word up to a full sentence. If the statement *She graduated with highest honors* is responded to with *Yes, I know,* an entire sentence, which otherwise would be embedded after *know,* has been deleted. Obviously this can occur only in an environment where the hearer can tell immediately what has been left out. Other examples:

1. "Why did you do it?"—"Because I wanted to *(do it).*"

2. "I hope he'll be there!"—"I'm sure he will *(be there).*"

3. They got sore at me, but I don't know why *(they got sore at me).*

4. "He's heading off tomorrow."—"Oh? Where *(is he heading off)?*"

5. I thought she would be there, and she was *(there).*

These show the commonest deletions: after the *to* of the infinitive, after auxiliary verbs (*will, may, can,* and so forth), after interrogatives (*why, where, who, when,* and so forth), and after *to be.* Imperatives more often delete their subjects than not: *(You) stand here.* Almost equally common is the deletion of both subject and auxiliary verb at the beginning of a question. This is especially frequent when the subject—just as in the imperative—is *you: (Do you) want a bite?* Deletion is also frequent when two sentences are conjoined: *June wanted to leave last night but (June) couldn't (leave last night).* In this example one can also think of *but couldn't* as a reduction from a replacement, *but she couldn't.*

Addition usually comes about when sentences grow so complex that function words have to be inserted to keep the relationships clear. The passive sentence *This truck is powered by a diesel engine* contains a form of the verb *to be* and a preposition *by* which do not appear in the active *A diesel engine powers this truck.* Most embeddings involve an addition of some sort—for example, the addition of *that* when one sentence is put in apposition to a noun in another sentence: *I heard the report + The market had advanced* ⟶ *I heard the report that the market had advanced.* The same happens when direct discourse is changed to indirect: *John explained, "Those measures were necessary"* becomes *John explained that those measures were necessary.* If the quotation is a command, *to* is added; if a yes–no question, *if* or *whether: John said, "Leave right now"* ⟶ *John said to leave right now; Jennifer asked, "Were they gone?"* ⟶ *Jennifer asked if (whether) they were gone.*

The grammatical morphemes that are added in this way have sometimes been called "transformationally introduced particles," suggesting that they add nothing to the meaning. It was thought for some time that no transformational changes had any semantic effect. And when we compare any two sentences for which it would be reasonable to posit a single underlying source it does appear that they are the same. In fact, the main reason for using the term *transformation* is that the sentences seemed to be paraphrases of each other, just different ways of saying the same thing. But their sameness generally turns out to be of a special kind: not identity in the fullest sense but just a mutual truth value. *Came the dawn* and *The dawn came* are logical equivalents—if one is true the other has to be true, and if one is false so is the other. But language is more than logic and meaning is more than truth, and to exclude other values is to insist that language is nothing but a transmission belt for factual knowledge. The sentence *Came the dawn,* with its initial verb and its postposed subject, is intended to set a scene and *present* something on it. The word order signals that presentational intent, which is absent in *The dawn came* but is found in other sentences using the same device of order: *Up stood the witness, On came the storm, Away flew my handkerchief, There rang out a strange sound, There emerged another mutant species, There appeared several new models.* Predictably, *Came the dawn* and *Up stood the witness* have verbs that are suitable for bringing-onto-the-scene. Other verbs are not acceptable in this construction: **Sailed the ship, *Up gave the enemy, *There will help another attempt.* But we can say *There froze a great glacier,* because freezing brings the glacier into existence; and we can say ***There waved a flag,*** because waving is what flags do, and saying that one is waving is a way of saying that one is there. With careful probing, other similarly elusive meanings can probably be found in every transformational change. A good working principle is that language does not waste its resources, and every difference makes a difference.

Transformations then are a way of *relating* structures that have features in common. If they share all but one, the transformation helps to focus on that one. We are then in a better position to hypothesize a meaning for it.

Deep structure

Possible answers to ***Will you go?*** include ***I will not go, I won't go, I will not,*** and ***I won't.*** They are all appropriate under the circumstances, they share the same elements, and they have the same truth value. Accordingly they are good candidates for derivation from the same source. But what source? ***I will not go*** gives everything that is needed to derive the three others, but then we find that a mere ***No*** is just as good an answer and has no obvious representation in ***I will not go.*** Still another kind of answer that it would be nice to account for is ***Not this time.***

The appropriateness of a simple ***No*** suggests that the meaning of negation is somehow logically outside the rest of the sentence—that the two main constituents are ***no*** and ***I will go,*** where ***no*** denies everything else. The fact that it is physically *inside* the sentence ***I will not go*** thus appears to be the result of some transformation. If so, none of the four sentences can be regarded as basic, and the underlying sentence from which all are derived must be represented in more abstract form. This is the *deep structure* of those sentences, and is the syntactic analog of the underlying forms discussed in Chapter 4. In transformational grammar, every sentence has an underlying deep structure that is acted upon by transformations to produce a *surface structure*, which is the syntactic form of what is actually said. ***No*** is a surface structure from which a transformation has deleted everything except 'negation.' ***I won't*** is a surface structure in which the negation has been moved in and attached to the auxiliary, and ***go*** has been deleted.

The completeness or straightforwardness of one member of a set of surface structures often makes it look as if it ought to be the transformational source of the others, as appeared to be the case with ***I will not go.*** But if deep structures are necessary for some cases they are best assumed for all. A seemingly more basic surface sentence ***(The dawn came)*** has merely been acted on by fewer transformations than its counterpart ***(Came the dawn).***

A deep structure can be shown with the same formalism employed for constituent analysis—which of course it is, in the most fundamental sense. So, for our negative answers, a crude representation is

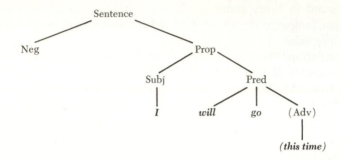

Prop is the proposition, what it is that the sentence negates. Providing the slot Adv—in parentheses to show that it is optional—makes it possible to derive *Not this time, Not yet,* and other such answers from the same deep structure.

We have already seen some of the transformations that are needed to produce the example sentences from this one deep structure. Most of them require that *not* be moved in next to the auxiliary, and two require an additional morphological transformation that reduces *not* to *-n't.* But what about Neg? This is an abstract element that is "realized" as *no* when everything else is deleted, but as *not* otherwise. The generating of either *no* or *not* under Neg must then be "sensitive" to the other transformations; otherwise we might get the unacceptable answers *°No this time* or simply *°Not,* and would not be able to generate *never* from *not ever.* Not only must Neg be sensitive to the other transformations; they in turn must be sensitive to Neg. Suppose instead of *Will you go?* our original question had been *Did you go?* The answers would have had *did* for every instance of *will,* but the plain *No* answer seems to be a denial of *I went,* where no *did* appears. But since with plain *No* everything else is deleted anyway, we can just as well assume that whenever Neg appears, a form of *do* will automatically appear with any verb that does not already have some other auxiliary. The verb form is thus sensitive to the presence of Neg. We see this whenever someone denies a proposition: "You say he *went.* I say he *didn't go.*"

An analysis proves its value if it helps to solve other puzzles besides the one for which it was designed. Consider the following examples:

How I did yearn for them!

I do so want you to be happy!

"Do you deny that you were there?"—"I do indeed deny that I was there."

"I wish he had been more considerate."—"He did apologize, you know."

Here we have forms of *do* again, and now they are keyed to affirmation. There are of course various ways of showing affirmation—a nod of the head, an assertion with emphatic intonation, as in "Why didn't you go?" —"*I went,* you idiot!" But when affirmation (or negation) is made *verbally* explicit, the effect is to introduce a form of *do* if no other auxiliary is already present. And since questions of the *Did you go?* type also call for an explicit *Yes* or *No,* they too introduce a *do.* So our diagram can be revised slightly:

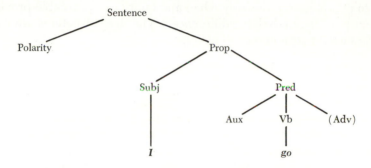

Polarity is realized as Neg, Aff (affirmative), or Q (question), and Q may be combined with Neg or with Aff:

$$\text{Polarity} \longrightarrow \quad (Q) \quad \left(\left\{ \begin{matrix} \text{Neg} \\ \text{Aff} \end{matrix} \right\} \right)$$

Comment: Choose at least one.

The parentheses indicate an optional choice, "either Q or Neg–Aff or both"; the braces indicate a forced choice, "Neg or Aff but not both." From this deep structure we can derive *I did go* (with Aff), *I didn't go* (with Neg), *Did I go?* (with Aff + Q), and *Didn't I go?* (with Neg + Q), and of course the other possibilities by deleting one or more elements. The form *I went* would not have this deep structure; it fails to make Polarity explicit. As already mentioned, the effect of Polarity if there is nothing already under Aux is to put a *do* there. But suppose the auxiliary *can* is already there. Then the effect with either Aff or Neg is to produce the full form of *can* rather than the reduced form *c'n.* Thus *I can* /kæn/ *go* is explicitly affirmative, *I can* /kən/ *go* is merely affirmative, with no focusing or emphasis on affirmation. A good deal more would have to be added to develop all the implications, but the main advantage is apparent: this kind of representation enables us to bring together all the types involving explicit affirmation and explicit negation, which obviously belong together because of certain equal effects that they have.

In the example with Polarity there is a one-to-many relationship between deep and surface structure. The same technique can be used to illuminate a many-to-one relationship, in which two or more deep structures correspond to a single surface sentence. When this happens we call the surface sentence "structurally ambiguous" (not quite the same as "ambiguous" applied to two different homonyms, like **sale–sail, beer–bier**). The sentence **I cooked the meat dry** may mean that I used a dry-cooking process, adding no liquid ('I cooked the meat when the meat was dry'), or it may mean that I cooked the meat till it was dry. (Our being able to paraphrase in this way when ambiguity causes trouble proves our awareness of the underlying difference.) The deep structures are not the same, as can be seen in the following:

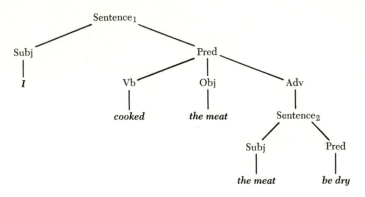

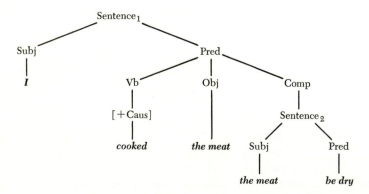

For the meaning 'cooked till it was dry' the deep structure adds a feature to the verb, [+Caus] or causative: the cooking caused the meat to be dry. The causing has **be dry** as its complement (Comp). This feature is needed for a variety of verbs, some of which are always causative in particular senses: *to convert, to make, to turn.* It is even combined with the resultant condition in one group of verbs, which typically has the causative suffix *-en: to whiten, to lighten, to soften, to madden, to sicken, to sharpen.* Noting this and other similar phenomena, one group of linguists has undertaken to fit the meanings of individual words into the same structural scheme used for phrases and sentences. Thus the deep structure of *John sharpened the knife* would be something like

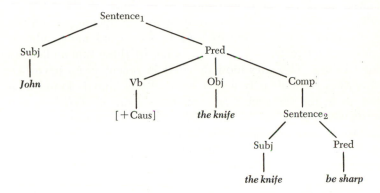

If we were to put the verb *to whet* under [+Caus], the result would be *John whetted the knife sharp.* (A transformation erases Sentence₂ and "moves up" the constituents *knife* and *sharp* into the higher sentence; the second *knife* is then deleted by another transformation.) But with no verb specified under [+Caus], the causative suffix *-en* is generated and attached by a transformation to *sharp,* which has already been moved up by another transformation. The correctness of using the same deep structure for both *John sharpened the knife* and *John whetted the knife sharp* can be seen in another transformation that often takes place when the objects of verbs are extremely long. Instead of *John whetted every knife that he could lay his hands on sharp* we may say *John whetted sharp every knife that he could lay his hands on.* We could almost hyphenate the verb and the adjective: *whetted-sharp. Sharp* belongs to the verb as much as to the noun: *whet-sharp = sharp-en by whetting.*

Thus a number of things dovetail when a model of this kind is used, which confirms its correctness: (1) causatives are needed elsewhere as much as they are needed here; (2) apparently different but actually synonymous sentences are reconciled; (3) a peculiarity of sentence order is shown to result from the same kind of movement transformation that creates a single word form. Deep-structure analysis does not answer all the questions of syntax, but it does well enough with some of the most important ones.

These examples also show how the richest syntactic resource of a language is built into its structure: the recursive adding of sentences to sentences. The Comp in these cases is itself a sentence. The knife *was* sharp, the meat *was* dry, at the end of the process.

Hidden sentences, higher and lower

Contained sentences may lose more than most of their bulk. Some virtually lose their identity, and only with the opening of the door to deep structure, which seems to lead to more and more subterranean galleries waiting to be explored, are some of these mummified remains coming to light. The ones most debated in recent years have been the *performatives.* Occasionally a specimen of this kind is found alive and kicking, as in the sentence *I tell you he did say it! Tell* here is a performative verb, so called because the saying of it performs the act that it refers to: if I say *I tell you* then I'm telling you, not like saying *I smoke cigars,* where the saying is not the same as the smoking. The expression *hereby* often marks a performative verb: *I hereby pronounce you man and wife.* The performatives of most interest to linguists are the ones that use expressions of saying: *declare, ask, command,* and their synonyms. When instead of speaking performatively we *report* someone else's assertion, request, or order it is necessary to use one of these expressions explicitly: *He declared (said, asserted, remarked, observed, told me, announced, claimed) that he didn't care how the election turned out.* So it is fair to ask whether the same expressions are present in direct discourse. When I say *I don't care how the election turns out,* perhaps I am really saying *I declare that I don't care how the election turns out.*

It has been argued that this is indeed the case,[16] and certain remains of performatives in larger sentences seem to confirm it. *John incidentally was one of those rejected* does not mean that John's rejection was incidental but that the speaker is making an incidental remark: *I incidentally tell you that John was one of those rejected.* Other adverbs that are often used this way are *frankly, definitely, positively, truthfully, emphatically, honestly.* They are among the ones often called *sentence adverbs,* which modify whole sentences and not smaller parts. (For another kind of sentence adverb, compare *The play ended happily* and *The play ended, happily;* the first *happily* is a descriptive adverb, and the second is a sentence adverb meaning 'it is a happy fact that.') They are *outside* the sentence proper, and so can be analyzed as higher sentences, sentences which have others subordinate to them. The deep structure of *It honestly didn't work* would then be:

---

[16] See Ross 1970.

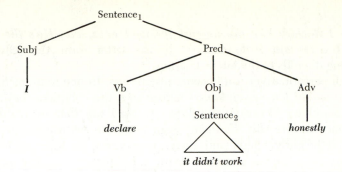

One reason why certain performatives escape notice is that when most of their structure is stripped away and the remnant—in this case an adverb—moves inside what was once a subordinate sentence, peculiar things begin to happen. The adverb gets attracted to some element in the subordinate structure and comes to be felt as a modifier of it rather than of any vanished higher verb. We can see this happening in stepwise fashion:

Truly Mary is nice.

Mary **truly** is nice.

Mary is **truly** nice.

The closer **truly** gets to **nice** the more the meaning seems to be 'very nice.' The adverb **really** has not only passed through these stages but shows the final change in structure by a change in its form from **really** to **real:**

Really Mary is nice.

Mary **really** is nice.

Mary is **really** nice.

Mary is **real** nice.

As we saw earlier, this is the process by which **very** became the intensifier that it is today. The regularity with which the same process repeats itself with one adverb after another suggests that when speakers actually use these particular performatives they do not usually intend them to refer to an act of saying but to the truth of what they say: 'I say truly' is rather 'It is true that' or even 'I say that it is true that,' with two higher sentences.[17] The verb **declare** has this intensifying use with no need of any

---

[17] Consider a remark such as **I don't (just) say he's big, he is big,** where the performative is qualified and the truth is affirmed.

adverb: *I declare he's the biggest fellow I ever saw; He's the biggest fellow I ever saw, I do declare.* In the latter form, the affirmation-specifying *do* adds to the intensification.

Not all performatives can become intensifiers. In one sense of *Knowing John, he would have complained before this,* the complete sentence has to be something like *Knowing John, I (can) say that he would have complained before this. Knowing John* is not an intensifier, but it does have a sufficiently vague and general reference to take on the loose functions of a sentence adverb with no reference to any particular speaker: *Knowing John I (we, you, anybody) can say. . . .*

But the question of higher sentences has more interesting consequences than just whether one always means 'I declare' when one declares. There are many other such higher verbs that leave a residue when they disappear. In the sentence *John is here, because his car is outside,* we know that his car being outside is not why he is here—that is why the normal cause-effect order in **Because his car is outside John is here* sounds wrong. But if *I can tell* is added, then either order is possible: *I can tell, because his car is outside, John is here; I can tell John is here because his car is outside.* The *because* modifies the higher verb *to tell* (*know, detect,* or whatever). These higher verbs are all of a type: they concern the manipulation of information—having it, getting it, giving it, explaining it, seeking it. They are already half-adverbial in their habits even when they are fully expressed, as can be seen by the fact that they are never quite sure where they belong. The expression *I suppose* can occupy the same positions as *supposedly* in the following:

> *I suppose* you were looking for a job.
>
> You *I suppose* were looking for a job.
>
> You were *I suppose* looking for a job.
>
> You were looking *I suppose* for a job.
>
> You were looking for a job *I suppose.*

The higher verbs in the following can all be moved somewhere else:

> The first one, *I mean,* was not intended for you.
>
> Were the voting machines out of whack, *I wonder?*
>
> Marie *it appears* had a few qualms of conscience.
>
> Has he made reservations yet, *do you know?*
>
> Where *do you think* she lives?

The same footloose character can be seen in other insertions that cue the hearer on how he is supposed to take the sentence. Affirmation, negation, and interrogation are in a way themselves higher sentences, as might be inferred from their position all the way to the left in the structure trees of the preceding section. So it is natural for them sometimes to take up positions outside the sentence proper, and when they do, they tend to amalgamate with other higher sentences occupying the same position. This leads to a phenomenon that some grammarians have called "negative transportation." In place of *I suppose he doesn't care,* which contains the higher sentence *I suppose* plus a Neg that has been moved inside *He cares* to give *He doesn't care,* the Neg can be combined with *I suppose: I don't suppose he cares.* This does not deny the supposition so much as the caring. One also has the option of saying *He doesn't care, I don't suppose,* which shows where the negation really belongs and illustrates the other "outside" position, at the very end. But "transportation" covers more than negation. With Aff, *I think he really likes it* can become *I really think he likes it.* And with Q one may have *Do you suppose it's safe?* alternating with *Is it safe, do you suppose?* where the interrogative inversion is attached to the higher sentence. Both negation and interrogation can combine: *Don't you think it's nice? Isn't it nice, don't you think?*

Certain auxiliary verbs—particularly *must, could, may,* and *might*—are very often remnants of higher sentences. When we say *John must be careful* we mean that he is under obligation to be careful; but when we say *John must be sick* we mean 'It must be that John is sick.' Like the sentence adverbs, these modal elements have been absorbed in the lower sentence. Sometimes they create odd results. In *I must have heard you and didn't know what I heard* the expected form would be *I must have heard you and not known what I heard,* with the *must have* coupled to *known* as well as *heard.* But since in the interpretation intended there is only one higher sentence, *It must be that I heard you and didn't know what I heard,* the speaker feels that it is enough to have the *must* affect just one verb, the first one. The same goes when the higher sentence is a question: *Was he there and didn't realize what was going on?* meaning *Is the explanation that he was there and didn't realize what was going on?* Here there is no way out. We cannot say *Was he there and didn't he realize what was going on?* because that would destroy the connection between the two events.

The farther back one stands from particular instances of higher sentences the clearer it becomes that syntax involves not just what is said but what is said or implied *about* what is said. The sentence *If you do that you'll see what happens* has the form of a prediction but the sense of a warning; and the reply *You just try showing me* has the form of a command but the sense of a threat. The person who says *Please, it's hot enough in here already!* is probably asking someone not to turn up the heat. In these three examples there are still linguistic elements that suggest how the utterance is to be taken: the future is loosely involved in warnings, the word *just* with threats (joined to imperatives, especially imperatives with the subject *you* expressed), and *please* of course is explicit for requests. But entire utterances may have such an aura: **John, look at the time!** would hardly ever have the same intention as **John, look at that beautiful bird!** At its most tenuous, the clue may come entirely from the nonverbal setting: **I brought you some flowers** may mean 'Please forgive me for the way I quarreled with you last night.' Speakers have grammaticized the commonest instances of this-is-how-I-want-you-to-take-what-I-am-saying, but the rest—the majority—are left to the imagination and whatever help it can get from the outside.

Thus far all the examples of sentences that get lost in the shuffle have been of higher sentences. But lower sentences may suffer the same fate. This is especially true of *existence predicates*. Speakers often bring something in by merely assuming that it is there, without according it a proper introduction. In the sentence **Snow is possible tonight** we have an adjective, **possible**, apparently describing **snow**. The forecaster can even say **Possible snow tonight**, putting the adjective directly in front of the noun. But while a suitable description for **snow** may be **white, crystalline, powdery**, or **stark and beautiful, possible** hardly qualifies. So the sentence must be represented in deep structure by something like **(That there be snow tonight) is possible.** Similarly in **The blighting is caused by insufficient water** we seem to be saying, rather incoherently, that some kind of water is causing the blight. What we intend of course is **The blighting is caused by (there is insufficient water).** There are many such **there be**'s lying around, and no doubt countless other syntactic orphans, if we could recognize them.

SYNTAX BEYOND THE SENTENCE

Sentences containing reduced higher sentences are already one step beyond the tightest definition of a single sentence, because they shade off into explicit combinations of sentences tied together by conjunctions, plus their verbal and nonverbal indicators of intent. Also, much of what is found in such complex sentences can be found in combinations of simple ones, where relationships are not specified by grammatical operators but left to be inferred. The relationship between these separate sentences is called *paratactic*—a "side-by-side" *(para-)* arrangement rather than a "with" *(syn-)* arrangement. Instead of **It's raining, so I'm coming in,** one can say **It's raining. I'm coming in.** The specific function word **so**, showing 'consequence,' is omitted. In **I wanted to help him. Unfortunately it was too late.** there is an "adversative" relationship which can be expressed by joining the two sentences with **but: I wanted to help him, but unfortunately it was too late.** The three sentences **He came in.**

He looked around. He sat down. imply a coordination that can be made explicit, in a single sentence, with *and: He came in, (and) (he) looked around, and (he) sat down.*

Besides paratactic relationships there are others that tie sentences together. One is *co-reference*—an element in one sentence refers to an element in another. Pronouns are the most familiar examples:

"Why don't you use your credit card?"—"I don't have *one.*"

"Didn't you have to dodge the cars?"—"There weren't *any.*"

He couldn't open the door. *It* was locked tight.

They didn't just fine him. *That* would have been too easy.

There are other pro-words too:

"Weren't they the right size?"—"I thought *so,* but they turned out to be too big."

"Are you going back to Gray's Lake?"—"I hate *the place.*"

"Shall we invite Swerdloff?"—"I can't stand *the man.*"

And since deletions are done usually "under identity," omitting something from a construction is generally a guarantee that the missing element is somewhere in the context. So, for comparatives:

"Did she get there at six?"—"No, (she got there) earlier (than six)."

"Why don't you take this one?"—"It isn't as nice (as that one [referred to still earlier])."

Other deletions:

He's tall.—(He's tall) And handsome.

"I don't want to take that stuff."—"You don't have to (take that stuff)."

This is evidence for inter-sentence links. It is also evidence for a type of organization that might be called conversational ping-pong. Most spoken language consists of *dialog,* that may take the form of simple pairs where an answer closes off a question but just as often stretches out in chains of responses and responses to responses. Generally no one speaker holds the floor long enough for there to be any hint of a still higher level of organization, of something more than a succession of gives and takes.

But an eloquent speaker does sometimes launch into a monolog— more often in a story-telling culture than in a TV-watching one—and writers do compose paragraphs which are sometimes read aloud. Are there markers of *closure* for paragraphs, similar to the ones we found for sentences—pause, intonation, and typical structures?

Unquestionably, paragraphs are marked by pause and intonation, just as sentences are (see page 59). A statement normally has a terminal fall; this is "finality" in both a logical and an affective sense: the speaker has "finished" that much of his subject and stops momentarily for breath. Each connected sentence tends to drop a little lower, and the lowest pitch of all is attained at the end of the series. Occasionally a word such as *finally* will identify the last sentence.

But our awareness of paragraphs in English is due more to their semantic content than to any formal indicators. The most readable prose is the kind that provides for some kind of logical transition at the beginning. The commonest device is the topic sentence. There are hackneyed ways of introducing it—*Next I want to speak of . . . ; We turn now to . . . ; Leaving that for the moment, what can we say of. . . .* And sometimes a writer or speaker will number his paragraphs. But as a rule, nothing in particular, least of all syntactic, labels either the beginning or the end.

Not all languages leave paragraph divisions so much to chance. In Yagua, a language of Peru, narrative paragraphs tend to begin with a statement of action that carries a particular emphatic suffix.[18] An even tighter scheme is found in certain "chaining" languages of New Guinea—for example Fore, which has distinctive suffixes for "final verbs" and "medial verbs," the former occurring at the end of a unit which, for length and content, is best regarded as a paragraph.[19]

As for still more inclusive units of organization—entire themes or discourses or stories—it is doubtful that any grammatical signs of closure can be found. Such units are at the highest level of awareness and are most apt to be announced and concluded with verbal formulas: *. . . and now my story's begun; . . . and now my story's done.* But whole texts do have their system, and the system is being investigated. We must have light on it to understand the relationship between linguistics and literature.[20]

Syntax and invention

If the traffic department of a large modern city wants to find out in the most painless way whether some proposed change in the direction, signal-

---

[18] Powlinson 1965, p. 109.

[19] Longacre 1970.

[20] See van Dijk 1972 and Pavel 1973.

ing, speed, number of lanes, and lane width of a flow of traffic will move the cars and trucks more smoothly or jam them up, it resorts to a simulation: the conditions are pre-set and a computer sends pretended vehicles along imaginary streets to reproduce the movements and interferences that would occur in reality. It is not necessary to erect the signals, re-route the lanes, and alter the face of the city to find out whether or not the new arrangement will work.

The mechanism of syntax is like the computer. In our advance scheming for good and bad ends, we try out alternatives in a simulated program to see how close we can come to predicting what the results would be if the plans were actually carried out. In part this is possible because we can pre-set the words in the program and then sit back and watch the fun. Will the semantic features clash or blend? Will they weave themselves into amusing or startling or suggestive patterns? What we think of as the free play of ideas is to some extent pure frolicking with the semantic features of words, which the syntax of our language permits us to do.

The bars to incompatibility then are let down—words join that would only clash in reports of the real world; but the grammatical framework stands, for it corresponds to the built-in characteristics of the computer. And computer programs have been devised that will write a crude novel, by pre-setting certain conditions and allowing events as they occur to serve as partial input to succeeding events, much as an amateur story teller makes up a plot as he goes along.[21]

Dreams are perhaps the extreme of this freewheeling use of language—the restraints on semantic features are lowered but most of the grammatical ones remain intact. One attested dream sequence was the following: *How to write* (not *ride*)*a creeping doorcan bicycle.* Everything here is according to rule—*how to* is a normal beginning for a set of directions, *write* follows in the normal spot for a verb, the *-ing* form *creeping* is used in its normal way as a modifier, *doorcan* is a normal compound on the order of *doorway* or *ashcan* used normally as a modifier, and *bicycle* occupies the normal slot for the noun. The design of poetry is similar, except that it is contrived and not random. The poet may even alter some of the less secure grammatical features. He is not concerned that the verb *unfurl* takes inanimate objects when he describes a lanky and attitudinizing man as *unfurling himself.*

Being able to put words together free of the dead weight of things is a first step to invention. The verb *to fly* has as one of its semantic features the possession of wings. Human beings have no wings, but that was no bar to simulating them verbally and in the end concretely.

---

[21] Klein et al. 1973.

ADDITIONAL REMARKS
AND APPLICATIONS

1. During the Second World War, transmitters were said to **observe radio silence** when transmissions were stopped to prevent detection. If you wanted to sleep and your roommate had his record player on, would you be apt to ask him to **observe record player silence?** Explain your answer as a problem of the line between syntax and morphology.

2. Similar to the example *I went to check on the dry clothes* given in the text (page 137) is the following from a television ad: **How to stop a leaky basement.**[22] Discuss its formation, and compare it with the following:

   a. How to stop a runny nose.

   b. How to cure a runny nose.

   c. How to cure a nose that's runny.

   d. How to stop a basement that's leaky.

   e. How to stop a nose that's runny.

   f. How to stop a nose running.

   Some of these will probably sound better to you than others. Among those that sound more or less acceptable, does it seem as if there might be a certain amount of blending, so that we no longer think of **leaky basement** necessarily as 'a basement that leaks' but as 'a leak in a basement'? If there is such an actual change in the meaning, would you then think it unnecessary to try to generate such a sentence from a more logical deep structure such as **How to stop a basement from leaking?** Consider as part of your evidence other sentences with a similar "event" sense:

   a. I want to get rid of this leaky basement.

   b. A leaky basement doesn't happen too often.

   c. [Forced busing] will create people who will leave the city.[23]

---

[22] Channel 56, Boston, 28 September 1972.
[23] Station WEEI, Boston, 1 December 1972.

3. Deduce as much as you can about the words and structure of the following nonsense:

> Degressably, the slem that Quisian had arvingly craduced thrammed a ranglin through both markles of wismy cluff so hort that umbody flapsed. Thereupon, the dramp nording the wendorous plorin stambored its tilfored cormel aside hypaxically till all the bohams could prentiously desorm.

If you had to decide at gunpoint between calling it English and calling it a foreign language, which would you choose? Why?

4. What kind of transformation has been responsible for the most notable feature of the second sentence in the following?

> It required a larger daily allowance [of alcohol] to keep her misty-minded. Too little and she was aching melancholy.[24]

5. The radio comedian Fibber McGee once said *to waste a guy like me's time*,[25] fumbling over the phrase intentionally. What was the point of the joke? Express this as a restriction on the formation of the possessive, which also excludes *all of them's money, *both of us's friends. Could the latter be expressed as *both of our friends?* What do you make of the following, from a literary magazine?—*They* [two veteran Hollywood chaps] *are William Demarest and Raymond Walburn, both of whose talents have long been recognized.*[26]

6. Most sentences in English and related languages have a favored accent pattern, consisting of two major prominences, one close to the beginning and one close to the end:

> *thieves*   *ca*
> The   were ᵗʳʸing to es
>   pe.

> *What*   *tha*
>   on earth is   t?

>   *Hen*
> But   ry diₙ,ₜ ob cᵗ!
>   je

---

[24] Dorothy Parker, "Big Blonde," in Sally Arteseros (ed.), *First Prize Stories, 1919–1960* (Garden City, N.Y.: Doubleday, 1960).

[25] "Fibber McGee and Molly," 2 March 1948.

[26] *Saturday Review of Literature* (30 June 1951), p. 22.

Given that nouns are more likely to occur toward the beginning of a sentence and verbs toward the end, does it seem likely that this pattern helps to "push" the stress of nouns to the left and verbs to right, accounting for the tendency toward end-prominence in verbs that was noted in the text (pages 145–46)? Listen to people who are talking emphatically and see if you note instances like the following:

> You will receive pinking shears just for seeing the machine demonstráted. (TV announcer)[27]
>
> Everything he looks at he'll photográph. (newsfilm announcer)[28]
>
> With the microscope we explore the minutest organísms. (TV announcer)[29]

7. Do you associate mass nouns with a kind of meaning? Some speakers are uncomfortable with saying either of the following:

> The doctor wanted to know how many vegetables I eat, because he said I was not getting enough roughage.
>
> The doctor wanted to know how much vegetables I eat, because he said I was not getting enough roughage.

The second is somewhat worse than the first, but the first is unsatisfactory too. Why? Compare the following:

> He takes too much pains with his work.
> He takes too many pains with his work.
> How much dried milk solids does it contain?
> How many dried milk solids does it contain?

Does the meaning seem to want one thing and the grammar another? Would the paraphrase *How much do you eat in the way of vegetables?* be a way of getting around the problem?

8. Classify the following as mass or count: *evidence, clue; quarrel, strife; client, clientele; vocabulary, verbiage; ectoplasm, ghost.* Classify the following as intensifiable or unintensifiable: *to seize, to grip; to prance, to walk; sociable, social; a jailbird, a criminal; provably, probably.*

9. Do you restrict *less* to mass and use only *fewer* with count? Judge

---

[27] Channel 2, Denver, 13 December 1962.

[28] "Sports in Action," Astor Theater, Boston, 19 March 1964.

[29] Truman Bradley, announcer for "Science Fiction Theater," Channel 38, Boston, 3 April 1966.

the sentence *I've seen him less times this year*. Does your use of the word *majority* reflect the mass–count contrast? Judge the following:

> The majority of the people were opposed.
> The majority of the loss was in municipal bonds.
> The majority of the sugar was lost in transit.

10. Consider the following as an example of "transitivity" in nouns:

> "What sort of dog is that?"—"It's a hybrid."
>   —"*It's a cross."
>   —"It's a cross between a bulldog
>   and a mastiff."

What is wrong with the sentences *John is a denizen* and *John is a frequenter?*

11. William Styron wrote *Did they too taste the mouth go dry at thought of the coming slaughter?*[30] Is this way of using the sensory verb *taste* normal for you? What about the following, from Sir Walter Scott?—*I strained my eye on vacant space, as if to descry the fair huntress again descend like an apparition from the hill.*[31] Does this construction of sensory verb plus bare infinitive (*go, descend*) refer primarily to things or to events? Test your answer against your reaction to the following:

> "Did you see Joe?"
>   —"Yes, I saw him eat a watermelon."
>   —"Yes, I saw him eating a watermelon."

Are the two answers equally appropriate?

12. What kind of expression are *to lift a finger* and *to bat an eye?* Judge the following:

> He lifted a finger to help me.
> He didn't lift a finger to help me.
> When I told him he batted an eye.
> When I told him he didn't bat an eye.

What about *to say boo?* Can you think of others?

---

[30] *The Confessions of Nat Turner* (London: Cox and Wyman, Panther Book, 1968), p. 326.
[31] *Rob Roy* (London: Everyman, 1963), p. 363.

Are there affirmatively biased words? See if you reject any of the following four possibilities with *bit* and *little:*

"Would you give me some of that?"

—"OK, I guess I can spare a bit (a little) of it."

—"Sorry, I can't spare a bit (a little) of it."

13. Is there a negative bias in *to hurt* when it is used with an inanimate object? Compare **It hurt the cargo, It didn't hurt the cargo.**

14. The text mentions that some expressions only half belong to the negatively biased category. Would this be true, in your speech, of **to hack it?** Try yourself on the following:

    a. He just can't hack it.

    b. I didn't hack it in that job.

    c. Oh, he hacks it just fine.

    d. He can hack it as well as you can.

Rather than being negatively biased, is **hack it** perhaps like **afford,** which requires an implication of 'being able'? (See page 199).

15. *Abstract* and *concrete* are sometimes recognized as two opposing classes, like mass and count. Study the following, decide which sentences are acceptable to you, and see if the abstract–concrete distinction has anything to do with it. (Imagine the sentences as answers to some such question as **Are you going to do so-and-so?** or **Why didn't you do so-and-so?**)

    a. I didn't have the money to.

    b. I didn't have the dollars to.

    c. I didn't have the mental equipment to.

    d. I didn't have the electrical equipment to.

    e. I don't have the willpower to.

    f. I don't have the horsepower to.

    g. I don't have the power to.

    h. I don't have the gasoline to.

    i. He doesn't have the right preparation to.

    j. He doesn't have the right tools to.

Think up other examples.

16. Examine the following sentences to see whether something is necessarily implied as to the truth or falsity of the embedded sentence:

    a. Jack forgot to call. (Did he call?)

    b. Jill neglected to sign the check.

    c. Jill was unwilling to sign the check.

    d. Jill was reluctant to sign the check.

    e. Mary just had to speak out.

    f. Mary was determined to speak out.

    g. Louise had a sudden impulse to slap him.

    h. Louise had an irresistible impulse to slap him.

    i. I restrained Louise from slapping him.

Does it seem reasonable to set up a class or classes of verbs or governing expressions according to what is implied in the embedded sentences? Think up some additional governing expressions and see how they affect what follows them, and also whether negating them makes a difference. For example, *I was sorry he died* and *I wasn't sorry he died* both assume that he died; but what about *He balked at doing what he was told* and *He didn't balk at doing what he was told?*[32]

17. Assuming that you understand the sentence *He threw me a cheerful greet as I came in,* what is nevertheless wrong with it? State your answer in terms of word classes. Do the same with *How many centuries ancient is it?* (Suggestion: Consider a class of words including *old, heavy, deep, long, wide,* and so forth, which have a property that is lacking in *ancient, weighty, profound, lengthy, spacious,* and so on. Do the antonyms *young, light, shallow, short,* and *narrow* have this same property? Can you say *How many feet narrow is it?*)

18. Assume that of the following three sentences two are closer together *grammatically* and two are closer together *psychologically.* See if you can match them up. (Re-read pages 154–55).

    a. Nobody was there that I knew.

    b. Nobody that I knew was there.

    c. Nobody who was there did I know.

19. What is there about the interpersonal situation in which sentences

---

[32] If the book is available, see Abraham 1974.

such as *Want a bite?* and *Sit down!* are used that makes it easy to omit *you?* Can you think of similar situations where *I* is left out? Relate your observations to the general concept of *redundancy* (the amount of explicitness needed to avoid ambiguity).

20. Compare the following sentences:

> If it's going to rain, I wish it would rain.
> If it's going to rain, I wish it would.

In the second, *rain* is transformationally deleted because it is the same as the preceding *rain* ("deletion under identity"). Do the two sentences mean the same? See if the following implications are equally applicable to both sentences:

> desire for the rain
> impatience at the rain's inability to make up its mind

In the following two sentences, decide whether the implications of (a) acceptance or determination and (b) resignation are equally applicable to both:

> If I have to drive it in, I'll drive it in.
> If I have to drive it in, I will.

Does it appear that even with as simple a transformation as deletion we cannot be sure that there will not be some change in meaning?

21. There is a type of conditional construction involving *do* and other auxiliaries that is still used (more in writing than in speech), though it is becoming obsolete. Examples:

    a. Did so much as a breath of criticism touch him, he complained.
    b. Were I to say that, I would suffer for it.
    c. Could we but try our hand, we would manage.
    d. Should you need me, I'll be ready.

Compare the word order with that in yes–no questions. Is there a similarity in meaning between questions and conditions? Would it be reasonable to add "Cond" (condition) to Neg, Aff, and Q in the Polarity scheme? (See pages 162–64).

22. Some transformations are held to be obligatory. An example is the reflexive transformation, whereby a deep structure such as *Beatrice loves Beatrice* has to be transformed to *Beatrice loves herself.* Following are three violations of that rule. See what if anything

justifies them, and consider whether they suggest a need to keep meaning in mind at all times:

  a. *We* call upon *us* all to act without violence.[33]

  b. I don't see how *you* can resist *you*. (Wife to hero in a movie, who has just spilled perfume on his clothes.)[34]

  c. (An item from the Boston *Globe*):[35]

"Rusty, if you were sitting at your trial, would *you* find *yourself* guilty?" Bailey recalled asking Calley as he spoke last night before several hundred Yale University students. Calley, whom Bailey described as "a pretty honest fellow," replied, "*I* would find *me* guilty of manslaughter," Bailey said.

23. We have seen how adverbs are often retained from performative verbs *(I frankly don't know = I tell you frankly I don't know)*. Some performative verbs themselves have become virtual adverbs. See what evidence you can find for this in the way the verb *guess* is used. First, imagine that you are in a guessing game, where *guess* has its literal meaning, and you are required to estimate the number of pellets in a glass jar. You say *Since it's my turn to guess, I guess that it's 1649*. Would it be normal for you to say *Since it's my turn to guess, it's 1649, I guess?* Now suppose that you are not in a guessing game but are just expressing a casual supposition: *I guess we'd better go*. In this case might you say *We'd better go, I guess?* Notice the *that (I guess that)* in the first example. Would it be just as natural to insert a *that* in the corresponding place in the second example? Where would a *that* be used—after something felt to be fully a verb, or after something less? And which would be more likely to move around, a verb or an adverb?

24. Given a question–answer pair such as *"Why do you insist he did it?"* *—"Because I'm stubborn,"* decide whether something is wrong with this one: *"Why do you suppose he came?"—"Because I'm well-informed."*

25. Discuss the status of *parenthetically* and the status of *wonder* in the following: *This fact leads me parenthetically to wonder whether we have recently stated what the deadlines are.*[36]

---

[33] War Resisters League circular, March 1970.

[34] *Rally Round the Flag, Boys*, 1959.

[35] 4 October 1971, p. 10.

[36] Personal letter, 1971.

26. Discuss the status of *morally* in *Morally it makes no difference.* Explain how *practically* became an intensifier in *It makes practically no difference.*

27. Does negation sometimes belong to a higher sentence when it actually appears in a lower one? Consider the following interpretations:

"Why didn't she buy it?"—"She didn't have the money."

    a. It was the case that she didn't have the money.

    b. It wasn't the case that she had the money.

"Why do you hate me?"—"I don't hate you!"

    a. It is the case that I don't hate you!

    b. It isn't the case that I hate you!

28. Discuss the expression *Let's face it* as a possible higher sentence. First, what does it mean? Second, what is its relationship to what follows that makes it viewable as a higher sentence?

29. What does the sentence *I can't seem to do it* illustrate about negation?

30. What has happened in the following, and what does it illustrate about a transformational relationship between statements and questions?

    "Did they suffer?"—"Terribly."
    "Did it work?"—"Perfectly."
    "Was he tall?"—"Incredibly."

31. A falling intonation is often a cue to the meaning 'I am saying this' and a rising intonation to 'I am asking this.' Can intonation then be regarded as a kind of performative? Can it even reverse another performative, as in *I assure you he's your friend,* spoken ironically? Consider the following:

    The sermon in *Tristram Shandy* . . . progresses from an initial indicative assertion of trust to a final statement of doubt, while the intonation begins by questioning the assertion and ends by affirming the doubt.[37]

32. Discuss sentence a, after comparing it with b and c:

    a. I never thought that it made any difference.
    b. I thought that it never made any difference.
    c. I didn't think that it ever made any difference.

---

[37] Dolores M. Burton. 1971. *MLA Abstracts* 3, "Linguistics," Item 687.

33. The following was part of a radio ad: *That's all it can take to [pro-duce a bad effect]*,[38] meaning 'Nothing more is needed to produce a bad effect.' What has happened to *can?*

34. An office worker was overheard saying on the telephone: *Did he hurt himself at one time and not be able to do anything?* Discuss the problem. (Would you say *Did he not be able to do anything?*)

35. *Mind you* is a higher sentence that directs the hearer as to how to take the sentence that it accompanies. Which of the following comes closest to its meaning?
    Bear in mind that . . .
    Remember . . .
    Obviously . . .
    I say this to warn you against drawing any false conclusions . . .
    It is an unexpected fact that . . .

36. How is it possible to answer the question *Are you sure you wouldn't like to see that program?* with either *Yes* or *No* (in both cases with a "firm" falling intonation) and mean the same thing?

37. The columnist James J. Kilpatrick, complaining of the problems he encountered in incorporating himself in order to save on income taxes, wrote the following: *Last week we ran out of walking-around money and had to get an advance on expenses. It seemed ridiculous for we to sign a check made out to us, so we asked our secretary to sign it.*[39] Discuss the second *we*. Would an *us* have been satisfactory? Does this suggest anything about the tendency for grammatical and logical functions to coincide?

38. Certain word games use random combinations with interesting results. One such game is the "Minister's Wife." The players take the frame sentence *The minister's wife is a _____ wife* and fill the blank with any adjective they can think of starting with a given letter —first *a*, then *b*, and so on through the alphabet. One word is supplied with each player's turn. A point is lost when a player is unable to think of any additional adjective starting with that particular letter, and after each such loss the next letter is begun. Play the game, and notice how the natural reaction to any speech sequence is to assume that it is meaningful and to try to make sense out of it, which of course is why the game is entertaining.

---

[38] Station WEEI, Boston, April 1971.
[39] Palo Alto *Times* (25 July 1974), p. 25.

References

Abraham, Werner. 1974. "Karttunen's Types of Implication in English and German: A Contrastive Study," in S. P. Corder and E. Roulet (eds.), *Linguistic Insights in Applied Linguistics* (Brussels: Aimav, and Paris: Didier).

Algeo, John. 1972. *Problems in the Origins and Development of the English Language,* 2nd ed. (New York: Harcourt Brace Jovanovich).

Bolinger, Dwight. 1971. "Intensification in English," *Language Sciences* 16: 1–5.

Boxwell, Maurice. 1967. "Weri Pronoun System," *Linguistics* 29:34–43.

Friedrich, Paul. 1972. "Shape Categories in Grammar," *Linguistics* 77:5–21.

Iannucci, James E. 1952. *Lexical Number in Spanish Nouns* (Philadelphia: University of Pennsylvania Press).

Keller, Kathryn C. 1955. "The Chontal (Mayan) Numeral System," *International Journal of American Linguistics* 21:258–75.

Klein, Sheldon, et al. 1973. "Automatic Novel Writing, a Status Report." Department of Computer Sciences, University of Wisconsin, Technical Report No. 186.

Longacre, Robert E. 1970. "Paragraph and Sentence Structure in New Guinea Highlands Languages," *Kivung* 3:150–63.

Osgood, Charles E. 1971. "Explorations in Semantic Space: A Personal Diary," *Journal of Social Issues* 27:5–64.

Pavel, Thomas G. 1973. "*Phèdre:* Outline of a Narrative Grammar," *Language Sciences* 28:1–6.

Powlinson, Paul S. 1965. "A Paragraph Analysis of a Yagua Folktale," *International Journal of American Linguistics* 31:109–18.

Quirk, Randolph; Sidney Greenbaum; Geoffrey Leech; and Jan Svartvik. 1972. *A Grammar of Contemporary English* (New York and London: Seminar Press).

Ross, John R. 1970. "On Declarative Sentences," in R. Jacobs and P. Rosenbaum (eds.), *Readings in English Transformational Grammar* (Boston: Ginn).

Tervoort, Bernard Th. 1968. "You Me Downtown Movie Fun?" *Lingua* 21: 455–65.

van Dijk, Teun A. 1972. *Some Aspects of Text Grammars* (The Hague: Mouton).

Welmers, William E. 1950. "Notes on Two Languages in the Senufo Group," *Language* 26:126–46.

MEANING 7

At what point does language break free? Distinctive features make phonemes, phonemes make morphemes, morphemes words, words sentences, sentences discourses, discourses monologs or dialogs or stories or whatever, and these are puffed or puffable into novels, trilogies, encyclopedias, or higher units as large as one may please. Looking up and down the stairway it seems as if there is no escape. Yet at some point—and it surely is not necessarily the last and highest—language must make contact with the outside world. This contact is what we call meaning.

The term *meaning* is used in many ways, not all of them equally relevant to language. Saying *I didn't mean to hurt him* or exclaiming indignantly *What is the meaning of this!* refers to an intention. *Another child means an extra mouth to feed* or *Smoke means fire* signifies an inference. *The German* **hund** *means 'dog'* is a translation. And so on. The meaning of "meaning" that, while not itself linguistic, is closest to language is that of the example *A red light means 'Stop.'* It is not quite the same as *Smoke means fire.* We do not make smoke in order to mean fire with it. Traffic lights, like words, are part of a communicative system with arbitrary values. We infer the meanings because we put them there ourselves; we only get back our investment. It is the same with language. The linguistic counterpart of *A red light means 'Stop'* is *X linguistic form has 'Y' meaning,* for it expresses the value of the code, the price tag that we have attached. (It may be that psychologically *A red light means 'Stop'* and *Smoke means fire* are identical, the code having been so thor-

185

oughly assimilated that we react to the warning of the color red as if it were a natural phenomenon. But this is not a question for linguists.)

Traffic signals are like linguistic signs the way counting on two fingers is like calculating with a computer. Traffic signals are ordinarily one for one: red for stop, yellow for caution, green for go. Only rarely do two or more together have a special meaning, as in Massachusetts, where red plus yellow means 'Walk.' Linguistic signs are built of units built of units. Not all levels are penetrated equally by meaning.

It is pointless to look for meaning in distinctive features, phonemes, and syllables, for these are members of the phonological hierarchy and are meaningless by definition (pages 23, 35, 59, 78), though we did observe a curious relationship between vowels and the notion of size (Chapter 2, pages 24, 25). With morphemes we begin to find units to which meanings are attached, and this carries on through words and sentences. So the question comes down to which of these levels—from morpheme upward—is the real tie with the outside world.

The answer must depend on how we picture the outside world. If it is a kind of idealized collection of entities that keep their shapes no matter what kaleidoscopic patterns they take whenever they are shaken up, our choice will fall on morphemes or words. If it is the patterns themselves, it will fall on sentences. This is because a sentence—a particular sentence, not a sentence type—does not mean in the same way that a word means. The meaning of a sentence is something in the outside world at a given time and in relationship to given persons, qualities, and objects. The meaning of a word is potential, like that of a dollar bill before it is involved in a transaction. The statement **X** *word means* '**Y**' carries a prediction of how a speaker will use **X** word. To make it refer to a real event we must turn it into a sentence—an exclamation like *John!* when we unexpectedly see a friend or *Run!* when danger threatens. The same is true of sentence forms, though not of sentences themselves: the sentences *Boy meets girl* and *Girl meets boy* involve the same forms, including that of **X**-as-subject, which suggests something about who takes the initiative. A speaker will use this or any other form in an actual sentence to match some real event, but the arrangement is only a linguistic potential, a bit of linguistic substance with a meaning that tends to remain constant.

The problem of meaning, then, is one of fitting together the partially (but never firmly) fixed semantic entities that we carry in our heads, tied to the words and forms of sentences, to approximate the way reality is fitted together as it comes to us from moment to moment. The entities are the world reduced to its parts and secured in our minds; they are a purse of coins in our pocket with values to match whatever combination of bargains, fines, and imposts is likely to come our way. The problem of meaning is how the linguistic potential is brought in line with nonlinguistic reality whenever a speaker creates an utterance, or even—since we manipulate our environment almost as readily as our language—how the real is brought in line with the potential. (This has the ring of the philosophical dispute that shook the Schoolmen of the Middle Ages: which is primary, the things in the world to which we merely give names, or the entities in our minds that we project outward? The answer seems to depend on whether we stand on the linguistic or the non-linguistic side of meaning.)

THE SEGMENTATION OF REALITY

The expression *outside world* does not mean what is "outside us" but what is "outside language." It may well be inside us. If I say I have a headache, or that I saw you with a red hat in my dream last night, I am relating something that no one else can observe, yet I put it into words as readily as I refer to the weather or to the day's major league baseball scores.

This is the sense in which we must take the term *reality*, for it includes what is viewable only from within as well as what can be seen by anyone. In fact, the inner view is more important for most of the things adults talk about. Utterances that comment on what is going on at the moment, like **Now I get up, now I walk to the window, now I look out,** are exceptional; more usual are **Last night I got up because I couldn't sleep** or **If you'll hand me that wire I'll attach this hook,** where we look inward on our memories or our plans. Whatever it is that represents these past and future or imagined events in our minds is the main part, if not the whole, of reality as we grasp it. The link to meaning is there—beyond the reach of any instruments we now have. As one team of psychologists sees it, meaning is the part of language that is least understood "because in all probability it reflects the principles of neural organization in the cerebral hemisphere."[1]

What conditions need to be met for the signs of language, limited in number, to designate reality, which is infinite? The first condition is that reality must be *segmented*. Whenever we manipulate an object we separate it from its environment. Part of the act of separating it is the act of naming it: a cumulus cloud, a wall, a stick, a laugh. Language gives us a map of reality in which everything is covered but much detail is left out. The second condition, necessary for the first, is that the segments must be *repeatable* and that we must have some mechanism to recognize similarity between one appearance and the next so as to call the two by the

---

[1] Locke, Caplan, and Kellar 1973, p. 10.

same name. A wall in the dark must still be a wall in the daylight. The third condition is built-in *vagueness;* absolute identity of segments cannot be required, for dealing with the continuum of experience would then be impossible; explicitly or implicitly we have to be able to say *X is Y* and mean '*X* is a kind of *Y*,' '*X* is like *Y*.' Otherwise we might learn to apply the name *dog* to Fido but could never extend it to other dogs (and might even fail to apply it to Fido when we saw him a second or third time). A fourth condition is simply *memory,* which is not specific to language; there must be provision for storing the linguistic units to make them available for future use.

How is the connection between linguistic unit and segment of reality made, so that when the segment presents itself the speaker will respond with the unit—or, in the role of hearer or under some form of self-stimulation, so that when the unit is presented the segment will be invoked? The basis for this is the permeation we noted earlier (Chapter 1, page 2). It may be that as we grow expert in the use of language, "outside world" is to be taken in a less and less material sense; but in the beginning it is concrete—the child learns to make verbal responses to things in a way that embodies those responses as part of the complex manifestations of the things themselves. For a dog to become a recognizable and repeatable segment of reality, the child needs to make enveloping contacts with it—feel the hair, see the tail wag, watch the fawning behavior, hear the bark—and hear, whenever older children or adults are about, utterances replete with a certain pattern of sounds, /dɔg/. The attributes of a particular dog are not only a texture of hair and a certain size and shape and color of eyes; they include also the name *dog.* It is true that the color of eyes and texture of hair are "always there" and the name *dog* is intermittent, but the dog's bark is intermittent too and is nevertheless a characteristic. Continuity is not a requirement; we can identify a dog by his bark as readily as by his size and shape; all that is necessary is a predictable relationship, and just as under predictable conditions of excitement the dog will bark, so under predictable conditions of conversation he will be referred to as a dog.

Given permeation, we need one more psychological mechanism: an instinct for taking the part for the whole. This is characteristic of all human behavior. A mother is identified by a voice or the touch of a hand; a glimpse of a face is enough to identify the man behind it. If through permeation the name of a thing becomes part of the complex that to our minds is the thing, the name can then be abstracted to stand for it. Sentence patterns as well as words are names in this respect. There are only two differences between linguistic units and other identifying features: the linguistic units are put there in order to be abstracted later, and human beings vocalize them.

The child's first experiences, with assistance from parents and playmates, make it possible for the first abstracting to be done from objects that can be seen, touched, heard, tasted, and smelled. But not much of the vast complex of language, least of all the parts that direct its own functioning, can be learned in this way. Very soon it is the verbal object that has to be manipulated and abstracted not from the flow of events but from the flow of words. If this had to be done completely out of touch with solid objects the child could not build on the foundation he already has; fortunately most early talk is about visible and tangible things and about the here and now. When words that signify relations are first slipped in, what they relate is part of the world of direct experience, and the relationship can be sensed. Contexts are not an unfamiliar blur, but contain words that are already known, and are uttered in settings that define their terms.

As time goes on, more and more segmentation takes place inside language, with new meanings feeding on old ones. The raw material is now the unending string of sentences that the child hears, and instead of recurring events with their more or less stable aspects, there are recurring words with their more or less stable contexts, all tending to focus on particular characteristics of the concepts behind the words.

The word *boy* makes a good example of how a meaning is abstracted. The first step is from concrete reference—the child hears the word applied to an individual, perhaps to himself. For all he can tell, *boy* could be a proper name. A later concrete application to another individual does not necessarily dispel this impression—more than one man is called *Jack,* more than one boy can be called *boy.* But two Jacks together are seldom referred to by an adult speaker in any such terms as **Look at those two Jacks,* nor one as **He is a Jack,* though children will try to generalize *Jack* as soon as they learn to generalize *boy.*[2] The context of numerals and articles plus one appropriate situation after another establishes a distinction between a name that can apply to any individual with the necessary traits and a name that applies arbitrarily to just one or a very few. The child now perhaps formulates a theory: "Boy means 'male' (like me, or like Jack) and 'young' (like me, or like Jane)." This leaves out 'human,' which is apt to be taken for granted, and for the time being no conflict arises when a parent says *Come here, boy* to a dog. But this will be discarded as it comes clear once again that *Bowser is a boy* is never heard; *boy* in this case is relegated to the category of nicknames. Meanwhile other contexts are building up, establishing a category of 'human' within which *boy* is consistently applied, and the crude theory

---

[2] One child at two years and six months: *That's a Fifi here.* (Weir 1962, p. 111.) Another at two years and ten months:

INTERVIEWER: I'm Joe.
CHRISTY: No you don't. You're a Wick. (Miller 1973, p. 386.)

FIGURE 7–1
Features of the Meaning of <u>Boy</u>

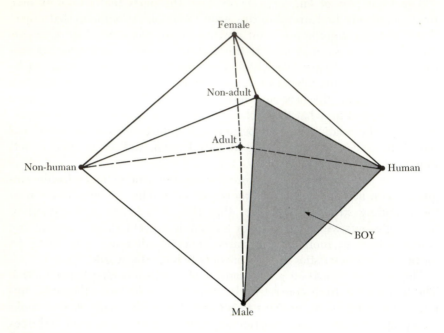

is refined till it fits within a matrix of features of meaning, as in Figure 7–1. Nearly all utterances in which *boy* occurs will be consistent with this scheme. But a few will not—for example, ***The boys are out for a good time tonight,*** where *boys* refers to men. The unusual nature of such utterances will show not only in their low frequency but in the special circumstances of their use: always playful, seldom or never in a context like **The boys are at work today.* A kind of vague association is set up whereby 'play' of any kind partly neutralizes 'non-adult.' The other features stay fairly clear; nature makes sharp distinctions between human and non-human, male and female. But adult and non-adult may give some contrary readings, and the least adult of all will not give any reading whatever—that is, no speaker will be heard to say ***Look at that boy over there!*** referring to a three-month-old infant. Here it will always be qualified: ***Look at that baby boy over there!*** So the child comes to a kind of relative concept of boyness in which 'male' and 'human' are set but 'non-adult' is elastic at both ends. At age ten a boy is more a boy than at age three months or age nineteen.

No one term is abstracted in a vacuum. ***Boy, girl, man, woman, child, baby,*** and later ***youth, adolescent, young man, young woman,*** all abut or overlap in a self-limiting scheme of shared features that does more to define the meaning of each member than any experience of one term alone.

The more abstracting we do, the more general our vocabulary becomes, and the better adapted to coping with unforeseen circumstances. But we cling to the more concrete and specific meanings too—our memories are vast, and need not give up one hold on reality to acquire another. It is hard to prove sometimes whether there is a single very abstract meaning or a set of relatively more concrete ones tied together in a bundle. Take the word *own,* which might be encountered in any of the following three situations, each of which imposes a different interpretation:

1. A customer goes to a roadside stand to buy vegetables. He points to some heads of cabbage and says, *Are these your own?* Interpretation: 'Did you grow them yourself?'

2. A census taker queries a householder: *Is this house your own?* Interpretation: 'Do you have title to it?'

3. A den mother at a Boy Scout jamboree where there are several other den mothers, each with her flock of boys, points to two boys and asks one of the other den mothers, *Are these your own?* Interpretation: 'Are these your offspring?'

By leaving out *own,* we can test the meanings of possession. In the first, *Are these yours?* might be used, but could be taken in the sense 'Are they your property?' In the second, *Is this house yours?* is possible, but could be taken as 'Is this where you live?' And the third, with *Are these yours?* could mean 'Are these two among the boys assigned to you?' So we have the option of defining *one's own* less abstractly in two senses: 'that to which one has title as against that to which one does not' (second situation) and 'that which one has produced as against that which one has not' (first and third). Or we can opt for the extreme of abstractness and say that *own* simply intensifies possession, adding to whatever degree of it there may be when *own* is absent. This has the advantage of fitting *own* into a scale of intensification: *my book, my own book, my very own book, my very very own book, my very very own personal book, my very very own personal particular book,* and so on.

A test for the more abstract interpretation is to see whether a finer degree of possession can be inserted between two of the degrees given in the examples and still elicit *own.* Suppose that den mother A is given charge of another pack as well as her original pack to take to a general rally. And suppose that den mother B points to one of the boys and asks *Is this one yours?* The question could be taken to mean 'Is this one of the total group of which you are in charge?' Den mother B might then point to another boy and ask *Is this one your own?* meaning 'Does he belong to your original group?' This is a less intense possession than 'Is he your offspring?' and confirms the abstract meaning of *own.*

Own is a function word, and function words tend to acquire abstract, homogeneous meanings. A better example to show a bundle of relatively disconnected fibers might be an ordinary noun or verb. Take the verb *to kick.* A bicyclist is heard to say *I find that the easiest way to shift gears is just to kick the trigger,* accompanying the statement with a gesture of his hand simulating the fingers holding on to the handlebar with the wrist twisting up to the left. Why *kick,* which ordinarily refers to a blow with the foot?

We have to imagine what the choices are. *To hit* suggests a motion in which hand and arm swing free. *To push* suggests a steady pressure. *To punch* is a motion outward from the body. *To whack* is delivered with a flat surface. *Kick* avoids these inappropriate meanings, suggests 'sudden motion after which the moving organ returns to rest,' carries a hint of an upward motion like that of a kick with the foot, and already has certain mechanical associations, such as the kick of a gun and of a motor. *To kick with the hand* is not a use of the verb within a well-defined semantic area like that of *own,* but is an extrapolation from various different relatively concrete uses, tied together by a literal or metaphorical association with the physical sensations of kicking. There is no continuum of kicking as there is of possessing, and a new use of *kick* is arrived at by taking a new position relative to a number of old ones, within a field hedged in by all the verb's synonyms.

There is some abstracting with *kick,* of course, but no master plan as with *own.* We operate both abstractly and concretely. One is as much a part of our stored capacities as the other.

THE ANALYSIS OF MEANING

Semantic features

Our words come so naturally and unconsciously that they seem rather simple tokens of reality. This is partly because on the few occasions when we do think about the relationship between words and things we almost always pick the simplest category, that of nouns, and the simplest examples from the category: *dog, toy, sun, page, house.* Yet the truth is that literally any combination of things, traits, or ideas can be segmented.

If we should ever need to talk regularly and frequently about independently operated sawmills from which striking workers are locked out on Thursday when the temperature is between 50° and 60°F, we would find a concise way to do it. Of course, it is no small accomplishment for our language to be able to perform that segmentation in the way just illustrated—by accumulating segments already named, which intersect at the desired point. Sometimes the accumulation—if it is not too long— becomes a set unit, and we forget or only dimly remember its former associations. This is true of compounds (see pages 111–12).

But it is not necessary that a linguistic unit be morphologically complex—like a compound—in order to be semantically complex. Some of the simplest words harbor an amazingly explicit set of wayward traits, of which we are almost never aware until someone misuses them. Digging them out, classifying them, and showing their relationships is termed *componential analysis* or *feature analysis*, and the traits themselves are *semantic features*, which supposedly do the same for meaning that distinctive features do for phonology. Dictionary makers have struggled with this problem for centuries. It is obviously to their interest to reduce the meanings of words to the simplest possible terms consistent with what they can expect of their readers. The latter condition limits their aims, which many linguists in the past couple of decades have hoped to improve on by giving the terms a scientific polish and refining them to the point where they cannot be refined further.

The diagram for *boy* is a sample of how the semantic atoms of a word can be spelled out. The abstract features [+Human +Young +Male] have to be used to analyze a great many words and accordingly have a claim to being the kind of irreducible component that one hopes to find. Other words incorporating [+Young] are *child, cub, litter, calf, sapling.* Others with [+Male] are *boar, gander, stamen, testosterone, tenor.* And others with [+Human] are *corpse* (as against *carcass*), *tresses* (as against *mane*), *tell, talk* (as against *bray, cackle, trumpet*), and countless other things that only humans can be or do.

In the last chapter we saw that grammatical classes themselves can be treated as features of meaning (see Chapter 6, page 156). If we note that *Smith is a bigger quack than Jones* can mean that he is more of a quack, while *Smith is a bigger headshrinker than Jones* can refer only to his size or importance, we can say that *quack* "belongs to the class of intensifiable words," or "has the feature [+Intensifiable]" (and *headshrinker* has the feature [−Intensifiable]). It is a common practice to adopt these grammatical features as the ones that are stated first—just as most dictionaries tell you that a word is a noun or an adjective before they tell you what else it is—and then add the rest. So *dog* might have the display

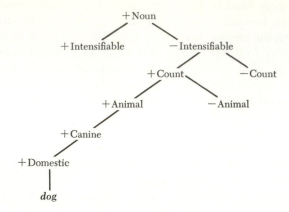

Feature analysis got its most recent impetus from anthropologists, who have used it to describe kinship. Family relationships are sharply defined (when not complicated by too much intermarriage), but cultures differ in what degrees and directions of kinship are to have separate names. In English we have two words for 'sibling,' **brother** and **sister,** where sex is the distinguishing feature. Among the Black Tai of Vietnam and Laos the prime separation is by age: 'older than self' and 'younger than self.' In Greek the same word is used for both 'brother' and 'sister' with an inflection for gender. English has something similar with **cousin,** where the same word is used for both sexes (though **boy-cousin** and **girl-cousin** are virtual compounds, since we are unlikely to say *man-cousin or *woman-cousin, regardless of age). **Aunts** and **uncles** are distinguished for sex, but in Italian the same word is used, with a gender ending: **zio, zia.** Figure 7–2 shows the Black Tai nuclear family, with self, parents, older siblings (**pi⁵**), younger siblings (nɔŋ⁶), and in-laws. (The super-script numbers are tone markers.) The equal sign means 'spouse of'; the triangle is 'male' and the circle 'female.'

Most human institutions and artifacts can be spread out semantically in this fashion. A manufactured object is made up of predetermined parts and has predetermined functions. With the features [Keyboard Percussion String Reed Wind Bellows Manual] one can define **piano, accordion, harmonium, flute** ([−Keyboard −Percussion −String +Reed +Wind −Bellows −Manual]), and so forth.

Away from the safe area of things that are easy for humans to define because humans are responsible for them, semantic features become more elusive. It could hardly be otherwise, for a word that is very easy to define is a word that we can get along without—instead of the word itself we can use the definition (for technical purposes, **male sibling** is

FIGURE 7–2
The Black Tai Nuclear Family

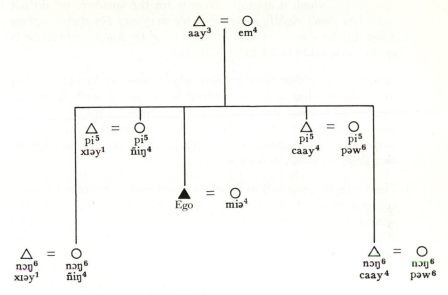

SOURCE: Adapted from Fippinger 1971, p. 78.

better than *brother*). Some examples will show the great variety of features that we build into the words that segment nature in all its variety:[3]

1. Some such feature as 'entity in its own right' is needed to distinguish *disease* from *illness* and *ailment.* Diseases are classified and labeled, and a disease can be "caught"; we do not ordinarily say *catch an illness* or *catch an ailment.*

2. A feature of 'belongingness' distinguishes *to return,* when it takes an object, from *to take back.* *We took Junior back to the zoo* might refer to letting him visit the place again, but *We returned Junior to the zoo* calls him an inmate.

3. A feature 'enemy' distinguished *U-boat* from the neutral *submarine* in the First World War.[4]

---

[3] Since linguists would not necessarily agree on whether to regard these meanings as formal features, the bracketed plus and minus signs will not be used for them.

[4] Barber 1964, p. 100.

4. A feature 'referring to speaker' is needed to distinguish *rightly* from *exactly* in a sentence such as *I don't rightly know.* It is half-apologetic, which is appropriate only for the speaker: we do not say **You don't rightly know,* but we may say *He didn't rightly know* in the sense 'He said he didn't rightly know,' where *he* is again the speaker in the lower sentence.

5. Whatever it is that most typifies adjectives—say 'quality' rather than 'object'—has to be recognized for nouns as well. If we say *The sword has lost its tip* we refer to an object, a material part of the sword. But if we say *The sword has lost its point* we may mean that it has become dull. Similarly, if we say *Put an edge on that knife* we mean 'make it sharp.'

6. The verbs *to warp* and *to bend, to kneel* and *to genuflect* show a contrast in which the first member of each pair emphasizes the retaining of a condition or a position. Something that is warped stays that way till it is repaired; one who kneels stays in that position till the purpose of kneeling (to pray, to receive the crown) is fulfilled. But bending can as easily be followed by automatic springing back, and genuflecting normally includes straightening up again. Some such feature as 'goal' or 'completion' is involved in *warp* and *kneel.*

Features are useful for analysis only if they are shared—the more widely the better. At least some of the ones just cited do appear in other words. 'Goal,' for instance, is what distinguishes *arrive* and *reach* from *leave* and *depart.* It also tells *I went home* from *I headed home* and *I contributed it* from *I offered it.* 'Space' and 'time' are needed to separate certain prepositions: *until* refers only to time, *underneath* only to space, while *before* and *after* are indifferent; and the same two features distinguish *long* and *far* as adverbs *(How long did you stay? How far did you go?), now* and *here, when* and *where,* and many other pairs. 'Referring to speaker' is all-important in pronouns and demonstratives: it determines the orientation of *this* and *here* against *that* and *there* and marks *I, me,* and *mine* off from *you, his,* and so forth. 'Belongingness' is necessary for *steal, borrow, property, bequeath,* and *trespass.*

Given the huge size of the lexicon in any language it might actually be hard to find many features that were absolutely unique to particular words. Perhaps the question ought to be turned around. Is the proportion of features that are really widespread and stable high enough to justify the notion that with a comparatively small number (say a few hundred, contrasted with words in the thousands) the whole lexicon can be accounted for?

On the question of how stable a feature is, take that of 'goal.' *He managed to do it* tells us that the goal was attained: he did it. *He was able to show them that he was innocent* has the 'goal' feature, but more weakly: it depends on context. Here the goal seems to have been attained. *He was finally able to show them* hardly leaves any doubt. But it is possible to say *He was able to show them but he didn't try.* A similar verb is *to phone.* One is unlikely to say *I phoned him yesterday* unless the connection was completed (with *I called him yesterday* it would make no difference). But while **I phoned him yesterday. He wasn't in,* expressed as two sentences, is unusual, the two can be combined: *I phoned him yesterday but he wasn't in.* If goal-attainment is embodied in both the verb and the context it is assured; otherwise not.

For features that seem too restricted to be worth much attention, take the synonyms *clothes* and *clothing.* We say *I haven't put my clothes on yet,* not **I haven't put my clothing on yet.* On the other hand a dealer would probably say *I have my clothing locked in the safe,* not **I have my clothes locked in the safe.* Some such feature as 'more personal' or 'more closely referred to the wearer' distinguishes *clothes.*

Or take *person* and *people.* One would not be apt to say to a friend, pointing to a group standing nearby, **Have you met those persons? People* would be normal—and so would *persons* if the reference were to individuals 'not present': *I had never met those persons.*

The pair *lonely* and *lonesome* illustrates both doubtful generality and doubtful stability. For most of us the two are close synonyms. Both **One lonely person stood up and protested* and **One lonesome person stood up and protested* strike us as inappropriate for the meaning 'one lone person,' though *lonesome* is worse than *lonely.* But if on leaving someone a woman were to say *Don't be lonely,* we would probably take her to mean 'Go out and get some company,' whereas *Don't be lonesome* could only be a command to suppress our feelings. A feature of 'aloneness' attaches tightly to *lone* and loosely to *lonely,* but is only inferred with *lonesome.*

It may be that these apparently over-specific features are not so in reality, but are cases of something more general that can only be discovered by digging our well of meaning deeper. And of course we have no way of knowing, with such a meager selection of cases, whether the too-specific features outnumber the general ones. On the other hand, perhaps it is what the *culture* packs in a word that really counts, not what features already happen to be floating around in the language and gravitate together. In that case all the language does is name the cultural totality, not by any regular analytic-synthetic procedure but by throwing together whatever resources it has in a way that tends to be more regular than irregular, but could never be predicted no matter how thorough our foreknowledge of the possibilities.

In spite of the uncertainties, it is still possible to use a feature approach to teach a great deal, in a simplified way, about a large part of the lexicon.

Field relationships

Feature analysis makes a fundamental assumption about meaning that is highly debatable: that features are *contained in* words. It is no coincidence that in every case it has been necessary to contrast two or more words to decide what a given feature is. So perhaps, as some linguists have argued, the way to treat meaning is not with features but with relationships or "oppositions" in a field. A word would have meanings according to the whole semantic range of its field and how its functions are shared with all the other words in the same field. Circumstances could then account for a good deal of trading back and forth, which would take care of apparent instability, and also for the development of meanings that are more the property of the field than of any word in it. This sort of relativity is familiar enough with words that signify opposites. **Hot** and **cold** as primary sensations are more or less absolute; we learn them in association with two kinds of discomfort. But in their field relationships they crowd each other now toward one extreme and now toward the other. A **cold meal** may actually be fairly warm; it is simply one that is minus-hot. The words for dimensions provide a more complicated example. It is sometimes pointed out that with length, breadth, width, height, and depth, **length** always has to represent the maximum dimension. We would not say **The rectangle is 2 feet long and 10 feet wide.* Likewise inside a house we would not say **That wall is 4 feet long and 7 feet high*—we would replace **long** with **wide**. But speaking of the façade of a building we probably would prefer **It is 40 feet long and 90 feet high** to *?It is 40 feet wide and 90 feet high*. Width is not apt to be selected because buildings create a special set of relationships in which the maximum *horizontal* dimension gets called 'long.' A low building could be described as **100 feet wide, 50 feet deep, and 40 feet high,** or as **100 feet long, 50 feet wide, and 40 feet high,** though with **long** preferred because it is *along* the base; and this can be stretched to cover buildings that are slightly higher than they are "long," and easily made to cover façades where depth is irrelevant. The field relationships give options to suit our point of view.

A fair example of a feature within a field that can come and go for a word in the middle of the field is found among the words **coax, persuade,** and **convince.** It is our old friend 'goal,' which is clinched with **convince:** **I was convincing him to go** would not be used except to imply success— he eventually did go. But with **persuade** it depends on the context:

I persuaded him to go implies that he went, but *I was persuading him to go* leaves some doubt. We cannot say **I convinced him and convinced him but he wouldn't do it,* but *I persuaded him and persuaded him but he wouldn't do it* is possible. At the other extreme, *coax* tells us nothing about whether he went, even in *I coaxed him to go. I coaxed him to go but he wouldn't* is a normal sentence.

In the set *fall, topple, collapse* we have what appears to be 'unintentionality.' Lacking any indication to the contrary we would assume that *John fell* meant that it happened without his intending it. Yet this feature is not permanently stuck to *fall,* though it is to the two other verbs: we can say *He fell on purpose* but not **He toppled on purpose. Topple* is completely unintentional, *fall* is just mostly so.

It takes more than a little ingenuity sometimes to unravel the field relationships that have led to the choice of a particular expression. The verb *to stuff* has become more or less standard in the office routine of putting a heavy mailing into envelopes. Since it normally means 'to cram,' and stuffing envelopes does not necessarily mean packing them full, why was *stuff* chosen rather than the more neutral *fill?* Apparently because it represents a convergence of incidental characteristics of plurality and muscularity, set against an unwanted incidental characteristic of the other verb. One would not say *He stuffed the envelope* referring to a single letter going into a single envelope. But the mass operation involves a lot of stuff, put in with as much effort as if a single container were crammed to the full. So *stuff* is favored, and *fill* is disfavored because it is frequent in contexts that involve no pushing at all—pouring, for example, as in *The pharmacist filled the envelope with the powders.*

Field relationships are not confined to sets of synonyms. They may reach out to a feature of the landscape that is required to be present for a certain word to be used, even though it would seem strange to think of a matching feature in the word itself. We saw this with expressions which though not explicitly negative are always or almost always used when a negative (or an interrogative or a conditional) is somewhere in the environment (see Chapter 6, page 150). The verb *to afford* establishes exactly the same kind of connection with 'possibility' that *budge, much, far,* and so forth establish with 'negation.' In its usual sense, 'to have the (economic) means for,' or 'not to lose by,' there is generally a *can, be able,* or *be possible* in the context. But all that is necessary is that such a meaning be implied. Though we do not say **I afford a house like that* or **I afford to offend him,* we can readily say *I afford a house like that?!! Is there a chance of your affording it?* or *When it comes to affording something like that . . .* (speaker shakes his head).

Except for their comparatively narrow range, these restrictions which cause words to cluster in sets—'negation,' 'possibility,' 'intentionality,' and the like—are the same as others that operate on a grander scale. The grammatical classes are only the most obvious cases—noun, verb, and so on. There are others just as comprehensive, though not as visible. Some are linked to the social code in which we happen to be functioning at the moment of speaking (more will be said on this subject in Chapter 11). An example is the expressions *at this time* and *right now.* The first is aloof and formal, the second informal and relaxed: *The doctor can't see you at this time (right now).* One of the most pervasive features is emotional loading: the speaker betrays an attitude of approval or disapproval. The adverbs *soundly* and *roundly* are synonymous, but in *He soundly berated them* the speaker indicates his approval of the action, while *He roundly berated them* is neutral. Some more obvious pairs, with the neutral term first and the loaded one second, are *big–overgrown, sweet–cloying, uninformed–ignorant, odor–fragrance.* Otherwise innocent-looking' words may be classed for occupation, geographical area, age of speaker—any basis whatever that is part of the reality of our lives. The word *village,* for instance, has a technical use in the United States (contrasting with *town* in a legal sense), but for most speakers it is not a term that would be used to refer to a settled area in this country. One may talk of a village in France but not a village in Kansas, regardless of the fitness in terms of size, industry, architecture, or whatever.

Dynamic relationships

If the connectivity of meanings is partly determined by field relationships, it is no less so by the dynamic relationships in a sentence. The first tells us what features are potential, the second what ones are actual. Such interplay is to be expected, considering that potential features were abstracted from actual sentences in the first place, and that whole chunks up to sentence size persist in memory. Take the meaning of the verb *to wear.* It is in a field relationship with *to have* and *to carry* in the following:

> John has long hair.
>
> John wears a sweater.
>
> John carries a gun.

These are ranged according to intimacy. What is inalienably John's, his hair, is normally expressed with *have* (though *have* is used with other kinds of possession too); clothing goes with *wear,* and accouterments such as canes, umbrellas, guns, and swords most often go with *carry.* Depending on the point of view (closeness to the body) one may refer to wearing a gun or a sword. But *wear* is not apt to invade the territory of *have.* In spite of this, it can do so if the dynamics of the sentence permit it:

That's the latest way to wear hair.

That's the latest way to wear your hair.

The first sentence is apt to refer to a wig; this is a normal use of **wear.** The second, with **your** added to emphasize inalienable possession, is most apt to refer to one's own hair. Both **wear** and **your** thus gain by the dynamics of the sentence. **Hair** does not *have* to refer to inalienable possession—*your hair* could refer to a wig. But in its most usual sense **hair** refers to a natural growth, and this fact reinforces and is reinforced by **your.** In the process, a meaning is squeezed out of **wear** that is not central to it at all: 'to have in a certain style, to sport.'

Faced with a sentence to interpret, a listener implicitly puts the problem this way: "What I have just heard is intended to convey a message; under the circumstances that I see before me, what meanings do I assign so as to justify the speaker's intention?" Hearing the phrase **apple trees heavy with fruit** the listener will picture fruit-laden trees, in a total impression of an apple orchard at harvest time. But if he hears **apple trees heavy with their fruit** he has to justify **their.** Since apple trees can't be heavy with pears, it makes no sense to take **their** as specifying 'apples,' so he assigns a broader interpretation than 'generically apple' to the basic sense of 'typical of an apple tree,' perhaps something to do with the typical qualities of the fruit, thus portraying the apples for themselves: big, red, juicy, dangling from the limbs. But suppose the phrase is **Joshua trees heavy with their fruit** (or **Osage orange trees** or any other tree bearing inedible fruit). If the speaker had said **Joshua trees heavy with fruit,** the impression would be that the fruit is edible—that was the earliest defining trait of **fruit** when we learned the word as children, though with our scientific education it has now receded somewhat. By adding **their** the speaker has suggested 'typical of Joshua trees': inedible.

The dynamics of the sentence may even reverse the direction of certain measure words, making them go opposite to the way they usually go. Thus **young** normally moves away from **old,** but if we say **There were several young girls there,** we probably refer to girls in their teens (it would seem odd to say *?She's a young girl of four*); **young** makes **girl** older. For another example, *Webster's Third New International Dictionary* defines **grain** as 'a small, hard particle.' Since particles are normally small, why use the term? The problem is that particles are too small. If **grain** were defined as 'a hard particle' it might be taken to mean a **minute** particle.[5] **Small** makes it larger. What the sentence form is able

---

[5] **Minute particle** illustrates what one linguist terms "salient feature copying." Other examples are **high mountain, sharp knife, heavy load, strong ox.** The adjective repeats an unmarked feature of the noun, one that is expected to be there unless there is some indication to the contrary. See Maher 1974, p. 38.

to do here of course depends on the field relationships between *young* and *little (a little girl of four)* and *small* and *minute.*

This "inferential strategy" on the part of the hearer is illustrated in a study of verbs of perception (*see, hear, smell,* and so forth).[6] Take the two sentences

> We saw her just sit there.

> We saw her just sitting there.

Why do we infer in the first but not in the second that sitting is a course of action that has been decided on (she is too stubborn, or perhaps disconsolate, to do anything else)? The construction with the simple form of the verb (*sit* rather than *sitting*) is used only with happenings for which we imply a terminus; she must therefore have some such terminus in mind, and that means not aimless sitting but sitting as a result of a decision to sit. A decision implies a motive. The motive—most likely stubbornness—then becomes the most important part of the meaning of the sentence.

Other factors

There is more to the interpretation of a sentence than the dynamic interrelationships of its words and their field relationships with other words. The crudest outside factor is the physical setting. If someone says of a girl running along the beach *She likes the sun and air,* the utterance is not apt to be interpreted as *She likes the son and heir.* This elimination of irrelevant meanings has been given the unprepossessing name of *disambiguation.* Here the setting has cleared up the ambiguity. If we saw the sentence written, the spelling would clear it up. When Groucho Marx heard someone remark sympathetically *It must be tough to lose a wife,* he chimed in with *Yes, it's practically impossible,* disambiguating the ambiguity by using a word *(impossible)* whose features are compatible with only one sense of *tough.* In more subtle ways, our whole world view adds to or trims off the excess fat of ambiguity. If we hear two such sentences as

> They heard Bill from the floor above.

> They saw Bill from the floor above.

we are apt to feel that the first can be taken two ways (either Bill is on the floor above or they are), the second in only one (they are on the

---

[6] Kirsner and Thompson 1975.

floor above).[7] The reason is probably the way we have learned to conceptualize seeing and hearing, and is related to the fact that the first of the following two sentences strikes us as normal and the second as strange:

They heard Bill's sound (noise, clatter, racket) from the floor above.

?They saw Bill's image from the floor above.

Long experience has impressed on us that sound has a staying power that light lacks: a sound can echo and reverberate for an appreciable amount of time. This is reflected in the large number of names for sounds and the virtual lack of them for sights (we could not even use *sight* in this sentence: **They saw Bill's sight from the floor above*). With **sound** having this concrete a manifestation, we have a clue to the underlying grammatical constituents. *They heard Bill from the floor above* can refer to hearing *Bill's-sound-from-the-floor-above*—the prepositional phrase modifies the understood word *sound*—but *They saw Bill from the floor above* can only be taken as *see-from-the-floor-above*—the prepositional phrase modifies the verb.

Why should disambiguation be necessary? Why not simply have one word for one meaning, one meaning for one word? Two things make it impossible. First, speakers' brains do not interlock like electrical power grids, and what goes on in one never quite matches what goes on in another. Even if we could freeze a word-meaning relationship at some point, the friction between one mind and another would soon thaw it; meanings never remain the same. Second, there is simply too much to verbalize. The situation is the same as with phonemes. By re-using words in patterns of repetition and combination it is possible to get along with a number much smaller than the totality of meanings that we have to come up with in a lifetime. Most words embody meanings that radiate from a central core, so that a bit of context is enough to determine which branch to follow. Take the word *cell*. In the phrase *cells of the body* we are off on one track; with *cells of the honeycomb* we take another; and with *cells of a battery* we take a third. As one of our earlier discussions indicated (see pages 99–107), we cannot be sure that these contexts are not part of collocations that are themselves semi-fixed ridges on the landscape—hearers do not have to make a fresh start interpreting *cell of the body* every time they hear it. On the other hand, even if the senses of a word are unrelated to one another, having them all bundled together makes storing them easier. Not every filing system is totally logical; memory works in strange ways.

---

[7] Example suggested by Timothy Shopen, private communication.

The number and variety of factors that finally yield an interpretation of a sentence shows how the lexicon has to be stretched to cover everything, and the holes in the fabric that must be closed by the inferences that we plan for our hearers to draw when we speak. The holes have been called "inferential gaps."[8] In the process of filling a gap we often read new features into words which then become more or less permanent —part of the *reference* of the word rather than an inference based on its relationships. This accounts for differences among speakers, some of whom at a given time may already view a feature as referential—that is, as *in* the word—while others take it still as inferential. An example of an inferential meaning that has now become referential for everyone is the sense 'desire' for *want.* At one time *to want* signified merely 'to lack' (as it still does in **They were tried and found wanting**). But **I want it** was used so often as a polite hint, just as today we might say **I don't have any butter** to imply 'I desire some butter,' that the inferred meaning became the central one. An example of a meaning that is still not settled for all speakers is that of **convince,** cited earlier in this chapter as having the feature 'goal.' We understand **I convinced him to go** as meaning that he went. But for those who accept **I convinced him to go but at the last minute he was unable to,** the 'goal' meaning of the shorter sentence is an inference. The referential meaning is that I gained his will; once that is gained, it is assumed that his compliance is gained as well.

Inferences take the shape of "if he says *that,* he must mean *this,*" and *that* and *this* must be related, somehow, in our experience. It may be through connections in the real world. Someone ordered to **Turn the cereal off** understands it to mean 'Turn the gas (or electricity) off at the burner under the cereal.' When a lawyer advises a client that he need not pay because **the statute of limitations has expired on that bill,** he does not mean that the statute of limitations is no longer in force but that the period of time during which according to the statute of limitations the bill was legally collectable has expired. In both these examples the meaning intended is several steps away from the meaning expressed. If we could not take such metaphorical shortcuts, communication would bog down in legalistic formulas. The metaphorical gap may be wide or narrow. It is narrow in **Don't eat with your knife.** Since people eat with knives, forks, and spoons, this injunction makes no sense unless we interpret *to eat* in part-for-whole terms as 'to put food in the mouth.' Similarly with **What time is it in the kitchen?** where **What time is it?** stands for the related question **What does the clock say?** The gap is wide in **I cut all the flagstones,** where the speaker intended *cut* as 'cleared by cutting' and *flagstones* as 'grass around the flagstones.' Typically expansive terms are the personal pronouns, which are often used to cover not

---

8 Kirsner and Thompson 1975.

just the individual but anything associated with him or her at the moment. At the counter of a market a father, his son, and some purchases were being checked through. The clerk was not sure who went with what. The father made a sweeping gesture and said *We're all here.* If *we* had been merely personal, it would have had to be *We're both here; We're all* included the groceries.

The analytical strategies of inference and disambiguation may not always be called for. If an utterance, or part of one, matches closely enough with some remembered formula, it may be captured directly— collocations again. Our minds are probably equipped to handle both processes at the same time. It would be hard to decide which is uppermost in our understanding of a sentence like *They set the clocks and put out the lights before going to bed.* If our minds are already calculating by the time we hit the verb *set,* then the process is one of keeping two alternatives before us—*did set* or *do set?*—not committing ourselves until a decisive word comes along. But if we automatically jump to conclusions, then we will not wait until all the parts are arrayed in front of us but will simply take the verbs *set* and *put* one way or the other, past or present, and hope for the best. The analytical process will not be invoked unless we strike a snag—we might, for instance, have taken the sentence to mean that they always do those things before going to bed, and then the speaker goes on to add *but forgot to lock the doors,* which forces us to reassess the verb and pick a different meaning. This would seem to be more efficient and is probably the way things happen, especially as ambiguity is rarely so complete as in the example just quoted and our guess is more likely to be right than wrong. It may well be based on the statistical probabilities that we learn to sense through long experience with the language. Someone hearing *Did you see that gull?* would guess the highly frequent meaning 'bird' rather than the infrequent 'gullible person,' and no mental switching would be called for unless he was wrong, which would not be too often.

Meanings that are inside and central, meanings that are inside but peripheral, meanings that hover on the outside like hungry flies—a word is anything but the tight package of form and meaning that it is usually thought to be. Yet meanings are stable—just stable enough to make inference possible, not so stable as to make it unnecessary. Given nature's size, language otherwise could not reach around it.

MAPS OF SEMANTIC SPACE

Pity the poor analyst, who has to do the best he can with meanings that are as elusive as a piece of wet soap in a bathtub. He would like to take a definite feature, say [+Human], and tie it to definite verbs, say *study, think, murder,* or *invent (Bell invented the telephone, *The cow in-vented the milking machine).* But it slips out of his grasp. *The girls left,* **The fog left, The fog went away*—so far so good; but what about *The train left*—or *the mail, the bus, the cargo, the ship?* "Human" is too specific for *leave,* which requires instead something like "routinely mov-ing under human control."[9] Plucking a word out of a sentence is like plucking a morpheme out of a word. One is never sure whether the excised organ has enough vitality of its own to survive the operation. Words are environmentally conditioned just as morphemes are, though less drastically. If we fail to detect a loss or specialization of meaning, it may be due to the bluntness of our tools.

But business goes on, and if we shut our eyes to the indeterminacy that we know is there, semantic space can be sketched or modeled in fairly obvious ways. This is especially true if the area chosen is well de-fined, as it is with kinship terms, and if the features are chosen to fit the case and not to fit everything else in the world. Figure 7–2 showed a tree diagram of family relationships. Another device is the grid, or matrix, in which features are set out in coordinates. A good example is one that shows how foods are prepared (see Table 7–1).

If the field is restricted to the meanings of a particular word, the simplest diagram is the branching tree, like the one used on page 194 in abbreviated form to analyze *dog.* Different senses are shown by separate branchings. The diagram that follows shows three senses of the word *nectar,* in a descending hierarchy of categories or features:[10]

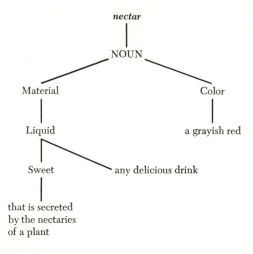

---

[9] *Routinely* because while we might say *The rig that was moving the house left early,* we would not say **The house that was being moved by the rig left early.*

[10] Bolinger 1965, p. 557.

TABLE 7–1
Culinary Semantics

	Non-fat liquid	Fat	Direct heat	Vigorous action	Long cooking time	Large amount of special substance	Kind of utensil	Special ingredient	Additional special purpose	Liquids	Solids
							Other relevant parameters			Collocates with	
cook₃										+	+
boil₁	+	−								+	+
boil₂	+	−		+						+	+
simmer	+	−		−						+	+
stew	+	−		−	+				+ soften	−	+
poach	+	−		−					+ preserve shape	−	+
braise	+	−		−			+ lid			−	+
parboil	+	−			−					−	+
steam	+	−		+			+ rack, sieve, etc.			−	+
reduce	+	−		+					+ reduce bulk	+	−
fry	−	+					+ frying pan			−	+
sauté	−	+				−				−	+
pan-fry	−	+					+ frying pan			−	+
French-fry	−	+				+				−	+
deep-fry	−	+				+				−	+
broil	−	−	+							−	+
grill	−	−	+				?(griddle)			−	+
barbecue	−	−	+°					+ BarBQ sauce		−	+
charcoal	−	−	+°							−	+
plank	−	−	+				+ wooden board			−	+
bake₂	−	−	−							−	+
roast	−	−	±							−	+
shirr	−	−	−	−			+ small dish			−	+
scallop	−	−	−				+ shell	+ cream sauce		−	+
brown	−								+ brown surface	−	+
burn	−				+					−	+
toast	−	−	+						+ brown	−	+
rissoler	−	+			+				+ brown	−	+
sear	−	+		−					+ brown	−	+
parch	−	−	−						+ brown	−	+
flamber	−	−	+					+ alcohol	+ brown	−	+
steam-bake	+	−	−							−	+
pot-roast	+	−		−			(?) lid			−	+
oven-poach	+	−	−							−	+
pan-broil	−	−	+				+ frying pan			−	+
oven-fry	−	+	−							−	+

SOURCE: Adapted from Lehrer 1969, p. 49.

° 'Hot coals.'

Here we do find an attempt to lay hold of universals—'material' presumably subsumes everything that can be directly perceived through the senses. The main difficulty with such a scheme is that features are split off which ought to remain together. For example, a 'delicious drink' may well be 'sweet,' but the diagram suggests that sweetness is restricted to the other branch. Another disadvantage is the implication that all the meanings of a single word constitute a "field" in some useful sense. Honey is made from nectar, so that *honey* and *nectar* would seem to have a closer field relationship than *nectar* and, say, *goat's milk,* which could be allowed as a 'delicious drink' if one feels that way about it; yet there is no place where *honey* could be fitted in. Here we see again how meaning can be cast adrift from form. On the basis of any fancied resemblance a word can migrate to a new territory, marry, and settle down. No one could predict that *nectar* would end up designating a color, but the color family raised no objections to the match.

Some of the disadvantages of trees can be overcome by using overlapping circles. Figure 7–3 shows two diagrams for the senses of *bachelor,* a tree diagram and a circle diagram. The circle diagram makes it possible to show low-level features that are shared between meanings (for example, 'young' does not have to be repeated as it does in the tree diagram). It also does not make the apparent assumption that 'human' versus 'animal' is more basic than 'male' versus 'female.'

Only a tremendously complicated multidimensional model—possibly nothing less than a map of the neural connections in the brain—will do full justice to the network of meaning. Till that is attainable we have to be content with partial and rather trivial samples of this or that small patch of the fabric.

"Something like"

The main fault of tree diagrams and similar representations is that they are designed to deal directly with external reality rather than with the way language mirrors external reality. When a zoologist looks at his subject he is not interested in how speakers of any particular language view the animal world as revealed in the names and concepts they use to classify and subclassify. Like other scientists he cannot trust field relationships, sentence dynamics, physical setting, or any of the other incidental aids that everyday communication depends on to narrow the general meanings of words to fit particular situations. For him, everything must be precisely defined at the level of words, and he will redraw the lines and assign new names wherever necessary. He may use some popular terms for convenience, but as a member of his international scientific community the zoologist shuns them.

FIGURE 7–3
The Tree Diagram Versus the Circle Diagram*

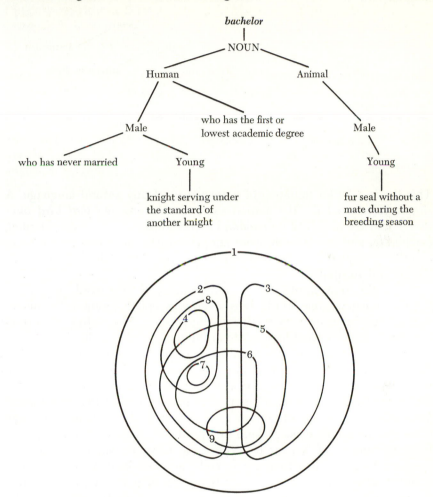

SOURCE: Adapted from Hill 1973, pp. 274–75.

*In the circle diagram, the first circle represents *noun,* which includes all senses of the word. The second circle represents all uses which apply to human beings, and the third represents the only sense which is animal. Circle 4 represents 'holder of the lowest academic degree,' and circle 5 gives all senses of the word which designate males. Circle 6 gives the senses which designate young adults, whether human or animal. Circle 7 represents 'knight serving under the standard of another knight,' and circle 8, which encircles both 4 and 7, is a circle designating the meaning 'apprentice,' or lowest in a hierarchy. Finally, circle 9 encloses the two instances of unmated males, one human, the other 'unmated fur seal.'

When the linguist tries to emulate the zoologist he brings out tree diagrams like the one that follows:

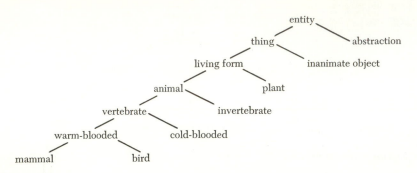

This too is a better imitation of nature than of any natural language. A simple test is to take the normal sentence *Do you see that bird over there?* and try to substitute *mammal* or *vertebrate.* The words *mammal, vertebrate,* and *invertebrate* were adopted in the early part of the nineteenth century as scientific terms and have still not made their way into the general vocabulary.

A scientific term must meet the requirement of "one word, one meaning; one meaning, one word." It is a requirement that cannot be met in natural language, for reasons that we have seen. The history of *sort of* and *kind of* shows what happens to all hierarchies that ordinary speakers bandy about in an ordinary way. In one experiment in which subjects were required to build hierarchies for certain concepts, the term *pop* was offered by the experimenters as a stage above *Coca-Cola.*[11] It is true that *Coca-Cola* is a "kind of" pop, but how did the subjects interpret *kind of?*—as 'a variety of pop' or as 'a pop, sort of'? Ordinary language takes the hierarchic concept 'kind of, species of, variety of' and reshapes it as a synonym of 'similar to.' The same elasticity shows in the way speakers behave when they are forced—in some kind of test—to play scientist by classifying and subclassifying sets of nouns; they are unable to do it consistently.[12] As one team of anthropologists points out, the difficulty of tree-style hierarchies is that they have "no way of indicating when an item is classified in a certain way because it is 'like' another item which is more central" to its domain.[13] They illustrate this "something like" with the words that are the closest equivalents to the English *tree* and *bush* in two northwest California languages, Yurok and Smith River. Neither word exactly means 'tree' or 'bush.' In both languages the word for 'tree' more precisely means 'fir tree,' but loosely embraces other

[11] Smith, Shoben, and Rips 1974, Table 3.

[12] Freedle 1970, pp. 63–64.

[13] Bright and Bright 1965.

kinds of trees. Similarly in Yurok the term for 'lilac' is taken as basic for bushes in general, which are referred to as 'lilac-like.' The something-like principle is a linguistic universal, for all that we like to quip, sometimes, "He thinks a tomato is a vegetable. Ha, ha!"

Words with shared features: synonyms and antonyms

The two words *peel* and *skin* can be used as either noun or verb:

> an orange peel, a snake skin

> to peel an orange, to skin a snake

But whereas we can say **Peel off the skin** or **His skin peeled,** we cannot say *Skin off the peel* nor *The peel skinned.* In some sense *peel* is more inclusive than *skin* when used as a verb. Probably it reflects the effort involved in removing a peel, which is more than enough to skin something, while the relatively easy operation of skinning does not necessarily suffice for peeling. However that may be, **to skin** and **to peel** are in the same field, and *peel* seems to occupy more of it than *skin.* It is not quite that *peel* completely surrounds *skin,* for in that case it would be possible to say *peel a snake, *peel a rabbit.* Nor is it that an intersecting category, say 'fruit,' makes an essential·difference, for one can either peel or skin a banana. And there are grammatical differences. **Skin** requires a complement if it is used intransitively: *He skinned, He skinned out of his shirt;* whereas **He peeled** might be used if he removed all his clothing, but otherwise requires an object plus **off: He peeled off his shirt.** The relationships are complex and most likely unique to this one field.

For practical purposes we cut through the complexity and simply say that **to peel** and **to skin** are *synonyms.* This means that they are close enough to allow the speaker a choice between them in a significant number of contexts. The measure of synonymy is replaceability. Two terms may share all but some small part of a field, but they are not synonyms unless one can be used instead of the other. Thus **man** and **boy** share practically an entire field except for the feature of 'age,' but are still kept well apart unless the speaker himself is unsure of his meaning. The reason is that it is precisely the age difference that we want to emphasize.

The companion term for synonym is *antonym,* and the same measure of replaceability applies, except that now it is between *A* and not-*A*. In answer to **Is it wet?** one has a choice between **No, it isn't wet** and **No, it's dry.** There are of course other kinds of not-*A*; for example, *pernicious* is not-*A* with respect to **wet**—but it is also irrelevant. It is not-*A* because **wet** and *pernicious* are not even in the same field. For one term to replace another, with or without **not,** it is obvious that they must be in a close field relationship to each other. Not-*A* plus a field relationship is a "contrary" in logic; not-*A* minus a field relationship is a "contradictory." The contrary opposition between **wet** and **dry,** within a field of 'presence of moisture,' can be shown diagrammatically:

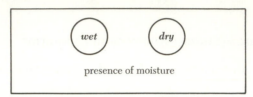

The effect of adding **not** is to make the areas cross. In the diagram below we see the antonymic pair **wet–dry** included within the overlapping ovals **not-dry** and **not-wet.** Along with **wet** is shown its synonym **moist,** and a synonym of the synonym, **dampish.** The reason **not-wet** and **not-dry** overlap is that it is possible for something to be both things at the same time, as in sentence d of the following set (the meanings of a through d are located on the diagram):

    a. It is quite moist—in fact, it is rather wet.
    b. It's not wet, just moist.
    c. It is somewhere around moist or dampish.
    d. It is neither wet nor dry, just dampish.

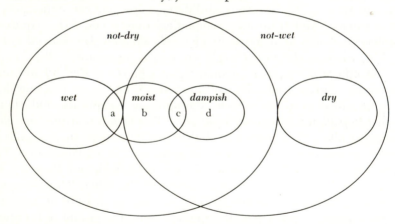

Overlapping is characteristic of contraries—there is usually a middle ground. With some antonyms it is spaced out quite neatly: *large–medium–small, right–center–left, open–ajar–shut.* There may even be inner and outer antonymic terms: in *always–often–seldom–never, never* equals *not-ever* (the older sense of *ever* is *always: forever = for always*) and *seldom* equals *not-often.* Similarly with *hot–warm–cool–cold* and *good–fair–poor–bad.* Even in some such semantic field as 'having control over something,' with its antonyms *to keep* and *to dispose of,* it is possible to squeeze in a fence-sitter: *He neither kept it nor disposed of it; it was stolen.* It may be that there is always a middle ground except in some artificially designed human activity where doubts are settled by definition. Between *fair weather* and *foul weather* there is the possibility of *middling weather,* but between *fair ball* and *foul ball* there is no *middling ball,* no matter how ardently an umpire might desire it. Between them, *fair ball* and *foul ball* make a clean sweep of the field of 'batted ball':

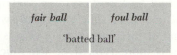

There is no restriction on the other semantic ingredients nor on the grammatical features that can be shared by an antonymic set. *To hurry* and *to go at a leisurely pace* are antonyms differing in grammatical form, though of course both are verb phrases. *Always–often–seldom–never* and *hot–warm–cool–cold* resemble each other in having a pair of enclosed antonyms; but while the enclosed antonyms can take grammatical comparison—we can say *more often, more seldom, warmer,* and *cooler*—two of the enclosing ones can (*hotter* and *colder*) and two cannot (**more always,* **more never*). But if we were to fit *tepid* between *warm* and *cool* and *occasionally* between *often* and *seldom,* we would have terms in both sets that are not normally compared: **more tepid, *more occasionally.* Some pairs of antonyms are opposed in terms of more than one set of features: *to work* and *to rest* are antonyms on the basis of 'presence or absence of productive activity'; *to work* and *to loaf* are opposed on the same basis plus the basis of 'concern versus indifference.' The basis of antonymy between *noise* and *silence* is not the same as that between *noise* and *music.* Words from all major categories can form pairs: nouns such as *good* and *evil;* adjectives such as *good* and *bad;* adverbs such as *fast* and *slow;* prepositions such as *out* and *in;* pronouns such as *his* and *hers.*

Since both antonyms and synonyms occupy the same field, it is possible for the same pair of words to be both synonymous and antonymous. This should not be surprising, because we have already seen many instances where a given meaning can be foregrounded at the expense of other meanings. As was noted earlier, *peel* and *skin* are synonyms in *to peel (to skin) a banana.* They are antonyms in *You have to peel a raw potato but you can skin a boiled one.* There is still a third relationship that has already been mentioned: the meaning of *to skin* in some situations is included within that of *to peel.* This is a special kind of synonymy called *hyponymy:*

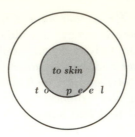

If we say *You can peel off bark and you can peel off a rind, and you can also skin off bark, but you can't skin off a rind,* we are saying in effect that in terms of 'amount of force needed,' *to skin* is enclosed in the range of *to peel.* Hyponymy is more typical of scientific terminology than of everyday language. The term *vertebrate* is *defined* so as to include *fish, reptile, mammal,* and other categories of the same phylum.

And the truth is that synonymy and antonymy in general are less scientific than stylistic. "Speaker's choice" has to do with meeting communicative emergencies as they come up. Sometimes it is a matter of precision. A writer or speaker is about to say *He delivered a lengthy apology* and realizes that he may be taken to mean an excuse and not a justification, which he intended; so he uses *justification* instead. At other times it is a matter of contrast, of finding something that sounds different. This is often necessary to keep from attracting our hearer's attention to the words we use instead of their meaning. Our stock of phonemes is not unlimited and now and then plays us false by serving up two words that sound so much alike—they may even be identical— that if we use them together we are liable to be misunderstood or thought to be making a pun: *That was a fine fine you had to pay! The painter succeeded in painting the pain on her face all too plainly; That weakness is one that he does not to my knowledge acknowledge.* If we replace the second *fine* with *penalty,* the *pain* with *anguish,* and the *acknowledge* with *admit to,* the problem is avoided.

These cases—and the ambiguity of *apology* as well (the fact that the "one word" *apology* has two senses creates the same problem as do "two words" such as *fair* and *fare*)—are just a mild case of a kind of conflict that sometimes causes words to disappear (see pages 439– 40). Instead of being virtually driven out of the language, as *niggardly* has been, *fine, pain,* and *acknowledge* are simply driven out of the immediate context where they cause trouble. There is also a more subtle form, where contrast is a matter of semantic shading, of avoiding the repetition of the same word with the same sound when it is supposed to have a different meaning even though both meanings may be well within the normal range of the word. The first sentence of the second paragraph of this chapter was originally written "The word *meaning* is used in many ways. . . ." When the line was edited it appeared that *word* might be taken in the sense that it had at the beginning of the preceding paragraph, namely words as a level in linguistics. To avoid this it was replaced with *term.* It was not so much that either *word* or *term* could not be used in either sense as that, by not repeating, the reader would be warned away from assuming a repetition of the same meaning. The need to do this is often erroneously treated in books of rhetoric and elsewhere as just a mechanical avoidance of repeating the same word, and some unwary writers take this advice seriously and write sentences like *Shakespeare's The Tempest is his most enthralling work; in it the great dramatist pours out an emotive force that is missing elsewhere. How well the genius of the English stage knew his public,* with the metamorphosis of *Shakespeare* continuing through *the prince of European letters, the creator of Hamlet, the Bard of Avon,* and so on. Sometimes these excesses are justified, for example in obituaries: *beloved father, dear uncle, devoted grandfather.*[14] The real stylistic problem in the avoidance of repetition is the need in every context to define terms in such a way that if the least contrast is intended it will be physically manifest in the words we choose. This is the beauty of having synonyms with a certain amount of give-and-take in their semantic field. If there is no prefabricated contrast among the synonyms at our disposal, we can make one to order and let the dynamics of the sentence define it for us.

Other word sets

Synonyms and antonyms are not the only sets of words that are joined through shared or opposed semantic features. There is probably no limit to the groupings that would make sense for one purpose or another. Examples of these types of semantic fields:

1. Converses: *come–go, buy–sell, read–write, give–receive.* These are close enough to each other to be expressed sometimes by the same word: *The landlord rents the house to me, I rent the house from the landlord.* The sentence *Gangs or crews of such native labor were usually placed in charge of American enlisted men*[15] was intended to mean that the enlisted men were responsible for the native labor, but *in charge of* could be taken the other way.

2. Characteristic object: *eat–food, drink–beverage, hear–sound, spell–word, harvest–crop*

---

[14] Example from David Gold, private communication.
[15] *American Speech* 23 (1948), p. 223.

3. Cognate object: *wrap–package, ask–question, run–race, live–life, bequeath–bequest.* Literally a cognate object must have the same historical derivation as its verb *(live a life, bequeath a bequest),* but more freely it is used for any object that is the necessary result of the action of the verb; the existence of the object implies in turn that the action took place.

4. Characteristic action: *heart–beat, mind–think, fire–burn, wind–blow, rain–fall*

5. Cognate subject, action, object: *employer–employ–employee; donor–donate–donation; inventor–invent–invention; thief–steal–loot; preacher–preach–sermon;* and with an indirect object added, *payer–pay–payment–payee; giver–give–gift–receiver.* As is evident from these examples, the semantic sharing is often matched by a sharing of morphemes. In certain sets a member may be semantically defective: so in the set comprising *drunkard, go on,* and *binge,* the verb *go on* is less explicit than *pay,* for example, with reference to its co-members *payer* and *payee;* similarly with *commit* in *criminal–commit–crime.*

6. Characteristic quality: *water–wet, summer–warm, feather–light, prairie–flat*

7. Symptom and state: *smile–happiness, smoke–fire, groan–pain*

8. Co-hyponyms: *matter* includes its hyponym *solid,* but also includes *liquid* and *gas;* the included terms are *co-hyponyms.* Other examples: H_2O includes *ice, water, vapor; color* includes *red, yellow, orange,* and so on; *member* includes *arm, leg, head; organ* includes *stomach, heart, liver; school larnin'* includes *readin', writin', 'rithmetic.* Here belong all the groupings not only of nature but also of our occupations and daily associations: *curriculum* includes *mathematics, history, chemistry; baseball scores* include *hits, runs, errors; church service* includes *prelude, offertory, sermon, doxology.*

Certain of these sets are themselves related and tell us something about the classes to which their members belong. Characteristic object and cognate object differ only slightly. The verbs in the first are just a shade "more transitive" than those in the second. How transitive a verb is can be viewed as its freedom to take objects. *To live* can only take *life* or a synonym of *life* such as *existence, one's days, experiences,* and similar expressions. One *eats* food, but there are many foods, and people have been known to eat non-foods. One can only *speak* a language, but there are many languages, and people sometimes speak gibberish. *To taste* can be said of anything with a flavor, and *to touch* can be said of any material object. *To touch* contains fewer features than *to eat* (compare *He didn't eat, He didn't touch his food*): it seems that a feature-deprived verb is like an unattached atom, with an appetite for any object it can lay hold of; the fewer features it has, the more transitive it is. Grammarians have been prone to treat transitivity like pregnancy—a verb cannot be a little bit that way. The truth is that everything in language is a little bit of something other than it is.

ARBITRARINESS: ICONS AND SYMBOLS

If the history of writing gives hints about the history of language, the first forms of communication must have been imitative. The use of pictograms to convey messages long before the development of syllabaries and alphabets—not to mention the universality of imitative and expressive gesture —seems so natural that we can only suppose a primitive stage in which sounds were related to sense. The imitation need not have been perfect— in fact, the very difficulty of copying the sounds of nature with the human voice would have been an advantage because speakers would have had to ignore imperfections and accept substitutions that were less and less like the originals—but mimicry there must have been.

Meanings in which form imitates nature are called *iconic,* and the forms are *icons.* Meanings that are arbitrary and conventional are called *symbolic,* and their forms are *symbols.* Everything points to icons as more primitive than symbols. Children invent them. Two speakers without a common language resort to them for communication. But however vivid the beginnings, the color has long since faded to a uniform gray. As we saw earlier (pages 22–23), even in our common onomatopoetic words the imitation must give way to the system of sounds that the language imposes. The result is almost always an imperfect copy. If we listen to the note of the whippoorwill we observe an appreciable pause between *whip* and *poor: whip-poorwill, whip-poorwill.* But English has the habit of reducing interior syllables and clicking them off at a faster rate; the result is that we say something like *whipperwill.*

But if through the centuries our art has declined, our apparent sophistication has grown. We are not bothered by imperfect copies. Until someone calls them to our attention we do not even notice them. This is the effect of permeation. Language has become an almost purely conventional code, with a few exceptions listed as curiosities. Certainly there is no essential relationship between the sound of any phoneme, or the combined sounds within any word, and any event beyond language, barring the frayed remnants of an occasional onomatope.

But how is it then that language can express reality? Does not this rough denial of expressiveness do language an injustice? If we look at the stippling in a picture or the grain in a photograph, we note an equal lack of correspondence between dots or grains and the flesh of the human face, whose image is nevertheless clearly reproduced. What if words are only the grain of language and the non-arbitrary picture is filled out at a higher level, becoming more and more iconic the farther up one goes?

The sense in which language is most iconic and least arbitrary, according to Roman Jakobson,[16] is in its status as an elaborate diagram. The lowest common denominator of a diagram is simple togetherness. If two things react upon each other in our experience and we want to talk about them, whatever the device that is normally used for one (say, X) or for the other (say, Y), the result in what we say is going to be an XY or a YX. The words *cat, bite,* and *dog* may be arbitrary, but if a dog bites a cat we can reasonably expect that these words will keep close company in what we say about it. This of course is non-arbitrary, because the togetherness of the words reflects the togetherness of the things and events. Actually, the diagrams of a language are far more iconic than this, for its devices have little purpose except to talk about things and events. If when a particular event occurs we can predict with some certainty what is going to be said about it—and our daily experience proves that we can, even with events that have never occurred before—then we know that the correspondence of the points on our diagram to the externals that they stand for is anything but arbitrary. Language uses arbitrary units to sketch non-arbitrary pictures.

Phonesthemes

Though the system in all its smaller parts may be more symbolic than iconic, we sense it as iconic, and treat it so in daily small acts of creation and readjustment. More of this will come in the chapters on variation, where it will be seen that most change in language that is not due to accident arises from the underlying iconic drive to make sound conform to sense. When a child says *gooder* instead of *better,* it is only because *good* has been learned as the proper symbol for 'good' and any deviation from it adds to the arbitrariness—makes it less iconic. Whenever a speaker uses a metaphor—speaks of *following suit, playing into someone's hand, trumping the other fellow's ace,* or *getting a raw deal*—he makes or repeats an icon.

Even the symbols themselves turn out to be somewhat less arbitrary than they appear at first sight if we look beyond just the primary association of word and thing. Given a particular word for a particular thing, if other words for similar things come to resemble that word in sound, then no matter how arbitrary the relationship between sound and sense was to begin with, the sense is now obviously tied to the sound. The relation-

---

[16] Jakobson 1965.

ship between sound and sense is still arbitrary as far as the outside world is concerned (and would appear that way absolutely to a foreigner), but within the system it is no longer so.

Something of this nature must have happened with those two past-tense endings, -/d/ and -/t/, that have begun to cluster around opposite meanings: -/d/ for 'relatively gradual,' -/t/ for 'relatively abrupt.' Even speakers who use only one of them—Britishers favor -/t/, Americans -/d/—still sense the difference. *Spilled* seems more natural than *spilt* in *The water spilled drop by drop over the rim; spilt* more natural than *spilled* in *The milk spilt all over the floor when she dropped the pitcher.*[17] Of course it helps when there is a suggestion of sound-symbolism. The voiced sound of /d/ is less abrupt than the voiceless sound of /t/ (compare *jolt, volt, bolt, halt, dealt* [a blow]). But associations of this kind do not depend on sound-symbolism alone. *Demoniacal* is a more menacing word than *demoniac,* probably because it echoes *maniacal.* To call an accusation *baseless* is more telling than to call it *groundless,* probably because it echoes *base* with its meaning of 'low, contemptible' (and also because the initial [b] makes a lip gesture possible).

Often we find words clustering in groups with a vague resemblance in sound—too hazy to carve out as a definite morpheme—to which has been given the name *phonestheme.* Most of the words ending in *-ump* suggest heaviness and bluntness: *rump, dump, hump, mump, lump, stump, chump, thump, bump.* Children sense these associative possibilities and coin words with them: *If the house is as old as that it's raggy, shaggy, and daggy,* remarked one seven-year-old; and referring to the muck at the bottom of an excavation the same speaker said *It's all gushy—it's like mushy dushy.* The makers of multiple-choice tests find phonesthemes useful as distractors for their questions; if *twisted* is offered as an equivalent for *knurled,* as was done in one test, it is on the assumption that persons not fully acquainted with *knurl* will assume that it is related to *twirl, whirl, birl, tirl, furl,* and *gnarl.* Shifts of meaning often go in the direction of a family of words having phonesthematic ties. The word *bolster* no longer suggests a padded and comparatively soft support but rather a stiff and rigid one, because of the attraction of *brace, bolt, buttress.* (Of seventeen persons tested on this point, thirteen voted for 'rigid.') Phonesthemes are often a principal ingredient of new words: *hassle* probably follows from *tussle, bustle, wrestle.* One anthropological linguist holds that connections of this kind may be part of our innate equipment for learning our native language—an indispensable aid to memory.[18]

---

[17] See Quirk 1970.
[18] Durbin 1973.

If words become parts of things to our minds, as they must if language is to do its job efficiently (in spite of our trying, in philosophical moments, to break the bondage), at least a partial association of sound and sense can hardly be avoided. When other aspects of things hit our eyes we do not hesitate to infer a kinship in the things if we detect a similarity in the aspects, and it is only natural for us to do the same with words: no two girls ever toss their heads in the same way, but one's doing it should mean somewhat the same as another's; two words such as *flout* and *flaunt* are not identical, but they are similar enough so that they *ought* to be related in meaning. We feel a lurking sympathy for the seventeen-year-old who produced the following definitions:

> *Ossify:* this means to astonish, to frighten to death.
>
> *Palpable:* good to the taste, good to eat.
>
> *Pander:* that means run fast, panting down the track, thundering down, you know, pander, pander, pander, that's the way it sounds.
>
> *Pariah:* that's the black pariah, the wagon that takes away the drunks.
>
> *Platitude:* that's how high aviators get into the air.
>
> *Aptitude:* that is the feelings you have about something. Your father says, "I don't like your aptitude toward using the car."
>
> *Brandish:* that is what you have in restaurants sometimes, brandish cherries. They burn with ice cream.
>
> *Henchmen:* those are the guys that sit on the bench, I suppose, the ones the coach never uses.
>
> *Flagrant:* that is the way flowers smell, or a field of daisies.[19]

Not all of us go so far in blurring the arbitrariness of language with this kind of poetic truth, but the outlines are never perfectly sharp for any of us. Who nowadays feels comfortable with *disinterested* as a synonym of *impartial?*

LINGUISTS AND MEANING

To give meaning its place in the linguist's world, one must see how things were and how they are.

---

[19] Downes and Schuman 1955.

Until about 1965 it was a history of constant postponement. Things were cozy inside the formal system, with *-emes* and structures of various sorts all ticketed and orderly, and no rowdy elements were to be allowed on the premises. Meaning, as we have seen, is an exceedingly ill-assorted fellow. One can scarcely invite him into the house without admitting at the same time one or more of his drunken friends. The technique was either to lock him out or to demand a password and slam the door shut the moment the legitimate guest was inside, which not infrequently cost him part of an arm or a leg.

Not that linguists were averse to keeping company with meaning when first making their way through the dark streets of a new language. He was the one familiar face in a crowd of strangers, a handy guide and a prompter of hunches. But once the preliminary acquaintances were made and the moment of high theory had arrived, he had to show his credentials or stay out.

In theory—though not always in practice—American linguists until very recently have kept their investment in meaning as low as possible by dealing with it in one of three ways: admitting only a well-defined minimum of it; not admitting it from outside but pretending it was already there (that is, carrying on with its ghost); or admitting all of it and telling it to keep quiet.

The first approach was an outgrowth of field work and made use of "differential meaning." This is the minimal sort of meaning that an informant relies upon when we ask him whether **uru** and **ulu** are the same in meaning or different. We have heard him say both and we want to know whether [l] and [r] in his language are distinct phonemes or allophones of one phoneme. Unless we are the victims of an unlucky coincidence (as with English **vial** and **phial**; see Chapter 3, page 62), the response "same" or "different" ought to settle the question.

Differential meaning crops up at a higher level in the use of *paraphrase*. To determine whether two surface structures have the same deep structure, one relies on an informant (or on one's intuitions) to say whether they have the same meaning. Paraphrase has pretty solid justification in the way we behave in responding to a question such as **What did he say?** Suppose the original speaker's actual words were **The committee chairman subpoenaed the firm's records.** We interpret the **what** of the question to refer to the *content* of what was said, not to the words, and our reply may take any one of several forms, including **He said that the records of the firm were subpoenaed by the chairman of the committee,** where three of the original structures have been transformed. Instead of quoting we regenerate.

Differential meaning was indispensable but not sufficient. In practice the field worker always leaned on other aspects of meaning, sometimes less, sometimes more. Suppose two informants disagree on "same" or "different." The only way to settle the argument is to try to find exactly what the words do mean; and this is referential meaning, not just differential. Suppose the informant is not bilingual and fails to understand the question posed in our language, and we are unable to pose it in his— there is no way even to ask, "Is this the same or is it different?" We must then appeal to objects, pantomime, or whatever kind of dumb play two persons use when they have to communicate without language. But worst of all—and this is where the breakdown comes in theory—suppose we intend the question on one level of language and the informant infers it on another. We have assumed that one can sensibly ask "same or different?" as if these notions were a kind of absolute instead of being conditioned by the structure of the language, which is the very thing we are trying to find out. *Seal* and *seal* are the same, phonologically, but our informant may think we are talking about a seal on an envelope in the first instance and a seal in the ocean in the second, and so answer "different." *The boy walked to the school* and *The man plodded from the station* are the same syntactically, but if it is not understood that we are talking about syntax then an informant is going to call them different.[20] It is pretty generally admitted nowadays that more than differential meaning is needed to analyze a language, even at just the level of the phoneme.

As for paraphrase, we saw some of its limitations in the last chapter. It overemphasizes truth values. And it is incapable of dealing with the inferential strategies outlined in this chapter. When we read a sentence like this one from a popular magazine—*Sitting around these days in a large group of our friends without having memories of a contessa to draw on is a little like being the only one without shoes on*[21]—we know that *without shoes on* is a paraphrase of *with shoes off*, but using the latter in this passage would destroy the effect. Beyond its truth value, the sentence conveys an *expectation*.

Differential meaning was an attempt to set limits on how far one should go with meaning for certain purposes. It was not intended as a definition or description of meaning from a linguistic standpoint. That is the aim of the second approach, which undertakes to deal with meaning without going outside language. It is a refined version of the idea that "context determines meaning"—if we know the company that a word keeps within the society of words, then we know what it means.

But now context must be taken in a large sense. It is not enough to look to the immediate context. One could encounter the word *rhizome* over and over—*He pulled up the rhizome, The cow ate the rhizome, The rhizome crept under the ground, It was a tender rhizome*—and still not learn what it is. So one must reach far afield: "Let us assume that the

---

[20] Paraphrased from Pike 1954, pp. 23–24.
[21] Shirley Jackson, *The Saturday Evening Post* (6 June 1964), p. 8.

total and potentially infinite set of utterances containing a given lexical item exactly specifies the meaning of that lexical item."[22] Meaning is to be expressed in terms of "collocations"[23] or "the intralingual relations contracted by linguistic units."[24]

The difficulty with theories of meaning that play only with associations within language and seal themselves off from the outside world is that they are ultimately circular. Take a simple instance like **He strummed the guitar.** If we do not know the meaning of **guitar,** the context tells us that it must be a musical instrument because only musical instruments are strummed. If we do not know the meaning of **strum,** the context tells us that it is most likely a form of playing because that is what one normally does with musical instruments. But what if we do not know either **strum** or **guitar?** A dependence on context has to assume that we know everything except the one item in question, but if we do not know that item, and context is a string of interdependencies, then we cannot be sure that we know the context either. At some point it is necessary to break out of the circle, to get a foothold outside language. A word is like Antaeus, revitalized by each contact with the earth. "Every language provides ways to extricate itself from bondage to its own commitments in the formal registration of meanings."[25]

The third approach was that of transformational grammar in its early stages. Meaning at last was to come into its own. It was given great honors and a new name: *the semantic component.* Once the ceremonies were over and meaning was conveniently locked in the throne room, the more important business of the syntactic component and the phonological component was free to go ahead as usual. So matters stood till a rescue operation was carried out in the late 1960s.

Now meaning has moved center stage. There is renewed cooperation between linguists and logicians in studying the special part of meaning that deals with internal consistency, "operators" such as **any, some, every, all,** and forms of discourse. Equally significant is the discovery that much of experimental psychology is actually experimental linguistics. If we cannot see inside the human head to test how meanings are organized, we can have subjects classify them, test their reaction times to see how close two meanings are, and so on. Sociologists too are making their bid, reminding linguists that intentions and expectations are as important as semantic features.

There is still the abiding danger that the techniques developed in dealing more or less successfully with some other part of language will be

---

[22] Miron and Archer 1965, p. 43.

[23] Joos 1958.

[24] Wyatt 1965, p. 505.

[25] Ray 1962, p. 323.

pushed into a new area where they do not fit. The attitudes that grew
up around the hard sciences both aided and impeded progress in the
soft sciences. In linguistics there was for a time a determined effort to
analyze syntax according to habits that were formed in analyzing phonology—sentences, phrases, compounds, even words were to be delimited by
audible signals, such as the stresses and junctures we touched on earlier
(page 59). That effort had only a very limited success and was replaced by techniques designed specifically for syntax. Similarly now we
are witnessing attempts by the "generative semanticists" to extend these
syntactic techniques to cover meaning (see pages 165, 540–46). Perhaps
they will have better luck. On the other hand they may represent, in the
words of one critic, an "impossible ambition."[26]

One potential actor is still waiting in the wings: the lexicographer. He
is an unpretentious fellow, and perhaps that is why he has been there
so long. If only he were not such a dilettante—insisting on looking at
every wayward sense and anecdote, at frequencies and usages, at the
whole of meaning instead of some theoretically important part . . .

---

[26] Gray 1974, p. 4.

ADDITIONAL REMARKS AND APPLICATIONS

1. Comment on the meaning of *meaning* in the following:

   Seven o'clock *means* breakfast in our household.

   Keep out. This *means* you.

   Do you *mean* to wait?

   Without love, life would have no *meaning*.

2. Do traffic and other such signs have, in addition to their one-to-one relationship to what they mean, a tendency to be suggestive or pictorial? Would green for 'Stop' and red for 'Go' be just as good as the reverse? What is the sign used in many communities that means 'Watch out, children playing'?

3. Explain the difference between a syllable and a morpheme.

4. Seeing similarities is sometimes linked to being able to abstract, supposedly a higher intellectual faculty. Consider a child who has had only cats as pets and on seeing a dog calls it a cat. Or a child who on seeing a strange man calls him Daddy. Is this a kind of abstraction, or is it a lack of ability to discriminate? How is it necessary for language?

5. The color of fire boxes is red, part of the complex of features that we recognize as a fire box. How is it analogous to the names that we give to segments of reality so as later to abstract the names to stand for the segments?

6. A little girl writes in a letter, *They treated us like one of the family.* What has happened here?

7. A little girl's teacher—in the second grade—asks her what she is afraid of, and she replies *It!* The teacher wants to know what *it* is, and the child replies that that is just what frightens her so, she doesn't know—maybe it's a punishment, or a disease, or a big animal that will get her if she misbehaves. She has lain awake nights worrying about *it* and what "she will get." After talking with the child's

mother the teacher finds the answer: at home she has been scolded with **You'll get it!** whenever she does something wrong.[27] What does this tell us about the way in which early meanings are acquired?

8. If you decide in the middle of the day to take a nap, which would you be more likely to say: **I'm going to lie down for a while** or **I'm going to bed for a while** (assuming that bed is where you actually do go)? If you prefer the former, what is there about the meaning of *go to bed* that caused you to reject it? What does that tell you about how the expression *to go to bed* is learned? Suppose you were taken suddenly ill. Is *to go to bed* appropriate now? Is there a feature here similar to that for *to kneel* mentioned in the text (page 196)?

9. A doctor, giving treatment for a cold, says **Don't eat too much but drink plenty of liquids.** Since it is highly probable that if the patient drinks it will be a liquid, why bother to say it? Why not **Don't eat too much but drink plenty** or **Don't do too much eating but do plenty of drinking?** Explain the doctor's orders as a problem of how we learn the verb *to drink* in context.

10. Can the verb *to bake* be given a suitable abstract definition, without reference to concrete instances? Consider the following examples:

    a. She baked (?roasted) the ham.

    b. She roasted (*baked) the prime ribs.

    c. I'm going to bake (fry, *roast) some pancakes for breakfast tomorrow.

    d. She baked (*roasted) a cake.

    e. She baked (roasted) the chicken.

    f. We baked (roasted) the potatoes in the hot ashes.

11. Which of these two sentences would you prefer, referring to an old TV program?

    I've seen it before but I'm watching it again.
    I've watched it before but I'm seeing it again.

Account for your preference in terms of semantic features.

12. Might it be said that the meanings of words like **unique, perfect, unparalleled, full, empty, complete** and **unsaturated** have an 'abso-

---

27 Engel 1975.

lute' feature? What happens to them when intensifiers are added—
very unique, highly unsaturated, most perfect?

13. There are several number paradigms:

    a. one, two, three, four . . .
    b. first, second, third, fourth . . .
    c. all, half, third, fourth . . . twenty-first . . .
    d. single, double (dual), treble (triple), quadruple, quin-
       tuple . . .
    e. once, twice, thrice, four times . . .

What are the semantic features of each set?

14. *Odd* and *strange* are synonyms. Judge the following for acceptability,
    and see if you can determine in what respect they are different:

    a. John is rather odd (strange) today.
    b. It was odd (strange) of John to lose a leg.
    c. It was odd (strange) of Mary to say that.
    d. Mary looked at me oddly (strangely), as if she had never
       seen me before.
    e. Mary looked at me oddly (strangely), as if she had had some
       sudden misgiving.
    f. Mary's oddity (strangeness) is her love for cats.

15. If certain function words, say prepositions, are taken to have stable
    meanings, it is possible to determine certain features of the words
    they go with. Take the prepositions that can be used with *world* and
    *earth (through the world, through the earth, in the world, in the
    earth, *on the world, on the earth)* and try to determine how *world*
    and *earth* differ in their features.[28]

16. A feature that is assumed to be present unless otherwise specified
    is called *unmarked;* if it needs to be specified it is *marked.* (The
    "unmarked value" is the *usual* value of a term.) Decide which of the
    two features 'dead' and 'living' is unmarked in *coral* and in *tree.*

17. There is a class of verbs that has been termed *factive.* These verbs
    imply that the fact described in their complements is true. Decide

---

[28] See Shopen 1974.

which of the verbs in the following sentences have the factive feature
and which do not:

    a. I*'m sorry* that you have a toothache.

    b. He *said* that he had a toothache.

    c. I *hope* he has a toothache.

    d. They *know* he has a toothache.

    e. They*'re sure* he has a toothache.

    f. She *forgot* that she had a toothache.

    g. He *revealed* that he had a toothache.

    h. He *admitted* that he had a toothache.

18. What is there about the meaning of prepositions that makes *the tree
    beside the lake* and *the money inside the box* more usual than *the
    lake beside the tree* and *the box around the money?*

19. Is there a kind of word magic in the way we conceptualize adjec-
    tives? When we say *Rhubarb leaves are poisonous* do we represent a
    "feature of" rhubarb leaves the same way we do when we say
    Rhubarb leaves are green? Does this tell us that semantic features
    belong to the meanings of things, to their representations in our
    minds, rather than to the things themselves?

20. The names given to features are themselves words. Does this mean
    that we cannot get outside the words of a language so as to set up a
    special language for the purpose of scientific description? Study and
    discuss the following passage: "Semantic components are not part
    of the vocabulary of the language itself, but rather theoretical ele-
    ments, postulated in order to describe the semantic relations between
    the lexical elements of a given language."[29]

21. The following two sentences are equally unambiguous, assuming a
    heterosexual relationship:

    A student loves a girl-student.
    A student loves a boy-student.

    Are the two equally acceptable to you? If not, what can you say
    about marked and unmarked features?[30]

---

[29] Bierwisch 1970, p. 169.

[30] A translation from the German, where the unambiguous **Student** and **Studentin**
are used, solved this with **A student loves a co-ed.** But the problem of attachability
of features still remains.

22. The following verbs have a 'causative' feature (see pages 164–65): *to blush, to redden, to flush.* A separate feature in each is the nature of the cause. Identify it. (Try adding such phrases as **with anger, with running, with embarrassment, with pleasure, with alcohol.**)

23. Decide on the acceptability of the following:

> We spent six years of our lives there.
> We spent six days of our lives there.

Explain the relative acceptability in terms of the meanings that the parts of the sentence impose on each other.

24. A linguistic study explains that the sentence *John has finished the peas and Mary (has finished) the potatoes* "requires a similar deleted verb in each of the coordinated parts"—for example, he and she were eating, he and she were preparing, harvesting, etc., but not he was eating the peas and she was peeling the potatoes.[31] Would the same be true of *John has finished his peas and Mary her potatoes?* If not, why not?

25. The sentence *I got a good price for it* can be rephrased as *I got a high price for it;* and *I got it at a good price* can be rephrased as *I got it at a low price.* Does this mean that *good* has developed two opposing senses, 'high' and 'low'?

26. In an article criticizing certain dictionary definitions, it was asserted that to define *inspect* as 'to examine carefully' is inaccurate, because *to inspect carelessly* is a normal English phrase. Is this a fair criticism?

27. Discuss the use of *minimally* in the following, from a study of graduate education: *Casual inspection reveals that most schools of education are overwhelmed with the magnitude of keeping the schools minimally staffed.*

28. Is *They could smell Bill from the floor above* ambiguous (like *hear* in the text, pages 202–03)? Why? Are there many different names for smells?

29. There are two persons in a car, the driver and a passenger. The car is going rather fast. The passenger says to the driver *Aren't you going*

---

[31] Dixon 1970, p. 11.

over seventy? As both driver and passenger are moving at the same speed, why this rather than *Aren't we going over seventy?*

30. Comment on the following sentences, keeping in mind the central meanings of the words in heavy type:

    a. Don't *eat with* your knife.

    b. A dictionary—you consult it but don't *read* it.

    c. I'm *cooking* four things: cereal, eggs, coffee, and *toast.*

    d. These apples are for cooking, not *eating.*

    e. Burn lamp *upside down* (directions on a lamp that is supposed to be mounted bulb-down).

31. A medicine advertises that it *helps your pain while you sleep.* Most people would rather have their pain hindered than helped; explain the apparent anomaly. Is there something similar in the following question-and-answer pair? *"How's your headache?"—"It's better now."*

32. A popular magazine carried a cartoon showing a junior official who has just discovered a microphone hidden in his office. He is exclaiming *Somebody cares! I've been bugged!*[32] Compare this with the example *We're all here* in the text (page 205), and comment on the meaning of the pronoun *I.* Comment also on the meaning of *you* in the sentence *Did you rain all the way in?* spoken by someone meeting a commuter getting off a bus on a rainy day.[33]

33. Make up a set of features that will account for the meanings of the following words: *clock, watch, sundial, hourglass, timepiece, chronometer, clepsydra, horologe.* Display them on a grid like that of Table 7–1.

34. A modification of the branching tree can be used to show the semantic relationships between kindred words in two or more languages. A simple example is the following, in which there are two trees laid on their sides, illustrating the primary and secondary senses of the English noun *virtue* and its cognates in three Romance languages. The solid lines are for the primary senses, the broken lines for the secondary ones:

---

[32] *The Saturday Evening Post* (24 October 1964).

[33] Example from Erica García, transmitted by Roberst Kirsner.

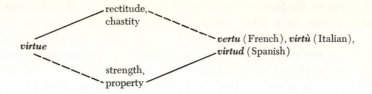

Make a similar double tree for some other English word and a cognate in another language.

35. See if in your speech the following can be arranged in an age sequence from youngest to oldest, and discuss the relationship of this arrangement to the meanings of the individual words:

baby boy   young boy
man   little boy
boy   young man

(You may need to try each in some such context as *I saw a* _____ *sitting there.*) Is there a difference when the expressions are used to refer to someone within his hearing? (For example, *This* _____ *would like a ticket to the show.*)

36. The word *sweet* is sometimes paired antonymously with *sour*, sometimes with *bitter*. Does this make *sour* and *bitter* synonyms? If not, why not?

37. Does English have formal ways of building antonyms? Name the antonyms of the following words: *decent, likely, pro-French, to trust, clockwise*. Compare the use of *not* in the following pairs of sentences: *He is trustworthy, He is not trustworthy; He is American, He is not American.* See if you can replace the *not* with *un-*.

38. Do we generally try to avoid rimes and alliteration in making phrases? Consider whether the following are normal; if any are not, what do we usually do about it? *mighty mild, mighty miffed, pretty prim, awful lawful, very various, very varied, really reedy, quite quiet.*

39. Someone is about to use the sentence *What right do you have to complain about his not telling you things when you make a scene when he does?* but is dissatisfied with it. How can it be improved from the standpoint of contrast? (Suggestion: A near-synonym can be substituted for a repeated function word, in either of two positions.)

40. *A* plans to fly from Chicago to St. Louis to visit *B* and return with him a few days later when *B* drives from St. Louis to Chicago for a brief stay there on business. Meanwhile *A* finds it impossible to make the plane trip originally planned. "Never mind," *A* says. "I'll *go back (return)* with *B* when he leaves for St. Louis and have my visit there a few days late, and then *return (come back)* by plane." Comment on the use of *go (come) back* and *return*.

41. The following onomatopoetic words in Japanese were part of a list that was given to a group of native speakers of French to try to identify. They did so quite successfully. Try your luck, and look for the equivalents in the footnote:[34]

    chirin-chirin   kokekokko   wã-wã   nyao

42. If you were asked which of the two words *coins* and *cash* more strongly suggested 'noisy bits and pieces' which would you pick? Can you relate your choice to a phonesthematic family? Do related sounds always suggest related senses? What about *pill, pile, pole, poll, pal, pool, pull, peel, pale, pall, pell?*

43. Use differential meaning to identify certain phonemes in the following pairs: *say-stay; sigh-die; fuss-fuzz.* Could one also use differential meaning to identify a morpheme in the phrases *two dogs, two cats, two churches, two bridges?*

44. Consider the following conversation:

> "What ever happened to Myna Evans? Has she gone into an eclipse like all the other actresses of the 1930s?"
> "It looks like it. I don't think *she's been heard from* since the charity work she did around 1952."

In transformational grammar the expression in boldface type would be taken to have the same deep structure as that of a or b (or possibly c) below. Can you substitute any of them for the original without a change in the meaning?

    a. anybody has heard from her
    b. people have heard from her
    c. we've heard from her

Would *people have heard about her* be closer than a, b, or c to the original meaning? If so, what conclusions can you draw about the tendency of semantic contrasts to seep into any contrast of form?

---

[34] In this order: 'ringing of a bell,' 'cock's cry (cock-a-doodle-doo),' 'bow-wow,' 'mewing of a cat (meow).' From Frei n.d.

45. There is a rhythm rule in English whereby successions of *content* words are not apt to occur when they result in a succession of accented syllables; for example, we prefer *quite a tall girl* to *a quite tall girl* (but there are many exceptions). One result is that certain words preserve two forms, one that is used after *to be* and its synonyms (*They were content*) and another that is used as a pre-modifier and may or may not be used after *to be* (*a contented cow*—compare **a content cow*). For at least some speakers, *drunk* and *drunken* are a similar pair. But is the distinction between them purely rhythmic? You probably would not say **a drunk bum*; but if you did, which would suggest 'habitually so' to your mind, *drunk* or *drunken?* How does this fit the expression *drunk driver?*

46. A friend of a barber comes into the barbershop and uses the washbasin to wash his hair. He complains that the water from the "hot" tap is cold. The barber says *Let it run a minute and it will hot up.* Is *to hot up* a familiar expression to you? If not, do you understand it nevertheless? Assuming you do, explain from the standpoint of field relationships how it is possible. Consider in particular the relationships among *hot, warm, heat up,* and *warm up.* See if you make a contrast now between *hot up* and *heat up.* (Would you say *Give the oven a minute to hot up* as readily as *Give the water in the tap a minute to hot up?*)

References

Barber, Charles. 1964. *Linguistic Change in Present-day English* (University, Ala.: University of Alabama Press).

Bierwisch, Manfred. 1970. "Semantics," in John Lyons (ed.), *New Horizons in Linguistics* (Harmondsworth, England: Penguins).

Bolinger, Dwight. 1965. "The Atomization of Meaning," *Language* 41:555–73.

Bright, J. O., and W. Bright. 1965. "Semantic Structures in Northwestern California and the Sapir-Whorf Hypothesis," *American Anthropologist* 67. Special publication.

Dixon, R. M. W. 1970. "Syntactic Orientation as a Semantic Property." Report no. NSF-24, Computation Laboratory, Harvard University, pp. 1–22.

Downes, Mildred, and Rita S. Schuman. 1955. "Pathogenesis of Reading Disability," *New England Journal of Medicine* 252:6.

Durbin, Marshall. 1973. "Sound Symbolism in the Mayan Language Family," in Munro S. Edmonson (ed.), *Meaning in Mayan Languages: Ethnolinguistic Studies* (The Hague: Mouton).

Engel, Walburga von Raffler. 1975. "The Correlation of Gestures and Vocalizations in First Language Acquisition," in Adam Kendon, Mary Ritchie Key, and Richard M. Harris (eds.), *Organization of Behavior in Face-to-Face Interaction* (The Hague: Mouton).

Fippinger, Dorothy Crawford. 1971. "Kinship Terms of the Black Tai People," *Journal of the Siam Society* 59:65–82.

Freedle, Roy. 1970. "Some Relations Among Nouns: The Pursuit of Semantic Markers," in *Proceedings of the Seventy-eighth Annual Convention, American Psychological Association,* pp. 63–64.

Frei, Henri. n.d. "Cinquante ononamopées japonaises," in David Cohen (ed.), *Mélanges Marcel Cohen* (The Hague: Mouton).

Gray, Bennison. 1974. "Toward a Semi-revolution in Grammar," *Language Sciences* 29:1–12.

Hill, A. A. 1973. "Some Thoughts on Segmentation of Lexical Meaning," *Annals of the New York Academy of Sciences* 211:269–78.

Jakobson, Roman. 1965. "A la recherche de l'essence du langage," *Diogène* 51:22–38.'

Joos, Martin. 1958. "Semology: A Linguistic Theory of Meaning," *Studies in Linguistics* 13:53–70.

Kirsner, Robert S., and Sandra A. Thompson. 1975. "The Role of Pragmatic Inference in Semantics: A Study of Sensory Verb Complements in English." Manuscript.

Lehrer, Adrienne. 1969. "Semantic Cuisine," *Journal of Linguistics* 5:39–55.

Locke, Simeon; David Caplan; and Lucia Kellar. 1973. *A Study in Neurolinguistics* (Springfield, Ill.: Charles C Thomas). Reviewed by P. G. Patel, *Canadian Journal of Linguistics* 20 (1975).

Maher, J. P. 1974. "Medieval Culture and Technology in Comparative Romance Linguistics; Some Unsuspected French Cognates of Iberian and Italian **Bravo: Brouette** 'Wheelbarrow,' **Rabrouer** 'to Treat Rudely,' **S'ébrouer** 'to Snort.' " Manuscript.

Miller, Wick. 1973. "The Acquisition of Grammatical Rules by Children," in Charles A. Ferguson and Dan I. Slobin (eds.), *Studies of Child Language Development* (New York: Holt, Rinehart and Winston).

Miron, Murray S., and William K. Archer. 1965. "Qualification in Natural Language," *Linguistics* 11:30–49.

Pike, K. L. 1954. *Language in Relation to a Unified Theory of the Structure of Human Behavior* (Glendale, Calif.: Summer Institute of Linguistics).

Quirk, Randolph. 1970. "Taking a Deep Smell," *Journal of Linguistics* 6:119–24.

Ray, Punya Sloka. 1962. "The Formation of Prose," *Word* 18:313–25.

Shopen, Timothy. 1974. "Main Verb Arguments Versus Adverbs and Adjuncts —a Problem in Defining the Meaning of the Sentence as the Sum of Its Parts." Preprint.

Smith, Edward E.; Edward J. Shoben; and Lance J. Rips. 1974. "Structure and Process in Semantic Memory: A Featural Model for Semantic Decisions," *Psychological Review* 81:214–41.

Weir, Ruth Hirsch. 1962. *Language in the Crib* (The Hague: Mouton).

Wyatt, William F., Jr. 1965. Review of John Lyons, *Structural Semantics: An Analysis of Part of the Vocabulary of Plato.* In *Language* 41:504–12.

MIND IN THE GRIP OF LANGUAGE 8

A little girl asks, "What does the wind do when it doesn't blow?" or "Where did I live before I was born?" and we smile at her naiveté. But if she asks, "Where will I live after I die?" most people in our culture will take her seriously, though it will cost them to find an answer.

The idea embodied in these questions has weighed on linguists and on philosophers and psychologists working at the borders of linguistics for a long time: How is our thinking influenced by the language we use? Is thinking even possible without language? The second question is broadly psychological and philosophical; the first has sociological overtones as well, for it involves not only such passive things as our world view and our attitudes toward others as their language affects us, but the active arts of persuasion: if a government can change economic behavior by tampering with the monetary system, it can also implant thoughts and influence actions by tampering with language—and this invokes the great questions of truth, reform, and propaganda. Nor are governments without company: every argument between individuals is in some measure an attempt to influence thinking through language.

LANGUAGE AND THOUGHT

No one denies that language and thought are related. The question is how and how closely. The ultimate in closeness was claimed by a now outmoded school of psychology which held that thinking is merely talking to oneself, in an implicit sub-vocal way.[1] The opposite view was expressed by W. D. Whitney a century ago: "Language is the spoken means whereby thought is communicated, and it is only that"[2]—thoughts are generated in their own sphere and then formulated in language. A more comfortable position is somewhere between the two extremes: language is a tool in the way an arm with its hand is a tool, something to work with like any other tool and at the same time *part of* the mechanism that drives tools, part of *us*. Language is not only necessary for the formulation of thought but is part of the thinking process itself. Two famous metaphors describe the relationship: "Talking about language is building a fire in a wooden stove"; "Talking about knowledge or science is rebuilding a boat plank by plank while staying afloat in it."[3] We cannot get outside language to reach thought, nor outside thought to reach language.

Thinking is not done in a vacuum, but is always about something. What is the nature of an object of thought? It is rarely the image of a material thing standing before us; most often it is recalled from past experience or transmitted from the experience of others. In the latter case it almost inevitably comes via language. We could imagine of course that when we learn, from what someone tells us or from what we read in a book, that Pluto lies at the outward bounds of the solar system, the linguistic information is translated into some kind of mind-stuff before being filed for future reference. But no one knows what such a recording substance would be like, and it is simpler to assume that what is stored away is a set of appropriate sentences. Memory of our own past experience too is largely possible because we have put that experience into words. Any writer who has ever needed to consult a thesaurus has had the joyless task of trying to pin down an idea which refused to materialize until the word for it came to mind.

The most primitive act of thought is that of focusing on an object and distinguishing it from the blur that surrounds it. A child accomplishes this literally by feel—picking up and handling, reinforced by sight,

---

[1] See Watson 1919, Ch. 9.

[2] Silverstein 1971, p. 100. Whitney was not denying all forms of interdependence. He later went on to say (p. 101) that "there are grades of thought, spheres of ratiocination, where our minds could hardly work at all without the direct aid of language." But these aids are more in the nature of cue cards or promptings, to help us arrange our thoughts and keep track of where we are.

[3] Attributed by Quine 1960 to Otto Neurath.

sound, smell, and taste. Handling is a self-directed gesture language. The same movements will be gone through another time when the object is handled again, and by provoking this reaction the movements become part of the representation of the object. Even adults feel at a loss when describing a physical object if they are forbidden to use their hands to describe its shape. In Chapter 10 we shall see how an earlier gesture language was probably transferred to a spoken one. Words are not the first associations that we have of things which then come to serve as representations of them, but they are substituted so early and implanted so deeply that it is almost as difficult to think of a cow without thinking the word *cow* as to hear or use the word without thinking of the animal. And even if we accomplish this difficult task it is usually with the aid of some other verbal trick such as **milk-giver, bovine animal, moo,** or **brindle.** And when we imagine that we have captured a wordless thought we may only be fooling ourselves—the words perhaps are hovering in the background.[4]

As for any kind of thinking that is more complicated than simple identification and naming, a well-known linguistic philosopher gives this view of the structure that underlies it: "What comes of the association of sentences with sentences is a vast verbal structure which, primarily as a whole, is multifariously linked to non-verbal stimulation. These links attach to separate sentences (for each person), but the same sentences are so bound up in turn with one another and with further sentences that the non-verbal attachments themselves may stretch or give way under strain. In an obvious way this structure of interconnected sentences is a single connected fabric including all sciences, and indeed everything we ever say about the world, for the logical truths at least, and no doubt many more commonplace sentences too, are germane to all topics and thus provide connections."[5]

LANGUAGE AND LOGIC

Linguistics is a science, and sciences are by definition logical systems. A language may be treated as data for descriptions that can be tested for truth or falsity. But is a language in itself a logical system? This one

---

[4] The imaging of *individual* persons and things—for which we have proper rather than common nouns—is probably a different matter. Suppose you see the face of a young actress who reminds you of an old-time actress whose face, as you think of her, is clear in your mind—you may be able to say, "She has larger eyes than this actress has." Later perhaps you recapture the name; but the image came first. What words—loosely, common nouns—help us to do is to abstract and generalize; and that kind of thinking is word-dependent, at least to a much higher degree.

[5] Quine 1960, p. 12. Elsewhere (p. 3) he says, "Conceptualization on any considerable scale is inseparable from language."

question is two in disguise: does a language contain devices that are like the ones used in formal logic, and is it the purpose of language to be logical?

Aristotle assigned to language a position superior to logic, that of *meaningful expression* in general. Logic is the restricted language of affirmation and negation, of propositions which are true or false. A modern logician would include more than this—for example, what is probable. But language still includes not only propositions but fantasy (in poetry and fable) and expressions of desire: we do not say *I want a beer* to acquaint the hearer with the logical truth of our existence and our desire but to get the desired object. Language, linked to a modicum of direct experience, is what gives us our knowledge of the world; what we do with it—grasp a part of the world through it, reweave it in imagination, or express its truths in propositions—answers to our intentions. Language is the uncommitted means for everything.[6]

Obviously if language is to serve logic as well as poetics and pragmatics, the devices used by the logician must already inhere in it. The fact is that the processes of most importance to logicians are also very general linguistic processes: for example, affirmation and negation, conjunction and disjunction, definiteness and indefiniteness, condition and concession, which are loosely embodied in the words **yes** and **no, and** and **or, the** and **a,** and **if** and **although.** (We have to say *loosely* because logic must always define its terms more exactly than they are used in natural language—what we infer from *a person I didn't like and I had every reason to like* would be more logically expressed as *a person I didn't like even though I had every reason to like him.* We use **and** pretty freely.) An example of how the meaning of such a linguistic form can be explained by a logical proposition is the word **unless,** which is defined by *Webster's Third New International Dictionary* as 'under any other circumstances than that.' *If not* is sometimes given as the equivalent, but the two are not quite the same: ***Professor Arid will pass you in Linguistics 123 if you don't fail the final exam and if you don't make less than a C on your term paper*** is an acceptable sentence, but ****Professor Arid will pass you in Linguistics 123 unless you fail the final exam and unless you make less than a C on your term paper*** is not—**unless** implies a unique circumstance whereas **if not** includes the possibility of two or more. The proposition defining **unless** is thus worded as follows: "There exists a unique circumstance Q, such that for all circumstances C, if $C \neq Q$, then C implies P."[7] (The symbol $\neq$ means 'not equal to.')

---

[6] See Coseriu 1958.

[7] Proposition and examples are from Geis 1973. Actually the "uniqueness" applies only within a given semantic universe. We can have two *unless*'s provided their circumstances are semantically unrelated:

Logic is a specialized language dealing with the relationships of truth and falsity within language. Another specialized language, which points outward to the external world rather than inward, is mathematics. Its specialty is making precise the way we deal with things in space— amorphous space, where we group things together by addition and multiplication, separate them by subtraction and division, and compare them for equality and inequality; and structured space, where we locate them in geometrical ways. Mathematics is less language-dependent than logic is; in fact, it is an alternate route to a special part of the real world. Of course, one must resort to language whenever mathematical symbols are verbalized, but the symbols are more directly meaningful, like traffic signs. What logic and mathematics share is a precise notation, which is a reflection of precise definition, and is to be found to some degree in all sciences.

It is possible, using the special languages of logic and mathematics and adding some specific content, to engineer a robot that will perform in ways strikingly like a human being in accepting instructions and solving problems. Simulating "a network form for the representation of knowledge in the mind" is one of many ways in which computers have been applied to the study of language.[8] What gave computational linguistics its start was the hope of creating a translation machine that would make scientific work published in one language easily and quickly available in others. That proved more difficult than was expected (largely because, as we saw, words are not fully detachable units—see pages 99– 107), and though work continues in some quarters, most computational linguists are now engaged in other tasks. An instance of the kind of robot just mentioned is one that would learn how to drive a car. It is given a basic vocabulary, or "primitives," such as *turn, push, brake, accelerator, left, right, front, behind.* It analyzes commands and translates them into its control program. Some commands can be obeyed directly, such as *Push accelerator.* Others depend on having "condition" built into the program: *If speedometer high, push brake.* Still others require a comparison of the state of the car with the state of the highway. Comparisons may reveal conflicts which will require internally generated commands that must be analyzed and effected in their turn— a kind of "thinking" that will change the robot's memory structure.[9] Characteristically the situations in which such a device can be successful

---

I won't go swimming unless the water's warm and unless I won't look silly at my age. (Unrelated universes, one unique circumstance in each.)

* I won't go swimming unless the water's warm and unless I won't have to wear trunks. (Same universe, hence neither circumstance is unique.)

[8] For a brief survey of other applications, especially to dictionaries, see Kučera 1969.

[9] Furugori 1974.

have a limited and highly predictable range of objects and events. It may turn out that the chasm between the human brain and mechanical simulations of it is that between finiteness and virtual infinity: the network in the brain and the intricacy of its interconnections are astronomical. Nevertheless, computer models are about the only way of experimentally testing theories of how the brain operates. One computational linguist sees a two-way relationship between the fields, with linguistics contributing as much to computer theory as computation contributes to linguistics, especially as more sophisticated computers are designed with strata resembling those of language.[10] Computers are already engaged in tasks as various as testing grammar theories, reconstructing prehistoric languages, editing bilingual dictionaries, studying the perception of sounds, simulating the memorization of meanings, making Braille translators for the blind, and analyzing Latin hexameter verse.

CONTROL BY LANGUAGE

The general question of the interdependence of thought and language yields to the particular one of fluidity and rigidity. Mind and spirit have always been conceived (at least in our culture) as a kind of ectoplasm, formless in itself but freely shaped by the act of thinking. Nothing is impervious to it; it penetrates all walls and envelopes all concepts. Language has never had this reputation. It is a structure, warping whatever filters through it. The problem of rigidity was first popularized in the 1930s by a school of philosophy, still active, known as *general semantics,* which saw in our use of *words* a kind of surrender of the flexibility and refinement of thought for the sake of traffic in verbal *things.* Much was made of the uncritical use of generalizations, of the difficulty of pinning a statement like the following down to a set of precise referents: "It is the ability of a community to achieve consensus on the great issues and compromise on the lesser issues which lies at the heart of the democratic process. . . ."[11] The critical reader must ask: Can communities as a whole have abilities? Can the difference between great and small issues be recognized? Is there ever consensus without compromise? Is democracy a process? And so on.[12]

---

[10] Hays 1973.

[11] Speech by W. W. Rostow of the Department of State, 26 January 1964.

[12] For a more recent statement of the general semanticist's position see Hayakawa 1972.

The Whorf hypothesis

It remained for a linguist, Benjamin Lee Whorf, to turn the question away from individual words and toward the framework of whole languages. He was not the first to take this step—Fritz Mauthner in 1902 declared that "if Aristotle had spoken Chinese or Dakota, his logic and his categories would have been different."[13] Others, including Wilhelm von Humboldt (page 508) and Whorf's own teacher Edward Sapir, held similar opinions. But Whorf was the most successful in dramatizing it. Since every language has a form and no two forms are the same, it follows that no two cultures having different languages can have identical views of the world. Instead of a perfectly flexible rubber mask that shapes itself to reality, each language is somewhat like a Greek mask, with its own built-in scowl or grin. Whorf's perception of language as a pair of glasses with more or less warped lenses through which we view our surroundings was sharpened by his work with a language about as different from English as any language can be—that of the Hopi, a tribe of Pueblo Indians living in Arizona. Whorf had what Archimedes demanded in order to move the world—a place to stand; and he maintained that French or German or Russian was no good as a platform, since in fundamental structure these languages—in common with others of Indo-European stock—are the same.

One of the chief things that English and its sister languages fasten upon the experience of all their speakers is a prior categorization of the reality outside us into nouns and verbs. The noun pictures things as detached from the processes that surround them, making it possible to say *The wind blows* or *The light flashes,* though wind cannot exist apart from blowing nor flashing apart from light. Not only does it *enable* us to say such things, it *forces* us to: by itself, *snowing,* as our English teacher said, "is not a sentence"; where no subject is handy, we must throw in a plug for one: *It is snowing.* Whorf writes:

> English terms, like *sky, hill, swamp,* persuade us to regard some elusive aspect of nature's endless variety as a distinct *thing,* almost like a table or chair.... The real question is: What do different languages do, not with ... artificially isolated objects but with the flowing face of nature in its motion, color, and changing form; with clouds, beaches, and yonder flight of birds? For as goes our segmentation in the face of nature, so goes our physics of the cosmos.[14]

Two examples will suffice to show the arbitrariness of this segmentation, its dependence upon the local interests and transitory needs of

---

[13] Cited in Coseriu 1958, p. 7.
[14] Whorf 1941.

the culture that attempts it. The word *vitamin*, coined in 1912 to designate a group of substances supposed at the time to be amines, covers such a strange agglomeration of chemicals that *Webster's Third New International Dictionary* requires fourteen lines to define it, in spite of the fact that it is given only one sense. Yet to the average user of the term it seems to name something as clear and definite as the house next door. 'A thing in nature' becomes 'a thing in commerce,' and the pill-taker is not concerned with what it "really is." Similarly, the term *complex* was applied around 1910 to a combination of psychological factors that, as the name implies, were difficult to separate and simplify; but the existence of the term, and the identification of some particular ailment as a "complex," gave all that was needed for a new entry among our realities.

Coupled with a categorization of "thingness" in nouns is a categorization of "substance" in the subgrouping of mass nouns. English and related languages have a special technique of combining these with certain formalized "counters" in order to carve out segments: *a piece of meat, a glass of water, a blade of grass, a grain (bushel) of corn, a stalk of celery.* The resulting picture is one of a universe filled with taffy-like aggregations that can be clipped into pieces by our scheme of numbers: *earth, air, stone, iron, light, shade, fire, disease,* even—and especially—abstractions like *love, honor, dismay, courage, dictatorship,* and *accuracy.*

Out of this substance-operated-on-by-numbers, this notion of *jewels* as "contained in" *jewelry* and *guns* as "contained in" *artillery,* our language has evolved an elaborate vocabulary having to do with an all-containing *space*—the term *space* itself is a mass noun that subsumes in an abstract way all other mass nouns. And here is where the world view of our language departs most radically from that of the Hopi: our concepts of space are so pervasive that we are able to transfer them almost totally to *time.* We treat time as a mass, and carve it into units and count them: *five hours.* For it we use the same prepositions: *before, after, in, at;* the same adjectives: *long, short, same, different, right, wrong, hard, nice, more, less;* and many of the same nouns: *stretch* of time, *segment* of time, *amount* of time. And, of course, we capture events in our space-like nouns—the word *event* itself, plus *rain, dance, movement, stir, riot, invasion, courtship,* and countless others. This, Whorf points out, is almost never done in Hopi:

> Our own "time" differs markedly from Hopi "duration." It is conceived as like a space of strictly limited dimensions, or sometimes as like a motion upon such a space. . . . Hopi "duration" seems to be inconceivable in terms of space or motion, being the mode in which life differs from form, and consciousness *in toto* from the spatial elements of consciousness. . . . Our "matter" is the physical sub-type of "substance" or "stuff," which is conceived as the formless extensional item that must be joined with form

before there can be any real existence. In Hopi there seems to be nothing corresponding to it; there are no formless extensional items; existence may or may not have form, but what it also has, with or without form, is intensity and duration, these being non-extensional and at bottom the same.

Our custom of quantifying time is illustrated by the sentence ***Ten days is greater than nine days,*** which contrasts with the Hopi expression of the same idea in terms of duration, ***The tenth day is later than the ninth.***[15] Events of brief duration cannot be captured as nouns in Hopi: "lightning, wave, flame, meteor, puff of smoke, pulsation, are verbs."[16]

So where Western philosophers—from Plato and Aristotle with their concepts of matter and form to Kant with his *a priori* space and time— have imagined that they were intuiting general laws that applied to all of nature or at least to all of mankind, what they actually were doing was exteriorizing a way of looking at things that they inherited from their language. Much that is difficult in recent physics as well as in philosophy and logic has been the struggle to climb out of this rut, all the harder to escape because we are in it, unconsciously, from the moment we begin to speak. Whorf surmised that a world view such as that of the Hopi might be more congenial to the concepts of modern physics than the languages of Western Europe. In a similar vein, Y. R. Chao has argued that Chinese is more congenial than English to certain approaches of symbolic logic.[17] For example, the normal Chinese ***Yeou de ren shuo jen huah*** 'There are men who tell the truth' is closer to the logical formula than is the normal English ***Some men tell the truth.***

Partial escape from the trap

Linguists now feel that Whorf's position was exaggerated. Western philosophers and physicists *did* evolve their analyses in spite of their language; Whorf *does* explain his position in English, implying that a reader of English can grasp the concepts that English presumably fails to embody in its structure; ***There are men who tell the truth*** *is* an English sentence, almost as commonplace as ***Some men tell the truth;*** and in some ways language answers to nature rather than the other way around.[18] It must be, then, that languages are more pluralistic than a catalog of their bulkier categories seems to suggest. English escapes from its hidebound

---

[15] Whorf 1949, pp. 37 and 24.

[16] Whorf 1957, p. 215.

[17] Chao 1955.

[18] Bull 1960 argues that this is even true of time, all languages being constrained by the nature of time (or man's view of it) to express certain relationships in similar ways.

subject-predicate, noun-verb formulas in the construction ***There's singing at the church,*** using an *-ing* form whose *raison d'être* is precisely that it does blur the line between noun and verb, and omits the subject. Another example is inceptiveness, the "get-going" phase of a continuing action, which many languages categorize sharply (Latin, for example, with the suffix *-escere*); to the casual outsider it might appear that English lacks suitable means for expressing this. But the lack is handily made up by liberal use of the verb *start*—in ***He came in and called me names*** we have the sensation of something left out; generally we want ***He came in and started calling me names.*** To take another example: the Romance languages divide sentences into two broad classes, those which merely *convey* to the hearer what is in someone else's mind—mental pictures that may be dream or reality and may be intense or dim—and those which show the *volitional involvement* of the other person, his willing or commanding or other emotional filtering of what the sentence says. The two categories are called *indicative* and *subjunctive* and are shown in the endings of verbs. It might seem that English speakers, lacking the forms, must also lack the appreciation; but the identical distinction crops up in the freedom, or lack of it, with which English allows a main verb to skip over a subordinate verb: ***He was here, I suppose*** represents the indicative, ***°He was here, I regret*** represents the subjunctive.[19] The Romance indicative–subjunctive contrast thus has the same performative function as the explicit higher sentences in English (see pages 166–70).

Recent studies of the categories themselves show that they are not as compact and exclusive as we have been accustomed to think. Even among such things as nouns there are some that are "nounier" than others, more central to what are felt to be the defining characteristics of nouns. In the old view the main parts of speech could be pictured as abruptly distinct, like a new staircase:

Instead it has been proposed that they shade into one another, like a worn staircase:[20]

[19] Bolinger 1968. See also Hooper 1975.

[20] See Ross 1972.

The same may be true of all the categories into which we divide up the world. A sparrow is "birdier" than a chicken—if you are talking about birds and ask your companion which ones are his favorites, you will sense nothing amiss if he replies, "My favorites are the robins," but it will surprise you if he says, "My favorites are chickens," and you will feel that something is downright wrong if he says, "My favorites are the chickens" (the definite article is a subcategorizing device here). These and other examples suggest that the differences between languages are not so much in kind as in explicitness and degree. What one language builds into the broadest layers of its structure another expresses informally and sporadically; but both have it.

All the same, this does not mean that some very common category in our language will not magnify certain of our ways of seeing things and diminish others. Better examples than those in comparisons of structure can be found in comparisons of lexical equivalence; for we do unquestionably "structure" our universe when we apply words to it, sometimes— especially when the phenomena are continuous and do not exhibit seams and sutures—quite arbitrarily.

The example most frequently cited is that of colors. The visual spectrum is a continuum which English parcels out into six segments: *purple, blue, green, yellow, orange,* and *red.* Of course painters, interior decorators, and others concerned with finer shades and saturations employ a more elaborate vocabulary; but the additional words are generally defined with those six as reference points: *turquoise* is 'between blue and green'; *reseda* is 'between green and yellow'; *saffron* is 'between yellow and orange'; *crimson* is 'a shade of red'; *emerald* is 'a shade of green.' In Zuni, orange and yellow are combined into a single range named *łupzʔinna* (whose borders are not necessarily the red end of orange and the green end of yellow—all we can say is that *łupzʔinna* roughly coincides with our orange plus our yellow). In Navaho, the two colors *łičiíʔ* and *łico* divide somewhere between red and orange-yellow. How these different habits of naming can affect our "thinking"—symptomized by the efficiency with which we communicate—can be shown through recognition tests: the monolingual Zuni, presented with a small set of different colors and then asked after a brief period to pick out the ones he saw from a much larger collection, will have trouble recognizing the ones for which his language does not have convenient names.[21] Young Wolof children can more easily discriminate colors for which their language has names, though adult Wolof monolinguals are not limited in this way.[22] It would seem that whatever initial advantage a concentration on one part of the color spectrum may produce is reduced later as more possi-

---

[21] See Landar, Ervin, and Horowitz 1960.
[22] Greenfield and Bruner 1971.

bilities of naming and categorizing are opened up. Other continuums present the same problem across languages—temperature, for example, where English *hot–warm–cool–cold* do not coincide lexically or grammatically with the corresponding terms in other languages.[23] Even with continuums, however, linguistic relativism is not absolute. A study of color categories in numerous languages has revealed that they fall into a rather definite evolutionary sequence. *Black* and *white* are basic and always to be found. Next is *red,* followed by *green* and *yellow,* singly or together; after that *blue,* then *brown,* and finally any combination of *pink, purple, orange,* and *gray.*[24]

According to the authors of the Wolof study, more important than mere naming to the influence of language on thinking is how deeply a language organizes concepts into hierarchies:

> In a way quite different from that envisaged by Whorf, we seem to have found an important correspondence between linguistic and conceptual structure. But it relates not to words in isolation but to their depth of hierarchical imbedding both in language and in thought. This correspondence has to do with the presence or absence of higher-order words that can be used to integrate different domains of words and objects into structures.[25]

Schooling supplies some of this hierarchical organization through displacement (talking about things not present) and writing (which frees words from things), thus providing words that elicit other words and concepts that elicit other concepts. This in turn will "push a certain form of cognitive growth better, earlier and longer than others. . . . Less technical societies do not produce so much symbolic imbedding nor so many ways of looking and thinking."[26] As an example, children who had, as part of their language, a concept such as 'color' were able to classify objects (in tests administered to them) at the same conceptual level in terms of 'shape' and 'use' as well as 'color.' But children who started out by using a lower conceptual level than 'color'—for example, the specific colors 'red' and 'blue'—were unable to use the higher, more abstract classifications.[27] By insisting overmuch on *grammatical* relativism and picking only superficial examples of *lexical* relativism, linguists and anthropologists have perhaps missed the most important cognitive mani-

---

[23] See Prator 1963.

[24] Berlin and Kay 1969. See review by George A. Collier in *Language* 49 (1973), 245–48.

[25] Greenfield and Bruner 1971, p. 77.

[26] Ibid., p. 79.

[27] Ibid., p. 76.

festation of all, the intricacy of lexical organization. It is an area that is only beginning to be studied.

The "semantic differential"

If the lenses of our language that stand between us and reality are slightly warped, they are also tinted. It is one thing to see a certain kind of fish narrowed down to *eel;* it is something slightly different to see eels as repulsive creatures. Yet our language—plus other associations that we *act out* in connection with eels under the tutelage of fellow members of our culture—decrees both things: the focus and the affect. Every term we use apparently has the power to sway us in one direction or another. Experiments on this semantic differential, as it is called by the psychologist Charles E. Osgood and his co-workers, show that persons presented with pairs of antonyms such as *wise–foolish, good–bad, deep–shallow, light–heavy,* and the like will relate other terms in rather consistent ways to each of these extremes, even when there seems to be no logical connection. The technique is to draw a seven-point scale with the antonyms at either end, for example

light  *heavy*

and to give subjects a term such as *skittish* with instructions to locate it at one of the points. While it would not be surprising, in view of associations with other terms such as *lightheaded,* if everyone agreed that *skittish* ought to go well over to the "light" end, what is surprising is that subjects will even agree on where to locate something as apparently outlandish as *wood* on a scale between *severe* and *lenient.*[28]

Osgood has found a number of affective dimensions to which concepts can be related in this way, but the most consistent ones in the more than twenty languages tested are three, which he has labeled "evaluation," "potency," and "activity." Evaluation is by all odds the most predictable: virtually every term and its associated concept seems to attract or repel, however slightly.[29] English even formalizes this to some extent in its system of lexical intensifiers, where *well* and *badly* figure as synonyms of *very (well thought out, well out of danger, well ready, well sufficient; badly bungled, badly needed, badly lacking, badly upset).* Figure 8–1 shows a three-dimensional plot of the three factors E (evaluation), P (potency), and A (activity), on which the antonyms *kind* and *cruel*

---

[28] See Osgood, Suci, and Tannenbaum 1957, and Weinreich 1958.
[29] Osgood 1971.

FIGURE 8–1
Affective Dimensions of <u>Kind</u>, <u>Cruel</u>, and <u>Coward</u>

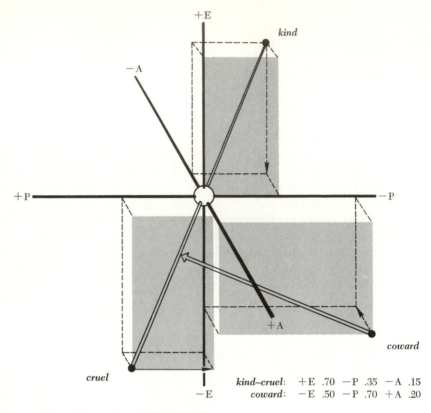

kind–cruel: +E .70 −P .35 −A .15
coward: −E .50 −P .70 +A .20

SOURCE: Adapted from Osgood 1971, p. 15.

and the noun *coward* have been projected. Since **kind** and **cruel** are measurable in terms of all three (**kind** for example is +E, −P, and −A), and *coward* also can be located in the same space, it follows that *coward* can be located with reference to *kind* and *cruel.* In a forced-choice test, we would expect subjects to judge a coward to be slightly cruel, as the arrow in Figure 8–1 indicates.

Does this mean that, in addition to making us see reality in certain shapes and sizes, our language is also one of the most powerful factors in forcing us to take sides? If all the speakers of a given language share a prejudice, language will transmit it. Take for example the associations of insanity. Most of them are "funny": **crazy, nutty, loony, daffy, half-witted, harebrained, loopy,** and so on. They reflect a culture in which psychopathological states are not diseases to be treated but deviations to be laughed at. It has required a vigorous reorientation of our attitudes to put mental disease on a footing other than ridicule or shame so that it *could* be treated. We can excuse language by saying that people use words, words don't use people. But this is like saying that people use guns, guns don't use people—the *availability* of guns is one factor in their use.

The evils of word availability have been impressed on us ever since the women's liberation movement first drew attention to them at the beginning of the 1970s. Language consecrates the subordinate role of women in the loss of surnames at marriage, in the labeling of wed or unwed status by **Mrs.** and **Miss** (marital-status labeling is not required of men), in the greater caution expected of women in speech (women are more "polite" than men), in the many opprobrious names for women[30] (**slut, gossip, crone, hoyden, slattern**—the list is endless), in the contempt attached to **spinster** but not to **bachelor,** and in hosts of other ways. Even an epithet for males is an indirect slap at a female: **son of a bitch.** The network of associations among these verbal habits traps us in a set of attitudes from which we can extricate ourselves only by earnest attention to both the attitudes and the words.

We have learned the dangers of acquiescing in defamation in the past decade or two from the upward struggle of minority groups. This has bred an awareness—and conscious avoidance—of the *unintentional* use of the most obvious slurs, such as the noun **nigger** and the verb **to Jew down.** Hardly anyone in an urban community would unthinkingly call a Brazil nut a **niggertoe.** The taboo extends even to unrelated homophonous terms—for example, **niggardly.** But this is a superficial awareness, and we are only beginning to examine other usages that betray—and at the same time help to transmit—uncritical prior judgments. The white (honky?) who would never think of using the word **nigger** may give himself away by venturing opinions on **the negro problem.** The presupposition here of course is that problems are to be identified and defined in white terms—the speaker who uses this phrase is shocked if someone retorts that it is rather **a white problem.** At the same time there are growing signs of a deeper understanding. The very existence of such an expression as **If you're not part of the solution you're part of the problem** shows an awareness of the impertinence of assuming that one has the right to stand outside the process and judge it or manipulate it. The mere presence in the language of the phrase **self-fulfilling prophecy** shows an acceptance of the theory that it is possible, by predicting an event, to influence behavior in a way that will bring the event about. Language to some extent records our intellectual maturity.

---

[30] See Stanley 1972 (2).

In a society that accepts slavery as a normal condition of existence, terms for 'slave' and "low" forms of service will be used unthinkingly with opprobrious meanings: *slavey, caitiff, varlet, scullion, ragpicker, menial, lackey, flunkey, cad, churl, villain.* Such a society may even be enlightened by other standards; the democracy of ancient Greece, it has been said, was "carried on the backs of slaves." If the consensus within the society is such that the institution and the terms associated with it are never questioned, the two will perpetuate each other and language will help to mold the attitudes of its users. On the other hand, a competitive society results in competing values, and some measure of neutrality is thereby achieved. Language is used by all parties to every controversy, Republicans and Communists, atheists and religionists, militarists and pacifists; by being pulled in all directions it is forced to remain more or less impartial.

A better term would be *potentially* impartial. If people use language to get the cooperation of their fellows, then little if anything that is ever said is entirely neutral; communication is more often to influence than to inform. From the orator or advertising man who calculatingly chooses expressions that will sway his audience to the scientist who in his enthusiasm over his discovery calls it *proof* or *an important departure,* every speaker is guilty of decorating his information. And since everyone does it, the devices for doing it inhere in the language and are hard to avoid even when we try.

If accusing language of this form of seduction seems a strange idea, we can trace our surprise once more to the false importance that our culture gives to writing. Some degree of impartiality can be achieved in print. But in speech we must contend with intonation and its running emotional commentary, insinuating whether we like what we say, whether it is said to persuade or command or to abase ourselves or overawe another; and some elements are always more highly colored and stand out as more important than others. Leaving this out, as writing manages to do in part, creates the illusion of uncolored fact. The colors are still there, only paler.

What distinguishes the world-view distortion that we saw in English versus Hopi from the suasive coloring that we are considering now is that the first manifested an indeterminacy of *things* with respect to *language,* while the second manifests an indeterminacy of *language* with respect to *things.* In the first, the very form and substance with which reality is revealed to us was affected; in the second, within a single language a given bit of reality can be *presented* in more than one way. Both processes are normally unconscious, but the first is seldom otherwise, while the second may be not only conscious but deliberately and often maliciously cultivated. The degree of consciousness corresponds fairly well with the grading of linguistic devices from crude to subtle, from straightforward lexical name-calling to the hidden bias of a syntactical construction.

CONTROL THROUGH LANGUAGE

Naming

As we inherit our nouns—and the categorizations of reality that they represent—we also inherit the right to *make* nouns, which is one of the few truly inventive privileges that our language affords us: anyone can make up a name for something and many people do, while inventing a new suffix or a new syntactic pattern is practically impossible.

The act of naming, with all we have seen it to imply in the way of solidifying and objectifying experience, becomes one of our most powerful suasive tools, enabling us to create entities practically out of nothing. The speaker who says *We want no undesirables around here* projects his inner dislikes onto the outer world. Turning *undesirable* into a noun makes it possible to avoid a clearly tautological *We don't want the people we don't want.* A noun tells us, "It is there; it is something that can or ought to be dealt with." As long as people were left to their own resources to find things to do, 'being without work' was generally a matter of choice or ability; when large numbers of people became dependent upon industry, the condition was objectified as *unemployment.* We are used to having *things* about us; naming reassures us that the elusive threat has been cornered:

> I learned a useful trick from a certain noted doctor. I wondered how he got by without the criticism I encountered when I failed in an attempt to get fluid from the pleural cavity. Occasionally, following pneumonia or pleurisy, fluid will accumulate between the lung and the chest wall, giving such discomfort that it must be drawn off. Whenever I tapped a side and failed to find what I was looking for, the patient or relatives would question my skill, but the noted doctor seemed to be able to create increased confidence, even if he failed to find the fluid.
>
> I finally learned his secret, when I had an opportunity to call him in consultation on a case of suspected pus in the pleural cavity. He asked for a hollow needle, and pierced the chest wall several times without getting a drop. With an air of satisfaction, he turned to the patient and parents, and exclaimed, "Ah, great! I've got it!"
>
> "What is it, doctor?" cried the interested ones.

"A dry tap! A dry tap! Splendid! Better than I expected!" The patient and relatives said, "Isn't it wonderful? A dry tap." Everybody was happy, and the noted doctor remained noted.[31]

The importance of the name, rather than the real virtues, of a commercial product is proved by the long record of litigation over trade names like *aspirin* and *cola.* One of the great triumphs of modern advertising has been to condition the public to accept the fabricated name-entities of commerce—to ask for Clorox rather than sodium hypochlorite, for Snarol instead of metaldehyde—or any other of those "active ingredients" that appear in microscopic yellow letters on an orange background at the low corner of the back label of the product. Consumer advocates have tried with some success to battle the advertisers in the drug industry by persuading doctors to use generic names in their prescriptions. All such efforts are handicapped by the unpronounceability of scientific terms. Advertising performs a service by cutting through the naming habits of scientists—at a price.

Favorable and unfavorable naming: epithets

Over and above the mere fact of naming—which already to some extent prejudices the case—is the clearly prejudicial application of epithets, terms that are crudely and frankly favorable or unfavorable. We find them in all four of the "content" parts of speech—nouns, adjectives, verbs, and adverbs—and they operate at all levels of awareness; but in general the adjective and adverb are more aboveboard than the noun or the verb. If someone says *That wretched picture bored me to death,* the hearer can deal with the detachable adjective and, if he likes, replace it: *I didn't think it was wretched; I thought it was interesting.* Similarly with *He deliberately insulted me*—the hearer is free to substitute *But perhaps he did it unintentionally.* The adjective and adverb are a kind of simile, an overt and explicit attachment of one idea to another. The noun and verb are metaphors: the comparison is smuggled in, the person or thing or act is not *like* something good or bad but *is* that something. It is no coincidence that many epithets actually are metaphors of fairly recent memory: *He is a bum, He is a prince, She is an angel, She is a tramp, She cackled, He brayed.*

Epithets form a special part of the lexicon not only because of their function—to insinuate a comparison without the hearer's being aware of it—but also because of their grammar. The sentence *The comedy displeased me* is normal because *comedy* designates something. The sen-

[31] J. A. Jerger, M.D., "City Doctor," *American Magazine* (February 1939).

tence *The folly displeased me* is not normal because *folly* does not designate, it only describes. *His folly displeased me* is normal because it contains a hidden sentence in which *folly* is the predicate: *his folly* = 'he did something that was folly (foolish).' The subjectiveness of epithets shows up in constructions with infinitives. We can say *He is a shyster to treat his friends that way,* since *shyster* embodies a subjective judgment. We do not say *He is a lawyer to treat his friends that way,* since that kind of statement is felt to be objective; but it becomes normal if something is added to show that it is an opinion, a subjective judgment, such as *must be, I would say he is,* or a very emphatic intonation: *He must be a lawyer to treat his friends that way.*[32]

The hidden temptations that the lexicon offers the average user of the language are practically irresistible. Most of the areas of our experience are mapped out epithetically, and the person who wants to steer a middle course has to keep his eye constantly on the narrow and shifting channel between good and bad. The most insidious examples are not the ordinary antonyms like *clumsy–graceful, easy–difficult,* or *democratic–fascistic* but terms that are synonyms in that they name the same objective fact, yet antonyms in the attitude that they solicit toward the fact:

Favorable	*Quasi-neutral*	*Unfavorable*
upright, righteous, virtuous		goody-goody, puritanical, sissy
conciliation		appeasement
patriotism		chauvinism, jingoism
defense		militarization
farsighted, man of vision		visionary, starry-eyed idealist
brilliant		show-off
smile		leer
indoctrination		brainwashing
man Friday	assistant	lackey
loyalty	adherence	partisanship
intercede	intervene	interfere, butt in
bachelor girl	single woman	old maid, spinster
the good things of life	luxuries	extravagances
venerable	old	old-fashioned, superannuated
innovative	new	newfangled

The hidden temptations are embraced openly in commerce and poli-

---

[32] See Bolinger 1972 and 1973.

tics. The following excerpt from a sales publication advises how to put
a customer's suspicions at rest:

> An alert real estate salesman should learn how to express himself and
> use psychology. . . . Don't say *down payment;* say *initial investment.* Don't
> ask for a listing; ask for an *authorization to sell.* Don't say *second mort-
> gage;* say *perhaps we can find additional financing.* Don't use the term
> *contract;* have them sign a *proposal* or *offer.* . . . Don't use the word *lot;*
> call it a *homesite.* Don't say *sign here;* say *write your name as you want it
> to appear on your deed.*[33]

As for politics, a study of some twenty thousand lines of Soviet newspaper text showed the highest frequency of concepts relating to the
Soviet bloc to be, in this order: *solidarity* (with various synonyms, such
as *unity* and *brotherhood), building the future, peace, growth (development,* etc.), *greatness, struggle,* and *tasks (obligations, historic mission);*
and the highest relating to the West to be *aggression (war-mongering),
colonization, imperialist, oppression, encroachment on freedom, international tension,* and *reactionary.*[34] On the other side of the world the
greatest flowering of scented words has been in connection with military
operations:

> Bombing is *protective reaction, precision bombing* is *surgical strikes,*
> concentration camps are *pacification centers* or *refugee camps.* . . . Bombs
> dropped outside the target area are *incontinent ordnance,* and those
> dropped on one of your own villages are excused as *friendly fire;* a bombed
> house becomes automatically a *military structure* and a lowly sampan
> sunk on the waterfront a *waterborne logistic craft.*[35]

Not all the self-serving uses of words are quite so Augean as these
examples, and of course politics is only one of the stables. When those
who opposed Hitlerism before 1941 were later dismissed as *premature
anti-fascists* the inspiration was political. But a school administration that
prefers not to pay the going rate for Ph.D.'s may persuade itself that
Ph.D.'s are *overqualified,* and the motive then is business. And when the
ordinary citizen excuses himself from nobility by saying that someone
who gives up his life for an ideal must have a *martyr complex,* the motive is personal. We are good at believing our own rationalizations.

---

[33] *The Sonoma County Realtor,* Santa Rosa, California. Quoted in *Consumer Reports*
 (October 1972), p. 626.

[34] Oppenheimer 1961–62.

[35] Commager 1972, p. 11.

Elevation and degradation

Since the epithet is language aimed at the heart of social action, it is bound to receive from the culture as well as give to it. While we are not concerned here with semantic change—that is a question of the evolution of language—but rather with the existence at any one time of linguistic forms that influence us, it is pertinent to note how the stock of terms with favorable or unfavorable connotations is maintained against the social realities that undermine it. Two processes are at work, or rather two directions of a single process, which are generally called *elevation* and *degradation*. If for reasons that have little or nothing to do with language a thing that has carried an unfavorable name begins to move up in the world, the name moves up with it. In religion, many once-opprobrious names have faded. Probably the majority of religious eponyms—names imitating the personal name of the founder—were to begin with unfavorable. But many were in time adopted by the followers of the religion (**Christian, Lutheran, Calvinist**); others have become milder (**Campbellite**); and few but the most recent might still be resented (**Russellite, Buchmanite**).

The opposite effect is observed in the negative associations of a term attached to something that moves down. The most prolific source of negative connotation and of the constant replacement of terms that are downgraded is the phenomenon of social *taboo*. The taboo against strong language results in minced oaths: **darn** for **damn, gee** for **Jesus.** The taboo against referring to certain bodily functions results in a succession of replacements, each term being discarded as it too vividly and nontechnically comes to suggest its referent: H. L. Mencken listed two pages of synonyms for **latrine,**[36] itself borrowed as a polite word from French (it originally meant the same as one of its modern substitutes, 'washroom'). What was a denatured term for one generation ceases to be for the next one, as the direct association with the buried taboo reasserts itself.

The denaturing process is called *euphemism* (see page 440). The most familiar examples are the political euphemisms, some of which have already been listed. When destroying a city is called **taking out** a city, an innocent term is substituted for a wicked one. Ordinary noncommercial and nonpolitical euphemisms, which cover our nakedness and other shortcomings, are often humorous: the plea is not to elevation but to tolerance. **Belly** becomes, besides the elevated **abdomen,** the facetious **paunch, corporation, bay window,** and **embonpoint. A libertine** is a **wolf.** The synonyms of **drunk** have proliferated to the point where a

---

[36] Mencken 1945, pp. 640–41.

nonsense word inserted in the blank of *He was just a little bit* _____ will suggest it.

Euphemism is not restricted to the lexicon. There are grammatical ways of toning something down without actually changing the content of the message. Take the two sentences *He has been known to take a bribe now and then* and *He is known to have taken a bribe now and then.* Both report the same events, and the verb *know* is "factive" in both cases—that is, it is not used unless the complement is regarded as true. Yet the first sentence, by suggesting less immediacy, is milder.

Hints and associations

The ordinary epithet or euphemism is a bludgeon. True finesse is found among the less obvious loaded terms that hint rather than designate. Here the semantic differential comes into its own. The associated term is not obviously epithetical and therefore gets past our guard; but it is colored, darkly or brightly, and the color rubs off.

The lexicon abounds in loosely associated semantic sets having intimate ties with codes and practices in society, which for lack of a better name will be called *norm classes.* They comprise a catalog of "fors" and "againsts" to which we pay unthinking and often ritualistic respect. The norm classes—the associated word sets—are enough by themselves to invoke this respect. Merely mentioning one of the words will command it.[37]

Since human circumstances are always particular, never general, the problem with any particular act, in order to give it a place in a well-regulated society, is to fit it to the proper symbol. The extreme case is that of interpretative law: a homicide has been committed; the jurors must determine whether it was *self-defense* or *murder. Self-defense* belongs to the norm class of *preservation of life, a man's house is his castle, resistance to aggression,* and so on. *Murder* belongs to that of *destruction of life, taking the law into one's own hands, disobedience to the Commandments,* and so on.

A less dramatic example is the norm class of *clothed (covered, decent, modest)* versus that of *naked (exposed, immodest, exhibitionist).* As beach attire has grown scantier and scantier, bathers can be said to be approaching a state of nakedness (as streakers can be said to have attained

---

[37] Mills 1940 dubbed the cruder manifestations of norm classes "vocabularies of motive." The ideas that embody or are embodied in the complex of norm classes and the social norms themselves were called "idols" by Francis Bacon, and more recently have been termed "symbols" by Franz Boas (*The Nation* [27 August 1938], p. 203), Howe Martin ("Symbolism in Advertising," *Frontier* [January 1967], pp. 9–11), and others.

it); yet the emphasis is on the fact that they do have something on, and this has usually been enough to prevent legal interference. And we may be sure that if ever the last vestige is permanently cast off, it will be in the name of *nature (Praxiteles, Michelangelo, the nobility of the human figure)*, not of *nakedness.*

Very early in life the child is made aware that he is expected to justify himself; in the average home, by the time he is able to talk, almost every youngster faces the inquisition of *Why did you do it?* after any willful act. Propriety is served almost as well, it would seem, by our picking the right norm class for what was done thoughtlessly as by thoughtfully choosing the right behavior in the first place; and in the course of time we become quite expert at it. If we admire Russian communism, we call it the Russian *experiment,* attaching it to the norm class of *scientific investigation, withholding judgment until results are in, condoning temporary mistakes,* and so on. If we disapprove of reparations payments to Cuba, we call them *ransom,* which suggests both *kidnaping* and *cowardice.* Where the American public might have condemned dispatching *troops* to Nicaragua in 1927, no excitement was aroused by the sending of *marines;* the word had romantic associations.[38] Hitting upon the right norm class gives the emotional release of discovery, and skill at doing it is esteemed: the person accused of running up a *white flag* wins the argument by saying that he ran up a *white banner.*

A frequently used shift of norm class involves substituting a *physical* context for a *social* one—an instance of the fallacy of reduction. A man interfering with police work by erasing the chalk marks left by a traffic officer might say that he was only *rubbing off white stuff;* one arrested for profanity might justify the offense as an act of *merely emitting sounds.* The classical example of the fallacy of reduction is *The table in front of you is only atoms.*

Code switching

A speaker may change styles—"switch codes"[39]—to put himself closer to his hearer. His purpose then is to get all the obstacles out of the path of his message. If I am an English-speaking Canadian who knows some French and live in a bilingual part of Canada I may use French even with French speakers who know English, if that will facilitate our communication. But not all instances of code switching are aimed at clearing the channel. Some may actually obstruct it, though they serve other pur-

---

[38] Frederick Alexander Kirkpatrick, *Latin America, a Brief History* (New York: Macmillan, 1939), p. 371.
[39] See pages 340–45 for discussion.

poses—solidarity, social distance, prestige, concealment, and so on. A speaker or writer may switch codes with deliberate intent to deceive. An instance—referred to at the time as a masterpiece of public-relations technique—occurred in the Second World War when General George Patton was criticized by his commander-in-chief, Dwight Eisenhower. A spokesman for Allied Headquarters in Algiers covered this up by announcing that "General Patton had never at any time been reprimanded by General Eisenhower." In the Army code, *to reprimand* is to administer an official rebuke as a punishment, and it follows strict rules of disciplinary procedure. Naturally the public took the word in its more general sense.

A more commonplace variety of code switching is designed not only to disguise but to impress. Sometimes what is disguised is mere emptyheadedness—one is expected to say something, and says nothing while making it sound like something. But often it is the unpalatability of the message, which is glossed over with high-sounding phrases, a kind of euphemism on a large scale. *Officialese* is the name usually given to this code as used by bureaucrats and writers of official reports, whose strivings yield such things as ***It is imperative that the present directive be effectuated expeditiously,*** where the meaning is ***Do it now.*** One famous example was the order concerning blackouts during the Second World War, submitted to President Roosevelt for his approval:

> Such preparations shall be made as will completely obscure all Federal buildings and non-Federal buildings occupied by the Federal Government during an air raid for any period of time from visibility by reason of internal or external illumination. Such obscuration may be obtained either by blackout construction or by termination of the illumination. This will, of course, require that in building areas in which production must continue during the blackout, construction must be provided that internal illumination may continue. Other areas, whether or not occupied by personnel, may be obscured by terminating the illumination.

The President amended this to:

> Tell them that in buildings where they have to keep the work going, to put something across the window. In buildings where they can afford to let the work stop for a while, turn out the lights.[40]

Theodore Roszak has this to say about officialese applied to unpalatable messages:

> When knowledgeable men talk, they no longer talk of substances and accidents, of being and spirit, of virtue and vice, of sin and salvation, of

---

[40] Associated Press dispatch (11 March 1942).

deities and demons. Instead, we have a vocabulary filled with nebulous quantities of things that have every appearance of precise calibration, and decorated with vaguely mechanistic-mathematical terms like *parameters, structures, variables, inputs* and *outputs, correlations, inventories, maximizations,* and *optimizations....* The more such language and numerology one packs into a document, the more 'objective' the document becomes— which normally means the less morally abrasive to the sources that have subsidized the research.[41]

Feeling that such obfuscatory codes were practically becoming institutionalized, the National Council of Teachers of English set up in 1972 a "Committee on Public Doublespeak" to try to do something about them. In 1974 it was searching for the coiners of such terms as *combat emplacement evacuator* ('shovel'), *civilian irregular defense soldier* ('mercenary'), *to destabilize* ('to subvert'), *pupil stations* ('desks'), and *learning resource centers* ('libraries') as possible recipients of an annual Orwellian Award.[42]

Americans have perhaps been more severely bitten by aspirations of grandeur than other speakers of English. At least, its symptoms have been with us for a long time and its condemnation likewise. James Fenimore Cooper remarked that the man of true breeding "does not say, in speaking of a dance, that 'the attire of the ladies was exceedingly elegant and peculiarly becoming at the late assembly,' but 'the women were well dressed at the last ball'; nor is he apt to remark, that 'the Rev. Mr. G_____ gave us an elegant and searching discourse the past sabbath,' but, that 'the parson preached a good sermon last Sunday.'"[43] Cooper himself was no angel of clarity. In *The Last of the Mohicans* he wrote, "Without any aid from the science of cookery, he was immediately employed, in common with his fellows, in gorging himself with this digestible sustenance." Mark Twain chided him:

> This was a mere statistic; just a mere cold, colorless statistic; yet you see Cooper has made a chromo out of it.... Cooper spent twenty-four words here on a thing not really worth more than eight. We will reduce the statistic to its proper proportions and state it this way: "He and the others ate the meat raw."[44]

---

[41] *The Making of a Counter Culture* (Garden City, N.Y.: Doubleday, Anchor Books, 1968), pp. 142–43.

[42] *Newsweek* (25 March 1974), p. 108.

[43] Quoted by Mathews 1961, p. 127. See also James Thurber, "The Psychosemanticist Will See You Now, Mr. Thurber," *New Yorker* (28 May 1955), pp. 28–31; and Ethel Strainchamps, "Caveat Scriptor," *Harper's Magazine* (August 1960), pp. 24–27.

[44] *Letters from the Earth* (New York: Harper & Row, 1962), p. 140.

Officialese has its stereotypes, which are designed to impress. But its success is also due to another quirk of human nature, our willingness to accept complication for profundity. Where profound thoughts make for hard words, hard words pass for profound thoughts.

Non-neutrality in grammar

Words are plentiful enough to supply all needs, suasive and other. We are not surprised when many turn out to have suasion as the main reason for their existence.

Grammar has too much else to do, and cannot be specialized for any non-neutral purpose. Nevertheless, certain grammatical devices lend themselves better than others to suasive language, mostly because of what they leave unsaid. This is especially true of what one linguist has termed *syntactic exploitation.*[45] Here are two examples:

1. The deleted agent of the passive. A well-known nature program on television has the slogan **Man protects threatened animals.** It does not say by what or by whom the animals are threatened, but the content of the program makes it clear that man himself is the threatener. The slogan gives credit while concealing blame. One English verb is even stereotyped in this way, without an agent: **to be supposed to,** as in **John was supposed to be here at ten o'clock.** By whom was he supposed? We are expected to assume some Higher Obligation, transcending the whims of mere individuals. Newspaper headlines take advantage of the absence of the agent to slant a piece of news: instead of **Board Member Accuses Principal of Misconduct,** the item is made to sound more sinister by being worded **Principal Accused of Misconduct**—the reader infers that the principal is being accused by more than just one person.

2. "Experiencer deletion."[46] Certain impersonal verbs carry with them a reference to a personal standpoint, that of the one who undergoes the experience. Typical verbs are *seem, appear,* and *strike*—for example, **It strikes me that he is asking too much.** *Strike* requires that the experiencer be named: we cannot say **It strikes that he is asking too much.* But *seem* and *appear* offer a choice: **It seems (to me) that he is asking too much.** Not mentioning the experiencer may make it appear that indefinite numbers of experiencers are involved. And by the device of "subject raising" a human subject may be promoted in place of *it* and the

---

[45] See Stanley 1972 (1).
[46] Smith 1974.

responsibility placed on him rather than on the experiencer: *It seems to me that John is lying* becomes *John seems to be lying,* and *It is certain* (in my view) *that John is lying* becomes *John is certain to be lying.* Other examples: *It is obvious* (to whom?) *that . . . , It is a known fact* (known to whom?) *that, Clearly she . . .*

Suasive syntax exploits many other forms, innocent and necessary in themselves but deceptive when misapplied. The subject of a sentence is the *actor* often enough to create an expectation, and this enables speakers to excuse themselves from responsibility by getting out of the actor slot and putting something or someone else there. *This thing won't work* (*fit,* etc.) is a common way of referring to one's own ineptitude with a physical or mechanical object. In describing an automobile accident a speaker may say *I was driving down the street when all of a sudden that other guy drove right across my path,* or *I was driving along when all of a sudden that other guy came right at me from a side street;* either way the speaker wins—the responsibility is on the other fellow. In some places the lexicon dovetails with the grammar in letting us off the hook. There are pairs like *fall–drop* and *escape–forget:* instead of *I dropped it* and *I forgot it* we can say *It fell* (out of my hands) and *It escaped me* (slipped my mind). Many verbs give a choice between transitive and intransitive, making it possible to say *It broke* (on me) and *It tripped me* instead of *I broke it* and *I tripped over it.* The *get* passive is often used in this way: *The dishes got broken* rather than *I broke the dishes.* The Mexican-American writer Enrique López points out the standard way in Spanish of avoiding responsibility. He calls it the "exculpatory reflexive": *Se me hizo tarde,* said by someone late for an appointment, literally means 'It got late on me.'[47] One child psychologist advises saying such things as *I see the milk is spilled* rather than *You spilled the milk,* which puts the child too much on the defensive.[48]

Hidden sentences are another complex of devices necessary to economy in language but open to deceptive use, comprising various sorts of unstated propositions. We have already seen one—and its possibilities for deception—in the grammar of epithets: *He hired a fool* does not mean that he hired a person belonging to a recognized class of fools the way *He hired a mechanic* means that he hired a person belonging to the recognized class of mechanics—rather it means that he hired 'someone who was a fool.' The speaker does not come out and frankly state his case but cuts corners and assumes that his hearer will agree with him. In a sentence such as *Did you see that pornographic movie?* the modifier *pornographic* says something about *movie* which is left implicit: that the

---

[47] Guadalajara, Mexico, newspaper (March 1974).

[48] Haim G. Ginott, *Between Parent and Child* (New York: Macmillan, 1965), pp. 44–45. Reference from Robert Kirsner.

movie *is* pornographic. When we do not have to be explicit about our propositions we may be too relaxed about where we put them; we attach a modifier at the most obvious grammatical juncture and trust to luck that the hearer will understand where it belongs: **She's lost her first tooth** for 'She's had her first loss of a tooth,' **Put on some warm clothing** for 'Put on some clothing that will keep you warm,' or **There is a definite shortage** for 'There is definitely a shortage.' This makes it possible to refer to a **careless mistake** and spare the feelings of a **careless person** who makes a mistake, or to say **uncertain origin** when we want to gloss over the fact that origins are never uncertain but people are often uncertain about them.

Grammatical ambiguity can be of many kinds, and is heavily relied upon in dishonest advertising. In a sentence such as **Athletes have found chewing a natural aid to high-speed effort** the indefinite subject can be taken to mean either 'some athletes' or 'all athletes'; the advertiser is legally protected by the first meaning and lets us infer the second. Lexical ambiguities lend themselves to the same kind of abuse. One refiner has taken advantage of the fact that there is no legal definition of **brown sugar,** only a general understanding that it is made from cane, in order to market a brown-*colored* beet sugar.

Little needs to be said about the suasive use of elements smaller than words—contributions to this level are actually to the lexicon of epithets. Certain affixes are used mainly in coining words that are epithetical, and a few of them are so clearly identified with this use that they have graduated to the status of words themselves: the **pros,** the **antis,** and **ism,** alongside of the properly affixal use in such words as **pro-Arab, anti-religion, McCarthyism.** One suffix that can hardly be identified with suasion but is much used in epithets, especially in connection with a certain type of compound, is **-er** (alternative **-or**). The epithetical use trades on a fraudulent association. Most often this suffix means 'a professional, habitual agent':[49] a **singer** is one who sings professionally, an **actor** one who acts, a **bookseller** one who sells books. The epithet adopts this for things that are not occupations, implying that the person stigmatized does them as consistently as if they were: **woman-chaser, hymnsinger, troublemaker, Bible-banger, mudslinger.** Typically these epithets are parasynthetic compounds, formed by composition **(Bible + bang)** and derivation **(bang + -er)** at the same time. They are not all suasive— **mountain-climber** and **moneylender** are neutral—but enough of them are to encourage the constant creation of new ones when we feel like calling someone a bad name. Now and then an **-er** word is applied to someone who is guilty of only a single act, as if to imply 'This act, like an occupation, brands indelibly.' So a person who deserts just once is a

---

[49] Marchand 1966, p. 138.

deserter or a *defector;* one who commits only one murder is a *murderer.*

Though it is out of place here, we may note an identical use of the perfect tense, which is normally 'indefinite' as to time and whose indefiniteness is capitalized upon to suggest persistence of effects. Of a man who was in jail once, we say *He has been in jail,* no matter how long ago it was. We would not say *He is suing because he has been turned away from that hotel* if the situation is that he was turned away two years ago; but we might well say *He is suing because he has been accused of disloyalty* when the accusation was two years in the past— that is something that puts its brand on a person.

If we look beyond words and propositions to the non-verbal parts of communicative acts we find much in gesture that is suasive and even more in intonation. Questions and commands solicit actions on the part of others, and are the utterances most clearly demarcated by intonation; but statements too may insist or wheedle.

Truth

A study of the uses of suasion makes us realize that probably the most important ingredient of communication is the attitude of the communicators toward each other: an intention on the part of the speaker not to misinform, and good will on the part of the hearer in trying to interpret as the speaker intends. Literal truth is not enough, if for no other reason than because there is so much about language that is always present but only vaguely inferred and scarcely subject to definition. Take for example the simple matter of coordination in a sentence and the matter of the sequence of the items coordinated, and what we infer from those two things. Coordination implies 'These items are on the same level': we do not say *°He is an embezzler and a lover of horses,* even though each part of the coordination taken separately may be true. As for sequence, if there is a possibility of inferring one item from another we normally place first the one on which the inference can be based: *The clock is accurate and dependable* is more likely than *The clock is dependable and accurate; The house is broken down and uninhabitable* is more likely than *The house is uninhabitable and broken down.* So when a certain brand of meal puts on its package the statement *Enriched and degerminated,* it is falsifying on both counts. Enrichment and degermination do not belong on the same level, and nothing about degermination can be inferred from enrichment. The reader is tricked into regarding degermination, which he only vaguely grasps anyway, as a virtue. A truthful statement would read, "We are ashamed to say that in order to keep the stuff from spoiling we had to remove the germ, but we *did* add some synthetic vitamins to compensate for the loss."

There was a time not long ago when a noted linguist could declare, "The grammatical rules of a language are independent of any scale of values, logical, esthetic, or ethical."[50] That was before students of language became interested in what lies beyond the sentence; we now realize that understanding language includes understanding the circumstances of its use. The question of appropriateness to external facts is as relevant as that of appropriateness to classes of speakers or appropriateness to the occasion of speaking. If one were to state rules defining an appropriate conversational situation, two of them would have to be that a speaker assumes that his hearer will believe what he says, and the corollary that the hearer expects what is being communicated to be true.[51] There are monologs, such as the telling of jokes, and interchanges, such as coercive interrogation, where the rules are suspended; but these are not conversations. What modern linguistics makes clear is that a new definition of truth is in order. We know the many ways in which sentences can be tucked away in other sentences so that they communicate almost subliminally; and we know the many faces of ambiguity, and how they can be turned into disguises. The only sensible definition of a lie is an utterance that is intended to deceive, and the best definition of truth is that which is intended not to deceive (and is not simply erroneous). This brings truth down from the stratosphere and makes it a product of our efforts.

Not that our instincts are always a help to our better selves. A language that would enable us to report things as they are and that would be used by speakers without the infusion of their own personalities and prejudices is the ideal of every science; and every science has to some extent developed a denatured language to make this possible. But whether our human condition will permit it to be realized generally is doubtful. If Whorf was right, we do not grasp things as they are but always to some extent as our language presents them to us—or, in broader terms, as our society incorporates them in terms of all its habits of acting and talking. And as for avoiding the body heat of our likes and dislikes, the irony is that scientific language itself takes on authoritative overtones. The moment it finds its way into general use, we are plagued as much by pseudo-scientific pretentiousness as by any other form of non-neutrality. It would seem that language is bound to be suasive as long as it is human, that the effort to be neutral cannot be carried out in the language as a whole but must represent a will and a purpose in each small act of speech.

---

[50] Hjelmslev 1961, p. 110.
[51] Lakoff 1972, p. 916.

ADDITIONAL REMARKS AND APPLICATIONS

1. Discuss the question reportedly asked by a little girl, **What if they gave a war and nobody came?**

2. How important is naming something to knowledge of it? Imagine yourself having the following experience that most people have at some time or other. You are tramping through the woods and come across a flower that you admire but can't name. You feel frustrated and reproach yourself for "ignorance of" the flower. You are free to examine it closely and perhaps to describe it more fully than any layman ever has before, yet you still feel that something vital is missing. Describe your predicament in terms of names as part of an organized system.

3. How might language be one basis for animistic religion? What would be the concluding sentence in the following proportion?

   The man moves   :   The man sleeps   : :   The sun moves   :

4. Does the grammar of the word **truth** reveal anything about the way we view it as an entity? Decide which of the following are normal and see what conclusions you can draw:

   "Why do you believe it?"—"Because it is a fact."

   —"Because it is a truth."

   —"Because it is the fact."

   —"Because it is the truth."

5. When a complex issue presents itself and we say **What's the answer?** does the use of **the** perpetuate an oversimplification?

6. As an example of the thingness of nouns, take the word *language.* See if you agree with one linguist who warns against

   the unrealistic assumption that a language is a "thing," a quasi-physical object floating around in space, clearly bounded and relatively stable. Observe how we metaphorically set off one language against another, saying that languages can displace each other, retreat, get mixed; on the other hand, they can also "drift," like a river; we "acquire" and "handle" a language, switch from one to another, etc.[53]

7. Compare the following two statements and comment on the view of time and activity they imply:

    a. He gave me more time to finish the work.

    b. He allowed me to consummate later.

8. Even where a category thoroughly permeates a language structure, it may have little or no semantic value. In the Romance languages, for example, *gender* affects nouns and adjectives and has a certain semantic basis in words that actually discriminate according to sex (*mother,* feminine; *soldier,* masculine). For speakers of these languages would words like *table, house, vision,* which are feminine, or *foot, tree, danger,* which are masculine, carry a sexual connotation?

9. Claims are often made about the "genius of a language," based on trivial differences in vocabulary. A British poet residing in Japan wrote a pleasant essay, "First Times for the Japanese," picturing them as having a quaint special regard for first encounters (like the storekeeper who gives superstitious attention to his first customer). He drew his conclusions from the frequency with which *first time* appears in Japanese and in English translations from Japanese.[53] Actually the Japanese expression, *Hajimete-desu-ka*—literally 'first time/be/question,' or 'Is this the first time . . . ?'—is the equivalent of English *Have you ever . . . ?*[54] Does the fact that South Americans call a screwdriver *atornillador* ('screw-driver') while Spaniards call it *destornillador* ('screw-remover') prove that South Americans are more constructive?

10. Imagine that a visitor from Manchester, England, is involved in a traffic accident in Los Angeles, California, and has to explain his actions to a policeman. In some ways they understand each other, but communication is imperfect. Explain what makes it possible for them to communicate, and also what makes it difficult in some respects. Do not be satisfied with a simplistic answer such as "They both speak English." What is there about sharing our worlds that makes language work at all? How do we arrive at approximations of the "same

---

[52] Pap 1972.

[53] James Kirkup, *The Year of Japan* (Tokyo: Asahi Press, 1971), pp. 27–37.

[54] Reference and comment from Kazuo Kato, personal communication.

meanings"? How much can a translator of the *Aeneid* give of what a Roman felt who read those lines?

Take a paragraph from a newspaper and pick out words and expressions that only someone familiar with your culture (town, state, region, country) could grasp in their entirety.[55]

11. See if you can find sets like *stand–sit–lie, walk–run, fog–mist–drizzle–sprinkle–rain–downpour–deluge,* where another language would be likely to carve up the continuum in a different way.

12. How do you feel about the insistence of women's liberation on replacing *Mrs.* and *Miss* with *Ms.?* How does the repetition of *he or she* instead of the "common gender" *he* strike you, as in *Everybody is entitled to do as he or she thinks right?* Instead of admiring someone's *horsemanship* should we admire his or her *horsepersonship*— or is this a snide question? Even before women's liberation, what had already happened to such terms as *authoress, schoolmistress,* and *aviatrix?* Why do you suppose the same thing has not happened to *actress*—or would you perhaps even here say *She is a good actor?* (Or would you say both *She is a good actor* and *She is a good actress,* with a difference—has the taboo caused a split in the meaning?)

13. Comment on the following names given to non-industrialized societies or nations: *savage, uncivilized, backward, underdeveloped, developing, emerging.* The term for lower-priced passage on common carriers used to be *second class.* What is it now? Why the change? Check the relationship between *third class* and *steerage.*

14. A number of colleges and universities are abandoning the system of academic "credits" as a way of measuring the work done by students. What might some of their objections be to keeping *credit* as an entity among our realities? Since credits were said to be "earned" and money is also "earned," can similar objections be raised to *money?*

15. As a way of bringing psychological abnormalities down to earth, where they could be treated medically, people were encouraged to regard "lunatics" as "the mentally ill." One term that was pressed into use was *sick,* replacing *crazy, loony,* etc. What has happened to *sick* as a result? (Suppose someone is annoyed with your attitude and says *Oh, you're sick!*)

---

[55] See Lakoff 1975.

16. A decorated Vietnam soldier who had deserted the army and gone to Canada declared on a radio talk show (San Francisco, 29 August 1974), *I am not a deserter, I deserted.* What is the linguistic basis for his claim?

17. Comment on the following: "When a crime is committed by someone else, the average citizen wants to know all about it; he calls that Free Press. But when he himself is involved in a crime, the average citizen wants it kept out of the papers; he calls that Fair Trial."[56]

18. On 8 August 1974 callers on radio talk shows had much to say about the future of Richard Nixon. Two opposite themes kept recurring: *equal justice under law* and *Don't kick a man when he's down.* What do these themes represent, and how were they being used?

19. Discuss how the norm class of "teamwork" and "cooperation" is used suasively. Does the person who says *We want you to cooperate with us* really mean that he wants to reciprocate by cooperating with you? What does *cooperate* literally mean?

20. Are *commitment* (promise) and *truth* associated in the same norm class in our society? If someone promises you to do something and does not keep his promise, might you say to him *You lied to me— you said you were going to and you didn't?* Consider the ingredients of a promise as a *prediction* (of one's future action) and an *intention* (of performing it). Is there a difference between this and other meanings of *truth?*

21. Comment on the words *conscript–draftee–trainee–selectee* as an attempt to sweeten compulsory military service. What is each new term an instance of?

22. Read the following passage and see if you can restate it briefly and intelligibly:

> Skills constitute the manipulative techniques of human goal attainment and control in relation to the physical world, so far as artifacts or machines especially designed as tools do not yet supplement them. Truly human skills are guided by organized and codified *knowledge* of both the things to be manipulated and the human capacities that are used to manipulate them. Such knowledge is an aspect of cultural-level symbolic processes, and, like other aspects to be discussed presently, requires the capacities of the human central nervous

---

[56] *The Nation* (11 April 1966), p. 421.

system, particularly the brain. This organic system is clearly essential to all of the symbolic processes.[57]

23. Translate the following sentences into ordinary English:

   a. The major limitation on the exchange programs of the Department of State appears to be their chronic fiscal starvation.

   b. The principal use of federal funds today is to accelerate the development of particular university resources when university priorities in on-going programs do not accord with national needs.[58]

24. Following are two of the general rules observed by the editors of *United Nations World* magazine. Relate them to syntactic exploitation:

   a. There is no place in the world *distant* or *far.*

   b. No place, culture, custom, or people is *strange, exotic, queer,* or *bizarre.*

25. Discuss the expression in boldface type in the following: "As a white housewife in a Birmingham supermarket told Robert Baker of the *Washington Post* (September 19), it [the retaliation against blacks] was 'terrible' but 'that's what they get for trying to force their way where *they're not wanted.*' "[59] Compare the term *undesirables* (page 251). Discuss this sentence: "In the fifth century the *known world* was limited to Europe and small parts of Asia and Africa."

26. Discuss the word *unwelcome* in *I rejected his unwelcome suggestion* as a hidden sentence. Find other examples of how we exploit syntactic disguises for ulterior purposes.

27. A savings and loan association in California advertised *We pay the highest interest rates on insured savings.* As a superlative, *highest* has to mean a comparison with something. At the time the ad was being used, the federal government had imposed certain "highest" rates that a savings and loan association might pay, in terms of the length

---

[57] The citation is from a review of Stanislav Andreski's book *Social Sciences as Sorcery* (London: Andre Deutsch, 1972) that appeared in *Time* ([25 September 1972], p. 71). In his book, Andreski criticizes the officialese of other social scientists. See the review in *Time* for one restatement of the paragraph.

[58] These two passages are from Harold Boeschenstein et al., *The University and World Affairs* (New York: Ford Foundation, 1960).

[59] *I. F. Stone's Bi-Weekly* (30 September 1963), p. 8.

of time that the depositor decided to commit his deposit (any such association was free to pay less if it chose). Is there another meaning of *highest* which the advertiser was probably trading on?

28. Discuss the nature of the ambiguities in the following sentences and why it was possible to exploit them:

    a. The oil utilities, in an area where they had to compete with natural gas, promoted the slogan *No heat costs less than oil heat.*

    b. The milk industry, caught in a dangerous misstatement when it promoted the slogan *Milk is good for every body* (some people are allergic to cow's milk), switched to *Milk has something for every body.*[60]

29. Comment on the following:

    a. My memory played a trick on me.
    b. Smith gives the impression that he doesn't care.
    c. You have drawn a foolish conclusion.
    d. He is rumored to be in love with his neighbor's wife.
    e. Appetite improves 100 percent with Polyvims.
    f. She can't vote because she has been convicted of a felony.

30. Consider what is wrong with the following example, what syntactic principle is involved, and how it might be exploited: *The jester and the king left the room.*[61]

31. Decide which of the following seem most natural and see if you can determine what makes the difference:

    a. "What is he?"—"He's a crooked lawyer."
    b. "What is he?"—"He's a crooked preacher."
    c. "What is he?"—"He's a dangerous radical."
    d. "What is he?"—"He's a dangerous communist."
    e. Look at that crazy teenager!
    f. Look at that crazy lifeguard!
    g. Who's that crazy girl?
    h. Who's that crazy boy?

    Try *politician* and *judge* in a and b.

---

[60] Example from William Bright, private communication.
[61] Example from Robert Kirsner, private communication.

References

Berlin, Brent, and Paul Kay. 1969. *Basic Color Terms: Their Universality and Evolution* (Berkeley and Los Angeles: University of California Press).

Bolinger, Dwight. 1968. "Postposed Main Phrases: An English Rule for the Romance Subjunctive," *Canadian Journal of Linguistics* 14:3–30.

———. 1972. *Degree Words* (The Hague: Mouton).

———. 1973. "Objective and Subjective: Sentences Without Performatives," *Linguistic Inquiry* 4:414–17.

Bull, W. E. 1960. *Time, Tense, and the Verb* (Berkeley and Los Angeles: University of California Press).

Chao, Y. R. 1955. "Notes on Chinese Grammar and Logic," *Philosophy East and West* 5:31–41.

Commager, Henry Steele. 1972. "The Defeat of America," *New York Review of Books* (5 October), 7–13.

Coseriu, Eugenio. 1958. *Logicismo y antilogicismo en la gramática*, 2nd ed. (Montevideo: Universidad de la República).

Furugori, Teiji. 1974. "Pass the Car in Front of You: A Simulation of Cognitive Processes for Understanding," in *Proceedings of the Association for Computer Machinery*, Annual Conference, November, pp. 380–86.

Geis, Michael L. 1973. "*If* and *Unless*," in Braj B. Kachru et al. (eds.), *Issues in Linguistics: Papers in Honor of Henry and Renée Kahane* (Urbana: University of Illinois Press).

Greenfield, Patricia M., and Jerome S. Bruner. 1971. "Learning and Language," *Psychology Today* 5:40–43, 74–79.

Hayakawa, S. I. 1972. *Language in Thought and Action,* 3rd ed. (New York: Harcourt Brace Jovanovich).

Hays, David G. 1973. "Linguistics and the Future of Computation," *National Computer Conference*, pp. 1–8.

Hjelmslev, Louis. 1961. *Prolegomena to a Theory of Language,* trans. by Francis J. Whitfield. (Madison: University of Wisconsin Press).

Hooper, Joan B. 1975. "On Assertive Predicates," in John Kimball (ed.), *Syntax and Semantics IV* (New York: Academic Press).

Kučera, Henry. 1969. "Computers in Language Analysis and in Lexicography," in *The American Heritage Dictionary of the English Language* (New York: American Heritage, and Boston: Houghton Mifflin).

Lakoff, Robin. 1972. "Language in Context," *Language* 48:907–27.

———. 1975. "Contextual Change and Historical Change: The Translator as Time Machine," in Mario Saltarelli and Dieter Wanner (eds.), *Diachronic Studies in Romance Linguistics* (The Hague: Mouton).

Landar, Herbert J.; Susan M. Ervin; and Arnold E. Horowitz. 1960. "Navaho Color Categories," *Language* 36:368–82.

Marchand, Hans. 1966. Review of Karl E. Zimmer, *Affixal Negation in English and Other Languages. Language* 42:134–42.

Mathews, Mitford M. 1961. *The Beginnings of American English* (Chicago: University of Chicago Press).

Mencken, H. L. 1945. *The American Language,* suppl. I (New York: Alfred A. Knopf).

Mills, C. Wright. 1940. "Vocabularies of Motive," *American Sociological Review* 5:904–13.

Oppenheimer, Max, Jr. 1961–62. "Some Linguistic Aspects of Mind-Conditioning by the Soviet Press," *Journal of Human Relations* 10:21–31.

Osgood, Charles E. 1971. "Exploration in Semantic Space: A Personal Diary," *Journal of Social Issues* 27:5–64.

———; George J. Suci; and Percy H. Tannenbaum. 1957. *The Measurement of Meaning* (Urbana: University of Illinois Press).

Pap, Leo. 1972. "Linguistic Terminology as a Source of Verbal Fictions." Paper read at Third International Congress of Applied Linguistics, Copenhagen, 22 August.

Prator, Clifford H. 1963. "Adjectives of Temperature," *English Language Teaching* 17:158–64.

Quine, W. V. 1960. *Word and Object*. (Cambridge, Mass.: Technology Press of M.I.T., and New York: Wiley).

Ross, J. R. 1972. "The Category Squish: Endstation Hauptwort," in Paul M. Peranteau, Judith N. Levi, and Gloria C. Phares (eds.), *Papers from the Eighth Regional Meeting of the Chicago Linguistic Society*.

Silverstein, Michael (ed). 1971. *Whitney on Language*. (Cambridge, Mass.: M.I.T. Press).

Smith, Donald. 1974. "Experiencer Deletion." Preprint.

Stanley, Julia P. 1972 (1). "Syntactic Exploitation: Passive Adjectives in English." Paper read at meeting of Southeastern Conference on Linguistics VII, 21 April.

———. 1972 (2). "The Semantic Features of the Machismo Ethic in English." Paper read at meeting of South Atlantic Modern Language Association, 3 November.

Watson, John B. 1919. *Psychology from the Standpoint of a Behaviorist* (Philadelphia and London: J. B. Lippincott).

Weinreich, Uriel. 1958. "Travels Through Semantic Space," *Word* 14:346–66.

Whorf, Benjamin Lee. 1941. "Languages and Logic," *Technology Review* (April).

———. 1949. "The Relation of Habitual Thought and Behavior to Language," in *Four Articles on Metalinguistics* (Washington, D.C.: Foreign Service Institute, Department of State).

———. 1957. "Science and Linguistics," in John B. Carroll (ed.), *Language, Thought, and Reality* (Cambridge, Mass.: The Technology Press of M.I.T.).

PSYCHOLOGY AND LANGUAGE LEARNING 9

No two disciplines are more closely related than linguistics and psychology. Both deal with language, one by definition and the other by necessity. It is so hard to keep language and mind apart that some early behaviorist psychologists, as we noted in the last chapter, simply gave up trying and affirmed that thinking was silent speech. Psychological tests are usually based on language, language gives the earliest and most easily identified symptoms of mental disturbance, and of course how we learn to speak is one of the most fundamental and fascinating problems of human behavior.

Psychologists were a little late in accepting the *nature* of language as a concern of theirs because it once seemed to belong more to sociology. As long as language was viewed as nothing but a social heritage, psychologists could see little more in how we learn it than in how we learn anything else, except for its complexity. The same conditioning mechanisms could be assumed for everything. What made this believable was the great diversity among languages. How could there be an instinct for language in any but the most trivial sense with people everywhere doing such different things? American linguists for years abetted this view by emphasizing differences more than similarities.

Two developments in linguistics shook psychologists out of their indifference. The first was the blow to their professional pride on seeing linguists grow more and more confident in their descriptions. A psychologist likes to be able to predict behavior, and linguists were gaining an uncomfortable lead, not only claiming that language was "rule-governed behavior" but getting better and better at stating the rules. The other development was the increasing awareness of universals. The differences among languages began to seem superficial, like the difference in mating rituals between two tribes where the fundamental sex drive remains the same. Psychologists felt that they had to join with linguists in resolving this apparent conflict between our genetic and our social heritage. As members of one department acknowledged, "We believe the coming focus of psychology will be language—the learning of a child's first language, learning a second language, and the relation between language and thought."[1]

IS LANGUAGE LEARNED OR INHERITED?

The original question was whether human beings come already equipped with a genetic plan for language. As early as 1887 the ethnologist Horatio Hale declared that young children have an instinct for language.[2] But he went too far: he theorized that the instinct is not just one for quickly grasping and internalizing whatever existing language a child is exposed to, but one that would enable two children to invent a language out of nothing. We know there is some equipment at birth, or we could never learn to speak. But how explicit is it?

Part of the answer can be inferred from those resemblances—we call them universals in this context—that are so widespread among cultures everywhere as to make it unthinkable that they arose by accident. Two striking examples are intonation and sound-symbolism.

We know two things about intonation. It is the first part of language that a child learns (see page 5), and it patterns in similar ways in languages all over the world. An example was given earlier (page 52) of some intonation patterns that are shared by English and Kuni-maipa. The similarities are so prevalent that when they are not found one is prone to think that something interfered with their realization, not that the potentiality for them was absent. There is evidence for this in certain tone languages. Given a universal tendency for yes–no questions to have a rise in pitch at the end, what happens if an end syllable is required to carry a low tone? Here is a description of such a situation in the Chengtu dialect of Chinese. (*Naming tone* refers to the shape of the tone when there is no conflict with intonation or with other tones.)

---

[1] *Pomona Today* (February 1974), p. 15.
[2] Cited in Langer 1948, p. 86.

Naming tone	*Effect when combined with question*
High-rising	Remains high-rising and often ends higher than usual
Low-falling	Becomes low-level
High-falling	Becomes high-level
Low-falling-rising	Becomes low-rising

In each case, the question manages to raise the pitch in some way. As if this were not enough, there are particles like [a], [san], [mə], [le], [lo], otherwise meaningless, which can be added at the end to carry a high or rising intonation free of any interference by phonemic tone.[3]

Resemblances in sound-symbolism of the type mentioned on page 24 are equally widespread. In one study of 136 languages, 38 were found to have clear evidence of the representation of smallness by means of particular sounds, most often by front and high vowels, and in some tone languages by high tone. The number is greater if one includes the languages that have distance symbolism ("nearness" resembles "smallness").[4]

Striking as the specific language-to-language resemblances in intonation and sound-symbolism are, they do not prove very much about any supposed linguistic inheritance, for both are a kind of gesture. The mouth shape for high-front vowels shows a narrow opening between tongue and palate; the analogy with both smallness and nearness is obvious. Intonation is even more deeply entrenched. It is gestural in some respects, as when a downward dip of pitch accompanies a submissive or placating bow of the head. But it is also connected with the physiology of speech and with the nervous system in general. The universal lowering of pitch toward the end of unexcited discourse results automatically from running out of lung power: subglottal pressure raises and lowers pitch, other things being equal. The equally universal raising of pitch for questions and other keyed-up utterances is probably the result of higher nervous tension in the body as a whole, which has the local effect of tensing the vocal cords. Given such beginnings, it was only natural for these audible effects to be simulated. If lowered pitch is the normal thing when one is "through," one can adopt it as a gesture to symbolize finality and fake it when necessary. This "innate referential breath group," as the terminal falling pattern has been called, is adopted by children as the phonetic marker of complete sentences.[5] As for nervous tension, it is raw material with a communicative potential so obvious

---

[3] Chang 1972, pp. 408–09.

[4] See Ultan 1970; Tanz 1971; and Nichols 1971 (especially pp. 826, 828, and 833).

[5] Lieberman 1967, p. 47.

that it was bound to be used in identical ways again and again in the languages of the world, which could happen without there being any specific inheritance of intonational patterns. Of course this does not rule out some specific capacity of children to hear and develop intonational patterns sooner than phonemic ones. It simply fails to prove the linguistic independence of any such capacity. It is probably musical as much as linguistic.[6]

Nevertheless it is clear that human beings in some sense are programmed for language. The proofs are indirect, but there are too many to be ignored. The psychologist Eric Lenneberg sums them up:[7]

1. Speech, which requires infinitely precise and swift movements of the tongue and lips, all well coordinated with laryngeal and respiratory motor systems, is all but fully developed when most other mechanical skills are far below their levels of future accomplishment.

2. Certain diseases, such as muscular atrophy, affect other motor skills but do not necessarily delay language.

3. The stages of development are relatively clear-cut and are found in children everywhere in the world.

4. Children of deaf parents go through the same stages of pre-language vocalization as other children, even though their parents are unable to respond.

5. Deaf children vocalize in the early stages of childhood as much as hearing children do.

6. At least in the early stages, progress from one stage to the next does not require practice. Children who have been prevented from babbling (for example, by surgery) will babble spontaneously, as other children do, once the physical damage is repaired.

The convinced "nativist" is not satisfied to interpret these facts modestly but claims that children actually inherit certain grammatical patterns, or at least a very definite predisposition to them. Since a child acquires his native language "at a point in his life when his general ability to acquire abstract systems is not particularly highly developed" and "with access only to fragmentary and degenerate data,"[8] it follows that the inherited language capacity must be highly specific. These two arguments require

---

[6] Van Lancker 1974 reviews the literature on this.

[7] Lenneberg 1967, pp. 131–40.

[8] Ritchie 1974.

explanation. The grammar of a language is held to contain an extremely elaborate abstract system of rules. If the child is too young to form such rules, then he must inherit them in some form or other. And to counter the opposing argument that even with feeble abstracting powers the child still might build the rules from observation, it is pointed out that what he hears is too defective to serve as a model. Accepting this reasoning, one can admit almost any degree of explicitness in the language capacity that comes packed in our genes. We can view everything that a child hears his parents say as mere "raw material,"[9] affecting the appearance of a language much as the kind and amount of nutrients will affect the appearance of a plant, without altering its essential structure.

An example from English grammar is the rather remarkable fact that when children learn English as a first language they never seem to make any mistake in the use of the progressive *-ing,* always attaching it to just the right verbs (for example, *walking* in *He is walking,* but not *owning* in **He is owning*), though they make plenty of mistakes with other verb forms. Roger Brown describes how this might happen from the nativist point of view, which assumes an inborn knowledge of the appropriate verb classes. The child presumably would already be using the verbs onto which he must later attach the *-ing.* He detects a difference between two classes of verbs: "state" verbs, such as *own, know, understand, be wet, be blue,* and "process" verbs, such as *run, live, work, be* ('behave') *stubborn, be impertinent.* What he has to avoid later of course is forming sentences like the following:

*He is owning a house.

*She is knowing that it's no use.

*The dress is being blue.

—while still forming others such as

They are living in Detroit.

The child is being stubborn.

You are being impertinent.

If, when the verbs are first learned, the child grasps not only their individual meanings but their underlying kinships, each verb will be properly tagged as "state" or "process" (along with all the other class labels that we dealt with in Chapter 6). Then when the first progressives are formed the ground has already been laid for attaching *-ing* only where it belongs.

---

[9] Lenneberg 1967, p. 375.

The child hears other people using the progressive appropriately and notes that *-ing* in this construction is attached to just those forms which he has already categorized in his mind as "process verbs." He does not have to experiment, and makes no mistakes.[10] The nativist thus assumes that we are born with some capacity to sense the division of verbs into process verbs and state verbs. Another example is the "Complex Noun Phrase Constraint," which accounts for the difference in acceptability between the following two sentences:

    a. Who does John believe that Harry saw?

    b. *Who does John believe the claim that Harry saw?

The rule here is that the interrogative *who* cannot be pulled out of a clause that modifies a noun. In this case the *who* of the b sentence has been pulled forward from the clause *that Harry saw* which modifies the noun *claim: John believes the claim that Harry saw who?*[11] As the rule appears to be quite general, we can safely assume that "when a child acquires English as his native language he knows without having to learn it that a and b will differ in degree of grammaticality since b violates a universal constraint that a does not violate."[12] (This is a rule that would have to lie fallow till late childhood; a and b, the sentences in question, are too complex for very young children. But that too is allowed for—the rule is "there," waiting to be discovered.)

A considerable edifice has been built here on a rather fragile foundation. In the first place we do not know very much about a child's ability to learn abstract systems other than language, since until he learns language he is in no position to talk about them. In the second place the data on which the child builds his formulations is not really degenerate. It is true that there are many false starts and other mistakes in the speech that a child hears; but he learns to ignore them because they are random. The structures that he learns are the ones that are repeated.[13] Besides, parents direct a good deal of exaggeratedly correct and repetitive speech at their infants, providing models that may make a deeper impression than undirected conversation. We do not know what a child uses as data or how he uses it.[14]

---

[10] Brown 1973, pp. 327–28.

[11] See Ross 1967, p. 127.

[12] Ritchie 1974, p. 325.

[13] Anderson 1972. See also Halliday 1970 for a criticism of the notion of "degenerate."

[14] Lamendella 1973, p. 8. For a similar criticism of claims about universals see Pulgram 1971, especially pp. 479–80.

Other kinds of potential universals are less persuasive; it is easier to see how they could simply have arisen in response to similar ways of living in different parts of the world. Take for example the particle *yo* in Japanese, which is added (in male speech) to an utterance to suggest that the speaker will show no patience toward any contrary assumptions on the part of his hearer: if it is a command or a statement he will brook no objection, and if it is a question he rejects the need to ask it.[15] There is a close parallel in Western languages in the use of certain exclamations. In English the closest is *for Christ's sake: It's raining, for Christ's sake* (so why are you stupidly planning to go out?); *Come here, for Christ's sake* (you shouldn't need to be told); *Am I going to help him, for Christ's sake?* (of course not, so why did you ask?). Impatience of this sort is to be found among all human speakers and must find some mode of linguistic expression. But the expression hardly predates the feeling.

The most convincing evidence for an inborn capacity for language is Lenneberg's third point, the developmental schedule in children.[16] All children pass through the same stages (not necessarily at the same rate), of which there are three if we start counting after one-word utterances have begun to be used. The first stage is that of basic semantic and grammatical relations. Verbs are there, though uninflected; so are descriptive adjectives; and nouns are discriminated for such functions as agent, direct object, and indirect object. This is basically a stage of two-word sentences,[17] though some longer combinations are found (see Table 9–1 for examples). The second stage brings in the elements most conspicuously lacking in the first, those essential grammatical morphemes with which meaning is modulated: inflections of the verb and noun, articles, prepositions, and auxiliary verbs.[18] See Table 9–2 for the order in which they are acquired. In the third stage the child advances to a complex grammatical interplay of which the best illustration is the ability to use tag questions correctly. At Stage 2 a child can express a tag question but only with some such stereotype as *hunh*—for example, *You like it, hunh?* —but at the third stage the proper selection is made: *You like it, don't you? He ate them, didn't he? She's here, isn't she?*[19] What determines the three-stage order is relative complexity of meaning and grammar.[20] It cannot be the frequency of individual forms in the adult speech heard by the child—if that were the case, *the, a, and,* and such things as inflectional endings would appear first, whereas in fact certain of these forms,

---

[15] Lakoff 1972, pp. 920–21.

[16] Most of what follows is based on Brown 1973.

[17] Ibid., p. 249.

[18] Ibid., p. 208.

[19] Ibid., pp. 403–04.

[20] Ibid., p. 58.

TABLE 9–1
Sentence Types at the Stage of Prevailing Two-Word Sentences

Ordered Constituents Present	Constituents Omitted	Example
Agent-action-dative-object-locative	None	*Mother gave John lunch in the kitchen.* (non-occurring)°
Agent-action	Object	*Mommy fix.*
Agent-object	Action	*Mommy pumpkin. (is cutting a)*
Agent-locative	Action	*Baby table. (is eating at a)*
Action-dative	Agent, object	*Give doggie. (you give it to)*
Action-object	Agent	*Hit ball. (I)*
	Agent, locative	*Put light. (I, there)*
Action-locative	Agent-object	*Put floor. (I, it, on)*
Agent-action-object	None	*I ride horsie.*
Agent-action-locative	None	*Tractor go floor.*
Action-dative-object	Agent	*Give doggie paper.*
Action-object-locative	Agent	*Put truck window.*
Agent-action-object-locative	None	*Adam put it box.*

SOURCE: Adapted from p. 205 of *A First Language: The Early Stages*, by Roger Brown. © 1973 by the President and Fellows of Harvard College.

° No actual examples of this occurred in the study from which the other examples were taken. In the other examples the words in parentheses are needed to complete the child's meaning as the experimenter observed it.

such as *and, but,* and *because,* are not fully understood until early adolescence.[21]

The scholar responsible for assembling the evidence for these regularities, the psycholinguist Roger Brown, agrees that they are impressive, but does not accept the nativist argument:

> Linguists and psycholinguists when they discover facts that are at all general have, nowadays, a tendency to predict that they will prove to be universal and must, "therefore," be considered innate. The Stage 1 meanings have proved to have some generality . . . and I do feel tempted to hypothesize universality. But not innateness . . . because . . . it is my impression that the first meanings are an extension of the kind of intelligence that Jean Piaget calls sensorimotor. And Piaget has shown that sensori-

[21] Ibid., p. 30.

TABLE 9–2
Mean Order in Which Three Children Acquired
Fourteen Grammatical Morphemes

	Morpheme	Example	Average Rank
1.	Present progressive	-ing (as in *Mama talking*)	2.33
2–3.	*in, on*	*on table*	2.50
4.	Plural	-s (*shoes*)	3.00
5.	Past irregular	*went, broke*	6.00
6.	Possessive	-'s (*Pat's hair*)	6.33
7.	Uncontractable copula	*is*	6.50
8.	Articles	*the, a, an*	7.00
9.	Past regular	-ed (*played*)	9.00
10.	Third person regular	-s (*plays*)	9.66
11.	Third-person irregular	-s (*does, has*)	10.83
12.	Uncontractable auxiliary	*is* (*is working*)	11.66
13.	Contractable copula	's (*Pat's funny*)	12.66
14.	Contractable auxiliary	's (*Pat's going*)	14.00

SOURCE: Adapted from p. 274 of *A First Language: The Early Stages*, by Roger Brown. © 1973 by the President and Fellows of Harvard College.

motor intelligence develops out of the infant's commerce with objects and persons during the first 18–24 months of life . . . an essentially practical intelligence that is acted out rather than thought. . . . Let us consider some of the intellectual prerequisites of Stage I meanings. Nomination [*this, that, see, here, there*] and recurrence [*more, another*] both presume the ability to recognize objects and actions. Nonexistence [*all gone, no more, no*] presumes the ability to anticipate objects and actions from various naturally recurring signs and also to notice when such anticipations of appearance or existence are not confirmed. . . . Piaget's description of the time when each thing is conceived by the child in terms of the schemas into which it can enter—as "graspable," "suckable," "scratchable," and so on—is irresistibly suggestive of the development of lexical entries for nouns and verbs which describe the combinations in which they can enter. Which is not to say that the sensorimotor process is linguistic but that the linguistic process does not start from nothing and can build on data that are not linguistic.[22]

This parallel development of motor skill and language skill is shown in Table 9–3. Grammatical relations, of course, are not the same thing as

---

[22] Ibid., pp. 198–200.

TABLE 9–3
Developmental Milestones in Motor and Language Development

At the Completion of:	Motor Development
12 weeks	Supports head when in prone position; weight is on elbows; hands mostly open; no grasp reflex
16 weeks	Plays with rattle placed in hands (by shaking it and staring at it); head self-supported; tonic neck reflex subsiding
20 weeks	Sits with props
6 months	Sitting: bends forward and uses hands for support; can bear weight when put into standing position, but cannot yet stand without holding on. Reaching: unilateral. Grasp: no thumb apposition yet; releases cube when given another
8 months	Stands holding on; grasps with thumb apposition; picks up pellet with thumb and finger tips
10 months	Creeps efficiently; takes side-steps, holding on; pulls to standing position
12 months	Walks when held by one hand; walks on feet and hands—knees in air; mouthing of objects almost stopped; seats self on floor
18 months	Grasp, prehension, and release fully developed; gait stiff, propulsive, and precipitated; sits on child's chair with only fair aim; creeps downstairs backward; has difficulty building tower of three cubes
24 months	Runs, but falls in sudden turns; can quickly alternate between sitting and stance; walks stairs up or down, one foot forward only
30 months	Jumps up into air with both feet; stands on one foot for about two seconds; takes a few steps on tiptoe; jumps from chair; good hand and finger coordination; can move digits independently; manipulation of objects much improved; builds tower of six cubes
3 years	Tiptoes 3 yards; runs smoothly with acceleration and deceleration; negotiates sharp and fast curves without difficulty; walks stairs by alternating feet; jumps 12 inches; can operate tricycle
4 years	Jumps over rope; hops on right foot; catches ball in arms; walks line

SOURCE: Adapted from Lenneberg 1967, pp. 128–30.

Vocalization and Language

Markedly less crying than at 8 weeks; when talked to and nodded at, smiles, followed by squealing-gurgling sounds usually called *cooing*, which is vowel-like in character and pitch-modulated; sustains cooing for 15–20 seconds

Responds to human sounds more definitely; turns head; eyes seem to search for speaker; occasionally some chuckling sounds

The vowel-like cooing sounds begin to be interspersed with more consonantal sounds: labial fricatives, spirants, and nasals are common; acoustically, all vocalizations are very different from the sounds of the mature language of the environment

Cooing changing into babbling resembling one-syllable utterances; neither vowels nor consonants have very fixed recurrences; most common utterances sound somewhat like *ma, mu, da,* or *di*

Reduplication (or more continuous repetitions) becomes frequent; intonation patterns become distinct; utterances can signal emphasis and emotions

Vocalizations are mixed with sound-play such as gurgling or bubble-blowing; appears to wish to imitate sounds, but the imitations are never quite successful; beginning to differentiate between words heard by making differential adjustment

Identical sound sequences are replicated with higher relative frequency of occurrence, and words *(mamma* or *dadda)* are emerging; definite signs of understanding some words and simple commands *(Show me your eyes)*

Has a definite repertoire of words—more than three, but less than fifty; still much babbling but now of several syllables, with intricate intonation pattern; no attempt at communicating information and no frustration at not being understood; words may include items such as *thank you* or *come here*, but there is little ability to join any of the lexical items into spontaneous two-item phrases; understanding progressing rapidly

Vocabulary of more than fifty items (some children seem to be able to name everything in environment); begins spontaneously to join vocabulary items into two-word phrases; all phrases appear to be own creations; definite increase in communicative behavior and interest in language

Fastest increase in vocabulary, with many new additions every day; no babbling at all; utterances have communicative intent; frustrated if not understood by adults; utterances consist of at least two words—many have three or even five words; sentences and phrases have characteristic child grammar—that is, are rarely verbatim repetitions of an adult utterance; intelligibility not very good yet, though there is great variation among children; seems to understand everything said within hearing and directed to self

Vocabulary of some one thousand words; about 80 percent of utterances intelligible even to strangers; grammatical complexity of utterances roughly that of colloquial adult language, although mistakes still occur

Language well established; deviations from the adult norm tend to be more in style than in grammar

playing with objects, and clearly there is *something* about language that goes beyond sensorimotor intelligence. But there is no way at present to test whether it is innate or learned.[23]

Another fact that works against the idea that we are born with rules in our head is the way children waver when they first begin to apply a rule. If the rule is already there, we should not have to learn it, we would *discover* it, and the hesitations that accompany learning should not plague us. But children do have "a considerable period . . . in which production-where-required is probabilistic" in their use of grammatical forms,[24] which is to say that for a time they seem not to know quite how to get things right.

The nativist theory has found many adherents among linguists, particularly those who follow Noam Chomsky. There is no question that human infants come into the world with vastly more preformed capacity for language than used to be thought possible. There is evidence that even a four-week-old infant is especially tuned to react to speech sounds as against other sounds.[25] But whether or not the genetic design contains elements that are explicitly linguistic hinges on the overall question of explicitness. There is so much interdependence in the unfolding of our capacities that we cannot be sure that the linguistic ones do not start as nonlinguistic, only to be made linguistic by features of the environment. Suppose that language and tool using have the same basic mechanisms, as some anthropologists maintain (see pages 312–13). At a certain point the infant discovers that he has a right hand and a left hand, and he discovers objects. This is an event external to his brain, but at the same time it is inevitable, and along with other external events it molds capacities around the use of tools. At the same time or later the infant discovers words as objects. He is already equipped to use objects, and a simple transfer molds this capacity around a subject and a predicate—a thing and what you do to it. It is not necessary to have a predisposition to grammatical subjects and grammatical predicates; that can take shape from the objects that lie around the child as he matures, whether they are things of nature, cultural artifacts, or words.

THE SEVERAL GRAMMARS OF CHILDHOOD

If language is adaptive, and if children as they grow have different needs, then one can argue that the grammar used at any one age is perhaps the "best" grammar for that age. It follows that the way a child

---

[23] Ibid., p. 201.
[24] Ibid., p. 257.
[25] Mattingly 1973.

of three speaks is not just a bad imitation of the way an adult speaks, but is the way a three-year-old ought to speak. As one authority puts it, "The child approaches the language-learning task not once but several times; not with just one set of innate structures, but rather a succession of them corresponding to the developmental stages of human cognitive equipment."[26] When the child emerges from the home and socialization is under way, child language can be viewed as child dialect. A child speaking too much like an adult can be resented by other children as much as an adult is resented by other adults if he holds onto childish mannerisms. For all we know, children may sense and express things that are later lost, so that there is regression as well as progress in the ontogeny of language.

In Chapter 1 we distinguished four stages in the development of language: holophrastic (or one-word), joining, connective, and recursive. These will serve as labels for the grammars to be talked about here.

The grammar of the holophrastic stage is the lack of grammar. With only single words, nothing can be related within language. The only relation is the most important relationship of all, the one between language and situation. Very young children probably resort to naming "as an almost reflexive concomitant of perceptual identification"—that is, to help recognize and contemplate what they perceive.[27] One team of psychologists suggests how the child arrives at a concept of nounness and verbness. To begin with there is a repeated connection between the mother's voicing of something and the appearance of an attention-getting object. Many neurons are excited when this happens, and different groupings are excited at different times; but since the mother's vocalization is a constant, one set of neurons is repeatedly excited. This creates a neural assembly, which viewed subjectively is "the abstract idea of a name." The child then perceives two things on any such occasion: the particular word that the mother uses, which is a lower-order cognition, and the interconnection with other acts of naming, which is a higher-order cognition, an abstract sense of nounness—there is a double perception, half on the surface and half in depth. "Verbness" is acquired in the same way, and once the two classes are established directly the child has an indirect means as well as the direct one of putting new items in the proper category: if he knows the words *people, dog,* and *Bobby* and hears *People kivil, The dog kivils,* and *Bobby kivils,* the word *kivil* stands in the same relation to familiar nouns as do other verbs that are already known, and is properly categorized as a verb. Nounness and verbness become complementary abstractions.[28]

At the one-word stage there is nothing to suggest that the child dif-

---

[26] Lamendella 1973, p. 31.

[27] Flavell, Friedrichs, and Hoyt 1970, p. 338.

[28] Hebb, Lambert, and Tucker 1971, pp. 220–21.

ferentiates between noun and verb. Things and activities are both merely named. The grammar of the joining stage is the beginning of grammar proper, when two names are brought into relation with each other. How this happens has been described by tape-recording the utterances of two Hungarian-speaking children from the time they began to speak till they were ten years old and transcribing them phonetically.[29] The joining of two elements is revealed not to be something that happens in a flash and then is secure forever, but something that comes about many times by chance; the union may be as quickly dissolved, but is eventually cemented. One such happy collision of names occurred for the boy, Pierre:

> During the months of April and May (age one year and eight to nine months) we had the rare opportunity of recording through several repetitions the *progressive formation* of the bipolar phrase. In one of those historic moments, Pierre was busy looking at one of his favorite pictures, of a rider jumping his horse over a hedge. His reaction during the previous month had been to waver between saying *ló* (horse) and *ugrik* (jump), the two elements of the parental sentence **Look, the horse is jumping over the hedge.** He used one or the other expression indifferently, as if either were capable of representing the situation as a whole. But the day of our recording, May 29, he seemed attracted by the picture to the point of fascination. The one-word utterances *ló* and *ugrik* were repeated at rhythmic intervals and the pauses between them became shorter. The pitch curves, which had been independently parallel at first, became complementary (Figure 9–1), as if to express an awareness of their mutual existence and rapport, and finally, with the fifth repetition, the two expressions were joined in a single bipolar phrase (Figure 9–2).[30]

After this inspired beginning Pierre went back to his single repetitions, and many other such relapses occurred till well past the age of two. We cannot read the child's mind and know when he means a succession of two words to be taken as more than just a succession, but we can see how he joins them rhythmically and intonationally. There are four successive phases:

1. In the first phase, "the two expressions have parallel intonation curves, reaching about the same height and dropping to the same terminal level. Both expressions carry a heavy accent. Only their physical proximity reflects any relatedness."

2. In the second phase, "the two expressions are always separated by a pause and highlighted by equal accents, but the pitch re-

---

[29] Fónagy 1972.

[30] Ibid., pp. 41–43.

FIGURE 9–1
Two Instances of the Phrasal Pair <u>Ló</u> 'Horse' and Ugrik 'Jump'

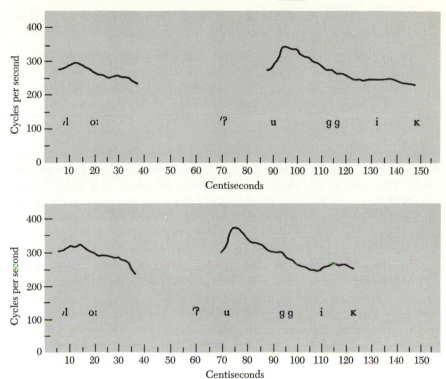

SOURCE: Adapted from Fónagy 1972, p. 42.

FIGURE 9–2
Fusion of the One-Word Utterances <u>Ló</u> 'Horse' and Ugrik 'Jump'*

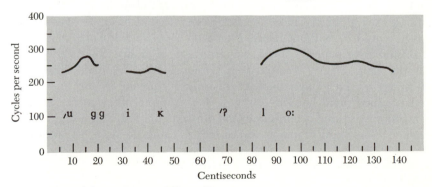

SOURCE: Adapted from Fónagy 1972, p. 43.

* The apparent break is due to the velar and glottal occlusion.

mains high at the end of the first and does not go down to terminal level until the end of the second."

3. "In the third phase, the accent on the first syllable is noticeably weaker and the pause separating the two expressions is reduced."

4. "In the fourth phase the pause disappears and the only sign of any remaining phrasal independence is the force of the two accents, the glottal stop that generally separates the two expressions, and the approximately equal rise of the intonation curve in each of them."[31]

The second grammar is a good working grammar, and if only two things had to be dealt with at a time it would probably serve us indefinitely. The shift to the third, or connective, grammar is a struggle for the child, not only because manipulating three or more things is much harder than manipulating two but because it marks the beginning of arbitrariness. The second grammar is the simplest and most logical: an invariant term is tied to a more or less stable concept. The learning of pure reference is the thread that the second grammar has in common with the first.[32] The only room for arbitrariness is in the order in which the elements occur, and in this respect children seem to imitate what they hear but without any strict necessity—they often reverse the sequence. In the third grammar the child would like to carry on with the one-to-one correspondence of form and meaning, and as we shall see (pages 403–05), it is his influence here that has "leveled" many unnecessary complications. But now he is forced to conform, and as he learns the grammatical morphemes, which are the symptoms of the third grammar, he masters forms from the standpoint of correctness as well as meaning. This goes hand-in-hand with juggling ever more complex utterances; in fact, the complexity is one motive for it, since an important use of the function words is to keep the interrelationships clear in a sentence containing several words. Headline English is a good example of what language would be without them: *Plymouth Rubber Net Falls,* announced a Boston newspaper.[33] (The net earnings of a firm called Plymouth Rubber had fallen.) Arbitrariness comes hard. The child grasps the meanings of the grammatical morphemes before he is able to organize and produce them himself—he will, for example, obey more readily a command expressed according to the adult model than one using childish syntax.[34] The third grammar forces him not only to have categories but

---

[31] Ibid., pp. 65–66.

[32] Scholes 1969.

[33] Boston *Globe* (27 February 1969).

[34] Shipley, Smith, and Gleitman 1969.

to mark them—nouns for plurality, verbs for agreement, adjectives for comparison, if the language is English—and to do so at times in inconsistent ways, as when the past of *go* is not admitted as *goed but has to be *went.* But this is incidental to the child's efforts to communicate in more and more complex situations, only certain aspects of which are embodied in the function elements. Mastering the third grammar extends well into middle childhood. The eight-year-old who says **I know whose girlfriend Bruce has* when he means 'I know who is Bruce's girlfriend' has yet to master possessives and relatives.

The fourth, or recursive, grammar might be termed the grammar grammar—the one in which grammar is not only used but used with some awareness of it as grammar. The foundations of course are laid in the preceding stage. The child is constantly being corrected—sometimes by others but mostly by his own observation—and when he is forced to substitute *deer* for *deers and *fought* for *fighted he sets up some kind of proportion such as "*deer* is to *deer* as *dog* is to *dogs*" or "*fight* is to *fought* as *work* is to *worked.*" He may at first learn *fought* and the plural *deer* as isolated words, but eventually the abstract proportion has to be mastered because otherwise it is impossible to handle such things as tag questions and negations: "*He hit me!*"—"*No he didn't!*"—"*Yes he did!*" presupposes a category of pastness to which *hit* and *did hit* both belong. The child who asks **I'm magic, amn't I?* has obviously learned a rule, not a word, for nobody says **amn't* and there is no model for him to imitate.[35] But the pattern does not come without a struggle. Here as in the other stages we see the physical event often preceding the cognitive grasp of it. In his second grammar, Pierre put words together before he actually caught on to the interesting possibilities of what he was doing. Similarly a child will often anticipate the third grammar by using a correct inflected form such as *fought* before he learns the rule for adding the past tense morpheme *-ed.* After he does learn the rule he may then shift to the incorrect *fighted for a time and not return to *fought* till the fourth grammar begins to set things right. The clearest sign of the fourth grammar emerges a little later: the child's ability to talk about what he does. By the age of four to six most children can pass fairly sophisticated judgments on some errors of syntax. Children start to do this at about the same time as they begin to be able to perform other "meta-cognitive" functions, such as explaining their judgments of space and number or working out strategies for remembering. One can take an even longer view of the child's new power and say that it consists in a detachment of language from the immediate situation, whereby it can be used not just for interaction with the present scene but for *control* of the environment, including control of itself—that is, use of those elements that relate one part to another and relate the whole to past and future as

---

[35] Bellugi 1970, p. 66.

well as present. The child controls his environment in the sense that he can bring the past alive (tell what happened yesterday), create the non-existent (tell stories), and plan what he is going to do. The last of these is as important for survival as communication: talking about doing something before doing it, using words to plan a strategy for action. If we lacked inner speech we could not act in an orderly manner.[36]

To illustrate talking about language, here is an interview between a mother (M) and her seven-year-old daughter (D). (The girl had played such games before and was quite adept.)

M: Are you ready to do some work?
D: Yes.
M: We're going to talk about sentences this morning. And I want your opinion about these sentences.
D: Yes, I know.
M: Are they good sentences, are they bad sentences, do they mean something, are they silly, whatever your opinions are.

Okay: *John and Mary went home.*
D: That's okay.
M: That's an okay sentence?
D: Yes.
M: Does it mean the same thing as: *John went home and Mary went home?*
D: Yes, but it's sort of a little different because they might be going to the same home—well, it's okay, because they both might mean that, so it's the same.
M: Here's another one: *Two and two are four.*
D: I think it sounds better *is.*
M: *Two and two is four?*
D: Am I right?
M: Well, people say it both ways. How about this one: *Claire and Eleanor is a sister.*
D: (laugh) *Claire and Eleanor* are *sisters.*
M: Well then, how come it's all right to say *Two and two is four?*
D: You can say different sentences different ways! (annoyed)
M: I see, does this mean the same thing: *Two is four and two is four?*
D: No, because *two and two are two and two* and *two and two is four.*
M: Isn't that a little funny?
D: *Two and two more is four,* also you can say that.
M: How about this one: *Boy is at the door.*
D: If his name is *Boy.* You should—the kid is named *John,* see? *John is at the door* or *A boy is at the door* or *He's knocking at the door.*
M: Okay, how about this one: *I saw the queen and you saw one.*
D: No, because you're saying that one person saw a queen and one person saw a one—ha ha—what's a one?
M: How about this one: *I am eating dinner.*

---

[36] See Luria and Yudovich 1971, especially pp. 52–53, 82–84, and 87.

D: Yeah, that's okay.

M: How about this one: *I am knowing your sister.*

D: No: *I know your sister.*

M: Why not *I am knowing your sister*—you can say *I am eating your dinner.*

D: It's different! (shouting) You say different sentences in different ways! Otherwise it wouldn't make sense!

M: I see, you mean you don't understand what that means, *I am knowing your sister.*

D: I don't understand what it means.

M: How about this: *Claire loves Claire.*

D: *Claire loves herself* sounds much better.

M: Would you ever say *Claire loves Claire?*

D: Well, if there's somebody Claire knows named Claire. I know somebody named Claire and maybe I'm named Claire.

M: And then you wouldn't say *Claire loves herself?*

D: No, because if it was another person named Claire—like if it was me and that other Claire I know, and somebody wanted to say that I loved that other Claire they'd say *Claire loves Claire.*

M: Okay, I see. How about this: *I do, too.*

D: It sounds okay but only if you explain what you're trying to say.

M: How about: *The color green frightens George.*

D: Doesn't frighten me, but it sounds okay.

M: How about this one: *George frightens the color green.*

D: Sounds okay, but it's stupid, it's stupid!

M: What's wrong with it?

D: The color green isn't even alive, so how can it be afraid of George?

M: Tell me, Claire, is this game getting boring to you?

D: Never-rrrrrrrrrrrrrrr.

M: Why do you like to play a game like this? What's the difference how you say things as long as people understand you?

D: It's a difference because people would stare at you (titter). No, but I think it's fun. Because I don't want somebody coming around and saying—correcting me.

M: Oh, so that's why you want to learn how to speak properly?

D: That's not the only reason.

M: Well, what is it?

D: Well, there's a lotta reasons, but I think this game is plain fun.

M: You want to go on playing?

D: Yeah, and after this let's do some spelling; I love spelling.[37]

Grammar that is conscious of itself is about as far as grammar can go. Even adults never fully complete the cycle—there are hidden connections that we use automatically without ever penetrating them. How many of us would recognize, let alone be able to formulate, what is going on in a sentence like the following? *I dreamed I was dreaming, and of course I had to wake up from my dream dream, and that woke*

---

[37] Gleitman, Gleitman, and Shipley 1973, pp. 148–51.

me out of my dream too. The person who said this formed the sequence *dream dream* with *dream* as a modifier. It is easy to do with *dream— dream book, dream interpretation, dream sequence;* it is not so easy with *vision, delusion,* or other synonyms of *dream.* Similarly *a love meet, a love sign, a love feast,* but not *an affection meet;* or *a pleasure spot, a pleasure trip, a pleasure dome, a pleasure car,* but not *an enjoyment spot.* There is buried somewhere in our subconsciousness a category of nouns that are used more freely than others as modifiers. And people differ in their ability to focus on questions like this. One series of tests reported striking differences among three adult populations, made up of persons with experience in graduate school, persons with college but no graduate study nor intention of it, and secretaries with high-school diplomas but no intention of going to college. They were given noun compounds to interpret, such things as *foot–house–bird, house–bird–thin, kill–house–bird,* with set stress patterns. The first group did best at interpreting according to the rules of noun compounding, and the third class did worst.[38] But we have to be careful in interpreting such data. Grammatical awareness may be to some extent a trick learned in school. Secretaries may be more cooperative than others, so that when they hear a silly-sounding expression like *house–bird–thin* they are motivated (as we all are at times with what strikes us as deviant) to imagine that the speaker was trying to say something sensible and was careless with his arrangements, and instead of venturing a "correct" interpretation such as 'a cracker shaped like a house-bird' they charitably help the speaker out with an "incorrect" one like 'a thin house-bird.' And there is a more insidious danger: the tester may be wrong in *his* grammatical assumptions!

In any event it is still probably true that the fullest potential of human language is realized when it becomes its own metalanguage: "All our discussion about language is carried on in that very medium. Can one talk about flatworm communication in the flatworm system? Can a chimpanzee . . . talk about talking?"[39]

The division into four grammars naturally makes things seem much tidier than they ever truly are. A later grammar does not supersede an earlier one; it incorporates it. And there are always tasks belonging to one stage that are never fully carried out till later. Even pronunciation problems drag on. A child of thirty months who can handle sentences of several words still has to struggle with certain difficult sounds such as [θ], [æ], and palatals other than [č] and may continue to substitute [b] for [v].[40] The conquest of speech advances on all fronts at the same time.

---

[38] Gleitman and Gleitman 1970.

[39] Bender 1973, p. 11.

[40] Weir 1962, p. 142.

OTHER PSYCHOLOGICAL CORRELATES OF LANGUAGE:
THE BRAIN

Like the chemist who seeks to understand the physical structure of chemical elements, the linguist would be happiest if he could catch a specimen of talking man with a transparent skull and feed him tracers that would impart a glow to the speech centers of the brain and make each transmission from neuron to neuron visible to the eye. As this physiological reduction of linguistic activity is still a few years off, we have to content ourselves with what can be reached indirectly. A lot can be inferred from the effects of surgery, from experiments that do not involve mutilation, and from close attention to behavior.

History mentions a number of personages who at some point—usually past the age of forty—have been "struck dumb" and afterwards, often very soon afterwards (so that no physical cause was suspected), recovered their speech. Thus the prophet Daniel "set his face toward the ground and became dumb" (Dan. 10:15). Speechlessness is a common symptom of stroke or apoplexy, which in time was to give anatomists their first clue to the localization of language in the brain. Along with inability to speak, some form of paralysis on the right side of the body often occurs: hand, whole arm or side, or perhaps just the facial muscles. Postmortem examination made it possible to correlate these external accidents with cerebral ones, and it was usually found that some trauma, such as a blood clot, had struck the left hemisphere of the brain. In 1861 the surgeon Paul Broca announced that speech was fixed in the left frontal region. Evidence has since accumulated showing that nearly all human beings have their language functions "lateralized" to the left, though some left-handers have them to the right. Damage to the right side of the brain does not usually result in severe language impairment. Damage to the left side generally has serious consequences after early childhood. Lateralization is under way by the age of two and complete at about the age of five, and from then on till puberty the left side of the brain continues to develop its language functions, but the right side is still "plastic" enough to take over if necessary. After puberty no one seems to be able to relearn a first language without some deficiency, usually very serious.[41]

Speech is not the only language function that can be tied with fair accuracy to a particular region of the brain. The person who is unable to speak as a result of a lesion in the left frontal region may still be able to understand, read, and write. If the damage is more to the side, there may be no loss of speech—the person may even become more voluble, but his speech tends to be dissociated from meaning: the words are there

---

[41] Krashen 1973.

and can be understood, but they are strung together in strange ways. A small lesion at any point on the left side may result in some loss of relevance in what is said without affecting the fluency with which it is spoken.[42] So it is clear that the whole of the left side of the cortex (surface area) of the main part of the brain is somehow involved in language.

Is it possible to pinpoint the exact spot that controls each language function—articulation, glottal excitation, storage of nouns or verbs, connecting up of sentences? Accustomed as we are to machines that have to be exquisitely specialized if they are to work at all, we expect a like arrangement in human anatomy, but the brain is not that kind of organ. A function may appear to be located in one part, but if that part is injured another part may take over. How the brain works is more a problem of fluid dynamics than one of ordinary mechanics. Some linguistic functions are more or less localized, particularly the ones that involve the perception of sounds and the muscular control of speech. But the cognitive functions—understanding, planning, and organizing— cannot be pinned down; locating them is "impossible by definition."[43]

Nevertheless, given approximate locations, it is possible to make some interesting correlations. One such is dynamic aphasia, resulting from an injury to the forward part of the left hemisphere. The victim is unable to answer questions, though he understands them perfectly well. He fumbles for words but cannot organize them. He can improvise a list of nouns fairly easily but has great difficulty with verbs. Experiments suggest that what he has lost is the power of "propositionizing," which is the stage between the idea of what is to be said and the production of the utterance; it is a kind of preliminary assembly around which the utterance is formed. All that is necessary to enable the victim to respond intelligibly is to give him some external references on which to hang the elements of his sentence—some blank pieces of paper are enough, to which he can point one by one as he brings out what he wants to say.[44]

The losses that occur when the left hemisphere is hurt are not typically in *amount* but in *kind*. The victim does not lose, say, 50 percent of his total language ability, but may lose 90 percent of one special ability and only 10 percent of another. He may be able to read a word aloud but not be able to say it when shown a picture of what it names, or vice versa; he may be able to understand a word on hearing it but not on reading it, or vice versa. One way of testing for differences in capability between the hemispheres is by experiments in "dichotic listening." Listeners are equipped with headphones into which stimuli can be fed that are not the same for one ear as for the other. It develops that we hear sounds related to certain functions of language better in the right ear than in the

---

[42] Lenneberg 1973, pp. 119–21.
[43] Lamendella 1975, Ch. 2, pp. 17–18.
[44] Luria and Tsvetkova 1970.

left—as might be expected from other correlations such as right-handedness. It is not the nature of the sounds themselves that makes the difference (hiss as against burst, pitch as against loudness, noise as against periodic vibration), but the part that they play in language organization. Some sounds—for example, musical melodies and environmental noises—may be heard better in the left ear; but when musical sounds are tested in a context where they serve not as music but as linguistic tone (words in the Thai language, for instance), or when musical melodies are tested on trained *musicians* (who are analytically minded), the right ear hears better.[45] Even when the stimuli are words, if they are the kind that we use thoughtlessly, such as greetings or swear words, neither ear makes more mistakes than the other. But the kinds of mistakes are not the same. A word misheard by the left ear is apt to be heard as a swear word or a command of the sort that is usually given without thinking. One misheard by the right ear is apt to be heard as one that we normally use when we speak thoughtfully. Thus *get up* in one test was taken for *fast, shit, dammit, stop,* and *get out* by the left ear, but for *thank you, enough, up, duck, get out, stop, doughnut, camp, gap, shut up,* and *can't* by the right.[46]

It is probably no coincidence that "propositional" language and right-handedness are housed in the same half of the brain. Tool using and verbal problem-solving may well be the same at bottom. It is as if all human activity were roughly divided between "holding" functions and manipulative ones, lateralized in separate halves of the brain. Each of us is perhaps not one spirit but two: the clever, talkative, intellectual, maze-threading, problem-solving genie sits on the left hand, and the artistic, intuitive, whole-seeing, and wordless but passionate genie sits on the right. But since for lack of words he is unable to tell us about himself, the genie on the right remains largely a mystery. His rival may even suppress him. Gabby people get ahead in a gabby world.[47]

The processing of speech

Baby chicks are precocious in their equipment for walking and pecking. Human infants are precocious in their equipment for talking. As we saw in Chapter 1, language has to be learned early. The ear and the organs of speech mature soon enough to take on the task. It would be delayed far too long if it had to depend on gesture or any other medium.

This explains why the responsibility falls on the tongue and ear, but how their activities are coordinated remains something of a riddle. The

---

[45] Van Lancker and Fromkin 1973; Bever and Chiarello 1974.

[46] Van Lancker 1974, Ch. 4, pp. 52–63.

[47] See Pines 1973, pp. 138–59. For left-handed persons the two genies may just switch places.

most favored theory is that of "analysis by synthesis." It goes more or less like this:

As sounds are produced there are two kinds of feedback, one from the sounds themselves, which are not only spoken but heard, and the other from the muscles that do the work and the neural mechanisms that control them. A link is established between the sound and the producing mechanism. In part the child may establish it experimentally: he plays with making sounds and tests the sensations of his efforts. Each sound in this way comes to be associated with a rather gross set of muscular movements. In producing an [i], for example, the tongue is fronted and raised. The physical code for [i] is thus "raise the tongue and front it." Since the configuration of movements for each sound is unique and fairly obvious, the child is able to store up a repertory of distinct sound-movements.

The next step is to run the process backwards: when the child hears the sound [i] he mentally runs through the movements that would have produced it had he been saying it himself. This constitutes his identification of the sound when it is spoken by someone else. One bit of evidence for this method of handling the incoming stimulus—not simply recognizing each sound directly as an acoustic configuration but first passing it through a part of the articulatory mechanism—is that the acoustic wave does not have the same one-to-one tie with its speech sound that the articulatory configuration has. Certain sounds—for example, those of /g/—have more than one acoustic pattern when viewed on a sound-spectrogram: they *look* different even though they *feel* the same when we make them, and our brain interprets them as the same.[48] Presumably if our ear interpreted the actual sounds of /g/ just as they are intercepted by the ear, there would seem to be more than one of them; they would "sound different."

This is a crude model of processing at the level of distinctive sounds. Later we learn more and more to bypass the muscular movements and depend on higher layers of neural organization.[49] The processing of "speech" becomes the processing of "language," about which no capsule statements can be made because it involves memory and other highly complex and largely inaccessible mechanisms.

Storage and resynthesis

How active a role does the speaker play in putting an utterance together? When he says *Good morning* to greet an acquaintance, is he

---

[48] Liberman 1956.
[49] Mattingly 1971.

resynthesizing old words into a new sentence by attaching the adjective *good* to the noun *morning?* We said no to this question in Chapter 5. *Good morning* is an idiom and is as much a unit as either *good* or *morning* taken separately. The tendency among American linguists has been to be as analytical as possible, and to regard phrases as whole chunks stored in long-term memory only when an analytical treatment makes no sense (see page 102). Thus *Hand me the pliers* is always thought of as resynthesized no matter how many millions of times it has been said, but *Shoot the works* is conceded to be a repetition because there is no way to rebuild it semantically out of *shoot* and *works,* and because with it the processes of synthesis do not work normally—that is, we are unlikely to say **He shot the works* and we cannot say **Fire the works,* **Shoot all the works,* and so on.

Looking back at the early grammars of childhood, we see that recall from memory—or retrieval from storage, to use the jargon of computers —is the first activity of intelligible language. When a child names an object that he sees, and later names an object that he wants to get, there is a one-to-one correspondence between the name and the thing or situation. The name has been stored in memory and can be evoked by the sight of the thing or can be used to evoke the thing. There is no synthesis, which has to wait for the second grammar; the only operation is retrieval. As the child develops, older grammars are incorporated in new grammars but are not abolished.[50] There is no reason to believe that speakers ever give up what they learned to do first of all, namely to apply some spoken unit to some unit of experience. So it is very likely that much more of the talk that goes on is "idiomatic" than just those utterances that can't be analyzed. The fact that we can analyze does not necessarily mean that we do.

The question is what and how much gets stored in memory. It is hardly likely that we store every sentence we hear on the chance that some day we may need that same sentence for our own purposes. It is more reasonable to suppose that we store units of smaller size, at least in that portion of our storage space to which we require ready access when we want to synthesize a new sentence. But that does not necessarily mean that sentences are not all stored *somewhere.* We need to retain traces of many sentences in order to extract the meaning of even a single term—for instance, *John fouled* plus its situation is not enough to lead us to the meaning of *foul,* as there are a number of ways to strike a foul ball. The chances are that our memories retain far more than we ever need to re-use, of which only part gets shaken down to something that may resemble a dictionary and a grammar.

If this is true, resynthesis and mere retrieval must overlap over the

---

[50] Lamendella 1975, Ch. 2, p. 12.

whole range, with resynthesis rarest at the level of words, but dominant above that level. As we saw in the treatment of morphemes (page 112), it may be that we store the prefix *de-* and re-use it to coin new words on the order of *de-bug, de-caffeinate;* but we do not do the same with *deduce* and *defer,* which are stored as units, to the chagrin of dictionary-makers and linguists, whose job would be easier if all such cases were predictable. On the other hand units of the size and repeatability of *down the road, here and there, over and above, patently absurd, I discovered to my dismay, to sully one's lips,* and others like them, while transparent and resynthesizable, are not always, perhaps not usually, resynthesized, but are pulled from storage as units when the occasion is right. They are collocations (see pages 99–107).

But the typical stored unit is the word. Our difficulty in synthesizing words from smaller units (see pages 108–11), plus the ease with which words can be retrieved, testifies to this. At the same time, vast amounts of information are stored alongside of words, aiding in their retrieval and guiding us in their use. This includes not only meanings of every description, but phonological information, synonyms, translations into another dialect or language, usage levels, appropriate syntactic contexts, and so on. If we do not have hovering in the back of our minds all the contexts in which we have ever encountered a word and everything about it that might be considered a resemblance to something else, it is not because we lack the capacity, in view of all that we do remember.

This comes to light whenever the retrieval mechanism breaks down. Everyone occasionally forgets a name, and in the gropings to remember we can observe the process in slow motion. Say you are watching an old movie on TV and you see an actor you knew years ago, Robert Benchley, but you can't remember his name. The first name that comes to mind is *Benjamin*—this has the same first syllable as the word you are looking for, and the same first segment, with voice added, in the second syllable. Then you think of *Robert Finch*—this supplies the given name but sacrifices part of the surname, though rectifying the mistake of /j/ for /č/. Eventually you alight on the proper form—and recognize it as such, which is another bit of information that has to be stored somewhere.

Names of people are usually captured in this way, by resemblances in sound. Common words are as readily called to mind through meaning and other associations. A linguist reported that after using the expression *utterance token* he caught himself thinking of a northern Indian or Alaskan carved figure. He then realized that the word *token* had made him think not of the precise form but of the meaning of a similar-sounding word: *totem.* The route thus passed from form to the meaning of a nearby form to the nearby form itself.

These are samples of how a stored item can be rather unsystematically cross-indexed. It is the systematic indexing that interests the linguist.

We know that *ark* is a noun and *come* is a verb and *easy* is an adjective—or rather we know that *ark* has to be used in ways that a grammarian refers to as "noun," and similarly for *come* and *easy*. These are the gross usage connections that we have for those words. We also know that *easy* has more than one meaning and that one of those meanings when combined with *be* is seldom if ever encountered except in the comparative degree (or rather, we know that it appears only as *easier* in contexts appropriate to that form of *easy*): *The patient was easier after the sedative*[51] (not likely **The patient was easy after the sedative*, though *The patient was comfortable after the sedative* is normal). With *feel* there is no such restriction to the comparative: *I'm not going to feel easy until all these precautions have been taken.* We know from our gross indexing of a word such as *work* that it can be either a noun or a verb, but we also know that as a verb it can apply to any task and that as a noun it can apply to any specific task *(This is the work I have to do this afternoon).* But in reference to a general occupation it can refer only to manual labor, at least for some speakers: *What kind of work do you do? I'm on my way to work.* For a professional person, possible alternatives are *What kind of job do you have?* and *I'm on my way to the office.*[52]

Each word is thus a mass of associations, of which grammars have seen fit to recognize only the topmost layer, which can be categorized as "parts of speech" or "selectional restrictions." There is a vast amount of grammatical detail still to be dug out of the lexicon—so much that by the time we are through there may be little point in talking about grammars and lexicons as if they were two different things.

Our initial question—how active a role the speaker plays in putting an utterance together—can now be partially answered. If we think only of the grosser links among words, such as the fact that one is a verb and another a noun, it seems that the speaker can intervene almost at will. There is little in any given situation which a speaker has to meet by verbalizing something that will trigger what he is to say. But if we think of all the other ties, the possibility of indirect as well as direct spontaneous triggering is very high. The speaker is probably free, but not as free as we have supposed. Some of his synthesizing is consciously controlled. Much of it is unthinking and automatic, in which situations evoke not only stored elements but also the potential linkages that bring them together.

---

[51] Example from *Webster's Third New International Dictionary*.

[52] Pointed out by J. D. McClure, private communication.

ADDITIONAL REMARKS AND APPLICATIONS

1. Is there something similar in English to the perturbations of tone by intonation in Chinese, which were cited to show how tenacious intonation is (page 275)? Consider the use of intonation to signal 'incompleteness' at the end of a non-final clause, as in the following answer to the question *What will you do if it rains?*

$$\text{If it } {}^{\text{rai}}{}^{\text{n}}{}^{\text{s}} \quad \text{I'll stay } {}^{\text{ho}}{}_{\text{m}}{}_{\text{e.}}$$

Now suppose that the question is *What are you planning to do tomorrow?* and the answer is

$$\text{If it } {}^{\text{ra}}{}^{\text{s}}{}_{\text{i}}{}^{\text{n}} \quad \text{I'll stay } {}^{\text{ho}}{}_{\text{m}}{}_{\text{e.}}$$

The different treatment of **rains** is due to the fact that in the first answer it is a repetition, whereas in the second it is a new idea. In spite of this difference, does the intonation (rise for incompleteness at the end of the first clause) still win through?

2. The ethnologist Horatio Hale maintained that it should be possible for two or more children, isolated from adult human companionship before they had learned their native language (and at the same time managing somehow to survive), to develop a language of their own. Otto Jespersen investigated the case of twins, badly neglected and left in the care of a deaf woman, whom he first met when they were obviously able to converse with each other but in a way that was unintelligible to adults. It was clear, however, that their language was *based* on Danish. Does this suggest that all that is needed is the barest push from outside to set the language-learning process going? Do you think that without this push it would start spontaneously?

3. Discuss the implications of the following statement: "Basic gram-

matical structures seem to be learned despite differences in the child's linguistic environment, whereas how children use language to express ideas may be more vulnerable to environmental variation."[53] (The evidence for this was a study of three children: the one who got a good command of inflections first was the one who had the least amount of correct modeling from parents or others using the inflections.)

4. All languages have nouns and verbs. Does it strike you that this reflects (1) an inborn tendency to use nouns and verbs, (2) the child's encounter with the natural world, or (3) the fact that languages started out (accidentally?) having nouns and verbs and have merely perpetuated them through social inertia? Or possibly some combination of 1, 2, and 3?

5. Listen to five minutes of relaxed conversation between two adult native speakers and try to calculate the proportion of "degenerate" utterances you hear. (Do not count as wrong anything that is customary at that level of communication, whether "correct" by puristic standards or not. Count as wrong only the expressions that you would expect the speakers to avoid without being told to do so). See how close your figure comes to an estimated 25 percent.

6. A child who substitutes [t] for [k], as in *tat* for *cat,* will also substitute [d] for [g], as in *doe* for *go.* Does this suggest that children develop the ability to discriminate between sounds before they develop the ability to reproduce them correctly?

7. Observe the speech of a two-to-five-year-old and note as many characteristics of the child's grammar as you can.

8. Consider the following incident, supplied by a linguist:

> During the day we rent out our garage to an architect. If I have taken the car and come back home, my wife will often ask me where I've parked. Once when I came in, and we were standing two feet from each other in the center of the living room, my wife asked me, "Are you in the garage?" Our four-year-old daughter, Rachel, said immediately, "Mommy! That's silly! Daddy is right there![54]

See page 205 for the meaning of *we,* similar to *you* in this story. Which of the four grammars is evidenced by Rachel's alertness? What in particular has she not learned yet?

---

[53] Cazden 1972, p. 122.

[54] From Robert Kirsner, private communication.

9. A child spontaneously produces *If you finish your eggs all up, Daddy, you can have your coffee,* and successfully imitates her new sentence when her father repeats it right after she first says it, but has trouble imitating it later when the intent that inspired the remark in the first place has faded.[55] What does this tell us about the child's ability to process something *as a linguistic item* rather than as a *message?*

10. Have you ever intercepted a bit of your own internal dialog in which you have said to yourself *I must do so-and-so* (but without any definite plan for doing it), then forgotten about it, and subsequently caught yourself carrying out the idea? Watch yourself for this or for some other evidence of the self-directing use of language.

11. In one psycholinguistic test, adults who responded to the command *Ask him what to eat* with *What do you (what does one) eat?* rather than with *What do I eat?* were judged in error. The tester was convinced that they were behaving as if *Ask him what to eat* were the same grammatically as *Tell him what to eat* (making *him* the subject of the infinitive in both cases). Is this necessarily true? If not, what does it suggest about the dangers of psycholinguistic tests?

12. *Dyslexia* (severe problems in learning to read) is sometimes associated with left-handedness. Why should there be any connection? Left-handedness or ambidexterity is also sometimes associated with difficulty in learning a second language. If your school has a foreign language requirement, find out whether any special provisions are made for this problem.

13. Speculate on the possible connection between the lateralization of the brain and the persistent dualisms that have cropped up in human thinking over the centuries: body and mind, substance and form, constancy and change, argument and function (in logic), topic and comment (in language). Think of others.

14. Can you see a connection between our vast memory for word associations and what poets call the evocative power of words? Here is how John Ciardi describes it:

> A poem does not set out toward a subject. Rather, it finds one. Let a man sit down with no intent but to describe an old family photo— say one of those faded sepia nineteenth-century stiff poses of a group of ancestral faces. He has no notion of being significant or far-reaching. He means only to make visual. By the time he has finished

---

[55] Cazden 1972, pp. 84–85.

a single paragraph aimed at visual accuracy (*and if he is word sensitive*), the words he has summoned in his effort to be accurate will have leaked a ghost that was nowhere in his mind at starting. That ghost (or those ghosts) once evoked, the rest of his writing is between him and those ghosts.[56]

Comment on the "ghost" that made Ciardi write *ancestral faces* rather than *quaint faces* or *patriarchal faces.* (Suggestions: Does *ancestral* connote dignity and stiffness? Does your recollection of the term *ancestor worship* have anything to do with it? Is there something purely in the sound—a stateliness about a word in which the first two syllables both contain full vowels?)

15. Do dreams give us some insight into the kinds of things that are stored in the brain? Try to recall some dreams that you have had and see if they are relevant to the question. Here is an example:

> Reading in a newspaper of a hotel that had its lobby on the eighth floor, I suddenly recalled I don't know how many dreams I have had in which I was trying to find my way in a hotel that had such an arrangement, or other peculiarity that had caused me to lose my way—uneven corridors ending in blank walls, floors that had no access to other floors except by climbing through windows and down bookshelves, people who were supposed to be in suites that weren't there—either the suites or the people, or both—and elevators that shot up past where they were supposed to go. All this melange was like random pathways across a kaleidoscope of stored information. But it also was as if not only direct experience but the chance experience of dreams unremembered till then were all filed away somewhere.

References

Anderson, Lloyd B. 1972. "Explanation, Abstractness, and Language Learning," in Paul M. Peranteau, Judith N. Levi, and Gloria C. Phares (eds.), *Papers from the Eighth Regional Meeting of the Chicago Linguistic Society.*

Bellugi, Ursula. 1970. "Learning the Language," *Psychology Today* 4:7.32–35, 66.

Bender, M. Lionel. 1973. "Linguistic Indeterminacy: Why You Cannot Reconstruct 'Proto-Human,'" *Language Sciences* 26:7–12.

Bever, Thomas G., and Robert J. Chiarello. 1974. "Cerebral Dominance in Musicians and Nonmusicians," *Science* 185:537–39.

Brown, Roger. 1973. *A First Language: The Early Stages* (Cambridge, Mass.: Harvard University Press).

---

[56] "Hanging Around Words," *Saturday Review* (11 March 1972), p. 14. Reference from Lurana Amis.

Cazden, Courtney B. 1972. *Child Language and Education* (New York: Holt, Rinehart and Winston).

Chang, Nien-Chuang T. 1972. "Tones and Intonation in the Chengtu Dialect," in D. Bolinger (ed.), *Intonation* (Harmondsworth, England: Penguins).

Flavell, John T.; Ann G. Friedrichs; and Jane D. Hoyt. 1970. "Developmental Changes in Memorization Processes," *Cognitive Psychology* 1:324–40.

Fónagy, Ivan. 1972. "A propos de la genèse de la phrase enfantine," *Lingua* 30:31–74.

Gleitman, Lila R., and Henry Gleitman. 1970. *Phrase and Paraphrase: Some Innovative Uses of Language* (New York: W. W. Norton).

———; Henry Gleitman; and Elizabeth F. Shipley. 1973. "The Emergence of the Child as Grammarian," *Cognition: International Journal of Cognitive Psychology* 1:137–64.

Halliday, M. A. K. 1970. "Functional Diversity in Language as Seen from a Consideration of Modality and Mood in English," *Foundations of Language* 6:322–61.

Hebb, D. O.; W. E. Lambert; and G. R. Tucker. 1971. "Language, Thought, and Experience," *Modern Language Journal* 55:212–22.

Krashen, Stephen D. 1973. "Lateralization, Language Learning, and the Critical Period: Some New Evidence," *Language Learning* 23:63–74.

Lakoff, Robin. 1972. "Language in Context," *Language* 48:907–27.

Lamendella, John T. 1973. "Innateness Claims in Psycholinguistics." Preprint.

———. 1975. *Introduction to the Neuropsychology of Language.* (Rowley, Mass.: Newbury House). Page references are to the manuscript.

Langer, Susanne K. 1948. *Philosophy in a New Key* (New York: New American Library).

Lenneberg, Eric H. 1967. *Biological Foundations of Language* (New York: Wiley).

———. 1973. "The Neurology of Language," *Daedalus* 102:3.115–33.

Liberman, Alvin M. 1956. "Some Results of Research on Speech Perception," *Journal of the Acoustical Society of America* 29:117–23.

Lieberman, Philip. 1967. *Intonation, Perception, and Language.* Research Monograph No. 38. (Cambridge, Mass.: M.I.T. Press).

Luria, A. R., and L. S. Tsvetkova. 1970. "The Mechanism of 'Dynamic Aphasia,'" in Manfred Bierwisch and Karl Erich Heidolph (eds.), *Progress in Linguistics* (The Hague: Mouton).

———, and F. Ia. Yudovich. 1971. *Speech and the Development of Mental Processes in the Child* (Harmondsworth, England: Penguins).

Mattingly, Ignatius G. 1971. "Reading, the Linguistic Process, and Linguistic Awareness." *Haskins Laboratories Status Report on Speech Research* (July–September), 23–34.

———. 1973. "Phonetic Prerequisites for First-Language Acquisition." *Haskins Laboratories Status Report on Speech Research* (April–June), 65–69.

Nichols, Johanna. 1971. "Diminutive Consonant Symbolism in Western North America," *Language* 47:826–48.

Pines, Maya. 1973. *The Brain Changers* (New York: Harcourt Brace Jovanovich).

Pulgram, Ernst. 1971. Review of N. Chomsky, *Language and Mind* (New York: Harcourt Brace Jovanovich, 1968). In *Modern Language Journal* 55:474–80.

Ritchie, William C. 1974. "An Explanatory Framework for the Study of Adult Language Acquisition," in Roger W. Shuy and Charles-James N. Bailey (eds.), *Towards Tomorrow's Linguistics* (Washington, D.C.: Georgetown University Press).

Ross, J. R. 1967. *Constraints on Variables in Syntax*. Ph.D. dissertation, Massachusetts Institute of Technology.

Scholes, Robert J. 1969. "On Functors and Contentives in Children's Imitations." Communication Sciences Laboratory Quarterly Report, Department of Speech, University of Florida 7:3.

Shipley, Elizabeth F.; Carlota S. Smith; and Lila R. Gleitman. 1969. "A Study on the Acquisition of Language: Free Responses to Commands," *Language* 45:322–42.

Tanz, Christine. 1971. "Sound Symbolism in Words Relating to Proximity and Distance," *Language and Speech* 14:266–76.

Ultan, Russell. 1970. "Size–Sound Symbolism," *Working Papers on Language Universals*, Stanford University, No. 3, pp. S1–S31.

Van Lancker, Diana. 1974. *Heterogeneity in Language and Speech: Neurolinguistic Studies*. Ph.D. dissertation, Brown University.

———, and Victoria Fromkin. 1973. "Hemispheric Specialization for Pitch and Tone: Evidence from Thai." *Journal of Phonetics* 1:101–09.

Weir, Ruth Hirsch. 1962. *Language in the Crib* (The Hague: Mouton).

THE ORIGIN OF LANGUAGE 10

Not many years ago this chapter would have been forbidden ground. Origins were not to be talked about because they could not be investigated, only guessed at. Known linguistic traces go back to about 5000 B.C., but beyond that nothing is recoverable. So linguists had better leave the subject alone. The Linguistic Society of Paris outlawed it in 1866 and reaffirmed its action in 1911. One occasionally hears the same view repeated today: "Speculation about the prehistoric beginnings of language is not a respectable activity."[1]

Anthropologists and anatomists have not been so easily put off, and since about 1965 there has been a growing interest in the evidence—mostly from outside linguistics—for at least some notion of when human beings started to speak and how they did it. Various lines of investigation have converged: observations of young children, whose speech has primitive beginnings very like what can be supposed for early language and may "recapitulate" it; measurement of human skeletons to see whether they had the anatomical prerequisites for speaking; investigations of non-speech systems, such as the sign language of the deaf, to see how necessary actual speech is to the process; the study of natural animal communication; experiments in teaching apes to communicate, to ascertain whether language requires fully developed human intelligence;

---

[1] Brown 1973, p. 63.

and of course the excavation of archeological remains, especially of tools, which have their own peculiar relationship to language.

It almost goes without saying that *the* primordial language, meaning the first that was ever spoken, can never be reconstructed in the way we can reconstruct much of Indo-European from bits and pieces of its descendants. According to one view, the rate of change observed in all living languages, if it operated in the past as it does today, would have wiped out traces of any language spoken 30,000 years ago; any similarities that might be found would then simply be due to chance. But there is reason to believe that language much as we know it today existed thousands of years earlier. So the best we can do is to make some informed guesses about what early stages of language were like, not what they were in fact.[2]

What most older theories about origins had in common was a tacit belief in the existence of language as something separate from people. For the Bible it lies at the root of creation: **In the beginning was the Word.** For the eighteenth-century philosophers it was invented; man was there beforehand, accoutered with all the powers that he has today except for speech. For speculative linguists it was discovered, in a kind of how-to way: you can bark like a dog to represent 'dog,' go *ding-dong* to represent 'bell,' and say *ta-ta* on leaving a friend, "waving" good-bye to him with your tongue. (One still hears echoes of the discovery theory, modified to mean that man discovers what is already in his head. See Chapter 9, pages 276–84.) The insights of the theory of evolution came a century late: it took that long to realize that language was simply part of the development of the human race, inseparable from other physical and mental powers, modifying and being modified by them. All life forms transmit. Some use sounds, others smell, touch, taste, movement, temperature changes, or electrical charges. Their messages maintain social unity, warn off predators, attract mates, point to sources of food, and otherwise help keep the species going.[3] As Darwin made clear a century ago, the facial expressions that back up much of human language are an extension of those used by all the primates.[4] There was probably no quantum break with this past; too much of it is still with us. But there must have emerged a succession of differences, important enough to select for survival only those human beings who possessed them to a higher and higher degree.

The first great barrier in animal communication that had to be surmounted was *fixity of reference*. Most animal messages are connected

---

[2] See Bender 1973.

[3] See Sebeok 1969.

[4] Darwin 1913.

with just one thing in the real world: a growl is a warning to an enemy; a particular scent is an attraction to a mate; a cluck is a summons to a brood of chicks. A dog does not come to his master and growl to indicate that there is an enemy approaching; the growl is *at* what stimulates it. But transferred meanings are the rule in human language. Basically one steals a purse or a paycheck, but one may also steal a base or steal the limelight. Form and meaning are detached from each other and to some extent go their own ways. It would be unfair to other species to say that no such detachment is to be found in the non-human world. There are birds that appear to vary their song in ways that are not instinctively predetermined, and neighboring species of fireflies do not all use the same courtship flashes.[5] But this degree of freedom is rare. It is also rare in the human young up to a certain age. But children soon learn that *orange* not only means a particular piece of fruit regardless of what position or condition of lighting it is seen in, but can also be used of an entire class of similar objects.

The second barrier that had to be surmounted was *holophrasis,* the emitting of just one independent signaling unit at a time. Animal communication appears to lack syntax. Without it, propositional language is impossible—one cannot say anything *about* anything, but is limited to command-like or exclamation-like utterances, and those in turn are limited to the here and now: the tribe can be warned of an approaching danger but not reminded of what precautions were taken at the last encounter. Again, human infants lack syntax up to about the age of two, but eventually get the hang of putting words together (see Chapter 9, pages 286–87).

There were further barriers, but these two had to be leveled first, and we must ask why all the life forms on earth had to wait millions of years for *Homo* to do it. Was it because a certain level of intelligence had to be developed first? But how could that be, when intelligence seems so dependent on language? Language could hardly have been a precondition for language.

The answer seems to be that something a step lower than human intelligence is enough to surmount the first two barriers. Here we can learn from the experiments with two famous chimpanzees, Washoe and Sarah. Washoe learned the American Sign Language to the point of transmitting not only one-word messages but messages using combinations as well, and the signs that she used acquired the same flexibility that human words have. For example, she learned the sign for 'more' as a way to get her trainers to keep tickling her, but then transferred the sign to a game of being pushed in a laundry cart, and afterwards extended it spontaneously to swinging by the arms and eventually to ask for the continuation of any activity. Examples of two-word sign-sentences

---

[5] Jakobson 1969.

that she invented were 'Open food-drink' for 'Open the refrigerator'—
her trainers had regularly used 'cold box' for 'refrigerator'—and 'Open
flower' for a request to be led through a gate to a flower garden.[6] As for
Sarah, she used visual signs also, but in place of movements of the hands
and fingers she was given plastic tokens of various shapes and colors.
These she learned to a point where she was able to interpret fairly complex commands, amounting, for example, to compound sentences. In one
experiment, after being taught to respond correctly to 'Sarah insert apple
pail,' 'Sarah insert banana pail,' 'Sarah insert apple dish,' and 'Sarah
insert banana dish,' she was confronted with 'Sarah insert apple pail
Sarah insert banana dish,' which she duly obeyed; and finally the redundant words were omitted so that the command read 'Sarah insert
apple pail banana dish,' and again she responded correctly. To do so
she had to recognize that 'banana' went with 'dish' and not with 'pail,'
despite the fact that it was between the names of the two receptacles.[7]
Sarah's accomplishments have been replicated by Lana, who punches her
symbols on a computer and manages to keep in the news with her expanding vocabulary.[8] Whether these chimps will be able to go on to
higher things no one knows—one critic feels that Sarah "is near the limit
of her abilities, even with clever stage managing"[9]—but both Sarah and
Washoe have matched the language ability of a four-year-old child and
have proved that creatures other than humans had the intelligence to
transfer meaning and to create syntax.

In a more recent experiment, the trainers of Washoe have worked
with a very young chimpanzee, Moja, who at six months already had
command of fifteen signs and was putting two of them together to say
Gimme more![10] This precociousness suggests one reason for the lower
development of chimpanzees: a complete language system is so complex
that it requires a prolonged period of plasticity to acquire it. Chimpanzees grow up too fast.

The fact that chimpanzees had the intelligence to create syntax does
not of course prove that they did create it, or even that what the present
generation of clever chimpanzees have learned can be transmitted from
ape to ape; perhaps only the determination and diligence of human
trainers could bring it off. But the brain capacity is there.

The third barrier in communication was *lack of metalanguage*. Until
elements of language were introduced that referred to language, it was
not possible to turn syntax inward and enable it to build on itself. Take

---

[6] Gardner and Gardner 1969.

[7] Premack and Premack 1972.

[8] Associated Press dispatch, Los Angeles *Times* (29 January 1974), p. 12; New York
Times (4 December 1974), p. 45.

[9] Bender 1973, p. 9.

[10] *Signs for Our Times*, Gallaudet College, Washington, D.C. (September 1973).

as simple an element as a relative pronoun. In a sentence such as **Do you know the man who wrote this?** the word *who* facilitates the concatenation of two sentences of which one defines an element in the other. It is not necessary to have a *word* for this—some languages may do it by position, as **Do you know the wrote-this man?**—but whether function word or function order, something has been devised to warn the hearer that one of the two sentences is not a statement in itself but part of a larger proposition. Syntax would be sterile if these inward-pointing elements—pronouns, conjunctions, prepositions, inflections of verbs, sentence adverbs—had not been added to the speaker's repertory.

Looking back at the three barriers we can see that the surmounting of each one was a further gain in recursiveness, in the power to limit the units at one level of language sufficiently to make them manageable and at the same time, at another level, to use them over and over in building larger units. The breakaway from holophrasis made words available not just for single referents but for classes of them. The attainment of syntax made words usable not just one at a time but in combination. The arrival of metalanguage redoubled syntax. Nor was all this movement in one direction. The pressure toward re-usability pushed down as well as up. Hearers can identify countless numbers of words not by following any particular guidelines but by recognizing their general phonic outlines, just as they can recognize faces by general impressions without digitizing them. But we don't have to produce faces and we do have to produce words, and we are not all artists. So out of sheer necessity, as the load grew heavier and heavier, there developed a system of phonological points. The worst amateur, no good at freehand speaking, could acquire a set of these through practice and make a good enough imitation of an artistically spoken word to get by.

The upward barriers must have been at least partially leveled before the downward one was breached. This raises the most hotly debated point of all: Was human language originally spoken? There are reasons to believe that it could not have been, but that it would never have developed as far as it has if it had not become so.

PREADAPTATION[11]

We cannot suppose that any (except perhaps the last) of the long series of evolutionary steps that led to language was actually *aimed* at what it eventually produced. Rather, like the swimming bladder that preceded

---

[11] The term is Darwin's, and is taken here from Lieberman 1974, on which the information in the first part of this section is based.

the lung, it was a mechanism that was on hand and could be adapted to a new use. The ancestors of the apes that first took to the trees to escape predators had to have the forelimb structure that made tree-climbing possible. That in turn created a selective pressure for still more specialized use of those limbs, and structures properly called "arms" were the result. With the descent from the trees, the specialization of arms from legs led in turn to the possibility of standing and walking erect. This made it useful to modify the position of the head, which had to be moved forward to direct the eyes properly. Some progress must already have been made in that direction during the tree-climbing years, since clinging to a vertical trunk to some extent forces an erect posture. As this posture became the normal one, the larynx was pushed down, changing the configuration of the vocal tract and providing for a wider range of vocal sounds. (See Figure 10–1 for a comparison of the adult human vocal tract with that of a newborn human infant, an adult chimpanzee, and Neanderthal man. The important difference is the right-angled bend in the human tract and the location of the long pharyngeal cavity *above* the voice box, or larynx, where the cavity can serve as a resonator.) The "origin" of language from these adaptive changes covers millions of years. But of course it is the later phases that interest us most, for it is only with the *use* of the apparatus to carry messages that language as we know it can be said to begin.

No other primate uses the vocal organs to communicate anything but rudimentary warnings and emotive cries. That is why earlier attempts to teach apes to communicate with human beings were failures, and why Washoe was taught a sign language. The normal channel with primates is the visual one. They cannot speak because their vocal mechanism does not permit it: they do not move their tongues during a cry, and the sounds that their larynx produces are mostly *aperiodic*—that is, the sounds are not melodic and cannot be modulated for fine pitch contrasts.[12]

Earlier human forms undoubtedly could manage better than a modern chimpanzee, but they too lacked the physical equipment to match the range of modern man. Reconstruction of skulls and vocal musculature reveals that Neanderthal man could not utter the three most stable vowels, [a], [i], and [u]; it would have been harder for him than for us to create sharply differentiated vowel sounds. He could have produced dental and labial consonants ([d b s z v f]), but may not have been able to make a contrast between nasal and non-nasal. Of course even with just two audible contrasts, a phoneme-like code is possible, as any digital computer will tell you—apes could talk if they knew how. But the fewer the contrasts that can be made, the more laborious the coding becomes,

---

[12] Lieberman 1972, p. 35.

FIGURE 10–1
Air Passages of the Adult Chimpanzee, the Newborn Human,
Neanderthal Man, and the Adult Human*

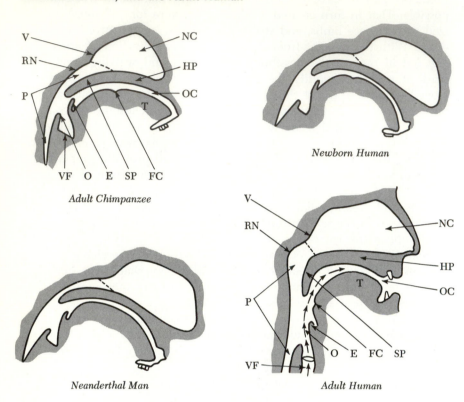

Adult Chimpanzee

Newborn Human

Neanderthal Man

Adult Human

SOURCE: Adapted from Lieberman 1972, p. 109.

* The anatomical details are as follows: P = pharynx, RN = roof of nasopharynx, V = vomer bone, NC = nasal cavity, HP = hard palate, OC = oral cavity, T = tongue, FC = foramen cecum, SP = soft palate, E = epiglottis, O = opening of larynx into pharynx, and VF = level of vocal folds.

so primates would have required greater intellectual powers, not weaker ones. We can conclude that while the lower range of sounds possible for Neanderthal would not have precluded his talking, they required too high a grade of intelligence for him to do much of it. The drive toward vocal expression had begun, but still had a long way to go.

Meanwhile, as a basis for what was to become spoken language, a fairly elaborate system of gesture must have been in use.[13] Culture was

---

[13] See especially Hewes 1971 and 1973. Most of the discussion here is based on Hewes.

already too far advanced at a time when *Homo* still did not have the power of speech for there not to have been some way of handing skills down from one generation to the next—literally handing, for tool using was the most important skill and is best taught by demonstration, just as it is today. Washoe's trainers found that "a particularly effective and convenient method of shaping [the signs] consisted of holding Washoe's hands, forming them into a configuration, and putting them through the movements of a sign."[14] There is no great distance between signing how to use a tool and signing other meanings; manual shaping is the easiest way to do it. It would be easier to teach children to speak if we could reach into their mouths and mold their tongues. Even now it is the sounds that children can see that they learn most easily (such as the labials [b p m]) and the most difficult widely used sound is one that is both invisible and involves an unusual percussion movement which might be helped if it could be seen and manually shaped: the tapped or trilled *r* sound.

Could a gesture language have become as expressive a medium of communication as spoken language? Today, among the congenitally deaf, it is very nearly so. The American Sign Language has its own scheme of arbitrary units, roughly corresponding to a syllabary in spoken language, which is to say that it is not merely a form of pantomime. The signs doubtless are somewhat more iconic than spoken syllables (see page 217), but memory tests suggest that the deaf have a store of visual and kinesthetic impressions of components of their signs rather like those stored up by the non-deaf of their phonemes. And sign language is akin to speech in other ways. Though it was invented, it is now handed down by tradition and is undergoing the same kinds of changes as natural language. It is somewhat like a pidgin language, first imposed by necessity and then going native, becoming "creolized." An example of internal change is the word for 'sweetheart,' which half a century ago was formed by bringing the hands together at the edge of the little fingers and cupping the heart, but now is formed with all the fingers in contact except the thumb, more in keeping with other signs in the system. The word has been "leveled," as when a child alters **broke** to **breaked** to conform to other *-ed* words.[15]

Whether sign language as elaborate as this could have been developed without being preceded by spoken language, or whether deaf people even today could survive if they were not sheltered by a society that mostly uses talk, are unanswered questions that may raise some doubts. But then it is not necessary to suppose that primitive sign languages were quite so advanced. It is enough to assume that there was gesture,

---

[14] Gardner and Gardner 1969, p. 672.
[15] Based on Bellugi and Klima 1973, especially pp. 12, 83, 87.

that those skilled in using it had a better chance to survive, and therefore that any improvement in it would have been reinforced by natural selection. This set the intellectual stage for the transfer to speech, while the physiological stage was probably set by factors already mentioned— man's increasingly erect posture with its lowering of the larynx and the "bent tube" enlargement of the vocal tract. At the same time that the hands were no longer needed for locomotion and were free for tool using and for gestures, the vocal mechanism was as if by accident being prepared to take over. And skill with tools was making it easier to lay up a supply of food so as to restrict the need to chew to a few relatively brief periods, which in turn freed the mouth and tongue for more verbal play.

These advances were reflected in a more complex social organization. If skill with tools is to be transmitted continuously it requires more than the tradition of a single family. As social interdependence increased, dependence on instincts was lessened, and this made for greater resilience in adapting to the environment. An ice age would not wipe out a race that could keep warm by clothing itself rather than having to pass through the tedious evolutionary stages that might develop more "natural" modes of protection such as body hair. Instinctive behavior receded farther and farther into the background, and what we call intelligence superseded it. Mere input-output sensory processing was no longer enough; as early as the beginning of tree-living, it was necessary to have a sharp visual pattern–identifying ability.[16] From this there arose a conceptual level of reality in which human beings acquired a "holistic awareness of entities generically categorized in terms of both their physical attributes and capacity for action."[17] Such categories were ripe for naming. As they were shaped in contact with things, gestural naming was a natural first step.

What makes it seem the more likely that the skills of tool using and language were tied together in man's prehistory is that the brain itself houses them in the same general region. As we saw in the last chapter, the human brain is lateralized, with functions calling for analysis—tool using, language, symbolic behavior in general—largely confined to one side (the left, for most people, which controls the *right* side of the body), and space perception, environmental sensitivities, and holistic appreciation confined to the other or more evenly distributed between the two. One can see certain analogies in this kind of brain specialization between the special ways that tools are used and sentences are constructed. With tools, the left hand develops a holding grip while the right develops various precision grips—it "does something to" what is held in the left

---

[16] Lieberman 1974, p. 60.
[17] Lamendella 1975, Ch. 2, p. 31.

hand. A propositional sentence contains a topic (usually the grammatical subject) and a comment (usually the grammatical predicate), which does something to or tells something about the topic (see page 155). In a discourse, the topic is often "held over"—our imagery suggests the analogy with handedness.

Whereas language and tool using are related in the brain, language and primitive cries are not. In man an electrical stimulus on the cortex—the region of highest organization—will cause vocalization; in animals the stimulus generally has to be applied below the cortex.[18] This makes it highly unlikely that there was any direct transition from emotional noises to propositional language.

If tool using enabled gesture to become practical as well as emotional and provided the push for a systematic gestural language (probably a little more subtle than Washoe's accomplishments with sign language thus far), it also helped to pave the way for the transfer to speech. One can explain the use of a tool through gesture only up to a point; beyond that, especially as tools themselves become more complex, using the hands for explanation interferes with using them for manipulation. Even an accidental sound might have been seized upon under those circumstances, but there were undoubtedly already many that were not accidental, such as vocal signs of approval or disapproval, warnings, persuasions—a great part, probably, of what still constitutes the emotive part of language—not to mention signals used in hunting, where concealment (and hence invisibility) would have inhibited the use of gesture. Besides, even now there remains a good deal of gesture in the use of sound, especially intonation—we can often predict a facial expression if we hear a speech melody. So sound and gesture were already overlapping, and the advantages of sound would have reinforced its use: no interference with other activities of the hands and arms, the possibility of communication out of sight of one's hearer and in darkness, and increased speed—even with a sign language designed as efficiently as possible, the deaf today are held to a comparatively slow rate.[19]

Here is how Morris Swadesh describes the possible origin of one vocalized meaning that must have overlapped most of the long period when gesture was the prevailing mode of communication:

> The use of nasal phonemes in the negative in so many languages of the world must in some way be related to the prevailing nasal character of the grunt. In English, the vocable of denial is almost always nasal; but it can vary from a nasalized vowel to any of the three nasal consonants: *ã!ã*, *ẽ!ẽ*, *õ!õ*, *m!m*, *n!n*, *ŋ!ŋ*. . . . Why is nasality so common? Surely because it

---

[18] Van Lancker 1974, Ch. 5, p. 5.
[19] Bellugi and Klima 1973, p. 88.

results from the relaxation of the velum; . . . the most usual position of the velum is down, and the most relaxed form of grunt is nasal. The prevalence of nasals in the negative . . . may therefore be due to the fact that they are based on grunts.[20]

. . .

Simple nasality expressed relaxation and contentment. Joined with laryngeal constriction, it signified rather displeasure or frustration.[21]

Once the voice had assumed the major burden of communication, the subsequent refinement of language was largely a matter of cognitive growth which, like a liberated slave, demanded more and more of the freedom that an ever more finely tuned vocal apparatus made possible. The change to speech was not merely a recoding, vocally, of units already present in gesture. Vast new possibilities were engendered. The advantages of skilled sound-making redounded on the physical mechanism, which was steadily adapted to language and specialized away from digestion. Linguists of the extreme "language is but a cultural artifact" persuasion have argued that speech is merely an *overlaid* function, making an artificial use of organs that were designed by nature for the intake of food. But the human speech-and-digestive organs have developed traits in their later evolution that are not advantageous for eating. The shift of the larynx that made for better sound production "has the disadvantage of greatly increasing the chances of choking to death when a swallowed object gets caught in the pharynx. . . . The only function for which the adult human vocal tract is better suited is speech."[22] Human beings have *evolved* as speakers. In the process, the many dimensions in which the sound wave could be modified multiplied the number of distinguishable sounds that could be transmitted, and an ever more agile tongue increased the speed of transmission, thus placing a heavier burden on memory and a higher premium on cognition. This had a drastic effect on the linguistic units themselves, which were able to become increasingly condensed and automatic. In leaping from idea to idea we can no more give conscious thought to speech movements than we can pay attention to our feet when we walk or dance. Such watchfulness may be necessary for learning but is a hindrance in performing.

We can assume that the first vocal units were primarily consonantal— the instability of early vowels has already been noted (see page 311)— and independently meaningful.[23] While the idea of a language with words in which vowels have little or no function except as a transition from one consonant to the next or for affective connotations may seem

---

[20] Swadesh 1971, p. 193. The exclamation point symbolizes a glottal stop: [ʔ].

[21] Ibid., p. 200.

[22] Lieberman 1972, p. 94.

[23] What follows is based partly on Wescott 1967; Swadesh 1971; and Kuipers 1968.

strange, the fact is that such languages still exist—for example, Kabardian in the northern Caucasus and Bella Coola in coastal British Columbia. As the main burden was on single consonants, there were probably more consonantal contrasts than a language would show today. But as more and more meanings had to be expressed, it became increasingly difficult to add more consonants, and some other device was needed. That of doubling consonants (to express plurality or repetition) had probably already been in use, and could most readily be extended to other meanings; and the splitting off of transitional vowels would have occurred also, making vowels distinctive within syllables. Sentence-like combinations of consonant-words would also have provided the raw material for more complex words. In any case, there was probably a stage in which words were made up of two consonants with or without a vowel contrast. For the first time, distinctive units were on the way to becoming meaningless, but they were probably larger than the units that we regard as distinctive today—roughly, syllables rather than phonemes.[24] As long as the total stock of words was not too large, it was possible for speakers to remember how to produce them as wholes. Words were mostly of one syllable and were to a large degree "transparent"—that is, the meanings of their component sounds were still partially preserved. But the syllable was now ready to fade out its meaning and become a mere building block. How this can happen is illustrated with the suffix *-let* in English, which is transparently 'small' in **rivulet,** but in **bracelet** and **bullet** merely serves to flesh out the words—the connection with **brace** and **ball** has been lost. The fact that the earliest forms of sound-writing (which represents words by their sounds rather than by pictures of their meaning) were syllabic (see pages 484–88) makes it clear that the syllable was the arbitrary unit of which speakers had become most conscious, though by that time the phonemes were there in latent form.

The phonemic stage probably came as a result of the increasing number of syllabic units as vocabularies grew larger and larger. The problem would not have been with *recognizing* words; our memories are capable of storing vast quantities of images configurationally, and we recognize faces and voices with no difficulty, and probably process words the same way when we *hear* them. *Saying* them so that someone else can recognize them is a different matter. Word-speaking and syllable-speaking are like freehand drawing. When there are not too many pictures to draw, one can store the instructions in an informal way: "Put that curl a little over to the left and slant the eye down a bit but not too much." The difficulty of making even two hundred pictures in this way is obvious, and the number of words in all living languages runs to thousands. So it

---

[24] Wescott 1967, p. 72, dates the syllabic period from about 300,000 to about 50,000 B.C., and the phonemic period from then on, with phonemes becoming completely meaningless about 10,000 years ago.

happened that formerly meaningful sounds were downgraded to a set of phonetic instructions. Instead of "put this curl a little to the left," children learn to "hit the /t/ phoneme in second position in this word"—like following a diagram numbered to guide the amateur's hand in drawing the picture of a face.

The beauty of this is that speakers can not only draw words as effectively as if they were real word-artists, but can exploit to the best advantage the limited range of their vocal apparatus. Only a comparatively small number of phonemes are needed; it is not necessary to crowd them; they can be made sharply distinct. Instead of five or six positions along the palatal ridge, two or three suffice, a good distance apart. Instead of a dozen tongue heights, three to five are enough. Even though you miss the target a bit, it is still easy to make each unit distinct from the rest.

This brought language to the stage where all the components it has today were either realized or on the verge. Complete realization was again adaptive. It meant the power to outwit natural enemies. It made possible a new kind of teamwork. Imagine it in operation in driving off or capturing a predator. Complex messages could be transmitted instantly to give precise instructions and keep members of the team informed of directions, locations, and movements. In competition with another tribe it spelt the difference between survival and extinction. Languages—if they and their speakers were to exist at all—had to reach the same level of sophistication in rather short order. For this reason it is not necessary to imagine that all human beings at one time in the past spoke a single language. All that was required was that whatever languages there were should become equally efficient.

VARIATION

The preceding stages can be thought of as the evolution *toward* languages. Subsequent developments are the evolution *of* language. There is undoubtedly movement in some direction, as there always is; but we are too close to it, and seem rather to be drifting in circles. It is a commonplace among most linguists, for example, that "no twentieth-century language is any more advanced than ancient Greek." If we knew what the outcome of the next ten thousand years of evolution was to be, we could measure the factors existing now that are leading to it; but in our ignorance we are unable to mark the signals that are the signs of progress. In any case, it is as if for the whole of recorded history, and no one knows how many hundreds of years before that, languages have merely reshuffled the game-pieces that they inherited from an unread past in an endless array of assortments without any difference in the rules of the game.

What we are most conscious of is that endless array, and the apparent change-without-progress kind of evolution whereby a given language at one stage is converted into a different language at a later stage. What causes it? There are millions of little causes, but the cornerstone of the Tower of Babel was that "ultimate" achievement of an almost meaningless layer, first of syllables and then of phonemes. It increased the symbolizing power of language geometrically, but sacrificed nearly every remnant of mutual intelligibility between dialects from tribe to tribe. Concept and symbol were "freed from each other to the extent that change could modify either one without affecting the other."[25] Change can be fairly rapid, and when groups of speakers are separated for any length of time they end up by not understanding one another, especially if they come into steady contact with speakers of some other language and there is extensive cultural and linguistic intermixture. There is also a certain tendency toward private language that aggravates this—not all speakers at all times *want* their language to be understood by others. In Ojibwa there is a fairly elaborate etiquette on how not to inform a questioner if his questions are unnecessary or impertinent or if the proper ground has not been laid for them by certain initial formalities.[26] In the Second World War Japanese cryptographers were baffled by an apparently unbreakable code being used in American military communications. They were not aware that Navaho Indians had been recruited to transmit the messages, which were undecipherable because they had no structural relationship with English. But mostly, unintelligibility is not intentional and results instead from the fact that sounds can evolve on their own without destroying meaning, so long as meaning is free to marry itself to any sound. This freedom is not quite total, but it is nearly enough so to have created an enormous variety of languages. Later chapters will deal with some of the ways in which change operates.

Monogenesis or polygenesis?

Some hints have already been dropped about whether all of today's languages are traceable to a common ancestor. The legend of a single primordial language persists like the legend of Adam and Eve, the single pair from whom all other human beings have sprung. The fact that we can trace many divergent languages today back to one ancestor—Russian and Czech, for example, to common Slavic—suggests that if one were to go back far enough all lines would converge. In the same way, allowing for intermarriage, only two individuals at the outset could account for the whole human family tree. Yet if all life forms as we know them

---

[25] Chafe 1970, p. 31.
[26] Black 1973, p. 19.

have evolved from earlier forms, it would be strange if at every evolutionary juncture just one pair, conveniently of opposite sexes, should have come into existence to serve as the ancestors of all later forms of that species. It would be just as strange if there had been a moment at which language emerged as the possession of just one society which thereafter transmitted it to its descendants and perhaps to imitators in other societies. Far more likely would be the presence of about as many languages as there were societies, rivaling one another in efficiency and improving through competition. The similarities that are often cited as indications of common source are as easily explained by the fact that human beings are built alike, live out their lives in the same world, and confront the same kinds of problems, and are often in close contact with one another, so that one society borrows from another even though their cultures may earlier have been quite dissimilar. All languages are apt to avoid an initial [fš] cluster because an [f] in that position would scarcely be audible, unlike the medial [fš] in *offshoot.* This is in the nature of the speech and hearing mechanism. All languages will have nouns because nature confronts us with recurring entities that have to be named and dealt with. And when Chinese cooking is imitated, **chow mein** and **foo yong** are borrowed along with it.

But there is another side to the question of monogenesis. Even granting that at no time was there just one language, it would still be possible for all the languages spoken today to have descended from a single ancestor, and it is still more possible, even probable, that all those spoken today are descendants of a relatively few of those spoken in the past—in other words, that today's languages have a higher degree of kinship than we have imagined. Figure 10–2 shows how this could have happened.[27]

The pessimistic statement at the beginning of this chapter, that *the primordial language can never be reconstructed,* thus needs to be qualified. We probably can never reconstruct a common ancestor for languages *A* through *H* (if indeed they had one), but it may still be possible to reach far back into prehistory and recapture an early dialect of language *E*—which could even turn out to be the ancestor of all living languages, assuming that language *B* had no survivors. One comparatist who believes that something like this may be possible is Mary LeCron Foster, who sees kinships among Asiatic and New World languages, along with proto-Indo-European, that have never been considered to be related. Her technique is to hypothesize sound-changes that will account

---

[27] Even this representation is oversimplified, because it fails to show intertwinings. One of the branches of *F,* for example, might have come in contact with the ancestor of E_5 before expiring and contributed elements to the latter language which live on. It is hard to write an epitaph for a language.

FIGURE 10–2
Hypothetical Genealogy of Modern Languages*

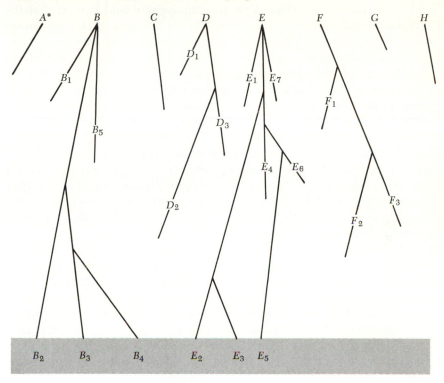

* Languages *A* through *H* represent possible original languages of man; the shaded area encloses the surviving descendants.

for differences in primitive roots, and to test the resulting model for consistency and productivity. As with all theoretical models, there comes a point where the predictive power can hardly be due to chance, and then we can be fairly sure that we have at least a shadow of the truth.[28]

A LOOK AHEAD

There is no more reason for us to suppose that language has played out its evolution than there would have been for a Neanderthal philosopher to assume that he was at the summit of human perfection with no greater

---

[28] See Foster 1975, and Swadesh 1966, especially p. 34.

achievement to be foreseen or imagined. What will be the key to the next surge—social regimentation? International communication? More and more compact societies? One anthropologist would have it that the "graphic period" already marks an epoch, with language change slowed down by writing, and that we are now in the throes of another, a "telecommunicative period," with rate of change retarded still further as recorded models of older speech are imitated.[29] But styles in writing evolve too, and the Network Standard is not apt to affect much besides pronunciation. Whatever will mark the new period is here now, in disguise. Like the Promised One, he is among us and we know him not.

Perhaps his name is Implicitness. If meaningful sounds, meaningful syllables, and meaningful words have been successively downgraded to serve as raw material for something yet more intricate, perhaps we are now unconsciously witnessing more and more the downgrading of higher sentences to form implicit elements in macrosentences, as we noted in the chapter on syntax. With the word *hopefully* in **Hopefully it will be tomorrow,** the speaker enshrines a whole sentence in one word—a sentence which if it were expressed would have to be a *main* sentence, which the speaker wants to subdue: **It is to be hoped that. . . .** Another example is *reportedly,* as in **Agnew was reportedly incensed at the charge,** where the complete form would be something like **Somebody issued a report; the report said that Agnew was incensed at the charge.** The reduction of sentences has been going on for a long time and may be on the increase, with the result that we shall end by implying more than we say—a fitting development in societies where people know more and more about their neighbors' affairs.

Or perhaps a more sweeping change will intervene, not in the structure of language but in its decreasing variety. The density of population makes some means of world communication more and more imperative, and a drift may be setting in—not yet toward just one language for everyone, but toward a universal second language that in time could become the first. A few altruistic scholars have looked for ways of speeding up the trend by constructing an interlanguage. But that is a story for a later chapter (see pages 580–82).

In any case, the time is past when it was not respectable to speculate on origins or try to forecast the future. Not being required to explain a miracle—the supposed quantum leap from no language to language—we can work comfortably with whatever evolutionary explanations our information will allow. Language was not stumbled on, invented, or given by the gods. It grows with us, almost as intimately as our arms and legs.

---

[29] Wescott 1967, pp. 72–73.

ADDITIONAL REMARKS
AND APPLICATIONS

1. Given the way language developed in the course of human evolution, how plausible are speculations on Martian or other extraterrestrial language?

2. Of the four shapes in Figure 10–1 (page 312), which two are most strikingly similar? Does the similarity support the notion of biological recapitulation?

3. What facial expressions with their related emotions strike you as similar between man and other animals? Consult the illustrations in Darwin 1913 (if you can obtain the book).

4. Do the emotions conveyed by facial expressions in human beings still have "fixity of reference"? Or is this really two questions? (1. Does a smile, for example, indicate 'happiness'? 2. If a person smiles, is he necessarily happy?) What has happened with all the expressions of emotion in human beings? How does this relate to the concept of *sincerity?*

5. Relate the evolutionary stages of holophrasis and metalanguage to the developmental stages in children (see pages 284–92). Is there a hint of recapitulation here?

6. A dog understands and obeys when his master says **Go get my hat.** Would you say that understanding the words involves segmenting them into distinctive sounds, or reacting to some overall or particularly salient feature? Give reasons for your answer.

7. Why is a completely vowel-less language practically unthinkable, even granting that there are languages that have no vowel *contrasts?* (See pages 37–38.)

8. There are probably remnants of facial gestures in some of the phonesthematic sets mentioned on pages 218–19. Do you sense something of this kind in *vicious, venomous, vitriolic, vixen, vituperative, vile, viper, vilify, vim, vital, vigorous, virile, vivid, vivacious, vindictive, vindicate?* What about the [p] of *yep* and *nope?* (Is this [p] ever released?)

9. What do the act of speaking and the act of throwing a stone have in common in the demands that they make on physical and mental evolution?

10. How might the fact that food came to be *prepared*—cooked, concentrated, and softened—have facilitated speech?

References

Bellugi, Ursula, and Edward S. Klima. 1973. "Formational Constraints on Language in a Visual Mode." Proposal to National Science Foundation from the Salk Institute for Biological Studies.

Bender, M. Lionel. 1973. "Linguistic Indeterminacy: Why You Cannot Reconstruct 'Proto-Human,'" *Language Sciences* 26:7–12.

Black, Mary B. 1973. "Ojibwa Questioning Etiquette and Use of Ambiguity," *Studies in Linguistics* 23:13–19.

Brown, Roger W. 1973. *A First Language: The Early Stages* (Cambridge, Mass.: Harvard University Press).

Chafe, Wallace. 1970. *Meaning and the Structure of Language* (Chicago: University of Chicago Press).

Darwin, Charles. 1913. *The Expression of the Emotions in Man and Animals* (New York: Appleton).

Foster, Mary LeCron. 1975. "The Symbolic Structure of Primordial Language," in Sherwood Washburn and Elizabeth R. McCown (eds.), *Perspectives in Human Evolution IV* (New York: Holt, Rinehart and Winston).

Gardner, R. Allen, and Beatrice T. Gardner. 1969. "Teaching Sign Language to a Chimpanzee," *Science* 165:664–72.

Hewes, Gordon W. 1971. *Language Origins: A Bibliography*. Department of Anthropology, University of Colorado.

———. 1973. "An Explicit Formulation of the Relationship Between Tool-Using, Tool-Making and the Emergence of Language," *Visible Language* 7:101–27.

Jakobson, Roman. 1969. "Linguistics in Its Relation to Other Sciences," in *Actes du Xᵉ Congrès International des Linguistes, Bucarest, 28 Août–2 Septembre 1967* (Bucarest: Editions de l'Academie de la République Socialiste de Roumanie).

Kuipers, A. H. 1968. "Unique Types and Typological Universals," in *Pratidānam: Indian, Iranian and Indo-European Studies Presented to Franciscus Bernardus Jacobus Kuiper on His Sixtieth Birthday* (The Hague: Mouton).

Lamendella, John T. 1975. *Introduction to the Neuropsychology of Language*. (Rowley, Mass.: Newbury House). Page references are to the manuscript.

Lieberman, Philip. 1972. *The Speech of Primates* (The Hague: Mouton).

———. 1974. "On the Evolution of Language: A Unified View," *Cognition* 2:59–94.

Premack, Ann James, and David Premack. 1972. "Teaching Language to an Ape," *Scientific American* 227:92–99.

Sebeok, Thomas A. 1969. "Semiotics and Ethology," *The Linguistic Reporter*, Suppl. 22, October, 9–15.

Swadesh, Morris. 1966. *El lenguaje y la vida humana* (Mexico City: Fondo de Cultura Económica).

———. 1971. *The Origin and Diversification of Language* (Chicago: Aldine Atherton).

Van Lancker, Diana. 1974. *Heterogeneity in Language and Speech: Neuro-linguistic Studies*. Ph.D. dissertation, Brown University.

Wescott, Roger W. 1967. "The Evolution of Language: Reopening a Closed Subject," *Studies in Linguistics* 19:67–81.

VARIATION IN SPACE 11

A woman who was born in Vermont but has lived many years in England returns for a visit. Looking for Church Street she misses her way and asks a Vermonter who happens to be walking in the opposite direction, "Can you tell me where Church Street is?" He answers "Yup" and walks on.

The visitor is willing to accept *yup* for *yes* because she has lived there before, but not the literal answer which omits the information she needs, and which she is fairly sure her non-informant knew that she needed. Is her annoyance due to a *linguistic* misinterpretation on his part—that is, has such a question as **Can you tell me where Church Street is?** ceased to be a yes–no question? Not quite, for a simple *no* answer would be appropriate if one lacked the information—followed, of course, with an apology. The fault lies in the neglect of *compliance* in a social situation that clearly called for more than the laconic affirmative.

This incident, with its stereotype of the down-easter, illustrates three things about the relationship between language and the world around it. First, the same meanings are expressed in different ways from area to area: **yup** and **yes** are only two of the variants that also include the Scotsman's **aye** and the Connecticuter's **eeyuh**, the German's **ja** and the Russian's **da**, and the countless forms that serve the same purpose in "other languages." Second, what is said has to be appropriate to the relationships between one speaker and another within a communicative

326

situation; the rules of speaking involve more than a simple interpretation of grammatical correctness. The realities of place-to-place and person-to-person-to-situation can be pictured as two kinds of space, geographical and social. What these signify for *meaning* is the third point: we learn the rules of space just as we learn those of grammar. "People not only know their language, they know how to use it."[1] Whether or not a given expression will be appropriate in a given situation, both of which we know from past experience, is part of our knowledge of the language and becomes one of the hovering meanings of the expression, like the inferential ones described in Chapter 7. In fact, the example used there (page 204) of the verb *want* in *I want something to eat* for 'I lack something to eat' shows just such a social meaning gravitating inward and becoming part of the lexical meaning of the word. In a broad sense, *all* of meaning responds to social space, since it is used in communicating with people and mostly about people. But a great deal of meaning responds directly to the interaction among speakers when they speak. Some of these keenly immediate meanings infuse the lexicon itself; others linger at the borders. *Want* is an extreme case of actual shift, but there are many others like it. The verbs *to come* and *to bring* retain their primary meanings of 'approach speaker' (*The train is coming*) and 'transport toward speaker' (*It is bringing my mother-in-law*); but for reasons of courtesy, secondary meanings have been added whereby the speaker can take the point of view of his hearer: *I'm coming to your party and bringing you a nice present.* One who *comes* to a party expects to be there as a more or less willing participant and probably as an invited guest; *I'm going to your party* would seem perfunctory if not rude. *I'm coming* violates the primary rule, since the approach is not toward where the speaker is; but a secondary rule supplants it within the social situation. It takes children quite a while to untangle these complications because they first have to grasp the role-playing involved.[2]

Grammatical rules can be affected as easily as lexical ones. Most languages have some manifestation of a non-present tense, usually associated with what has happened in the past. By being 'non-present' it is also in a sense 'unreal,' and this makes it suitable to soften a request or blunt a criticism. The clerk in a store is more apt to ask a customer *Did you want something?* than *Do you want something?*—the "past" tense does not confront the hearer quite so boldly. This of course burdens the grammar with a new meaning of *past,* and complicates such things as the auxiliary system, where the verb *owe,* for example, surrenders its past tense *ought* entirely to such courtesy uses and compels the

[1] Teeter 1973, p. 95.
[2] Keller-Cohen 1973.

language to create a new way of expressing pastness: we can say *You were under obligation to do it,* using simple *were;* but with the courtesy-oriented *ought* we must add another auxiliary: *You ought to have done it.*

On the other hand, the hovering social meaning need not actually affect a grammatical form. A nurse in a hospital brings two urns, one with coffee and one with tea, to the door of a patient's room. She wants to ask *Will you have coffee or tea?* As an alternative question, this is normally spoken

$$\text{Will you have } {}^{co}\!f\!f^{ee} \text{ or } t_{e_{a_?}}$$

But saying it that way would be rude, for it would close the door to a third alternative, which is to have neither. So she says

$$\text{Will you have } {}_{co}f\!f^{ee} \text{ }{}^{or} \text{ }te^{a^?}$$

a normal yes–no question, leaving it up to the hearer to supply, after *yes,* the additional information of which one, or perhaps both.

Straddling the line between lexicon and grammar are many of the expressions that were dealt with in Chapter 6, those signals that a speaker gives of how his hearer is supposed to understand what he is saying or is about to say or do. *See here* is a way of pointing out some object of interest that is near the speaker; but it also announces a reprimand: *Now see here! You had no business talking to her that way! Pardon me* to begin with is a command; at first remove it is a request to excuse some offense or inconvenience to the person spoken to; at second remove it is a request to be *allowed* to inconvenience someone, as in *Pardon me, may I get by?* *Now then* is a turn of the conversational wheel, dismissing all preliminaries and getting down to business.

The social meanings that are most firmly embedded of all in the grammar of a language are the sentence types themselves, which as we saw earlier (page 157) answer to communicative purposes: statements, questions, and commands. Basically a yes–no question subordinates the speaker to the hearer; there is a temporary *dependency* relationship. The command does the opposite. The normal intonation curves show this clearly: the question moves up, the command moves down. Statements answer to varying degrees of appeal or authoritativeness. The important thing is that a social criterion establishes a grammatical class. Once grammaticized—as was emphasized earlier—the social functions in turn become more elaborate, for one can use a question to express a command, mitigating the force of it just as by using a more wheedling intonation. The protocols of using one type of sentence or another become quite elaborate.[3] One would not, for instance, step into a room and immediately launch into an answer-type sentence such as *I took John to the movies last night.* No question has been asked, so it is necessary to pretend one or to make some other appeal to the hearer's attention: *Know what? (Guess what!) I took John to the movies last night.* A more formal introduction might be something like **Miss Mayberry, I have an item of possible interest to you: I took John to the movies last night.**

So much for the tangled web that binds words and grammar to social meanings. It affords a rather different view from the popular one that language is a mere exchange of information; instead it is the means of cultural interaction, of which exchange of information is only a part.[4]

"Social space" and "geographical space" help to describe *synchronic* linguistics, distinguishing it from *diachronic* linguistics—the first referring to the way languages differ from languages and dialects from dialects at a given point in time, the second to the changes that take place in the course of evolution. But a slight redefinition is in order, to make it clear that geography in a literal sense has nothing to do with the matter. A tribe can strike its tents and move a thousand miles, and if its members stick together and avoid contact with speakers of any other language, the new location will be the same as the old as far as the language is concerned. The movement relative to mountain chains and rivers is as irrelevant to the language as the external drift of the solar system is to life on earth (except only that as new *things* are encountered new *names* will have to be provided—but that can happen to stay-at-homes too). So rather than geography we should think of membership within a speech community, which usually, though not necessarily, corresponds to some bounded area. It is easy to take geography too literally and miss the fact that ghetto speakers speak as they do just as much because of where they are in a linguistic sense as Southern States speakers do. The fact that one place is a kind of social prison while the boundaries of the other are open does not make one more or less of a speech community than the other.

The important distinction is between where one "belongs" and what one does. People can be seen as victims—willing or unwilling or unwitting members of the communities where they were born or confined—

---

[3] See Grayshon 1974.
[4] Kirch 1973, p. 341.

or as actors who are privileged to adopt more than one role. A careful student of social variation says, of the latter view, "As far as we can see, there are no single-style speakers."[5] At the very least we have one style of speaking at home and another style in the market place, both within a single speech community. As a rule there is no sharp line between informal and formal but a gradation that extends through several degrees of familiarity within the home (sister to sister, mother to daughter, daughter to mother), up a ladder with rungs for friend to friend, adult to child, boss to assistant, parishioner to priest, and ends in the frigid and rigid formality of envoy to monarch. The metaphor of "up" reveals the value that speakers place on these levels. Formal speech is esteemed either because it is associated with a dominant social class or because it is a mark of respect or both.

Where people belong as speakers—that is, the existence of communities—may of course condition the adoption of roles. A social worker who has several styles within her own community and assumes different roles when interacting with her superior or with her fellow workers may adopt the norms of ghetto speech in order to communicate better with the people she ministers to or because she feels genuine solidarity with them. There is no difference between this and learning an entirely different language when living abroad. Sub-communities of various kinds exist in every complex society, and not every speaker participates in all of them, but every speaker participates in more than one according to age, sex, profession, and voluntary or involuntary association—from military encampment to sorority or fraternal lodge. There is a sports community, and the professionals belong in it and use its jargon—they are more or less trapped; but the amateurs join it now and then and play the role.

Each of the two ways of looking at variation in space has its specialists. Those who concentrate on where speakers belong follow the lead of classical sociology. They are interested in populations and statistics, in the assimilation of minorities and broad-scale language policy. The mapping of dialect areas is their oldest specialty—Southern States speech, North Midland speech, Tidewater Area speech, and so on. Those who concentrate on what speakers do follow the lead of social anthropology. Their concern is with the "ethnography of speaking,"[6] described as the "interrelations of speaker, addressee, audience, topic, channel, and setting."[7] The average speaker may be conscious of the difference between the two viewpoints when someone he talks to behaves in an unexpected way. If the other person is being served in our house and

---

[5] Labov 1970, p. 46.

[6] Hymes 1962.

[7] Labov 1970, p. 30. See also Hannerz 1970.

refers to the food as *grub,* we may object to his behavior or his attitude; the occasion (or our self-esteem) calls for more formality. But if he calls it *vittles* we are more apt to think of him as a hick or an old-timer: where is he from, what group does he belong to?

One particular kind of role-playing deserves to be elaborated on ahead of all the rest because the nature of language forces it on us: everyone behaves now as speaker, now as listener. Interest has focused excessively on the speaker's role; this is clear in the general use of the word *speaker* where 'user of the language' is intended. The reasons why speaking gets the most attention are obvious. In phonetics it involves articulation, the only kind of processing that is open to easy observation. In grammar it covers what we hear people say, and can record or write down to analyze later. And it is limited in scope: we know this much at least about our ability to understand, that it is vastly greater than our ability to produce. The order of magnitude is approximately that of how many paintings an amateur can recognize as against how many he can paint himself. The speaker's grammar is relatively compact. It is part of his identity; he is not expected to be other than what he is, unless he is an actor, and great versatility is not demanded of him. But he has to interact with others who are what they are, and whose idiosyncrasies he must somehow surmount. We saw on pages 54–56 how within a fairly short while a listener can set up a series of correspondences to match what he hears with what he himself does. The more such adjustments he makes the larger his listening grammar becomes.

Since the speaker and hearer roles are the most fundamental of all, they have the profoundest effect on the grammars that correspond to them. In a sense, the speaking grammar is a derivative of the listening one. If we understand speakers who use sounds, words, and rules that we do not use, and at the same time accept these ways of speaking as perfectly valid representatives of our language, it must be because we have a more inclusive consciousness of the total grammar than just of the part that corresponds to our own way of expressing ourselves. As one observer puts it, "After a child has been well exposed to a few critical lects he formulates an internal grammar fairly close to a panlectal grammar of his native language."[8] This is to say that one who has had to interpret a representative variety of lects (speaking grammars) will formulate a general grammar of the language from which the special cases can be deduced—including his own.

The notion of the panlectal grammar helps to explain something that appeared to be little more than a curiosity when it was first brought up: the many striking ways in which transformational derivation and his-

---

[8] Bailey 1970.

torical derivation resemble each other. Suppose we hear someone say
Hit don't make no difference, and have to accommodate our listener's
grammar to include *hit* as a variant of our speaking grammar's form *it.*
We might observe that *Hit don't make no difference* bears the same
relationship to *I don't like it* that *He beat me* bears to *I hate 'im:* in both
cases an /h/ that is initial in the sentence is lost when the pronoun
is used unemphatically in the interior of the sentence. So we have a
correspondence rule which might read something like "We both have
an /h/ which is lost in interior position, but mine is lost with *it*
initially as well, though not with *he, him, his,* or *her.*" This interdialectal
rule mirrors the historical one: there was an /h/ in those forms which
was lost first in unemphatic position and then, for *it* (which was unemphatic most of the time anyway), in all positions. To the extent that
the existing forms in a language are derived from a common base, it can
easily happen that the best deductive rule for tying them together in
our heads is one that traces them to a form that duplicates a previously
existing one.

If among roles those of speaker and hearer occupy a special place,
among communities there is a community that is just as special: the
Community of One. Every speaker has an *idiolect,* just as every collec-
tivity of speakers has a *dialect.* We are most conscious of this in the
pet words and expressions that individuals use. Theodore Roosevelt
salted his speech with the word *strenuous,* which caught on as a result.
Mark Twain enjoyed the sound of *mephitic.* The senator from Maine
for many years, Owen Brewster, continually used the expression *on
that score.* Idiosyncrasies of speech can be used to caricature a person
as effectively as the jut of a chin or the bulge of a nose—as with
Richard Nixon's *I want to make one thing perfectly clear.* Idiolects
differ from dialects just as dialects differ from languages: the range of
variation in either case is narrower. That is why we can single out
pet expressions—the narrow range favors a relatively higher frequency
of the relatively fewer things that are said, by comparison with the
larger group. This also makes it possible to do something with individuals that everybody enjoys doing with groups but that gets more
and more dangerous the larger the group: to look for personality traits
in the way language is used. There are undoubtedly characteristics of
whole communities that are revealed through language. Many Spanish
males accentuate their masculinity by glottalizing their speech, a trait
that Latin Americans find extremely funny. With individuals, traits of
speech are interpreted quite directly as indicators of personality. In TV
broadcasts during 1964 and 1965, Harry Truman repeatedly used the
phrase *That's all there was to it,* which was typical of his downright
temperament. In one experiment with voice types, using criteria of

speed and loudness, judges had no difficulty rating the personalities of a hundred or so male college students as "bright, self-sufficient, resourceful" (for loud-fast), "bright, aggressive, competitive, confident, self-secure, radical, self-sufficient, resourceful" (for loud-slow), and so on.[9] Voice quality and choice of words are easy and spontaneous indicators. Syntax is less obvious, at least in speech. In written language it leads to questions of style, and that in turn to an art that may conceal as much as it reveals about the personality. In any case it is a subject to itself.

SPEECH COMMUNITIES

Though *where* a community is does not necessarily count for much in the effect it has on the language used, it is traditional to distinguish between groupings in a society that are anchored to a location and groupings that are not. The study of dialectal variation got its start in countries with fairly stable populations where the most interesting differences were those associated with particular localities. The result has been an *areal linguistics* that has accumulated a great body of literature, and that can be separated, for convenience, from the study of other communities. But we will look at the latter first.

Non-areal communities

There is no limit to the ways in which human beings league themselves together for self-identification, security, gain, amusement, worship, or any of the other purposes that are held in common; consequently there is no limit to the number and variety of speech communities that are to be found in a society.

First are the communities to which society assigns us because of the value it places on some biological classification, especially sex and age. At the outset both sex and age represent biological facts, not speech communities. Males and females have a different linguistic birthright. Females are almost never dyslexic, which suggests a more stable genetic equipment for language: reading problems and speech problems affect the male half of the population. Females learn to talk earlier, learn foreign languages faster and better, and do more talking in their lifetime than males do, though social factors join biological ones in the

---

[9] Markel, Phillis, Vargas, and Howard 1972.

later developments. The anthropologist Gordon Hewes states the evolutionary background for the differences:

> No one seriously supposes that the consistent precocity of girls in acquiring speech, and their lower incidence of speech defects, can be attributed to cultural learning differences. . . . The point is that [the observed differences between girls and boys] are compatible with our reconstructions of early hominid behavior, in which males would have been the principal hunters, trackers, and protectors of the group—with a survival premium on ability to analyze environmental noises, as well as spatial and constructional abilities—whereas females, as the main transmitters of speech to infants, as well as the sex with the greater need to detect the emotional overtones of vocal messages, could be expected to be more precocious in language-learning and less prone to speech defects. . . .[10]

We might add that in spite of the failure of society to educate them in any field, women from Sappho through Teresa de Ávila to modern times have become brilliant poets and novelists, while women mathematicians and composers have been few.

Age differences show biological factors even more clearly. We are not born with language, and all the successive grammars sketched in Chapter 9 are correlated with biological growth. Adulthood also has its biological trademark. The brain internalizes language at an ever slowing rate, with the result that an elderly person gradually loses the capacity to absorb new data and ends by speaking in ways that identify him as old, even if he stays clear of the society of other old people. There are also some less important physiological differences, such as pitch: male speakers show a gradual lowering of pitch from preadolescence to around forty years of age, a level (relatively speaking) until around sixty, and then a rise.[11]

With the biological foundation to build on, and social structures that tend to throw women into the company of other women and children into the company of playmates, it is not surprising that the communities of sex and age come to rank among those with the most clearly marked linguistic differences. After the first few months children learn more language from other children than from adults. Even some of the traits of early childhood grammars that were noted in Chapter 9 may be transmitted from child to child as much as they are re-formed with each generation: such things as the past tense forms *throwed, fighted, runned.* We judge these as "nonstandard" because children are forced to *un*learn them; but there are other things that make up the pool of childish expressions which children learn from children and then simply

---

[10] Hewes 1973, p. 115.
[11] Hollien and Shipp 1972.

lay aside or forget later. The verb *to stand* is—or was—common in children's contests—for example, *Johnny and me'll stand you three*—but is not even recorded in the principal English dictionaries. *All right for you* is a child's resentful dismissal of someone who has failed him. *Get* with an infinitive complement, while used somewhat nowadays by adults, is more usual with children: *He gets to go but I don't.* Rather than a linguistic heritage this perhaps reflects a child's greater dependence on permission to do things. The most thoroughly documented case for the transmission of language from children to children, very largely by-passing the older generation, is that of Black English. In one study of selected features of Black English, those who used the forms most consistently were children up to the age of five. Between five and eight the children shift to predominantly standard forms, though around ten there is a slight reversion, presumably an assertion of identity.[12] Later the standard comes to prevail more and more.[13]

The transmission of child language is not concerted by society; it just happens. Age-related varieties that are a part of adulthood are more apt to be deliberately cultivated, even ritualistic. Children of the Cham villages in Vietnam speak like their mothers, whose pronunciation differs in several ways from that of their fathers. But the boys, as they grow older and study the Cham writing, adopt the pronunciation of their fathers.[14] This is of course a sex-and-age distinction. Among the Ainu of Northern Japan there is a purely age-related elderly speech that "persists in its own right and is adopted by younger people as they gradually mature"—an "old speech" which does not itself grow old and die out.[15]

Probably all societies institutionalize the differences between male speech and female speech at least to some extent. Sex differences in speech have been noted by writers in English since at least the sixteenth century, and were recorded for Carib in Wilhelm Bréton's dictionary published in 1664.[16] In Koasati, an Indian language spoken in Louisiana, there are morphological differences between words when used by men and when used by women. Roughly they involve the addition or substitution of an [s] in men's speech at the end of words that lack it in women's speech. The distinction is now fading, with women adopting men's forms. There apparently was no stigma attached to the women's forms, though, as male speakers were heard to admire it and to be

---

[12] Hall and Freedle 1975.

[13] See especially the work of William Labov—for example, the age comparisons in Labov 1972, p. 807.

[14] Blood 1961.

[15] Hattori 1964.

[16] Data from Key 1972, p. 15.

annoyed by all the hissing in their own speech.[17] Sex differences have captured attention in recent years through the protests of women's liberation, which has campaigned for the abolition of differences that denigrate women. There are perhaps more of these in language *about* women than in language *of* women—some of them were mentioned in an earlier chapter (see page 249). But women's actual usage often reflects the same subordination. There is a great deal in women's speech in English that reflects extra politeness, one aspect of which is "leaving a decision open, not imposing your mind, or views, or claims, on anyone else." Two patterns reveal this decisively: the abundance of tag questions (*The war in Vietnam is terrible, isn't it?*) and the high frequency of a rising intonation on utterances that are not syntactically questions, as when a woman responds to her husband's question *When will dinner be ready?* with

$$O^{hh} \quad\quad\quad six \; o^{'clock?^{18}}$$
$$around$$

How much of women's speech is unjustly different and how much is simply different would be hard to decide and of course is irrelevant to the general question. In the role that they have traditionally played (whether the tradition is a just one or not—societies only sporadically get around to the question of justice), women have been the peace-keepers and socializers at home and the ingratiators elsewhere. This has caused them to avoid using "rough" language, and to be the first to say exaggeratedly nice things. The latter is one reason for the greater abundance of intensifiers. Women were probably the ones who turned *rather* and *quite* into pure expressions of degree. Their influence can be seen in the evolution of *such* and *so* from correlating determiners to plain intensifiers. Conservative male usage still requires that these words be followed by *that* or *as*, or have a *that* or *as* clearly implied by the context: *He is such a tall fellow (he is so tall) that he practically tops the basket,* but not *He is such a tall fellow!* nor *He is so tall!* It is easy to recognize many other differences in vocabulary between men and women. A man is free to use expletives like *shit* and *bastard* among men; women till recently were limited to such exclamations as *fudge* and *oh, dear.* A woman may say *The wall is mauve,* but if a man says it, "one might well conclude that he was either imitating a woman sarcastically,

---

[17] Haas 1964.
[18] The observation and the examples are from Lakoff 1973, pp. 54–57.

or was a homosexual, or an interior decorator"—fine color discriminations are for women.[19]

Unless it is continuously re-created, a distinct female speech is hard
to maintain because with their traditional custody of children women
transmit their speech characteristics to their male offspring. This is
happening with the young male speakers of Cham, mentioned above,
who neglect to learn the Cham script. In a study of pronunciation in
Mexico City it was found that a rather sudden change had taken place
in the past forty years, spreading across socioeconomic groups and age
groups, in the pronunciation of the trilled [rr]. Women apparently
started the fashion of assibilating it (making it like an [s]), and
children imitated their mothers.[20]

It is difficult to speak of sex differences without mixing the community and role approaches that we are trying to keep apart. If a child
talks like an adult we are more apt to praise than blame him. If a
woman talks like a man, both men and women may look askance.
Lawyers talk like lawyers when in the presence of lawyers: the community is sustained from within. Women talk like women when in the
presence of men as well as among themselves: the pressure is from
without as well as from within. A woman is constrained to play her role
in ways that a lawyer is not.

English-speaking societies are no exception; in fact, they are free by
comparison with certain others. In Japan the underlying concept of
dependency affects a much broader range of communities—the dependency of

> the child on the parents, the employee on the employer, the poor on the
> rich, the student on the teacher . . . ; the female is considered as depend-
> ing on the male for her own identity and existence, and as such inferior in
> the social scale of value, and hence clearly marked in the system of speech
> levels.[21]

If biology has some slight but genuine influence in setting apart the
speech communities of young and old, male and female, its only value
where Black English is concerned is in calling attention to it. The
historical basis for Black English is the African pidgin that was used
in the slave trade and was the only language available to blacks sometimes deliberately thrown together from different language backgrounds
to keep them from communicating effectively with one another. As with
all pidgins—which are discussed later in this chapter—the nuisance

---

[19] Lakoff 1973, p. 49.
[20] Perissinotto 1972.
[21] Saint-Jacques 1973, p. 93.

TABLE 11–1
Some Examples of Syntactic Differences Between Standard and Non-standard English

Variable	Standard English	Black Non-standard English
Linking verb (copula)	He *is* going.	He ——— goin'.
Possessive marker	John*'s* cousin.	John ——— cousin.
Plural marker	I have five cent*s*.	I got five cent ———.
Third-person singular (verb agreement)	He live*s* in New York.	He live ——— in New York.
Past marker	Yesterday he walk*ed* home.	Yesterday he walk ——— home.
'If' construction	I asked *if he did it.*	I ask *did he do it.*
Negation	I *don't* have *any.*	I *don't* got *none.*
Use of 'be'	*Statement:* He is here *all the time.*	*Statement:* He *be* here.
Subject expression	John moved.	John, *he* move.
Verb form	I *drank* the milk.	I *drunk* the milk.
Future form	I *will go* home.	*I'ma* go home.
Indefinite article	I want *an* apple.	I want *a* apple.
Pronoun form	*We* have to do it.	*Us* got to do it.
Pronoun expressing possession	*His* book.	*He* book.
Preposition	He is over *at* John's house.	He over *to* John house.
	He teaches *at* Francis Pool.	He teach ——— Francis Pool.
Use of 'do'	*Contradiction:* No, he *isn't.*	*Contradiction:* No, he *don't.*

SOURCE: From Hall and Freedle 1973, p. 445. By permission of S. Karger AG, Basel, Switzerland. Adapted from J. C. Baratz 1969, "A Bi-dialectal Task for Determining Language Proficiency in Economically Disadvantaged Negro Children," *Child Development* 40:99–100. While all the items in the third column are undoubtedly more frequent in black non-standard, not all are exclusive to it. *I ask did he do it* is cited for the *did he do it* part (the *ask* for *asked* is irrelevant here), but such questions are common in standard English and seem to be gaining ground. Similarly *John, he moved* and *I want a apple,* while not standard, are common among many speakers other than blacks.

irregularities of morphology were discarded and syntax was simplified. The result was that as blacks gradually rebuilt a speech community in the lands to which they were transported, they had to reconstitute the grammar, which retained certain features of the pidgin even while it was being "relexified" with words taken in constantly from the standard (see Table 11–1). The result is that unlike the differences that set other

FIGURE 11–1
Tense in Black English

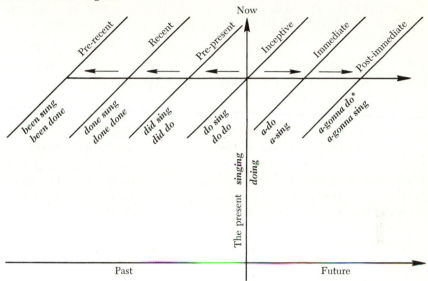

SOURCE: Adapted from Fickett 1972, p. 18. Reprinted by permission of the *Journal of English Linguistics.*

* The indefinite **gonna do, gonna sing** does not appear because it has no fixed relation to the other forms.

non-standard dialects apart, a number of the ones that distinguish Black English are in the grammatical signals rather than in the lexicon.[22] Two of the most striking are the non-use of the copula *to be* under some conditions and the system of tenses. The fact that the copula is often a grammatical luxury has been brought out before (see page 157). Black English sensibly omits it when it is superfluous: ***They sick.***[23] As for the tenses, they are elaborately systematized, as can be seen in Figure 11–1. *I singing* represents action in progress at the present moment. As for the tenses and aspects,

> ***I do see him*** is just anterior to the present and intrudes upon it, and is therefore the *past inceptive tense.* ***I did see him*** is slightly longer ago, or the *pre-present tense.* ***I done seen him*** is still further ago, or the *recent past.* ***I been seen him*** is even farther ago and is designated as the *pre-*

---

[22] Stewart 1968. For a full discussion see Dillard 1972.

[23] The example is from Dillard 1972, p. 53. The black speaker—aiming at the standard—may also say ***Im is sick;*** and there are other mixtures due to code switching.

recent past. Moving ahead from the present, if someone says *I'm a-do it,* he will do it in approximately 30 seconds, or in the *immediate future.* If someone says *I'm a-gonna do it,* he will do it soon, that is, in the *post-immediate future.* If he says *I gonna do it,* however, the execution may be indefinitely delayed.[24]

The phonology of Black English is equally distinctive. We have already seen that one of the offshoots of African pidgin has a most un-English feature, phonemic tone (see page 45); the same importation of tonal contrasts from African languages influenced the intonation of the black dialect called Gullah, spoken on the Sea Islands of Georgia and South Carolina and the nearby mainland coast.[25] Black English in general seems to have been affected to the point of having sharper pitch variations than the standard, and this according to one theory may partly account for the fact that Black English has more pauses at wide intonation breaks and divides sentences into shorter clause groups.[26]

The African origin of Black English has been the focus of a controversy, some traditional dialectologists tending to regard it as little more than a special variety of Southern States English, others emphasizing the African heritage. As with all encounters between speakers of different languages, exchanges have gone both ways. Probably much of what gives standard American Southern its flavor—at least in pronunciation—comes from Black English. "In Charleston and other Tidewater centers, educated white speakers employ a variety of English quite similar to their counterparts in Barbados, Trinidad, and elsewhere in the Caribbean,"[27] where the influence of the language spoken by the slaves is unmistakable. In the early years of the American colonies the English spoken was fairly uniform. But with black nurses in charge of white children in their formative years, and particularly with children of both races playing together rather freely up to a certain age, imitation of the phonological features was inevitable, repeating what happened on a larger scale with Anglo-Saxon nurses and Norman French children and their playmates in the England of the twelfth and thirteenth centuries.

We turn now to communities that people can more or less voluntarily *join.* The language variety here can be properly called a *code,* though the term is loosely used of any variety (including the ones already described) that a speaker feels free to adopt for a particular purpose.

---

[24] Fickett 1972, p. 19.

[25] Turner 1949, chapter on Gullah intonation.

[26] Engel 1972.

[27] Bailey 1974, p. 15.

Codes are often referred to as jargons, especially by outsiders who have difficulty understanding them, and indeed we have already seen some of the social dangers of the kind of linguistic isolationism that jargons may lead to (see pages 257–59). Private groups too easily insulate themselves from the ordinary correctives for idiocy and falsehood, which need to be understood if they are to be laughed or driven out of court. There is an enormous amount of sheer dead weight in the special vocabularies of certain professions or occupations—horses do not need to be measured in *hands,* distances at sea by *leagues,* depths by *fathoms;* a *two-syllable* word does not have to be called *dissyllabic,* nor does *soldier* have to be called a *troop (**He had 800 troops under his command**),* especially when a troop is also a whole company. No sports announcer will use the same word for 'defeat' twice in succession if he can avoid it, and most use the same tone of voice, a kind of half-high-pitched hurried monotone. The most famous example of over-extended specificity is the terms for 'group of birds or animals,' attributed to Joseph Strutt's *Sports and Pastimes of the People of England,* where the terms are explained as "a peculiar kind of language invented by the sportsmen of the middle ages, which it was necessary for every lover of the chase to be acquainted with":[28]

a sege of herons and bitterns
a herd of swans, cranes and curlews
a dopping of sheldrakes
a spring of teals
a covert of coots
a gaggle of geese
a skein of geese (flying)
a bevy of quails
a covey of partridges
a congregation of plovers
a walk (or wisp) of snipe
a fall of woodcocks
a murmuration of starlings
an exaltation of larks
a watch of nightingales
a badelynge of ducks
a sord (or sute) of mallards
a muster of peacocks
a flight of doves and swallows
a building of rooks
a brood of hens
a host of sparrows

a nye of pheasants
a cast of hawks
a plump of wildfowl
a desert of lapwings
a company of widgeon
a chattering of choughs
a pride of lions
a lepe of leopards
a herd of harts, bucks, and
    all sorts of deer
a bevy of roes
a sloth of bears
a singular of boars
a sownder of wild swine
a dryft of tame swine
a route of wolves
a harras of horses
a rag of colts
a stud of mares
a pace of asses
a baren of mules
a drove of kine

[28] From *Word Study* (February 1942), reprinted from *The Week-End Book* (Harmondsworth, England: Penguins, 1938).

a flock of sheep   a nest of rabbits
a tribe of goats   a clownder of cats
a sculk of foxes   a kendel of young cats
a cete of badgers   a shrewdness of apes
a richesse of martens   a labour of moles
a fesynes of ferrets   a mute of hounds
a huske (or down) of hares   a cowardice of curs
a dule of turtle

On the other hand, highly specialized activities in a technical field require special ways of talking. How this affects one part of the medical profession has been described as follows:

> How did the surgeon acquire his knowledge of the structure of the human body? In part this comes from the surgeon's firsthand experience during his long training. But what made this experience fruitful was the surgeon's earlier training, the distillation of generations of past experience which was transmitted to the surgeon in his anatomy classes. It has taken hundreds of years and millions of dissections to build up the detailed and accurate picture of the structure of the human body that enables the surgeon to know where to cut. A highly specialized sublanguage has evolved for the sole purpose of describing this structure. The surgeon had to learn this jargon of anatomy before the anatomical facts could be effectively transmitted to him. Thus, underlying the "effective action" of the surgeon is an "effective language."[29]

Occupational codes are distinguished chiefly by their vocabulary. The carpenter, the physician, the mechanic, the farmer—each has his particular objects and operations to name. But certain occupations—especially the ones whose operations are mostly verbal—develop other linguistic peculiarities as well. The intonation of sports announcers has already been mentioned. That of politicians is typical enough to caricature:

I know that I speak for every
                                        loyal A
                                              merican. . . .

That of old-time preachers was described by Mark Twain in the fifth chapter of *Tom Sawyer:* "His voice began on a medium key and climbed steadily up till it reached a certain point, where it bore with strong emphasis upon the topmost word and then plunged down as if from a spring-board":

----

[29] Bross 1973, p. 217.

Shall I be carried toe the skies, on flow'ry beds of ease,

Whilst others fight to win the prize, and sail thro' blood-y seas?[30]

While professional jargons may fail to be understood by default, there are other jargons that are not understood by design. Their speakers use them for concealment, and they are typical of communities that want to shut the rest of the world out. They may be casual communities—no more, perhaps, than groups of children trying to fool other children by talking in pig Latin—but more usually they are communities that make fairly consistent use of their secret language to further private or antisocial activities. Among the Walbiri of Central Australia there is a kind of male-status secret language called tᵛiliwiri, which boys start learning at thirteen. It consists in substituting words that are contrary in meaning in one semantic feature: 'hot' for 'cold,' 'flat ground' for 'hole,' 'older brother' for 'younger brother,' and so on (but not, for example, 'older brother' for 'younger sister,' which would differ by two features). Adult males can speak at normal rates and be understood.[31] The Hanunóo of the Philippines have an approved way of talking during courtship that calls for a high degree of skill in keeping messages from being understood by others, particularly by rivals and older adults. It may involve only certain mechanics—for instance, barely audible whispering, an extremely rapid rate of speaking, falsetto, or activation of sounds by inhaling rather than by exhaling. It may also involve a complicated rearrangement of the sounds, or the partial substitution of other sounds, in a word. For example, the word **rignuk** 'tame' may appear as **nugrik, rignuŋ, qayrig,** or **rinsiŋ,** or it may be spelled out according to the Hanunóo syllabary. The secret language is part of a pattern of concealment that includes clandestine trysts and disguises.[32] The most furtive

---

[30] Reprinted by permission of Harper & Row, Publishers.
[31] Cazden 1972, reporting Kenneth Hale.
[32] Conklin 1959.

activity of all is that of criminals, and the most practical criminal jargon is that of pickpockets, who have to be able to transmit signals in full hearing of their victims without being detected. Here are some examples:

> When the tool locates the victim's bankroll or wallet he may name that location to the stalls in argot. That is, he may say in an undertone *Left bridge* or *Right bridge,* or *Kiss the dog,* or whatever instructions may be necessary to inform the stalls, so that they can put the victim into position for the tool to work. The tool may likewise communicate with the stalls during the theft, giving them instructions such as *Raust* or *Come through,* or *Stick,* or *Stick and split me out* or *Turn him for a pit,* etc. All tools give the stalls an *office* or signal when they take the wallet. . . . It seems incredible that the victim does not register this dialogue centered so personally upon him, but I do not know of any court case where the victim either caught the pickpockets in the act or became suspicious as they rifled his pockets, in which the victim reported hearing any of this interchange. . . .[33]

One finds an element of concealment, or at least of exclusiveness, in any jargon, professional or popular, that makes for identity or cohesiveness within the community. Being able to talk the lingo of sociologists is a badge of membership in the guild. College slang is to some extent a way of closing the doors on conventional speakers, while the educational establishment is supposedly trying to open doors a crack in the opposite direction: "There is reason to believe that this is exactly the success that education is after, for it serves to mark many people as unsuccessful and to let into the club only those who are willing to play the success games that the class in control asks them to play."[34] Language provides both its direct and its reverse snob appeal and snob identification.

There are secret languages that do not aim at concealment so much as at mystery, which come mainly in two kinds, incantations and glossolalia. Both have magical and religious ties. The spells of witchcraft and the esoteric speech of a medium at a seance are examples of the first. "Speaking in tongues" is another term for the second, which has long been associated with ecstatic religious experience. In Acts of the Apostles, 19:6, we read that "when Paul had laid his hands upon them, the Holy Spirit came on them; and they spake with tongues, and prophesied." The speaker is supposed not to be in control of what he is saying, and while the sounds generally conform to those of his language, his utterance is not intelligible unless the hearer can match it with a similar occult power of interpretation. Glossolalia was formerly restricted in the United States to minor Protestant groups but in recent years has spread to some of the larger denominations. Though social

---

[33] Maurer 1955, pp. 53–54.
[34] O'Neil 1970, p. 2.

scientists have taken it to be a symptom of some form of mental disturbance, in one test the glossolalists turned out to be somewhat less neurotic than a control group from a conventional church.[35]

Areal communities

The largest areal communities are simply those that speak a distinct language—most often within a single geographical area but, as with Latin in the third century and English today, sometimes flung wide across the world and with discontinuities between. But what is a different language? And how large is large? Some mutually unintelligible languages are spoken by only a few hundred people, and the distance to the next language may only be over the hill in either direction (see page 13). Intelligibility is as hard to pin down as difference and size: if we can make adjustments in our listener's grammar that expand it to include many speaker's grammars, we can do the same with a neighboring language if it is not too much unlike our own. There is no really satisfactory definition of *language* that will distinguish it from *dialect*.[36] Political boundaries force people on either side to turn their backs on each other most of the time, but even there one finds a gradation, albeit steeper than anything within the borders. What most distinguishes areal communities from non-areal ones is the relationship of inclusion: we speak of dialects *of* English and modern dialects *of* Latin, the latter referring to ways of speaking as diverse as French, Rumanian, and Portuguese, each of which has dialects of its own and subdialects within dialects. A mechanic who belongs to the Methodist church and the Masonic lodge and coaches a Little League team on weekends belongs to four non-areal communities, not counting his other memberships—sex, age, politics, and so on. He is less apt to belong to two different areal communities, though even this overlap is common enough in parts of the world that still bear the marks of recent conquest, as happens throughout Latin America, where many speakers belong to the community of Spanish or Portuguese and to that of one or more native languages as well. Map 11–1 gives an idea of the enormous linguistic diversity in Middle America (Mexico and Central America) that is more or less superficially overlaid by Spanish. A milder version

---

[35] Wolfram 1973, p. 39.

[36] One has been proposed, which is that if two varieties have the same underlying forms, they are dialects of a single language; if not, they are different languages even though they may be mutually intelligible. The example given is the Spanish of Spain and that of Latin America, which together represent numerous dialects of one language, as against either of these when compared with the Spanish of the Sephardic Jews, a different language. See Agard 1971. The difficulty with this definition is that getting agreement on the underlying forms may be just the same problem under another name.

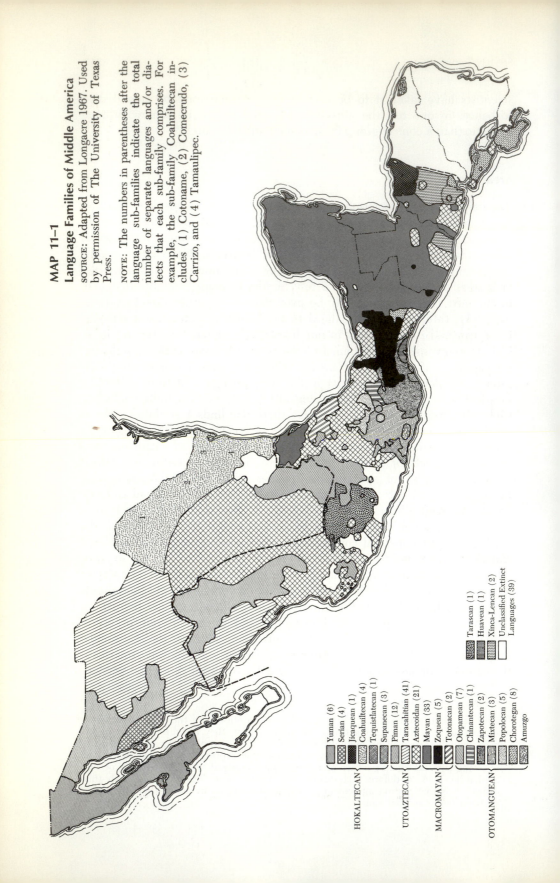

MAP 11-1
Language Families of Middle America

SOURCE: Adapted from Longacre 1967. Used by permission of The University of Texas Press.

NOTE: The numbers in parentheses after the language sub-families indicate the total number of separate languages and/or dialects that each sub-family comprises. For example, the sub-family Coahuiltecan includes (1) Cotoname, (2) Comecrudo, (3) Carrizo, and (4) Tamaulipec.

HOKALTECAN
- Yuman (6)
- Serian (4)
- Jicaquean (1)
- Coahuiltecan (4)
- Tequistlatecan (1)
- Supanecan (3)

UTOAZTECAN
- Piman (12)
- Tarachitian (41)
- Aztecoidan (21)

MACROMAYAN
- Mayan (33)
- Zoquean (5)

OTOMANGUEAN
- Totonacan (2)
- Otopamean (7)
- Chinantecan (1)
- Zapotecan (2)
- Mixtecan (3)
- Popolocan (5)
- Chorotegan (8)
- Amuzgo

- Tarascan (1)
- Huavean (1)
- Xinca-Lencan (2)
- Unclassified Extinct Languages (39)

of this is found in more homogeneous areas where a generalized variety of a language is used for official communication and a local variety for most other purposes. The official variety may or may not at the same time be the local variety for some fortunate segment of the population (the ruling class, as with Southern British, or the ruling area, as with Parisian French), but as it tends to be associated with literature and hence to preserve older forms, it is convenient to use as a point of reference in describing varieties. These can be studied as variants *of* the standard. This would ordinarily be done anyway, as the standard represents the seat of power. And such was the setting for the earliest work on dialects, which looked at local varieties not so much in terms of their own structure as in terms of the quaint differences from the standard. For many non-linguists the word *dialect* still carries the stigma of that association. Figure 11–2 shows, along the vertical or time dimension, the real historical development over the centuries, and also shows the fictitious derivation, as a kind of reflection in the horizontal plane of the present, with the standard masquerading as the source of the dialects. Ideally the historical source and the standard would coincide, just as underlying forms ideally converge with historically original forms (see pages 80–82).

Serious investigation of geographical dialects began in the latter part of the nineteenth century. The first comprehensive study was made in North and Central Germany by Georg Wenker. A smaller study followed in Denmark, and between 1902 and 1908 Jules Gilliéron published his *Atlas Linguistique de la France,* the most influential work of its kind. Since the turn of the century materials have been collected for similar atlases all over the world. In the United States the model has been the *Linguistic Atlas of New England,* directed by Hans Kurath and published between 1939 and 1943. Other regional atlases have followed, the most recent being the *Linguistic Atlas of the Upper Midwest,* by Harold B. Allen, already partly published and scheduled for completion in 1976. Fieldworkers are now investigating the English of the Deep South of the United States. The resulting *Linguistic Atlas of the Gulf States* will show at least eleven regional dialects.[37] Canada is the most important area in North America yet to be mapped for English. The work has already begun under the direction of H. M. Scargill (Scargill 1973).

As the name implies, a linguistic atlas is a collection of maps showing the prevalence of particular speech forms in particular areas. What the dialect geographer most often selects to mark off a dialect area is simply its preference for certain words. Differences in pronunciation or syntax yield a more reliable measure, but words are easier to work with; information can even be gathered by mail through a questionnaire that asks

---

[37] Pederson 1971.

FIGURE 11–2
Diachronic and Synchronic "Derivation"

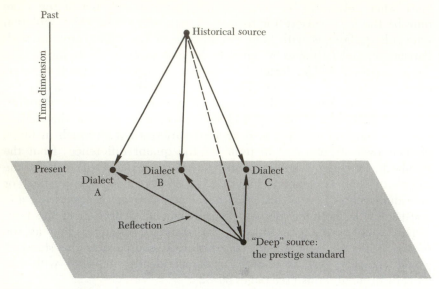

what words a speaker uses for particular meanings: is a field enclosure made of stone called a *stone wall,* a *stone fence,* a *rock wall,* or a *rock fence?* Are drains that take rainwater off a roof called *eaves troughs, water spouting, gutters,* or *rain spouts?* For greater accuracy, detailed phonetic information is needed. Trained interviewers must be sent to the scene and may spend hours with a single informant. Does he pronounce *soot* to rime with *boot* or with *put?* Is his final consonant in *with* like that of *bath* or that of *bathe?* Does his pronunciation of *tomato* end with the same vowel sound as *panda,* or is it like *grotto?* The Swiss German atlas, published in 1962, was based on a questionnaire containing 2600 items, which took from four to eight days to administer. Its phonetic discriminations were exquisite—as many as twenty-one different tongue heights, for example, in front unrounded vowels.[38] Items chosen to test differences in vocabulary, pronunciation, and syntax are the ones most likely to reveal the peculiarities of everyday speech: names of household objects, foods, parts of the body, weather phenomena, numbers, and so on.

Unless he is combining his interest as a linguist with an extracurricular one as a folklorist or sociologist, the dialect geographer is less concerned with the items in a questionnaire for their own sake than as indicators of where to draw the boundary lines and how to trace the routes of speakers who have migrated from one area to another. The

---

[38] Moulton 1963.

MAP 11–2
**Seven Heterophonic Lines Dividing West from East
In Southern England***

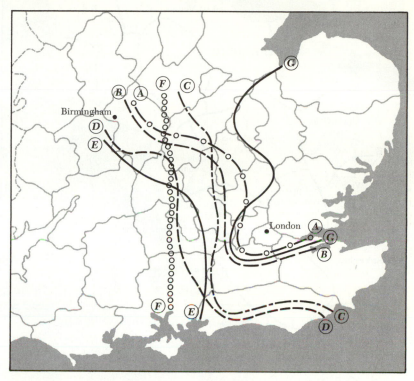

SOURCE: Adapted from Kurath and Loman 1970, p. 34. Used by permission of The University of Alabama Press. © 1970.

* The lines separate two different pronunciations of the following: Ⓐ *ear,* Ⓑ *law,* Ⓒ *lane,* Ⓓ *three,* Ⓔ *cow,* Ⓕ *new,* and Ⓖ *apple.*

latter—the fanning out of dialects from their original centers and their crisscrossing and blending as the wave moves outward—is of special significance in a country like the United States, with its extraordinarily mobile population.

Boundaries are set by mapping the farthest points to which a given form has penetrated. When a line—termed an *isogloss* if it has to do with words, an *isophone* if with sounds—is drawn connecting these points, it is usually found to lie close to the lines drawn for other forms—for instance, the same speakers who say **snake feeder** for 'dragonfly' are also apt to pronounce the word **greasy** as **greazy.** The interlocking lines form a bundle of isoglosses (or isophones) and represent the frontier of the dialect in question. In Map 11–2 we see seven isophones (called *hetero-*

MAP 11–3
Word Geography of the Eastern States

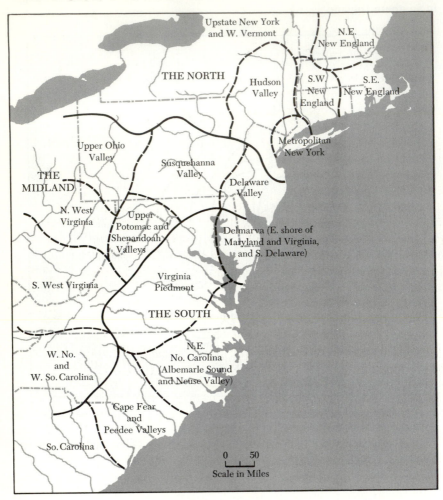

Upstate New York
and W. Vermont

N.E.
New England

THE NORTH

Hudson
Valley

S.W.
New
England

S.E.
New England

Metropolitan
New York

Upper Ohio
Valley

Susquehanna
Valley

THE
MIDLAND

Delaware
Valley

N. West
Virginia

Upper
Potomac and
Shenandoah
Valleys

Delmarva (E. shore of
Maryland and Virginia,
and S. Delaware)

S. West Virginia

Virginia
Piedmont

THE SOUTH

N.E.
No. Carolina
(Albemarle Sound
and Neuse Valley)

W. No.
and
W. So. Carolina

Cape Fear
and
Peedee Valleys

So. Carolina

0   50
Scale in Miles

SOURCE: Adapted from Kurath 1949. Used by permission of The University of
Michigan Press.

phonic lines here because they represent pairs of oppositions such as
[a] versus [æ] in *apple*) that show how Southern England is divided into
two main dialect areas, roughly along a line from London to Birmingham.

In the eastern part of the United States, English divides rather clearly
into three grand dialect areas. They reflect the settlement of those areas
by early migrants from England who brought their dialects with them.
One such dialectal transplant from England is the vowel in words

like *half, bath, aunt, glass,* and *laugh.* We easily recognize one way of pronouncing these words as a feature of cultivated speech in the East and of over-cultivated speech elsewhere. It is by no means uniform (in Eastern Virginia, for example, it will be heard in *master* and *aunt* but not in many other words), and represents one side of a split that took place in the eastern counties of England before the American Revolution. The /a/ was transplanted from those counties as folk speech by immigrants to New England, but it also took root in London and so became established as fashionable speech in the parts of the country that maintained the closest ties with England.[39] Map 11-3 shows the three areas (plus subdialectal sections) known, from their geographical position, as Northern, Midland, and Southern.

As the population spread westward the boundaries became more and more blurred. The earlier, more gradual movement extended them fairly evenly as far as the Mississippi. Maps 11-4 and 11-5 show the northern limit of certain Midland terms and the southern limit of certain Northern terms, as this rather complex bundle of isoglosses traversed the states of Ohio, Indiana, and Illinois. By the time the migrants had flowed up against the Rocky Mountains, the three tides had broken into a series of rivulets and eddies. Where a given area was settled mainly by speakers of a given dialect, that dialect of course prevailed. The area around Hayden, Colorado, was turned into a kind of Northern island by a group of women schoolteachers who came out from Ann Arbor, Michigan, and married ranchers there. Later, as younger speakers grew up and intermarried, Northern and Midland traits were blended (see Map 11-6). California is where the greatest amount of leveling out of differences has occurred, because of the in-migration from other areas.[40]

Dialect blending is not confined to the West but goes on wherever the streams of communication, which seem to grow swifter every day, overflow the earlier lines. In northern Illinois, for example, which Maps 11-4 and 11-5 divide between a Northern and a Midland dialect area, the lines again are growing dim. The following list—of interest also as a sample of the kind of vocabulary used—enumerates words that are receding in the predominantly Midland area of Illinois, even though half of them were Midland to begin with:

1. *window blind* 'shade for a window, on a spring roller' (Midland)

2. *woodshed*

3. *pigpen*

---

[39] Kurath 1965, pp. 239-40.
[40] Metcalf 1972.

MAP 11–4
Midland Terms, Northern Limit, in Ohio, Indiana, and Illinois

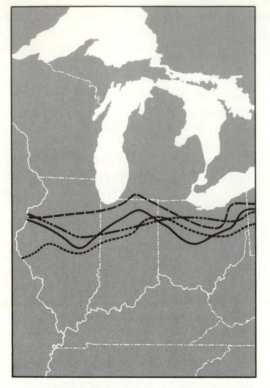

Grea[z]y ──────────

Snake feeder ── ── ── ──

Sook, so ──·····──·····──
   (call to cows)

Sugar tree ·············

SOURCE: Adapted from Marckwardt 1957, pp. 10–11. Used by permission of The University of Alabama Press. © 1957.

4. ***pulley bone*** 'breastbone of a chicken, wishbone' (Southern, South Midland)

5. ***light bread*** 'bread made with yeast' (Southern, South Midland)

6. ***hay doodle*** 'small pile of hay' (Midland)

7. ***trestle*** 'saw horse with an X-frame'

8. ***poo-wee!*** a call to hogs

9. ***poison vine*** 'poison ivy'

10. ***cement road*** 'concrete road'

11. ***to favor*** 'to resemble,' as in ***John favors his father***

MAP 11–5
Northern Terms, Southern Limit, in Ohio, Indiana, and Illinois

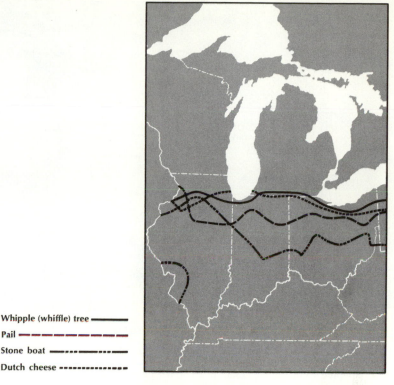

Whipple (whiffle) tree ━━━━━
Pail ━ ━ ━ ━ ━ ━ ━ ━ ━
Stone boat ━ ‒‒ ━ ‒‒ ━
Dutch cheese ‒‒‒‒‒‒‒‒‒‒‒‒‒

SOURCE: Adapted from Marckwardt 1957, pp. 10–11. Used by permission of The University of Alabama Press. © 1957.

12. **baby cab**   'baby carriage' (Midland)

13. **belling**   'shivaree' (Midland)

14. **belly buster**   'dive in coasting prone on a sled, belly flop' (Midland)[41]

Two metaphors describe the extremes of diffusion. One is the relay race, the other the cross-country. In the first, a speaker picks up something from his neighbor to the east and runs with it as far as his neighbor to the west, always staying between them. In the second, a speaker breaks loose from the paternal neighborhood and travels to all points of

---

[41] Shuy 1962, p. 59. Professor Shuy was kind enough to provide definitions.

MAP 11–6
Northern–Midland Mixture in Colorado, Younger Informants

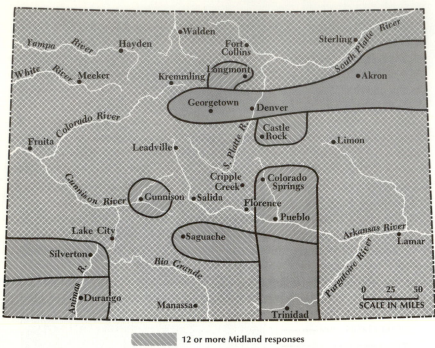

■ 12 or more Midland responses

■ 11 or more Northern responses

SOURCE: Adapted from Hankey 1960, p. 24. Used by permission of The University of Alabama Press. © 1960.

the compass, picking up pieces at each stop and dropping them all along the way. The latter is the kind of diffusion that makes dialectology a hazardous business. As Robert Louis Stevenson wrote in *The Amateur Emigrant,*

> I knew I liked Mr. Jones from the moment I saw him. I thought him by his face to be Scottish; nor could his accent undeceive me. For as there is a *lingua franca* of many tongues on the moles and in the feluccas of the Mediterranean, so there is a free or common accent among English-speaking men who follow the sea. They catch a twang of a New England port, from a cockney skipper, even a Scotsman sometimes learns to drop an *h*; a word of a dialect is picked up from another hand in the forecastle; until often the result is undecipherable, and you have to ask for a man's place of birth.[42]

---

[42] *South Seas Edition* (New York: Charles Scribner's Sons, 1925), p. 9.

The compilers of the new *Dictionary of American Regional English* are at present editing the most comprehensive survey ever made of recorded speech, covering dialects of the United States from Florida to Alaska, for which they have tried "to collect the greater part . . . of the words and phrases, pronunciations, spellings, and meanings used . . . up to the present time."[43] Besides bringing to light the quantities of unregistered written forms in obscure places, this project will rescue uncounted expressions that would otherwise be lost as their users died away because the forms existed only in the spoken language. The estimated five million entries are being processed by computers. (The compilers of the vast *Oxford English Dictionary* assembled three and a half million entries by hand.)

In Europe, dialect geography lacks much of the here-and-now flavor that it has in the United States. With a more stable population and with more radical linguistic as well as geographical and political barriers to surmount, European dialects are bound more tightly to their localities and have more to tell us about events long ago than about recent ones.

The most thoroughly investigated dialects anywhere in the world are those of the Romance languages, which are themselves, of course, just dialects of Latin that drifted apart in the early years of the Christian era. Since more is known about Latin—thanks partly to the very dialectal facts that it helps to illuminate—than about any other ancient language, dialectology in the Romance area has closer ties to historical linguistics than it has anywhere else.

The dialectologist who looked most consistently to geography as a key to the history of dialects was the Italian Matteo Bàrtoli. It should be possible, he thought, to correlate the past evolution of dialects with their positions relative to one another, and he expressed the correlation in a set of four "areal norms":

1. Norm of the isolated area: an area that is cut off and shielded from communication tends to retain older forms.

2. Norm of the lateral area: where a central area is wedged into the middle of a zone that presumably was once homogeneous, the edges of that area tend to retain older forms.

3. Norm of the principal area: if a zone is split into two segments, the larger one tends to retain the older forms. (This is in partial conflict with norms 1 and 2.)

4. Norm of the later area: an area that has been overrun—as by conquest—at a more recent date tends to retain older forms.

---

[43] Cassidy 1967, p. 14.

The norm of the lateral area is the most picturesque, with its suggestion of an adventurous dialect driving across the territory of a sedentary one and overspreading it everywhere except at the edges. Using the Romance languages in their present state as evidence of what probably happened while the speakers of Vulgar Latin were still more or less in touch with Rome, we can see in Table 11–2 the effect of continued contact in France and Italy as against interrupted contact, and hence the retention of older forms, in Spain and Rumania.

The norm of the lateral area explains how it can happen that countries as far apart as Rumania and Spain share forms and meanings that are missing in the areas that lie between. But why, if all these languages have a common source, should they be so different today? Mostly because the Romans, in their expeditions, made contact with speakers of other languages and for a time spoke some form of mixed language with them. This raises the question of a special kind of areal community mentioned earlier in connection with Black English, that of contact languages, or pidgins. Wherever speakers of different languages are thrown together, whether at trading posts or slave stations or on the battlefield, they devise a compromise language to deal with the essentials. African pidgin was one such. Another, often mixed with it in North America, was the pidgin used to communicate with Indian tribes. The Portuguese in their trades, travels, and conquests established pidgins around the world, including an African pidgin of their own that influenced the language of blacks in both English-speaking and Spanish-speaking America.[44] The English-based pidgin of Melanesia (New Guinea, the Bismarck Archipelago, the Solomon Islands, and other areas) was important enough in the Second World War for the United States Armed Forces Institute to publish a manual for its use.[45] Examples: *Bimeby leg belong you he-all-right 'gain* 'Your leg will get well again'; *Sick he-down-im me* ('sickness downs me') 'I am sick'; *Me like-im sauce-pan belong cook-im bread* 'I want a pan for cooking bread.'

A pidgin may continue as a mere trade language and vanish when trade is cut off, or events may cause it to survive as the only language its users have available to them.[46] This happened with the pidgin ancestor of Black English, and also with the French-based pidgin in Haiti. The result then is that the pidgin is learned as a native language, and the process of *creolization* begins: the children do their work, and the creole evolves like any other language. Haitian was a pidgin that has become a creole; so is Gullah, and so is Police Motu, a pidgin in

---

[44] Granda 1970.

[45] Hall 1943.

[46] Hall 1962.

TABLE 11–2
Equivalent Terms in Four Romance Languages

Spain	*France*	*Italy*	*Rumania*
hermoso	beau	bello	frumos
mesa	table	tavola	masa
hervir	bouillir	bollire	a fierbe
entonces	alors	allora	atunci
día	jour	giorno	zi
más	plus	più	mai

SOURCE: Adapted from Coseriu 1956, p. 38.

the early stages of creolization in the neighborhood of Port Moresby in New Guinea, which is based not on English but on Motu, a Malayo-Polynesian language.[47] In a broad sense we all speak creoles, for all languages are mixed.

The variety of data in this section reveals why linguists for years resisted tackling problems of sociolinguistics and why many still do. Once the gate is open an uncontrollable flood of issues, questions, and controversies comes pouring in, many of them having little or nothing to do with language as a reasonably well-defined object of study. The difficulty is the same as with meaning, only on a larger scale. We saw how hard it is to tell when we have laid hold of the meaning *of* a term rather than a meaning that is a hanger-on and may be valid for some, invalid for others, present on one occasion, absent on another. A linguist ought to be able to occupy himself with what is *in* a language, not with everything else in the world. The American who sees a sign in an Aberdeen shop window reading **Cook by gas** assumes that this is a dialectal difference between Scots and American English. But is it? Suppose that **by** and **with** in both dialects retain their normal ties to the meaning of 'agency' and 'means' (or 'accompaniment'), and the difference is due to a different *attitude* toward the operation of certain mechanical things (the American **It is run by electricity** perhaps reveals the same animistic viewpoint toward a source of power). Is **cook by gas** then a linguistic question or a cultural one? The nature of language makes it an uncomfortable field for people who like precision.

---

[47] Hooley 1965.

REGISTERS, REPERTORIES, ROLES, AND REPUTATIONS

A *register* is a variety that is not typically identified with any particular speech community but is tied to the communicative occasion. It would be odd to think of people-at-home as a community, yet speech-at-home may be as different from speech-with-strangers as a local dialect is from the standard. One cannot be dogmatic about this because registers can easily become identified with particular groups. Speech-with-one's-friends is a register midway between speech-at-home and speech-with-formal-acquaintances; but if one's friends all belong to Hell's Angels the register acquires community ties.

A speaker's *repertory* is the set of linguistic varieties that he has at his command, each of which enables him to play a *role* defined within a speech community or a social situation. He may play the sycophant to a superior—a socially determined role that will lead him to use ingratiating mannerisms and flattering language; he will choose words from a particular register. Or he may meet with members of his union to discuss a strike; the language he uses will be that of his occupational community.

The *reputation* of a variety is the value placed on it by society. Not all roles are freely played. Some are forced on their users. One variety may capture the schools. Another may be actively campaigned against and marked for extinction.

Registers

> What the [New York] *Times* calls *a reproof* or a *remonstrance,* the *News* calls a *belch* or a *beef.* A rash of strikes is described by the *Times* as a *plethora,* by the *News* as a *bellyfull.* When the *Times* becomes *indignant,* it *deplores;* when the *News* gets *sore,* it says, *Nuts.*[48]
>
> While shouts of *Amen!, Right on!,* or *Tell it like it is!* would be appropriate to spur on the minister of a revival meeting in a small Southern church, the professor giving a lecture on astrophysics at a university would be surprised to receive encouragement in such a form, even though he may be just as desirous of attentiveness from his audience as the minister is from his.[49]

These quotes make it clear that everyone is conscious of the appropriateness, or lack of it, between language on the one hand and occasion, audience, or channel on the other. Mostly it is a question of various degrees of formality, at least some of which can be found in any com-

---

[48] *The New Yorker* (31 May 1947), p. 31.
[49] Di Pietro 1973, p. 20.

munity, areal or non-areal. Even though Manchester or Chicago English may not consider itself in the prestige class of Southern British, there nevertheless are more formal or less formal varieties of each, with the formal varieties tending to be more alike from place to place than the informal ones; and within a religious community a conversation between lay brothers is likely to be more relaxed than one between a brother and a superior.

For convenience one may divide the up-and-down continuum of formality and familiarity into levels, as two linguists have done, recognizing the following five: (1) oratorical, or frozen; (2) deliberative, or formal; (3) consultative; (4) casual; (5) intimate.[50] The oratorical register is used by professional speakers; it is a self-conscious form of public address. The deliberative register is aimed at any audience too large for effective interchange with the speaker. Both oratorical and deliberative tend to be monologs, though deliberative is not polished as an art form. Consultative is typically dialog, at the level where words still have to be chosen with some care; most business is transacted in this register. Casual implies the absence of any social barriers—the relationship, for example, between fellow students. Intimate adds kinship or close friendship.

Most writing is addressed to audiences that cannot talk back, and accordingly tends to be upgraded to the deliberative level (the written counterpart of oratorical is poetry or poetic prose). This is true even in narrations. Raymond Chandler recorded the impression that Dashiell Hammett made by breaking with this tradition: "A rather revolutionary debunking of both the language and material of fiction had been going on for some time. . . . Hammett applied it to the detective story, and this, because of its heavy crust of English gentility and American pseudo-gentility, was pretty hard to get moving." It was hard to put people down on paper as they were, and "make them talk and think in the language they customarily used."[51]

The relative formality of writing of course reflects the fact that it is always more or less grafted onto the language that we learn first as children and that always remains for us the warmest and most interior part. The bookish overlay is cold and unexpressive, as one inner-city schoolchild revealed in the following interchange with the teacher:

> STUDENT (reading from an autobiographical essay): This lady didn't have no sense.
> TEACHER: What would be the standard English alternate for this sentence?

---

[50] Joos 1967, and Gleason 1965, pp. 357–61.
[51] *Pocket Atlantic* (New York: Pocket Books, 1946), pp. 209–10.

STUDENT: She didn't have any sense. But not this lady: *she didn't have no sense.*[52]

Since registers are social phenomena, they are manifested in other ways besides the strictly linguistic: by deferential or respectful or domineering mannerisms, gestures, and tone of voice. But linguistic behavior shows them most unmistakably, and there are forms of speech that are clearly identified with particular registers. The example most often cited is that of forms of address. In most if not all societies the ways of saying 'you' must be watched with care; it is the word that most intimately *hits* the person, next to his own name, with which it shares some of the same taboo character (see pages 440–41). Even in the English of the United States, to address someone with **Hey, you!** is insulting by comparison with the familiar **Hey, bud!** Most if not all European languages have, or have had, two or more forms of 'you' for different registers—in French **tu** and **vous,** in German **Du** and **Sie,** familiar and formal respectively. The formal maintains a certain social distance, for whatever reason—newness of acquaintance, respect, hostility; the familiar is used when the distance has been bridged. English no longer requires that a formal **ye, you** be distinguished from a familiar **thou, thee; you** has been generalized. But at the top register we still address a judge as **your honor** and a cardinal as **your eminence,** with the added courtesy of the third singular form of the verb instead of the form directly associated with **you.** Another way of avoiding the threat of **you** is to use an exclusive **we** ('you and I'), which nurses in hospitals have the reputation of favoring. An example is the following, said by a nineteen-year-old American student to her five-year-old Japanese tutee, who was delaying things by insisting on tying his shoes: **Why don't we not worry about your shoes, OK?**[53] Besides the dodging of **you,** we see here three other components of courtesy behavior: a negative, to suggest rather than to command; a question, likewise; and the addition of a question tag, leaving acceptance of the suggestion open to the hearer.

The French **tu–vous** distinction, informal versus formal, is the prevailing type in Europe, but there are more complex systems. One that is more complex by just one step is that of Uruguay, where a once-snobbish **tú** (from standard Spanish) has wedged itself between the familiar **vos** and the formal **usted,** so that nowadays a young man is apt to call his closest male friends **vos** but use the **tú** as a casual form with women friends; women may respond in the same way, though they tend

---

[52] Grimshaw 1973, p. 33, quoting John J. Gumperz.
[53] Videotape shown at Stanford University, 4 December 1973, to Language Teaching Study Group from the People's Republic of China.

to generalize *tú* for both intimate and casual.[54] The seventeenth century Spanish dramatist Lope de Vega puts a discussion of the 'you' forms in one of his dramas. Angela has just been told that Leonardo, whom she loves, is really her brother. To put distance between them, she shifts from addressing him as *tú* and uses the extra-courteous *vuesa merced* ('your grace'). He complains of her coldness, and a friend chimes in with the tongue-in-cheek argument that with all the pleasant connotations of 'grace' he ought to be flattered. Meanwhile, responding to his sweetheart's *vuesa merced,* he has had to shift from *tú* to the formal *vos.* (*Vos* had not yet been downgraded to the meaning it now has in Uruguay). The discussion characterizes *tú* as the form used with those we love—and with coachmen and other inferiors.[55] Italian and German had a similar three-point system, which is declining now as it has in standard Spanish, but Catalan maintains it: the middle term, *vós,* is used "among equals who have known each other for a long time, as a sign of respect; and also to speak with peasants."[56] Japanese has a much more complex scheme in which four levels of formality intersect with two levels of respect, the latter expressed by forms of the verb. The levels of formality, which are identified as *informal, polite, superpolite,* and *formal writing,* can be illustrated by the ways of expressing 'yes': *un, ee, hai,* and *sikari,* respectively.[57]

The Japanese system extends register distinctions beyond forms of address, and other languages do the same, more or less consistently. The ways of saying *yes* in English are not so strictly formalized as in Japanese, but even more delicate distinctions can be drawn with intonation. As for *no,* it is particularly sensitive to register, and is regulated not only by intonation but by a wide choice of expressions. If a person is being served at table, rather than *No more, please* it may be considered better manners to say *Thank you* with a headshake or a gesture of the hand. In expressing disbelief it is often better to start with *Well* and then hesitate than to use an outright negation. Instead of *I disagree* it is usually preferable to say *I don't know* and then state one's own opinion. In Mernkwen, a language spoken in the Cameroons, it is enough to say *ngang wa,* with *ngang* meaning 'no' and *wa* being a formalized expression of respect. But intonation and gesture are so important in this that if a girl's

---

[54] Ricci and Ricci 1962–63. The *vos* is better known as an areal problem. See Rona 1967.

[55] Lope de Vega Carpio, *¿De cuándo acá nos vino?* in his *Obras,* new ed. (Madrid: Real Academia Española, 1929), p. 692. The reference is thanks to Joseph Silverman.

[56] Corominas 1954; see the entry "Vos."

[57] Kuno 1973, pp. 19–22.

parents ask her if she would like to marry a particular suitor and she says not *ngang wa* but simply *ngang* accompanied by a deep sigh, her 'no' means 'yes.'[58]

It is not unusual for syntax to be affected as well. In Chinese, the idea that one group of officials (A) is more numerous than another group (B) is expressed in a lecture as

A	*dwō*	*yú*	*B*
A	numerous	than	B

and in a conversation as

A	*bǐ*	*B*	*dwō*
A	compared to	B	numerous[59]

Syntactic differences in English are to be found at one extreme in the dropping or contraction of words at the beginning of utterances *(Taste good?* for *Does it taste good? Nat a good orange?* for *Isn't that a good orange?)* and at the other extreme in special writing styles—for example, the substitution in newspaper headlines of the present tense for the present perfect *(Heath Resigns* for *Heath Has Resigned).*[60] There may even be a register restriction that hampers a speaker in expressing a particular meaning. This has happened with the phrase *sure enough,* which is informal and yet is the only way we have of expressing 'this proposition confirms a prior expectation' *(I was hoping he would be there by noon and sure enough he showed up at twelve on the dot);* the French, Italian and Spanish expressions (French *en effet*) are not branded for register. Vocabulary is where the richest spread of differences can be found. The following scale gives some approximations:

Intimate	*Casual*	*Consultative*	*Formal*	*Frozen*
cute	pretty	attractive		comely
to guzzle	to swig	to drink	to imbibe	to quaff
nutty	crazy	insane	demented	mad
	scared	frightened	apprehensive	affrighted
slanted	catercorner	diagonal	oblique	
on the ball	smart	intelligent	perceptive	astute
to play like (he was dead)	to act like	to pretend		to feign (death)

---

[58] Grayshon 1973.
[59] De Francis 1951, p. 50.
[60] Greenbaum 1975.

It is not easy to fill out a chart of this sort because other meanings besides those of register usually intervene. *Intelligent* and *perceptive,* for example, are not exactly as shown here, but differ also in terms of a feature of sensitivity that attaches to *perceptive;* and the levels may switch. All the same, *perceptive* tends to be a shade higher than *intelligent.* Another interfering factor is that of slang, which always belongs in the two bottom levels but does not define them. Thus *tipsy* and *crocked* are equally casual but *crocked* would be felt as more slangy.

Register distinctions in pronunciation are more apt to show themselves as "misses" rather than "differences"—that is, the speaker takes less care or more care to articulate distinctly, but the phonemes are the same. Where there are phonemic differences they tend to attach themselves to particular words; thus a person who always refers to his *mother* when talking outside the family may refer to her as *muvver* to a close relative, retaining an infantile pronunciation that is sanctioned in the family. The supposed cultural preeminence of Britain and later of Boston and environs has led to many socially marked pronunciations: [áyðər] for [íðər], [vázəz] for [vésəz], [ánvəlop] for [ɛ́nvəlop], [əsyúm] for [əsúm], and so on; many of these are modeled on French.

The register levels are complicated by overlappings from various speech communities. A street gang almost by definition uses forms from casual, though it has forms that set it apart from other communities at whatever register. A society of chemists would for the most part hold its meetings and transact its business using consultative or formal. Here again we find socially marked forms. In everyday usage *iodine* is pronounced [ayədayn] by most Americans, but a chemist may call it [ayɔdin], to match the pronunciation of the other halogens, *fluorine, chlorine, bromine,* and *astatine.* The *aluminum* of commerce is the *aluminium* of chemistry. A sailor's *below* is a landlubber's *downstairs.*

Repertories and roles

A speaker's repertory typically includes varieties of a single language, but it is not unusual for one or more of the "varieties" to be in some additional language. This does not mean that problems of speech community—German versus Czech, or English versus Italian, say—supersede those of register. In parts of the world where conquest has imposed a language from outside, after a time the older and the newer languages may achieve a modus vivendi that is termed *stable bilingualism,* with one language serving in one capacity and the other in another, often with register distinctions. In Paraguay the majority of urban families are bilingual, using Spanish for official purposes and Guaraní among equals in the home and with friends; in some families "it is considered lacking in respect for a child to address an older person in Guaraní," though he normally uses it with his playmates.[61] Even where two rival varieties represent the "same language" they may differ quite radically, as happens with the standard language and the local dialects in Norway: two students home for a vacation will use the standard when talking about school matters but will switch to dialect to talk about other topics.[62] This illustrates another point: how difficult it is to separate attitudes toward speakers from attitudes toward subjects. Even though the students may be close friends, their academic identity submerges their relation of intimacy, and they choose their roles accordingly.

The kind and degree of bilingualism reflects the nature and organization of society. If speakers of various languages or dialects are brought so closely together that they have to intercommunicate, and yet no group yields to any other, the result is some form of common speech that is not native to anyone. This is the case of modern standard Arabic, which is taught in the schools and is used in communicating across dialects. It was also the situation in Europe for several hundred years after Latin had ceased to be a colloquial language but was maintained for high-level communication.[63] (A pidgin is also a non-native shared language, but results from inter-societal rather than intra-societal contacts—see pages 356–57.) At the other extreme there have been societies so rigidly stratified linguistically as well as socially that bilingualism was the exception—the elites used one language for their intra-group communication, the masses another; this was true of several pre–First World War European countries.[64]

The more usual situation with bilingualism is that only a part of the population—generally a minority with little power—is obliged to play a role in more than one language. The majority speech is compulsory, with compulsion often backed by law, but the minority one is kept up, with varying success. This has happened repeatedly in the United States as waves of Germans, Italians, Poles, Swedes, and others have immigrated and created their own close-knit settlements. In time the minority is usually absorbed and its language disappears. At present the minority that has attracted the greatest attention is the Chicano population in the American Southwest, along with its Puerto Rican counterpart in the Northeast. In Chicano bilingual speech one finds several kinds of language mixing, including, of course, code switching. Thus if both speakers know both languages, one of them may say one sentence in Spanish

---

[61] Morínigo 1931, p. 30.

[62] Cazden 1972, p. 152.

[63] Kaye 1972.

[64] See Fishman 1967.

and the next in English and then switch back; one language may simply be more convenient for a particular topic than the other.

If the minority wields political power or possesses the outer size and inner strength to maintain an ethnic identity, the community may remain bilingual indefinitely, or even reassert its own native speech. That is the situation in French Canada. In other parts of the world—Switzerland, for example—bilingualism is a natural consequence of a federation of minorities. One has to interact with speakers of other languages and learns to switch codes with relative ease.

If one does not have to shift to a second language but only to another variety or another register, code switching is just one of many aspects of normal, painless communication. But sometimes it is coerced, and if the difficulties are not understood the social consequences can be serious. As we have seen, the differences between Black English and the standard taught in the schools are not numerous but do lie in some of the fundamentals. The black child might be better off if he spoke with a foreign accent, for then allowances would be made; but since others generally understand him they think he ought to "know better" than to talk the way he does, and if he uses forms that are not understood, he is blamed for his hearer's ignorance. What happens in the schools is that a white teacher who is faced with white pupils who do not use the standard and black pupils who do not use it, more often than not can understand the non-standard of the white but not that of the black (see Figure 11–3). The result is that the black child has the choice of being misunderstood or of being constantly on his guard to use the standard in all communication with whites. If in addition the black non-standard has a low reputation, the child is "disadvantaged" in the worst sense of the term.[65]

Conflict between one register and another is usually less painful, but just as real. Two speakers may operate across essentially the same range, but one with home base, so to speak, closer to casual and the other with home base closer to formal. When they communicate they are liable to exaggerate the distance between them. Hearing A's average formal-like speech, B will interpret it as affectation; hearing B's average casual-like speech, A will interpret it as condescension—assuming, of course, that he regards B as an equal and does not put the whole thing down to vulgarity. The farther apart the home bases are, the wider the imagined distance and the greater the potential for misunderstanding—so long as they remain on shared ground (see Figure 11–4). If the two speakers do not share the same range of socially interpretable language and behavior, this particular source of conflict is absent. So one gets the paradox of misunderstanding growing out of understanding. A human being

---

[65] See Arthur 1971, pp. 5–8.

FIGURE 11–3
The American Teacher's Acquaintance with Non-standard English

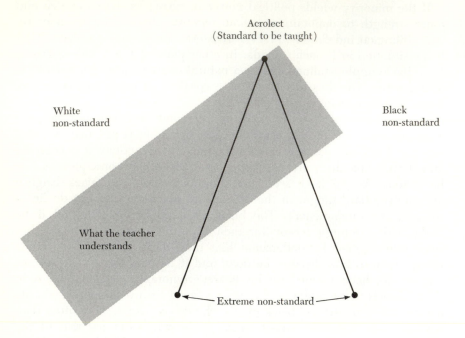

SOURCE: Based on Arthur 1971.

can accept a horse as a horse, however unlike a person; but something that pretends to be human had better be human, like me.[66]

Reputations

The social status of words such as **shanty, hooligan, shebang, slug** (of liquor), **slew** (of stuff), **gob** (as in **shut your gob**), **puss** ('face'), **shindig, dornick,** and **shenanigans** provides us with a record of socially devalued speech, that of Irish immigrants in the nineteenth century: all are either from, or influenced by, the Gaelic second language of the English-speaking Irish who were the original occupants of ghettoes—called **shanty-towns**—in large Eastern cities. Where a community is looked down upon, its speech is likewise, and the speakers themselves may accept the de-

---

[66] "If the learner of a sociolinguistic system makes an error that falls within [the] range of interpretable shifts, he may constantly exchange predictably faulty social meanings" (Ervin-Tripp 1973, p. 319).

FIGURE 11–4
Cross-Perceptions of Repertory Ranges

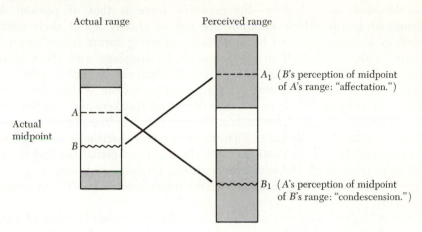

SOURCE: Adapted from Grimshaw 1973, p. 32.

* The unshaded area is the range controlled by all members of the speech community. The actual range shared (*left*) is wider, and the range not shared is narrower, than either seems to be when viewed from an off-center position (*right*).

valuation and try to exchange their old ways for new: "When Mrs. Murphy became Mrs. Murfree, she left the distinguishing mark of her earlier dialect to the Irish of shantytown, and branded their use as below her or her children."[67]

Every immigrant group has to contend with linguistic hostility. As the group is assimilated the problem disappears, but with other speech communities it remains, as a class stigma. We have seen that the technical jargon of scientists and literary people tends to be seen at the level of formal register, hence looked up to. But the technical talk of farmers and mechanics is not, even though some of it may be as esoteric to the average speaker as terms from physics or canon law. It is not the language that is primarily devalued, but the speakers, and the language is a handy way of telling which individuals to consider inferior to oneself.

One reaction to linguistic conflict is submission, usually after a period of resistance on the part of older speakers; this has been the fate of most ethnic minorities in the United States. Another reaction is a reassertion of the native variety and an attempt to purge it of influences from outside. When the influx of tourists into Martha's Vineyard threatened to submerge the local community, the response of the latter was

---

[67] See Hutson 1947.

to speed up certain changes in the pronunciation of the vowels, to make the local speech distinct from that of the mainlanders.[68] In either case —submission or resistance—the cohesive force is that of *purism*. A dominant group, whose children are not as choosy about their companions as they ought to be and start importing forms from "below," senses a threat to itself in the threat to its language and takes arms against Franglish, Spanglish, slanguage, or whatever corruption rears its ugly head. A minority group, building resistance from within, does the same, claiming preeminence for its writers and speakers and warding off the infiltrations from above as best it can. This has been the history of Czech "closure" to German, Flemish to French, Afrikaans to English, Catalan and Basque to Castilian, with the less prestigious standing up to the more prestigious, and with every national language opposing the popularizing trends that emerge along with the unpredictable loyalties of young speakers.[69]

What has to be appreciated in this is the close identification of language with self. The advocate of the "let 'em learn English" philosophy displays a monolithic monolingual ignorance of the sacrifice. It is asking a millionaire to give up his fortune and start again without a penny in his pocket. Our language is part of us—far more than a symbol of ethnic identity, it is the warp of a fabric whose weft is our innermost being and our hold on reality. For an adult speaker to surrender it is to put himself at the mercy of others who comprehend his handicap far less than if he were crippled or blind.

Less out of charity than practicality, the efforts of the dominant society to preserve the standard are therefore aimed at the young. The aims are seen as humanitarian, "to give every child an equal opportunity"— to acquire a standard that a few have acquired at no cost by choosing the right parents. Even so, this may be the best way out of a dilemma. Two concepts of linguistic democracy are in potential conflict. One, fostered by social activists and aided by sociolinguists who properly emphasize that every code has its points and one has as much right to attention as another, is that linguistic variety should be encouraged. The other, the traditional melting-pot view, is that every *individual* in the society has a right to his share, which he can only get by demanding it in fluent Standard—and it is therefore the duty of the schools to teach it to him. There is a compromise, for which linguists can claim credit, largely through what has been learned in the initiatives taken by the Summer Institute of Linguistics in bringing literacy to various parts of the world. Those missionary linguists realized years ago that for speakers of a non-standard the schools had to represent a period of transition in which the child was first taught to read and write in the language or

---

[68] Labov 1963.

[69] See Wexler 1971.

dialect native to him. Then, with literacy established, the standard could be learned and literacy transferred to it, with the child's own cultural heritage all the while respected and maintained. This kind of enlightened bidialectalism is coming more and more to be official policy.[70]

Language devalued to the point of complete suppression comes under the heading of *taboo*. For the most part taboo is fragmentary, affecting words that relate to behavior that is not approved of. This will be dealt with in the next chapter. But a more sweeping kind of taboo is found where an entire segment of society is required to use a special language, which differs in lexicon or grammar, though rarely (and only superficially) in phonology, from that of the rest of the society. Among certain native Australian languages until recently there were two forms of speech, *guwal* and *dyalŋuy*, the latter having the same grammar and phonology as the former but a completely different vocabulary. It was required to be used with and in the presence of certain taboo relatives; in the Dyirbal tribe these included mother-in-law, father-in-law, paternal aunt's daughter, and maternal uncle's daughter (but not maternal aunt's daughter), among others:

> The relation was transitive: if X is taboo to Y, then Y is taboo to X. In fact a taboo relative would seldom be spoken to directly; if a woman were in the room with her father-in-law and another person (she would never be alone with her father-in-law) she would talk in dyalŋuy to the third person, telling them anything she wanted to communicate to her father-in-law.[71]

ANALYSIS

A celebrated definition of the central aim of linguistics, which has guided a generation of researchers, is the following, by Noam Chomsky:

> Linguistic theory is concerned primarily with an ideal speaker-listener, in a completely homogeneous speech community, who knows its language perfectly and is unaffected by such grammatically irrelevant conditions as memory limitations, distractions, shifts of attention and interest, and errors (random or characteristic) in applying his knowledge of the language in actual performance.[72]

---

[70] Or, as one sociolinguist calls it, "biregistralism," pointing out that the best compromise would be to give registers preference over varieties—to recognize, for example, a separate prestige level for Black English which users of that variety could aim at without the extra burden of switching to white standard. Differences between varieties would iron themselves out in the long run. See Houston 1969.

[71] Dixon 1972, pp. 32–33, 292–93. The quotation is from the preliminary edition, 1967, pp. 230–31.

[72] Chomsky 1965, p. 3.

With minor qualifications the latter part of Chomsky's definition is still valid, but as the material covered in this chapter implies, the first part is no longer generally accepted. It is not just that there never is nor has been such an idealized person or community (there is no ideal gas either, but idealization is basic to kinetics and thermodynamics), but that such an assumption obscures rather than clarifies our understanding of natural language, whether in equilibrium or undergoing change. The condition of a gas can be stabilized experimentally to allow for observation; a language cannot. It exists only in converse with an environment and can be studied only in connection with it. The study of variation, properly conceived, "adds to our knowledge of linguistic structure, and simplifies the situation."[73]

At the same time, not all parts of language are equally affected by its dynamics, and a shift from an idealized to a social point of view does not necessarily invalidate work already done. In particular, techniques of handling data have been developed that are too valuable to be cast aside. We have seen how at least one such technique, that of positing underlying forms, turned out to correlate with historical change. How make the best use of practices already in vogue?

One procedure that sociolinguists have adopted is to take older generative rules and rewrite them as *variable rules* that are sensitive to social contexts. Originally, transformational rules applied either categorically or optionally; in the one case speakers had to follow the rule, in the other they might or might not—but nothing was said about the conditions under which the "might or might not" applied. Sociolinguistics elected itself to make that condition explicit. An example of an optional rule is the following, applied to contraction in such forms as *He's there, I'm going, You're right:*

$$\ni \longrightarrow (\emptyset) \ / \ \# \# \ [\text{\_\_\_\_\_}, +T] \ C \ \# \#$$

The parentheses mean 'optionally,' so that the interpretation up to the diagonal means 'shwa optionally goes to zero.' After the diagonal, the double double-crosses mean 'word boundary,' the $+T$ means a positive tense feature (that is, the word in question is a verb in either the present or the past tense), and the C means a single consonant. The underlined blank space is where the segment under consideration—that is, the shwa—would go if it were there. So altogether we are told that an auxiliary whose only vowel is a shwa, which has no initial consonant, and which has a single end-consonant, may lose its shwa. This applies to *am, are, is,* and also to *have, had, will,* and *would* when they lose their initial consonant—for example, *He had been there* may be

---

[73] Labov 1969, p. 737.

expressed with a full *had* /hæd/, or with *had* without its initial /h/ and
/æ/ reduced to shwa /əd/, or with this last form changed by the rule
to /d/: *He'd been there.*

It remains now to see if the "optional" can be defined. What conditions induce the speaker to exercise his option? One is the presence
of a pronoun rather than a noun preceding the verb. We are more apt
to say *I'll do it* than to say *The boy'll do it,* and we would not say *The
data're compiled* at all. Another is having the verb followed by another
verb rather than by a noun or an adjective: *He's going* would almost
always be contracted, *He is wise* less necessarily so. These facts can be
incorporated in a variable rule to show that the presence of the preceding pronoun and that of the following verb affect the outcome:

$$\text{ə} \longrightarrow (\emptyset) \; / \; [\beta\text{Pro}] \; \# \# \; [\underline{\hspace{2cm}}, +\text{T}] \; \text{C} \; \# \# \; [\alpha\text{Vb}]$$

The Greek letters allow for the pronoun (Pro) and verb (Vb) features
to be plus or minus without destroying the rule—they indicate that if
the value is plus, the rule is more apt to apply, but if it is minus, it still
may apply.[74]

Any variable can be written into a variable rule—including whether or
not the speakers have a college education.[75]

A variable rule implies something for the form to vary *from.* The
basis for variation, like that for other transformations, is some real or
posited style or form of the language that will best explain all the variations. In the rule just cited, there is a form *with* shwa that is the spring-
board for the one without. Similarly there is a form with a full vowel
that is the springboard for the one with shwa: we would "derive"
Who'd gone? from *Who 'ad gone?* /hu əd gɔn/ and that in turn from
Who had gone? The most conservative, deliberately pronounced form
is used as the basis. We saw earlier in this chapter how the listener's
grammar probably sorts out all the variants and ties them together under
some such relationship as this, with something that approximates the
most conservative variety subtending the others. So it happens that a
given dialect, alive or dead, can be seen as basic to the description of
an entire language. The researcher considers himself fortunate if he
can find such a dialect actually preserved for him. An instance of this
kind of lucky survival, matching that of Latin in the West, is that of
Kannada in India, the literary form of which has been preserved for
prestige purposes and can be used for generating the colloquial dialects.[76]

---

[74] Ibid., pp. 737, 739.

[75] See the Linguistic Society of America's *Meeting Handbook* (December 1973),
p. 103.

[76] Bright 1969.

ADDITIONAL REMARKS
AND APPLICATIONS

1. In October 1974 the buses in Aberdeen, Scotland, carried the sign *Stop road accidents in Aberdeen—drive carefully.* While this is perfectly intelligible to a speaker of American English, there is something a bit unfamiliar in one of its collocations. See if you can find the difference; then check the footnote.[77]

2. The following is one of the worksheets used in preparing the *Linguistic Atlas of the Gulf States*.[78] See what your own choices would be. If you have others, state them. (The asterisk indicates a possible choice, not an incorrect form.)

    a. She likes to)   dress up *dike up, *rig up, *slick up, *prink up, *doll up, *dike out /different terms for men? different terms for women putting on make up?/
When a girl goes out to a party, in getting ready, you say she likes to _____.
If a girl likes to put on her mother's clothes, she likes to _____.
If a girl spends all her time in front of a mirror making herself look pretty, you say she likes to _____.
If a woman likes to put on good clothes, you say she likes to _____.

    b. *purse* /for coins/ *pocketbook
What do you call the small leather container with a clasp on it that women carry money in?
Small thing you take to church to carry coins?
What do you put your money into in your pocket?
Something you would carry your money in is a _____.
If it was small and had a clasp on it for carrying coins, you would call it a _____.

    c. *bracelet*
What does a woman wear around her wrist?

---

[77] *Road accidents* would probably be called *traffic accidents.*
[78] Pederson, McDavid, Foster, and Billiard 1972, pp. 128–29.

d. ***string of beads***   *pair of beads
Suppose there are a lot of little things strung up together and used to go around your neck as an ornament, what would you call these?

e. ***suspenders***   *galluses, *braces
What do men wear to hold up their trousers?

f. an old)   ***umbrella***
What do you hold over you when it rains?

g. ***bedspread***   *coverlet, *coverlid, *counterpane
What is the last thing you put on a bed? The fancy top cover.

h. ***pillow***   *piller, *pillow slip, *pillowcase, *pillow bier
At the head of the bed you put your head on a _____.

i. ***bolster***   /a large pillow/; it goes)   clear (across the bed
*clean, *plum, *slam, *jam
Do you remember using anything at the head of the bed that was about twice as long as a pillow?
That bolster didn't go part way across the bed; it went _____.

3. In a state such as California, populated by persons from all areas to the east, what competing forms are likely to be the most successful, those widely and generally used elsewhere or those restricted in their distribution? Take the expression ***hot cake.*** As a folk term, in the East this expression is centered in Eastern Pennsylvania. But somehow it has found its way into formal English: "In parts of the Middle West . . . one is likely to make ***pancakes*** at home, but to order ***hot cakes*** in a restaurant."[79] In California, ***hot cake*** is more general than ***pancake.*** Is it more likely taken from the Pennsylvania or from the formal usage?

4. Test your reactions toward some other dialect of English. If you are a Northern (or Southern) speaker do you find a Southern (or Northern) accent irritating? How do you react toward a speaker of British Standard (Southern British, or "Received Pronunciation")? Does it make a difference whether the other speaker is of the same sex as you, or the opposite sex?

5. If you are a native speaker of American English, see if you can classify your own dialect by the following list of words:

---

[79] Reed 1954, p. 8.

Northern	Midland	Southern
cherry pit	piece 'distance'	corn shucks
pail	green beans	you-all
comforter	wait on 'wait for'	snap beans
stoop 'porch'	quarter till	pallet
clapboards 'siding'	want off 'want to	chitlins 'hogs'
angleworm	get off'	intestines'
swill 'slop'	blinds 'shades'	light bread 'white
brook 'creek'	poke 'sack'	bread raised
hadn't ought	all the better	with yeast'
teeter-totter	(That's all the	tote 'carry'
eaves troughs	better he can	jackleg 'untrained
fried cake 'dough-	do it.)	person'
nut'	you-uns	clabber cheese 'cot-
johnnycake 'corn-	spouts 'gutters'	tage cheese'
bread'	snake feeder	mouth harp
spider 'skillet'	'dragonfly'	'harmonica'
darning needle		croker sack 'burlap
'dragonfly'		bag'
Dutch cheese 'cot-		carry (someone
tage cheese'		home) 'escort'
		branch 'small
		stream'
		pulley bone
		'wishbone'
		hants 'ghosts'

SOURCE: Adapted from Babington and Atwood 1961. Used by permission of The University of Alabama Press. © 1961.

If you are like many other speakers of American English, you may find that you use words from all three lists. Try to relate them to different contacts during your life—residence in particular areas or close association with certain speakers.

6. Dialect atlas materials have various applications in linguistics. One, suggested by William G. Moulton, is as a test of the hypothesis of "phonological space," which is that phonemes tend to be distributed more or less evenly relative to one another. For example, if we imagine the tongue positions in the mouth to represent a sort of continuum (see pages 43–44), each vowel will tend to be about as far from its neighbor in one direction as from its neighbor in another. As a corollary to this, the more tightly packed the continuum is (that is, the more vowels there are), the less free any vowel will be to have a wide range of allophones—speakers will have to be more precise in their pronunciation. Moulton finds this hypothesis largely

confirmed in the dialect atlas of Swiss German.[80] Assume that there is a phonemic system in which, for one reason or another, this even distribution does not obtain, and two vowels are very close together. If not too many words depend on the distinction, what is apt to happen? Apply this to the contrast in such pairs as *sot–sought, tot–taught,* etc.

7. Are there dialect problems among minority groups in your public school system? If so, see if you can identify some of the forms used. They may be phonological (*house* pronounced [hʌws], *pen* pronounced like *pin*), morphological (verb forms like *dove* or *might could,* or switching of preterit and participle forms like **He done it, He seen them, They had went, Somebody had stole it**), or syntactic (adjectives used as adverbs, as in **He did it easy;** non-standard clauses, as in **This is a recipe that if you don't do it right you won't like it;** interchange of cases, as in **Him and me don't like it,** or its opposite, by overcompensation, **It's for he and I**). Where are the speakers from? Are the forms they use standard in those areas? Do you use similar forms sometimes (for example, **Whom shall I say is calling,** an overcompensation)?

8. Judge each of the following as to (1) whether you would say it yourself and (2) whether you can readily imagine someone else saying it. If the answer to (1) is no but to (2) is yes, discuss what this means in terms of the kind of grammatical knowledge you have, especially as regards a panlectal grammar:

    a. He's the kind of fellow that you can talk to him.
    b. He's the kind of fellow that you talk to him.
    c. He's a fellow that you don't like him.
    d. He's a fellow that you have trouble liking him.

Assume that you found b and c impossible but a and d possible for some speaker. Can you formulate a rule for this speaker's grammar to account for the difference?

9. Discuss the Spanish expression *Allá voy,* literally 'There I'm going,' which translates the English *I'm coming* in answer to a summons. Which language has the more complicated rule for the use of the verb meaning basically 'to proceed to a point other than the locus of the speaker' (compare **He comes here, He goes there, *He goes here**)?

---

[80] Moulton 1962.

10. Countless words in German, Dutch, English, Danish, and Swedish resemble one another as closely as similar sets in French, Spanish, Italian, and Rumanian. Yet there exists no written record, like Latin, which can be assumed as a source and to which the forms can be traced. How does what we know about dialectology justify the assumption that there was a primitive Germanic language that split into dialects that become the parents of these languages?

11. A pidgin exists to be understood with the least possible effort. See if you can interpret the following from Melanesian Pidgin:

    a. Suppose man he-die, alltogether man he-make-im sing-sing 'long em.

    b. Cut-im grass belong head belong me.

    c. Bone belong dis-fellow man he all-same water.[81]

12. English has overwhelmed most of the creoles in the Caribbean area. What has happened to the creole spoken on the island of Curaçao? See Wood 1972.

13. A caller on a radio talk show[82] said *It's laid out so perfectly that you can do so much work with it!* Do you think the caller was a man or a woman? On a television program,[83] the actor playing the role of a policeman was given the line *Jeannie's blossomed into such a lovely lady!* Comment.

14. In a study of French, men and women were found to speak at about the same rate but women's utterances tended to be longer than men's (an average of 6.8 syllables as against 6.3). Also, older speakers were found to speak more slowly and to use shorter utterances.[84] See if you can detect similar differences among speakers of English.

15. Note some instances of slang in your speech and that of your friends and see if older speakers know what the slang means and also how they react to it. How would you feel about older speakers using such expressions?

16. What do the expressions *swarm* of bees, *pod* of whales, *hill (colony)* of ants, *crew* of sailors, *gang* of thieves, and *chorus* of singers illus-

---

[81] These examples are from Hall 1943.

[82] San Francisco radio broadcast, 1 September 1973.

[83] "The Streets of San Francisco," 30 August 1973.

[84] Malécot, Johnston, and Kizziar 1972.

trate? Are some or all of these justifiable because of the nature of what they designate?

17. The doctor makes a *prognosis,* the weatherman a *forecast,* the scientist a *prediction,* the soothsayer an *augury,* and the prophet a *prophecy* or *vaticination.* Think of some other set of words having a constant meaning and differing only by some such social reference.

18. If it is understandable that technical fields such as physics and surgery require a technical jargon, is the same true of technical fields dealing with the public, such as law and social services? If so, do these fields require a special effort to achieve clarity? Discuss.

19. Look up the synonyms of *crazy* in Roget's *Thesaurus.* Do they show differences in register? Discuss.

20. Classify the following for register, and make any comment you consider relevant:

    a. *Broad and Alien Is the World* (title of a book by Ciro Alegría)

    b. "How Stands Our Press?" (title of a pamphlet by O. G. Villard)

    c. The same goes for him and his ideas.

    d. How fatigued I am!

    e. I gottagetoff.

Find an equivalent for each of the above in a different register.

21. What are some of the syntactic and lexical marks of oratorical or frozen register in the following passage?

> And myth is . . .? For me, it is a story, a story of epic proportions in which natural and preternatural forces join to symbolize the essential realities of man in his world. In such a story, man's world of sight merges with his world of insight; the impalpable of his world of imagination becomes as real as the feel of the sword in his hand. Here, then, is narrative partaking of philosophy, and therefore containing within it the seeming mutually-exclusive elements of the magical and the mundane, the sense of immediate reality and the apochryphal, the social discord and the harmony, destruction and—the phoenix.[85]

22. Is there anything wrong with either of the following two sentences? If so, explain:

---

[85] Kenneth Lash in *The New Mexico Quarterly Review* (Spring 1947).

      a. Let's show 'em.
      b. Let's reveal 'em.

Are the following two acceptable? If not, what would you do to make them right?

      c. Let's pray. (minister at a church service)
      d. All seniors will please get up. (college president about to confer degrees)

23. Rate the following as casual or consultative:

      a. He grew steadily worse.
      b. He grew worse and worse.
      c. She's all the time complaining.
      d. She's constantly complaining.
      e. I told him right there.
      f. I promptly told him.

Do your decisions suggest anything about a register distinction for the *-ly* adverb standing before the verb?

24. A recently employed radio newscaster announced a portion of his broadcast with the words *Now for you cats with money, here's the stock market.*[86] Comment.

25. In class, a girl who had been heard to say *Won't say a word about it* to her boyfriend, quoted herself insistently as having said *I won't say a word about it.*[87] Discuss the nature of her claim and the motive for it.

26. One reason for the esteem in which consultative or formal register is held is that more people understand it than understand casual or intimate. What causes this? Relate your answer to social factors such as the media, mobility of speakers, and so on.

27. Discuss the problem that a schoolchild has in class on first being required to present something in deliberative register, when all his previous experience in communication has been in more intimate registers where there is immediate feedback from hearers.[88]

28. Do all three of the following compounds exist in everyday English: *child-abuse, wife-abuse, husband-abuse?* If not, comment.

---

[86] Reported on San Francisco radio, 15 September 1974.
[87] From Gleason 1965, p. 360.
[88] Ibid., p. 361.

29. Norman Podhoretz had this to say about class dialect in America:[89]

> Accent in America has more than a psychological or spiritual significance. "Her kerbstone English," said Henry Higgins of Eliza Doolittle [in G. B. Shaw's *Pygmalion*], "will keep her in the gutter to the end of her days." Most Americans probably respond with a sense of amused democratic superiority to the idea of a society in which so trivial a thing as accent can keep a man down, and it is a good measure of our blindness to the pervasive operations of class that there has been so little consciousness of the fact that America itself is such a society.

Read the rest of the article and discuss.

What relevance does the following passage have to the Podhoretz quotation?

> We find . . . that separate languages maintain themselves most readily in closed tribal systems, in which kinship dominates all activities. Linguistically distinct special parlances, on the other hand, appear most fully developed in highly stratified societies, where the division of labor is maintained by rigidly defined barriers of ascribed status.[90]

30. At the University of Oregon, sixty-one students were given the following sentences and asked to rate them:

a. He wants help from the Administration, so he is trying to please it.

b. He wants help from the Administration, so he is trying to please them.

c. He opposes the Administration, so he is trying to destroy it.

d. He opposes the Administration, so he is trying to destroy them.

What would you guess the ratings to be? Why?[91]

31. Comment on the expression *Oh, I don't know* as a response to someone who has voiced an opinion with which you disagree. Do the same with *If I were you*, a formula that is found in many languages.

32. Since an opinion is usually either right or wrong, what is the point

---

[89] "Making It: The Brutal Bargain," *Harper's Magazine* (December 1967), p. 66.

[90] Gumperz 1971, pp. 126–27.

[91] The majority favored b over a and c over d. A favorable attitude leads to thinking of the Administration as individuals rather than as an impersonal entity. From Greenbaum 1975.

of saying *rightly or wrongly* in a sentence such as the following?
She believes, rightly or wrongly, that they meant to cheat her.

33. You are wakened at 3 A.M. by the ringing of the telephone and you
say angrily, **Who's calling me at this hour?** Is the purpose of the
question to find out the name of the caller? If not, what is its social
meaning?

References

Agard, Frederick B. 1971. "Language and Dialect: Some Tentative Postulates,"
Linguistics 65:5–24.

Allen, Harold B. 1973–. *The Linguistic Atlas of the Upper Midwest*, vol. 1
(Minneapolis: University of Minnesota Press).

Arthur, Bradford. 1971. "The Interaction of Dialect and Style in Urban American English," in *UCLA Work Papers in Teaching English as a Second
Language* 5:1–18.

Babington, Mima, and E. Bagby Atwood. 1961. "Lexical Usage in Southern
Louisiana," *Publication of the American Dialect Society*, No. 36, November, pp. 1–24.

Bailey, Charles-James N. 1970. "The Integration of Linguistic Theory: Internal Reconstruction and the Comparative Method in Descriptive Linguistics," *Working Papers in Linguistics*, University of Hawaii, 2:93–102.

———. 1974. *Old and New Views on Language History and Language Relationships.* Manuscript.

Blood, Doris, 1961. "Women's Speech Characteristics in Cham," *Asian Culture*
3:139–43.

Bright, William. 1969. "Phonological Rules in Literary and Colloquial Kannada," *Working Papers in Linguistics*, University of Hawaii, 11:75–90.

Bross I. D. J. 1973. "Languages in Cancer Research," in Edwin A. Mirand et
al. (eds.), *Perspectives in Cancer Research and Treatment* (New York:
Alan R. Liss).

Cassidy, Frederic G. 1967. "American Regionalism and the Harmless Drudge,"
Publications of the Modern Language Association 82:12–19.

Cazden, Courtney B. 1972. *Child Language and Education* (New York: Holt,
Rinehart and Winston).

Chomsky, A. N. 1965. *Aspects of the Theory of Syntax* (Cambridge, Mass.:
M.I.T. Press).

Conklin, Harold C. 1959. "Linguistic Play in Its Cultural Context," *Language*
35:631–36.

Corominas, J. 1954. *Diccionario crítico etimológico de la lengua castellana*
(Bern: Editorial Francke).

Coseriu, Eugenio. 1956. *La geografía lingüística* (Montevideo: Instituto de
Filología).

De Francis, John. 1951. "Aspects of Linguistic Structure," in *Georgetown University Monograph Series on Languages and Linguistics* 1:48–51.

Dillard, J. L. 1972. *Black English* (New York: Random House).

Di Pietro, Robert J. 1973. "Language Creativity," *Pennsylvania State Modern Language Association Bulletin* 52:16–21.

Dixon, R. M. W. 1972. *The Dyirbal Language of North Queensland* (London: Cambridge University Press).

Engel, Walburga von Raffler. 1972. "Some Phono-stylistic Features of Black English," *Phonetica* 25:53–64.

Ervin-Tripp, Susan. 1973. *Language Acquisition and Communicative Choice* (Stanford, Calif.: Stanford University Press).

Fickett, Joan G. 1972. "Tense and Aspect in Black English," *Journal of English Linguistics* 6:17–19.

Fishman, Joshua A. 1967. "Bilingualism With and Without Diglossia; Diglossia With and Without Bilingualism," *Journal of Social Issues* 23:29–38.

Gleason, H. A. 1965. *Linguistics and English Grammar* (New York: Holt, Rinehart and Winston).

Granda, Germán de. 1970. "Cimarronismo, palenques y hablas 'criollas' en Hispanoamérica," *Boletín del Instituto Caro y Cuervo* 25:448–69.

Grayshon, M. C. 1973. "On Saying *No*," *The Nottingham Linguistic Circular* 3:40–45.

———. 1974. "Toward a Social Grammar of Language." Preprint.

Greenbaum, Sidney. 1975. "Grammar and the Foreign Language Teacher," in *On TESOL 74* (Washington, D.C.: Teachers of English to Speakers of Other Languages).

Grimshaw, Allen D. 1973. Review of John J. Gumperz, *Language in Social Groups,* ed. by Anwar S. Dil (Stanford, Calif.: Stanford University Press, 1971). In *Language Sciences* 27:29–37.

Gumperz, John J. 1971. *Language in Social Groups* (Stanford, Calif.: Stanford University Press).

Haas, Mary R. 1964. "Men's and Women's Speech in Koasati," in Dell Hymes (ed.), *Language in Culture and Society* (New York: Harper & Row), 228–33.

Hall, Robert A., Jr. 1943. *Melanesian Pidgin Phrase-Book and Vocabulary.* (Linguistic Society of America, Special Publication).

———. 1962. "The Life Cycle of Pidgin Languages," *Lingua* 11:151–56.

Hall, William S., and Roy O. Freedle. 1973. "A Developmental Investigation of Standard and Nonstandard English Among Black and White Children," *Human Development* 16:440–64.

———. 1975. *Culture and Language: The Black American Experience* (Washington, D.C.: Hemisphere Publishing).

Hankey, Clyde T. 1960. "A Colorado Word Geography," *Publication of the Amerian Dialect Society,* No. 34.

Hannerz, Ulf. 1970. "Language Variation and Social Relationships," *Studia Linguistica* 24:128–51.

Hattori, Shiro. 1964. "A Special Language of the Older Generations Among the Ainu," *General Linguistics* 6:43–58.

Hewes, Gordon W. 1973. "An Explicit Formulation of the Relationship Between Tool-Using, Tool-Making, and the Emergence of Language," *Visible Language* 7:101–27.

Hollien, Harry, and Thomas Shipp. 1972. "Speaking Fundamental Frequency and Chronological Age in Males," *Journal of Speech and Hearing Research* 15:155–59.

Hooley, Bruce A. 1965. Review of S. A. Wurm and J. H. Harris, *Police Motu: An Introduction to the Trade Language of Papua* (Canberra, Australia: Linguistic Circle of Canberra, 1963). In *Language* 41:168–70.

Houston, Susan A. 1969. "A Sociolinguistic Consideration of the Black English of Children in Northern Florida," *Language* 45:599–607.

Hutson, Arthur E. 1947. "Gaelic Loan-Words in America," *American Speech* 22:18–23.

Hymes, Dell. 1962. "The Ethnography of Speaking," in Thomas Gladwin and William C. Sturtevant (eds.), *Anthropology and Human Behavior* (Washington, D.C.: The Anthropological Society of Washington).

Joos, Martin. 1967. *The Five Clocks* (New York: Harcourt Brace Jovanovich).

Kaye, Alan S. 1972. "Remarks on Diglossia in Arabic," *Linguistics* 81:32–48.

Keller-Cohen, Deborah. 1973. "Deictic Reference in Children's Speech." Paper read at Linguistic Society of America, San Diego, 29 December.

Key, Mary Ritchie. 1972. "Linguistic Behavior of Male and Female," *Linguistics* 88:15–31.

Kirch, Max S. 1973. "Language, Communication, and Culture," *Modern Language Journal* 57:340–43.

Kuno, Susumu. 1973. *The Structure of the Japanese Language* (Cambridge, Mass.: M.I.T. Press).

Kurath, Hans. 1949. *A Word Geography of the Eastern United States* (Ann Arbor: University of Michigan Press).

––––––. 1965. "Some Aspects of Atlantic Seaboard English Considered in Their Connections with British English," in *Communications et rapports du Premier Congrès International de Dialectologie Générale,* Louvain, Belgium, pp. 236–40.

–––––– and Guy S. Loman, Jr. 1970. "The Dialectal Structure of Southern England: Phonological Evidence," *Publication of the American Dialect Society,* No. 54.

Labov, William. 1963. "The Social Motivation of a Sound Change," *Word* 19:273–309.

––––––. 1969. "Contraction, Deletion, and Inherent Variability of the English Copula," *Language* 45:715–62.

––––––. 1970. "The Study of Language in Its Social Context," *Studium Generale* 23:30–87.

––––––. 1972. "Negative Attraction and Negative Concord," *Language* 48:773–818.

Lakoff, Robin. 1973. "Language and Woman's Place," *Language in Society* 2:45–79.

Longacre, Robert E. 1967. "Systemic Comparison and Reconstruction," in Norman A. McQuown (ed.), *Handbook of Middle American Indians.* Linguistics, vol. 5 (Austin: University of Texas Press).

Malécot, André; R. Johnston; and P.-A. Kizziar. 1972. "Syllabic Rate and Utterance Length in French," *Phonetica* 26:235–51.

Marckwardt, Albert H. 1957. "Principal and Subsidiary Dialect Areas in the

North Central States," *Publication of the American Dialect Society*, No. 27.

Markel, Norman N.; Judith A. Phillis; Robert Vargas; and Kenneth Howard. 1972. "Personality Traits Associated with Voice Types," *Journal of Psycholinguistic Research* 1:249–55.

Maurer, D. W. 1955. "Whiz Mob," *Publication of the American Dialect Society*, No. 24.

Metcalf, Allan A. 1972. "Directions of Change in Southern California English," *Journal of English Linguistics* 6:28–34.

Morínigo, Marcos A. 1931. *Hispanismos en el guaraní* (Buenos Aires: J. Peuser).

Moulton, William. 1962. "Dialect Geography and the Concept of Phonological Space," *Word* 18:23–32.

———. 1963. Review in *Journal of English and Germanic Philology* 62:828–37.

O'Neil, Wayne. 1970. "Comes the Revolution," *Harvard Graduate School of Education Bulletin* 14:3.2–3.

Pederson, Lee. 1971. "Southern Speech and the LAGS Project," *Orbis* 20:79–89.

———; Raven I. McDavid, Jr.; Charles W. Foster; and Charles E. Billiard (eds.). 1972. *A Manual for Dialect Research in the Southern States* (Atlanta: Georgia State University).

Perissinotto, Giorgio. 1972. "Distribución demográfica de la asibilación de vibrantes en el habla de la Ciudad de México," *Nueva Revista de Filología Hispánica* 21:71–79.

Reed, David W. 1954. "Eastern Dialect Words in California," *Publication of the American Dialect Society* 21:3–15.

Ricci, Julio, and Iris Malan de Ricci. 1962–63. "Anotaciones sobre el uso de los pronombres *tú* y *vos* en el español de Uruguay," *Anales del Instituto de Profesores Artigas* 7–8.

Rona, José Pedro. 1967. *Geografía y morfología del 'voseo'* (Pôrto Alegre, Brazil: Pontifícia Universidade Católica do Rio Grande do Sul).

Saint-Jacques, Bernard. 1973. "Sex, Dependency, and Language," *La Linguistique* 9:89–96.

Scargill, H. M. 1973. *A Survey of Canadian English* (Toronto: Canadian Council of Teachers).

Shuy, Roger W. 1962. "The Northern-Midland Dialect Boundary in Illinois," *Publication of the American Dialect Society*, No. 38.

Stewart, William A. 1968. "Continuity and Change in American Negro Dialects," *The Florida FL Reporter* (Spring 1968), 3, 4, 14–18.

Teeter, Karl V. 1973. "Linguistics and Anthropology," *Daedalus* 102:87–98.

Turner, Lorenzo. 1949. *Africanisms in the Gullah Dialect* (Chicago: University of Chicago Press).

Wexler, Paul. 1971. "Diglossia, Language Standardization, and Purism: Parameters for a Typology of Literary Language," *Lingua* 27:330–54.

Wolfram, Walt. 1973. Review of William J. Samarin, *Tongues of Men and Angels* (New York: Macmillan, 1972). In *Language Sciences* 27:37–40.

Wood, Richard E. 1972. "The Hispanization of a Creole Language: Papiamentu," *Hispania* 55:857–64.

VARIATION IN TIME: SOURCES OF VARIATION 12

Among the slang terms used on one college campus in the early 1970s were the following: *bennies* 'Benzedrine, speed'; *chucker* 'a person who slicks his hair back and wears skin-tight pants and pointed shoes or heavy boots'; *dexies* 'Dexedrine, speed'; *doof* 'a bumbling fool'; *icky* 'foul-looking or -smelling'; *kerky-jerkies* 'butterflies, nervousness, mistakes made from nervousness'; *nurd* 'a slow-witted person'; *rip off* 'to steal from'; and *zilch* 'none, nothing.'[1] Whatever the ultimate fate of these terms (*rip off* at least appears to be here to stay—it supplies a need for a term to cover any and every sort of theft), it is clear that they increase the bulk of English words. Two of them, *bennies* and *dexies,* point to another area that expands almost as fast as slang: the vocabulary of the natural sciences.

A language *grows* in the number of its words as the societies that use it create new entities that have to be named. Some of the ways of building new words were summarized in Chapter 5. There we saw that newness is relative: neologisms almost never result from a random combination of sounds—random, that is, except for the fact that they must always satisfy the phonological requirements of the language; instead they are built of partially formed old morphological material. All the same, they are new configurations that stand for fresh concepts.

---

[1] "Slang at the University of Vermont," *Current Slang* 5 (1971).

A language also *dies* bit by bit as words grow obsolete and pass from use. But obituaries are harder to write than birth notices. Old words can be revived—a historical novel reaches into the past and brings back not only archaic terms but also, for flavor, some hint of archaic grammar. Short of social collapse, vocabularies show a net increase over the years.

But expansion in the number of word forms is only one kind of change. Most speakers hardly know more than a fraction of them anyway, and not the same fraction that other speakers know; yet they communicate on all matters of common concern and would be surprised if they were accused of speaking a different language. Differences in vocabulary are important for describing variation in space—dialects and codes can be largely delimited by them. But for variation in time, the dense core of sound and grammar is a better index.

The two great approaches to language are the descriptive and the historical, technically the *synchronic* and the *diachronic*. The content of all the chapters up to this one has been largely synchronic. Yet the two cannot really be pulled apart; the separation is mainly for convenience. As an American linguist said a century ago, "The traditional transmission of language is but the same process of teaching children to speak."[2] With old speakers and young speakers coexisting and communicating, both the past and the future are with us in the present. Synchrony is a two-dimensional picture that flattens out the dimension of change and commands the sun to stand still. Our failure to see the stirrings going on around us is due to the brief sampling of time that even the longest human life encompasses. For one thing, change is seldom on a noticeable scale. For another, we can ignore it and still make ourselves understood.

Now and then we do become aware of some shift of grammar or pronunciation within our lifetime. Perhaps we see a rule taking shape as individual words one by one shift their allegiance and move into a new category. One example is what continues to happen to the adjective forms based on the names of states. We no longer call peanuts grown in Virginia **Virginian peanuts,* though we unhesitatingly call pineapple grown in Hawaii *Hawaiian pineapple.* An earthquake in California is never a **Californian earthquake,* though one in Alaska might be called an *Alaskan earthquake.* The **Iowan landscape* is impossible, but the *New Mexican landscape* seems natural. What we are witnessing is a gradual restriction of these adjectives to the status of names of the state's inhabitants: an Iowan, a Californian, a Virginian. With the newest states this has not yet been fully accomplished. A few generations ago we spoke of *Californian gold* just as we speak of *African gold* today.

---

[2] Silverstein 1971, p. 39.

Another example is the changing rule for the possessive. Some older speakers still tend to avoid expressions like *the college's president, the garden's fertility,* and few if any younger ones would yet say °*Spanish's words* or °*Italian's derivations.* The old rule limited possessives to persons or to what could be easily personified; the new rule admits them for purely relational purposes, where an *of* phrase would have been used before: *the president of the college, the fertility of the garden.* This change has been going on for a long time. It also illustrates a reversal in the fortunes of war: the *-'s* form was the only one in Old English, but was gradually replaced by *of* phrases in Middle English until by the time of Chaucer most remaining instances were found with personal nouns,[3] even though inanimate *its* holds its own to this day: we may not be able to say °*German's words* but *its words* is perfectly normal.

More often the only visible change is a gain or a loss in some already existing rule. Earlier (pages 145–46) we saw a tendency for verbs of more than one syllable to be marked by having their last syllable more prominent than the last syllable of corresponding adjectives and nouns— for example, *supplement* pronounced /sʌpləmɛnt/ and /sʌpləmənt/. That process continues to affect more and more words. Those ending in *-ate* are typical. A speaker who still pronounces the ending as -/et/ with the noun *candidate* may already have shifted to -/ət/ with the nouns *graduate, associate,* and *affiliate,* and will almost certainly never have said anything but -/ət/ with the noun *duplicate;* but with all these words he will have retained -/et/ for the verb.

Many changes slip by unobserved—often simply because our spelling habits keep our minds in the old groove. For example, if someone were to ask, "Is there such a word as *maybe?*" we would have to answer yes. The process that converted *It may be* to *may be, may-be, maybe,* and *mebbe* took a couple of hundred years, but it is finished. If someone were to ask, "Is there such a word as *could-be?*" the answer would come harder, for there is no such spelling. Yet we readily drop the *it* from *It could be* and assign a definite intonation,

$$\text{Could} \quad \overset{\text{be}}{\frown}$$

which is never done with *It might be. Could-be* is a word in the making.[4]

There are structural changes in progress too, just as obvious if we

---

[3] The proportion of *-'s* to *of* with inanimate nouns in Chaucer is 137 to 531 in verse but only 2 to 564 in prose, which reflects everyday usage more faithfully. See Mustanoja 1960, p. 74.

[4] *Maybe* can still have the intonation shown for *could be,* but otherwise has established its one-word status by its freedom to move about like an adverb. We can say *He maybe smokes a pipe* or *He smokes a pipe maybe,* which is not yet possible with *could be.* See Greenbaum 1969, p. 109.

can forget the pigeonholes of high-school grammars. The verb *see* of course refers to vision. But it also long ago became a function word in causative constructions like *I saw him home, See that he is taken care of.* And now, almost on the sly, it has become a complementizer in constructions like *I hate to see you waste your money like that,* which is in the same family as *I hate to have you waste your money like that* and *I hate for you to waste your money like that.*

Visible change is the tip of the iceberg. Every alteration that eventually establishes itself had to exist formerly as a choice. And this means that the seedbed for variation in time is simply the whole landscape of variation in space that we traveled over in the last chapter. If speakers migrate from one community to another they adopt the ways of the new community, and those of the old fall into disuse. If political upheavals abolish certain class distinctions, the vocabularies of superiority and submission vanish along with the roles they served. If religious ties are weakened, certain old forms will no longer be reverenced and will be forgotten. All such *if*'s are apt to be overdrawn. No social revolutions are necessary for linguistic change, though of course they speed things up; it is enough for speakers to decide for whatever reason that one variant is worth adopting instead of another, and the course is set.[5]

How variants come on the scene in the first place of course is another question. Some are the result of mistakes, such as slips of the tongue. Or the mistakes may be logical ones. A child is given models to imitate that do not represent a genuine sampling of the grammatical competence of his elders. He builds a grammar to account for what he *hears,* which may be slightly different from the grammar that his parents *know.* Consider the preposition *for* in *for free,* which was originally a non-standard blend of *free* and *for nothing.* Many speakers, partly because *free* alone is slightly ambiguous and partly to be humorous,[6] adopted the two-word phrase, until by the mid 1940s more and more children who only heard the form and could not appreciate the joke were adopting *for free* as their standard. The grammar of *for* with adjectives *(for good, for certain, for sure)* was thus extended.

Some innovative forces are within the language mechanism itself; the speaker makes mistakes, but they are due to complexities in the system. In every act of speech a number of things go on at once. We organize our sentences into patterns of sound that signal to the hearer how he is to decode them so as to represent the individual words and their connections in his mind. To this we add an intonation contour, with peaks of accent, to convey our feelings and our sense of the important. Around this we wrap a gestural envelope: a facial expression is often

---

[5] See Householder 1972.

[6] A humor that for its effect depends on the change being felt as deviant. See Fónagy 1971, especially pp. 209–15.

our only clue to the difference between a statement and a question. Sometimes these levels interfere with one another. The [p] of *yep* and *nope* is the result of shutting the mouth in self-satisfied finality at the end of an utterance. The gesture affects the word. Someone who says *Now wa-a-it a MIN-ute!* makes his sentence more spirited by putting an extra accent on *minute* even though there is no question of 'minute, not second'—the normal way of saying *Wait a minute* is with only one accent, on *wait*. Since most English words have a fixed or lexical stress, this example illustrates a certain amount of friction between the lexical level—the forms of words—and the intonational level—the orchestration of sentences to make them sound effective. The result is like what happens when someone tries to eat and speak at the same time; the same organs are involved in both activities and each must yield a bit. One characteristic of intonational rhythm in English is that of placing a major accent close to the end of a sentence. Sometimes this leads to alternating pronunciations of the same word or even—with words most often used at the end of a phrase—to a permanent change. Take the suffix *-able*. Though normally when added to a verb it does not shift the stress (*permít, permíssible; cúltivate, cúltivatable; mínimize, mínimizable*), a good many speakers tend to move the stress to the right in longer forms, especially those with *-ize* or *-fy: réalize, realízable; vérify, verifíable; idéntify, identifíable.*

These are cases of interference in the act of speaking. Other kinds of interference go deeper. There is a psychological interference that stems from the mere existence of more than one choice for roughly the same purpose; the result is that two get confused and produce a third, called a *blend*. And in a language such as English there is a conflict between written and spoken language that has led to countless changes in pronunciation.

Often the precipitating cause is imposed from outside. Any change in the style of living brings a new mix in the elements of language, which are then assigned their values and adopted or ignored. A convicted man is thrown into a prison which has strict rules forbidding conversation at certain periods. He soon acquires the habit of speaking out of the side of his mouth and suppressing the movement of his lips. This distorts the sounds of his vowels and his labial consonants, /p b m f v/. There is little danger that prison life will affect the language of those on the outside, but similar drastic changes in the life of a society do have their effects. When the Norman invasion brought to English many words containing the phoneme /v/—*vile, very, vale, vain, venial, venom*—English altered its phonemic system just enough to turn the sound of [v], which it already had as an allophone of /f/, into a new phoneme. The same thing happened with /z/.[7]

---

[7] Vachek 1965, pp. 53–54.

WHERE THE VARIANTS COME FROM

It is impossible to enumerate, let alone treat, all the forces of change, whether they reside in the language or impinge from outside. Variation is infinite and its causes likewise. We are limited to the conspicuous and the typical. And we must keep in mind that the thousands of deviations that are ground out by this or that force or combination of forces are only raw material. Most of them come to nothing—mispronunciations, mistakes in grammar, artificial coinages, importations, attempts at verbal humor, poetic distortions, novel assignments of meaning—the majority pass unnoticed, or are noticed and disregarded, or are briefly taken up but no sooner bloom than they fade. It is only by being noticed, appreciated, and adopted that a few make their way in to stay.

Speakers' errors: the confusion of sound and sense

The most commonplace of all mistakes, in speech as well as in writing, are those caused by some malfunctioning in the neural commands that tell our vocal organs or our finger muscles what to do. A command may not be fully carried out. Or it may be carried out, but in the wrong sequence. Or it may trip another command which replaces it or is added to it. The trouble may be either at the coding end (for example, the commands are issued in the wrong order) or at the receiving end (the muscles try their best, but get in one another's way). Back of it there is usually a higher failure: the speaker is in a hurry, or feels that under the circumstances he can afford to be careless, and he neglects to pay close attention to what he is saying.[8]

Loss   A command is not fully executed. This is often a matter of timing. Carefully pronounced, the word *temperature* has four syllables, but the second, being a syllabic /r/, can be speeded up to the point that it forms a cluster with /p/ and one syllable is lost. This happens usually next to a stressed syllable, which robs its neighbors of some of their length. The initial loss may materialize as the reduction of a vowel, as when *schirreve* (the *reeve,* or king's officer, of the *shire*) had its second vowel reduced to shwa, giving the modern *sheriff,* which in turn many of the younger generation are pronouncing [šɛrf]. In the adjective *crooked* (a *crooked* stick) only the vowel reduction has occurred, though for many speakers the majority of such *-ed* adjectives have lost the vowel: *an aged woman* pronounced /eɪd/ rather than /eɪəd/. In

---

[8] "Slips of the tongue are predictable natural processes introduced in the absence of close monitoring" (Bailey 1974, p. 19).

mirror pronounced like *mere,* and *cabinet* pronounced as *cabnet,* both
steps have occurred. For most Americans *laboratory* is *lábratory* and
for most Britishers it is *labóratry,* but both have lost a syllable (as
happened also in Portuguese, giving us *Labrador*). The loss of the /t/ in
postpone and of the /t/ and one /s/ in *postscript* is due to muscular
inertia—/s/ and /t/ have the same point of articulation—but we still
monitor *post-war* and *postfix* carefully enough to keep both sounds. Not
only whole syllables may go, as in *'Deed I do* for *Indeed I do,* but whole
words, typically unaccented function words. *You like it?* is perfectly acceptable for *Do you like it?* and is a reduction of the latter, not a declara-
tive-type question such as *He likes it?* Very young speakers carry this
kind of pruning to an extreme; with less speech control than adults, they
tend to hit the stressed syllables of a word and let the rest go: *'pression*
for *expression* and *'raff* for *giraffe.*[9] Most of our nicknames— *Fred* for
Frederick, Will for *William, Angie* for *Angela, Chris* for *Christopher*—
are the happy result of childhood's refusal to carry a burden of unnecessary syllables. We tolerate a great deal of such telegraphic reduction so
long as it does not interfere too much with sense. The words *and, in,
than,* and *an* are all reduced to /n/ in rapid speech: *The pen 'n' pencil
'n the drawer are better 'n a typewriter to copy 'n easy thing like that.*

Assimilation   A command (or its execution) is improperly timed.
It comes too early or too late. The result is that a feature belonging to
one phoneme is carried over to another. In rapid speech, expressions
such as *tin box, manpower, gunboat,* and *in place* are apt to become
timbox, mampower, gumboat, and *implace:* the bilabial feature of the
/b/ or /p/ is anticipated and converts the /n/ to /m/. This is what
operated in Latin to change the *in-* prefix to *im-* and, in reverse, the
com- prefix to *con-,* as can be seen in many English borrowings: *indent*
and *intend* but *impress* and *immense; compel* and *commence* but *condign*
and *contend.* One common type of assimilation is the voicing of voiceless consonants when they occur between vowels. Vowels are practically
always voiced, and the speaker fails to shut off the voicing when he gets
to the consonant or begins it too soon before he reaches the next vowel.
This is one of the reasons why a voiced flap replaces [t] in American
English in such expressions as *latter, better, atom, get 'im.* One even
hears a /ǰ/ in place of a /č/ now and then—for example, *congratulate*
pronounced as if it were spelled *congradulate.* Assimilation often creates
an intrusive sound that may later show up in the spelling. In pronouncing the word *gamel* speakers tended to raise the velum a little too
quickly in pronouncing the /m/, with the result that the latter half of

---

[9] Examples are from Brown and Bellugi 1964.

the /m/ was pronounced with the velum up, automatically creating a /b/ and producing the modern form *gamble.* The same process gave the /d/ in *thunder* and *tender* and the /b/ in the substandard pronunciation *fambly* for *family.* If the following sound is not only non-nasal but also voiceless, two features may be anticipated. The word *youngster* is often heard as *younkster:* the velum is raised too soon, and this would convert the /ŋ/ to /g/ except that the voicelessness of the /s/ also jumps the gun and changes the still unpronounced /g/ to a /k/. The same process inserted a /p/ after the /m/ in *empty* and *Thompson.*

There are also cases of reciprocal assimilation. Two adjoining sounds borrow features from each other. In the words *seven* and *eleven,* many speakers carry the labiodental articulation of the /v/ over to the /n/, which becomes a labiodental /n/; but that is felt as an /m/, which then reacts on the /v/ to produce /b/. The result is *sebm, elebm.* Mutual assimilation of this sort has been responsible for the creation of new sounds that have become phonemes in their own right. Palatals are typical. In the word *cordial* the /d/ was drawn toward the position of the /y/, and the /y/ picked up the tighter closure of the /d/; the blending of the two resulted in /ǰ/. Related processes gave us the modern pronunciations of *capture, righteous, pinion, million, fissure, mission, Asian,* and the high-speed pronunciations *gotcha* for *got you, hadja* for *had you,* /mɪšə/ for *miss you,* and so on.

All the examples up to this point have been of *contact* assimilation—that is, the segments affected stand side by side. There is also *distance* assimilation, which is most apt to occur when two sounds not too far separated happen to have most of their features in common. When the speaker codes the utterance preparatory to speaking it he misplaces a feature. A college teacher intending to say *discussing shortly* came out with *discushing;* the palatal feature in the initial sound of *shortly* was anticipated in the second /s/ of *discussing.* A distance assimilation is more apt to be spotted as a lapse and corrected on the spot. But not always. Many speakers have habitually pronounced **Confound it!** as **Counfound it!** anticipating the offglide in the second syllable. This kind of distance assimilation, involving vowels, is common enough to have given rise to the phenomenon of *vowel harmony* in a number of languages. In Finnish there is a case ending *-hen,* whose vowel *e* assimilates to the preceding vowel: *pää-hän* 'head,' *päi-hin* 'heads,' *puu-hun* 'tree,' *maa-han* 'land,' *suo-hon* 'bog,' *kyy-hyn* 'viper,' *yö-hön* 'night,' *tie-hen* 'road.'[10] This assimilation involves lag: the feature is prolonged when it should be cut off. Most assimilation involves anticipation: the feature is turned on too soon.

Old assimilations are sometimes evidence of the former presence of

_____

[10] Example from Anttila 1972, p. 73.

sounds that have since disappeared. For example, we expect a /z/ to result when an /s/ comes directly before a voiced consonant in the same word, as happens with *cosmic, Moslem, lesbian;* but *isthmus* has /s/, and the spelling confirms that the /s/ formerly stood before a /t/ and has not yet taken on the new voicing assimilation to the /m/.

Metathesis   Sometimes whole segments are moved around, a kind of wholesale assimilation that involves not a borrowing but an outright theft. We call this *metathesis.* The resemblance to assimilation can be seen in errors like *I slaw Sloane* for *I saw Sloane;* as a pure metathesis this would be *I slaw Soane,* with the /l/ moved from one position to the other, rather than a mere borrowing of its features, with the cluster /sl/ replacing /s/. The same physiological processes are involved in both metathesis and assimilation: articulations are shifted about, whether because of miscoding or of mistiming. Since metathesis is on a larger scale than assimilation, it is usually caught and corrected—one can easily tell that *snop-shats* for *snap-shots* is a mistake. But some cases of metathesis survive, especially with difficult combinations of sounds, where many speakers tend to make the same adjustments. The word *uncomfortable* is commonly pronounced *uncomfterble,* with the /r/ moved to the following syllable. The clusters /ks/ and /sk/ are typical shifters. Many people say *asteriks* for *asterisk,* and the standard pronunciation *ask* goes back to a former *aks* that still survives dialectally. The two words *tax* and *task* come from the same source and still show a certain similarity in meaning: *They taxed him with his failures = They took him to task for his failures.* Metatheses tend to go in the direction of favored sequences of sound.

A special kind of metathesis that usually involves coding at a higher level than mere sounds is the *spoonerism,* named after William A. Spooner, an English divine whose slips of the tongue were legendary: *Is the bean dizzy?* for *Is the dean busy? Let me sew you to your sheet* for *Let me show you to your seat.* They are among the funniest of lapses because they involve more than an interchange of sounds. The typical spoonerism is not *Dend a spollar* for *Spend a dollar* or *Nend a berve* for *Bend a nerve,* but such things as *Blake the grass* for *Break the glass* or *It doesn't one right the first time* for *It wasn't done right the first time.* The switches tend to be into well-worn grooves—more often than not at least one of the altered forms already exists as a word. That is true of all such lapses, whether they make a perfect spoonerism or not— for example, *an assign assailum* for *an insane asylum.* One would not be likely to hear *Wum the gurks* for *Gum the works,* since *wum,* though phonologically possible in English, does not sound like an English word. Nor would one be likely to hear *to fight the band that heeds you* for *to bite the hand that feeds you,* since this is a set phrase; the more automatic the expression, the less likely it is to be scrambled. For the same reason function words are seldom if ever involved in spoonerisms: *Hold my books* would probably never be said as *Mold high books* or *Hold by mooks.* Spoonerisms are the result of higher-level coding falling back on lower-level coding—the less habitual is snared by the more habitual. The mixup is at two or more levels,[11] unlike other metatheses, which are only at the level of sound, and unlike blends (to be discussed shortly), where the confusion is at the level of meaning (though they too result in a new configuration of sound). Since spoonerisms almost always yield utterances that are ludicrously inappropriate, they have little or no historical effect.

Dissimilation   When a pianist has to hit the same key twice in succession he gets around the difficulty by using one finger one time and another the next. It is hard to get the same neural assembly to fire twice in quick succession. Since speech has nothing so handy as two different tongues to execute the same maneuver, it sometimes avoids the trouble by changing or dropping one of the repeated sounds. In the sentence *Our time is up in five minutes* we have no difficulty pronouncing the first word as /awr/, though we tend to prefer the simplified /ar/. But in *Our hour is up in five minutes,* we would be sure to say /ar/ to avoid the repetition of /aw/. Some sounds are more susceptible than others. In many languages dissimilation affects /r/ and /l/ especially. The word *grammar* has two /r/'s; for some speakers in Middle English times this was unsatisfactory, and they changed it to *glamor,* which has survived with a different meaning. The word *purpre* was changed to the modern *purple,* though *purpure* survives in heraldry. In the word *February* the first /r/ is simply dissimilated out for most speakers at least part of the time. Dissimilation often touches higher cognitive levels than most of the other changes discussed here. Over and over we have seen the importance of *contrast* as a linguistic principle. When two sounds or two syllables or two words are repeated, there is a loss of contrast, and we feel a need to omit the repetition or to substitute something else for it. So when a linguist writes *This strikes me about as hopeful a project as an analysis of the food values of manna,* omitting the *as* after *strikes me,* it is probably because he has already programmed two more *as*'s to follow.[12] Another linguist was heard to say *The follow-*

---

[11] Syntax is probably involved also. *Sold my hocks* for *Hold my socks* is a more likely spoonerism than *Bold my hooks* for *Hold my books* because the latter replaces a verb with an adjective.

[12] Example quoted by Walt Wolfram in *Language Sciences* 27 (1973), p. 39.

ing example, for ex-, for exam-, for instance, is . . ., manifesting in his struggle the pains we take to avoid this kind of repetition. Although **He braved the dangers bravely** and **He braved the dangers intrepidly** are equally inane, the first *sounds* inane and we avoid it.

Addition   We have already seen how certain kinds of dissimilation can result in the addition of a sound: *fumble, humble,* and *grumble* all resulted from anticipating the non-nasality of /l/, causing the /m/ to split into an /m/ half and a /b/ half. Other additions occur as a way of easing difficult sequences of sounds. Consonant clusters tend to be troublesome, though languages vary in which ones they reject. In the Romance-speaking area that now covers France and Spain the Latin initial clusters with /s/ were unacceptable to the pre-Roman population, which split them into two syllables by adding an initial /e/. So we get Old French *estudie* (modern *étude*), Spanish *estudio,* and Portuguese *estudo,* where Italian has **studio,** all from Latin **studium.** Japanese does an even more thorough job of breaking up clusters, as can be seen in the words that it borrows—a **strike** in baseball is **sutoraiku.** The substandard forms **ellum** for **elm** and **athalete** for **athlete** are sometimes heard in English, where the clusters /lm/ and /θl/ have been broken up by the insertion of shwa.

Many of the observations in this section are a restatement of facts already studied in Chapters 3 and 4. In a broad sense most allophones of the phonemes are the result of assimilation. They are "conditioned" by neighboring sounds or neighboring events, which is to say that they pick up some features from their surroundings. Even the aspiration of voiceless stops before full vowels, as in **timber** and **intake,** can be thought of as a borrowing of extra time within a longer syllable, and if the word **stop** is pronounced with an unreleased /p/ at the end of a sentence, that feature can be regarded as an assimilation to the mouth closure that often goes with a speaker's coming to the end of his speech (which also creates the spurious [p] in **yep** and **nope**). More commonplace examples are the palatal allophone of /n/ in **pinch,** the dental allophone of /l/ in **filth,** the labiodental allophone of /m/ in **amphitheater,** and the fricative allophone of /k/ in **packhorse,** each of which is an assimilation to the consonant immediately following. Allomorphs too—those that are "phonologically conditioned"—are mostly traceable to assimilation. The plural endings in English (and the possessives of nouns and third-person-singular endings of verbs)—/s/ in **cats** but /z/ in **dogs** and **toys**—retain these features because of assimilation to the preceding sound. The /v/ of **wives,** the first /z/ of **houses,** and the /ð/ of **paths** are assimilations too. In Old English the sounds [f v], [s z], and [θ ð] were allophonic pairs. The plural ending caused the consonant to fall between two vowels, and it became voiced by assimilation, as in the example *congradulate* mentioned earlier. Thus the singular *hlāf* 'loaf' had the plural *hlāfas* 'loaves,' where /f/, with a vowel on either side, was sounded as [v], as shown in the modern spelling.

But allophones have little importance in themselves. They become important for historical change only when they are *chosen* for a communicative purpose, and by that time they have ceased to be mere allophones and are on their way to becoming phonemes in their own right. We have seen how the influx of Norman French words, in which /f/ and /v/ were distinct phonemes, helped to raise the status of the two sounds in English. In that case the "phonemic split" was the result of a foreign invasion. Just as often it comes about through some accidental loss in the language itself. In the word *stronger,* the old /n/ phoneme had a velar allophone [ŋ] through assimilation to the following /g/. But in the base form *strong* the /g/ was lost, as it has been in all such words still spelled with *-ng.* Had the /n/ reverted to its alveolar pronunciation, there would have been nothing to distinguish *sung, king,* and *fang* from *sun, kin,* and *fan;* a host of homonyms would have been created. Probably to avoid this confusion speakers held on to the velar allophone, which by definition then became a new phoneme.[13]

Toward the end of the last century, when interest in historical linguistics was at its peak, there was a lively controversy over whether the changes in sound that languages undergo were necessarily always regular. Some of them were so to such a majestic degree that they were elevated into *laws,*[14] and the champions of regularity felt that what appeared to be exceptions were mostly due to insufficient evidence or faulty analysis. We know now that the regularity of changes in sounds is due to more or less consistent behavior of the human speech mechanism. Speech is a code, expressed by means of sound-units integrated into a steady flow, and the fact that the process has to be made automatic causes certain predictable effects of unconscious planning, timing, and inertia.

But not all the problems of turning out a well-rounded sentence stem from a misalignment of automatic behavior. Nor are the automatic errors always purely so. Intellectual choices have to be made and intellectual confusions may be incurred. Mistakes at this level are from a wide range of faculties and their interaction often produces whimsical results. "Sporadic changes" is what they used to be called. Three of them

---

[13] That, at least, is the linguistic way of describing the events. Psychologically listeners were probably already paying as much attention to the velar [ŋ] as to the /g/ in distinguishing between *sung* and *sun;* but since it makes for a more economical description to say that the /g/ was what counted and the velarity of [ŋ] was only an automatic consequence of the /n/'s being where it was, that is how the facts are represented.

[14] A term that today's linguists avoid because it is pretentious and because it puts language on the same footing as the physical sciences.

will be treated here: blends, malapropisms, and spelling pronunciations. (Other high-level disturbances that are less concerned with the scrambling of sounds will be looked at later.)

Blends   Suppose someone is about to say **A spurious scarcity of goods led to high prices:**

> A spurious (a) scarcity of goods . . .
>   (b) shortage
>   (c) sparseness
>   (d) lack
>   (e) dearth
>
>   .
>   .
>   .

If he says a **curious spaircity of goods** we know that he has confused two things, both of which he intended to say: **spurious** and **scarcity.** This is little more than a metathesis (it is a *little* more because he has said **curious** and not **scurious**—an existing word is always favored, even if wrong in sense). But if he says **a spurious sparsity of goods** he is probably confusing two things, only one of which he would want to say in a single breath: **scarcity** and **sparseness.** Enough speakers have made this confusion over the years so that **sparsity** is recognized (**sparseness** appeared in the early part of the nineteenth century, **sparsity** in the latter half). **Sparsity** is a *blend.*

The column (a) to (e) shows the dimension in which blends occur: it is paradigmatic, involving sets within the language (in this case, sets of synonyms), rather than syntagmatic, involving the horizontal axis of items in the spoken chain. It is also at a high cognitive level: the speaker is making one of the freest choices that a speaker can make, between two words that are nearly the same in meaning. Blends do not necessarily result in new configurations of sound—the speaker who meant to say either **She was on the verge of a crackup** or **She was on the verge of a breakdown** and came out with **She was on the verge of a crackdown** did not create a new word—but when they do, the creation frequently sticks. This could not happen unless speaker and hearer somehow thought alike; it is as if the existing stock of words were ours as raw material to reshape, with the assurance of some degree of acceptance by others, depending of course on the degree of appropriateness that the new expression seems to have. Many blends are as inappropriate as most spoonerisms. A college professor, intending to compliment a committee that had worked on the status of women on the faculty, was caught between saying **who have helped us so unstintingly** (or

unselfishly) and *who have helped us so generously,* and was morti-
fied to hear himself saying *who have helped us so ungenerously.* In
the same category falls the welcome-aboard speech of an airline
stewardess whose mind flitted between *trip* and *flight* and tricked her
into saying *I hope you have a pleasant flip.* But other blends deserve and occasionally enjoy a lease on life. *Glob* combines *gob* and
blob in a nice union of form and meaning. *Rampacious* joins *ram-
pageous* to *rapacious. Riffle* is semantically a blend of *ripple* and *shuffle,*
although the word form existed previously in another meaning. These
creations are in the standard dictionaries, though others lack sufficient
currency, such as *portentious (portentous + pretentious)*[15] and *protru-
berant (protuberant + protrude).* Others with a promising look but no
currency are *to slag (to lag + to sag* or *to slacken,* with a suggestion
of *laggard* and *sluggard);*[16] *to stample (to trample + to stamp on);*[17]
and *spinwheels (pinwheel + spin).* Since blends are drawn from
paradigms with multiple members—usually a word has more than one
synonym—it is nothing unusual for three or more alternatives to contribute. A speaker was heard to say *He plays the straight-pan type,*
combining *straight man + straight face + dead pan.* Another was heard
to say *The department is underhandicapped* meaning *understaffed*
and *handicapped,* but also *underhanded* in the unusual sense of 'having
too few hands,' where *hand* means 'worker.' Other things besides words
can be blended: *I should say not* and *I should say so,* expressions of
negation and affirmation which are diffident as far as their words are
concerned, have been blended with the intonation of other much more
assertive affirmations and negations such as *You're darned right* or *Hell,
no.*

The kind of blend that is most apt to persist is the one built of loose
elements—phrases rather than single words; we tend not to monitor
them quite as carefully. A good many set phrases in fairly common use
are composites of this kind. It is not easy to be sure, but the following
are probably as represented:

rarely ever = rarely + hardly ever

every now and then = ever and anon + now and then

---

[15] *Bernard Reder's portentious trifles at the Whitney,* sentence from *The Nation*
(23 December 1961), p. 500; *Equally portentious is the reduction of Federal
funds,* from *Publications of the Modern Language Association* 83 (1968), p. 524.
This latter is more likely a malapropism for just *portentous.*

[16] *Their French work slagged all week,* from a report by an instructor reporting on a
Harvard class.

[17] *If they spread their nets there people would stample them,* heard on a San Francisco
radio station.

most everywhere = most places + almost everywhere

twenty-some-odd = twenty-some + twenty-odd

He didn't stay any longer than he could help = He didn't stay any longer that ('so far as') he could help + He didn't stay any longer than he had to[18]

There's no use getting there before eight = It's no use getting there before eight + There's no use in getting there before eight

prices from $6.50 and up = prices $6.50 and up + prices from $6.50 up

equally as good = equally good + just as good

Blends like these occur constantly and for the most part die aborning: *I must take umbrage to Dr. Lee's letter (take umbrage at + take exception to);*[19] *that's the way they're like (that's what they're like + that's the way they are); to keep track on them (to keep tabs on them + to keep track of them).* But the syntactic blends that have the greatest potential for linguistic change are the ones that alter the relations in highly productive patterns. It is commonplace to hear sentences like *He is one of those who does it best,* where the plural *those* is left high and dry as a result of blending *He is one who does it best* with *He is one of those who do it best.* In a sentence such as *It's been nine hours since I've eaten anything* the tense relationships are disrupted by a blend between *It's been nine hours since I ate anything* and *It's been nine hours that I've not eaten anything.*[20] The use of *if* clauses as if they were noun clauses is practically standard: *It would help if we did it* blends the meaning of *Our doing it would help* with that of *If we did it the result would be helpful.* The section on hidden sentences in Chapter 6 (pages 166–70) might have included instances such as these to show the possibility of having two hidden sentences of equal rank.

Again, syntactic blends are the gravitational result of a vast submerged bulk of constructions that do not appear physically in utterances but only reveal their existence by the perturbations they cause. As an example of such crisscrossing forces we can take some constructions with the verb *to see.* In certain sentences there are two passives—for example, *He was seen to go* and *He was seen go*—which on first examination do not appear to contrast with each other, yet which have different outlying associations. The first is used with constructions embodying such

---

[18] See Long 1959, p. 76, for the illogicality of this expression.

[19] *Boston Globe* (13 November 1971), p. 10.

[20] See Long 1959, p. 124.

verbs as *think, believe, guess, know,* as in *She was believed (guessed, known) to be the one,* whose corresponding active is *They believed her to be the one.* The second is found with constructions using verbs of perception, as in *She was heard leave,* with corresponding actives *They saw her go, They heard her leave, They watched it happen.* Some of these constructions, however, are not very firmly established, which makes them susceptible to fairly weak pressures from related constructions. We can say *She was believed to represent the other tradition,* but not very easily the active *?They believed her to represent the other tradition;* the active works well only with the verb *to be.* The verb *to see,* already only shakily a member of the *think, believe* set, cannot enter at all beyond the verb *to be: They saw her to be the one,* but not **They saw her to represent the other tradition:* the influence of the "perception" uses is too strong. On the other side, the passive of perception verbs is not well entrenched either: *They heard her go, She was heard go,* and *They watched her go,* but not **She was watched go.* So even *see* gets into trouble in the passive: *She was seen go,* but not **She was seen write a letter,* nor **She was seen crack a nut.* For many persons even *She was seen go* and *She was heard leave* are probably marginal. The problem is simply that the speaker has to thread his way among several constructions (*She was heard leaving* is also involved in this) that resemble one another in much of their lexical content and that contrast in very subtle ways, and he tends to avoid sentences that in the fast interplay of conversation may be taken the wrong way. Two related constructions using much the same material may blend—that is one solution; or they may repel each other because of the ambiguity they create. This may spell the doom of one or the other or of both. There are always alternatives: *They saw that she went* expresses the factual knowledge and *They saw her go* the action, without any practical need to resort to the passive or the *to* infinitive.

Malapropisms   A malapropism is a special kind of uneducated blend. It is named for a character in an eighteenth-century play, Mrs. Malaprop, who was afflicted with chronic word trouble (her language was *malapropos*). Instead of two (or more) expressions, either of which would be appropriate under the circumstances and both of which appear physically in the result (this is the ordinary blend), there is a confusion between two, of which one is clearly inappropriate, and that is the one that is spoken. The result is not a new word form but a shift in meaning. Mayor Richard Daley of Chicago is a celebrated modern practitioner: "*harassing* the atom," "rising to higher *platitudes* of achievement" (probably blending *planes* and *altitudes*). A political writer says: "A man *aggregates* to himself the right," intending *arrogates.* A weatherman predicts: "Five below zero, *nominally* a safe temperature for driving," intending *normally.* A linguist *hypothecates* ('pawns') a hypothesis instead of *hypothesizing* it. What probably was a malapropism in the Watergate transcripts was editorialized on as follows in a Washington newspaper:

> The President had been sounding out Haldeman, Ehrlichman and Ziegler on the possibility of dumping John Dean:
>
> P. I wonder . . . what it is worth to us to get him out of the damned office. I relieve him of his duties?
> E. Well, the alternative is somehow or other to pass the word to everybody in the place that he's a piranha. I don't know how you do that.
>
> A *piranha?* Was Ehrlichman suggesting that Dean be regarded as a particularly voracious South American freshwater fish? Or did he mean a *pariah,* a person rejected or despised? Posterity . . . will have to decide.[21]

The mental twists that underlie a malapropism are often quite intricate. Senator Alan Bible of Nevada, announcing that a parcel of land had been put in trust for the Washoe Indians, said, "I hope this action *harks* a new era in stability and prosperity for these fine people."[22] This creates a kind of *°hark forward* on the basis of *hark back,* but the correct verb is *herald,* which probably made the leap to *hark* by way of the line from the Christmas hymn *"Hark, the Herald* Angels Sing," helped out by the verb *to mark* in *to mark a new era.* The pathological malapropist has been described as follows: "He is sure that *acumen* means 'omen,' that *bucolic* means 'colic,' that *cupidity* has to do with *love,* that *jaunty* means a gay picnic, that *hybrid* means 'aristocratic,' that *incongruous* means a time when Congress is not in session, that *frugal* means 'fruitful.'[23] The odds against widespread acceptance of any of these pieces of false coin are high, but now and then the inspectors are fooled. *Mitigate* in the sense of *militate* continues to crop up sporadically; during the Dominican intervention in 1965 it was reported that "time mitigated against President Johnson's consulting the ministers of the OAS." Where the terms confused are more or less synonymous, chances of survival are better. *To comprise* means almost the same as *to be composed of,* and many say or write *to be comprised of. To career* for *to career* meaning 'to rush headlong' is another example: a vehicle

---

[21] *Washington Star-News* (18 May 1974), p. A-10.

[22] *The Valley Journal,* Sunnyvale, California (24 July 1970). Conceivably the senator said *marks,* and the transformation occurred in the brain or finger of a reporter or a typesetter.

[23] Downes 1957, p. 203. This reference thanks to William Perry.

careering down a road is apt to careen—lurch from side to side; for most American speakers of English, *careen* has replaced *career.*

Spelling pronunciation   When someone pronounces *pulpit* to rime with *gulp it,* it is a fair inference that he did not acquire the word from hearing it (though ten years from now, as others imitate his pronunciation, this may no longer be true). Learning words from the oral tradition offers the opportunity, though not the guarantee, of saying them as they are customarily said. Guessing at them from reading, in a language that uses an alphabetic system of writing, provides as many chances of breaking with this tradition as there are unreasonable spellings. Left to guesswork, *hypocrite* will come out sounding something like *cryolite,* and *epitome* like *metronome.* This is the penalty for not spelling them *hippocrit* and *epitomy,* for those are the more regular spellings of the sounds in question. Of course, if the writing system is not alphabetic— if it is divorced from sound as it is in Chinese—false associations of precisely this kind do not occur. English spelling might conceivably be so remote from pronunciation that we would throw up our hands and look for no connection at all. As it is, it is just remote enough to ensure a maximum of interference.

The influence of spelling on pronunciation is twofold. First, there is the initial encounter: our introduction to a new word is probably more often through print than by ear, especially as the words we do not already know are most apt to be of a literary or scientific or other specialized sort that is written more often than spoken. We then may want to say it, and we guess at what the letters represent. Second, there is the continual impression of visual images of words on our minds, the familiar ones as well as the unfamiliar ones. A spelling may make us question an authentic pronunciation if the latter is not very firmly established in the first place.

The influence of writing on the spoken language is a hazard of literate societies. One linguist ventures the opinion that "it has probably been the greatest single cause of phonological change in modern English, both British and American."[24] Universal literacy is too recent a phenomenon to reveal long-range effects, but it seems reasonable to suppose that one such effect will be the slowing down of change. Reading is more widely shared over a longer period of time than any form of listening: we "hear" an author of a hundred years ago as clearly as we hear one today, if we read him, and the cultivation of classics ensures that we will. Words, images, and turns of phrase that might otherwise pass from the

---

[24] Householder 1971, p. 69. See also his Chapter 13, "The Primacy of Writing," pp. 244–64.

scene acquire a firmer hold, and become the property of all who share the culture.

Within this broader tendency toward uniformity, spelling pronunciations are both a confirmation and a contradiction. When spellings serve as reminders of how things are pronounced today, pronunciation is less apt to change: when we see *policeman* we are not so inclined to say *pleeceman.* Here spelling is merely conservative. When spellings lead to the revival of a pronunciation long since given up, their force is not conservative but reactionary. In Southern Britain the word *often* is coming more and more to be pronounced with a [t] and with the *o* of *odd.* When a spelling leads to a pronunciation that never existed, its influence is neither conservative nor reactionary but subversive. Many words that had long been spelled and pronounced with simple *t* were respelled with *th* by writers who enjoyed showing off their etymological erudition. One by one such words have taken on a pronunciation that they never had, suggested by the *th: theater, Catholic, author, Theodore.* The latest addition for many speakers is *thyme.* Somehow *Thomas* managed to escape—no doubt because there were more Toms among the common speakers and fewer among the idle intelligentsia.[25]

Nicknames are often an indication of older pronunciations—*Ted* for *Theodore, Kate* for *Katherine, Tony* for *Anthony, Dick* for *Richard* (which, besides the [k], suggests an earlier apical flap for [ɾ], the only /r/ sound apt to be imitated by a child as [d]). A large family of words spelled with *o* traditionally pronounced [ʌ] has been changing the [ʌ] year by year to [a]. The older pronunciation survives in *ton, honey, money, company, stomach,* and *onion;* the new one is triumphant in *combat, common, honest,* and *astonish. Comrade* still had the older pronunciation till about the middle of the last century. *Constable* can still be heard with [ʌ] among conservative speakers. A radio announcer recently said [kampəs] for *compass.*

Other influences may reinforce a spelling pronunciation. A broad *a* seems more elegant to some people, and a safer guess if the word looks at all like something imported from Continental Europe, so we get *Mazda, plaza, patio, Copenhagen, Bahamas,* and many others pronounced with [a] instead of the traditional [æ] or [e]. An *i* also sometimes gets a Continental pronunciation: one persistent guesser on a San Francisco radio station was heard to say [fləbitəs] for *phlebitis* [fləbaytəs]. Any more or less unusual spelling is a temptation. One foreign correspondent consistently pronounces *sortie* as *sore tea. Capri* is pronounced as if spelled *Capree* instead of [káprɨ]; *Fatima* becomes [fətímə] instead of [fǽtəmə]. These cases attest to our having in

---

[25] Jespersen 1909, para. 2.622.

English "two subsystems of correspondences between phonemes and graphemes, one characteristic of the synchronically domestic, the other for synchronically foreign lexicon."[26]

Spelling pronunciations are not a new phenomenon. Some of them date back to the beginnings of general literacy. The written diphthong *oi* is often cited. One still finds now and then, in dialectal writings, *jine* for *join,* *rile* for *roil,* and *pint* for *point.* These dialectal spellings represent a pronunciation that, except for the influence of the spelling *oi,* would probably be standard today.[27]

Speakers' errors: overgeneralization

It takes a child a long time to learn restrictions on usage, many of which make little sense anyway, and during his period of happy innocence he says many things that adults avoid saying. Two terms—*overgeneralization* and *analogical creation*—have been used for this special source of variant forms; the first views them as mistakes, the second as something more or less inspired.

Overgeneralization is characteristic of the third and fourth grammars described in Chapter 9 (pages 287–90). The use of **goed* instead of *went* is an extension, by analogy, of the past tense of regular verbs: *go* is to *goed* as *play* is to *played.* Past-tense forms such as **drinked, *falled, *feeled,* and **hurted,* and plurals such as **dirts, *milks, *knifes,* and **childs* are commonplace in children's speech,[28] and many of them eventually take hold: *worked* has replaced *wrought, beseeched* is replacing *besought, slayed* is threatening *slew.*

Applied to morphology, overgeneralization is often termed *leveling.* There is a "paradigmatic pressure" toward conjugating all the verbs the same way, having a uniform declension for nouns and adjectives, and bringing all other such tightly compacted sets—such as numerals, calendar periods, and times a day—into close alignment. The change is not always in the direction of the most regular overarching pattern. There may be an irregular pattern with more local influence, either because it is attached to some highly frequent form or because through meaning or some other association it is more closely related to the form that undergoes the change. The fairly new verb *to fit*[29] with its past *fitted* has such a close resemblance to *put* (past *put*), *set* (past *set*), *bite*

---

[26] Vachek 1973, p. 55.

[27] Ibid., pp. 41–44.

[28] See Brown 1973, pp. 325–26.

[29] It probably dates from the late sixteenth century.

(past *bit*), **spread** (past *spread*), and other one-syllable verbs with one-syllable past forms that for many speakers it has taken on the irregular past *fit:* "Gabrielle . . . shook her head No to everything we asked, whether the answer *fit* or didn't."[30] The same happened much earlier to the verb **to spit,** which now has *spit* (as well as *spat,* actually from another verb) as standard; we would regard *spitted* as a mistake. A final *-t* or *-d* is a temptation to drop the *-ed.* A hardware store in Los Angeles displayed a sign reading **Pipe cut and <u>thread.</u>**

The local influence is more in evidence where no paradigm is involved, only some powerful grammatical analogy or synonymy. The modifier **close** is not properly speaking a preposition, yet the association with **near** is such that it is sometimes used prepositionally if an adverb follows: **close home, closer there.** The verb **to avert** shares certain constructions with **to prevent: They averted a fuel shortage** and **They prevented a fuel shortage** may report the same event, although all that the first tells us is that they kept out of its way. This was no deterrent to the radio announcer who said, "It will help avert a fuel shortage from becoming a fuel crisis," giving **avert** a sentential object. An adolescent speaker was heard to say **It's up to how much time I have. To be up to** and **to depend on** are close synonyms: **Whether I can accept the job is up to my mother; Whether I can accept the job depends on my mother.** But **to be up to** refers to a decision and is normally restricted to human objects: **It's up to you, It's up to the President,** not °**It's up to the weather** or °**It's up to how soon they get married.**

Sometimes a shift and the adjustments it entails call for a stairway of analogical steps. It is impossible to reconstruct with any certainty, for no log is kept as words travel through conversational space, and by the time the effects find their way into print the original events are beyond observing. As a fair guess, take the expression **He's a wrong guy.** The first step may have involved the compound **all right,** which, along with **awake, asleep, amiss, akin, apart, alive,** and others, belongs to a class of adjectives that we have already met, which obeys the rule of position that they must appear in the predicate but not directly before a noun—we say **Two things were amiss** or **Two boys were asleep** but not °**two amiss things** nor °**two asleep boys.** But analogy is undermining the class:

> The guy is good : He's a good guy : :
> The guy is all right : He's an all right guy

shows how analogy with the synonym **good** is able to bring **all right** in front of the noun. The second step could have been like this:

---

[30] Dashiell Hammett, *The Dain Curse* (New York: Pocket Books, 1954), p. 150.

The guys are alike : Like guys flock together : :
The guys are alive : Live guys flock together : :
The guys are all right : Right guys flock together

whereby **all right** loses **all.** Meanwhile, other speakers may have accomplished the same result in the predicate simply by dropping the **all:**

The guys are all (completely) bad : The guys are bad : :
The guys are all right : The guys are right

This use of **right** in the sense of 'trustworthy' has been known in underworld usage since the early 1920s. With these two possible sources of **right** in a new sense now leading in the same direction, the stage is set for giving **wrong,** its antonym, the contrary new meaning, 'untrustworthy':

He's the right guy : He's the wrong guy : :
He's a right guy : He's a wrong guy

from one direction, and

The guy is right (not mistaken) : The guy is wrong (mistaken) : :
The guy is right (trustworthy) : The guy is wrong (untrustworthy)

from the other.

Reinterpretation: errors of the hearer

The raw material for building a grammar and a vocabulary are what a child hears, or thinks he hears, and what an adult hears or reads, or thinks he hears or reads. If our hearing were flawless and we could read the minds of those who speak to us and around us, no language would change as a result of channel noise. But children especially, and adults too sometimes, often mishear and occasionally misinterpret.

A child cannot seek out the facts from which he constructs his grammar and vocabulary. He depends on others to supply them for him. If they neglect to give him some important bit of evidence, his vision of the language at that point is bound to be different from theirs. We saw this with **for free** (page 387): when adults played with it, the child took it seriously and drew the only conclusion he could. A freshman class is assigned to write a theme in response to a story called "The Petrified Giant," about a large rock formation and how it affected the people who lived nearby. One student complains: "This story doesn't make sense because a giant is bigger and stronger than anybody so why should he be petrified." The teacher asks her what *petrified* means. She replies, "Scared—you know, petrified; like when you're petrified."[31] Her parents and at least some of her friends undoubtedly knew the literal meaning of the word, but never favored her with an example of it. Again, she draws the only inference possible.

More often the evidence is there, but is ambiguous. English has a great many compound nouns ending in an adverbial particle: *runoff, turnaround, shootout, playback, shakedown.* It also has numerous verbs made up the same way. A child comes into a store on an errand for his mother, buys something, and asks, "Will I get any change back?" apparently using the verb *to get* (something) *back.* The storekeeper says yes and completes the transaction, unaware that the child understands *changeback* as a compound noun, and that he is asking, essentially, "Will I get any change?" He is unaware, that is, until one day the child asks, "Will I get any changeback back?"[32] The reinterpretation gets by because it does not interfere with communication.

Folk etymology   Niccolò Tucci writes of his childhood:

> What the priest had told them was that my mother was an *Orthodox* Catholic. The Italian word for 'Orthodox' is *Ortodosso,* which in its feminine form, *Ortodossa,* sounds rather ominous to illiterate ears, because *un orto d'ossa* means a yard full of bones. This phonetic coincidence was enough to make the peasants connect my mother with some diabolical cult, and the feud dividing us from the people of Albiano became even deeper.[33]

A folk etymology is a kind of auditory malapropism. The hearer encounters an unfamiliar term, assumes it ought to be familiar, and proceeds to associate it with something he already knows. The confusion may lead to a mental change in the grammatical construction, as with *ortodossa.* It may change the form of a word, as when a sixteen-year-old girl writes, "It's the *upmost,*" meaning 'It's tops, it's the best,' reinterpreting the *ut-* of *utmost* as the more familiar *up.* Or it may merely change the meaning of a word, as when *hollow victory,* which originally meant 'complete victory,' came to be taken in the sense 'empty victory.'

---

[31] From Morse 1974, p. 545.

[32] Example from Richard Siegel.

[33] *The New Yorker* (14 January 1950), p. 29.

The term itself shows the linguist's preconception, like the play-wright's "All the world's a stage" or the con man's "Everybody has an angle." It seems as if the folk were trying to etymologize words, a game that should be left to experts. But folk etymology is not the same as the guesstymologies sometimes invented by etymologists when they are not sure how to account for a word. *Catnip,* for example, means the same as *catmint,* and the phonetic differences could be explained by a combination of assimilation, metathesis, and dissimilation—the /t/ becomes /p/ by contact with the /m/; the /n/ dissimilates from the other nasal (/m/) by disappearing; the /p/ and /t/ change places; and the resulting /tm/ becomes /tn/ by assimilation: *catmint* $\longrightarrow$ *capmint* $\longrightarrow$ *capmit* $\longrightarrow$ *catmip* $\longrightarrow$ *catnip.* But not all that is plausible is true. *Catnip* really comes from *cat* + *nep, nep* being another name for the same plant.

It is not necessary that the new interpretation make sense, only that it be somehow more plausible than what it replaces. This is especially clear in the folk etymologies invented by children. One child was convinced that *bakin' powder* was *bacon powder,*[34] another that *ice cream cone* was *ice cream comb.* For one six-year-old discussing *chicken pox* with another, the name was *chicken pots;* for the other it was *chicken fox.* But as a rule the substitute form is more intelligible as well as more plausible. A speaker was heard to say, referring to a tree that had blown over, "We could have saved it by using *guide wires.*" The term is *guy wires,* but *guide* is more obviously meaningful than *guy.* Many who heard the term *renegade* applied to some sort of outlaw and who lacked the verb *to renege* as part of their vocabularies established instead a connection with *run* and *gate* ('road, way'), because renegades were generally fugitives; *renegade* became *runagate.* The adjective *secrétive* was originally stressed on its second syllable, but so many speakers have associated it with *sécret* that now *sécretive* is more general. The past-tense form *shined* was once looked upon as substandard, but enough people have assumed that it ought to be related to the noun *shine* (as in 'to give a *shine* to') so that now it is respectable to distinguish between *The sun shone* and *He shined his shoes.*

Evidence for folk etymology is sometimes roundabout. When someone calls for a *slam* or *belt* of liquor we can guess that he has thought of *slug of liquor* as if *slug* were the *slug* of boxing and not from the Irish *slog* 'swallow.'[35] One can sometimes detect a folk etymology through a kind of spelling pronunciation—the error itself has been caused by

---

[34] Example from Fred W. Householder, Jr., personal communication.
[35] Hutson 1947, p. 20.

thoughtless reading. Most people saying aloud the Eugene O'Neill title
Mourning Becomes Electra will probably say

Mourning
be^{comes} E ^{lec}
tra.

as if it meant the nonsensical 'Mourning turns into Electra,' instead of
the proper 'Mourning looks good on Electra'

comes
Mourning be
Electra.

because they assume that *becomes* has its more usual sense. During the
1960s there was a popular television show titled "That Was the Week
That Was," based on a British original. Americans hearing the title
and not understanding the British idiom (generally used by Americans
only in an ironic, not an enthusiastic, sense: *You're a fine person, you
are! That's just great, that is!*) folk-etymologized the *that* to a relative
and gave the second *was* an existential sense. The fact that the result
was slightly mystifying may have lent to its appeal.

There may be a change in form so slight that it passes unnoticed. So
much confusion already exists between *wh-* and *w-* (most Southern
Britishers, and many others, drop the /h/ in *where, which, while,* and
so on) that when some speakers heard "He's a *wiz* (= wizard) at math"
they thought it referred to intellectual quickness, to whizzing through
a problem; *wiz* became *whiz.* The extreme case is found where there is
no difference in form at all and we are unaware of any change until we
see it written. There is no audible difference between "to give something *free rein*" and "to give it *free reign*," but the latter, rather common, spelling reveals what has happened in the writer's mind. Some other
examples:

> Purgatoire River ⟶ Picket Wire River
> Fontainebleau Hotel ⟶ Fountain Blue Hotel
> doughface 'mask' ⟶ doughface 'easily molded person'[36]
> sluice box (for washing gravel from gold) ⟶ slush box
> spit and image (of someone) ⟶ spittin' image
> pride of India 'chinaberry tree' ⟶ piney windy

---

[36] Sperber and Tidwell 1950, p. 98.

(take it to) the cleaner's (his place of business) $\longrightarrow$
(take it to) the cleaners

Fusion and downgrading   A doctoral candidate writes *thus far* consistently as *thusfar* in her thesis. Obviously *thus* and *far* have ceased for her to be separately meaningful, and *thusfar* has joined the ranks of *whatsoever, nevertheless, underway, notwithstanding,* and many other such grammaticized combinations.

All that it takes to create a fusion is two or more meaningful elements side by side and a disposition to take them as a unit rather than separately. The disposition may be a certain degree of unfamiliarity of one of the elements; this was true of *thus far,* where *thus* is now a low-frequency word and is virtually restricted as a modifier to this one phrase (we now say *this much* and *this bold* instead of *thus much* and *thus bold*). Or it may be the clear-cut singleness of the meaning plus high frequency. Within the past few years such expressions as *There is no way that such a thing can be proved,* quite often divided between question and answer as in *"Can it be proved?"—"There is no way,"* have been reduced to simple *no way,* with the result that *no way* has become an emphatic negative and may end by being written *noway.*[37] A woman offers a child some *little bits of* candies. For her, *little bits of* is analytically clear. For the child it is a unit, and soon the adjective *little-bitty,* or *itty-bitty* or *itsy-bitsy,* is established as a synonym of *tiny.* When we say *Yes, truly* we make a clear comma break between the words; but when we say *Yes, indeed* we run them together in spite of the printer's comma, and playful variants such as *yes indeedy* show what has happened.

Fusion is a much more pervasive phenomenon than these examples suggest. It underlies the whole process of compounding. One can detect its work in the relative speed with which certain compounds are pronounced. We say *borderline* faster than we say *border zone.* We can detect it in vowel reduction: *fireman* is more fused for most speakers than *trashman;* the first has /mən/, the second /mæn/. And it shows up in the regularizing of inflections: *babysitted* instead of *babysat, pinch-hitted* and *broadcasted* as the past tense of *pinch-hit* and *broadcast*—if we did not feel that *to babysit* is a fused verb we would not treat it differently from *to sit.* No matter how a compound is written, if it is truly a compound it will be fused to the point where there is some reluctance, however slight, to break it up. If one goes to the counter in a library, hands a borrowed book to the librarian, and asks to have it renewed because one wants to make a *book report* on it, we can be

---

[37] Not the same as the older *noway* 'in no way.'

sure that *book report* is a unit, for otherwise it would have been more natural to say "make a *report* on it"—under the circumstances, *book* is obvious. Many expressions that we still write as separate words are really compounds, fused in pronunciation and meaning. *Ill at ease* embodies a use of *ill* rarely encountered anywhere else. *Nice and hot, good and tired* show by their occasional spelling how *nice'n* and *good'n* have been converted to adverbs. Using *good* and *for* in the usual meanings of these two words, we can form *That would be good for the interests of all classes,* meaning that the interests would find it good. But in *That would be good for you* we immediately infer something to do with physical or personal well-being. In the first sentence *good* can easily be replaced with *best;* in the second it would force a change in meaning.

Fusion is even more. It is the unifying principle of collocations (see pages 99–107). Whenever a combination of words comes to be used again and again in reference to a particular thing or situation, it develops a kind of connective tissue. The example *good for* just cited is midway between a collocation and a compound. Its verbal make-up is unusual for a compound, but it leans toward compounding stress: the first syllable is strongly accented and the rest are huddled together (*góod for you*), as in *jáck-in-the-box.* Sometimes we can tell a collocational fusion by the fact that it shelters words or constructions that are no longer current. *He gave of himself* contains an old partitive, also preserved in *partake of* but obsolete in *They ate of the meat. He is to blame* contains an old passive that is still found occasionally elsewhere (*These jobs are still to do* for *still to be done*). Other collocations can be seen by some unusual feature of their construction. The verb *is* has become fused to preceding expressions using *what* in such a way that *is* may be said twice. The basis is probably sentences like *What I want to know is, is he really like that?* where each *is* has its own function; but now one often hears *What he says is, is that nobody is like that.* The noun phrase *the matter* has been so tightly fused within the larger collocation *to be the matter* that it is virtually an adjective. The steps are as follows:

1. *What's the matter?* ('What is the concern?')

2. *Nothing is the matter.* ('The matter—concern—is nothing.')

3. *There is nothing (that is) the matter.*

4. *There is nothing the matter.* (**There is nothing the concern.*)

5. *Is anything the matter?* ('Is anything wrong?')

The inclusive collocation itself, *What's the matter?* is now fused to the point that the direct-question form is usually carried over into indirect questions: *He wanted to know what was the matter* rather than *He wanted to know what the matter was.* Analogy added to fusion has caused a number of collocations of verb plus adjective and verb plus noun to take on the function of transitive verbs with *that* clauses: *I am confident that he will* is the same as *I trust that he will.* Some are barely detectible. *We have a good time listening to our favorite program* brings an idiom, *to have a good time,* into the slot of *enjoy*—it is not just 'We have a good time *when* we listen'; rather, the feeling is projected on the event, as in *we relish.* The same is found, though perhaps to a lesser extent, in *We take pleasure listening to our favorite program,* though hardly at all in *We find enjoyment listening to our favorite program*—here we are passively absorbing the enjoyment instead of actively engaging in it.

Fusion results in what is sometimes termed *opaqueness.* The opposite, *transparency,* is supposed to be the quality of expressions that speakers can easily "see through." For a speaker of English, *getatable* is transparent, *accessible* opaque, though a Roman would have penetrated *accessible* with no trouble. German is said to be more transparent than English because it builds more of its words out of native material: *vorzeigen* reveals the verb *zeigen* 'to show' whereas English *exhibit* reveals nothing. In a psychological sense it is doubtful that speakers often penetrate these associations. We are more apt to pass them over unconsciously—*to be tied up* and unable to keep an appointment, *to have one's hands full* with a job to do, *to keep one's shirt on* when there is cause for impatience—these are clear enough if we stop to think about them, but we seldom do and are often surprised when their literal meaning suddenly strikes us. It is enough for an expression to be semantically and functionally fused for it to be psychologically opaque.

Fusion is the growing end of linguistic arbitrariness, the process which by heavier and heavier compacting from above has yielded the meaningless sub-units that give language its enormous power. The distinctive sounds in all likelihood had individual meanings eons ago. As they were combined to form compounds of various sorts they sacrificed their individuality and were downgraded to phonemes: two levels existed where before was one. Words in turn were further compounded, and a system of affixes was born, which were partially meaningful but as we have seen always tended to merge their identity with that of the higher unit. The downgrading made possible by fusion has provided a continuous supply of inflectional material. It is possible that the reconstructed *es-mi* for 'I am' in Indo-European is a combination of *es* for the verb and *mi* for the person. The Modern French *finirai* 'I'll finish' was originally *finir* + *ai*, from Latin *finire habeo* 'I have to finish.' The Russian passive-reflexive suffix *-sja*, as in *obvinjat'sja* 'to be accused,' was originally the same as the reflexive pronoun *sebja* in *obvinjat' sebja* 'to accuse oneself.' The Uzbek (Turkic) *ëzaëtirman* 'I am writing' was originally *ëza-ëtirman* 'I writing lie.'[38]

It is fortunate that we can forget, that it is no longer necessary to think of **chilblains** as 'blains caused by chills,' of *How do you do?* as an inquiry about how one does, of *never mind* as an injunction not to notice something. New associations create new meanings, and language continues to build level on level.

Metanalysis   Though fusion is the normal direction of change as words are hammered together, sometimes the opposite takes place. A division is made where there was none before. The following exchange was heard between an uncle and his nine-year-old nephew:

> UNCLE: No, she's never ridden one.
> NEPHEW: I've never rid on one either.

In this example the false division has created an extra word. More frequently there is just a slippage in where an already existing separation ought to go. Otto Jespersen, who coined the term *metanalysis,* gives many examples of both kinds from the history of English, including the following:[39]

> *a nadder* ⟶ *an adder*
> *a napron* ⟶ *an apron*
> *richesse* ⟶ *rich-es*
> *pease* (mass) ⟶ *pea-s* (count, plural)
> *cherris* ⟶ *cherr-ies*
> *bod-ice* (old plural of *body*) ⟶ *bodices* (new word, new plural)

As the examples suggest, the division between the *an* form of the indefinite article and the noun that follows, and the one between a plural or fancied plural ending and the noun stem that precedes, are where such false divisions are most apt to be made. *Richesse, pease,* and *cherris* were originally mass nouns (like *wealth, corn,* and *fruit*) that just happened to have what sounded like a plural ending.

The *nadder–adder* type of change could occur with scarcely a ripple elsewhere, but the reformulated plurals—*cherries, peas,* and so on— required a new conception of the things named. One would no more pluralize *pease* than one would say *°corns* or *°wheats* (unless to refer

---

[38] Examples from Žirmunskij 1966, pp. 86–87, and Bidwell 1965–66, p. 45.

[39] Jespersen 1914, paras. 5.6–5.7.

to several species of corn or wheat). But *pease* was being pulled in another direction. A pea is about the size of a bean and as easy to think of individually as a bean is; and *bean* is a count noun: *bean, beans.* So children drew the obvious analogy: *pease* is to X as *beans* is to *bean.*

A special kind of metanalysis which has its own special name is *back formation.* The "singularizing" of *pease* is a back formation created by analogizing *pease* with *beans* and clipping off the end of *pease* to make the singular *pea.* Back formation is metanalysis combined with over-generalization. The hearer makes a false division and associates part of it with a morphological element—usually a genuine suffix but sometimes a spurious one—which seems to be more or less independent. The reasoning goes like this: if a *seller* is a person who *sells,* then an *usher* should be a person who °*ushes* and a *proctor* should be a person who °*procts.* So, on the basis of the adjective *sedative* we have formed the verb *to sedate,* analogizing with *relative–relate, denotative–denotate,* and other such pairs. (The reverse process then gave *calmative* based on *to calm.*) The verb *to televise* is based on *television,* with a strong push from the suffix *-ise, -ize.* Often a sort of fusion has to precede the back formation. From *applied linguistics,* meaning 'linguistics that is applied,' we get *applied linguist,* which cannot mean °'linguist who is applied,' but only makes sense if *appliedlinguistics* is taken as a fused unit. Sometimes the result of a back formation shows up not in the independent creation of the shorter form but in something else based on it. When people began using the term *motorcade* it was apparent that they had back-formed *caval-* from *cavalcade* in the process of splitting *-cade* off from it. This was easy to do, since we already had *cavalry.* Similarly the existence of a word *ham* referring to meat made it easier to split *-burger* off from *hamburger* and create the suffix-like element found in *nutburger, meatburger, Gainesburger, cheeseburger,* and many other recent coinages.

Reinduction   The subclassifications used in this section have somewhat artificially distinguished between errors typical of speakers and errors typical of listeners. There is no clear division between the individual's two roles when he blunders, only a slightly more conspicuous involvement of one than the other. Speakers monitor by ear everything they say, so a mistake in speaking is also a mistake in hearing. And no mistake in hearing is observable until someone gives evidence of it by speaking.

Reinduction is where we see the two roles most evenly balanced. The individual takes in the evidence by ear, digests it, forms a rule by abduction (a plausible guess on the basis of evidence), applies it by deduction, produces an utterance, sees what the reaction of hearers is, and by alternately testing and correcting, *induces* a final form of his rule that works. This is no different from what happens when he produces a *correct* rule. Reinduction figures in this section only because the resulting rule is one that deviates in some respect from the norm and produces a variant.

Suppose we hear someone say *Them ain't no good.* This outrages our grammatical sensibilities and we assume that it is simply wrong, a manifestation of unsystem, the product of ignorance if not stupidity. Our prejudice is confirmed if we then hear him say *They ain't here.* "This person simply mixes things up; he has no idea of a distinction between *they* and *them*," we think. But if we listen a little more closely we may realize that he is using *them* to refer to things and *they* to refer to people.[40] Given the model sentences that he has heard as a child, this may be a perfectly reasonable induction. The correct rule (by our present standards) of course is that *they* is a subject pronoun and *them* is an object pronoun, without regard to things and people. But at one point in the singular the situation is exactly reversed: *it* refers to things, and now it is the question of subjects versus objects that makes no difference: *It is useful, I need it. He* and *she* as subjects are matched by *him* and *her* as objects. So we get the following realignment:

	Subject	*Object*
Human	he, she	him, her
	they	them
Non-human	it	it
	they ⟶ them	them

The non-human pronouns are regularized to have *them* uniformly for things plural, agreeing with *it* for things singular. The special treatment for humans creates no problem, for they get special treatment in many other ways. And if it seems puzzling that the same pronoun *them* should be used for human objects, that can be sensed as reflecting the fact that when human beings are objects of verbs, most of the time they are not in a typically human role—they are being pushed around, treated like things, especially in the plural, where individuality tends to disappear. Of course not all sentences that the learner hears will conform to his reduction. *They're no good* can be said for things. So he may feel that he needs a special rule, perhaps "Use *they* when things somehow count as just as important as humans." He does not have to sacrifice his fundamental rule, only watch out for special occasions. He may even catch on to what the "correct" fundamental rule is and

---

[40] Example thanks to J. P. Maher, personal communication.

FIGURE 12–1
Abduction and Deduction in the Acquisition of Language

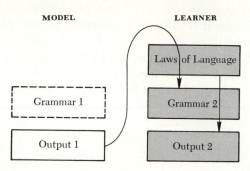

SOURCE: Adapted from Andersen 1973, p. 778.

use it when dealing with certain people—to that extent he is bidialectal;
but he will not use it when he is relaxed, at home, being taken as a
model by his children.

The transition from model grammar to reinduced grammar can be
seen in Figure 12–1. Grammar 1 is inaccessible—it is in the mind of
whoever is speaking. Only what the learner hears—Output 1—is available for processing through his innate capacities (Laws of Language).
From this, by abduction and deduction, he formulates his own grammar and produces his own output, which is available as a model for
the next generation of learners.

The combination of fundamental rules and special rules (exceptions)
explains how changes in grammar can be both sudden and gradual at
the same time. The new grammar that a child forms is discontinuous
with the grammar of his parents; this is a sudden change. But the dis-
crepancies are masked—and hence escape detection and correction—by
the concessions made with the special rules. And these, like all burden-
some exceptions, tend to be eliminated with time. Basically all linguistic
change is of this kind, and it bears a more than accidental resemblance
to other changes in our social habits. The new generation forms its own
convictions about politeness and rudeness and virtue and vice, but conforms outwardly—perhaps even unconsciously—by going through the
old motions when survival or comfort demand it. Only later, when the
lid is off, are we aware of what has happened.[41]

Inductions and special rules are able to coexist because together they
make up the filing system that brings order to the endless supply of
model sentences that come our way. The extreme of the special rule is
the collocation (Chapter 5), which is a rule unto itself. The two ex-

---

[41] The discussion is based on Andersen 1973.

tremes, rule and collocation, are in a tug of war. The collocation represents what we are used to. The rule represents our freedom to invent. Each is carried in our minds as a criterion of correctness. We may reject an expression because it is ill-formed according to our rules—an impulse to say *°better enough* on the analogy of *good enough* is throttled because our rule does not permit *enough* to follow a comparative. Or we may accept or reject on the basis of sheer familiarity. The peculiar grammar of many idioms does not bother us because we are accustomed to them: *to know better, to come a cropper, to make no bones about something.* On the other hand, we may reject a perfectly well formed expression if it is very low in frequency; we readily say *all day, all week, all year,* but *all hour* seems wrong and is apt to be replaced by *the whole hour.*[42]

Word meanings are reinduced too. The example *for free* was mentioned earlier—not being able to read their parents' minds (where *for free* is labeled "joke"), children take it as a sober, ordinary equivalent for plain *free.* One area in which meaning is constantly changing by reinduction is that of explicitness, especially explicitness leaning toward exaggeration. In place of *disliking* spinach we *hate* it. The child sees no

---

[42] The following occurred in a letter from a teacher: *The students were quite jolted when I talked Spanish with them all hour.* It is not a deviant sentence, as can be seen by checking the time expressions other than *hour* with which *all* can be used without adding *that:*

all day	°all decade
all week	°all century
all year	°all minute
all month	

The prerequisites seem to be two. First, the unit has to be great enough for its duration to seem long. *°All minute* is excluded because hardly anything we might do in just a minute's time would seem to be worth a remark about how long it took. The result is that *°all minute* has had no opportunity to become a familiar expression, and we reject it even when it might be appropriate—as in a fairy story, say of Lilliputians whose sense of time is on a smaller scale than ours: instead of *°They worked at it all minute* we would have our Lilliputian say *They worked at it that whole minute* or *all that minute.* On the other hand, *°all century* has plenty of duration, which brings up the second prerequisite. Units of time function in two separate ways: one is to express measurement, the other to express an established period for an activity. We schedule particular days, weeks, and years for things we do (this is the context where *all* is used with a unit of time and no article), but not particular centuries and certainly not particular minutes. That "particularizing" is involved is apparent when we compare a sentence such as *They worked at it all day* with one such as *They worked at it for a whole day*—the speaker has a particular day in mind. This is confirmed when we see how the definite article might be used: while we would no longer say in English *°They worked at it all the day,* we have a choice between *They worked at it all day long* and *They worked at it all the day long.* In addition we would find that in other languages related to English the definite article actually appears: *all day* in French is *toute la journée.* Now we can check the example with *hour.* For a class in school, it is an established period. And from the students' standpoint it can last unconscionably long. So *all hour* fits the rule. We are merely not quite used to it as a collocation.

real evidence of strong emotion and concludes that *hate* represents something less than abomination. The common practice of adding unnecessarily specific or emphatic modifiers puts a parasitic growth on otherwise healthy nouns and verbs. An airline stewardess advises passengers to check for their *personal belongings;* belongings are normally personal, and become something less by this process, just as *unique* has been robbed of its uniqueness by speakers who habitually say *very unique.* This is why the professional exaggerator is unable to wield an influence much beyond his own generation. Those for whom the word has connotations of disgrace may allow themselves to be swayed on hearing a reputable person called a *jailbird.* But the child, inducing the meaning from what he sees, quite innocently and correctly reads the word in the light of the evidence, not the evidence in the light—or the dark—of the word. Lies and misrepresentations are self-liquidating and have to be constantly reinvented, though at what cost to the stability of language we can only guess.

The changing world

Language is not the only thing that moves. Sometimes it stands still, relatively speaking, and the world moves. This is the source of most collocations. The clearest examples are the compounds that start out as syntactic constructions. There is a grammatical rule in English that allows us to build sub-sentences by attaching an *-ing* verb to a noun. We can say "I couldn't sleep because of the incessant *horn-blowing* going on next door," or "What was all that *dirt-throwing* about?" In the middle years of the American Civil War, General John H. Morgan was operating in Kentucky preparatory to making his famous raid into Indiana and Ohio. The success of the raid depended in part on intercepting enemy telegrams. One of Morgan's officers gave the following account: "Without delay we passed through Springfield and Bardstown, crossing the Louisville and Nashville at Lebanon Junction, thirty miles from Louisville on the 6th. . . . Tapping the wires at Lebanon Junction, we learned from intercepted despatches that the garrison at Louisville was much alarmed, and in expectation of immediate attack."[43] *Tapping the wires* is a grammatical construction. So, *at that time,* would *wiretapping* have been. Over the years, as the custom of tapping wires became established, *wiretapping* was infused with a specific content and became "a word." *Horn-blowing* is not a word in this sense; *firefighting* is.

---

[43] From Tamony 1973, pp. 1–2.

We see the most typical effect of a changing world in the constellation of meanings around a word, where lights flicker out and others brighten as energy is cut off from one or more senses and flows elsewhere. Most people would be puzzled today at the expression *rickety children,* failing to make the obvious connection with rickets. As the disease became less and less prevalent, the transferred sense of 'shaky, tottering, feeble' was left without its home base and became the central meaning of the word. The variant *rachitic* has taken over the original meaning. The scientific environment is in flux too. Take the word *light.* Light was, by definition, that which made things visible. At one time such an idea as "invisible light" would have been an absurdity, like joyous dirges or circular squares. But when the physical basis of light became known, it was natural to transfer the meaning to the *energy* that produces light, and from there to the "same" energy that lies beyond the range of the visible—with the discovery of infrared and ultraviolet, *invisible light* was no longer a mystery. Nor is *inaudible sound.*

Among the names of tools and appliances, a change in material culture often widens a split that is always latently present in such words. An icebox is a box for ice—that is its material side. It is also a place to keep things cold—that is its function. With the advent of mechanical refrigeration ice became superfluous, yet many people kept the name, preserving the function but ignoring the material. Nowadays we drink through *straws* often made of glass, from *glasses* sometimes made of plastic, and wipe our mouths afterward on *napkins* made of paper (*nappe* 'linen cloth'). A language is like a miserly housekeeper who clings to every dress form, sprung cushion, and moldy piece of luggage, looking for the day when it can be put to use again. But unlike most attic storerooms, that of language is never a clutter; nearly always a use *is* found for everything.

Sometimes a material change is matched by a material change in language. As more and more women have taken up activities formerly reserved for men, languages that make gender distinctions in their nouns have had to accommodate their occupational titles. As long as it was unthinkable for anybody but a man to be a doctor, the word for 'doctor' could remain comfortably masculine. But the new state of affairs forced a decision: either feminines had to be coined to match every masculine, or the gender of the noun had to become a formality. The languages facing this problem—Polish, for example—are still trying to decide in each case which of two variant forms to adopt.[44]

Changes in the material world can be sudden. The semantic reactions can be equally sudden. So change in meaning is more unpredictable than any other kind of change.

---

[44] See Nalobow 1971.

Bilingualism

The most revolutionary cause of change is the forced encounter between one culture and another. It need not be violent. It may well be cooperative, as when seamen from various lands man a single ship, or mixed armies fight a common foe. Whatever brings two speakers of different languages into contact and makes them communicate with each other counts as a force for change. In Chapter 11 we saw this manifested in pidgins and creoles. But the proliferation of variants as a result of bilingualism need not be on quite so grand a scale in order to effect quite considerable changes in either or both of two languages in contact. There may be an inpouring of commercial goods with their inventories, assembling instructions, and service manuals packed with terms that have no equivalents in the native language but must be adopted if the goods are to be put to use. The "foreign" language may be old rather than new: religious tradition often preserves a contact that otherwise would have faded, as when Latin was maintained in the Western church and Church Slavonic in large parts of the Eastern, as ritual languages. Fashion may be responsible, as when Paris established itself as arbiter in the nineteenth century and poured its genteelisms into all the languages of Europe. Whenever for any reason a person learns or half-learns a second language, he will mix some of it with the language he already knows, and others who are not bilingual, or are less so, will follow him if doing so seems to lead them where they want to go.

Borrowings are concentrated in the areas where contact is most intense. So it is not surprising that science and technology lead the field nowadays, with sports and tourism close behind. In Hungarian, for example, English sporting terms were taken in wholesale for half a century—four or five hundred of them, even including some numerals, especially in tennis.[45] But contacts have grown so close in recent times, with press, radio, television, and international travel, that a kind of universal diffusion is taking place.[46]

Typically the flow is greater in one direction than in the other. The speaker of a language regarded for any reason as socially or culturally superior does not feel under any compulsion to learn a language regarded as inferior, though he may condescend to pick up an occasional word that saves him the trouble of inventing one himself. That is often the fate of contact languages that have been brought low by conquest. English shows little trace of the dozens of Indian languages that were once—and in many cases still are—spoken between the Atlantic and

---

[45] Csapó 1971.
[46] See Peruzzi 1958.

Pacific, except for the numerous geographical names such as *Mississippi,*
Oklahoma, Topeka, and *Shawnee,* and a few names for material objects
like *tobacco, chocolate, hammock, potato, skunk, raccoon, lagniappe*—
and even these were often taken from French or Spanish, which had
borrowed them first. Nothing so deep within the structure of the
language as a pronoun or a verb ending or a phoneme or a particular
order of words was affected in any serious way. On the other hand,
borrowings *from* English in the lands under British and American rule
have been vast, if not devastating. Words have been taken in by the
hundreds, and here and there the deeper levels have been affected. In
Chamorro, the language spoken on Guam, the phoneme /r/ has been
introduced from English, as have certain consonant clusters that were
not previously permitted and shifts of accent to vowels that could not
formerly carry it.[47] In the Sicilian spoken in the United States, similar
changes have taken place in the phonemic system, and other changes
have occurred as well; for example, borrowed nouns and verbs have
been limited to a few grammatical classes whose size is thereby swollen,
and word order has been influenced by the borrowing of many adjectives that invariably precede the noun.[48] Naturally, other politically or
economically dominant languages have made equally deep inroads into
the native languages of the areas they overran. Tagalog, one of the
languages of the Philippines, adopted so many Spanish loanwords that
it had to augment its vowel system from three to five; and other equally
penetrating changes have occurred.[49]

Enforced bilingualism can be disruptive. In the Swiss village of Bonaduz, where speakers went from Romansh to German in a relatively
short period of time (in 1900, 63 percent classified themselves as
Romansh-speaking, 37 percent as German-speaking; ten years later the
proportions were reversed: 31 percent and 69 percent), the German
that was learned was picked up from several different dialects and resulted in such a conglomeration that speakers differed widely in the
rules of their grammar.[50] But more commonly the defenses are stronger,
a single language is held on to, and what is accepted from outside is
rather carefully filtered. Borrowing is made as painless as possible. Words
are affected first, grammar last. The borrowing language often develops
a kind of grammatical receptacle whereby foreign words can come in
and cause the least trouble. An example is the two frames in which
Chicano Spanish admits English verbs. One is *Hizo* _____ *mucho,* as
in *Hizo improve mucho* (literally, 'She did [made] improve a lot'). The
other is *Está* _____*-ing mucho,* as in *Está improving mucho* ('She is

---

[47] Topping 1962.

[48] Di Pietro 1961.

[49] See Bowen 1971, especially pp. 946–47.

[50] Moulton 1971, pp. 942–43.

improving a lot').[51] The ongoing system of the borrowing language is always to be reckoned with. It can reject a sound or a word form as quite indigestible. Or it can assimilate it quickly and easily. An example of the latter is the word *mandarin,* ultimately from Sanskrit *mantrin* 'counselor' (and akin to English *mind*—a counselor is a person who makes one think). It was taken into Portuguese as *mandarim,* and from there spread to other Western languages. In English it connotes a bureaucrat, usually a reactionary one, and it has overtones of supposedly oriental pretentiousness. But in Portuguese it immediately attached itself to the verb *mandar* 'to command' and came to signify a 'bossy person.'

Lexical borrowings have been classified in various ways. The following is proposed by Einar Haugen:

1. *Loanword:* both form and meaning are borrowed, with whatever degree of adaptation to the phonology of the borrowing language. Examples: *chic, blitzkrieg, tea.*

2. *Loanblend:* part of the form is native and part is borrowed, but the meaning is fully borrowed. Examples: Pennsylvania German *bassig* 'bossy,' with borrowed stem and native suffix; American Portuguese *alvachus* 'overshoes,' with native prefix *al-* displacing part of *over.*

3. *Loanshift:* the meaning is borrowed but the form is native. Examples: Italian *ponte* 'bridge' in the literal sense, for 'bridge' as a game, with its meaning borrowed from English; *to gainsay* 'against-say,' translating Latin *contra-dicere,* later also borrowed as a loanword, *contradict.*[52]

Less spectacular (and less noticed) than bilingual borrowing is bidialectal borrowing. A loanshift of sorts occurs whenever we "learn a new meaning for a word"—the meaning had to be part of someone else's speech for us to acquire it, and our acquiring it is to a certain extent learning just so much of another dialect. In fact, the whole process of language learning is one of bringing our personal ways of talking and comprehending in line first with those of other individuals at close range and then with expanding circles of speech communities outward to the limits of our reach in society.

But dialect borrowing is generally thought of as the picking up of items that have been identified as typical of some speech community other than the one to which the speaker most intimately belongs. Any form of bidialectalism can be the carrier. In North Carolina, a region

---

[51] From Reyes 1975.

[52] The classification and part of the examples are from Haugen 1972, pp. 79–109.

where some Northern pronunciations have found their way in, along with Northern perceptions of some Southern pronunciations, the local variety remains with one meaning and the new comes in with another. (The spellings of the last two examples represent what a Northerner thinks he hears.)

> A woman who is *whipped* is 'ugly'; one who is *whupped* is 'real ugly.'
>
> One who is *ruined* is verily so; one who is *ruint* is trivially so.
>
> One who is *poor* is moderately so; one who is *real pore* is poverty-stricken (often used ironically).
>
> One who is *fired* can be rehired; one who is *farred* is out.[53]

The schools are often responsible for splits of this kind. They try to suppress an undesirable variant, but the miscreant almost always escapes by putting on a disguise. Not that contrariness is necessarily involved—any variant from another dialect may gain acceptance just as easily:

> "He's an igernut, durn fool," said the mountaineer when my sister mentioned a local character.
> "He certainly sounds ignorant," she agreed, thinking to correct his pronunciation diplomatically.
> "Oh, he ain't ignorant," the man retorted. "Lotsa folks is ignorant and can't help it. But he's just plain igernut. He don't want to learn nothin'. Them's two different words, you know."[54]

Devotees of westerns never confuse a *pardner* with a *partner,* a *critter* with a *creature,* or a *greazer* with a *greaser.* Many speakers nowadays would find **Whip him well** a poor substitute for **Whip him good,** though some of them would refuse to accept the adjective *good* for the adverb *well* elsewhere.

Invention

There is some originality in every act of speech. Language in action is the fitting of linguistic material to aspects of reality, and the fit is one that has to be improvised in however slight a degree. In referring to

---

[53] Examples thanks to Walter Beale and David Moore, personal communication. What is called "eye dialect" may be involved in *pore* and *farred.* The Northern comic strip artist thinks he hears *pore,* and puts it in the mouth of his illiterate characters; the Southerner reads the comics, and exaggerates *pore* for effect.

[54] *Reader's Digest* (April 1947), p. 90.

something as a *dog* we assume that the token animal we see is covered by a term learned in relation to other tokens. Most of the time it is automatic; it is not a *logical* assumption because we do not think about it. But now and then we are confronted with something for which our automatic responses do not suffice, and then we have to cast about for a form and a meaning that will come sufficiently close, given a bit of stretching or paraphrasing and a dash of imagination on the part of our hearer.

A three-year-old girl does not know the word *to dream.* In reporting a dream she tells of what she *saw in her pillow.* A four-year-old, unable to manage a phrase such as *to look seriously at someone,* says she will *make her face mad at someone.* This is familiar material used to cope with a new situation. Its motivation is the same as when Sir Humphrey Davy in 1807 needed a name for a new element he had discovered, and called it *potassium,* inventing a Latinized form of *potash,* originally *pot-ashes,* from which the hydroxide was extracted. Some form of analogy is always involved. The speaker looks for a relatedness in language that corresponds to the relatedness in the real world. Ordinarily the machinery of language gives it to us quickly, but sometimes the problem has to be addressed deliberately. And in between are the times when we are just a little bit unsure—perhaps there is exactly the right expression for our needs out there somewhere, but we forget it. Such was probably the case with the speaker on a talk show who referred to the *wiseness* of doing something, instead of the *wisdom* of doing it— normally *wiseness* would be 'state of being wise,' not the content of what makes one wise, but the analogy of *foolishness* is so strong—where no such distinction is made—that *wise* and *-ness* are readily thrown together for the purpose. When an airline promises to "make your flight as smooth and quiet and *on time* as possible," we recognize an improvised adjective replacing *punctual,* which in this context would have too personal a ring. The hearer has no trouble interpreting these flashes of linguistic insight because he makes the same analogies. When he hears a medical association warning about "the amount of unburned particles *exhausted* in the air" he knows precisely what the intention of the verb is because he relates it to the noun *exhaust* (of a car) and is familiar with the thousands of cases in English where noun and verb are the same in form.

When the analogy in the real world is striking enough to be noticed, we call the result a *metaphor.* A couple of hundred years ago some sailor likened long-winded storytellers to spinners of yarn. This is how a figurative *He likes to spin yarns* was reinterpreted as meaning literally *He likes to tell yarns,* and *yarn* became a synonym of *story.* Countless present meanings are embalmed metaphors: *to lie low, to walk out on something, to raise the roof, to go ahead full steam.* Most of our abstractions are borrowed metaphors from Greek or Latin: *to insult* means 'to jump on,' *eccentric* is 'off center,' a *hyperbole* is 'a throwing beyond.' The something-like principle (pages 208–11) is a way of saying that every time we speak we metaphorize. "Metaphor," says one linguist-stylistician, "is not a figure of speech among the others, but a basic grammatical category."[55]

---

[55] Valesio 1974, p. 17.

ADDITIONAL REMARKS AND APPLICATIONS

1. How do you pronounce *heaven?* In the light of what often happens to *seven* and *eleven,* how might you expect some speakers to pronounce it? Explain the process. See if this kind of assimilation is apt to occur with equal readiness in all of the following, and try to account for any differences:

   > seven boys and seven girls
   > seven or eight
   > I have seven

   Would the *yep* and *nope* phenomenon (see page 21) suggest anything about this last example?

2. How do you pronounce the following expressions? Discuss any differences between the first column and the second in the sounds represented by the italicized letters:

a. brea*d*	brea*d*th
b. *k*eel	*c*ool
c. *in*finite	*in*timate
d. mis*t*er	mis*ch*ief
e. *th*ree	a*g*ree
f. We've go*t t*wo runs.	We've go*t t*o run.

3. In the word *lapboard* there is little or no accommodation between the /p/ and the /b/; both are articulated in almost the normal way. But the combination is a difficult one, and in the word *cupboard* it is possible to see what may some day happen to *lapboard* (compare also *clapboard* when it is pronounced the same as *clabbered*). Describe the steps that may bring about the same change in the pronunciation of *lapboard.*

4. In the name *Saint Paul* there is—for many if not most speakers— a kind of double assimilation. See if you have it in your speech, and if so, describe it.[56]

---

[56] Example suggested by Sidney Greenbaum.

5. A speaker who as a child pronounced *catch* as *ketch* but has subsequently changed to standard [kæč] comes out with *This is the
best place to ketch a cab.* What phonetic reason might there be for
his reverting to his childhood pronunciation?

6. Do any of the following sentences seem unacceptable to you?

    a. Being tired, I decided not to go out.
    b. As I was tired, I decided not to go out.
    c. Being busy with my writing, I didn't hear the doorbell.
    d. As I was writing, I didn't hear the doorbell.
    e. Being writing, I didn't hear the doorbell.

If you find that one is worse than the rest, what is a possible
reason for your dislike of it?

7. In the rapid pronunciation of *investment,* do you articulate the first
/t/? If not, is one of its features retained in an adjoining sound?
Explain. Discuss the same phenomenon in the word *Christmas.*

8. *Webster's Third New International Dictionary* records *coppice* and
copse as identical in meaning. Account for what appears to have
happened phonologically.

9. A speaker is heard to say *I would never let my membership lasp.*
What has happened?

10. What is the term for the change exemplified in *liberry* for *library?*
In making *hors d'œuvre* rime with *nerve?*

11. The words *dubious* and *chimney* for some speakers take the forms
jubous and *chimbley* (the latter sometimes *chimley*).[57] In each, two
events have taken place. Try to identify them.

12. Trace the series of changes that reduced the pronunciation of
government to *gubment.*

13. What sort of metathesis is *civics* for *physics?* Does it underscore
the need to take account of elements other than phonemes? Is the
same true of the spoonerism *mutts* and *dolts* for *nuts* and *bolts?*

14. Identify the phonetic alterations in the following: *pram* for *peram-
bulator; glanders,* related ultimately to Latin *glandula; sprite,* a

[57] Foster 1971, pp. 18, 22.

form of *spirit; bird,* from Old English *brid; number,* related to German *Nummer;* dialectal *fillum* for *film; tremble,* ultimately from Latin *tremulus.* The Latin word *poenitentia* gave us *penitence,* with little change except in the ending. What additional change produced *(re)pentance? penance?* (For the latter, pretend that *penitence* and *penance* were spelled as they sounded, *penitents* and *penants.*)

15. Is *You can rub that scrug* a likely spoonerism? What about *Bill the speans* and *Pill the sbeans?*

16. A typist, intending to write *Henry should be too,* types *Henry should bee to.* Is this similar to lapses that occur in speech? Explain.

17. Analyze the following blends, then check your answers with the footnote. (Your solutions may be better than the ones suggested.)

    a. Are we going to stand still and be laughed at as overgrown, stupid *clouts?* (from a foreign language magazine)

    b. a *skull and dugger* program (referring to a Disney television program)

    c. They'll *bustle* him off to a mental hospital.

    d. Now that you *rub around* with those people. . . .

    e. The singer had a *sachrymose* voice.

    f. Give them the tone with your *pitchfork.*

    g. They made up after their little *spiff.*

    h. The test will include *both* speaking *as well as* reading.

    i. It will go down *in posterity.*

    j. I've *gone through a lot of expense* to do this.

    k. She *isn't far from wrong.*[58]

18. What is the currently popular expression that results from blending *Who could care less?* with *She (he,* etc.) *couldn't care less?* Check the footnote when you have an answer.[59]

---

[58] a. *clod + lout;* b. *skulduggery + cloak and dagger;* c. *hustle + bundle;* d. *run around with + rub elbows with;* e. *saccharine + lachrymose;* f. *tuning fork + pitchpipe;* g. *spat + tiff;* h. *both X and Y + X as well as Y;* i. *in history + to posterity;* j. *to go through a lot + to go to a lot of expense;* k. *not to be far wrong + not to be far from the truth.*

[59] "The bank or collection agency often *could care less* that the goods are shoddy." From the Boston *Globe* (4 January 1972), p. 7.

19. Analyze the following rather common type of syntactic blend: *You're sure one woman who never gives up, do you?*

20. Some blends are deliberately coined (malapropisms too—Archie Bunker's lines in "All in the Family" are filled with them). An example is *smog* from *smoke* and *fog.* Find others.

21. A speaker was overheard to say *What a better place this world would be.* If it sounds strange to you, see if you can describe the grammatical restriction in your own speech that forbids it, and what has happened to cause the change. Do the same with *Everybody had been issued with temporary passes.*

22. Intending to write *19,* a typist writes *91.* Is this a purely mechanical sequencing mistake, or is there something in the language system that causes it? (Suggestion: compare the naming of the digits here with that of the digits, say, in *29.*)

23. Pick out the malapropisms in the following and analyze them. Check your results with the footnotes.

    a. Regretfully, Professor H. passed away shortly after submitting his contribution to this volume.[60]

    b. Davies described [Stalin] as a man of action, but of little formal education. As a prodigy of Lenin, Stalin earned a reputation as a man who could get things done. . . .[61]

    c. Thirty adults [on bicycles] showed up last Sunday in the sunshine and crisp breeze and sailed off on an 8.3-mile sojourn.[62]

24. Have you heard expressions such as *daylight savings time* and *You can make quite a savings on that purchase?* The standard, of course, is the singular *saving.* What do you suppose has happened?

25. Apparently intending *impedimenta,* Senator Howard Baker on a radio broadcast referred to *impedimentia* [ɪmpɛdəmɛnšə].[63] Discuss the nature of the substitution.

---

[60] *Regretfully* for *regrettably.* From Albert Valdman (ed.), *Papers in Linguistics and Phonetics to the Memory of Pierre Delattre* (The Hague: Mouton, 1972), p. 231, footnote.

[61] *Prodigy* for *protégé.* From a report on a lecture; Palo Alto, Calif., *Times* (9 October 1973), p. 7.

[62] *Sojourn* for *journey,* perhaps blended with *slow.* From the Boston *Traveler* (22 September 1964), p. 29.

[63] San Francisco radio station, 26 May 1974.

26. The word *substitute* has repeatedly been used with exactly the same syntax as that of *replace* ever since *substitute* was first introduced into English; for example, *A substitutes B* for *A replaces B* or *A is substituted for B.* Why do you think the confusion occurs? Would you regard *A substitutes B* as a malapropism? If you do, would you say that such a malapropism is quite properly condemned? Why?

27. Identify the correct forms to replace the following malapropisms:

  a. The issue would be more quickly enjoined.

  b. I made them a sincere offer but they flaunted it.

  c. He lives in Pepsi-Cola, Florida.

  d. She couldn't get into that college because they refused to waver the requirement.

28. Ted Baxter, the anchor man on the "Mary Tyler Moore" television show, relayed a piece of news from *a white-horse souse.* A San Francisco *Chronicle* writer referred to an *inter-uterine device.* Identify the nature of the error in each case.

29. If you found some quaint fictional character being made to say *I've lived here for nigh on to fifty years,* and then encountered the expression *nigh unto* as a literary archaism, what would you suspect had happened? What would you suspect if you heard some people pronouncing the first part of *hurricane* exactly like *hurry?*[64]

30. See if you can find the folk etymology in the following: "When finally, exhausted, I got to the bakers, I bought the largest fruitcake they had." Check the footnote after you have tried.[65]

31. The expression *to while away the time* dates from the early seventeenth century, and *to wile* ('beguile') *away the time* from the late eighteenth. Discuss what appears to have happened, and the phonological and semantic reasons for it.

32. In question 2, item g of the Additional Remarks and Applications of Chapter 11, the two forms *coverlet* and *coverlid* were given as synonyms of *bedspread.* What kind of form would you suspect *coverlid* to be, with reference to *coverlet?*

---

[64] "The higher, more advanced vowels may sometimes be heard in *hurricane*" (Alan F. Hubbell, *American Speech* 25 [1950], p. 109).

[65] Alice B. Toklas, *The New Republic* (18 August 1958), p. 8. The writer has taken the possessive *baker's* as a plural, or has imitated others who have done so.

33. Consider the following sentences:

    a. What do you figure (reckon, calculate) he wants?
    b. I didn't figure (calculate) to see you around here at this hour.
    c. I figure (reckon) it's too late for that.
    d. He figured (up) the accounts.
    e. They figured (calculated, reckoned) the balance.

    You will probably identify *reckon* and *calculate* as quaint or rustic in the sense of 'suppose,' and *figure* may strike you as slightly that way too. But the verb *to figure* has a long history in the sense 'to create a figure or image,' with the extended meaning 'to imagine' (in French *se figurer* is a common expression for 'guess, imagine'). Assuming that that was the source of *figure* as it is now used in sentences such as a, b, and c, what could have been the later semantic development involving *reckon* and *calculate,* and its influence on the way most people probably now think of *figure?*

34. Check your own pronunciations of the following words. Then look them up in an older dictionary (say one published between 1900 and 1910) and in as recent a one as possible. If you discern a pattern of change, account for it: *gynecology, conjurer, hover, dour, thence, chiropodist, chaise longue.* What further complication is there in the last example?

35. The words *diphtheria, naphtha,* and *diphthong* were traditionally pronounced with [p]. Does the insistence on [f] prove the maxim that a little learning is a dangerous thing?

36. See if you can find examples of alternate spellings of given names that may reveal the earlier pronunciations, such as *Rafe* for *Ralph* and *Ellen* for *Helen.*

37. A radio announcer pronounces *regatta* as if it were written *regotta,*[66] using what one linguist calls "the fine Italian [a]." What is the nature of the change?

38. The plurals of words like *basis, analysis,* and *crisis* are written *bases, analyses, crises,* with the last syllable pronounced like *ease.* Do you treat the plurals of words like *premise* and *process* in this way too? If so, what is the reason for it? Would you do the same with *mattress* and *promise?* If not, why not?

---

[66] San Francisco radio station, 26 May 1974.

39. A speaker who knows better and would ordinarily never make such a mistake is heard to say *I don't see how you standed me* for *I don't see how you stood* ('put up with') *me.* Is there anything in the situation that encourages the slip, perhaps something like what happens with *sweet tooths* and *snow mans?*

40. Look up the tense forms of the verb *to bring* in *Webster's Third New International Dictionary* and see if you can account for the forms labeled "substandard." Do the same with the forms labeled "dialectal" for the verbs *sneak, fight,* and *skin.*

41. Has the expression *I (we,* etc.) *might as well* become fused into a kind of collocation? Test, from the standpoint of meaning, the potential for abbreviation (dropping the *I,* for example) and the relative ease with which another auxiliary can be substituted for *might* (perhaps *could*). Do the same with *I might add that* (plus a clause)—is it more usual or frequent, for example, than *I will add that* or *I add that* or *Let me add that?*

42. Many speakers who say *He ups and hits me* in the present tense say *He up and hit me* instead of *He upped and hit me* in the past tense. Account for the change. What does it suggest about our willingness to accept a rather destructive change when the context overshadows the meanings of the individual words?

43. What do such plurals as *cloverleafs* (freeway intersections) and *brainchilds* tell us? The Scots novelist George Mackay Brown wrote the following: "For two hours the ebb would be rampant, draining the sea out of the Sound, leaving tooths of rock exposed."[67] Relate this to *sweet tooths.* How would you pronounce it?

44. Are the words *rather* and *better* verbs in English? The following was said by a television speaker: *They would have rather I didn't.*[68] The expression *You better* is common. Actually *better* and *rather* in such cases represent fusions with *would* and *had,* which formerly expressed such things as preference, potentiality, and desire. Compare *Would that it were true!* See if you can trace what happened.

45. Consider whether the speeding up that commonly goes with fusion is a manifestation of a more commonplace phenomenon, familiarity. If you live on the other side of a lake, and say *I've got to row home,*

---

[67] *Greenvoe* (London: Hogarth Press, 1972), p. 53. Example is from J. D. McClure.
[68] Paul Coates, Los Angeles, 22 September 1959.

would you normally say it as fast as *I've got to go home?* If you are at college with some students from Thailand and say *We have several Thais,* would you say it as fast as *We have several ties?* How does the degree of expectedness of what we say affect the speed with which we say it?

46. Among at least some workers in cinema and sound-recording one hears expressions such as *The sound track didn't get sunk up right,* meaning that film and sound were not properly synchronized. Describe the two things that have happened to yield *sunk.*

47. The word *buckaroo* (from Spanish *vaquero*) has yielded a suffix-like element that has been used in making a number of coinages in the last four or five decades. Explain why it was easy for this to happen and find some of the new words using the element.

48. Explain how *will* (originally referring to 'willing' and 'willingness') and *going to,* through reinduction, have come to be used to indicate the future.

49. One hears more and more utterances of the type *If we can just get a little clearer sense of where do we want to go*[69] instead of *If we can just get a little clearer sense of where we want to go.* The distinction between the two is, traditionally, the one between direct and indirect questions. Apparently there is a widespread reinduction in progress. Study the following sentences for the ones you think might be possible (and make up others), and see if you can arrive at some kind of rule for the reinduction:

    a. He wanted to know did I have any money.
    b. Just tell him who do you want to see.
    c. I know who does he want to see.
    d. I don't know does he have any money.
    e. Do the directors explain how are you supposed to do it?
    f. Will you please explain how am I supposed to do it?

50. For gradual semantic change—one feature at a time—consider the use of the word *majority.* Formerly it was and for many speakers still is a quantifier for countables only. We would say *The majority of the pencils were dull* but not **The majority of the paper was torn.* Yet now one hears such sentences as *My shoes got the majority of their wear on that hike across the island.* Does this

---

[69] This example was on a San Francisco radio broadcast, 26 May 1974.

strike you as acceptable? Is it for some semantic reason preferable to *My shoes got more than half of their wear on that hike?* What about *She spilled the majority of the sugar?* Assume that this last sentence is unacceptable but the one with *the majority of their wear* is acceptable, and put a check in each of the boxes below where *majority* now fits. Does this conform to your use of *majority?*

	abstract	concrete
mass		
count		

51. A phonemic split occurs when what was formerly a secondary signal becomes a primary one, as happened with the velarization of [n] before [g]. Consider the following similar situation, involving syntax rather than sounds: someone says *It isn't very good, do you think?* and you find that you can answer either yes or no and produce the same effect. Why is it possible, and what conveys the information in the answer?

52. If a child said to you *The sky was pitch black,* you would understand. Suppose the same child says later *The sky was pitch red.* Did your earlier understanding of *pitch black* imply that you both had the same conception of *pitch?* Does this indicate that we can get along with slight differences in our internal dictionaries?

53. The words *apart* and *alert* are not among those that had the prefix *a-* (= 'on') in English; they are borrowings from Romance languages. Yet they now behave like *awake, aside, akin, astride,* etc. (for example, they are seldom if ever used as modifiers before a noun). What has happened?

54. If you heard *That is a deadly poison* and *That is a very deadly poison* which would you take more seriously? What about *The wreck was a disaster* and *The wreck was a serious disaster?* What do these instances illustrate?

55. The words *candle, chandler,* and *chandelier* are all ultimately from a single Latin source. Look them up and trace the times and routes of the borrowing. (*The Shorter Oxford Dictionary* is adequate.) Do the same for *study, étude,* and *studio.*

56. A Frenchwoman who is fluent in English habitually says *Serve yourself* where native speakers of English say *Help yourself.* Classify this form of borrowing.

57. If any of the following occur in your speech, what are they probably instances of?

    a. I'm beat—I can't go another foot.

    b. Well I'll be blowed!

    c. I like reading whodunits.

    d. Lord, it's cold outside—I'm plumb froze.

    e. What are you all het up about?

    f. He just sort of snuck up on us.

Give the standard forms of the verbs.

58. With the aid of a good dictionary, look up the etymology of the word *gospel* and explain what kind of variant it is.

59. When a new phenomenon appears on the scene and we want to talk about it, do we generally coin an entirely new term or adapt an older one to the purpose? Consider what happened to the word *streaking* in early 1974. Think of other examples.

60. In Old Egyptian the word for 'million' originally meant 'tadpole' and the word for 'thousand' meant 'lotus.' In the Sepik Hill languages of New Guinea 'feather' is 'bird hair' and 'bark' is 'tree skin.' What universal principle do these examples illustrate?

61. What has happened to yield the boldface expression in "We spent a week *back-packing* in the Sierras"?

62. Look up the etymologies of the words *rogue, scamp, jerk, mischievous, naughty,* and *rascal.* Do they have something in common in the way of change of meaning? Has something similar happened to the expression *far out* in the last few years?

63. Trace the semantic development of the verb *to total,* referring to an object (especially an automobile) that is wrecked.

64. Would you be surprised to read or hear the statement *Those students need more tuition* in the sense 'need more instruction'? If so, give your idea of the meaning of *tuition* and account for it as a reinduction on the basis of contexts like *The tuition* (instruction) *is too high* (in price), *They paid my tuition* (like *They paid my trip*), *How much is tuition at that school?* and so on.

    Can you identify the changing circumstances that led to the phrase *horse cavalry,* despite the fact that *cavalry* (from *caballus* 'horse') were always traditionally mounted on horseback?

65. In the late 1960s, when members of the counter-culture began the style of highly individual dress and grooming, more conventional persons referred to them as *freaks,* which up to then had always been a term of contempt. What happened to the term when the "freaks" themselves adopted it?

66. When the mass nouns *pease* and *richesse* were reinterpreted as the plural count nouns *pea-s* and *rich-es,* the number of the verb was adjusted accordingly:

> His richesse *is* notorious. ⟶ His riches *are* notorious.
>
> Pease *is* easy to plant. ⟶ Peas *are* easy to plant.

But was the grammar in every case wholly shifted over to plural? Consider the following:

> How much pease does she have? ⟶ How many peas does she have?
>
> How much richesse do they have? ⟶ How many riches do they have?

Do you accept *how many riches?* Discuss the "grammatical lag" that may be involved, and the conceptual basis for it.

References

Andersen, Henning. 1973. "Abductive and Deductive Change," *Language* 49:765–93.

Anttila, Raimo. 1972. *An Introduction to Historical and Comparative Linguistics* (New York: Macmillan).

Bailey, Charles-James N. 1974. *Old and New Views on Language History and Language Relationships.* Manuscript.

Bidwell, Charles E. 1965–66. "The Reflexive Construction in Serbo-Croatian," *Studies in Linguistics* 18:37–47.

Bowen, J. Donald. 1971. "Hispanic Languages and Influence in Oceania," in Thomas A. Sebeok (ed.), *Current Trends in Linguistics.* Linguistics in Oceania, vol. 8 (The Hague: Mouton).

—— and Jacob Ornstein (eds.). 1975. *Studies on Southwest Spanish* (Rowley, Mass.: Newbury House).

Brown, Roger. 1973. *A First Language: The Early Stages* (Cambridge, Mass.: Harvard University Press).

—— and Ursula Bellugi. 1964. "Three Processes in the Child's Acquisition of Syntax," *Harvard Educational Review* 34:133–51.

Cavigelli, Pieder. 1969. *Die Germanisierung von Bonaduz in Geschichtlicher und Sprachlicher Schau* (Frauenfeld, Germany: Huber).

Csapó, József. 1971. "English Sporting Terms in Hungarian," *Hungarian Studies in English* 5:5–50.

Di Pietro, Robert J. 1961. "Borrowing: Its Effect as a Mechanism of Linguistic Change in American Sicilian," *General Linguistics* 5:30–36.

Downes, Mildred J. 1957. "The Unreader," *Language Arts* 32:202–04.

Fónagy, Ivan. 1971. "Double Coding in Speech," *Semiotica* 3:189–222.

Foster, Charles W. 1971. "The Phonology of the Conjure Tales of Charles W. Chestnutt," Publication of the American Dialect Society, No. 55, April.

Greenbaum, Sidney. 1969. *Studies in English Adverbial Usage* (London: Longmans).

Haugen, Einar. 1972. *The Ecology of Language* (Stanford, Calif.: Stanford University Press).

Householder, Fred W., Jr. 1971. *Linguistic Speculations* (Cambridge, England: Cambridge University Press).

———. 1972. "The Principal Step in Linguistic Change," *Language Sciences* 20:1–5.

Hutson, Arthur E. 1947. "Gaelic Loan-Words in American," *American Speech* 22:18–23.

Jespersen, Otto. 1909, 1914. *A Modern English Grammar on Historical Principles,* Parts I and II (New York: Barnes and Noble).

Long, Ralph B. 1959. *A Grammar of American English* (Austin, Texas: University Co-op).

Morse, J. Mitchell. 1974. "Race, Class, and Metaphor," *College English* 35:545–65.

Moulton, William G. 1971. Review of Pieder Cavigelli, *Die Germanisierung von Bonaduz in Geschichtlicher und Sprachlicher Schau* (Frauenfeld, Germany: Huber, 1969). In *Language* 47:938–43.

Mustanoja, Tauno F. 1960. *A Middle English Syntax.* Part I, *Parts of Speech* (Helsinki: Société Néophilologique).

Nalobow, Kenneth L. 1971. "The Gender of 'Professor Nowak' in Polish," *Polish Review* 16:71–78.

Peruzzi, Emilio. 1958. *Saggi di linguistica europea* (Salamanca, Spain: Consejo Superior de Investigaciones Científicas).

Reyes, Rogelio. 1975. "Language Mixing in Chicano Bilingual Speech," in J. Donald Bowen and Jacob Ornstein (eds.), *Studies on Southwest Spanish* (Rowley, Mass.: Newbury House).

Silverstein, Michael (ed.). 1971. *Whitney on Language* (Cambridge, Mass.: M.I.T. Press).

Sperber, Hans, and James N. Tidwell. 1950. "Words and Phrases in American Politics," *American Speech* 25:91–100.

Tamony, Peter. 1973. "Wiretapping and Bugging, 1863—Watergate 1972," in his *Americanisms: Content and Continuum,* No. 33, May.

Topping, Donald M. 1962. "Loanblends: A Tool for Linguists," *Language Learning* 12:281–87.

Vachek, Josef. 1965. "On the Internal and External Determination of Sound Laws," *Biuletyn Polskiego Towarzystwa Językoznawczego* 23:49–57.

———. 1973. *Written Language: General Problems and Problems of English* (The Hague: Mouton).

Valesio, Paolo. 1974. *Alliteration and the Grammar of Rhetoric.* Manuscript.

Žirmunskij, V. M. 1966. "The Word and Its Boundaries," *Linguistics* 27:65–91.

VARIATION IN TIME: THE OUTCOME OF VARIATION[1] 13

HOW THE VARIANTS ARE REACTED TO

Summing up all the hazards and speculations that were touched on in Chapter 12, we can appreciate the retort of a certain public figure on being advised to "watch out" when he expressed himself in language. "When I speak," he said, "let the language watch out."

The profusion of variants would have no effect if other persons besides their originators did not take them up. What fate lies between the source and the mainstream?

Resistance

Most resistance is passive. The variant serves an immediate purpose, but there is no continuity between the first occasion and the next oc-

---

[1] For brief histories of the English language the reader is referred to the following, in recent editions of three popular dictionaries: W. Nelson Francis, "The English Language and Its History," in *Webster's New Collegiate Dictionary* (Springfield, Mass.: G. and C. Merriam, 1973), pp. 20a–29a; Kemp Malone, "Historical Sketch of the English Language," in *Random House Dictionary of the English Language* (New York: Random House, 1971), pp. xv–xxi; Morton W. Bloomfield, "A Brief History of the English Language," pp. xiv–xviii, and Calvert Watkins, "The Indo-European Origin of English," pp. xix–xx, both in *The American Heritage Dictionary of the English Language* (New York: American Heritage, and Boston: Houghton Mifflin, 1969). A good brief treatment is also to be found in Chapter 8 of Margaret Schlauch's *The Gift of Language* (New York: Dover, 1955).

casion when it might be useful, and it is lost. Or it is recognized as a lapse, mentally (or actually) corrected, and ignored thereafter.

Some resistance is deliberate. Conservative speakers in every culture feel called upon to defend the bastions of purity and propriety—just as well perhaps, because too much change within a lifetime could interfere with communication. As long as old and young have to live together the checks are as important as the changes.

Resistance can also be active but unthinking. Something about a variant disqualifies it for adoption. Speakers may feel that a form that is all right otherwise (it fits, say, the phonological drift of the language) is unacceptable because it leaves too little meat in a word. In Castilian the Latin word *foedu* 'ugly' gave *feo* by one of the series of changes that nearly all words underwent, and would have given **eo* by a succeeding step; but "speakers shied away from the total stripping of an already meager sound structure."[2] Resistance to overly stripped-down forms may even lead to compensation in the other direction: *expanding* a form. We see this in the **Abel, Baker, Charlie** substitutes for **A, B, C.** Or speakers may have a dim awareness of some meaningful morphological element and avoid disfiguring it, in spite of the tendency of other words of similar shape to lose certain of their component sounds. In Portuguese, if Latin *regula* 'straightedge' had followed the line of least phonological resistance it would have ended up as **relha* (as *tegula* gave *telha* 'tile'), but instead it clung to a portion of its suffix and gave *régua*.[3] Instead of a definable morpheme, what is preserved may be some iconic value of the word. The sound symbolism that we saw earlier in connection with the high front vowels—*chip* versus *chop* and *freep* versus *frope* (page 24)—probably accounts for the form *peak* alongside of *pike* in reference to something pointed: a point is manifestly small (the name for the thirteenth-century pointed shoe was spelled both *piked* and *peked*). And there are a number of other such suspicious pairs, including *peep* for the *peeping* (also *piping*) of a bird, *seep* as a variant of *sipe*, and *teeny* alongside of *tiny*. One or more of them were probably ways of evading the Great Vowel Shift that changed the 'small'-sounding [i] to an unexpressive [ay] (see pages 452–53). The words *up, room,* and *stoop* would have had the same vowel sound as *out* if they had developed as other words did in English, but for some reason speakers rejected that shift whenever it would have given an /aw/ before a labial or velar consonant: English has no common words such as **goup* (compare *gout*), **towm* (compare *town*), **prouk* (compare *proud*).[4]

---

[2] Levy 1973, p. 206.

[3] Malkiel 1972, pp. 325–26.

[4] See Wang 1973, p. 105. But English does have one or two proper names: **Shoup,** pronounced [šawp] as well as [šup], and **Taub,** pronounced [tawb] as well as [tɔb].

Changing attitudes may diminish the value of a form. In this case it is the older variant that suffers. The verb *to discriminate* basically refers to making careful distinctions, but it came to be used more and more in connection with distinctions of the wrong kind, and now it would be a little chancy to call someone of refined tastes a *discriminating person.* Much the same has happened to the verb *segregate.* A degraded term may pass out of use entirely (see page 255) or only be restricted more narrowly in its use.

A more general and inclusive reason for resistance is conflict of homonyms. This is merely an acute form of the loss of contrast, a violation of the first law of language, which is that distinct functions are carried by distinct forms. The units at every level have to be chiseled as sharply as possible. If forces tend to deflect two or more of them toward each other so that they end by looking or sounding too much alike, speakers will try to avoid the debilitated contrast. If the distinction makes little or no difference, they will give it up: this is happening with the phonemic contrast between /a/ and /ɔ/ (page 44); it happened earlier in English with the two forms of the plural object pronoun, *hem* (surviving as *'em*) and *them* (of Scandinavian origin): they did not merge formally, but we now regard *'em* as a shortened form of *them.* If the contrast is important it will be strengthened. This is accomplished in various ways. A speaker may simply use a trick such as extra emphasis. A punster was heard to say, "He'll [*he* = 'the other fellow'] get the business, and *you*'ll get the *business*"—one will be helped and the other ruined.

With words, there is a kind of tradeoff between form and meaning. The closer two forms are related in sense, the less physical resemblance there needs to be for a conflict to be ignited between them. The words *to, too,* and *two* are phonologically identical, yet there is little conflict because they have completely different functions. (There is *some,* however: we can say *her very happy children* but not *°her too happy children*—it sounds too much like *her two happy children*). On the other hand, a resemblance can be much less than total and still bring anguish to the sensitive stylist. An example cited earlier was *The painter succeeded in painting the pain on her face all too plainly* (page 214). We obviously can't solve this kind of problem by abolishing one or more of the words from the language, but we can banish them from the immediate context by using a synonym or a paraphrase.

It sometimes happens that a conflict is so serious that it does result in the total loss of a form. The most famous example is the French word for *cock.* In southern France, the normal development of the expected Latin word, *gallus,* would have been *gat.* But in the same area the word *cattus* had an equal right to give *gat,* and it actually did produce that form. Had *gallus* been retained, the result would have been two meanings, 'cat' and 'cock,' both carried by the same form and both apt to occur in similar contexts where they would have caused confusion. One of them had to go, so speakers substituted other words for *gallus:* one meaning 'chicken,' one meaning 'pheasant,' and a third meaning, literally, 'priest.' In English the phrase *to wax and to wane* is common and causes no trouble, since *wax* coupled with *wane* is clear. But while we readily say *It waned* or *It is on the wane,* we avoid *It waxed* and cannot say **It is on the wax* at all. Conflict of homonyms forces us to say *It is on the increase.*

Fundamentally, there is no difference between collisions like these and one between antagonistic senses of a single word. A century ago a *saloon* was 'a large hall,' especially one for receptions or exhibits. But the proprietors of grog shops in the United States began to call their establishments saloons to raise them in the public esteem. The effect on the word, of course, was the opposite—it was lowered. As a result, one sense of the word has been relegated to history (including television westerns) and the other has been replaced by the French cognate *salon.*

There are other circumstances than being a stylist that create an aversion to forms that are too much alike even though not necessarily identical. The wind and weather on board ship, for example. The Old English word for the left-hand side of a ship looking forward was *backboard,* but there was also another: *ladeborde,* possibly meaning 'lading or loading side.' In time the latter was reinterpreted to eliminate any reference to loading, and the two words became rivals. *Ladeborde* won, helped by being transformed into *larboard,* a perfect mate for *starboard.* But what developed as a neat semantic analogy soon turned into a nuisance, not unlike the problem of a driver asking his companion, who is watching the signs, whether to turn left and getting the reply *Right,* meaning 'That's correct.' There must have been quite a few nautical accidents before a newly reinterpreted word, *port,* entered the competition and eliminated *larboard.*

A negative force even stronger than homonymic conflict is *taboo.* This we met before in connection with degradation (page 255), with the threat of *you* (page 360), and with family rules and their special vocabularies (page 369). If society regards something as unmentionable, and yet is forced to mention it, the name becomes the scapegoat for the thing. It has its "real" name, and that of course we secretly know, but never say. A substitute, termed a euphemism (see pages 255–56), is adopted to indicate the forbidden object without naming it. Of course, if the name is never, never said, the next generation has no opportunity to learn it. Then, since the object itself (which can be as sacred as Jahweh or as profane as human excrement) is still taboo, the substitute word is learned as the name, and in turn becomes taboo. The result is a continual succession of words marching to oblivion (or converted to other uses). The threat of *you,* for example, can extend to a personal name. In aboriginal Australian cultures, when a person died his name was buried with him and could not be exhumed for a certain length of time; not only his name but other words closely similar to it were temporarily abolished. The solution adopted by some tribes was to borrow substitute words from the language of a neighboring tribe.[5] In New Guinea there is not only a similar name taboo but also an entire substitute language that must be used on entering the tabooed area where the pandanus trees grow.[6]

If dropping words from one's own language and replacing them with words from another seems extreme, we can consider what happened at one time in Javanese. "Before the second world war it was not an uncommon fact in the higher strata of Javanese society that Javanese in conversation with other Javanese abandoned their native language, switching to Malay or Dutch in order to get rid of the burden of linguistic etiquette."[7]

Acceptance

Like most resistance, most acceptance is passive. The principle on which we all unconsciously operate is that *everything means something* and *everything different means something different.* If our interlocutor uses an expression that sounds strange to us, our first impulse is not to accuse him mentally of talking nonsense but to assume that he has merely missed his aim. We may even fail to hear the error.

But if the variant is conspicuous enough so that we cannot avoid noticing it, the tendency then is to assign it a value. The cheapest such added value is "his way of talking rather than mine." Hiking the price a little gives "their way of talking" or "the way of talking on X occasion," leading to the many restrictions of code and register. At the same time we are likely not to be satisfied with such a low level of contrast; we either abolish it or make something of it. The passenger on an airplane finds it superfluous to talk about *port* and *starboard* instead of *left* and *right,* and the old navigational terminology falls into disuse. We may for a time be willing to accept two pronunciations of *vase* (/ves/ or /vez/ in everyday parlance and /vaz/ in polite society), but we are not content to let it go at that indefinitely: an imaginative speaker is heard to say, "These small ones are my /vezəz/ but these big ones are my /vazəz/."[8] The word *rear* may be more elegant than the word *back,*

---

[5] Lamb 1974, p. 22.
[6] Franklin 1972.
[7] Uhlenbeck 1970, p. 441.
[8] Labov 1970, p. 77, footnote.

but *rear door* and *back door* have shifted from a mere register distinction to a technical one: the rear door of a building or institution or vehicle but the back door of a house. Luxury distinctions tend to become practical distinctions.

The same is true of dialect differences, as we saw earlier with *ignorant–igernut, poor–pore,* and *partner–pardner.* It is equally true of the differences that grow out of the variant grammars that result from reinduction. Suppose there comes a time when you are using *burnt* as the past of *burn* and I am using *burned.* Our conversation turns on the subject of something charred and you use your variant *burnt.* I suspect that you are in possession of a formula that I lack, whereby a thing gets burned and ends up burnt. Anything can tip the scales in the direction of a split like this—perhaps just the fact that *burned* takes longer to say and hence sounds like something going on, while *burnt* is short, like something finished.

Not even the variants within a paradigm are exempt. They too are luxuries—grammatical luxuries. Why should *went* and *gone* be so dissimilar to each other? So let's assign a distinction to them that is over and above the one of mere tense or aspect. *She probably went* refers to a goal—that is, 'went there'; *She must have gone* generally refers to a departure—that is, 'from here.' There is no such change in the verb *to leave: She probably left = She must have gone (left).* The past and past participle forms of many verbs have tended to bifurcate in much the same way: *struck–stricken, knitted–knit, worked–wrought, speeded–sped.*

The same happens with other paired expressions that supposedly have the same grammatical status. There is only one singular form *antenna,* and consequently it has to carry all the meanings of that word; but there are two plurals, *antennas* and *antennae,* and there the meanings have tended to split. The word *staff* and its plural variants is a mosaic of bifurcations:

staff–staves ⎱	'cudgel'
staff–staffs ⎰	
staff–staffs	'official personnel'
stave–staves	'barrel slats'
staff–staves ⎱	'lines for writing music'
stave–staves ⎰	

Actor and *actress* presumably have just the difference of sex, but when Carol Burnett says, *I am a better actor than I am an actress,* we know that something has been added. Any grammarian will tell you that *Thursday* when used as an adverb is the same as *on Thursday,* yet *We work Thursday* will be taken by many people to mean 'this coming Thursday' and *We work on Thursday* to mean any Thursday.

At any moment there are probably dozens of latent distinctions in the back of our minds, ready to crystallize by reinduction into unmistakable bifurcations once enough speakers develop similar leanings. Suppose you are in the habit of saying *C'mere* as a familiar way of asking someone to approach. This would be a normal phonetic reduction of *Come here* spoken on home grounds, where everyone already half-knows what is going to be said and where there is no need for ceremony. Equally normal under the same circumstances would be a sentence like *Tell him to c'mere.* But one day your spouse mentions a relative in Maine or California who plans a trip but is undecided where to go, and you say *Tell him to c'mere.* Something sounds wrong, and you correct it to *Tell him to come here.* On reflection you realize that *c'mere* is not appropriate for a two-thousand-mile trip. *Come here* in the altered form *c'mere* has been reinterpreted in your mind as the kind of coming that requires no more than a trip across the hall.

CUMULATIVE CHANGE

There is no question that language changes. But does it *evolve?* Evolution implies more than innumerable heterogeneous collisions, most of them canceling one another out. It implies a drift, a direction, almost a purpose. If we look only at meaning, the metaphorical leaps seem to take us in all directions. The ancestral form that gave the Greek word for 'fire,' *pyr* (which we have in *pyromaniac* and *funeral pyre*), also gave a Latin word *burrus,* 'fiery red.' This led to Romance forms meaning 'dark red' (Provençal *burel* was 'brownish red') and, in turn, Old French *buire,* with a variant *bure,* meaning 'dark brown.' The color was extended to a material of that color, baize, which was the sense that the word came to have in the Modern French form, *bureau.* This baize was used for covering writing desks, which in turn appropriated the name, extending it to articles of furniture. The writing desks were used in government offices, and our modern bureaucracies are a fitting climax to this bit of semasiological vagrancy. (*Semasiology* is the semantic history of word forms.)

But while such deflections of meaning would have been as hard to predict as the direction of a ricocheting bullet, the bullet itself—the bit of phonological stuff containing an initial bilabial stop and an /r/— remains more or less intact, flattened a bit but identifiable. Forms, unlike meanings, are stable enough to be projected backward into prehistory. Figure 13–1 shows the probable ancestry of the English words *hammer*

FIGURE 13–1
Probable Evolution of the Words Related to Hammer and Heaven

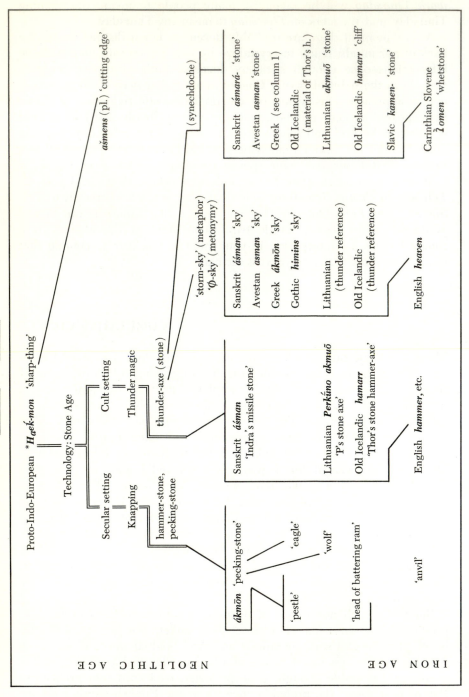

SOURCE: Adapted from Maher 1973, p. 451.

and **heaven,** traced back to a Stone Age form meaning 'something sharp,' and transformed semantically by a series of bold images that include interpreting the sharp thing as an ax, the ax as the source of the crash of thunder, the thunder as the sky, the sky as the abode of gods, and so on. The semantic shifts have to be treated with respect, for otherwise there would be no assurance that the similarity in form was not due to accident, but the form gives the historical linguist something to build on.

Comparative reconstruction

There are two ways of writing history: one by consulting documents, the other by collecting circumstantial evidence and hypothesizing a model. Historical linguistics uses both methods in varying degrees. If it wants to describe the development of Modern French, there is rich documentation all the way back to Latin. To do the same with any of the languages shown on Map 11–1 calls for using the knowledge of how languages develop in general plus comparison with sister languages, for there are practically no documents. This explains why the pedigrees of only a few of the great language families are known with any certainty. The greatest achievement of the comparative method has been the reconstruction of the ancestral language from which English and its Germanic relatives have descended, along with the Latin, Celtic, Indic, Slavic, and other sub-families of that vast fraternity—see Figure 13–2. A similar family tree for the Mayan languages is shown in Figure 13–3.

The written evidence left by the ancient world includes not only scribal accounts and inscriptions but a few actual comparisons between languages made on the scene for practical purposes. In the summer of 1973, the team of archeologists headed by Henri Metzger of Lyon University in France unearthed a stone slab in the south of Turkey on which there are parallel translations in Greek, Aramaic, and Lycian, engraved, according to Metzger, in the year 358 B.C. Its value, like that of other such finds (see pages 489–91), is that it provides the key to an only partially deciphered language, that of Lycia in Asia Minor; since Greek and Aramaic are well known, paleographers have a chance to cheat a bit on their decipherment.[9]

The Romance languages are a natural testing ground for theories of reconstruction because of the abundant literature of Classical Latin and the rich variety of sister tongues in Europe. An ancient form can be hypothesized to account for the variants found today in Italian, Portuguese, Catalan, French, Spanish, Rumanian, and other Romance dialects.

---

[9] Decoding the Language of Ancient Lycia," *Science News* (1 June 1974), p. 351.

FIGURE 13–2
Indo-European and Some of the Principal Languages
Descended from It

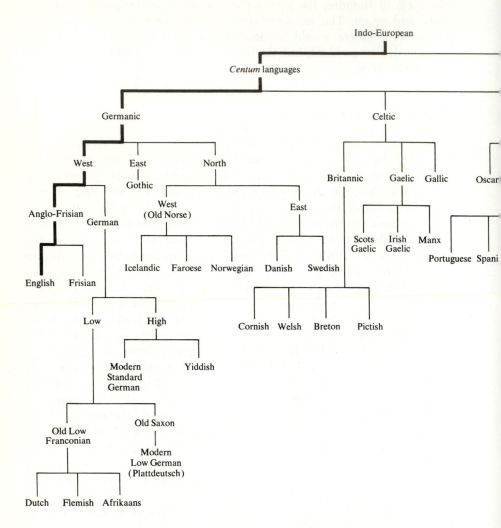

SOURCE: Slightly adapted from pp. 94–95 of *The Origins and Development of the English Language,* 2nd ed., by Thomas Pyles, copyright ©1964, 1971 by Harcourt Brace Jovanovich, Inc., and reproduced with their permission.

° *Centum* and *satem* are the words for 'one hundred' in Latin and Avestan respectively. They are used as tags for an early isophone of Indo-European that involved certain of the velar sounds. On one side of the boundary the [k] of such words as *centum* (*c* = [k]) remained [k]. On the other side the [k] became an alveolar (as in *satem*) or a palatal. In many of the *centum* languages the same thing happened but much later. Compare English *church* with the more archaic Scottish *kirk.*

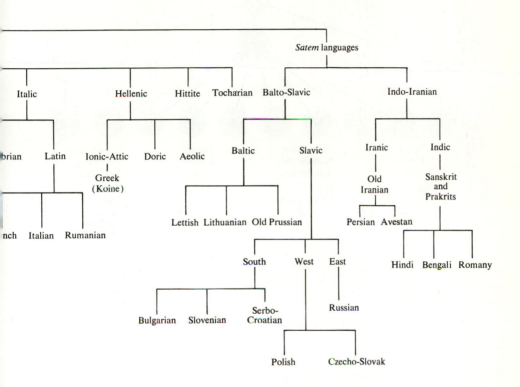

It can be checked against the known lexicon of Latin, and if an identical form is encountered, the hypothesis is confirmed. (The identity need not be perfect, because the Romance languages are descended from *spoken* Latin, and there are no records of that; but the differences are along familiar lines.) An example is the word for the human *chest:* Sardinian *pettus,* Rumanian *piépt,* Italian *pétto,* Rhaeto-Romance (Northeast Italy and Switzerland) *péč,* Old North French *píc,* Old Provençal *piéits,* Catalan *pít,* Old Spanish *pečos.* Positing a Proto-Romance *péktus* will account for all these in terms of the regular sound changes in each language, and *péktus* also coincides with the Classical Latin *pektus.*[10]

When the parent language was not written, the same hypothetical procedures are used to reconstruct it, though the reconstructed forms

---

[10] Adapted from Hall 1964, p. 306.

FIGURE 13–3
Mayan Family Tree

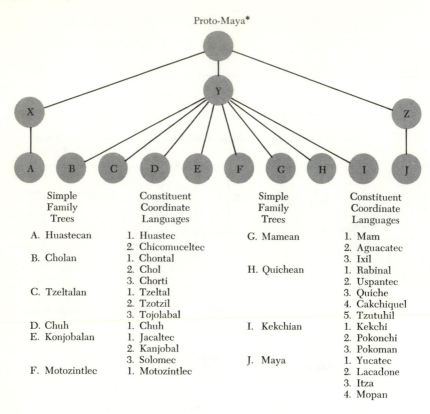

Proto-Maya*

Simple Family Trees	Constituent Coordinate Languages	Simple Family Trees	Constituent Coordinate Languages
A. Huastecan	1. Huastec	G. Mamean	1. Mam
	2. Chicomuceltec		2. Aguacatec
B. Cholan	1. Chontal		3. Ixil
	2. Chol	H. Quichean	1. Rabinal
	3. Chorti		2. Uspantec
C. Tzeltalan	1. Tzeltal		3. Quiche
	2. Tzotzil		4. Cakchiquel
	3. Tojolabal		5. Tzutuhil
D. Chuh	1. Chuh	I. Kekchian	1. Kekchi
E. Konjobalan	1. Jacaltec		2. Pokonchi
	2. Kanjobal		3. Pokoman
	3. Solomec	J. Maya	1. Yucatec
F. Motozintlec	1. Motozintlec		2. Lacadone
			3. Itza
			4. Mopan

SOURCE: Adapted from Diebold 1960, p. 8.
* X, Y, and Z represent intermediate proto-stages.

cannot actually be attested. The direct ancestor of the Germanic languages left no records, though it existed in historical times; the ancestor of that ancestor, proto-Indo-European, left none because writing had not been invented at the time it is supposed to have flourished, around the end of the last Ice Age.[11] But there is no question that there was a common language. Similarities like the following, in the words for 'brother' and 'eat,' are unmistakable:

[11] Lehmann gives evidence for assuming that the Indo-European speech community did not break up later than around 3000 B.C. The Hittite language of about 1950 B.C. had already substantially modified the original Indo-European and the Greek of 1450 B.C. had modified it even more. See Lehmann 1972, p. 991.

GREEK	*phrátēr* 'clansman'	*édomai* 'I shall eat'
LATIN	*frāter* 'brother'	*edō* 'I eat'
SANSKRIT	*bhrā́tā* 'brother'	*ád-mi* 'I eat'
GERMANIC	*broþar* 'brother'	*etan* 'eat' *(Old English)*
OLD CHURCH SLAVONIC	*bratrŭ* 'brother'	*jadętŭ* 'they eat'[12]

The words for numerals are equally convincing. In Table 13–1 they are shown with the reconstructed proto-Indo-European form, and—at the end, for contrast—with Hungarian, a non-Indo-European language. (In comparative reconstruction, an asterisk before a word or a letter indicates that it is a reconstructed, or hypothesized, element.) Perfect correspondence would be too much to ask; sporadic changes are bound to occur, even in word sets as important for communication as those of 'brother,' 'eat,' and the numerals. That is where looking for evidence from many sources proves its value. The Greek word for 'one' does not fit the pattern; but there was another form of 'one,' used on dice, which does fit: *oinós.* Sometimes the reason for the deviation is obvious within the word set itself: the Latin word for 'five' has an initial consonant that would be inexplicable if it were not clearly an assimilation to the initial of the second syllable (*quinque*), supported by the analogy with the preceding numeral in the series (*quattuor*).

Comparative reconstruction is exactly the same kind of task as that of discovering (or inventing) underlying forms for the morphemes of a single language, described in Chapter 4. Historical change creates the problems in both cases. It is fairly obvious that *calf* and *calve, half* and *halve, grief* and *grieve,* and many other such pairs are related not only in their identical parts, but also in the parts that distinguish them, /f/ versus /v/, which differ by just one feature (that of voice) and undoubtedly developed from a single sound. Similarly in the 'brother' set listed above, the /r/'s are practically constant, and the most conspicuous difference, that of the initials /b/, /f/, and aspirated /pʰ/ and /bʰ/, is with sounds all of which are labials. It is no coincidence that underlying forms often hark back to an earlier stage of the "same" language that is fully as different from the present stage as the latter is different from certain other now living languages of the same family. The underlying systematic phoneme /f/ that accounts for both phonemes /f/ and /v/ has the same status as the reconstructed */bh/ that accounts for the initial sounds in the words for 'brother.'

Of course the samenesses that point to a common ancestral form are not enough to establish what that form may have been. The differences have to be accounted for too. Here again the comparative method resembles that of positing underlying forms. The /f v/ alterna-

---

[12] Adapted from Lehmann 1973, p. 81.

TABLE 13–1
Words for Numerals in Proto-Indo-European, Five of Its Daughter Languages, and Hungarian

Proto-Indo-European	Sanskrit	Greek	Latin	Gothic	Old Irish	Hungarian
*oykos, *oynos	ékas	heĩs	ūnus	ains	oín	egy
*dwȭ(w)	dvaú	dúō	duo	twai	da	kettő
*treyes	tráyas	treĩs	trēs	* þreis	tri	három
*kʷetwǒres	catvā́ras	téttares	quattuor	fidwor	cethir	négy
*penkʷe	páñca	pénte	quinque	fimf	cóic	öt
*seks	ṣáṭ	héx	sex	saihs	sé	hat
*septm̥	saptá	heptá	septem	sibun	secht n-	hét
*oktȭ(w)	aṣṭaú	oktṓ	octō	ahtau	ocht n-	nyolc
*newm̥	náva	ennéa	novem	niun	noí n-	kilenc
*dekm̥	dáśa	déka	decem	taihun	deich n-	tíz

SOURCE: Adapted from Lockwood 1969, pp. 191–92.

tion did not happen by chance but was due originally to environmental conditioning (see Chapter 4, page 81). So in reconstructing a sound it is necessary to compare a number of word histories in which the hypothesized sound occurred in different environments. As an over-simplified example, take the supposed original */t/ as it appears in the five words and word sets of Table 13–2, in four languages that are widely enough separated to get a proper fix on the target. Except for 'come'–'go,' everything appears to be regular in Sanskrit, Greek, and Latin: all manifest the reconstructed */t/. And when other evidence than this is considered it turns out that the /s/ between vowels in Greek is conditioned by the following /i/: a /t/ can be posited as underlying the /s/ in **básis.** But Gothic matches this pattern only in 'is.' What we notice there is that the /t/ is protected by being the second member of an /st/ cluster: /s/ has the same point of articulation as /t/ and is also voiceless. So the retention of /t/ is conditioned by the /s/. In 'father,' the environment of the hypothesized sound has changed: it is non-initial and before an accented vowel (Sanskrit and Greek show where the accent was). In 'brother' it is after an accented vowel. In 'stand'–'stood,' though it occurs before what (in view of Sanskrit and Greek) must originally have been an accented vowel, as in 'father,' it has come to form part of a voiceless final cluster. In 'come'–'go' it again comes after an accented vowel, as in 'brother.' These conditioning

TABLE 13–2
Comparative Reconstruction of the Hypothesized Sound */t/ in Four Languages

	'is'			'father'			'brother'			'stand'–'stood'			'come'–'go'		
SANSKRIT	ás	t	i	pi	t	ā́	bhrā́	t	ā́	sthi	t	ás	ga	t	is
GREEK	es	t	í	pa	t	ér	phrā́	t	ēr	sta	t	ós	bá	s	is
LATIN	es	t		pa	t	er	frā	t	er	sta	t	us	-ven	t	iō
GOTHIC	is	t		fa	d	ar	brō	þ	ar	sta	þ	s	-qum	þ	s

SOURCE: Adapted from Anttila 1972, p. 246.

environments were responsible for the variations in Gothic and other Germanic languages. Other words that place the */t/ in the same environments have the same variants—the word for 'mother,' for example, puts it in non-initial position before an accented vowel, and the result in Gothic is again /d/: *mōdar.*[13]

Comparisons like these make it clear that what eventually became separate and distinct phonemes as languages evolved away from the parent language began with only allophonic variants. Sometimes the variant was established as a phoneme by the total loss of whatever it was that conditioned it as a variant. As we saw earlier in this chapter, when the /g/ of *wing,* which is preserved in the spelling, was still pronounced, the [ŋ] preceding it was only an allophone of /n/. But when the /g/ was dropped, the [ŋ] was all that was left to distinguish *wing* from *win,* and it took on phonemic status. At other times a phonemic split of this kind is helped along by words borrowed from other languages which already have the sounds as distinct phonemes. The influence of loanwords from French on the /f v/ split in English has already been mentioned.

A debate that rocked the linguistic world toward the end of the nineteenth century was whether "sound laws have no exceptions." Irregularities there were, aplenty, but when all the accidents and interruptions were cleared away—such refractory things as borrowings, analogies, and sound symbolisms—the core of authentically inherited words displayed a majestic progression of sounds in which every change

---

[13] Discussion based on Anttila 1972, pp. 245–47.

followed a predictable course. What this actually says is a truism: "There is no effect without a cause." If an exception is found, and later explained by modifying the rules, it ceases to be an exception; and presumably there is an explanation for everything if we can only find it. An example is the word *gulf,* from Latin *golfus.* The Latin is known to stem from the Greek word *kólpos* 'bosom, bay.' But the /f/ from a /p/ is exceptional. The probable explanation for it is found in certain Egyptian Greek spellings that had ø for *p.* The Greek speakers of the Mediterranean area habitually confused stops and fricatives; they not only used [ø] (a voiceless bilabial fricative) for [p] but also [θ] for [t], [x] for [k], and so on. Seafaring Greeks, the speakers most apt to implant a term such as 'gulf,' undoubtedly pronounced *kólpos* with a fricative—hence the Egyptian Greek spelling with ø; and the Romans, imitating this and following their custom of substituting the labiodental [f], their closest matching sound, for the Greek bilabial [ø], made it *golfus.*[14]

Though the "no exceptions" doctrine was an exaggeration, the regularities that did come to light needed no such justification to be truly impressive. What they proved was simply that sound systems have a reality of their own, apart from that of the words and sentences in which they occur. The English example that is most often cited is that of the Great Vowel Shift. From the time of Chaucer to the present, the long vowels have been changing from a set of values much like that of Latin to the values that they have now. Figure 13–4 shows the change in three steps. Between Middle English and Early Modern English (around the time of Shakespeare) there were extensive changes in pronunciation, though unit for unit the system remained the same for a great many speakers. For others, as the line connecting ɛ̄ and ī shows, two phonemes were tending to merge, and that merger is now complete in the standard language, though there is still much dialectal variation.

How inexorable the flow of change can be is seen in what happens to the streams that join it in mid-course. A loanword that enters after the epoch during which a particular shift takes place will not participate in the change, but will participate in all subsequent ones. The Latin word *titulum* was taken into Spanish three times: first as part of the native stock, then some time before the tenth century, and finally in modern times after all the intervening sound shifts had taken place. The last borrowing yielded *título,* which is Latin except for the ending. The original native form underwent one change, which was that of lowering the short vowel ĭ to *e,* to yield *tetlu* (the first *u* had already been dropped in spoken Latin), but the word then was forgotten; had it undergone the next change it would have yielded **tejo,* just as *mĭtulu* gave *-meja.* The borrowing in mid-course gave *tídulo* (later,

---

FIGURE 13–4
The Great English Vowel Shift

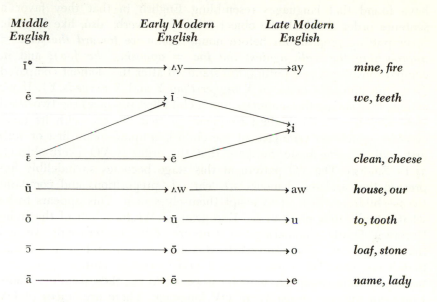

Middle English	Early Modern English	Late Modern English	
ī*	ʌy	ay	*mine, fire*
ē	ī		*we, teeth*
		i	
ɛ̄	ē		*clean, cheese*
ū	ʌw	aw	*house, our*
ō	ū	u	*to, tooth*
ɔ̄	ō	o	*loaf, stone*
ā	ē	e	*name, lady*

SOURCE: Adapted from *A Linguistic Introduction to the History of English*, by Morton W. Bloomfield and Leonard Newmark. Copyright © 1963 by Morton W. Bloomfield and Leonard Newmark. Reprinted by permission of Alfred A. Knopf, Inc.

* A line over a symbol is a sign of lengthening.

presumably, *tidlo* and *tildo,* and definitely the modern *tilde*); it was too late for the change from ĭ to *e,* but not too late for the voicing of intervocalic *t* to *d,* which occurred over a longer period of time.[15]

Sounds and words have been the passkey to history in the work of practically all comparatists up to the present. Syntax has hardly been used at all, for lack of knowing how to use it. Three converging developments are pushing it on the scene. First, there has been intensive work in the typology of languages, especially by Joseph Greenberg and his associates.[16] Obviously if we are to show historical relationships in syntax we have to know how to describe relationships in general, and that knowledge is becoming available. Second, psycholinguistics is giving us a better understanding of how children acquire language. This enables us to make predictions about change from one generation of learners to the next. Third, descriptive syntax has been delving into relationships among sentences that were overlooked before.

---

[15] Paraphrased from Menéndez Pidal 1958, p. 12.

[16] For example, Greenberg 1972 and other papers in this series.

An example of how syntax can be applied to history is that of the fundamental arrangement of elements in a sentence. Typological studies have found that languages resembling English in that they favor a sentence order in which the object follows the verb, also, like English, favor putting prepositions before nouns (compare *toward the wall* = *approaching the wall, against the foe* = *opposing the foe*); and in comparisons they favor putting the standard after the element compared (note the similarity between X *bigger than* Y and X *exceeds* Y). If we assume that among the sentences that a child first produces the two-word combination with the highest frequency is that of verb with its noun object,[17] whichever arrangement the child hits upon—noun first or verb first—will become basic. Suppose that the order is VO (verb-object), as in English. The VO pattern at this stage becomes so indelibly impressed that as later elements are learned—prepositions and comparatives—children will tend to adapt themselves to it. This appears to be what actually took place in the European, or Western, half of the Indo-European family. Comparing the structure of the Eastern half, we find that the opposite order prevailed—OV. Evidence from Hittite suggests that it too was OV, which makes it appear that if Hittite is an early branch of Indo-European, as it is supposed to be, then primitive Indo-European too was probably an OV language. There are traces of OV arrangements in the Western languages (such as *He worked the whole day through* for *He worked through the whole day*) that confirm this.[18]

Internal reconstruction

Conditions are ideal for describing the history of a language when written records go all the way back to the source. They are still good, though not ideal, when written records are lacking but a number of sister languages exist that provide a broad base for comparative reconstruction. Given neither of these advantages it might seem impossible to reach back, and yet it can be done, to some extent. This is because "most changes remain evident in the synchronic workings of a language for quite some time; a linguistic state is to a large degree a partial summary of the history of the language."[19] Most irregularities in a language are the ruins of past regularities, and by studying the rubble a great deal can be learned without going outside.

---

[17] Recall Pierre's pioneering sentence with verb and noun tossed together in either order (pp. 286–88).

[18] Based on Lehmann 1972.

[19] Anttila 1972, p. 84. See above, pages 331–32, for the resemblance between transformational and historical derivation.

This is *internal reconstruction,* and what clears the way is the partial victory, in each generation, of memorization over analysis. When a speaker uses analyzed units his utterances conform to active rules of his language, the ones that he has learned in the process of figuring out how things are put together and how they work. But when he merely repeats what he has heard, using a total expression holistically for a total situation and not synthesizing it from its parts, he is as apt as not to produce a fossil—something that conforms to rules once active but now dead. This is easiest to see in morphology. If we operated according to the living rules of English we would say **buyed, stealed,** and **eated.** But these three verbs are so high in frequency that they give us no real opportunity to reinduce them by our active rules; we memorize them as they are, and emit the product of rules that existed long ago.

It is the same in syntax. If there were no written records of English we might never be able to prove that the verb *divulge* was once a synonym of *publish.* But we might suspect it because of a syntactic restriction that it drags in its wake. Though *divulge* is now a synonym of *disclose* and *reveal,* and those two verbs can readily be used with *that* complements (as in **He revealed that he had taken part, He disclosed that he had taken part**), most speakers would feel at least a bit uncomfortable with *divulge:* *?He divulged that he had taken part.* Since *publish* has the same restriction (*He published that he had taken part*) and very few other verbs of this class do, we would at least suspect an earlier connection that is now lost.

Likewise with compounds and collocations—in fact, these are the principal stuff of the vast memory load that speakers carry, which they analyze only partially or not at all. It is essential to the growth of language that analysis be suspended part of the time, for otherwise the compacting of new forms, referred to earlier as downgrading, would be impossible. The word *cast* is very little used nowadays as a verb except in some rather tight collocations (*to cast aside* 'discard,' for example) or in highly restricted combinations with certain classes of objects *(to cast in a mold);* but it is found in numerous compounds: *castoff clothing, downcast eyes,* a *castaway* on an island. For the former central meaning of *cast* we now use *throw; cast* has largely become morphemic stuff for new and more complex memorized units. Much the same is true of the verb *to bear,* whose nerve center has been invaded by *to carry,* leaving *bear* dangling in the numerous memorized combinations that it once formed freely according to the rules of syntax. By studying the collocations and compounds that contain *cast* and *bear* it would be easy for us to deduce that they had once been freely usable verbs, even if there were no bygone writers whose works we could search for examples.

These are changes that are still in progress, and the earlier state of

affairs is easily recaptured. But it can still be done with changes that
are fully accomplished, by using indirect evidence. Take the progressive in English. Sentences such as *I was running* are straightforward
expressions of verbal aspect. There is nothing about the form *running*
to suggest that it is or ever was anything but an element of the compound verb. But then we observe a peculiar fact: the progressive can
be used in particular cases where other forms of the verb cannot. It
is normal to say *They're duck-hunting, He's trapshooting, I was trout-
fishing,* but not *°They will duck-hunt, °He trapshot, °I trout-fish every
summer.* Since *duck-hunting, trapshooting,* and *trout-fishing* can all be
used as nouns, and such nouns are quite freely formed *(Issue-raising is
a habit of politicians),* it appears as if the progressive form may have
been at one time some kind of noun. Other constructions point in the
same direction. For example, to refer back to a progressive a preposition
is used with a pronoun object: "He was working this morning and I
guess he's still *at it*"—pronouns normally stand in for nouns. To answer
What are you at these days? or *What are you up to?* we can say *I'm
preparing my finals,* as if to say *I am at preparing my finals.* If we conclude from this that the *-ing* form of the progressive was formerly a
noun serving as object of a preposition, we would be right, because the
older form of it was *I am on* (or *at*) *working,* just as we can still say
I am on the job or *I am at work.*

A similar use of indirect evidence we have already seen in the analysis of the phoneme /ŋ/. There is no /g/ any longer in *hang, string,* or
lung. But we know from the still active process of assimilation that when
an /n/ chances to fall before a velar, it velarizes: *in Greece* is apt to
be pronounced [ɪŋ gris]. Furthermore the distribution of /ŋ/ is odd: it
never occurs at the beginning of a word, and when it occurs at the end
of a syllable and there is no velar following, it is almost always at a
morpheme boundary. We don't have words like *°/ɔŋɨ/* or *°/bʌŋtrəm/*
but we do have lots like *Washington, slingshot, slangy, kingdom.* These
oddities are easily resolved if we assume that at one time another velar
consonant actually occurred after all instances of the velar nasal. The
omission of /ŋ/ from the table of systematic phonemes (page 79) was
just a bow in the direction of things-as-they-were. The velar nasal *is*
a phoneme in contemporary English; but we can dispense with it in the
table of systematic phonemes when we play the game of underlying
forms.

English spelling with its *g* of course confirms the reconstructed velar,
but that is evidence from outside. Likewise such dialectal utterances as
He went afishin', with its *a-* prefix, a relic of *on* or *at,* confirm the noun
status of the *-ing* of the progressive. But that, too, is not itself internal
reconstruction but comparative reconstruction: using a different dialect

is the same in principle as using a different language. On the other hand, a listener's grammar is always an infusion of many dialects (page 331), and that makes it impossible to say exactly where internal reconstruction leaves off and comparative reconstruction begins.

Language families

The Indo-European and Mayan genealogical trees shown in Figures 13–2 and 13–3 and the more general diagram on page 321 illustrate the "family" mold into which relationships among languages have been poured ever since people began thinking about them. It is an obvious and in many ways useful analogy, but a misleading one. The problem is much the same as with the semantic diagrams in Chapter 7 (see pages 206 and 209). Just as meanings do not really make clean separations that can be shown by lines splitting off from a single point, so languages seldom cut themselves off from one another but keep on intercommunicating, at least to some extent, and may renew old acquaintance with new intensity at any time. The lines not only divide but also recross, and are intersected in turn by lines from other sources. C.-J. N. Bailey offers the diagrams in Figure 13–5 to show the difference between oversimplified family trees (a) and (b)[20] and the more normal possibilities that result from contact, especially with an unrelated language. In (d), for example, an outside language collides with Baltic, causing it to split several ways and sending one offshoot back into Slavic. The last diagram shows a single outside language intersecting with two Indo-European lines and accounting for certain features that they have in common which are not shared by other Indo-European languages.

The dynamic mechanism of change can be seen more clearly as a wave model. Figure 13–6 portrays a single change in process. The vertical dimension is social space, the horizontal is geographical. The farther away one goes in either direction—toward a more distant social class or a more distant locale—the less effect the new change will have at a particular point in time. It is easy to imagine the kind of situation that would lead to "different languages." One would be that of having so many changes propagated at once that the center and the periphery become radically different. The other would be an expansion of the space—the outer speakers, say, migrate so far that it takes much longer for the new wave to reach them and a counterflow sets in: contact with an outside language creates a new center for change, and

---

[20] That of (b) assumes two dialects that continue in close contact for a time before separating.

FIGURE 13–5
Family Trees: The Ideal and the Real*

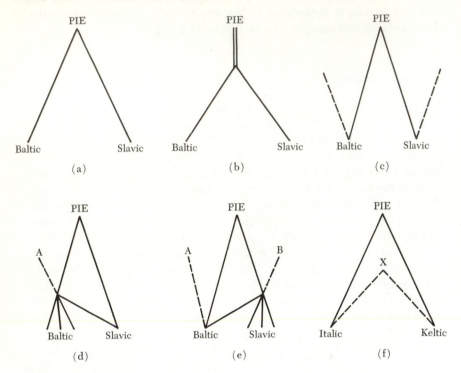

SOURCE: Adapted from Bailey 1974.

* Diagrams (a) and (b) show commonly popularized accounts of the evolution of languages. Diagrams (e) through (f) show what more likely happens, as outside languages (*dotted lines*) collide with evolving languages.

waves start moving in the opposite direction. The Scandinavian languages have undergone both kinds of alienation and fraternization in recent times:

> In terms of genetic relationship, Norwegian before the modern period would have been grouped with Icelandic and Faroese, but today the latter two (Insular Scandinavian) are mutually intelligible, but are no longer so with Norwegian, which has come to share intelligibility (or semi-intelligibility) with Danish and Swedish (Continental Scandinavian). It was during the modern period (1525 onward) that the Insular dialects became isolated from the Continental dialects which have come to enjoy continuous contact.[21]

---

[21] Voegelin 1973, p. 140.

FIGURE 13–6
Wave Model of Linguistic Change

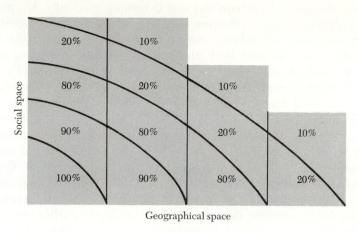

SOURCE: Adapted from Bailey 1973, p. 80.

Progress

All languages get better to the extent that they get worse. That is, when something happens to upset the equilibrium at some point in the vast system of contrasts that constitutes a language, something else happens to restore it. But that, if it can be called progress at all, is progress chasing its tail.

One of the great linguists of a generation ago, Otto Jespersen, felt that one sign of progress—particularly marked in languages like English and Chinese—is the discarding of "reminders." When we say *Mary is the sweetest, dearest, loveliest girl I know,* we express the one superlative idea three times in the suffix *-est,* as can be seen by factoring it out and saying instead *Mary is the most sweet, dear, lovely girl I know.* In the latter construction, supposedly typical of a later stage of language growth, we do not require an explicit superlative each time, but get the same results through the larger organization of the sentence. Jespersen was really reversing the older argument that Latin was a superior language because it was highly inflected.[22]

Jespersen did not have the benefit of recent thinking about redundancy, which holds that reminders are necessary. If a particular bit of information is expressed only once, it will not be intelligible unless all channels are functioning perfectly, free of noise and with undistracted

---

[22] See Jespersen 1894.

attention on the part of the hearer. Still, it may be that we need less redundancy than we needed before; there seldom are clean breaks in language change and perhaps this one is coming gradually. Unquestionably we depend as no civilization ever has before on communication in writing, and there redundancy can be cut to a minimum—if the reader misses the point, he goes back and re-reads. A tape recording can be replayed. And for centuries now it has been getting physically easier to communicate; speakers are less separated in space, they depend very little on hunting for a livelihood, and a shouted command in battle could probably not be heard above the din anyway. It is not so much that we have lost the power of communicating under adverse conditions as that we seldom need to and have developed easier ways of reaching one another that allow more information to be transmitted. Quantity has replaced quality, much as it did with the speedwriting of later medieval scribes before the invention of printing, whose scrawls are much harder to interpret than the careful lettering of earlier generations. Our sensitivity to contrasts is undoubtedly greater than that of our ancestors, and the tones need not be quite so sharp—more of them can be packed into a narrow space. Besides cutting down on the need for reminders this has probably subdued the fortis quality that earlier speech sounds may have had.

From the standpoint of a more complex civilization, there has been progress. Not all would agree that there can ever be progress in any absolute sense.

ADDITIONAL REMARKS
AND APPLICATIONS

1. Mixed metaphors (*The idea was no sooner born than it faded; The dark corners of their ignorance fell before her eloquence; As you go down the path of life, drink it to the full*) are condemned as bad style. What change have the expressions undergone that encourages speakers and writers to mix them?

2. Do you distinguish in pronunciation between *melee* and *Malay?* If so, what does this illustrate about the power of loanwords to introduce sound changes in a language?

3. In the United States the word *shivaree* has gradually crowded out its rival synonyms (*serenade, belling, bull band, horning, callathump, tin-panning, skimmerton*). Does the sound of *shivaree* in any way favor it? Compare words for other lively celebrations: *spree, corroboree, jubilee, husking bee, jamboree.*

4. See if you distinguish in pronunciation between verbs on the one hand and adjectives and nouns on the other in such words as the following, that end in *-ate: separate, certificate, correlate, intimate, animate, aggregate, predicate.* Think of some other examples. Are you conscious of having changed your pronunciation with any of these? If so, what caused you to change?

5. Look at the following doublets that are the result of dialect borrowing and explain the differences in meaning, if any: *girl, gal; curse, cuss; burst, bust; parcel, passel; vermin, varmint; saucy, sassy; ordinary, ornery; hoist, heist; rearing, rarin'; shaken up, shook up; slick, sleek; stamp, stomp.*

6. The verb *to bereave* has two past participles, *bereaved* and *bereft.* Do they mean the same? If not, what does this illustrate? Another example of a verb with two past participles comes from a conference report that contains the following phrase: *the way in which they are knit together* (referring to the condition of being in a tight relationship).[23] What would your sensation be if *knit* were replaced

---

[23] Northeast Conference on the Teaching of Foreign Languages, 1967.

by *knitted?* Compare this with *burned–burnt.* Are speakers tending to reinduce a new grammatical rule here, perhaps something on the order of "process versus result"?

7. The pronunciation [ɪnʲən] was once current for the word *Indian,* and survived at least until recently in the expression *honest Injun* ('I am telling the truth' or, as a question, 'Are you telling the truth?'). Explain how it came to be pronounced that way. Why do you suppose it no longer is?

8. Would *beau* be used nowadays for *boyfriend?* (And does a boy who has a friend who is a boy refer to his *boyfriend?*) Think of some other words that have become old-fashioned.

9. The following refers to unpaid workers: *Dozens of scholars worked free from 1888 to 1928 to prepare the [Oxford English] dictionary.*[24] This is a standard use of *free,* but does it strike you as normal? If not, why?

10. Three-fourths of a group of forty students marked one of the following as most unacceptable of the four sentences:

    a. That was a long fight.
    b. That was the longest fight I ever had.
    c. That was a long sore throat.
    d. That was the longest sore throat I ever had.

Would you agree in marking c as most unacceptable?

The question is perhaps not so much why c sounds bad as why d sounds fairly good, possibly by way of a blend with *That was the sore throat that I had the longest.* There is no **That was a sore throat that I had long* to bolster the other sentence; the closest parallel has to bring in the explicit word *time: That was a sore throat that I had a long time.*

What is there about the noun *fight* that makes b just as acceptable as a?

Give the same test to some of your friends, substituting *sprained knee* for *sore throat* to see if the results confirm those of this test. If they do not, this test (not yours, necessarily) is probably defective. Try to determine why.

---

[24] Hulon Willis, *Introductory Language Study* (Cambridge, Mass.: Schenkman Publishing, 1971), p. 110.

11. The normal development of *do you,* as in *Do you like it?* would be through [dyǝ] and eventually to [ǰǝ]. But this last step is avoided. Can you explain why? (Suggestion: if you heard [ǰǝ layk ǝt]—often written *Dja like it?*—what meaning would you assign to it?)

12. Look up the word *quean.* Note its pronunciation and its meaning. Why do you suppose it is no longer used? What do we call this phenomenon?[25]

13. The original sense of the word *familiar* was 'pertaining to a family.' The word *familial* was introduced around 1900 in this same sense. What happened to make the new coinage necessary?

14. If you were composing a title for an article on veterans who had lost the power of vision, you would probably choose "Blind Veterans" or possibly "Sightless Veterans." But if your article had to do with veterans who had lost the power to speak, what would you use? A solution adopted by one person was "Veterans Who Are Unable to Speak."[26] Why is such a roundabout wording necessary? Check your answer with the footnote.[27]

15. Agent nouns made from verbs regularly use the simple suffix *-er: brew, brewer; view, viewer; do, doer.* Can you think of a reason why *suer* from *sue* is now obsolete and *suitor* or *plaintiff* is used instead? Why is the word *succour* no longer used? A radio program used the expression *There's a fording place there.* Traditionally this would have been *There's a ford there.* Why the change?

16. Can you think of a reason why a word such as *support* might not undergo the change that seems to be threatening *police* (to yield *pleece*)? Does your answer suggest anything about why distinctive sounds are preserved?

17. The following occurred in a radio discussion of a new catechetical directory: "They identified persons from many disciplines—the sacred disciplines and what you might call the human disciplines."[28] The traditional antonym for *sacred* is not *human* but *profane.* Look

---

[25] If the book is available, see Williams 1944, pp. 83–89.

[26] Subtitle in *Nonverbal Components of Communication: Paralanguage, Kinesics, Proxemics.* Newsletter No. 6 (20 August 1973), p. 5.

[27] What would be the effect of using "Dumb Veterans"? Or "Speechless Veterans"? What about "Mute Veterans"?

[28] San Francisco radio station, 15 September 1974.

up the word *profane* for its various meanings. What was the probable reason for the speaker's avoiding it?

18. In what way do the social meanings affect our use or avoidance of the following terms?—*undertaker, mortician; wolf, Don Juan; cop, officer; servants, help.* Think of other examples, especially those involving occupations.

19. The following description is given of the Portuguese dialect of São Miguel in the Azores: "The vowels have moved up, with each vowel entering the space of its neighbor: [a] $\longrightarrow$ [ɔ] $\longrightarrow$ [o] $\longrightarrow$ [u]. Since [u] is the highest vowel it would seem to have nowhere to go to escape a merger with [o]. However, by moving forward as a rounded front vowel [ü], it continues to be distinct from [o]."[29] What change in English does this resemble? Does any part of it represent a phonemic change?

20. The word *light* comes directly from an Old English word related to German *licht*. In English we have *lucid,* from Latin, and *leucous,* from Greek. Would the resemblance among the originals of these words be further proof of kinship among these languages? See if you can find other examples.

21. Although *babe* in American English nowadays is a jocular nickname or a slang term for a girl, what earlier meaning would you reconstruct for it on the basis of the still-used collocations *babe in arms, babe in the manger,* and *babes in the woods?* Given the collocations *practical joke* and *practical nurse,* and knowing the meaning of the noun and verb *practice,* what earlier meaning would you reconstruct for the adjective *practical?* How do you account for the shift to the meaning it now has in *She is a practical person?*

22. The following passages are from the Dryden translation (Clough revision) of Plutarch's *Lives.* Point out the words and expressions that would not be used today, and give their modern equivalents:

> The ambassadors being departed, he withdrew his forces out of the Roman territory.
> The cities sent an embassy to Thebes, to desire succours and a general.
> Crassus durst not appear a candidate for the consulship before he had applied to Pompey.

---

[29] Lloyd 1973, p. 39.

23. At some time in the Middle English period, the phoneme /x/ (the final sound in Scottish *loch* or German *ach*) was lost in certain words, for example *right, brought, daughter, through, plough*. In others it was kept but changed: *laughter, enough, trough, rough*. What phoneme was substituted? Was the change abrupt or gradual, in articulatory terms? How do the two phonemes compare in the distinctive features that make them up?

24. The Zoquean languages (see Map 11–1, page 346) exhibit a typical instance of the "norm of the lateral area" (pages 355–56). Whereas the Zoque territory in general has voiceless intervocalic stops, the periphery—Mixe on the west, Northeast Zoque on the east, and Sierra Popoluca on the north—has a tendency toward the voicing of such stops. Would this provide some justification for reconstructing voiced allophones of intervocalic stops in the parent language, Proto-Zoque?[30] What does it tell us about the relevance of areal linguistics to comparative reconstruction?

References

Anttila, Raimo. 1972. *An Introduction to Historical and Comparative Linguistics* (New York: Macmillan).

Bailey, Charles-James N. 1973. *Variation and Linguistic Theory* (Arlington, Va.: Center for Applied Linguistics).

———. 1974. *Old and New Views on Language History and Language Relationships*. Manuscript.

Bloomfield, Morton W., and Leonard Newmark. 1963. *A Linguistic Introduction to the History of English* (New York: Alfred A. Knopf).

Diebold, A. Richard, Jr. 1960. "Determining the Centers of Dispersal of Language Groups," *International Journal of American Linguistics* 26:1–10.

Franklin, Karl J. 1972. "A Ritual Pandanus Language of New Guinea," *Oceania* 43:66–76.

Greenberg, Joseph H. 1972. "Numeral Classifiers and Substantival Number: Problems in the Genesis of a Linguistic Type," *Working Papers on Language Universals*, Stanford University, no. 9, pp. 1–116.

Hall, Robert A., Jr. 1964. *Introductory Linguistics* (Philadelphia: Chilton Books).

Jespersen, Otto. 1894. *Progress in Language, with Special Reference to English* (London: Swan Sonnenschein, and New York: Macmillan).

Kahane, Henry and Renée, and Angelina Pietrangeli. 1973. "Egyptian Papyri as a Tool in Romance Etymology, II *Gulf:* Hypercorrection or Dialect Borrowing?" *Romance Philology* 27:46–49.

---

[30] See Longacre 1967, p. 143.

Labov, William. 1970. "The Study of Language in Its Social Context," *Studium Generale* 23:30–87.

Lamb, David. 1974. "Linguists Find Twists in Aborigines' Tongue," *Los Angeles Times* (4 February), p. 22 (account of work of Summer Institute of Linguistics).

Lehmann, W. P. 1972. "Contemporary Linguistics and Indo-European Studies," *Publications of the Modern Language Association of America* 87:976–93.

———. 1973. *Historical Linguistics: An Introduction,* 2nd ed. (New York: Holt, Rinehart and Winston).

Levy, John F. 1973. "Tendential Transfer of Old Spanish *hedo* < *foedu* to the Family of *heder* < *foetēre,*" *Romance Philology* 27:204–10.

Lloyd, Paul M. 1973. "The Nature of Sound Change." Manuscript.

Lockwood, W. B. 1969. *Indo-European Philology* (London: Hutchinson University Library).

Longacre, Robert E. 1967. "Systemic Comparison and Reconstruction," in Norman A. McQuown (ed.), *Handbook of Middle American Indians.* Linguistics, vol. 5 (Austin: University of Texas Press).

Maher, J. Peter. 1973. "°H$_a$ekmon: '(stone) axe' and 'sky' in I-E/Battle-Axe Culture," *The Journal of Indo-European Studies* 1:441–62.

Malkiel, Yakov. 1972. "The Rise of the Nominal Augments in Romance," *Romance Philology* 26:306–34.

Menéndez Pidal, Ramón. 1958. *Manual de gramática histórica española* (Madrid: Espasa Calpe, S.A.).

Pyles, Thomas. 1971. *The Origins and Development of the English Language* (New York: Harcourt Brace Jovanovich).

Uhlenbeck, E. M. 1970. "The Use of Respect Forms in Javanese," in S. A. Wurm and D. C. Laycock (eds.), *Pacific Linguistic Studies in Honour of Arthur Capell* (Canberra, Australia: Linguistic Circle of Canberra).

Voegelin, C. F. and F. M. 1973. "Recent Classifications of Genetic Relationships," *Annual Review of Anthropology* 2:139–51.

Wang, William S.-Y. 1973. "Approaches to Phonology," in Thomas A. Sebeok (ed.), *Current Trends in Linguistics.* Linguistics in North America, vol. 10, part 2 (The Hague: Mouton).

Williams, Edna Rees. 1944. *The Conflict of Homonyms in English* (New Haven: Yale University Press).

WRITING AND READING 14

If the Aztecs before the time of Cortez had had schools with classes divided according to subject matter, a child taking instruction in language would have been taught the correct way to recite the texts of an oral tradition and might have been lectured on avoiding the Aztec slang of his day, but he would never have had to hand in a written composition and would never have been scolded for a misspelling. Writing, such as it was, would have been taught in his art class, and misspellings would have been impossible because there were no spellings, though there was something approaching it in the writing of proper names. Pictures, then as now, could tell a story, but they did so in their own way, not as marks that represented particular words or sounds. A picture of a man or of a man's head, or a stylized figure of a man, meant a man, a male being, an old boy, an adult person of the male sex, or a man by any other name one might choose. The symbol pictured the meaning directly, with no particular sounds as intermediary, unlike the written drawings in our modern culture, where the letter signs $m + a + n$ stand for a particular construct of sound that means one thing in the word *man* and something else in the word *mansion.*

Our own experience in school is so different that we are prone to think that writing *is* language and that speech is only a sort of replay of what is written, like a tape recording that is language in solid form but can be turned into sound if fed into a machine. We learned to speak so long ago that all the details have been forgotten, even if we could have been

467

self-conscious enough at that age to observe what we were doing. Our "language" class, therefore, did not teach us the sound or structure of English but concentrated on teaching us how to write; this is our most vivid recollection of language instruction, and it colors our notions of what constitutes language.

Yet the convergence of speech and writing—the use of writing to mediate language rather than to mediate ideas directly—was a process that took thousands of years. It is as if writing was fated to repeat—on a foreshortened time scale—the history of spoken language, starting with iconic signs similar to those of gesture (and, like gesture, *visual*), evolving through stages of greater and greater arbitrariness, and finally coupling itself to the fully arbitrary units that had already crystallized in speech.

The science and art of writing is so new that many of the world's cultures have still barely been touched by it. Advanced as the Aztecs were when Cortez invaded Mexico in 1519, they were centuries behind Europe in the development of writing and only a little more advanced than the nomadic tribes of Indians inhabiting what is now the United States and Canada. The Mayas were probably ahead of them: there is evidence that some of the Maya glyphs represented not exclusively words or ideas but sounds, which means that the Mayas had discovered the trick of "phonetism," of coupling their writing to the arbitrary units of speech and thereby tapping the resources of spoken language.[1] But the Mayas too were cut off from the written art of other lands, where the flow and counterflow of communication implanted the little innovations that led the cultures of the Old World to make great forward leaps in symbolization.

To understand the past of writing we must begin with the present, which we know best.

WRITING AND SPEECH

Convergence of writing and speech

Speech is prior to writing not only historically but also genetically and logically. Genetically we know that speech comes first because children who are blind have no difficulty in learning to speak but children who are deaf have great difficulty in learning to read[2]—shutting off the

---

[1] Voegelin 1961, p. 77, and Kellogg 1962, especially pp. 14, 15, 18.
[2] Mattingly 1971.

channels of sight has little effect on acquiring language, but shutting off those of sound is almost fatal to it. The take-off point for reading is located somewhere in the recursive grammar stage, the last of the four grammars described in Chapter 9 (pages 289–90). The child must not only be talking with a fair degree of fluency but must have an awareness of what he is doing, must be able to form an internal image of an utterance, especially of sounds and their relationships to word shapes. Until he has a sense of what a word is, a feel for such things as syllables and rime, a child is not ready to read. Readiness comes only when the child is able to recognize word segments and store them in short-term memory, in a kind of phonetic notation that matches what is stored when listening to speech. Interpretation and comprehension proceed from there, using the same mechanisms as language in general.[3]

As for learning to write, that comes much later, when the child has the power to coordinate other muscular activities as skillfully as his genetic equipment permitted him to control his speech organs while he was still an infant.

The logical primacy of speech can be seen in the form taken by all well-developed writing systems. Without exception they "cut in" at some point on the stream of spoken language. Some of them key their primary symbols to distinctive sounds; those systems are *alphabetic*. Others key them to syllables, and are accordingly *syllabic*; still others to words: these are *logographic* ('word-writing'). Psychologically the effect of cutting in at a lower level is to gain the advantage of the higher levels. Thus English writing is alphabetic, and we can, if we have to, assign values almost letter by letter and "sound out" words as we read or write. But—especially in reading—we see the letters in assemblies as well as one by one: we know what the syllable *Mc* in proper names looks like and react to it as a unit. At the level of words, whatever success the "whole word" method of learning to read may have had is due to our appreciation of visible word-shapes; 'languorous' is stored in our minds as ***languorous*** and does not have to be reconstituted from *l-a-n-g-u-o-r-o-u-s* every time we read it.

With these advantages it is no wonder that alphabets have become the most widespread of all forms of writing. They use symbols that with more or less refinement correspond to individual sounds, and the degree of refinement is measured by how close the correspondence comes to being one-to-one. A perfect correspondence, with each letter symbol standing for one and only one distinctive sound, would of course be a form of phonemic writing. Some modern writing systems come

---

[3] Mattingly and Kavanagh 1972.

very close to this ideal: Spanish, Czech, Finnish. Even the much-maligned English system allows us to interpret most spellings with confidence: we are safe in inferring that *sline,* if there were such a word, would be pronounced to rime with *fine,* not with *fin,* and that *wip* would rime with *rip,* not with *ripe.*

An alphabetic system has the capacity to become completely phonemic, and if it has failed to do so the reason is that writers have other needs and interests than that of making their writing a perfect image of the phonemic level of their speech. The needs are practical and the interests are both practical and esthetic. Among the needs are the functions that writing has fulfilled since its beginnings: communication across time (which until the invention of sound-recording devices was impossible for speech), communication across great distance (which likewise was impossible for speech until the appearance of the telephone), and communication to great numbers of people (which was closed to speech until the invention of radio). In modern times, the vastly greater size of the readership—for many publications, embracing readers of English from Tacoma to Calcutta—has made it necessary for writing to transcend local dialects and adhere to a standard that can be widely understood. A Southerner's **The poor roof bulged** would (in some areas) be transcribed /ðə poə ruf buljd/, and a Northerner's /ðə pʊr ruf bʌljd/; with both of them agreed on standard spellings, trouble is avoided. Almost all major languages—those that have succeeded in bringing within their fold great numbers of speakers over wide areas of the globe—tend to have greater uniformity in spelling than in pronunciation.

This uniformity reflects tradition, of course, and inertia. Adults have learned the system and see no need to change it. But it also reflects much of the real uniformity that underlies the comparatively superficial differences of pronunciation. It is no coincidence that the underlying forms described in Chapter 4 have traits that are preserved in spelling: the *g* of *resign,* the *n* of *damn,* the *t* of *intersection,* which emerge as phonemes in *resignation, damnation,* and *intersect.* If the history of words is in some way recapitulated in these derivations, then a spelling that was frozen at an early date and embodies the history will have some value in revealing the relationships between cognates. It unquestionably helps to have all the regular plurals in English spelled with *s* regardless of whether the pronunciation is [s] or [z]. The word *news* is spelled the same in **The news is good** and **I read the newspapers,** even though for many speakers the latter has /nus/ rather than /nuz/. We have to choose which level of language we want to represent most faithfully with our written symbols: distinctive sounds or morphemes. English spelling takes the first alternative, but with no great conviction: it is morphophonemic as well as phonemic.

Esthetic considerations, too, prevent a writing system from becoming fully phonemic and may even interfere at the morphophonemic level. There is hardly a town in the United States that does not boast at least one establishment with the sign *Ye Olde Tea* (or *Pottery* or *Antique* or *Curiosity*) *Shoppe.* Common English names are sometimes regarded as too common, and ambitious parents dress them up with exotic spellings: *Alyce* for *Alice, Bettye* for *Betty, Edythe* for *Edith*—a tendency that awaits the iconoclast who will dare to spell her name *Barrel* instead of *Beryl.* Some spellings are almost systematically prestigious—for example, the agentive suffix spelled *-or* rather than *-er: advisor,* not *adviser; expeditor,* not *expediter.* One esthetic attitude in particular has deflected writing away from speech and even created a counter-evolutionary trend: the deference that is felt in all societies, including our own, to the authority of the written word. For the Hindus, the Sanskrit writings embody "the language of the gods," and knowledge of Sanskrit and use of Sanskrit words has long been a prestige symbol in India.[4] In Ceylon a century ago, after a long period of foreign invasions and literary stagnation, there was such a desire to reassert the national identity that writers reached back to the form that the language had had four hundred years earlier. The result was a written language that was never spoken except when read aloud and that required special study to be understood.[5] In our society a respect for standard spellings is a requirement for social and economic advancement; the person who writes words with bad spellings in a letter of application will find it almost as hard to get a job as the one who has been caught writing bad checks. As a result, all spellings are locked in place and shielded from reform. Long after pronunciations have changed and speakers all over the English-speaking world have agreed on new ones, the old spellings live on, including some that did not exist historically but were introduced by pseudo-scholarship: the *h* of *rhyme,* the *c* of *indict,* the *g* of *feign.* Writing was for centuries the property of a priestly or scribal caste in a domain of occult powers, spells, and incantations. Modern writing has shaken off its ties with magic but has never fully lost its pretensions to erudition. We are no longer in fear of it, but we treat spellings as if they were the living bodies of words.

The convergence of writing and speech virtually stops at the level of morphemes. Ordinary writing does not show syntactic structure either by tree diagrams or by labeled bracketing—even though the latter is easy enough to set up typographically: [s[NP *The stuff that they served* NP] [VP *was awful* VP]s], which represents the same structure as the tree

---

[4] Sjoberg 1962, pp. 276–77.

[5] Sugathapala de Silva 1967.

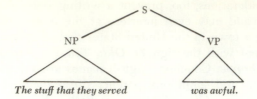

The deficiency here is that writing never really got around to providing a regular way of marking accent (writers can use italics, but good style allows them to use this device only very sparingly), and it has virtually disregarded rhythm and intonation. There is evidence that in certain medieval manuscripts spaces may have been left where pauses occur within compounds or between words, wider for longer pauses, narrower for shorter, as we might write today *wish ful* and *dish ful*, or *If you see him   when you get home   call me.*[6] In the example just diagrammed a wider space between *served* and *was* could represent the rhythmic interruption that—in speech—potentially marks the structural break. But the medieval tradition, if it existed, was lost. Punctuation and capitalization serve as a rough guide to some of the rhythmic and intonational contrasts in speech, but too much is left out and what is put in suffers from a confusion of two aims: the representations of the breaks that we *hear* and the divisions that logical-minded persons some-times insist that we *write*—the two usually agree, but not always. Con-sider the following sentence: *It is common knowledge that, if we are to learn to speak another language well, we must spend a great deal of time practicing it.* There is no comma after *knowledge,* where a pause would normally come, but there is one after *that,* where most speakers would not pause at all.[7]

In all this we can detect the hand of an ancient tradition: that writ-ing never fully symbolizes speech but serves as a prompter to what we want to say. The result is that writers have to make many choices that are not forced on them as speakers. An anecdote from the *Reader's Digest* shows the kind of compromise one must make because of the lack of markers for accent:

> We met frequently at the laundromat. "And where do you live?" I asked one evening while we were waiting out the cycles. "I *live* here," sighed the man. "But I have my meals and sleep in a bungalow a couple of blocks up the street with my wife and children."[8]

---

[6] Stevick 1967.

[7] Scott 1966, p. 540.

[8] (September 1960), p. 97.

Italicizing *live* was the best decision—even though *here* has a stronger accent—because it is the word on which a prominent accent is less expected:

$$\text{I } \text{li}_{\text{ve}} \;^{\text{he}}\text{r}_{\text{e.}}$$

The lack of markers for intonation is seen in the faux pas of the person who felt so warmly toward an invited speaker that in his later thank-you letter he wrote ***You would have been welcome if you had said nothing at all,*** neglecting to note that what he intended as

$$\text{You would have been }^{\text{welcome}}\text{ if you had said }_{\text{n}}\text{o}^{\text{thing}}\;^{\text{at}}\text{al}_{\text{l.}}$$

could be taken as

$$\text{You would have been }^{\text{wel}}\text{come if you had said nothing at }^{\text{a}}\text{l}_{\text{l.}}$$

In writing we must put *even if* in the first of these, to signal the intention.

The jockeying necessary to overcome the lack of accent and intonation markings calls for a high degree of skill, which is part of the equipment of every good writer. Sometimes nothing can remedy the defect. Lord Acton's phrase ***Compromise is the soul if not the whole of politics*** remains ambiguous; we shall never know whether he meant 'is the soul, nay, more, possibly the whole,' or 'if not the whole, at least the soul.' Sometimes a simple repetition—unnecessary in speech—will clear things up. So with the phrase *more or less:* in the question ***Are you more or less satisfied with the way things went?*** one of the meanings can be pinned down by writing ***Are you more satisfied or less satisfied . . . ?*** The accommodation most often called for is a change in word order, with or without a change in construction. A speaker wishing to reprove someone for shouting can say ***Is shóuting necessary?*** and be clearly understood if he puts the main accent on ***shouting*** and de-accents ***necessary;*** but if the sentence is written, the regularity with which main accents fall at the end will lead the reader to interpret it as *Is shouting nécessary?* A good writer will change the wording to get *shout* at the end: *Is it necessary to shout?*

Now and then we can make capital of a deficiency. Just as a piece of writing can—to advantage—span two or more dialects and so gain in universality, so by its very ambiguity it can at one and the same time embrace two or more actual utterances that we do not care to distinguish, and thereby gain in generality. At check-out counters in stores there used to be containers of free samples with a sign reading *Take one.* Ordinarily this would represent the utterance *Táke one.* But if a customer were to help himself to several, the storekeeper could point out that the sign read *Take óne.*

So we see both primary and secondary divergences between speech and writing: primary ones that are simply the lack on one side of some device that is present in the other—a graphic sign such as the apostrophe in writing, or a distinctive sound such as an accent in speech; and secondary ones that are the result of having to make alternative choices or arrangements in order to remedy a primary lack. There are vested interests in both.

Writing and speech as partially independent systems

The great nineteenth-century linguist Wilhelm von Humboldt expressed what he felt to be the true relationship between writing and speech: "language intrinsically lies in the act of its production in reality; . . . even its preservation in writing is only an incomplete mummified repository which needs, for full understanding, an imaginative oral reconstruction."[9] Most linguists over the years have agreed. Written language could never have come into existence and could not exist today without speech. But to say that it is *only* a mummified repository is not quite true; this is like the *only* of another famous reductionist claim that we saw earlier, that the speech organs are only organs of digestion: in the latter case we are saying that speech is only an overlaid function, and in the former we are saying the same about writing, when the fact is that both have branched off to some extent and achieved a new level of integration.

Writing speaks words to the mind in a voice of its own, sometimes more clearly than words spoken aloud. It is almost impossible, without help from written signs, to unravel the last line of the Carolyn West limerick:

---

[9] In Salus 1969, pp. 184–85.

> But I'd hate to relate
> What that fellow named Tate
> And his tête-a-tête ate at 8:08.

Everyone has had the experience of misunderstanding something heard and not getting it straight until seeing it written: *Peace Corps* interpreted as *P-Score, youth rehabilitation* as *U-3 habilitation.*[10] In one frustrating encounter a librarian spent the better part of an hour rounding up materials on *youth in Asia* for a high-school student who after a bewildered moment showed his assignment sheet with the word written out: *euthanasia.*[11] Many puns depend on an interference between visible and audible signals: the *robber barons* and all their little *robber bairns;* the estate called *Belleigh Acres;* and the *Akimbo Arms,* a Japanese motel. There are other intentional misspellings besides the *olde* and *Edythe* mentioned earlier: *goddamit* is softened as an oath by being written that way instead of *God damn it.* We even find a visual symbolism resembling the sound-symbolism of Chapter 7 (page 219). Readers asked to match 'pleasant' and 'unpleasant' to the spellings *grey* and *gray* tend to do it in that order, and to make such associations as *her lovely grey eyes* contrasting with *a gray gloomy day.* The *gh* of *ghastly, ghoulish, aghast,* and *ghost* marks—like a phonestheme—a kind of semantic constellation.[12]

Punctuation, too, may be short-circuited directly to meaning. The four expressions *my sister's friend's investments, my sisters' friends' investments, my sisters' friend's investments,* and *my sister's friends' investments* all sound identical but are clearly distinguished by the position of the apostrophe.

There are also structural correspondences, not sharply defined but statistically unmistakable. The most striking is the shortness of function words. Many of them have homonyms that are not function words, and if there is a difference in length, the function word is shorter:[13]

I–eye	to–two
so–sew	by–buy
be–bee	in–inn
we–wee	no–know
an–Ann	the–thee

---

[10] Example from Lee Hultzén, personal communication.
[11] Example from John Algeo, personal communication.
[12] Bolinger 1946, p. 336.
[13] Vachek 1973, p. 54, footnote 26.

Capitalization marks proper nouns and proper adjectives. But it is still used or omitted occasionally for other purposes that are directly related to meaning—omitted in e. e. cummings's verse for a kind of playing-down effect, added here and there in verse or prose to dignify or exaggerate: in Shakespeare's First Folio the tragedies consistently had more capitalization of common nouns than the comedies—a register distinction in writing.[14]

Figure 14–1 shows the relationship between writing and speech more or less as linguists used to think of it—an oversimplified conception that was partly a reaction to the equally oversimplified and exaggerated importance attached to writing by educators and the literate public in general. It allows for connections at only one level and in only one direction: grapheme[15] to phoneme. The relationship is not necessarily one to one, but is nevertheless expressible by rules. (*F* matches /f/, but so does *ph;* the *i* of *fine* matches /ay/, but the rule for this must take account of the presence of *e,* in view of what happens with *fin.* And so on.) The phonemic correspondences are the entry into the language system. A written message is interpreted phonemically and from there on the processing is the same as for speech.

Figure 14–2 shows the conception of speech and writing as more or less independent systems that tend to run parallel but converge more and more and finally intertwine. At the right and left extremes are elements that go directly to meaning without the intervention of arbitrary units such as phonemes and graphemes—one example on the graphic side is the numeral *2,* one on the spoken side a raising of the eyebrows for questioning. In the center each step along the graphic course marks an upward progression and at the same time a sidewise link to the concurring steps in speech. If we encounter the spelling *slough* we may have to sound out the word to tell which of the homographs is intended— /slʌf/, /slu/, or /slaw/; and if we find the word *read* with no indication of tense we may have to puzzle it out in terms of its morphophonemic makeup. But each graphic step likewise has the potential of going directly to meaning. The spelling *-que* just before a space tells us that the word of which it is a part is probably of French origin, just as an initial *ph, ps,* or *xy* indicates 'Greek,' along with connotations of learnedness. One can even go backward a step and find something like distinctive features. There are graphs that carry register distinctions: some forms of letters are more elegant than others.

---

[14] Tritt 1973, p. 47.

[15] The grapheme, like the phoneme, is a set of variants all of which have the same value. Thus the graphs *A, a,* and a are all allographs of the grapheme that represents the first letter of the alphabet.

FIGURE 14–1
Old-Fashioned Conception of the Relationship Between Writing and Speech

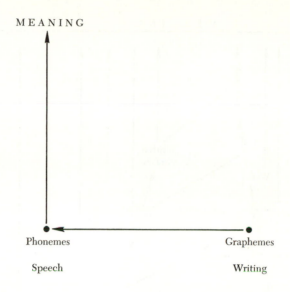

Each system, spoken and written, contributes its part. A speaker infected with literacy is no longer the same person. His brain is full of visual and auditory interminglings. Aware that a word may be misinterpreted, he may spell it out, as one TV interviewee did with the sentence *You just feel e-x-o-r-c-i-s-e-d.* Trying to remember the composer *César Franck,* the speaker may hit upon *Caesar Frank* and be totally baffled in spite of the phonological identity of *Frank* and *Franck,* until he visualizes the spelling with the letter *c.* He has become an expert *translator* from one mode to the other, as adept at interpreting from writing to speech and from speech to writing as he is in shifting from one register or spoken variety to another, with full awareness of the matching values in both systems.[16]

---

[16] For the concept of translation applied to writing and speech, see Haas 1973. Actually the translation, for all of us excepting a few professional transcribers (such as court reporters and biographers), nearly always goes in just one direction: writing → speech. Writing has always been more a device for noting down what is to be spoken later than for recording what has already been said. This may well be why—as one linguist has pointed out—it is simpler to set up rules for converting spellings to phonemes than the reverse. He argues that writing, for literate societies, serves as the backup to the standard, the master form to which all other forms are referred. See Householder 1971, Ch. 13, "The Primacy of Writing."

FIGURE 14–2
Speech and Writing as Semi-Independent Systems

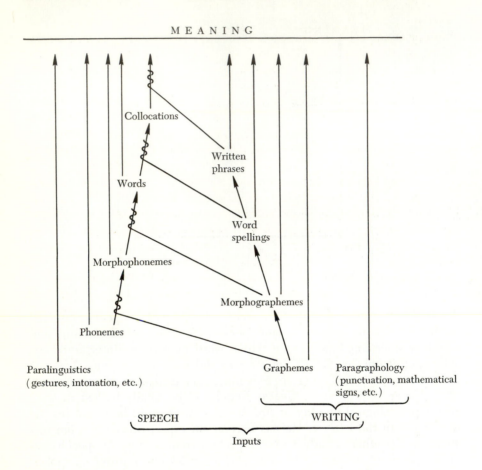

MEANING

Collocations

Written phrases

Words

Word spellings

Morphophonemes

Morphographemes

Phonemes

Paralinguistics
(gestures, intonation, etc.)

Graphemes

Paragraphology
(punctuation, mathematical signs, etc.)

SPEECH   WRITING

Inputs

Developed prose[17]

One of the earliest uses of writing was as a jog to memory. A series of visual symbols or written notes served the same purpose that outlines still serve today, as consecutive reminders in making a speech or telling a story. As long as writing was used in conjunction with speech there was no need for it to become fully emancipated. Yet by freeing speech from its absolute dependence on memory, visual symbols opened the way to an enrichment that was not possible before.

The more elaborate the speech or story and the more it is to escape

---

[17] See Ray 1963, p. 318.

from raw improvisation, the more exact, and hence elaborate, the notes must be. So in time the elaboration becomes the hallmark of the notes themselves. The speaker edits them at his pleasure, and if he has a fully developed writing system at his command they are no longer mere reminders but are the substance of what he plans to say: he can turn off his mind completely as he reads them aloud, doing the whole perform-ance as if by reflex, and still be understood. Or he can give them to some-one else to read. And if the purpose is silent reading he can make his sentences more complex, knowing that the reader who misses them the first time will go back. Writing is language in edited form, differing not just in the mechanics imposed by spelling and punctuation but in its polish and deliberation. "Developed prose" depends on our ability to write.

So writing enhances the possibilities of style. It is no longer something that issues from the mouth and vanishes with the air but is an object of art to be contemplated and worked upon at leisure. With less dependence on brute memory, the devices that an orator or a storyteller might have had to use to help him remember and to help his hearer follow become less necessary—such things as rimes, alliterations, and summations. Elab-orate language becomes less the province of a few; more intricate ideas can be grasped and more elegant expression attempted by every user of the language. The gap between writing and speech is widened. Writing creates a new environment with internal differences responsive to it. Some of them result from the display of words in space rather than in time: page references, words such as *former* and *latter* or *above* and *below.* Others reflect the conservatism and formality of writing. In conversation we would be apt to say that someone had *followed us around;* in formal prose this would probably be changed to *followed us about.* Above all, writing is characterized by amplification. One rarely finds parenthetical clauses in speech, but they are frequent in writing: *The President, who as we know has been under great pressure to re-duce three of his budgetary requests (the last having to do with public housing, but excepting the military), finally submitted a revised report, prepared by a specially appointed staff, to the joint meeting of the two committees last night.* There is no mistaking the lucubration of sentences like this.

Whereas oratory tended to lyricize language (rime, alliteration, and many other poetic figures of speech were probably mnemonic devices to begin with), developed prose intellectualizes it. It offers not only the mechanical possibilities of elaboration but also its own models for imitation (more permanent, and hence more influential, than oral ones) and the whole historical record to draw on as raw material—most writing is at least to some extent about what has already been written. Reality can be contemplated from more points of view. More and more inclusive concepts can be manipulated. The hierarchy reaches higher (see page 246).

Writing and speech are like two railroads with overlapping boards of directors that share, over part of the route, a single right of way. At times they seem to be the same, but there has never been a formal merger and their managements have too many ingrained rivalries now to approve one.

The efficiency of English spelling

No other spelling system in the world has been the occasion of so much amazement, frustration, irritation, sarcasm, and cold fury as that of English—a reflection as much of the large numbers of non-English-speaking people who have tried to learn it as of its own inherent refractoriness. British place names are the butt of the following riddle:

> *Problem:* How do you pronounce *athvrenzavce?*
>
> *Answer:* You don't pronounce it at all because they are all silent letters: *ath* as in *Strathaven; v* as in *Milngavie; ren* as in *Cirencester; z* as in *Culzean; av* as in *Abergavenny; ce* as in *Leicester.*

The tributes to other, more ordinary spellings have been just as heartfelt. Here is part of a poem composed by Richard Krogh:

> Beware of heard, a dreadful word
> That looks like beard and sounds like bird.
> And dead; it's said like bed, not bead;
> For goodness sake, don't call it deed!
> Watch out for meat and great and threat
> (They rhyme with suite and straight and debt).
> A moth is not a moth in Mother,
> Nor both in bother, broth in brother.

Reviewing these protests and experiencing the pain even as a native speaker of trying to learn how to spell a word and remember it afterward, one is astonished to read the claim, in a serious study of English sounds and spellings, that "conventional orthography is . . . a near optimal system for the lexical representation of English words."[18] It is necessary to consider this endorsement of the status quo in the light of the two sound-systems discussed in Chapters 3 and 4. From the standpoint of

---

[18] Chomsky and Halle 1968, p. 49. The same idea is paraphrased on page 184, footnote 19.

the *picture* stage, English orthography is a fright. From that of the *picture–pictorial–depict* stage, as we have seen, it has its points, for it gives a common spelling for words that stem from a common source.

The educational problem is obvious. The child beginning to learn to read still has a leg and a half firmly planted in the *picture* stage. He has learned some important morphophonemic alternations, probably including *fight–fought, bring–brought, think–thought* (but not *seek–sought*—he will not have learned *seek,* and when he does he may go on saying *seek–seeked* to the end of his days). These provide some justification for a uniform spelling for the past tense of those verbs, though a very weak justification for this particular spelling, which is both redundant and inconsistent with *teach–taught* and *catch–caught.* As for the alternations in *fine* and *finish, decide* and *decision, reside* and *residence,* the spellings are more consistently relatable but the words themselves are either not in the learner's vocabulary or are there but unrelated: a six-year-old is not ready to see a connection between *fine* and *finish,* even though he probably knows both words. To try to teach the words and connections in addition to the rules for reading is the same bad educational practice, though on a smaller scale, as trying to teach literacy in a foreign language (a Navaho child, for instance, being forced to learn to read in English, which he knows only imperfectly); each task is difficult enough by itself without mixing it with the other. What the child needs is the quickest possible entry for written symbols into the part of his language that he knows well, and the easiest match is through a writing system that is fairly close to the autonomous phonemes of the *picture* stage. In other words, if we consider only the problem of learning to read and leave other questions aside, including other educational ones, the best writing system is the one that comes closest to the simplistic diagram of Figure 14–1. Something of the kind is the basis for most styles of teaching beginners today. Even the Dick-and-Jane readers used reduced lists of words that had reasonably consistent spellings. The differences are mainly in where the entry into the spoken system is to be made. The whole-word method makes it at the level of words. Another method, not yet tried on any considerable scale, advocates making it at the level of the syllable.[19] The Initial Teaching Alphabet is a modified phonemic approach.

There remains the question, when the gates are opened to the flood of other considerations—the preservation of documents, the different pronunciations in different dialects, the direct spelling-to-meaning relationships diagrammed in Figure 14–2, the vested interest of the millions who already know the existing system—of whether English spelling

---

[19] Gleitman and Rozin 1973.

is efficient enough to be worth keeping as it is or should be mildly or drastically reformed. Reform is hardly unthinkable—the Dutch have done it every forty years or so.[20] The problem is one for society as a whole, and one thing can be said with certainty about it: the solution is not to be entrusted to linguists alone, who in matters of interference with language tend to take the attitude of a mother whose child has been accused of a crime. Scholars fall in love with the object of their attentions as easily as artists do.

With spoken language their affection may be justified. The sound-system, the words, and the syntax are under daily pressures of change, and a language at any given moment is probably the best communicative instrument its culture can have; indeed, by definition it is the only possible one. Writing lives in a cocoon. It is controlled by schools and copyeditors. There is no competition from millions of inventive writers who in the give-and-take of correspondence might attain something approaching the same kind of consensus that speakers attain in speech. A real written *language* has never existed; what we have is a code watched over by a priestly caste.

So for every argument that we ought to live with the system we have, there is a counter-argument that we ought to tear it down and build it up again. For example:

1. "English spelling shows underlying relationships. This is more important to readers than a faithful representation of sounds." The claim of relative importance may or may not be true, but it does not follow that dissimilar spellings cannot be easily related in our minds. If we can have suppletive forms in speech (*go–went, am–was, it–them*), we can endure them in writing, assuming there are other gains.

2. "Distinctive word-shapes are an advantage in rapid reading. We need cues to elements at least as large as words more than we need cues to sounds." This assumes that cues to sounds will necessarily interfere; there is no proof that they will, any more than there is proof that a more careful pronunciation of a sentence will make it harder to understand than a less careful one. No skilled reader computes the phonemic relationships of his words, except when he is learning new ones. He sees them as wholes. We have in our memory store as full an inventory of separate images for words as we would have if there were no individual letter signs at all.

3. "English writing, like Chinese, is interdialectal. Trying to make it fit any one dialect would hamper international communication and understanding." True, but no serious attempt has been made to strike

---

[20] Pointed out by Robert S. Kirsner, personal communication.

a balance among dialects and come up with a writing system to match it. Until some practical experiment is carried out, all we have is another plea for the status quo.

The reader can imagine this argument extending far into the night.

THE GROWTH OF WRITING[21]

The forerunners of our written signs were nearly all pictorial or diagrammatic. That is to say, they were *iconic,* in the sense explained on page 217. Primitive pictures conveyed messages in the same way as modern cartoons; the drawing of a man's figure might look more or less like an actual man, but its meaning depended on there being at least some resemblance. A diagram to point a direction really pointed in the direction intended, relative to the ground or to other points on a map. Notches on a stick to record the number of sheep sheared or soldiers recruited or vessels of oil delivered corresponded to the actual count. What men inscribed on wood or clay or graved on stone was intended to speak to the mind through the eye alone, not through the eye as a stimulus to the ear.

This is not to deny all connection with speech, nor to say that long strides were not taken toward an arbitrary system in representational drawing. Drawings could be arbitrary: if notches could represent recruits, clearly circles or dots would do just as well; nothing compelled the artist to include more detail than he was interested in. But always the potential of depicting an actual characteristic was there: a stick figure might be enough to represent a man, but a man with an arm missing would be shown by a stick with a missing arm. And connections with speech were often close: some designs were drawn to be translated aloud, either as reminders for those who drew them or as messages calling for an interpreter. But they differed from writing in having no fixed correspondence between the design and the language; the interpreter was free to ad-lib. A three-part drawing in which a king was shown first assembling his hosts, then laying waste an enemy land, then pausing to rest, might be read aloud as *After assembling his hosts and before pausing to rest, he laid waste the enemy land* or *In order to lay waste the enemy land he assembled his hosts, and afterward he rested* or *Before he rested he laid waste the enemy land with the hosts he had assembled* or in any number of other ways. The words could vary, and the actions did not need to be reported in the same sequence. Language, with its enormously greater resources, could run circles around the drawing, and

---

[21] This section for the most part follows Gelb 1963.

this explains why each step toward a symbolization of language rather than a direct symbolization of things and events was bound to mark a gain in communicative power.

The main steps were three: the writing of words, the writing of syllables, and the writing of distinctive sounds. Each stage overlapped the following one. Even Modern English writing has a few remnants of word signs and syllable signs: in **IOU** the letters stand for words; the symbol ¶ means 'paragraph' and § means 'section.' (We even use the primitive device of pluralizing symbols by doubling them: ¶¶, §§.) Mathematics, science, and engineering have many signs for words, including +, ÷, =, the numerals, ⋁⋁⋁ for 'resistor,' |ı for 'condenser,' |ı|ı for 'battery,' and so on. **Bar-b-q** uses *b* and *q* to stand for the syllables /bi/ and /kyu/, as **OK** stands for the syllables /o/ and /ke/.

Archeology enables us to estimate the dates of the three steps and credit their first appearance to particular societies, though we cannot be sure, even when a given piece of writing is assigned definitely to a given people, that some later archeological find will not reveal that the style was borrowed from a near neighbor who invented it a century or two earlier. Thus, while the Phoenicians seem entitled to credit for the second step, it could have been taken first by some other group in their general area. What is fairly certain, in view of a number of finds clustering near one another, is that it did occur in that area.

Word writing

While the interpreter of a pictorial message was usually free to ad-lib, a few of the signs must always have referred to individual persons or things that could be mentioned in speech by just one name. A drawing of a small bear could have been verbalized as **small bear, little bear,** or **bear cub,** but if it designated a person known as **Little Bear** only that reading would have been admissible. A semantic annotation might or might not be added to help the interpreter—say, a figure of a man to which the figure of the cub is attached; the result was necessarily that a particular sign called for a particular word or phrase.

Something similar must have happened with pictorial messages where the interpreter was theoretically free to ad-lib. If the message was to himself—a series of reminders, perhaps, for recounting a story—a timid person no doubt did as he would do today and memorized the text. In that case, when he came to deliver it, using his notes for added confidence, each symbol for a particular meaning would also have stood for a particular word or phrase. It is not difficult to imagine almost from the first a tendency to link a written sign to its meaning, not directly, but via a particular word or words. Any such tendency must have taken hold quickly, for it put all the resources of language at the command of the writer and reader. For the first time writing was *phonetized:* a given sign represented a given complex of sounds.

When this step was first taken is impossible to determine. One cannot tell by looking at the earliest pictorial messages whether they were interpreted idea by idea, with the words ad-libbed, or word by word. The signs might have been direct representations of concrete objects, or figurative representations of one notion through another (the sun for 'bright, brilliant, blinding'), or diagrams (an empty circle for 'empty, vacant, hollow')—nothing would prove that a word rather than a meaning was intended. Even an additional semantic indicator like the man beside the bear cub would not assure us that the sample was one of word writing, for the idea might be one that could be expressed by only one word anyway, such as the proper name **Little Bear,** and some semantic indicators would still leave room for ad-libbing: man plus mountain could stand for 'man from the mountain,' hence 'slave,' 'servant,' 'person of low birth.'

But somewhere in the word-writing stage an event took place that proved the word-by-word interpretation beyond a doubt. The pictorial stage would have found it very difficult to express abstract notions like tense and mood in the verb; so if we find *would be* symbolized by a drawing of a piece of wood and a drawing of a bee, we can be certain that the figures no longer stand for ideas. This is the *rebus;* something that we now associate with children's games was proof of the innovation of word writing.

Now nothing stood in the way of applying the same phonetic principle not just to whole words but to parts of words. Most languages contain words of more than one syllable, and often the syllables are the same in sound as certain one-syllable words. A slight extension of the rebus game enabled writers to use double characters for two-syllable words. In a modern rebus, *fancy* can be depicted by a fan and a sea, or *mumble* by a chrysanthemum and a bull. At first the sign-to-syllable relationship would not have been pure—a three-syllable word like *loggerhead* could have been represented by two signs, one for logger and one for head— but the basis for syllabic writing was laid, and the whole period of word writing was a mixture of word and syllable writing.[22]

The earliest developed form of word-syllabic writing was that of the Sumerians in Mesopotamia at the end of the fourth millennium B.C. The Egyptians had their own system within a century or so of this, but were probably influenced by the Sumerians.

Two samples of well-known syllabaries are shown in Figures 14–3 and 14–4.

---

[22] Gelb 1963, pp. 99–105.

FIGURE 14–3
The Japanese Katakana Syllabary

ア	カ	サ	タ	ナ	ハ	マ	ヤ	ラ	ワ		ガ	ザ	ダ	バ	パ
a	ka	sa	ta	na	ha	ma	ya	ra	wa		ga	za	da	ba	pa
イ	キ	シ	チ	ニ	ヒ	ミ		リ	ヰ		ギ	ジ	ヂ	ビ	ピ
i	ki	si	ti(tsi)	ni	hi	mi		ri	wi(i)		gi	zi	di	bi	pi
ウ	ク	ス	ツ	ヌ	フ	ム	ユ	ル			グ	ズ	ヅ	ブ	プ
u	ku	su	tu(tsu)	nu	hu	mu	yu	ru			gu	zu	du	bu	pu
ヱ	ケ	セ	テ	子	ヘ	メ	エ	レ	ヱ		ゲ	ゼ	デ	ベ	ヘ
e	ke	se	te	ne	he	me	ye	re	we(e)		ge	ze	de	be	pe
オ	コ	ソ	ト	ノ	ホ	モ	ヨ	ロ	ヲ		ゴ	ゾ	ド	ボ	ホ
o	ko	so	to	no	ho	mo	yo	ro	wo		go	zo	do	bo	po

ン (n)

SOURCE: Reprinted from *A Study of Writing*, by I. J. Gelb, © 1963, by permission of The University of Chicago Press. Adapted from Fossey, *Notices sur les caractères étrangers*, p. 314.

Syllable writing

Even after the knack of writing by syllables had been acquired, pure syllable writing was rather long in coming. The older word-signs were kept through tradition and inertia, and often a given word could be represented either by its own sign or by signs for its syllables. The second historical step—the discarding of all the word-signs and the adoption of a straightforward system of syllable writing—had to be taken by disrespectful foreigners who had no romantic attachments to the old signs and merely borrowed what was practical.[23] These were the Phoenicians. Other borrowers of other systems did the same, but the Phoenicians are most important to us because they stand in direct line with the later development of the alphabet.

The Egyptian table of syllable signs, or syllabary, contained two sets of figures, each representing a different kind of value. The figures of the first set represented particular consonants plus any vowel or no vowel at all: a single sign stood for *ma, me, mi, mu,* or *m,* or for *ta, te, ti, tu,* or *t.* The members of the second set were the same except that two consonants were involved; one sign, for example, stood for *tama, tame, tem, tma,* and so on.[24] The consistent omission of vowels was in line with the nature

---

[23] Ibid., p. 196.
[24] Ibid., pp. 75–78.

FIGURE 14–4   The Cherokee Syllabary*

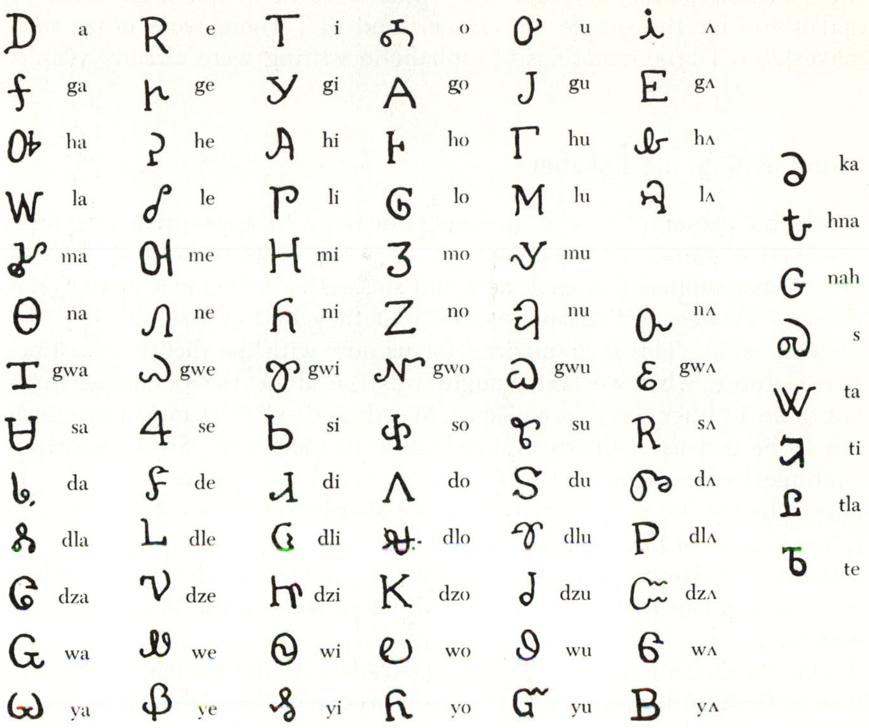

a	e	i	o	u	ʌ
D a	R e	T i	☉ o	Ɵ u	i ʌ
ga	ge	gi	go	gu	E gʌ
ha	he	hi	ho	hu	hʌ
la	le	li	lo	lu	lʌ
ma	me	mi	mo	mu	
na	ne	ni	no	nu	nʌ
gwa	gwe	gwi	gwo	gwu	gwʌ
sa	se	si	so	su	sʌ
da	de	di	do	du	dʌ
dla	dle	dli	dlo	dlu	dlʌ
dza	dze	dzi	dzo	dzu	dzʌ
wa	we	wi	wo	wu	wʌ
ya	ye	yi	yo	yu	yʌ

(additional signs at right): ka, hna, nah, s, ta, ti, tla, te

SOURCE: Adapted from p. 414 of *An Introduction to Descriptive Linguistics*, Revised Edition, by H. A. Gleason, Jr. Copyright © 1955, 1961 by Holt, Rinehart and Winston, Publishers. Reprinted by permission of Holt, Rinehart and Winston, Publishers.

* This syllabary was invented between 1809 and 1821 by Sequoya (George Guess) and used by the Cherokee people and missionaries working among them. It is partly an adaptation of Roman letters.

of the Semitic languages, where inflections are shown by internal changes instead of by affixes (like English **man–men** rather than **man–*mans** or **rise–rose** rather than **rise–*rised**); it was possible to sacrifice the vowels without losing the identity of the word, and thus make a saving in the number of different symbols written.

The Phoenicians entered the picture around the middle of the second millennium B.C. They imitated the one-consonant syllabary of the Egyptians, throwing out the rest. By about 1000 B.C. they had developed a completely syllabic form of writing with no word signs and no signs for more than one syllable. The vowels were still omitted, though where needed to avoid ambiguity they were often added in the form of consonants whose features resembled those of the desired vowel. For example, Semitic writing—including Phoenician—had syllabic signs for the semiconsonants /w/ and /y/ (plus a vowel), and used them as makeshifts for the simple vowels /u/ and /i/. There were other such makeshifts. The glimmerings of alphabetic writing were already visible.

Sound writing: the alphabet

It is a bit presumptuous of modern phonology to appropriate the term "distinctive sound" for its phonemes, as if the users of language would never have supposed at each new and successive refinement of the relationship between sound and symbol that they had at last hit upon the phonetic atom. This is dramatized for us now with the theory of distinctive features; what we had thought was the atom, the phoneme, turns out to be a rather complex molecule. Words and syllables must have been felt to be just as distinctively irreducible in their time. So if phonemes continue to be called distinctive sounds—and the phrase is too firmly entrenched to be got rid of easily—we should remember that the term refers to a set of phonetic features, at a certain level of refinement, which actually came into consciousness with the growth of alphabetic writing. For that we can thank mainly the Greeks of some three thousand years ago.

The Phoenicians were the seafaring traders of the ancient world and carried their writing wherever they went as one of the tools of their trade. It was probably in the ninth century B.C. that the form of Phoenician writing that was to become the Greek alphabet was planted along the western shores of the Aegean.[25]

The Greek innovation—and it was gradual, like all the others—was to do consistently what the Phoenicians had done sporadically: to add the interpretative vowel signs to all their syllables. What they themselves must have regarded still as a syllabary thus became an alphabet by accident. A sign signifying /mu/ (as well as /mi me ma/) would not have needed any /u/ after it if the context made it clear that /mu/ was intended. An English sentence written **Y** *mst* **b** *crfl* *wth* *sch* *ppl* would give us no trouble—*mst* here can only mean *must.* But when the symbol for any *m*-plus-vowel syllable was consistently accompanied by a sign for a particular vowel, it was natural for the next generation of scribes to forget that it stood for the syllable and take it for the consonant alone. Now it was possible to go on to a full specification of all the phonemes. This was the form of writing that captured the greatest number of languages around the world, including—with modifications—the Semitic itself, from which it was derived. We can never guess how far the progress and

---

[25] Ibid., pp. 178–81.

power of the Western world may have been due to the speedup of communication and the accumulation of recorded experience that was made possible when a quasi-phonemic writing that could be quickly learned took literacy away from a select priesthood and put it within reach of the general public.

Yet we need not be overly prideful of our Western accomplishment, for from the standpoint of sheer creativeness it was outdone by the Koreans some five hundred years ago. In 1446 King Sejong promulgated an alphabet—the date is still celebrated as a national holiday in Korea—in which certain strokes of the characters represented phonetic characteristics such as tongue position or force of articulation. The Koreans had had a good deal of practice with word and syllable writing using Chinese characters, and of course the whole evolution of alphabetic writing lay behind them, so they knew pretty much what they were doing in designing new forms; but their "visible speech," to borrow the name given to his own similar system four hundred years later by Alexander Melville Bell, was still a remarkable achievement. Unfortunately, it was slow in having the effect on education and general culture that the alphabet produced in the West, because the older system of writing continued to be used until after the Second World War; South Korea has still not gone over completely to the simplified alphabet.[26] A similar attempt around 1650, by Francis Lodwick in England, received some attention in its time but had no practical effect. Honorat Rambaud of Marseilles had also "invented an elaborate notation on comparable principles" a century earlier.[27]

The stages of development of writing are summarized in Table 14–1.

DECIPHERMENT

One of the most fascinating chapters in the recovery of the past is the interpretation of ancient writings on scattered, fragmentary, and often fragile artifacts that have come down to us. Much of our ability to read them is due to the continuity of certain cultures that developed a writing system at an early date and have kept their tradition sufficiently alive to our own day to give us a basis of comparison with earlier systems related to them. Foremost among these traditions are the Chinese, Hebrew, Sanskrit, Greco-Roman, and Persian, the last having been carried on in India by the Parsees, who fled there during the Mohammedan invasion of Persia in the eighth century. Now and then some precious bit of bilingual

---

[26] Fritz Vos, in Yamagiwa 1964; see McCawley 1966, p. 171.

[27] Abercrombie 1965, pp. 49–50.

TABLE 14–1
Stages of the Development of Writing

NO WRITING: *Pictures*

FORERUNNERS OF WRITING: *Semasiography*

    1. Descriptive-Representational Devices
    2. Identifying-Mnemonic Devices

FULL WRITING: *Phonography*

1. *Word-Syllabic:*	Sumerian (Akkadian)	Egyptian	Hittite (Aegean)	Chinese
2. *Syllabic:*	Elamite Hurrian etc.	West Semitic (Phoenician) (Hebrew) (Aramaic) etc.	Cypro- Minoan Cypriote Phaistos? Byblos?	Japanese
3. *Alphabetic:*		Greek Aramaic (vocalized)° Hebrew (vocalized)° Latin Indic° etc.		

SOURCE: Adapted from Gelb 1963, p. 191.
° Tentatively classed as alphabetic.

or multilingual evidence comes to light—a document such as the Rosetta stone, on which identical messages appear in two or more languages, at least one of which could already be read. The Rosetta stone contained inscriptions in two varieties of Egyptian writing, plus Greek. The most impressive multilingual record of all was the Persian inscriptions done at Bisutun by order of King Darius, with parallel texts in Persian, Elamite, and Assyrian (Babylonian).[28] The Persian empire embraced peoples

---

[28] Pedersen 1962, p. 155.

speaking these three principal languages, and other Persian inscriptions likewise are written in all three.

No two instances of decipherment are the same, but a close look at one will suggest some of the problems. The most recent—and among the most spectacular—is that of the Linear B tablets unearthed in Crete and on the Greek mainland in the southern peninsula of Peloponnesus. The man chiefly responsible for the discovery was the British architect and amateur cryptographer Michael Ventris, and the language, as it turned out, was a form of Greek about six hundred years older than any for which records had previously been known. The following is based on the account by John Chadwick, Ventris's closest co-worker.[29]

In one respect the Cretan and mainland finds were exceptional. Both had been stored at the site of ancient palaces that had subsequently been burned, with the result that large quantities of clay tablets containing the writing had been fired, just as brick and pottery are intentionally fired to harden them; had this not happened, the clay would long since have turned to mud. Ventris thus had several hundred tablets with which to work—the number of published texts is now about five thousand. This enabled him to ignore for the moment the question of what language he was dealing with and to concentrate instead on calculating the frequencies of the written symbols, making certain assumptions about what they were used for.

The first clue lay in the resemblance between Linear B and a much later form of writing from Cyprus that had already been deciphered. It was obvious that the two did not represent the same language, since when Linear B was given the Cypriote values the result made no sense, but it seemed likely that Linear B at least had the minimum similarity of being a related syllabary and not an alphabet. The assumption that it was similar led Ventris to look for certain signs nearly always found at the beginning of words and not in the middle. The reason for this was that in Cypriote the typical symbol stood for a consonant plus a vowel, as we have seen to be true of Semitic writing, and a word such as *sensible* would have had signs corresponding to *se-ne-si-bi-le*. But if a word *be-gan* with a vowel, a different kind of symbol would have had to be used. Such symbols were found.

A second successful guess involved a sign that was commonly used at the end of particular groups of signs that were found repeated elsewhere without that ending. It appeared that this might be some sort of conjunction like the Latin *-que* for 'and,' attached to the end of words.

A third deduction followed from mistakes that the scribes had made. In many places there were clear erasures, and what had first been inscribed and the correction written over it could both be read. In addi-

---

[29] Chadwick 1960.

tion there were words that almost invariably appeared in a certain form, but perhaps once or twice, in a context so similar that it almost had to be intended as the same form, a writing differing by one sign appeared. It seemed a safe guess that these infrequent changes were uncorrected mistakes. Since mistakes are generally made between forms that resemble one another, this made it possible to tabulate lists of forms assumed to be similar but not the same, like English *p* and *b* or *t* and *d*.

A fourth deduction followed from the assumption that the language was an inflected one. If it resembled Latin, one would expect forms like *domin-a*, *puell-a*, *bon-a*, and *serv-a*, in which the inflection is in the form of a characteristic vowel that alternates with some other ending such as *-us*. But if Linear B was syllabic it could not show these endings directly. It would have had to use one sign for *-na*, another for *-la*, another for *-va*, and so on. A study of the tablets showed that there were words that stayed the same at the beginning, like the *domi-* of *domina*, and that had variable endings. It also revealed a small number of words that remained the same when followed by words having these unstable endings and that might well be prepositions. On the hypothesis that a given preposition would usually govern the same case, the variable endings were assumed to stand for syllables all ending in the same vowel—this being the marker for case—but with different consonants.

The inflectional theory also made it possible to match the consonantal part of each sign with that of other signs. Given a form such as *domi-na* and *domi-nus*, we would recognize variants of the same word, identified by the *domi-* part, and would assign the *n* to the stem: *domin-*. Therefore, the syllabic sign for *-na* and the syllabic sign for *-nus* must contain the same consonant, *n*.

Finally, there was a hint of gender distinctions in the pictograms that accompanied the writing. If a tablet whose form indicated that it was a catalog of some kind also contained the figure of a woman, the chances were that lists of women were involved; therefore, the names were feminine and all had the same set of vowel endings.

Taking these assumptions together, Ventris set up a grid in which signs were lined up from left to right in terms of having the same supposed vowel and up and down in terms of having the same consonant. A sample provided by Chadwick 1960 from Ventris's later work notes is shown in Figure 14–5.[30]

Now began the task of trying to conjecture words. The tablets were clearly of a commercial nature, so it was likely that place names would figure, and Ventris plausibly reasoned that in the tablets unearthed at Knossos in Crete it was likely that both Knossos and the seaport town of Amnisos would be mentioned. The name of Amnisos was known from

---

[30] Ibid., p. 59.

FIGURE 14–5
Ventris's Grid*

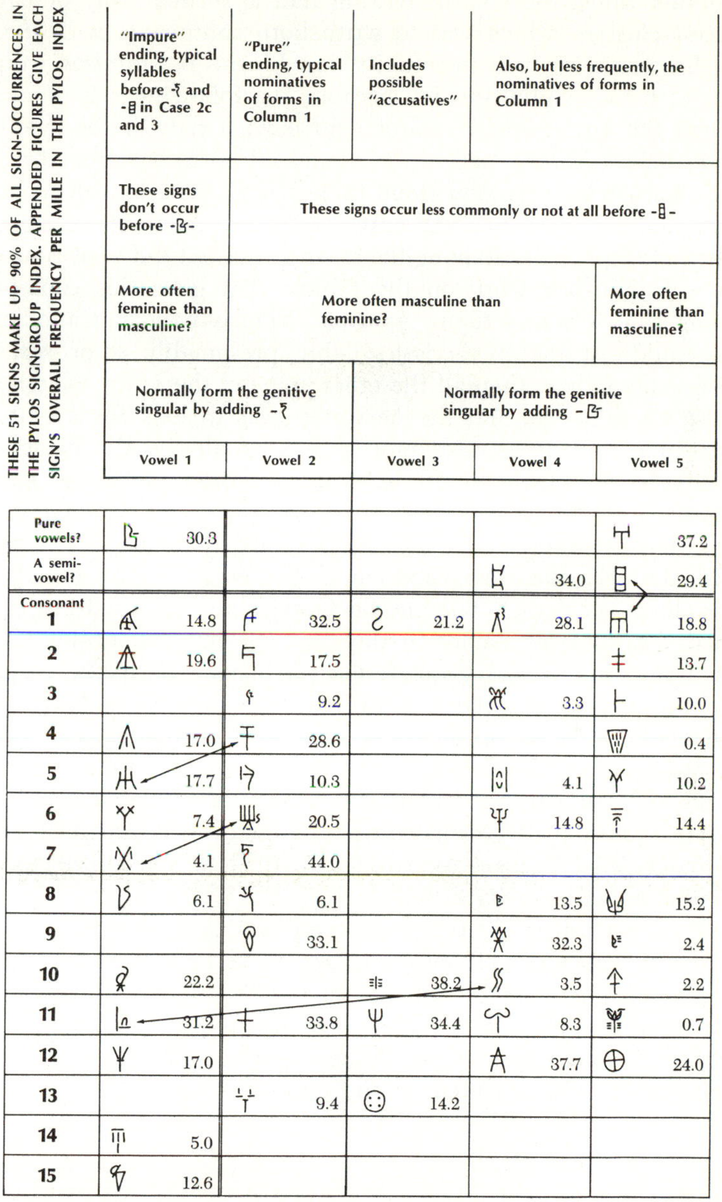

THESE 51 SIGNS MAKE UP 90% OF ALL SIGN-OCCURRENCES IN THE PYLOS SIGNGROUP INDEX. APPENDED FIGURES GIVE EACH SIGN'S OVERALL FREQUENCY PER MILLE IN THE PYLOS INDEX

	"Impure" ending, typical syllables before -? and -◻ in Case 2c and 3	"Pure" ending, typical nominatives of forms in Column 1	Includes possible "accusatives"	Also, but less frequently, the nominatives of forms in Column 1	
	These signs don't occur before -◻-	These signs occur less commonly or not at all before -◻-			
	More often feminine than masculine?	More often masculine than feminine?			More often feminine than masculine?
	Normally form the genitive singular by adding -?		Normally form the genitive singular by adding -◻		
	Vowel 1	Vowel 2	Vowel 3	Vowel 4	Vowel 5
Pure vowels?	30.3				37.2
A semi-vowel?				34.0	29.4
Consonant 1	14.8	32.5	21.2	28.1	18.8
2	19.6	17.5			13.7
3		9.2		3.3	10.0
4	17.0	28.6			0.4
5	17.7	10.3		4.1	10.2
6	7.4	20.5		14.8	14.4
7	4.1	44.0			
8	6.1	6.1		13.5	15.2
9		33.1		32.3	2.4
10	22.2		38.2	3.5	2.2
11	31.2	33.8	34.4	8.3	0.7
12	17.0			37.7	24.0
13		9.4	14.2		
14	5.0				
15	12.6				

SOURCE: Adapted from Michael Ventris, 28 September 1951.

* *Top:* A diagrammatic representation of the Linear B tablets; *bottom:* a diagnosis of consonant and vowel equations in the inflectional material from Pylos.

Homer and was a good candidate to work with because, for one thing, it had an initial vowel, and the vowel symbols had already been isolated. For another thing, the Cyprus writing had a peculiar way of handling consonant clusters, which was to write both consonants with the same vowel. So, assuming this peculiarity for Linear B, *Amnisos* would be written with the symbol for *-mi-* because the following syllable actually contained the vowel *i* and was of course written with the symbol for *-ni-: Am(i)nisos.* Ventris had already guessed correctly, from frequency counts, that a particular sign stood for *a-.* So now he looked for a word in which that sign came first and in which the second and third signs were already on his grid as containing the same vowel but different consonants. There was only one word on the tablets that gave this combination. Assuming that it was actually *Amnisos,* Ventris now had another sign that he could test, that of the last syllable, presumably *-so* or *-sos.* If this vowel was actually *o,* then all the other signs in the same column of the grid also contained *o,* and the next step was to look for a word containing three such signs and hope that it would be the name of the main city itself, which would have been written with the signs for *K(o)-no-so.*

It was not necessary to assume any particular language for names like *Amnisos* and *Knossos,* for place names are freely borrowed. But now Ventris did assume that it might be Greek and examined some of the inflected forms of the names in the light of that assumption. He also assumed that the syllabary might not have been perfectly adapted to Greek and that certain of the sounds, particularly certain syllable-final consonants, might have been omitted. This was his boldest guess and the luckiest one, for it developed that if one were free to add final consonants—and these turned out to be phonetically related consonants—the result would spell Greek words. Pictograms were again a help—a tablet on which a chariot appeared contained the word which Ventris had reconstructed as the Greek name for 'chariot.'

In 1953, a year after Ventris announced his discovery, new excavations at the site of the ancient city of Pylos brought to light a number of tablets on which his experimental syllabary could be tried out. Pictograms of vessels, identified by Greek names exactly as Ventris predicted they would be written, confirmed his solution beyond a doubt.

The Linear B syllabary is shown in Figure 14–6.

THE FUTURE OF WRITING

Literacy programs are expensive, and a third of the world's population is illiterate. UNESCO figures for 1970 were 2.3 billion total population,

FIGURE 14–6
The Linear B Syllabary*

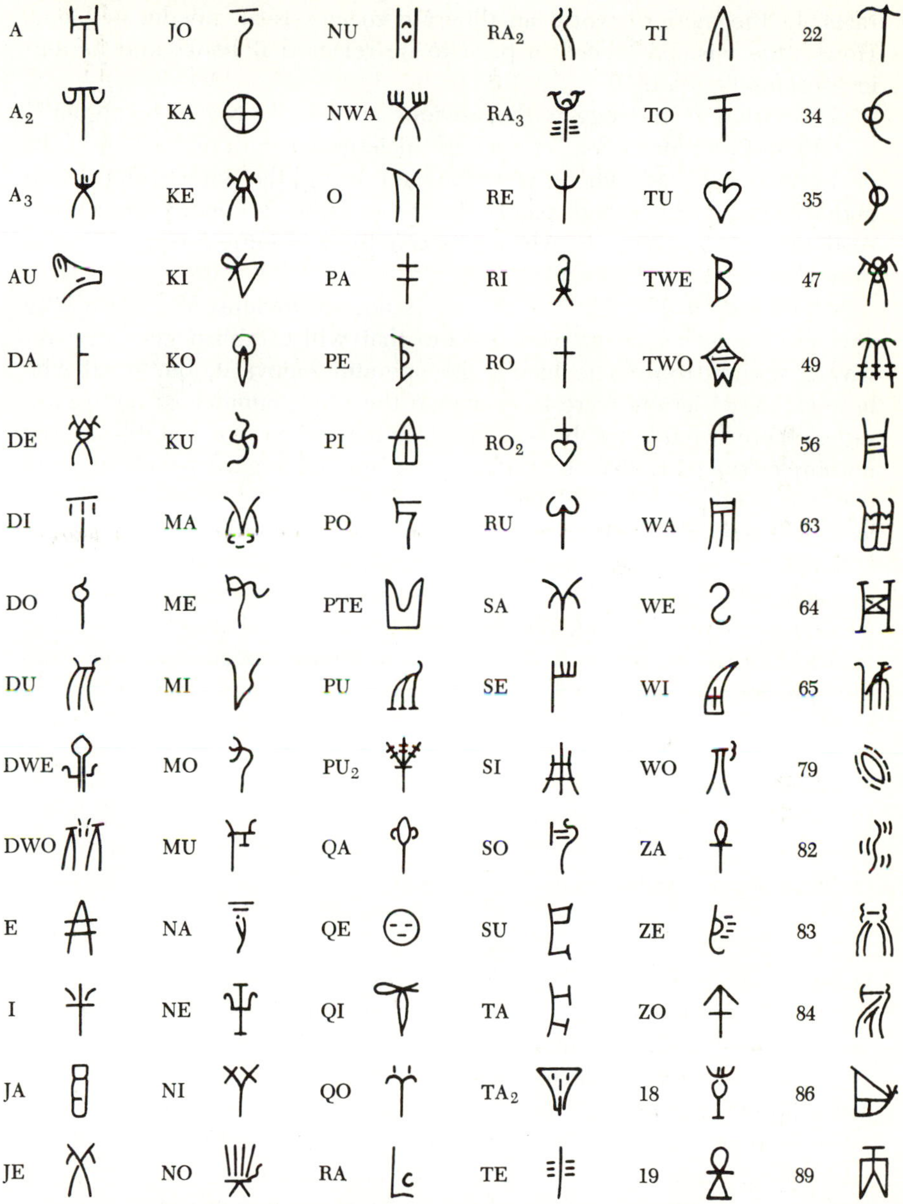

The table shows the Linear B syllabary signs arranged in columns, each sign paired with its phonetic value (or numeral for undeciphered signs):

A	JO	NU	RA₂		TI		22	
A₂	KA	NWA	RA₃		TO		34	
A₃	KE	O	RE		TU		35	
AU	KI	PA	RI		TWE		47	
DA	KO	PE	RO		TWO		49	
DE	KU	PI	RO₂		U		56	
DI	MA	PO	RU		WA		63	
DO	ME	PTE	SA		WE		64	
DU	MI	PU	SE		WI		65	
DWE	MO	PU₂	SI		WO		79	
DWO	MU	QA	SO		ZA		82	
E	NA	QE	SU		ZE		83	
I	NE	QI	TA		ZO		84	
JA	NI	QO	TA₂		18		86	
JE	NO	RA	TE		19		89	

SOURCE: Adapted from Chadwick 1972, p. 40.

* Ninety signs comprise the Linear B syllabary. Seventeen are not yet conclusively deciphered; numerals appear beside them. The vowel or vowel-consonant sounds of the other seventy-three signs are shown in alphabetical notation. Linear B also has 110 ideograms.

over 800 million illiterate—and though the percentage was being reduced, in absolute figures illiteracy was gaining because of high birth
rates. In the modern world an illiterate society is an uneducated one.
How is the wisdom locked in print to be released if books and periodicals cannot be read?

Audiovisual technology is the obvious answer. It has been argued[31]
that there is no need for "emerging" societies to endure the hardships
of learning to read when television can bring the same information
audibly, graphically, and painlessly: why build a nineteenth-century
road through a mountain when you can fly a twentieth-century plane
over it?

But on second thought the answer is not so obvious. We are a long
way from a television or even a radio that will establish genuine two-
way communication. The ham radio operator enjoys it, but if all who
now exchange letters were to exchange the same number of radio messages, there would not be enough frequencies to go around—to say
nothing of the cost. The advocates of the "media" regard people as mere
consumers of prepackaged messages, but there is a right to be heard
as well as a right to hear.

Suppose the difficulty could be hurdled by some great advance in
technology. Would reading and writing then go the way of the horse
and buggy? Probably not, for there are other costs that are higher still.
Consider four, which can be labeled archives, speed, symbols, and
fact, just for convenience.

Archives   The record of civilization is in print. To make it accessible
to everyone by ear might well cost more than all literacy programs for
a century. Besides, who is to interpret it? How easy would it be for
politicians to revise the past?

Speed   The average speaking rate is six syllables per second. A listener
can comprehend somewhat faster than that—which makes it possible to
speed up a recording slightly—but cannot approach the rate of the average reader. Another side to the question of speed is freedom to scan
and skip: by noting just a word here and there a reader can decide
whether there is anything on a page that interests him. Even if the
laborious process of rewinding and blindly hunting for the right spot
could be done away with (not, of course, by reading words written along-

---

[31] For example, by R. C. Theobald at the Fifth Waigani Seminar. See Gwyther-Jones
1971.

side the sound track!), scanning a tape would be extremely difficult, and
other forms of recording are not much better.

Symbols   Ordinary speech is not the only medium of communication
embodied in writing. The whole edifice of science and logic is built
on a tight system of mathematical symbols. It is possible of course to
verbalize an expression such as $\dfrac{\sqrt{(a^2 + b^2)}}{c}$ but next to impossible
to manipulate it if words have to be used; the practical value of it is in
avoiding words. Are we to forgo this kind of literacy too?

Fact   Writing is dispassionate. We saw this earlier as a liability: a great
part of the emotional content of speech is lost when it is put on paper.
Yet for transmitting *public* knowledge this can be an advantage, and
it is precisely the truth values that are least affected by it. If you read
Caspar submitted his report you know as much about what happened
as if someone spoke the same words, and you are not swayed by any
tone of enthusiasm or distaste in the voice of a speaker. And written
agreements are secure agreements; oral ones are not. To dispense with
literacy we would have to dispense with law and commerce.

There are cultures, not all of which are literate; but there is also a
world-wide culture of which writing is a part. Literacy, for better or for
worse, will have to be taught, for all of the foreseeable future.

But styles and systems of writing undoubtedly will change. Even as
simple a matter as the shapes of alphabetic letters is open to criticism.
Would-be readers who are dyslexic have great trouble with the letters
p, b, q, and *d,* which are identical in shape and differ only in their
orientation. Adopting characters with more contrast would be a great
help for a substantial segment of the population and some help to every
learner.[32]

One of the most interesting ideas on letter shapes comes from
generative phonology, where it has been suggested—at least for analytical purposes—that letters could be designed to indicate distinctive
features, in a style like that of Old Irish oghams: along a vertical line
a position is established for each feature, and a mark—a dot for 'minus'
and a line for 'plus'—indicates whether the feature is absent or present.
So, assigning positions from top to bottom to the features sonorance,

---

[32] Barber 1973.

nasality, voicedness, plosiveness, and coronality, the phonemes /t/ and /n/ will look as follows:[33]

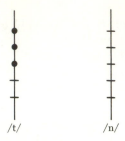

/t/   /n/

    If the past is any guide to the future, it will be events exterior to language that will lead to new experiments in writing, not efforts deliberately directed toward reform except as they may be part of more sweeping economic or political changes. The history of spelling reform in English has been the same as that of other piecemeal reforms where vested interests were at stake (such as Prohibition or truth in advertising): a long record of frustration. Shortly before and after the turn of the century, England and the United States witnessed a vigorous movement toward reform of spelling that enlisted many notable figures, including Charles Darwin, Alfred Lord Tennyson, and, more recently, George Bernard Shaw. For a time it even enjoyed an organization, the Simplified Spelling Board, with a subsidy of $25,000 a year from Andrew Carnegie and the official support of Theodore Roosevelt, who ordered the Government Printing Office to adopt some three hundred revised spellings. But, as H. L. Mencken pointed out, the effort to hasten things "aroused widespread opposition, and in a little while the spelling reform movement was the sport of the national wits."[34] Today one hardly ever hears of it, and spelling reformers are regarded as cranks.

---

[33] From Halle 1969.
[34] Mencken 1936, pp. 399–400.

ADDITIONAL REMARKS AND APPLICATIONS

1. Interpret the following figure, pretending first that you are reading it as a pictogram, then as a word symbol or logogram, then as a syllable symbol or syllabogram. What words might correspond to it as a pictogram? Of what words might it form part if it were a syllabogram?

2. List four letters which are fairly consistent in their phonemic values in English and four which are highly inconsistent. By and large, is it the vowel letters or the consonant letters that are more consistent?

3. List four words which have variant pronunciations in different parts of the United States but have a standard spelling. Writers of stories in dialect sometimes adapt their spellings to local pronunciations; give some examples.

4. Which would be more surprising, for someone to misspell *illegal* as *inlegal* (compare the same prefix in *indirect*) or to misspell *not bad at all* as *not bad a tall*? What does this suggest about our inclination to be swayed by morphemes rather than by sounds when we write?

5. In Chapter 13, pages 441–43, we noted that bifurcations in pronunciation enrich the language with new words. Are there also sometimes bifurcations in spelling, in which a word with more than one meaning comes to be spelled in different ways, though remaining the same in pronunciation? Look up the etymologies of the following pairs: *errant–arrant, crumby–crummy, coin–coign, born–borne.*

6. What has been the net effect of attempts at spelling reform in English? Consider the acceptability of variants like *color–colour, labor–labour, practice–practise, chastize–chastise, catalog–catalogue.*

7. The following sentences are from written sources. Each can be interpreted in two radically different ways. Read them aloud, adding the
unwritten elements (accents or intonations) that will make the
meanings clear:

   a. *Several cities have imported taxicabs propelled by light diesel*
      engines.
      Meanings: 'possess imported taxicabs'; 'have performed the
      action of importing cabs.'

   b. *Physics and biology surely provide basic stuff for the critical*
      mind of the humanist. Only science, to its own misfortune, is
      presently out of bounds for him. (Just the second sentence.)
      Meanings: 'but science'; 'science alone.'

   c. *Teixidor seems to feel that Ramírez himself would never*
      have consented.
      Meanings: 'Ramírez, as far as he himself was concerned'; 'not
      even as important a person as Ramírez.'

8. The following is from a scholarly essay by someone whose native
language was not English. What betrays this?

   By the way, between 1927 and "the sixties" Alejo Carpentier
   became one of the world's distinguished novelists.

9. Are there differences among the parts of speech in the ease with
which the meanings of the words in each of them can be shown by
representational drawing? If so, see if you can scale them for adjectives, verbs, and nouns. Between these three parts of speech on the
one hand and prepositions and conjunctions on the other, which
could be shown better by diagrams?

10. What is the significance of doubling in the signs *ff.* (after a page
number) and *et seqq.?* Identify some other signs that are doubled
for the same purpose and some that are not.

11. Contrast the stage at which a particular sign could be given the
interpretation 'peak, apex, vertex, top, cap, summit' with the stage
at which it could be given the interpretation 'peak, peek, pique,
Peke.'

12. Might the ultimate unintelligibility of pictograms have contributed to
their being interpreted arbitrarily—that is, being taken to stand for
sounds rather than for what they originally pictured? Consider the

development of the Sumerian word for 'hand' from the easily recognizable symbol on the left below to the cuneiform symbol on the right.[35]

Could the opposite also have happened, a loss of the original meaning leading to a carelessness with the form?

13. The units of writing, unlike those of speech, are often the creation of individuals. Consult any good encyclopedia, under *Cherokee* or *Sequoya,* for an account of the Cherokee syllabary (see page 487).

14. Do languages differ in the efficiency with which they can be written in syllables by contrast with distinctive sounds? Consider the variety of syllable types in English. Assume that each syllable (*ta, tab, tack, tam,* and so on) requires a separate and distinct symbol.

15. Long before it was suspected that Linear B might be related to Greek, historical linguists had made certain hypotheses about what an earlier form of Greek might be like. How would such hypotheses be of help in the decipherment? How would a successful decipherment help the hypotheses? (One hypothesis was that, although Classical Greek lacked them, an earlier form of the language must have had labiovelar sounds like the /kw gw/ of Latin **quis, pinguis.** These were found in Linear B.)

16. Young children must be taught to read, and they must also be taught words that they do not already know in their speech. Should these two things be combined in the initial steps of learning to read? Explain.

17. How does your school system teach reading, by the whole-word method, by phonics, or in some other way? Are slow readers a problem? Does your school have a program for teaching rapid reading? What devices are used?

18. If you know a system of shorthand, explain and demonstrate what kind of writing it is.

---

[35] Sturtevant 1947, p. 21.

19. Intending *Basque,* a typist writes *Bask.* Intending *weigh* the same typist writes *weight.* What two contrary tendencies do these misspellings represent?

20. Art Linkletter quoted someone as having written *He's such a good writer that he won the Pullet Surprise.*[36] Comment.

21. See if you can interpret the following sentence; if you have trouble try to decide what causes it. (The sentence *is* interpretable.) Consult the footnote after you have tried your hand:

   What has been said above of the presentations for which such physiological cortical processes lie at the bottom of these complex functions is still more valid of such universal "capacities."[37]

22. Make a list of homonymic pairs or sets such as *troupe–troop, review–revue, plum–plumb, use–ewes–youse–yews, seer–sear–cere–sere–Cyr,* and discuss the advantages and disadvantages of the spellings.

23. A long-established rule of English spelling has been to add a *k* to words ending in a *c* when a suffix starting with *e, i,* or *y* was attached—for example, *panic–panicky–panicking, frolic–frolicked, picnic–picnicking.* Watch for instances subject to this rule and see what is happening.[38]
   Another rule is that the plural of words ending in *-y* should be *-ies.* How do you account for the examples *the two Germanys*[39] and *By 1946 the New York Hootenannys were pretty widely known?*[40]
   Still another rule is that when a suffix starting with a vowel is attached to a word ending in a single consonant with the last syllable stressed (including any one-syllable word), the consonant must be doubled: *pen–penned, grub–grubby, rip–ripping, sic–sicced, revet–revetted, embed–embedded, compel–compelling, deter–deter-*

---

[36] Credited to Linkletter by Leo Rosten, *Rome Wasn't Burned in a Day* (Garden City, N.Y.: Doubleday, 1972), p. 50.

[37] The *which* is interrogative, not relative; in speech it would be marked by a higher pitch. The sentence is from Lenneberg 1973, p. 122.

[38] The following have been observed: *I've bivouaced under the stars* (*Writer's Digest* [April 1943], p. 20); *Democratic farm-blocers* (Los Angeles *Daily News* [16 April 1946], p. 16); *"I'm a Quebecer"* (*Harper's Magazine* [October 1964], p. 95); *crimson-tuniced bandmasters* (Sinclair Lewis, *It Can't Happen Here* [New York: Dell, 1961], p. 100).

[39] *The Nation* (11 November 1961), p. 369.

[40] *Western Folklore* 22 (1963), p. 168.

rent. Look up the forms of the verb *to chagrin* and see how they are spelled. If they violate the rule, could you reformulate it so as to eliminate *chagrin* as an exception? (Suggestion: look at the morphemic make-up.) Will your modified rule take care of all of the following?—*compellable, scrubbable, inferable, inferrible, conferrable, runnable, regrettable, barrable, strippable.* (These spellings are recognized by *Webster's Third New International Dictionary.*)

24. The verbs *to harass* and *to harry* are synonyms but not cognates. If spellings are to reveal underlying relationships, should these words be spelled as they are?

25. A native speaker of a Bantu tongue in Rhodesia was asked, "Does the fact that the tone in your language is not written make any problems when people read it?" He replied, "No, not at all. Everybody learns to read and has no problem." A second question followed: "But don't people sometimes have to read things twice? Once to know what it says and once to read it correctly?" The native speaker hesitated and then exclaimed, "Oh! Is that why we read our own language back and forth? We always say that we read our own language back and forth and back and forth, but that we read English straight along. We can read English in about half the time that it takes to read our own language, but I never knew before why."[41] Is there a possible moral in this for people who "have no trouble" reading English in its present orthography?

26. Discuss the following statement by the linguist Leonard Bloomfield:

Writing is merely a device for recording speech. A person is much the same and looks the same, whether he has ever had his picture taken or not. Only a vain beauty who sits for many photographs and carefully studies them may end by slightly changing her pose and expressions. It is much the same with languages and their written recording.[42]

27. The contemporaries of Saint Augustine in the fifth century A.D. marveled at his ability to read silently to himself, gleaning the sense without so much as moving his lips. How much of the speech process do we actually bypass in comprehending what we read to ourselves? Try to watch yourself as you read silently, to see whether you have any consciousness of sound-images or half-formed vocalizations.

---

[41] Recounted by Gudschinsky 1970, p. 24.
[42] Bloomfield and Barnhart 1961, p. 20.

References

Abercrombie, David. 1965. *Studies in Phonetics and Linguistics* (New York: Oxford University Press).

Barber, E. J. W. 1973. "The Formal Economy of Written Signs," *Visible Language* 7:155–66.

Bloomfield, Leonard, and Clarence L. Barnhart. 1961. *Let's Read: A Linguistic Approach* (Detroit: Wayne State University Press).

Bolinger, Dwight. 1946. "Visual Morphemes," *Language* 22:333–40.

Chadwick, John. 1960. *The Decipherment of Linear B* (London: Cambridge University Press).

———. 1972. "Life in Mycenaean Greece," *Scientific American* 227:4.36–49.

Chomsky, A. N., and Morris Halle. 1968. *The Sound Pattern of English* (New York: Harper & Row).

Gelb, I. J. 1963. *A Study of Writing*, rev. ed. (Chicago: University of Chicago Press).

Gleason, H. A. 1961. *An Introduction to Descriptive Linguistics*, rev. ed. (New York: Holt, Rinehart and Winston).

Gleitman, Lila R., and Paul Rozin. 1973. "Teaching Reading by Use of a Syllabary," *Reading Research Quarterly* 8:447–501.

Gudschinsky, Sarah C. 1970. "More on Formulating Efficient Orthographies," *The Bible Translator* 21:21–25.

Gwyther-Jones, Roy. 1971. "Vernacular Literacy, Bridge to a National Language," *Kivung* 4:161–70.

Haas, William. 1973. *Phono-graphic Translation* (Manchester, England: Manchester University Press).

Halle, Morris. 1969. "How Not to Measure Length of Lexical Representations and Other Matters," *Journal of Linguistics* 5:305–08.

Householder, Fred W., Jr. 1971. *Linguistic Speculations* (Cambridge, England: Cambridge University Press).

Kellogg, David H. 1962. "A History of the Decipherment of Maya Script," *Anthropological Linguistics* 4:1–48.

Lenneberg, Eric H. 1973. "The Neurology of Language," *Daedalus* 102:115–33.

Mattingly, Ignatius G. 1971. "Reading, the Linguistic Process, and Linguistic Awareness." *Haskins Laboratories Status Report on Speech Research* (July–September), 23–34.

——— and James F. Kavanagh. 1972. "The Relationship Between Speech and Reading," *The Linguistic Reporter* 14:5.1–4.

McCawley, James D. 1966. Review of Joseph K. Yamagiwa (ed.), *Papers of the CIC Far Eastern Language Institute* (Ann Arbor: University of Michigan Press, 1964). In *Language* 42:170–75.

Mencken, H. L. 1936. *The American Language*, 4th ed. (New York: Alfred A. Knopf).

Pedersen, Holger. 1962. *The Discovery of Language*, tr. John Webster Spargo (Bloomington: Indiana University Press).

Ray, Punya Sloka. 1962. "The Formation of Prose," *Word* 18:313–25.

Salus, Peter (ed.). 1969. *On Language: Plato to von Humboldt* (New York: Holt, Rinehart and Winston).

Scott, Charles T. 1966. "The Linguistic Basis for the Development of Reading Skill," *Modern Language Journal* 50:535–44.

Sjoberg, Andrée F. 1962. "Coexistent Phonemic Systems in Telugu," *Word* 18:269–79.

Stevick, Robert D. 1967. "Scribal Notation of Prosodic Features in *The Parker Chronicle*, Anno 894 [893]," *Journal of English Linguistics* 1:57–66.

Sturtevant, E. H. 1947. *An Introduction to Linguistic Science* (New Haven: Yale University Press).

Sugathapala de Silva, M. W. 1967. "Effects of Purism on the Evolution of the Written Language: Case History of the Situation in Sinhalese," *Linguistics* 36:5–17.

Tritt, Carleton S. 1973. "The Language of Capitalization in Shakespeare's First Folio," *Visible Language* 7:41–50.

Vachek, Josef. 1973. *Written Language: General Problems and Problems of English* (The Hague: Mouton).

Voegelin, C. F. 1961. "Typological Classification of Systems with Included, Excluded and Self-sufficient Alphabets," *Anthropological Linguistics* 3:55–96.

Yamagiwa, Joseph K. (ed.). 1964. *Papers of the CIC Far Eastern Language Institute* (Ann Arbor: University of Michigan Press).

SCHOOLS AND THEORIES 15

Talk about language is almost as old as language. When language gave the means for awareness of itself (pages 289–90), the resulting self-consciousness grew, first as verbal play and verbal magic, then as verbal philosophy. As for primitive verbal science, it had to wait for the invention of writing. If a specimen is to be studied it has to hold still—speech is too ephemeral. And there has to be a motive if one is to talk about language. This would have come as soon as the first writer of a text looked over what he had written and decided it was good, or corrected it, or threw it away. Editing leads to criticism leads to noting something about structure and rules.

However the first faltering steps may have gone, by about the time of Plato there was already in existence what some linguists of today regard as the best grammar that was ever written: the Sanskrit grammar compiled by Pāṇini. Though it was a detailed description of just one language, it implied general assumptions about sounds and morphemes that could have been made in our own time. Its purpose was practical rather than scientific; Sanskrit had ceased to be a vernacular language and needed to be taught with the aid of textbooks. Nearly all grammars since have been written with a similar purpose—to aid in mastering a second language. The earliest and still one of the best roads to linguistic understanding is through the comparison of one language with another.

As for the Greeks, their tradition was philosophical as well as grammatical. The great educators of the fifth century B.C. were the Sophists, who trained young men in the art of reasoned debate and were forced to do a certain amount of analyzing of the Greek language. Protagoras described the genders and verbal inflections. Later, Aristotle distinguished nouns, verbs, particles, and cases. But what gave the greatest stimulus to grammar in Western Classical times was the cultural adolescence of Rome and its dependence on Greek learning. The school grammar of Dionysius Thrax became popular with these eager learners of Greek and not only served as a model for later grammars but itself continued to be used for over a thousand years. Latin grammars copied the Greek terminology and more or less fixed a number of grammatical classifications that are still in use today.

If comparison on a small scale was the impetus for the first scientific descriptions of individual languages, comparison on a grand scale was what gave rise to linguistics as a science, and it was fitting that the Sanskrit and Greco-Roman traditions came together to bring it about, though the convergence was by hindsight and had to wait till the year 1786. Three years earlier the British poet, linguist, and professional jurist Sir William Jones went to Calcutta as judge of the supreme court. His ambition was to translate Indian legal writings into English so as to make it possible to govern India under its own laws; this forced him to learn Sanskrit as he had already learned Persian, Chinese, and several other languages.[1] As a translator he could not avoid being struck by the similarities between the Western languages that he knew and Sanskrit, and his knowledge of Chinese gave him the picture of what a really dissimilar language was like. The result was his famous "Third Anniversary Discourse" to the Asiatic Society of Bengal, in which he extolled the richness of Sanskrit and pointed out the unmistakable evidence of common origins in spite of geographical distance. Greek, Latin, and Sanskrit were offshoots of the same trunk.

This discovery led to more than a century of intensive historical-comparative work, the nature of which we studied in Chapter 13. It suited the Romantic temperament of the early nineteenth century to be delving into the past, and it also suited the passion for science that followed in the latter half of the century to be using objective evidence to build what would now be called a scientific model, the reconstructed language of the "Aryan" peoples. The Neogrammarians—those advocates of exceptionless laws mentioned earlier (pages 451–53)—were the first modern school of linguistic scientists.

As usually happens when partisans—including scientists—band together, pendulums began to swing. The historicists would have nothing

---

[1] Cannon 1971, p. 419.

to do with "merely" descriptive facts.[2] They turned away from the long tradition of writing textbooks of individual languages on Latin models and speculating about the universal traits of language with little more than Latin and Greek to go on. This was "unscientific," and for lack of scientific defenders it was discredited. Also, for lack of scientific critics, since the scientists merely dismissed and did not criticize, such work as was done in the old tradition during the nineteenth century was colored deeper than ever with the prescriptive bias that had always tinged it. Grammars were not records of what speakers did but models of what speakers, especially schoolboys, ought to do. The flavor of this can be got from the fulminations of a grammarian writing only about a hundred years ago against a construction that was being taken up by everyone, **The bridge was being built,** replacing **The bridge was building:**

> As to the notion of introducing a new and more complex passive form of conjugation, as, "The bridge *is being built,*" . . . it is one of the most absurd and monstrous innovations ever thought of. . . . This is certainly no better English than, "The work *was being published, has been being published, had been being published, shall or will be being published, shall or will have been being published;*" and so on, through all the moods and tenses. What a language shall we have when our verbs are thus conjugated![3]

The nineteenth century was, of course, not completely barren of workers on individual languages besides the textbook grammarians. One remarkable figure at the beginning of the century was the German statesman and philologist Wilhelm von Humboldt, whose insights were sharpened in the same way as those of modern descriptivists, by studying what would now be termed "exotic" languages—in his case, Basque and the Kawi language of Java. But it was not till the end of the century that the pendulum began to swing back. The most noteworthy figure in the return from historicism to description was Ferdinand de Saussure, who taught linguistics at the University of Geneva from 1906 to 1911. Saussure may have been led to his new conceptions by either or both of two other scholars, Georg von der Gabelentz and Hermann Paul,[4] but this is hard to determine because his own main work was not directly written by himself but put together posthumously by his students.[5] In any case Saussure got most of the credit—perhaps because he himself

---

[2] Vachek 1966, p. 16.

[3] Brown 1884, p. 379.

[4] Favored by Coseriu 1967 and Koerner 1972, respectively.

[5] Saussure 1959, p. xiv.

was primarily a historical linguist and his authority could not easily be questioned. He deplored the fanatical absorption with history and predicted that linguistics would have to "turn back to the static viewpoint of traditional grammar but in a new spirit and with other procedures."[6] Saussure envisioned languages as systems in stable equilibrium, but with emphasis on the equilibrium—the integral, self-contained, and seemingly arrested state that any language exhibits at a given period in its history. We have seen how change is necessarily built into the system regardless of where one cuts a cross section, but Saussure's overemphasis on *synchrony* as against *diachrony*[7] was necessary to get things back in balance. A diet of nothing but history was too much.

So now it was history's turn to take the shade. Descriptivism began to dominate the linguistic scene after the First World War and continued to attract the greatest number of young scholars up to the 1970s. The pendulum is poised to swing back, in part because of the slow realization that the present state of a language cannot be described in a vacuum: "We can never truly know what a construction is like today unless we know what it was like yesterday: the direction of its development is a part of its identity."[8] These words were prophetic of the recent work in underlying forms, which so often recapitulate historical developments (see pages 81–82). It would be rash to predict that the pendulum would swing all the way back. The clock itself may well be turned to face in another direction—sociolinguistics, for example, would regard any dispute between historical linguistics and descriptive linguistics as pointless. In that field, "distance" means much the same whether in space or time (page 459).

As twentieth-century linguistics has been almost completely dominated by descriptivism, we must try to grasp it as a whole before examining the separate approaches.

European descriptivism has tended toward the humanistic and literary, American toward the scientific in one guise or another. In an older land, one of rich cultures and varied languages, it was natural for the past to loom larger than it did in a country that was virtually monolingual save for languages with no literary background. In Europe, the scope if not the methods of traditional grammar prevailed. The languages chiefly studied were those that already had at least some history of analysis. Accordingly there was a basis for work at all levels— syntax as well as phonology and morphology.

The first infusion of science in American linguistics was from anthro-

---

[6] Ibid., pp. 82–83.

[7] *Synchrony:* phenomena as they appear at one point in time; *diachrony:* phenomena seen along the time axis. See page 385.

[8] Hatcher 1956, p. 43.

pology. It came in two waves. In the earlier the prime movers were the German-born anthropologist Franz Boas and his student Edward Sapir. Boas early realized that the language of a culture was its most distinctive creation, and while Sapir was a professional linguist in a sense that Boas was not, he too never lost the vision of language as inseparable from culture. To the inspiration of these two men was added the desperation of anthropologists to record American Indian data before it was too late—to find "enough scholars and enough time to accomplish all that needed to be done in a field where the extinction of languages is almost a yearly occurrence."[9] (Sometimes one can even fix the day when a living language dies; for example, the death of the Yahi dialect of the Yana language of California came with that of its last speaker on 25 March 1916.)[10]

It was no easy task that the anthropological linguists cut out for themselves:

> The New World is unique in the number and diversity of its native idioms. There are probably well over one thousand mutually unintelligible American Indian languages, which are customarily grouped into more than one hundred and fifty different families. In California alone, according to Sapir, "there are greater and more numerous linguistic extremes than can be illustrated in all the length and breadth of Europe. Such a group as German, French, Irish, Polish, Lithuanian, Albanian, Greek, Basque, Turkish, Hungarian, Finnish, and Circassian—to list European forms of speech with maximum distinctness—exhibits a lesser gamut of linguistic differences, as regards both phonetic elements and peculiarities of structure, than an equal number of languages that might be selected from among those spoken in California."[11]

It is little wonder that linguists in America were so caught up with the urgency of recording and analyzing native American languages that they had little time or patience for anything else.

The second wave in the growth of anthropological linguistics in the United States came in the early 1930s from religious missionaries. A number of Protestant denominations with extensive missions abroad established the Summer Institute of Linguistics, with two principal aims: the linguistic training of missionaries (originally in summer classes at the University of Oklahoma—hence the name) and the translation of the Bible. Since practically all the languages in question were without an alphabet, one of the first tasks the Institute faced was to "reduce the language to writing." (This is the common phrase, but it should not be

---

[9] Hoijer et al. 1954, p. 3.

[10] The moving story of that last speaker, Ishi, is told in Kroeber 1964.

[11] Hoijer et al. 1954, p. 3.

interpreted to mean that writing takes precedence over speech.) The Summer Institute has carried on a veritable linguistic conquest, for it has moved from small outposts among a few American Indian tribes to an operation that extends from Colombia to New Guinea and enlists the cooperation of government bureaus in twenty or more countries. In 1971 it began the study of its five hundredth language, and had trained more than twelve thousand students. Other religious organizations have been active too—for example, the Toronto Linguistics Institute and the Kennedy School of Missions of the Hartford Seminary Foundation in Connecticut. But the linguistic endeavors of missionaries go back many centuries. After the Spanish conquest of the Americas, the religious orders were charged with educating the Indians, and numerous grammars of Indian languages were written. In South America, the Jesuits even made two of the more generalized Indian languages—Guaraní and Quechua—their medium of instruction.

Linguistics under the influence of anthropology lived in a constant state of emergency. The anthropological linguists based in the universities were driven by the need to record the languages of cultures *in extremis*. The missionary linguists were driven by their calling to spread the Word. Urgency was stepped up to a frenzy when during the Second World War the American armed forces found themselves in the fearful situation of having to govern scores of Pacific enclaves with no one able to speak to the inhabitants, and they turned to the anthropological linguists to get a language program moving. Haste was the order of the day, and the climate of the 1930s and 1940s was wrong for profound reflection and all-encompassing theory.

It was partly the self-image of linguistics as a science that began to cut the ties with anthropology in the 1950s. The archetypal science is one that provides a free interplay between data and theory and does not hesitate to let theory leap ahead if it appears possible for data to catch up later. The anthropological linguists had been parsimonious with theory; they would have found model-building foreign to their methods—the facts should speak for themselves. The reaction when it came was abrupt and heavy with polemics. And for two decades the American scene became a battleground of competing Theories—not theories of this or that aspect of language that could be more or less easily verified, but Theories of the Whole.

It was an attempt that had to be made, bringing all of linguistics into a single tightly articulated deductive system, and it did not start with the Americans. In 1943 the Danish linguist Louis Hjelmslev published his *Prolegomena to a Theory of Language*,[12] expounding views that came to be known as *glossematics*. Hjelmslev's "empirical principle"

---

[12] English translations 1953 and 1961. See Hjelmslev 1961.

makes a good summary of the aims of all comprehensive theorists in linguistics: "The description shall be free of contradiction (self-consistent), exhaustive, and as simple as possible. The requirement of freedom from contradiction takes precedence over the requirement of exhaustive description. The requirement of exhaustive description takes precedence over the requirement of simplicity."[13] The first of the two hedges—the precedence of freedom from contradiction over exhaustive description—gives the linguist a license to shut out inconvenient data. The second hedge allows the description to be somewhat cumbersome in order to accommodate all the non-contradictory data.

Though Hjelmslev was first by right of discovery, it was not till the publication of Noam Chomsky's *Syntactic Structures*[14] in 1958 that theory came into its own. Several of Chomsky's contemporaries were elaborating other systems, some of which we will touch on later. Though these vied for attention, none had a success to match his. But the climax came quickly. By the late 1960s, Chomsky's own movement had split into rival camps. And while the contenders were rending one another, applied linguists were busy with concrete problems, and their work, especially in sociolinguistics and psycholinguistics, was threatening to overshadow that of the theorists. It was not that theory was frontally opposed; to some extent it was embraced, but mainly it was sidestepped. And the newer fields were attracting the recruits. By 1974 it was possible for one observer to say, "We have surely had enough of formalists for a while."[15]

Not every one of the groups to be discussed in this chapter has insisted on an all-encompassing theory. For some, principles and procedures were more important, though a determined theorist could probably find a theory lurking in the background. This tended to be the case with the groups engaged mainly in fieldwork and practical applications—the Firthians in England, the missionaries in the United States, and the American structuralists who taught in special programs for the military. It was also true of the Prague School, but for different reasons. The times were a factor. Theory was not in the wind till the 1950s, and for some groups it came as an afterthought. For others it was meat and drink.

The approaches that follow are more or less in chronological order, but all overlap—that is, each still has its adherents. For two reasons, historical linguistics is not included: first, it was given enough space in Chapter 13; second, in so far as it ever was a "school," its day is past—linguists of all persuasions can be historical linguists today.

---

[13] Hjelmslev 1961, p. 11.
[14] Chomsky 1958.
[15] Gray 1974, p. 12.

TRADITIONAL GRAMMAR

The traditional grammarian is an eclectic. If he has a theoretical preference it is likely to be an unconscious one. He is apt to be an *aficionado* in matters of language rather than a professional, though this at times shows more as an attitude than as any lack of dedication. He tends to view his descriptions as a means rather than an end: to aid in understanding texts, in learning a foreign language, in acquiring a better command of one's own language. (The second and third of these account for the prescriptive and puristic slant of much traditional writing on grammar.) There is no compulsion toward "total accountability"; if the practical aim is satisfied by a partial description, that is as far as it will go. Nor is there any fervent attachment to internal consistency. The arrangement will be for convenience, there is apt to be a certain amount of repetition, and much will be overlooked by way of interconnections and implications. But when the work is a comprehensive one, it will cover a wider range of topics than is possible for any point of view that has to decide beforehand what "is" or "is not" a part of language. English boasts some of the finest traditional grammars in existence. Three of them, all in multi-volume series, were published between 1909 and 1940. They are Otto Jespersen's *Modern English Grammar on Historical Principles,*[16] E. Kruisinga's *Handbook of Present-day English,*[17] and H. Poutsma's *Grammar of Late Modern English.*[18] As if to emphasize what was just said about the practical aim of most traditionalists, no one of these three authors was a native speaker of English and all aimed their grammars at least partly at foreign students. The earlier grammar of Henry Sweet[19] and the more recent one of George O. Curme[20] deserve mention, though they are less comprehensive. All those mentioned are descriptive rather than normative; Curme said pointedly that "any attempt to check the development of the language and give it a fixed, permanent form is misdirected energy."[21] The most recent English grammars that can be called traditional are those of Ralph and Dorothy Long, *The System of English Grammar,*[22] and Randolph Quirk et al., *A Grammar of Contemporary English.*[23] The Longs make no bones of their tra-

---

[16] Jespersen 1909–40.

[17] Kruisinga 1931–32.

[18] Poutsma 1914–29.

[19] Sweet 1898–1900.

[20] Curme 1931–35.

[21] Ibid., Part III, p. vii.

[22] Long 1971.

[23] Quirk, Greenbaum, Leech, and Svartvik 1972.

ditionalism: "The analysis presented in this book is traditional in procedure, terminology, and spirit."[24] The authors are skilled critics of the
contemporary scene who have exploited its findings but rejected its
biases. The Quirk grammar is on a scale comparable to those of Jespersen, Poutsma, and Kruisinga, and is the first to make use of a scientifically collected and vastly comprehensive corpus. The authors state
their independence: "We subscribe to no specific one of the current or
recently formulated linguistic theories."[25] At the same time they have
managed to take advantage of whatever insights those theories had to
offer.

Saussure's condemnation of traditional grammar makes it clear that
he was not speaking of the works mentioned in the last paragraph: "Traditional grammar neglects whole parts of language, such as word-formation; it is normative and assumes the role of prescribing rules, not of
recording facts; it lacks overall perspective; often it is unable to separate
the written from the spoken word. . . ."[26] What the up-to-date traditional grammars have done is to eliminate the law-giving tone of the
older works and to take full account of actual usage. But whether
normative or descriptive, the traditional grammar carries no burden of
explicit theory, and that justifies a common label for all its subspecies.

THE PRAGUE SCHOOL[27]

The Linguistic Circle of Prague was founded in 1926 by Vilém Mathe-
sius, who was a professor of English at Caroline University. The majority
of its members have been specialists in Slavic languages, English, and
to some extent Romance languages, which accounts for the humanistic
rather than anthropological cast of its research. No other European group
has wielded quite as much influence as this one. The Pragueans never
attempted to circumscribe the field of linguistics—no formal-deductive
system has emerged from their deliberations—but they produced a set
of principles that were pretty generally agreed upon by members of the
group and have been widely accepted elsewhere.

One of the earliest principles was that of the separation of phonetics
and phonology. The two were seen as complementary, but as having
different aims: phonetics studies the physics and physiology of sounds,
phonology looks at the function of sounds within a system, their pure

---

[24] Long 1971, p. v.

[25] Quirk, Greenbaum, Leech, and Svartvik 1972, p. vi.

[26] Saussure 1959, p. 82.

[27] This section largely follows Vachek 1966.

difference for the sake of being different. This separation is still regarded as fundamental by most linguists, and of course is essential to
the concept of the phoneme, which was in large measure another accomplishment of the Prague School. The analysis of the phoneme into
distinctive features is an even more direct product; it was formulated
by Roman Jakobson for a Czech encyclopedia in 1932.[28] The "minimal
pairs" test (pages 61–62) for establishing phonemes was first systematically applied by the Pragueans. They also developed the notion of "functional load"—the degree to which a language system utilizes a certain
contrast (for example, we saw earlier that the functional load of the
/a/–/ɔ/ contrast is so light, relatively speaking, that the two phonemes
are merging: *taught–tot, caught–cot*—see page 74).

The Prague group has influenced every important development in the
United States. For the American structuralists (see pages 517–20), the
point of contact was the phoneme. Though the approaches were different (the Americans tried to define the phoneme without recourse to
meaning; the Pragueans were not so puristic), the fundamental concept
was the same. Later, and especially with the advent of transformational-
generative grammar, the Praguean concepts of distinctive features,
markedness, underlying forms, and functional sentence perspective were
embraced one by one.

Distinctive features have already been mentioned, but it needs to
be added that "binarity" was also a Prague idea. Table 4–1 (page 79),
where the phonemes are specified by plusses and minuses applied to each
feature, illustrates this principle; when we say that "/t/ is minus-voiced" we
are saying that the feature of voice is absent. In terms of voice—or any
other feature—each phoneme can be described as either having it or
not having it. Binarity is what makes a grid of that kind possible. (See
also the grammatical features discussed in Chapter 6, page 156).

Markedness is a way of expressing the amount of information that is
coded in a form. The phoneme /d/ has one more plus value than /t/
has: it is voiced, /t/ is not. So in the phoneme pair /t/–/d/, /t/ is the
unmarked member, /d/ the marked member. It is not necessarily the
case that the unmarked member always *lacks* the phonic quality that
distinguishes the marked member; it may simply be indifferent to it.
Thus one could argue that in the word *gingham* the /ŋ/ is the marked
member in the contrasting phonemic pair /n/–/ŋ/, because its velarity
is essential (*It's a gingham* contrasts with *It's agin' 'em*); but in **ten
goals** there is an /n/ that may indifferently have the velar quality or
not—there is no contrast. This shows up more clearly in morphology
and semantics, where we find certain morphemes or words that are indifferent to a feature which may be vital to a companion morpheme or

---

[28] Vachek 1966, p. 46.

word. For example, *cat* is indifferent to 'male' or 'female,' whereas both *tom* and *tabby* have the sex of the cat as a marked feature. An even more complex manifestation is the one in which a word is normally unmarked but is defined by the situation as marked. An example is the word *goose.* In *That's a goose, not a chicken,* the word *goose* is unmarked for sex; in *That's a goose, not a gander, goose* is marked as 'female.'[29]

Related to markedness is the paired concept of "center" and "periphery." Linguistic categories are seen not as sharply defined sets but as agglomerations in which members at the center unmistakably belong but those farther out are less and less clearly within the family. The influence of this concept can be seen in a number of things mentioned in earlier chapters—for example, the notion of "more nouny" and "less nouny" (pages 244–45).

While the term "underlying form" does not derive from the Prague group, the basic principle does. The *morphophoneme* (or *morphoneme,* as the Pragueans sensibly abbreviate it) was a Prague concept by 1929. In English *keep* and *kept,* for example, there are what would be termed today two surface vowel phonemes but only one underlying morphophoneme.

The idea of functional sentence perspective identifies the Pragueans with an analysis of the sentence that was described on pages 154–55. Three ways of viewing sentences were mentioned there: grammatical, psychological, and logical. Functional sentence perspective takes the psychological view. In a sentence such as *Friends like him I don't need,* the grammatical subject is *I,* but the psychological subject—the *topic* about which the *comment* is made—is *friends like him.* (The Pragueans prefer the terms *theme* and *rheme* for *topic* and *comment.*) Functional sentence perspective is the study of how information is presented in the sentence, the relative semantic loading of theme and rheme and their parts.

A further seminal idea that has to be credited to the Pragueans, specifically to Sergeij Karcevskij, is that of the "something-like" principle explained on pages 208–11. Karcevskij put it this way: "Every time we apply a word . . . we transpose its semantic value."[30] It is in the nature of language for the relationship between form and meaning to be skewed. Old forms are used in new ways, never quite the same as before.

The Pragueans are notable for not mounting a single theoretical horse and riding it till it drops. Their openness is probably due in part to their functioning as a community of scholars rather than as a community of disciples.

---

[29] Markedness is studied as a language universal in Greenberg 1966.

[30] Karcevskij 1929. See Vachek 1964, p. 85.

AMERICAN STRUCTURALISM

The Pragueans regarded themselves as structuralists—that is, as advocates of the view that language is a structure with levels and interrelated parts, not an unanalyzable continuum nor a miscellaneous heap. In this sense nearly all of contemporary linguistics is structuralist; but the term has become identified with the group that first gave it prominence in America, chiefly the followers of Leonard Bloomfield from the late 1930s on.

Bloomfield was a Germanist who gave up European-style philology and became one of the early converts to the American Indianist movement fathered by Franz Boas. His first introductory text on language, published in 1914, was partially based on the psychology of Wilhelm Wundt; but with his abandonment of philology went also a rejection of any psychological starting point for describing language. He became an expert in the Algonkian family of languages in North America and, in common with other Indianists, who had to seek their data from informants rather than books, he believed that the most important thing was the material evidence in live speech. How he felt about writing we have already seen (page 503). Though he disavowed psychology, his attention to speech behavior and his anti-mentalism attracted him to behaviorism. His own viewpoint was mechanistic, which he believed was "the necessary form of scientific discourse."[31] His view of linguistics was broad enough to include those things that others felt had to be explained by recourse to mind, but he had a sense of the priorities: it was necessary first to study what could be described with the most certainty and precision. Correct usage, for example, was one of the things that would have to wait. He said of such questions as whether *ain't* is bad and *am not* is good: "This is only one of the problems of linguistics, and since it is not a fundamental one, it can be attacked only after many other things are known."[32]

Bloomfield influenced a generation of linguists both through his teaching and through his introductory textbook *Language* (1933). Even those who came after and felt they were repudiating him may have been most influenced by him because his primary intention was to make linguistics a science, and while the changing conceptions of science may have altered the approach they did not alter the goal.

Unlike the comparatively easygoing Pragueans, the American structuralists were determined to have a comprehensive and self-contained system. But they accepted Bloomfield's principle of first things first. Anything that could not be dealt with objectively had to be postponed.

---

[31] Bloomfield 1933, p. vii.
[32] Ibid., p. 22.

And "objectively" meant "physically manifested." Since speech sounds are the phenomena most accessible to direct observation, they naturally got the most attention. Language was split into levels, each higher level depending on the one below. Until the lower floors were put in order, the upper ones were not to be entered. The result was that in their theoretical work the structuralists gave great attention to phonology, a fair amount to morphology, very little to syntax, and practically none to meaning. Viewing the levels of language as uni-directionally dependent rather than interdependent made it impossible for them to see that it is no more feasible to describe the phonemes of a language without reference to the morphemes than to describe the morphemes without reference to the phonemes. A vast labor and ingenuity was expended in demonstrating, for example, that phonemes could be defined without any reference to meaning, merely by testing how sounds are distributed in an utterance; that is, one did not resort as the Pragueans did to saying that /m/ and /n/ are different phonemes because **sum** and **sun** have different meanings, but instead took account of the environments in which segments did or did not occur, in order to identify them.[33] The passion for using distribution and nothing else was such that it was even proposed to ignore the natural similarity among allophones when classing them into phonemes. For example, the sound [h] is always syllable-initial in English and the sound [ŋ] always syllable-final. What more logical then than to classify them as members of the same phoneme, since they were in complementary distribution and never contrasted? If a word had the sequence of sounds represented by [hæt] we could if we liked transcribe the initial phoneme as /ŋ/; its position would define it as [h]. This conception of identity was revealed by Jerry Lewis in an interview with Steve Allen: "I'm Kathryn Hepburn. How do you know I'm not? Did you ever see us together?"

The field work that almost every structuralist did as part of his apprenticeship reinforced the dogma of never "mixing levels." If you confront a language that you already know, as the Pragueans did, you can make your point of entry at any level. If you confront one that you not only do not know but that seems to be totally unlike any you have ever met before, such as an American Indian language, it will be all you can do to sort out the phonological signals. You will of course use everything you can lay hold of to make the identification, but there will be very little besides the sound-system and the most important morphological characteristics that you can describe scientifically for a long time. This was the common experience of young linguists in the field, including the missionaries whose main concern was to bring the Bible to language communities that had no writing system. As soon as the phonemes were

---

[33] Bloch 1948.

isolated, an alphabet could be set up and the biggest part of the linguistic job was done. What was left after the associations between the written symbols and the distinctive sounds had been established was less imperative, because the previously illiterate native speaker knew the syntax of his language and could unscramble a written sentence like *NobodyknowsthetroubleIseen* even if the linguist knew so little beyond the phonemes that he omitted the spaces.

Even historical linguistics helped to weight the scales—the great triumphs there had been in the laws of sound. Phonetics too: the field of electroacoustics was opened to analytical and experimental phonetics in the 1940s, and the way was at last clear to getting visual representations of ephemeral frequencies in the air.

A natural consequence, reinforced by habit and success, was that when things other than phonemes were tackled, phonemes still provided the model. They were the stuff of morphemes, they had been stunningly proved, and they were audible signaling units that could be isolated from the stream of sound; so perhaps other audible units could be found that would turn out to be the means of delimiting words—were there "-emes" of pause or stress that did this? For example, in a language where stress occupied a fixed position in a word, it would be possible to locate the word boundaries by counting syllables to the right or left of the stress. At the highest level, were there other "-emes" of rhythm or pitch that marked the beginning or end of clauses and sentences? Just enough evidence of this sort of thing did turn up to encourage the hope that the whole pattern would one day come clear, and we could speak as securely of the "sound" of a sentence or of a word as we can now relate sounds to phonemes. If this was ever more than a hope, it was abandoned almost before the search began, as aggressive younger doctrines gained hold and shamelessly mixed all the levels into one stew.

In morphology and syntax the structuralist style of analysis followed the one used with phonemes: it was a technique of *segmentation* and classification of segments. The distinctive sounds occur one after another in a stream of time; although there was admittedly a certain amount of simultaneity (intonation, for example, is overlaid on the segmental phonemes) and also a good deal of overlapping (as when a [t] and a [y] together produce a [č]), essentially the phonemes were viewed like beads on a string. So it was natural for words and sentences to be seen in the same way. The dividing of sentences into their linear constituents, with the hierarchy of immediate constituents, treated in Chapter 6 (pages 139–42), typified the structuralist approach to syntax. As for words, they too were chopped up from end to end, into their constituent morphemes. The word *them,* for example, was assumed to have an "objective" element *-m* also present in *him* and *whom.* As this analysis did nothing for *her* and *us* and not much for *me,* it was an open invitation to the sharp-eyed critics who later came on the scene and insisted that such "superficial" manifestations were not to be taken seriously; *them, her, us,* and the lot should be viewed as divisible only at a deeper level. But segmentation itself lives on, give or take a level or two. It is still pursued in syntax, and even in morphology it makes better sense in some languages than in others—agglutinative languages, for example (see page 28).

TAGMEMICS

We have already met the Summer Institute of Linguistics. Its theoretical position is an offshoot of American structuralism, but it early dissociated itself from certain of the doctrinaire precepts such as the non-mixing of levels,[34] and it has gone on developing at a time when the orthodox line could be pronounced virtually dead. The central figure in tagmemics is Kenneth Lee Pike, an ordained minister who has produced a number of devotional works besides his analytical studies, the latter culminating in a comprehensive theoretical work, *Language in Relation to a Unified Theory of Human Behavior,*[35] which portrayed all of human activity as patterned in much the same way as language, a point of view that developed quite naturally from the anthropological ties of American structuralism. (A recent exercise in this kind of relationship draws an analogy between language and a circus.[36]) Pike's work has been extended by another Summer Institute theorist, Robert E. Longacre, who has accommodated it to some extent with the viewpoints of transformational generative grammar.

Tagmemics[37] uses two main descriptive devices in its analysis of behavior, including linguistic behavior. The first makes the distinction between *etic* and *emic,* which Pike extended from phonology (taking the endings of *phonetics* and *phonemics* to name his terms) and applied universally: an emic unit is a formal unit within a closed system; an etic unit is a material manifestation that can be identified by any characteristic that strikes the eye. Thus we can speak of the segment [t] that is encountered in most of the languages of the world and has certain common traits of sound. That would be an etic unit, since it

---

[34] Pike 1947.

[35] Pike 1967.

[36] Bouissac 1970.

[37] The descriptive portion of this section is largely based on Sroka 1972 and Longacre 1971.

FIGURE 15-1
A Tagmemic Diagram

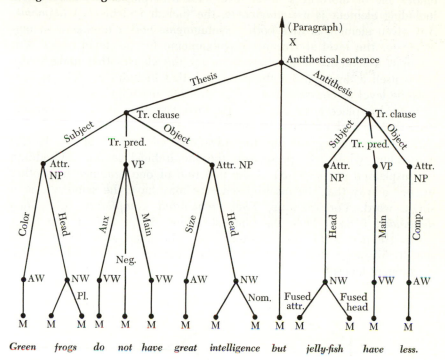

SOURCE: Adapted from Longacre 1971, p. 175.

is being described impressionistically and not assigned as part of the system of contrasts in any one language. We can also speak of the /t/ phoneme in English, which has particular allophones in particular environments. That is an emic unit.

The second descriptive device is the tagmemic hierarchy. Figure 15–1 portrays the grammar of the sentence **Green frogs do not have great intelligence but jelly-fish have less.** It starts with the zero level of morphemes (M) and moves up through the word level (AW = 'adjective word,' NW = 'noun word,' VW = 'verb word'), the phrase level, the clause level, and the sentence level.[38] The elements from level to level are related by

---

[38] Key to abbreviations in Figures 15–1 and 15–2 other than those already explained: Pred. 'predicate'; Attr. 'attributive'; Nom. 'nominalizer'; Comp. 'complement'; Aux. 'auxiliary'; Pr. W 'pronoun word'; Instr. 'instrumental' (in Figure 15–2, heads coming up is the instrument whereby one wins); Tr. 'transitive' (**win** implies an object even though none is mentioned); Mod. 'modifier'; Poss. 'possessive'; Pl. 'plural.'

inclusion—that is, one at a higher level (for example, a sentence) includes one or more at a lower level (for example, two clauses). The
including element is a *syntagmeme,* the included element a *tagmeme.*
Any given element is thus both a syntagmeme and a tagmeme—a tagmeme for the level above and a syntagmeme for the level below. For
example, a sentence is a syntagmeme for the clauses that make it up,
but is itself a tagmeme for the paragraph that includes it. (The highest
possible level of course is not a tagmeme for anything else, since there
is no further place to go; similarly the lowest level is not a syntagmeme,
since there is nothing that it includes.)

A tagmemic diagram has the advantage of being able to handle
embedding while still preserving the hierarchical levels. Embedding
was explained on page 153 as the insertion of one sentence in another
in such a way that the inserted sentence may have the same role as a
single word. For example, **They demanded compliance** and **They
demanded I do it,** have the same structure except that in the latter
a sub-sentence, **I do it,** is inserted where the noun goes. But this has
the disadvantage that it puts the main sentence and the sub-sentence
on different levels:

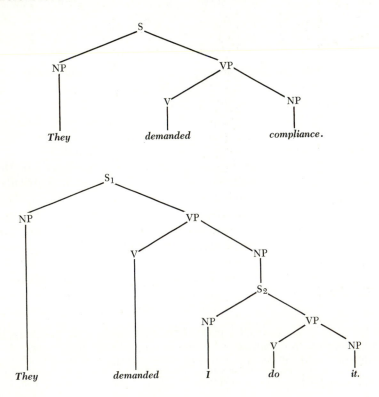

FIGURE 15–2
A Tagmemic Diagram with Looping of Embedded Sentences

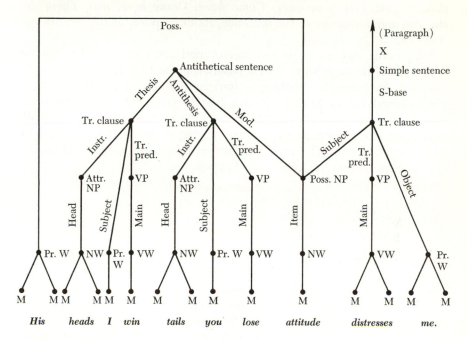

SOURCE: Adapted from Longacre 1971, p. 183.

That is all right as far as showing the inner structure of the whole complex sentence is concerned, but not if one wants to keep one typical level of structure visually distinct from another typical level in the diagram—sentences from phrases, phrases from words, and so on. By "looping," as shown in Figure 15–2 for the sentence *His heads I win tails you lose attitude distresses me,* the inner structure can be shown and at the same time sentences stay at one level, clauses at another, and so on. This is to say that a sentence is a sentence, whether it serves as a tagmeme for a paragraph or as a tagmeme for another sentence.

The hierarchy of levels shown in the diagrams implies a whole apparatus of analysis and definition which cannot be gone into here. Antithetical sentences must be distinguished from other types of sentences, main verbs from auxiliaries, subjects from objects, and so forth. And each of these must be described in terms of its variants. For example, a sentence as a syntagmeme must contain a subject and a predicate, which are its "feature mode" description, the component features it must have as an emic unit. But the features can change or be moved around—for instance, the command *You come here!* can take three forms: *You come here; Come here; Come here, you.* These are the etic manifestations of the sentence, its description in the "manifestation mode."

Supposedly any more or less stereotyped form of behavior can be analyzed in the same way, from a baseball game to a church service. In baseball, for example, "striking a foul ball" has two features: hitting the ball and failing to drive it in a line between third and first base. But it has numerous manifestations, including merely ticking the ball, driving it straight up in the air, or driving it to the left of third or to the right of first. The emic description tells *what* a foul ball is; the etic description tells the *ways* it can happen.

THE FIRTHIANS

The great stimulus to contemporary descriptive work came, in Britain as in America, from anthropology. The British counterpart of Franz Boas was Bronislaw Malinowski, whose field work among the Melanesians prepared him for linguistics as Boas was prepared by his work among the American Indians.[39] Among those who took part in Malinowski's seminars at the University of London was J. R. Firth, who developed Malinowski's later ideas about language and became the teacher of many of Britain's contemporary linguists. His position in Britain is like that of Bloomfield in America, and for similar reasons both gave their names to more or less coherent schools of thought. Likewise similarly, both were strongly behaviorist and anti-mentalist.

What strikes the reader accustomed to "pure" linguistics is the heavy social orientation not only of Malinowski—where it is to be expected, since he was a social anthropologist—but of Firth and his followers. They rejected introverted linguistics and have insisted on dealing with whole contexts, even in phonology. This distinguishes them not only from Bloomfield but also from his rebellious heirs, the generativists (excepting some of *their* rebellious heirs), and brings them close to sociolinguistics as it is practiced today in the United States. In fact, a British sociolinguist, Basil Bernstein, was a strong influence on the American trends. In addition it was Malinowski who conceived the notion of *phatic communion,* now generally accepted among sociolinguists: it holds that much of what passes for communication is rather

---

[39] The comments on Malinowski are based on Langendoen 1968.

the equivalent of a handclasp or an embrace; its purpose is sociability; as some have put it more recently, it is a way of "keeping the channels open" even when no information travels through.

Malinowski's early conception of society resembled Pike's in drawing a comparison between society and language: "In every act of tribal life, there is, first, the routine prescribed by custom and tradition, then there is the manner in which it is carried out, and lastly there is the commentary to it, contained in the natives' mind."[40] Substitute *emic* for *custom* and *etic* for *manner,* and you have Pike's vision of both society and language. (Or substitute *competence* and *performance* and you have the related dichotomy of Chomsky. One way or another, the human mind is fated to set up essences, underlying reality, and ideas in the mind of God on the one hand; and accidents, phenomena, manifestations, appearances, and shadows on the other.)

Malinowski's thinking naturally paralleled that of other linguists of his time and in some ways anticipated later thinking. His notion of meaning as a skewed relationship between sound and sense resembles that of Karcevskij referred to above: "If a word is used in a different context it cannot have the same meaning."[41] Like the psychologists Piaget and Osgood in our own day, he felt that children acquire language as a mode of action.[42] And he saw word classes as reflections of concrete experience, much as they have been described in this book (page 149).

Though Firth was a linguist by profession, which Malinowski was not, he was too deeply imbued with the spirit of British empiricism ever to shut out the rest of the world and evolve a theoretical system as self-sufficient as that of Hjelmslev or the other compactly designed schemes outlined later in this chapter. He felt toward language as he did toward human behavior in general: it

> is much more heterogeneous and disconnected than most of us would care to admit. We have, for instance, as many "sub-sets" as there are special systems of behaviour, special "sets" of social attitudes linked up with specialized languages. A man may have a bundle of assorted "sets," he may be at times a local peasant villager, at other times all the "set" of what is loosely called the educated class may take the stage.[43]

These words written in 1937 are closer to the heart of sociolinguistic

---

[40] Langendoen 1968, p. 13.
[41] Ibid., p. 31.
[42] Ibid., p. 26.
[43] Firth 1966, p. 92.

interests today than to any of the theoretical preoccupations between then and now.

Firth's conception of meaning, too, was social and behavioral. "Words become part of habitual action, and the only meanings they can have are the behaviour patterns, of which they are the co-ordinating function." Words refer to things and situations, of course, but in addition to this "directive reference" the meaning of a spoken word involves at least three additional things: attitudes toward the reference, attitudes toward the person addressed, and the purpose of the utterance; and these stand against a background of "the habitual verbalizations of the group." Firth rejected the attempt to analyze meaning strictly within the language system. To say that an imperative contains an "understood" *you* subject, for example, was for him an unsound analysis. The *you* is present in the situation and does not need to be duplicated in the utterance, since word and situation are part of a continuous whole; but if it is duplicated, there is a purpose: **Wait** and **You wait** are different sentences. "The use of such terms as 'contraction,' 'mutilation,' 'ellipsis' in describing normal speech habits is unscientific and unnecessary"—they presume an artificial standard in which forms are not contracted, not mutilated, and not elided.[44]

Unable or unwilling to abstract from the totality, Firth emphasized the whole, never the part. Though he made room for the atom in both his syntax and his phonology, it was always referred to the larger unit that contained it. In syntax his contribution was the notion of *collocations* that was explained in Chapter 5 (pages 99–107). In phonology he developed the concept of *prosodies*, not as the term relates to the structure of verse (or, more specifically, in linguistics, to such things as rhythm and intonation—see pages 46–52), but as a way of viewing units larger than the phoneme. He disliked the atomism of the phonemics of his time, and proposed instead to characterize units at least as large as the syllable. For example, to the phonemicist the phrase **Roman Meal** is a sequence of eight phonemes each of which is unique and has to be described separately—the initial /r/ segment is "voiced, apical, retroflex," the /o/ segment is "voiced, vocalic, mid, rounded," the /m/ is "voiced, bilabial, nasal," and so on. When we have finished this description we find that we have repeated the word "voiced" eight times. Either "voiced" is meaningless—that is, automatically conditioned by something or other and hence useless in distinguishing one phoneme from another—or it needs to be mentioned just once. It is a property that can be assigned to a sequence rather than (like bilabiality or apicality) phoneme by phoneme. Instead of reducing all units to some

---

[44] Ibid., pp. 174–77.

common denominator of length (such as the phoneme), Firth wanted to fit the levels of description to what he saw as the full-blown elements being described.[45]

Of the two concepts, prosody and collocation, the latter has proved the more fruitful. This may reflect the degree of compactness and arbitrariness of the levels that each attempts to describe. Atomization is appropriate to meaningless sub-units, and the phoneme has had the widest acceptance of any abstract unit in linguistics. So hardly anyone except those directly influenced by Firth has used prosodic analysis in the actual description of a language. But the notion of collocations is indispensable for tying meaning to form and in describing how children learn language.

Among those loosely regarded as followers of Firth (and called neo-Firthians) is a group that has attempted to do what Firth shunned: to set up a tightly integrated theory. The leading figure is M. A. K. Halliday, and his *systemic grammar* deserves attention in its own right.

The term *systemic* comes from the chief structural assumption of the theory, which is that a language consists of a network of systems. A system is defined as "a small number (usually two or three) of classes in contrast with one another."[46] For example, English has a class of clauses that are called "main" and another called "subordinate." The two are in contrast, and therefore constitute a system. If a structure in English is identified as a clause, that is the "entry condition" to the main-and-subordinate system: since the entry condition is satisfied, one of the alternatives in the system has to be chosen. This is merely to say that if we call something a "clause" we are obliged, in the next step, to choose either "main" or "subordinate." Suppose we choose "main." That becomes the entry condition to a lower (finer, "more delicate") system, which comprises the classes of main clauses that are in contrast with one another; these happen to be three: "declarative," "interrogative," and "imperative." The fact that making a choice in one system constitutes the entry condition into a lower system, and that one in turn the entry condition to a still lower system, and so on into

---

[45] See Hill 1966. Prosodic analysis is similar to the "long component" analysis proposed by Z. S. Harris; see Langendoen 1968, pp. 54–56. Rather than the **Roman Meal** example, we could choose one such as the sequence [ŋk], which shows how prosodic analysis handles "conditioning": the feature "velarity" covers both the nasal and the stop, and accordingly characterizes the sequence, not each individual phoneme in turn.

[46] Hudson 1972, p. 0.5. Halliday's own definition is typical of the many in linguistics that seem designed to frighten off the uninitiated: "A system is a set of features one, and only one, of which must be selected if the entry condition to that system is satisfied; any selection of features formed from a given system network constitutes the 'systemic description' of a class of items" (Halliday 1967, p. 37). Most of the discussion here is based on Hudson.

FIGURE 15–3
Conventions of the Systemic Method of Diagramming

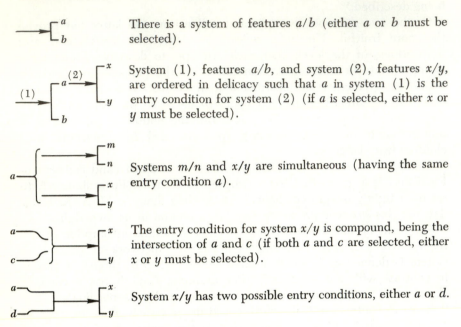

There is a system of features a/b (either a or b must be selected).

System (1), features a/b, and system (2), features x/y, are ordered in delicacy such that a in system (1) is the entry condition for system (2) (if a is selected, either x or y must be selected).

Systems m/n and x/y are simultaneous (having the same entry condition a).

The entry condition for system x/y is compound, being the intersection of a and c (if both a and c are selected, either x or y must be selected).

System x/y has two possible entry conditions, either a or d.

SOURCE: Adapted from Halliday 1967, p. 38. © 1967 Cambridge University Press.

finer and finer classes, is what gives the name *network* to the whole scheme. Figure 15–3 shows the main notational conventions (they are easier to understand if *class* is substituted for *feature*). The clause network can be used as an illustration if it is filled in a little more. Besides "main" and "subordinate," clauses are also either "active" or "passive," and either "positive" or "negative." There is thus an active–passive system to which "clause" is the entry condition, and a positive–negative system, in addition to the main–subordinate system. Elaborating a little further we get Figure 15–4. Included in the illustration is the "compound" condition negative plus interrogative: this combination is the entry condition to the conducive–plain system—that is, if a clause is both negative and interrogative, it must be either conducive or plain. An example of a conducive question is the remark **Isn't it sweet?** referring to the song of a bird—the speaker expects a "yes" answer. An example of a plain negative question is **Isn't it sweet?** in response to someone who has said **I don't like this lemonade.** The question is neutral

FIGURE 15–4
A Systemic Diagram of the Clause, with Key to the Diagramming of Some Specific Clauses

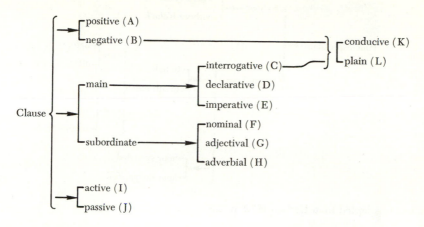

ACI *Do they eat?*	BDJ *They aren't eaten.*
ACJ *Are they eaten?*	BEI *Don't eat.*
ADI *They eat.*	BEJ *Don't be eaten.*
ADJ *They are eaten.*	BFI *(I know) that they don't eat.*
AEI *Eat.*	BFJ *(I know) that they aren't eaten.*
AEJ *Be eaten.*	BGI *(I discard the food) that they don't eat.*
AFI *(I know) that they eat.*	
AFJ *(I know) that they are eaten.*	BGJ *(I discard the food) that isn't eaten.*
AGI *(I bring the food) that they eat.*	BHI *(They're hungry) when they don't eat.*
AGJ *(I bring the food) that is eaten.*	BHJ *(They're thrown away) when they aren't eaten.*
AHI *(They wash) before they eat.*	K *Don't they eat?*
AHJ *(They are washed) before they are eaten.*	L *Don't they eat?*
BDI *They don't eat.*	*Do they not eat?*

SOURCE: Adapted from Hudson 1972, p. 1.5.

as to a "yes" or a "no" answer—it means 'Is the trouble the fact that it is not sweet?'[47]

An illustration of how a system network can describe compactly a set of syntactic structures is that of the classes of time expressions in

---

[47] Some speakers prefer *Is it not sweet?* for the latter meaning.

FIGURE 15–5
A Systemic Diagram of Time Expressions in English

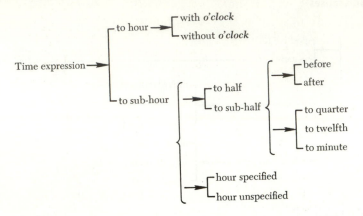

SOURCE: Adapted from Hudson 1972, p. 2.5.

English, as shown in Figure 15–5. It accurately characterizes the following, among an indefinitely large number of others:

1. Is it six yet?

2. I think it's about half past.

3. It was five after ten.

4. He got there at eight minutes before twelve.

5. *He got there at eight before twelve.

6. *It was half past ten o'clock.

Sentence number 1 is correct because if we go "to hour" we can choose
"without *o'clock*." Number 2 is correct because if we go "to sub-hour"
we can also go "to hour unspecified," and if "to half" is chosen, *past*
is automatic. Number 3 is correct because if we go "to sub-hour" and
then "to sub-half" and then "to twelfth" (= any twelfth part of the
hour, which means any multiple of five) we do not need to specify
minutes. Number 4 is correct and Number 5 is incorrect because if the
minute period is not a twelfth fraction of the hour, *minutes* has to be
added.[48] Number 6 is incorrect because if we go "to sub-hour" and then

---

[48] The rule for adding *minute* is a later step—a "realization" or "structure-building"
rule. All that the system network tells us is that something different has to be
done when the last choice is "minute" rather than "twelfth" or "quarter."

"to half" there is no "with *o'clock*" alternative—that comes only with the entry condition "to hour."

As the illustrations show, systemic grammar is an elaborate classification system that does not require a level of deep structure in syntax; it posits "a *single* structure that gives both 'deep' and 'surface' information about the sentence."[49] There is more to the apparatus than has been outlined here, of course, notably the "realization" rules that convert features to sentences. It is not enough to know that an item is a clause and subordinate and adjectival; we have to know also how to construct an adjective clause, including such things as relatives and their realization as *who, which,* and so forth.

STRATIFICATIONAL GRAMMAR[50]

There is a certain resemblance between stratificational grammar and systemic grammar. Both use networks and realization rules. Both are static systems—that is, they do not find it necessary to "derive" one layer of structure from another; it suffices to *relate* them. But there is also a close affinity between stratificational grammar and tagmemics, in the insistence on separate strata corresponding to the traditional levels of phonology, morphology, syntax, and semantics.

The central figure of stratificational grammar is Sydney M. Lamb, whose *Outline of Stratificational Grammar* first appeared in 1962.[51] While his practical interests are like those of Pike and other American structuralists, his theoretical debt, by his own acknowledgment, is to the Danish theoretician Louis Hjelmslev.[52] Like Hjelmslev, he views language as a system of relationships, not of entities or substances. There are not *things* in relation to one another as most other schemes visualize the linguistic universe, but relations that are related. A linguistic element is what it is by virtue of what it is connected to.[53]

Being a static system, stratificational grammar avoids what it criticizes as the "mutation rules" of transformational generative grammar; rather than arrows ("*x* gives *y*," to show equivalence or derivation) there are

---

[49] Hudson 1972, p. 0.4.

[50] This section is based chiefly on Lamb 1974. Professor Lamb kindly verified certain points but is not responsible for the sketchiness or possible deficiencies.

[51] Lamb 1966 (2).

[52] Hjelmslev's own Copenhagen School—that of "glossematics"—is not treated here, but an excellent appreciation can be found in Lamb 1966 (1).

[53] Lamb 1974, p. 198.

FIGURE 15–6
Types of Connections in the Relational Network of Stratificational Linguistics

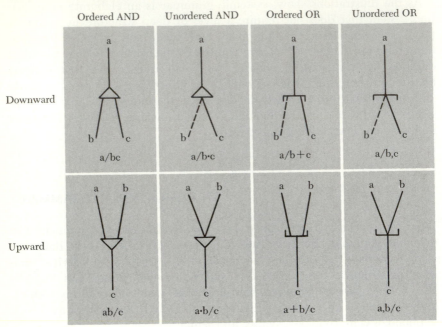

SOURCE: Adapted from Lamb 1974, p. 191.

linkages. Language is simply there, and any processes we find are in the act of using it, not in the system itself. Instead of transformations it has realizations. A thought, for example, which is captured on the meaning-unit or sememic stratum as a congeries of meanings, is realized on the word-unit or lexemic stratum by a clause. But one does not, as with transformations, leave the thought behind and "go to" a clause; both are present at the same time, along with the realization of the clause in the next stratum below, and so on. Processes—the real ones that go on when a speaker produces a sentence—involve the whole system at once, not separate codings first at one level and then at another.

The strata that give the system its name are, starting from the top, the conceptual, or *sememic,* the *lexemic,* the *morphemic,* and the *phonemic,* each with its grammar, or *tactics.* Most of what we have been calling syntax falls in the lexemic stratum as *lexotactics,* since it involves relationships among word classes. The relational network itself has a kind of abstract structure that can be applied at any level; it is illustrated in Figure 15–6. The "and" relationship means that an item is connected to two or more items which occur together—for example, **crumb** is connected upward to 'small,' 'piece,' 'bake,' and 'flour' (among other things) at the sememic level and downward to /k/, /r/, /ʌ/, and /m/ at the phonemic. The "or" relationship means that an item is connected to two or more items which occur as alternatives to one another; for example, the phoneme /t/ in final position is connected to the allophones [t] and [tʻ] (unreleased and released, respectively—see page 61). The "ands" and "ors" may be oriented either up or down, and may be ordered or unordered—for example, the connection between /t/ and its final allophones is an unordered one: the speaker may use either [t] or [tʻ] at any given time:[54]

But the relationship between **dog** and its phonemes is ordered—the phonemes have a set arrangement:

The network concept can be seen in the following diagram,[55] showing **well** connected downward to phonemes and upward to lexemes (**well** as a hole in the ground and **well** as an interjection, among other examples, with each of the latter having an intersecting *node* with a particular tactic category (the hole in the ground is a noun, the **well** in *She writes well* is an adverb, and so on):

---

[54] The two figures on this page are adapted from Lamb 1974, p. 190a.
[55] Adapted from Lamb 1974, p. 196a.

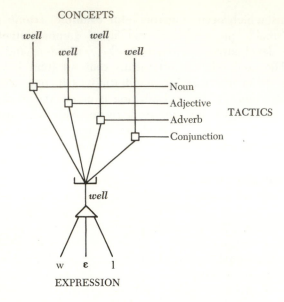

CONCEPTS

TACTICS

EXPRESSION

Stratificational grammar has not had a large number of practitioners, and this has led one sympathetic observer to remark that "the future of the theory is in doubt."[56] But it has been defended vigorously, among others by Adam Makkai, whose work with idioms has been in an area that stratificational grammar handles better than its major rival, and is not to be counted out.[57] It had the misfortune of being born at the wrong time, when students were flocking to transformationalism, and in the wrong place, practically in the shadow of the transformationalist citadel (Yale versus Harvard, with MIT standing in for Harvard).

TRANSFORMATIONAL-GENERATIVE GRAMMAR: THE MIT SCHOOL

In a sense, all grammar is generative: the ideal of grammatical rules is to describe the mechanism in the brain that generates sentences; but *generative* is identified with a single school of linguistics, that of Noam Chomsky, just as "structuralist" was attached to that of Bloomfield and his followers. More explicitly, Chomsky's movement has been called *transformational-generative*, or just *transformational*, recognizing the

---

[56] Francis 1973, p. 133.
[57] See especially Makkai 1972, "The Stratificational View of Language," pp. 58–116.

new "component" that most distinguishes it. Transformations had been adopted by Chomsky's teacher Z. S. Harris in 1952,[58] refined by him in 1957,[59] and passed on to Chomsky in conversations during the years between.[60] Adherents of the school are referred to as generativists or transformationalists.

The success of TG owes a great deal to the personality of Noam Chomsky. A rationalist to the core, he is as impatient with anti-mentalism in linguistics as he is with unreason in politics. He did not stop with repudiating behaviorism in linguistics but carried the war to the enemy's camp in psychology.[61] A shallow psychology and a shallow linguistics that excluded worlds of intuitive knowledge had dried up our resources for studying language; such knowledge would now be made explicit and embodied in a theory (and a theory of theories) capable of testing itself and detecting any false note by the sheer harmony of its inner logic. The promise of rational solutions that this vision held out attracted a powerful contingent of young talent that probably would have assured the success of any theory. TG had what every other school lacked: a corps of alert, zealous, militant workers who were not only quick to discover flaws but just as quick to prescribe remedies within the framework. The cohesiveness of the group made it possible for TG to undergo great internal changes without a change of label, rather like a corporation that after having established its name can change its product with impunity. The sameness of the doctrine resides in the sameness of the congregation. There was no conscious cultism in this, since viewed from within the enterprise was *the* theory of language, and if it was wrong it had to be fixed up, a process that no more entailed its being something other than what it was than altering one's beliefs from an anthropomorphic to an impersonal God makes one an atheist.

The notion of "generation" was borrowed from mathematics. There are two ways of describing a language, both as old as grammar itself. One is static; it assumes entities that are arranged in relation to one another. Stratificational grammar is a static model. So is something as simple as a paradigm: it displays a set of items that can interchange under certain conditions. The other approach is dynamic: a verb conjugation, for example, is viewed as a process of *adding* endings to a stem. The effectiveness of a generative model can be seen in a simple

---

[58] Harris 1952; see p. 18 for the term *transformation*.
[59] Harris 1957.
[60] See Harris 1957, especially p. 283, footnote 1.
[61] Chomsky 1959.

example from mathematics, say two number series like the following:

$$1, 7, 5, 11, 9, 15, 13, 19, 17, 23, 21 \ldots$$
$$2, 8, 6, 12, 10, 16, 14, 20, 18, 24, 22 \ldots$$

Inspection shows that in each series there are pairs *(1, 7; 5, 11)* that have a difference of 6 between their members, and that each such pair is larger than the preceding pair by a factor of 4. The static way of describing the series would be to list them, but this could only be partial because they run to infinity. The dynamic way is to pretend that you are *making* the series and to state the rule of operation. Probably the simplest rule here would be "Alternately add 6 and subtract 2." Generative grammar embraced the dynamic mode of description not only for those parts of language where things apparently "do happen" (as when a speaker substitutes a pronoun for a noun) but also for relationships that can just as easily be shown in a static way. One can say, for example, that a sentence in some sense "is" or "equals" a noun phrase plus a verb phrase $(S = NP + VP)$; that is static. Or one can say that a sentence "gives" a noun phrase plus a verb phrase $(S \longrightarrow NP + VP)$; that is dynamic—but of course is a fictitious dynamism, for descriptive purposes only.

Three stages mark the progress of TG. The first or pre-deep-structure stage extended from about 1955 to about 1964. Syntax was the main field of activity, and it operated with three entities, a set of phrase structure rules, a set of obligatory transformations, and a set of optional transformations. The phrase structure rules were "rewrite rules" of the following type:

$$S \longrightarrow NP + VP$$

$$VP \longrightarrow V + Comp$$

$$Comp \longrightarrow NP$$

$$V \longrightarrow Aux + Vb$$

$$NP \longrightarrow \begin{cases} N \\ Det + N \end{cases}$$

This particular set of rewrite rules (which is incomplete) can be expressed as a tree diagram:

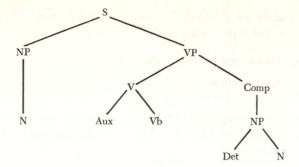

It represents the backbone of any simple declarative active sentence containing a transitive verb (with a proper noun as subject and a common noun as object), such as **Rome conquered the barbarians.** But to be a full representation of a sentence it requires that the elements be duly arranged and assigned their proper morphemes. For example, the verb must appear with its tense markers, contained in Aux, and if the tense is present or past the marker must be attached as a suffix. This is the function of the obligatory transformations—they do whatever is necessary to produce an actual spoken sentence of this simple type, which was termed a "kernel sentence." Once the kernel sentences are formed the optional transformations begin to apply. If it is desired to have a question, the question transformation generates a form of **do** for the example sentence, and again arranges the elements to produce **Did Rome conquer the barbarians?** Similarly the passive transformation produces **The barbarians were conquered by Rome.**

The phrase structure rules were the same in most essentials as the levels of analysis illustrated on pages 139–42; S ⟶ NP + VP, for example, is merely a dynamic representation of the immediate constituents of a sentence; so this much went very little beyond what structural grammar had been doing all along. But the addition of transformations made it possible to describe our intuitive knowledge that **Rome conquered the barbarians** and **The barbarians were conquered by Rome** are in some sense "the same." Such equivalence relationships, or paraphrases, have been the motive for most of the transformational work in syntax through all three stages.

The second stage began with the realization that the line between optional and obligatory transformations was impossible to keep straight. There seemed to be no good reason why one kind of structure should have the honor of serving as the source for others—a question is just as good as a statement; so it would be better if the source were conceived more abstractly, with *all* the forms that are actually spoken derived from it. Thus was born the idea of deep and surface structure, the brainchild mainly of Chomsky's associate Paul Postal.[62] What now emerged was a syntax consisting of the following:

1. A base containing two components:

    a. A set of categories, including such things as S, NP, Adv, etc. This is a "context-free" grammar.

    b. A lexical component, consisting of lexical entries each of which is a system of features (for example, Animate, Human, Abstract, etc.)

2. A transformational component, with rules for changing one structure to another

3. A semantic component, which assigns a meaning to deep structures and by implication to their derived surface structures

The interaction of the components was as follows:

1. The context-free grammar generates *phrase markers*. For example, the partial phrase marker

    represents—without any particular content—a sentence containing a transitive verb: the structure V + NP defines the verb as having a noun complement, hence as being transitive.

2. Lexical items are inserted to replace the feature sets that are the bottom level of the phrase marker. For example, the first NP might dominate a noun specified as minus-common (that is, proper), plus-concrete, minus-animate, and plus-count; such a word as **Rome** fits these specifications and can be inserted for that feature set in the phrase marker, and with other such insertions the deep structure of the sentence **Rome conquered the barbarians** will eventually result. After all the lexical insertions, the result is a particular deep structure.

3. The semantic component "interprets" the deep structure—assigns a meaning to it.

---

[62] See Postal 1964.

4. The transformational component converts the deep structure to a surface structure. For example, if the category symbol Question was part of the deep structure phrase marker, a question transformation will apply to produce, say, *Did Rome conquer the barbarians?*

In addition to the syntactic and semantic components there is a phonological component containing phonological rules that assign to the surface structure a phonetic representation in a universal phonetic alphabet (using distinctive features).[63] If a machine could be designed for the purpose, it would now be able to take that final representation and convert it to an intelligible sentence.

What had previously been optional transformations now became part of the base—a category symbol Q was added for questions, for example, and obligatorily triggered the question transformation. This met the criticism that questions are not "really" the same as statements, or the passive voice "really" the same as the active—they were different structures with different meanings and their differences were explicitly set forth in the deep structure before any transformation applied. The goal was to purify transformations of any semantic contamination. All the meaning there was had to be expressed in the base, and the function of transformations was merely to convert one phrase marker to another. A further change was the grammaticizing of the lexicon. Some way had to be found of expressing the unacceptability of a sentence such as *Sincerity admires John.* This was accomplished through the feature specifications on words. If the NP subject of a sentence is minus-human, it will clash with a plus-human verb. So by specifying *sincerity* as [− Human] and *admires* as [+ Human], and adding those features to the deep structure phrase marker, it became possible to block such a sentence and declare it not merely unacceptable but *ungrammatical:* it violates a grammatical rule, in this case a "selection restriction"— namely, that human subjects select verbs that can have human subjects, and similarly for non-human subjects. (A merely unacceptable and not ungrammatical sentence is, for example, one that overgenerates: *I saw the man that the girl that the boy that you mentioned likes called a fool.* Embedding rules allow one to do this, but there is a limit, albeit an elastic one.)[64]

Up through Stage II the disagreements among TGers were kept within the family. Stage III was different. It produced an open break. Though

---

[63] The foregoing is crudely paraphrased from Chomsky 1970, pp. 184–85.

[64] Here we see how TG shuns any consideration of frequency. A frequency measure built into the grammar would enable us to speak of sentences that are *gradiently* grammatical in a more efficient way. For the neglect of frequency in current descriptive work see Greenbaum 1974.

still acknowledging themselves as transformationalists, the rebels dubbed themselves *generative semanticists*. In keeping with its relative independence, generative semantics is given a separate section below, and only its makings are referred to here.

One thing that led to the schism was the grammaticizing of the lexicon. If meanings could be regarded as features so as to get them into the grammar, why not take the next step and view them as structured? Instead of a deep structure consisting of a phrase marker plus lexical insertions, there would be a *remote* structure consisting of meanings and their relationships; the old deep structure would either be done away with or would remain as merely one of the transformational steps between a remote structure and a surface structure. An example of a structured meaning is the meaning of the word *sick:* it is not only an adjective and [+ Animate], it is also the negation of *well,* and we should be able to express it as 'not well.' This idea had been suggested several years before, but seemed then no better than a reductio ad absurdum of the transformational approach. Now it looked attractive. But the keepers of the citadel, Chomsky included, would have none of it. They were "lexicalists"—defenders of the integrity of the lexicon. The disagreement became public, and by 1974 TG was on the defensive from attacks within its own erstwhile ranks as well as from outside. A German observer, surveying the concepts that TG had previously ignored but was now rediscovering, noted a growing "trend against formalism." "Students as well as scholars," he said, "are bored with learning new notations every day, only to find out that by the time they have acquired the technical skill to apply them, the theories behind the notations are no longer valid."[65] The effort of notation learning also partly explains something else. Having to work hard to learn a system produces a form of commitment that is not easily given up; the more complex and ramified it is, the more tenaciously it is held, and the breakaway when it comes is not apt to be gradual.

With the return of the pendulum it becomes too easy to discount the positive achievements of transformational-generative grammar. The fact that much of the description in this book is either taken from TG or directed at certain of its assumptions testifies to the impact it has had on linguistics. If it had not been for the concept of deep structure, we might not have been put on the track of hidden sentences (pages 166–70). If the notion of perfect paraphrase had not been pushed to the limit, we would probably know a great deal less about equivalences that are not quite perfect but come close to it. If it had not been assumed that language is homogeneous, the exceptions to homogeneity would not have been pursued so relentlessly and shown to be manifesta-

---

[65] Lipka 1975, p. 5 of the manuscript.

tions of a truly fundamental heterogeneity. If underlying forms had not been insisted on, our awareness that the "past is present" would not have been sharpened. But most of all, if linguistics had not been turned into a world of great expectations (some of them illusory), the hundreds of probing young minds that took it up would have employed themselves elsewhere and the truths as well as the errors would have lain uncovered.

GENERATIVE SEMANTICS, ALIAS ABSTRACT SYNTAX[66]

Structuralism foundered on relations of identity between structures which no simple static grammar could express but which transformations handled with ease. "Classical" TG has, in its turn, if not foundered, at least struck a snag in the form of structures that are beyond its powers, according to those transformationalists who have broken away from Chomsky after trying for years "to patch up the classical theory with one ad hoc device after another"[67] and finally giving up. Among the leading figures in the movement are George Lakoff, J. D. McCawley, Paul Postal, and John R. Ross.

As was mentioned earlier, the generative semanticists proposed to do away with one whole level of description, that of deep structure, and to generate sentences directly from meaning. There is good psychological evidence for the primacy of meaning over syntax—for example, in comprehension, which is a "sloppy process in which syntactic rules are used as a crutch to resolve conflicts when there are several possible semantic analyses, and are ignored when syntax and semantics disagree."[68] If it turns out that the lexicon has semantic underpinnings similar to the syntactic ones of phrase markers, then the same procedures can be used as before in one continuous set of operations. For example, the difference between the verbs in the following two sentences

John almost bought the house.

John almost wrecked the house.

shows that **buy** and **wreck** do not have the same semantic structure. The first one can only mean that no part of the action of buying really took place, while the second can mean either that no part of the act of

---

[66] This section is partly based on Pountain 1973.

[67] Lakoff 1970, p. 627.

[68] Hunt 1971, pp. 81–82, quoted in Patel 1973, p. 160.

wrecking took place (John flew his jetliner within ten yards of it but did no damage) or that some damage was incurred but not total damage (John in a fit of temper broke all the windows and smashed the furniture, but left the walls standing). The ambiguity in the second sentence can be shown by the remote structure underlying the two meanings:

John almost caused the house to become a wreck.

John caused the house to become almost a wreck.

To wreck, like other verbs of its type (causative verbs), can be decomposed into *do cause to become a wreck,* which makes it clear where *almost* belongs: with the action, or with the result.

By making words subject to rules similar to those of syntax, the old scheme of lexical insertion is done away with, and there is one continuous layer of lexical and syntactic rules. The generation of a sentence does not start with a syntactic structure but with a structured meaning, called the remote structure, which all the rules together then convert to a surface structure.

A fourth generative semanticist, Wallace Chafe, working independently of those named above, proposes the model in Figure 15–7 to show the steps in a derivation from meaning to form. Suppose we start with a representation in our minds—that is, the semantic structure—of what ultimately becomes the sentence *John has red hair.* The meaning 'red' is given there, but if it refers to naturally red hair the color is not precisely 'red' in the usual sense.[69] So let red_2 be the special contextualized sense and red_1 the more usual sense. Red_1 already has an established route through the grammar, and since the form is going to be the same anyway in the spoken output, we dress red_2 in the garb of red_1 and let it travel the same route. The conversion from red_2 to red_1 is a postsemantic process. The relationship between *John* and *hair,* furthermore, is a very special kind of "possession"—we could just as well express it with 'There is red hair with respect to John'; the embodiment of the meaning in the verb *have* is therefore another postsemantic process, as is the particular form that *have* takes with a singular subject, namely *has.* Once the surface structure has been formed, the rest proceeds more or less as in classical TG. How deep structure—which Chafe wants to avoid—sidetracks the whole process can be seen in Figure 15–8.

The concept of remote structure symptomizes the growing abstractness of description, the latest of the attempts, starting with deep structure, to push into the very heart of meaning. Patriotic TGers as well as generative semanticists have moved farther in this direction; both have put

---

[69] Chafe 1970, p. 42.

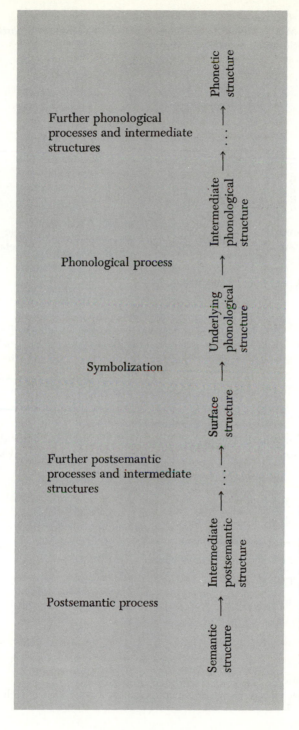

FIGURE 15–7
Derivation of a Sentence from Meaning to Speech According to One Version of Generative Semantics

SOURCE: Adapted from Chafe 1970, p. 56.

FIGURE 15–8
Derivation of a Sentence from Deep Structure to Speech According to
Transformational-Generative Grammar

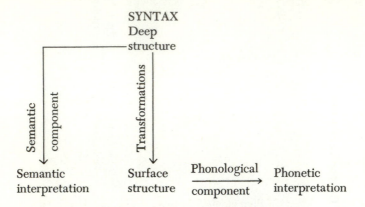

SOURCE: Adapted from Chafe 1970, p. 63.

on more of the fineries of logic and less of the homespun of verbal description (Lakoff calls the basis of his approach *natural logic*). Attempts to separate logical functions from other grammatical ones have even been made under the label of deep structure.[70] An example from within the TG fold is an analysis that was proposed for the sentence *The professors signed a petition.*[71] Such a sentence presupposes a number of entities at least equal to the number of items in it that can be contrastively accented. The bare bones of the sentence (capitalized below) merely relate a happening by something to something. When they are fleshed out they give more or less the following:

PERFORMER
of which we know (= *the*)
which were more than one (= *-s*)
who were of the professor class (= *professor-*)

AT A TIME
which was past (= *-ed*)

PERFORM AN ACT
which was to sign (= *sign-*)

---

[70] A well-reasoned example is Hetzron 1971.

[71] This is an elaboration of Pountain's example from Emmon Bach. See Pountain 1973, p. 14.

ON SOMETHING

which has not been previously identified ($= a$)

which is one in number ($= a$)

which was a petition ($= petition$)

By contrastively accenting in turn the words *the, professors, signed, a,* and *petition,* the basic entities of the sentence can be brought out. Accenting *professors* enucleates two of them—there is no way of separately accenting *-s* to highlight the number—and the same goes for *signed* and *a.* The presence of each underlying entity can be shown by a corresponding negation:

THE professors (we were talking about, not just any professors) signed a petition.

The PROFESSORS (as a whole group, not just one of them) signed a petition.

The PROFESSORS (not the janitors) signed a petition.

The professors SIGNED (yesterday—they are not signing it now) a petition.

The professors SIGNED a petition (they didn't just file it away).

The professors signed A petition (not THE petition that we were talking about before).

The professors signed A petition (not several petitions).

The professors signed a PETITION (not a death warrant).

This sort of analysis not only fixes the entities but makes it possible to separate the principal logical ones from the subordinate ones. The former are the *sentence* itself (S), its *arguments* (NPs), and its *predication* (V).[72] Ideally, meaning in remote structure is expressible in terms of symbolic logic.

The same abstractness and logicality can be seen in the studies of hidden sentences. It was a logician[73] who identified the performative sentences (pages 166–68) that were brought into linguistic description by Ross and others. The same workers are now trying to describe a kind of "fuzzy logic" that will account for the blurred outlines of what were formerly thought to be clear-cut entities: the category of nouns, for example, with its vague borders (some nouns are nounier than

---

[72] Lakoff 1972, p. 83.

[73] Austin 1970.

others, as we saw in Chapter 8—see pages 244–45). This kind of non-discrete analysis signals the return of statistics to language description; we shall have to know *how* nouny a noun is.[74]

Generative semantics is the most rapidly changing of the current theories that number a sizable membership. This reflects its newness, but is also a reaction against excessively rigid formalism. At the same time that it has explored the applications of logic it has welcomed research in areas to which no existing techniques or theories apply, in the hope that when they are understood their relationship to the familiar and the known will become clear, and better theories will result. This spirit has led to a deep interest not just in the content of speech but in its setting—the speaker's strategy in initiating a discourse, his intentions toward his hearer, his assumptions about the world, and other such questions of "pragmatics." The "keep out" signs have been removed and a line has been thrown to sociolinguistics. *Language* covers everything that ordinary speakers mean by the word.

Of course open-mindedness does not define a position, and there are still questions: how language learning is to be dealt with, how far the semantic analysis of the lexicon can be carried, how to handle the something-like skewed relationship between form and meaning, the neglect of which—"the dynamic nature of word meaning"—another linguist regards as one of the gravest shortcomings of transformational-generative grammar.[75]

CASE GRAMMAR[76]

Again we refer to the three ways of describing sentences that were outlined in Chapter 6 (pages 154–55). One was the traditional grammatical approach of subject–predicate and part of speech that has been practiced with ever increasing refinements since the time of

---

[74] Ross 1974 argues for "changing the theory of grammar from a discrete theory to a non-discrete one." It is wrong to claim that

> sentences are either well-formed or not; that constituents are either NPs or not; that NPs are either plural or not; that a sentence either does have a certain reading or does not have it; that elements either are or are not elements of different clauses; that groups of morphemes either are or are not idioms; that sentences are or are not related; etc., etc.

Generative semantics has been just as guilty as TG in working with discrete entities.

[75] Uhlenbeck 1973, p. 65.

[76] This section is based mostly on Fillmore 1968 and 1970.

Dionysius Thrax. Another was the psychological (topic–comment, theme–rheme) approach in which each part is assessed in terms of what it contributes to the sum total of information—how what we already know is balanced with what we are being told. The third was a functional approach that takes account of classes, events, and relations. Taking the sentence *The girl was delighted with Harry's gift* in each of these three ways, we might have something like the following:

1. *The girl* is the subject NP; the VP extends from *was* to *gift;* the construction is passive; there is a prepositional *with* phrase, etc.

2. *The girl* is the topic and we are told something about her. She is known to both interlocutors, and so is *Harry* (since he is referred to by name). Depending on the distribution of accents, *gift* may or may not be known.

3. *The girl* is the one experiencing the happening, *Harry* is the one causing it, and *gift* is the means or instrument.

Most of the theoretical positions we have described are identified with the grammatical approach. How a sentence is broken into its parts is central to traditional grammar, structural grammar, tagmemics, and stratificational and classical generative grammars. Each modifies the approach in its own way. TG, for example, defines categories configurationally: the rule VP $\longrightarrow$ Vb + NP says, by the position of NP relative to Vb, that NP is the object of Vb. As for the topic–comment approach, we have seen that it is identified most closely with the Prague School, though in keeping with their eclecticism the Pragueans have not pushed it to the exclusion of other approaches. The functional approach is typical of systemic grammar, of generative semantics in some of its aspects, and of *case grammar.* In systemic grammar the functional classes are worked out in a kind of pragmatic way, to fit the data of whatever sub-system of language is being described; we have seen how it can be applied to time expressions. In case grammar the classes are modeled on the predicate calculus of formal logic: in describing a sentence we look at the verb expression, which predicates something, and at who and what take part in it.[77] The term *case* is used because the functions are closely akin to the ones expressed in Latin-style declensions, which tend to show the different kinds of involvement that a participant might have in an action. A human participant, for example, might be the one responsible for initiating the event—that is, the agent—which

---

[77] For a criticism of case grammar, and an indication of similarities between it and systemic grammar, see Poldauf 1970.

was the Latin nominative; or the one benefiting (or losing) by it—that is, a beneficiary—the Latin dative. A non-human participant might for example be the means or instrument of the action, or the setting for it.

Case grammar dates from the mid-1960s and is an offshoot of transformational-generative grammar in the sense that it was a reaction against the failure of TG to distinguish the semantic roles of NPs in relation to their verbs from the positions that the NPs occupy in syntactic configurations. Though TGers felt the difference—they could see that "subject" ought to mean something besides just a slot for an NP—the question was never cleared up. The linguist who offered case grammar as a solution was Charles J. Fillmore; similar theoretical work has been done in Britain by John Anderson.

The predicate–calculus approach used by Fillmore is one that "presents, with each underlying predicate expression, an unordered set of argument slots, each of which is labeled according to its semantic role (or 'case' relationship) with the predicate word" (that is, loosely, with the verb).[78] The same "bare bones" reduction of the sentence is carried out as was mentioned on pages 544–45: first we have

Sentence $\longrightarrow$ Modality + Proposition

where Modality gets rid of such things as tense, verb aspect, and sentence type (question, command, statement)—those are left to be worked out by TG techniques. With attention focused just on the proposition, what is left is the predicate word and the arguments (participants with their roles), each designated as a particular case. The following cases were proposed (and room was made for others):

1. *Agentive* (A), the case of the typically animate perceived instigator of the action identified by the verb

2. *Instrumental* (I), the case of the inanimate force or object causally involved in the action or state identified by the verb

3. *Dative* (D), the case of the animate being affected by the state or action identified by the verb

4. *Factitive* (F), the case of the object or being resulting from the action or state identified by the verb, or understood as part of the meaning of the verb

5. *Locative* (L), the case which identifies the location or spatial orientation of the state or action identified by the verb

---

[78] Fillmore 1970, p. 41.

6. *Objective*[79] (O), the semantically most neutral case, the case of anything representable by a noun whose role in the action or state identified by the verb is identified by the semantic interpretation of the verb itself. Conceivably, the concept should be limited to things which are affected by the action or state identified by the verb. The term is not to be confused with the notion of direct object, nor with the name of the surface case synonymous with accusative.[80]

Analyzing the proposition in this fashion gives the "deep" relationships, which are then carried to the surface by what systemic and stratificational grammar would call realization rules. One such rule is the following: "If there is an A, it becomes the subject; otherwise if there is an I, it becomes the subject; otherwise the subject is the O."[81] This rule produces the following sentences:

John broke the window with a rock.

A rock broke the window.

The window broke.

The rule as given yields the "unmarked" choice of subject; this is to recognize what we noted on page 155, which was that the logical and grammatical categories tend to coincide: more often than not the subject is the agent. (All that "unmarked" means here is the more-to-be-expected thing.) The passive voice usually requires a "marked" choice of subject, and therefore a special rule. The realization operations themselves are worked out pretty much in accordance with TG.

Some of the advantages claimed for case grammar are the following:

1. It makes deep structure reflect meaning.

2. It makes it possible to analyze underlying semantic relations. For example, *persuade* and *believe* are revealed as synonyms differing only in that a proposition containing *persuade* must have one more participant (the agent).

3. It facilitates working with such things as performatives by requiring that participants in the speech act itself be identified.

4. It clarifies role relationships such as those found with the verbs *come* and *bring* (see page 327).

---

[79] Revised to *theme* in Fillmore 1970, p. 78.

[80] Fillmore 1968, pp. 24–25.

[81] Ibid., p. 33.

Anderson has made a special investigation of how spatial imagery gets implanted in grammar. He finds a general tendency among languages to develop grammatical cases of location and direction, which then fan out into a variety of semantic uses. We have seen one example in English (page 456), the underlying locative sense of the progressive: *I am working* means 'I am at the act of working,' with a locative preposition which is the same as in *I am at work.* (And we also notice how easily a progressive can be used to answer a *where* question: *"Where is he?"*—*"He's sleeping."*)[82]

The generative semanticists acknowledge their debt to case grammar, and the similarity between the two approaches is apparent in the fact that both generate from functions (meanings) rather than from structural configurations. If case grammar had not acquired a separate label, it could just as easily be counted as a special version of generative semantics.

AN EVALUATION OR TWO

No six-paragraph vignette could possibly do justice to any of the theoretical positions outlined in this chapter. All have depths of intricacy and compactness of thought that do credit to their originators but defy the summarizer, who is reduced to the role of caricaturist. Nor is it possible to include the broader approaches that dip into theoretical waters wherever it suits them but have no single anchorage of their own. This is true for example of sociolinguistics, which has reacted strongly against some of the assumptions of TG[83] but remains uncommitted to any of the more abstract deductive systems. Eclecticism is not only indulged but reveled in: "I welcome a classical balance of deduction and induction, universals and flux, intuitions and statistical evidence, mind and body . . . , private intention and social meaning . . . , explanatory theory and methodology of description. . . ."[84] This is natural and right in a field where scholars must climb periodically down from the ivory tower. The practical work of describing languages goes forward—to make dictionaries, assimilate minorities, provide bilingual instruction, train translators—with or without help from linguistic theory. Nothing has been said, for example, of new techniques of ex-

---

[82] See Anderson 1971 and 1973.

[83] On the notion of competence as rigidly separate from performance, for example, the sociolinguist maintains that "the conditions on the *use* of language (performance) are responsible for the *nature* of language" and the two must be taken together. The quotation is from Stampe 1973, p. 43.

[84] Bailey 1973, p. xiv.

perimental linguistics—such things as synthetic speech or the testing of informants in ways that will give more reliable data on which to build descriptions and theories.[85]

But enough has been said to cool the brow (or whip the flames) with the winds of controversy. The reader must decide whether to be filled with admiration or bewilderment. If he yields to the latter he will not be without company, even among linguists:

> Is there a true analogy ... between a "science" *like* linguistics and a "science" *like* physics? The problem is not that linguistics is at this stage "less advanced": will the descriptive linguist ever be able to propose an ordinary mathematical theory for a language, will he ever be able to falsify a "theory" by one observation, will he ever be able to construct an absolute test of his predictions? Surely we delude ourselves if we imagine that linguistics will be "like physics" sometime in the future.... [The problem] is rather that the extent of our data is in principle not precise. Languages change, and language interacts continuously with other forms of social behaviour.... We cannot even be expected to account for "all of the data," simply because we do not know what "all of the data" means![86]

And another, who at one time had toyed with the idea of becoming a convert to TG:

> I now believe that any approximation we can achieve on the assumption that language is well-defined is obtained by leaving out of account *just those properties of real languages that are most important*. For, at bottom, the productivity and power of language—our casual ability to say new things—would seem to stem exactly from the fact that languages are not well-defined, but merely characterized by certain degrees and kinds of *stability*. This view allows us to understand how language works, how language changes, and how humans using language have created the well-defined systems of mathematics....[87]

The difficulty is the mischievous set of assumptions put together by Hjelmslev: internal consistency, exhaustiveness, and simplicity. For these to hold, language must be reasonably homogeneous. In fact, for them to hold without a great deal of sweat and anguish on the part of the theorist, language must be *very* homogeneous, and that is just what it

---

[85] An example of the latter is Greenbaum and Quirk 1970.

[86] Matthews 1972, p. 77.

[87] Hockett 1967, p. 10. Italics in original. Hockett is referring to "well-defined" in the mathematical sense, and applying it specifically to transformational-generative grammar, but the same criticism applies to any deductive system based on the assumption that language is homogeneous.

has never proved to be. Each new theory has started with the brave impulse of rectifying the omissions of its predecessors, and then become so absorbed in the rectifications that nothing else seems to matter. Another blind man is describing the elephant. The comparison reflects no disrespect on the theorists who have labored on the description. They are anything but blind. The trouble is with the elephant. He is as big as creation. An overarching theory of language is practically an overarching theory of life, especially if one takes the lexicon fully into account (which is why so many theories, after taking a bite or two out of it, draw back with a severe case of indigestion).

The way around the difficulty has been to draw a line. On one side is what-I-choose-to-regard-as-language; on the other is what-is-beyond-the-pale. This, according to one linguist, is "a ploy common to grammarians of all schools, who regularly conclude that whatever their particular theory cannot handle is outside the proper concern of linguistics or else that it is trivial and uninteresting."[88] The dustbin into which the unwanted scraps are tossed has borne various labels: *style, performance, dialect,* even *ungrammaticality* (the latter applied at times to things that a native speaker is inconsiderate enough to regard as acceptable though they violate the rules). Deciding whether something is worth keeping in the first place—that is, whether it will fit and how and where to fit it—is equally troublesome, and has led to an excess of what one critic calls linguistic bookkeeping. In tackling a new problem the question of where it belongs in the total scheme of things becomes as important as what its internal make-up is. If the system were truly homogeneous (or if linguists were omniscient, which is perhaps the same thing) there would be nothing wrong with this—fitting a piece in properly would mean that we had the hang of it. But too often the procedure has led up blind alleys, because the parts to be fitted together were simply in different universes. We can take a fictitious example from the progressive construction in English:

1. Staring at me were two beady little eyes.

2. Charging us full tilt was an infuriated bull.

3. *Staring were two beady little eyes.

4. *Charging was an infuriated bull.

5. *Eating was my brother.

Here we seem to have a restriction based on two grammatical categories, progressive tenses and verb complements. The rule might be

---

[88] Algeo 1973, p. 8.

expressed like this (though suitably dressed up with algebraic symbols): "The progressive may appear initially, with inversion of *be* and *-ing*, only if the verb carries a complement." But such a rule makes no sense. What communicative purpose does it serve, and if the verb in the progressive requires a complement here, why not elsewhere? If the rule makes no sense it is probably not true, and with that suspicion we are motivated to look further. Are there examples that violate it?

6. Approaching was a strange sort of three-headed figure.

7. Emerging was a weird greenish vapor.

What the verbs in 6 and 7 have is exactly what those in 1 and 2 have when they carry a complement: they are directional. *At me* in 1 tells where the staring was pointed; *us* added to *charging* in 2 orients the motion of the bull. *Approaching* and *emerging* are directional by themselves, oriented toward the viewer; nothing has to be added. And now we realize that these progressive sentences are only a sub-type of the presentational ones that we saw on pages 160–61: **Charging was an infuriated bull* is bad for the same reason that **Walked a man* is bad, and *Charging us was an infuriated bull* and *In walked a man* are good for the same reason: they set a scene and present something on it, using locational expressions for the purpose. What brings about the restriction is not the encounter between one grammatical fact and another, but the encounter between a grammatical fact and a semantic one.

This is not an example of what a formal–deductive system is unable to do—details can always be fixed up—but it shows how vision can be dimmed by staring at the sun. The relevant theory is a modest one: presentational sentences, locational expressions. The grammatical universe of verbs and complementation is simply irrelevant. In small ways languages are highly patterned, but the total assemblage hangs together by a very weak gravitational force. "This is no grand indivisible unity," wrote the linguist W. D. Whitney a century ago; "it is an aggregation of particulars."[89]

If this is correct, then what linguistics will probably be looking for in the near future is more particular theories and less Theory. No science can do without theories of one caliber or another. There is nothing wrong with formal–deductive theories in tight systems—that is why the current ones have done fairly well in phonology, which is the most highly patterned and arbitrary part of language, and lends itself well to a mathematical analysis.[90] But there is another way, better suited

---

[89] Silverstein 1971, p. 12.
[90] See Arrowsmith 1974.

than mathematics to cope with the looser parts, at least until we know more about them. It is the *language of observation,* the kind of "discursive verbal description" that "makes no particular claim to theoretical sophistication" and "is neutral in relation to the various schools and their rival analyses." It is based on "fact," but that does not mean that it is not based on theory too, for "the theoretical statement of yesterday is the factual observation of today." It does not wrap things up; it is a prelude, but a time comes for preludes, after a long series of deafening grand finales.[91]

Linguistics is an adolescent science that has temporarily outgrown itself. There were no natural checks as there are in physics or aerodynamics, where a mistake may cause a plane to crash or a bridge to collapse. One sign of immaturity is the endless flow of terminology. The critical reader begins to wonder if some strange naming taboo attaches to the terms that a linguist uses, whereby when he dies they must be buried with him. As if *restrictive* clauses were not sufficiently named when they are also called *limiting, determinative,* and *specificative,* a well-known linguist renames them *partitive.* The Pragueans use (and carefully define) *theme* in relation to *rheme;* case grammar appropriates it as a substitute for *object. Phonesthemes* are *psycho-morphs. Yes–no* questions are *general* questions or *closed* questions. *Accent* is *stress. Morphophonemes* are *systematic phonemes.* And why, except for sheer mulishness, should the Prague *morphoneme* not have been universally adopted? With all due allowances for shades of meaning, and granting that any term becomes tinged to a certain extent with the shade of thought with which it is first associated, a tinge is not necessarily a taint, and the profusion of terms in linguistics is simply ridiculous. For a science *about* language, linguistics has been peculiarly insensitive to the importance *of* language in its own development.

These perhaps are growing pains. Adolescence is noted for appropriating the past and repudiating any debt to it, for discovering loyalty, faith, love, and the verities as if they had never existed before. As maturity comes we may hope to witness a greater continuity with the past. And with the future. It is not enough for the scientist when praised to demur modestly with the words, "I stand on the shoulders of a giant." He must have the humility to admit that where *he* stands is not the summit but only one more step up.

---

[91] The term *language of observation* and the quoted phrases are from Greenberg 1970. Greenberg is not suggesting that the language of observation replaces a theoretical calculus. Rather, it provides the axioms for a calculus. But in a longer view of science the surges of axiom and calculus can succeed one another at the hands of different investigators. This is especially true when the calculus attempts to encompass everything.

ADDITIONAL REMARKS AND APPLICATIONS

1. Structural linguists tended to be condescending, if not downright censorious, toward notions of correctness in language, and a certain amount of the "permissiveness" they inspired has seeped into the English classroom, arousing the ire of purists. Account for the linguists' attitudes in terms of their experience with linguistic change and widely divergent languages. How might their preoccupation with diversity also help to account for their neglect of universals?

2. Were the descriptivists who thought of words or morphemes as "made up of" phonemes deceiving themselves? A word is an element that has meaning, and when words are joined together to make a phrase or sentence, one can reasonably speak of the phrase or sentence as being "made up of" them. Phonemes are meaningless. Does a particular combination of phonemes such as one that constitutes a word have any function in the language if that word does not already exist, and does rearranging them mean anything? (Take the phoneme combinations *slart* and *starl,* for example.) What about similar combinations and rearrangements of words? (For example, *feathered horses* and *horsefeathers.*) Distinguish between meaninglessness *(slart)* and nonsense *(horsefeathers).*

3. Is the analogy between linguistic behavior and other behavior close enough to justify the comparison drawn in tagmemics? Compare the consequences of defying the conventions of breakfast-eating (for example, by dividing the meal into two snacks, the first at seven and the second at nine) and defying those of language (for example, by dividing a sentence so that another sentence comes between its first half and its second half). How does the fact that language is a system that points beyond itself, that has a *reference,* affect the consequences? Would it be appropriate to say that *ritualistic* behavior (eating a meal, playing a game) differs fundamentally from *symbolic* behavior?

4. Anthropological linguists have worked mainly on languages with which they are at least partly unfamiliar. (During the Second World War, certain exotic languages were even "taught" by linguists who did not know them; working with the class, the linguist analyzed

utterances elicited from a native speaker.) Formalists have worked mainly on languages with which they are completely familiar—they have "served as their own informants." Could this make a difference in how "deep" the analysis goes? How does it help to account for the sympathy that formalists feel toward a traditional grammarian such as Otto Jespersen?

5. Discuss the following claim: "Insightful analyses of natural language(s) simply cannot be performed if linguists do not have a proper understanding of their methods, techniques of inquiry, and methodological principles."[92]

6. Discuss the following claim, and compare it with the preceding one: "The exact means and procedures whereby [the phonologist] comes on his phonology is realized to be the subject matter of the psychology of invention, and not necessarily within the province of linguistic inquiry."[93]

7. In the writings of transformationalists one frequently encounters the following, or words to the same effect, as comments on something that seems to be an exception or counter-evidence to a particular claim: "These examples remain unexplained" (or "We are not yet equipped to deal with these matters"). What is implied as to the relationship between "unexplained" and "unexplainable," or "not yet able" and "not able"? How might a rival theorist view the matter?

8. Consider the following sentences:

   a. When I arrived he was paddling around in a pool.
   b. When I arrived he was paddling around in a pool they had there.
   c. When I arrived he was paddling around in a pool there was there.
   d. When I arrived he was paddling around in the pool.

   Try fitting each one in the blank in the following:

   I'd been wanting to visit with Grimsby for several days. That

---

[92] Botha 1974, p. 3.
[93] Wang 1973, pp. 109–10.

Wednesday morning looked like a good time so I went over to his place. _____. As soon as he saw me he climbed out, slipped into a robe, and we went in the house together.

Do you find one of the sentences less appropriate to the meaning than the others? If so, see if you can decide why. (The answer has to do with certain logical assumptions. After you have tried, look at the footnote. Don't worry about the technical terms; just try to get the idea.)[94]

9. What sort of problem do you suppose case grammar would face in dealing with a set of sentences such as the following?

   a. They painted the house.

   b. They applied a coat of paint to the house.

   c. They gave the house a coat of paint.

10. Would case grammar be in difficulties with a sentence such as *Europe saw millions die from the plague?* Consider the problems of dealing in a grammatical way with *Europe saw*, basically a metaphor replacing a locative, *in Europe.*

11. Transformational-generative grammar is required by its theoretical stance to be very explicit about all the structural relations in every sentence in deep structure. An example that is often cited is the contrast between *ask* and *tell: Ask her what to eat* is supposed to be the surface structure derived from a deep structure containing something like *You ask her* plus an embedded *What do I eat?* On the other hand, *Tell her what to eat* has something like *You tell her* plus *You eat such-and-such.* In both cases the second sentence is assigned a subject, even though it has none in surface structure. But suppose you are having trouble starting an engine and you want to know what to do about it. You send a friend to ask a mechanic, and your words to your friend are *Ask him what to use to start this engine.* The friend delivers the message to the mechanic

---

[94] Sentence a is inappropriate because it implies that we are going to talk about the pool, whereas in the situation as described the pool is only part of the background. To make it merely part of the background we have to add an "existence predicate" to show that it is simply there and is not a topic of conversation. *They had there,* with the indefinite *they,* has nothing to do with possession; it merely puts the pool on the scene. *There was there* does the same. In d the definite article implies that we already know about this particular pool, which again has the effect of merely reminding us of its existence.

as **What do you use to start that engine?** Should he have asked **What do I use?** (He is only the messenger, not the one having trouble; and the question is an impersonal one—what should *anyone* use under the circumstances?) A traditional grammarian might say that the infinitive in **Ask him what to use** has no subject, on the surface, down below, or anywhere else, but one is supplied from the context. What is your reaction?

12. A linguist in the camp of systemic grammar judges the sentence **They keep warm naked young** to be grammatical, and one in the transformational camp judges **I request that you believe the claim** to be ungrammatical ("One can request a person to do something but not to believe something"). How do you feel about these judgments? If you think they are wrong, what do you suppose might have led to them?

13. A discrete grammar has to make either/or choices not only between the classes that it sets up but also between grammatical and ungrammatical sentences. It is therefore not well adapted to coping with degrees of grammaticality or with analyzing sentences that are meaningful even though deviant in some way or other. Following is a problem in which you are asked to assign a meaning to an ungrammatical or semi-grammatical sentence. See if it can be done. Take the two sentences

   a. Do you mind if I am his friend?

   b. Do you mind if I be his friend?

Now take the two situations

   c. The speaker is not now the other's friend, but is wondering what the hearer's attitude will be if he seeks that person's friendship.

   d. The speaker actually is the other's friend, and is wondering what the hearer's attitude is toward that fact.

Assign c and d appropriately to a and b.

14. If you feel that you have succeeded in question 13, ask yourself what makes it possible for a deviant sentence to carry a meaning. Could it be through a resemblance to some normal sentence or family of sentences? (Try to think of other ways of asking b in which the form *be* appears.) Does this suggest a blending across constructions?

15. What difficulty might a discrete grammar have with such a sentence as **Kick him, why don't you?** pronounced

> Kick
>
> him, why don't you?

What difficulty would be posed by a sentence like **Let's you and him fight?** Is it a meaningless sentence?

16. Of the various schools discussed in this chapter, which one do you think may have the best answer to why one of the following sentences sounds so much worse than the others?

   a. John was peeved but I was madder.
   b. John was peeved all right but believe me I was madder than he was.
   c. John was peeved and I was mad too.
   d. John was peeved but I was even *more* angry.

After you have tried your hand, consult the footnote.[95]

17. It is possible to constrain a formal grammar in such a way as to block the asterisked sentences below, but the constraint would tell us nothing about *why* the sentences sound wrong even though they are perfectly logical and conform to all major rules. State the constraint and then see if you can explain the reason.

   a. I have trouble remembering the names of those people.
   b. I have trouble remembering those people's names.
   c. I have trouble remembering the name of those people (all members of the same family, with the same name).
   d. *I have trouble remembering those people's name.
   e. The achievements of those young athletes will never be surpassed.

---

[95] Probably the Pragueans would have the best answer, with their notion of functional sentence perspective. Sentence a puts *mad* in the position of the sentence accent, which suggests the highest degree of contrastive meaning; so we assume that *peeved* and *mad* are being offered as different concepts, though we know that they are the same. But in b, c, and d some other expression occupies the accent position, and *mad* and *angry* are not taken to be in contrast with *peeved* but to repeat the same idea. Try these two: **John was peeved but I was still madder; John was peeved but I was madder still.**

    f. Those young athletes' achievements will never be surpassed.

    g. The achievement of those young athletes will never be sur-
      passed.

    h. *Those young athletes' achievement will never be surpassed.

18. Why do you suppose the following two sentences

    j. I have trouble remembering the people's name.

    k. The young athletes' achievement will never be surpassed.

sound so much better than d and h in question 17? Does it have
something to do not with what is *in* the sentence but with what is
presupposed about it? Try your hand and then consult the footnote.[96]

19. What are the assumptions about the world and about one's interlocutor that make it possible to ask such a question as **Does she
have a temperature?** without sounding like an idiot? Would you
say that these assumptions, whatever they are, are more pertinent
to the first time one hears this expression than to later times? (Keep
in mind the nature of collocations.) Is it even possible that a child
will encounter *temperature* in this context sooner than in any other?
If so, how would it affect the making of the assumptions?

20. The following is to test whether it is necessary to adopt a theoretical
position in order to discover an interesting fact about language.
Study the two sets of sentences and mark in each set, with an
asterisk, the sentences that strike you as doubtful. Then compare
the two sets. You should find a correlation between them in regard
to certain of the words that are used. Try to make a generalization
about the class or classes of words involved; then check your answer
with footnote 98.

    a. I took that as an insult.

    b. I took that as an orange.

---

[96] The use of *those* in a through h tells us that the individuals being discussed have
not been previously identified; as a demonstrative, *those* points them out, introduces them. The article *the* in j and k tells us that the individuals have already
been identified. So j and k are not semantically overloaded; we already have the
information about who the young athletes are, for example, and all we are being
told is something about their achievement. In d and h the hearer is being forced
to digest two pieces of information at once, and in addition is being thrown a curve
in the ambiguity of *athlete's* and *athletes'*, which sound the same, before a singular noun (and a singular noun is rather unexpected in this context anyway). The
problem does not affect c and g because each item of information is in a separate
phrase.

    c. I took that as a sign of friendship.

    d. I took that belief as a comedy.

    e. I took that belief as a farce.

    (1) It was an insult what he said.[97]

    (2) It was an insult that he said.

    (3) It was an orange what he bit into.

    (4) It was an orange that he bit into.

    (5) It was a sign of friendship what he said.

    (6) It was a sign of friendship that he said.

    (7) It's a comedy what you're asking them to do.

    (8) It's a comedy that you're asking them to do.

    (9) It's a farce what you're asking them to do.

    (10) It's a farce that you're asking them to do.[98]

---

[97] In (1) through (10) the main accent is on the noun, and **what** (or **that**) and all following words are de-accented.

[98] Certain nouns are used more often than others to *describe* entities, rather than serving as names of entities in their own right. Thus we can call almost anything a *farce,* but *comedy* is generally reserved as a name for a stage piece. Similarly a great many things that someone might say or do can be construed as an **insult** or as a **sign of friendship,** whereas an **orange** is just an orange. **To take something as** is a construction that applies one of those descriptive nouns to some particular entity; so b and d, though possible as a kind of forced metaphor, are a little odd. In the numbered set we find that the descriptive noun works best with the **what** sentences, since **what** names a thing that can be described by such a noun. Of course most nouns are not restricted to either category, so we can use **farce,** for example, both as a descriptive noun ('something farcical or ridiculous') and as a name ('comedy, funny stage piece'). Is **comedy of errors** used as a descriptive noun more than **comedy** is? What do you suppose the function of metaphor may have been in establishing the descriptive use of a noun?

    You may also have noticed that the odd and even numbered sentences in (1) through (10) are grammatically different. Try putting a pause before **what,** and then try putting one before **that.** The **what** clauses are in apposition to **it,** whereas the **that** clauses are restrictive modifiers of **it:** **It that** (= that which) **you are asking them to do is a farce.**

References

Algeo, John. 1973. "Stratificational Grammar," in Adam Makkai and David G. Lockwood (eds.), *Readings in Stratificational Linguistics* (University, Ala.: University of Alabama Press, 1973).

Anderson, John M. 1971. *The Grammar of Case: Towards a Localistic Theory* (Cambridge, England: Cambridge University Press).

————. 1973. *An Essay Concerning Aspect* (The Hague: Mouton).

Arrowsmith, Gary. 1974. "A Mathematical Framework for Describing Speech and Language," *PASAA, Notes and News about Language Teaching and Linguistics in Thailand* 4:26–70.

Austin, J. L. 1970. *How to Do Things with Words*. William James Lectures, 1955 (New York: Oxford University Press).

Bailey, Charles-James N. (ed.). 1973. *New Ways of Analyzing Variation in English*. Eighth Southwestern Conference on Linguistics, Georgetown University, 1972 (Washington, D.C.: Georgetown University Press).

Bloch, Bernard. 1948. "A Set of Postulates for Phonemic Analysis," *Language* 24:3–46.

Bloomfield, Leonard. 1933. *Language* (New York: Holt, Rinehart and Winston).

Botha, Rudolph P. 1974. "Aims and Nature of Research Programme." Research proposal submitted. Mimeograph.

Bouissac, Paul A. R. 1970. "The Circus as a Multimedia Language," *Language Sciences* 11:1–7.

Brown, Goold. 1884. *The Grammar of English Grammars* (New York: William Wood).

Cannon, Garland. 1971. "Sir William Jones's Indian Studies," *Journal of the American Oriental Society* 91:418–25.

Chafe, Wallace. 1970. *Meaning and Structure of Language* (Chicago: University of Chicago Press).

Chomsky, A. N. 1958. *Syntactic Structures* (The Hague: Mouton).

————. 1959. Review of B. F. Skinner, *Verbal Behavior* (New York: Appleton-Century-Crofts, 1957). In *Language* 35:26–57.

————. 1970. "Remarks on Nominalization," in Roderick A. Jacobs and Peter S. Rosenbaum (eds.), *Readings in English Transformational Grammar* (Boston: Ginn, 1970), 184–221.

Coseriu, Eugenio. 1967. "Georg von der Gabelentz et la linguistique synchronique," *Word* 23:74–100.

Curme, George O. 1931–35. *A Grammar of the English Language*. Part II *Parts of Speech and Accidence* (1935); Part III, *Syntax* (1931) (Boston: D. C. Heath).

Fillmore, Charles J. 1968. "The Case for Case," in Emmon Bach and Robert T. Harms (eds.), *Universals in Linguistic Theory* (New York: Holt, Rinehart and Winston).

————. 1970. "Subjects, Speakers, and Roles," *Working Papers in Linguistics*. Technical Report 70-26, Computer and Information Science Research Center, Ohio State University, pp. 32–63.

Firth, J. R. 1966. *The Tongues of Men* and *Speech,* 2 bks. in 1 (London: Oxford University Press).

Francis, W. N. 1973. "Approaches to Grammar," in Thomas A. Sebeok (ed.), *Current Trends in Linguistics,* vol. 10, part 2 (The Hague: Mouton).

Gray, Bennison. 1974. "Toward a Semi-Revolution in Grammar," *Language Sciences* 29:1–12.

Greenbaum, Sidney. 1974. "Frequency and Acceptability." Manuscript.

———— and Randolph Quirk. 1970. *Elicitation Experiments in English* (Coral Gables, Fla.: University of Miami Press).

Greenberg, Joseph H. 1966. *Language Universals with Special Reference to Feature Hierarchies* (The Hague: Mouton).

————. 1970. "On the 'Language of Observation' in Linguistics," *Working Papers on Language Universals,* 4.G1–G15. Language Universals Project, Stanford University.

Halliday, M. A. K. 1967. "Notes on Transitivity and Theme in English," *Journal of Linguistics* 3:37–81.

Harris, Z. S. 1952. "Discourse Analysis," *Language* 28:1–30.

————. 1957. "Co-occurrence and Transformation in Linguistic Structure," *Language* 33:283–340.

Hatcher, Anna Granville. 1956. *Theme and Underlying Question, Word,* Monograph no. 3.

Hetzron, Robert. 1971. "The Deep Structure of the Statement," *Linguistics* 65:25–63.

Hill, T. 1966. "The Technique of Prosodic Analysis," in C. E. Bazell et al. (eds.), *In Memory of J. R. Firth* (London: Longmans).

Hjelmslev, Louis. 1961. *Prolegomena to a Theory of Language,* tr. Francis J. Whitfield (Madison: University of Wisconsin Press).

Hockett, Charles F. 1967. *Language, Mathematics, and Linguistics* (The Hague: Mouton).

Hoijer, Harry, et al. 1954. *Papers from the Symposium on American Indian Linguistics* (Berkeley: University of California Press).

Hudson, R. A. 1972. *Systemic Syntax Simplified.* Manuscript.

Hunt, E. 1971. "What Kind of Computer Is Man?" *Cognitive Psychology* 2:57–98.

Jacobs, Roderick A. and Peter S. Rosenbaum (eds.). 1970. *Readings in English Transformational Grammar* (Boston: Ginn).

Jespersen, Otto. 1909–40. *A Modern English Grammar on Historical Principles.* Vol. 1 (Heidelberg: Carl Winter, 1909); vol. 2 (id., 1914); vol. 3 (London: Allen and Unwin, 1928); vol. 4 (id., 1940); vol. 5 (Copenhagen: Einar Munksgaard, 1940).

Karcevskij, Sergeij. 1929. "Du dualisme asymétrique du signe linguistique," in Josef Vachek (ed.), *A Prague School Reader in Linguistics* (Bloomington: Indiana University Press, 1964).

Koerner, E. F. K. 1972. "Hermann Paul and Synchronic Linguistics," *Lingua* 29:274–307.

Kroeber, Theodora. 1964. *Ishi in Two Worlds* (Berkeley: University of California Press).

Kruisinga, E. 1931–32. *A Handbook of Present-day English: English Accidence and Syntax,* 5th ed. (Groningen, The Netherlands: P. Noordhoff).

Lakoff, George. 1970. "Global Rules," *Language* 46:627–39.

———. 1972. "The Arbitrary Basis of Transformational Grammar," *Language* 48:76–87.

Lamb, Sydney M. 1966 (1). "Epilegomena to a Theory of Language," *Romance Philology* 19:531–73.

———. 1966 (2). *Outline of Stratificational Grammar* (Washington, D.C.: Georgetown University Press).

———. 1974. "Dialogue with Sydney M. Lamb," in Herman Parret, *Discussing Language* (The Hague: Mouton, 1974).

Langendoen, D. T. 1968. *The London School of Linguistics: A Study of the Linguistic Theories of B. Malinowski and J. R. Firth.* Research Monograph no. 46 (Cambridge, Mass.: M.I.T. Press).

Lipka, Leonhard. 1975. "Re-discovery Procedures and the Lexicon." To appear in *Lingua.*

Long, Ralph and Dorothy. 1971. *The System of English Grammar* (Glenview, Ill., and London: Scott, Foresman).

Longacre, Robert E. 1971. "Hierarchy in Language," in Paul L. Garvin (ed.), *Method and Theory in Linguistics* (The Hague: Mouton).

Makkai, Adam. 1972. *Idiom Structure in English* (The Hague: Mouton).

——— and David G. Lockwood (eds.). 1973. *Readings in Stratificational Linguistics* (University, Ala.: University of Alabama Press).

Matthews, P. H. 1972. Review of Paul Garvin (ed.), *Method and Theory in Linguistics* (The Hague: Mouton, 1970). In *Lingua* 29:67–77.

Parret, Herman. 1974. *Discussing Language* (The Hague: Mouton).

Patel, P. G. 1973. "Perceptual Chunking, Processing Time and Semantic Information," *Folia Linguistica* 6:152–66.

Pike, Kenneth L. 1947. "Grammatical Prerequisites to Phonemic Analysis," *Word* 3:155–72.

———. 1967. *Language in Relation to a Unified Theory of the Structure of Human Behavior,* 2nd ed. (The Hague: Mouton).

Poldauf, Ivan. 1970. "Case in Contemporary English," *Philologica Pragensia,* No. 3, pp. 121–31.

Postal, Paul M. 1964. "Underlying and Superficial Linguistic Structure," *Harvard Educational Review* 34:246–66.

Pountain, Christopher. 1973. "Generative Semantics and Semantics," *The Nottingham Linguistic Circular,* University of Nottingham, 3:9–17.

Poutsma, H. 1914–29. *A Grammar of Late Modern English.* Vol. 1 (part 1, first half) (Groningen, The Netherlands: P. Noordhoff, 2nd ed., 1928); vol. 2 (part 1, second half) (id., 2nd ed., 1929); vol. 3 (part 2, 1A) (id., 1914); vol. 4 (part 2, 1B) (id., 1916); vol. 5 (part 2, 2) (id., 1926).

Quirk, Randolph; Sidney Greenbaum; Geoffrey Leech; and Jan Svartvik. 1972. *A Grammar of Contemporary English* (New York and London: Seminar Press).

Ross, John R. 1974. "Three Batons for Cognitive Psychology," in David Palermo and Walter Weimar (eds.), *Cognition and the Symbolic Processes* (New York: Halsted Press).

Saussure, Ferdinand de. 1959. *Course in General Linguistics*, tr. Wade Baskin (New York: Philosophical Library).

Silverstein, Michael (ed.). 1971. *Whitney on Language*. (Cambridge, Mass.: M.I.T. Press).

Sroka, Kazimierz A. 1972. Review of Kenneth L. Pike, *Language in Relation to a Unified Theory of the Structure of Human Behavior*, 2nd ed. (The Hague: Mouton, 1967). In *Linguistics* 85:72–103.

Stampe, David. 1973. *A Dissertation on Natural Phonology*. Ph.D. dissertation, University of Chicago.

Sweet, Henry. 1898–1900. *A New English Grammar*. Part 1 (Oxford, England: Clarendon Press, 1900); part 2 (id., 1898).

Uhlenbeck, E. M. 1973. *Critical Comments on Transformational-Generative Grammar 1962–1972* (The Hague: Smits, Drukkers-Uitgevers).

Vachek, Josef (ed.). 1964. *A Prague School Reader in Linguistics* (Bloomington: Indiana University Press).

———. 1966. *The Linguistic School of Prague* (Bloomington: Indiana University Press).

Wang, William S.-Y. 1973. "Approaches to Phonology," in Thomas A. Sebeok (ed.), *Current Trends in Linguistics. Linguistics in North America*, vol. 10, part 2 (The Hague: Mouton).

LANGUAGE
AND THE PUBLIC INTEREST 16

The linguist Leonard Bloomfield was interested in collecting what he called "tertiary responses" to language. These come after "secondary responses," which are the viewpoints that any person—from layman to linguist—expresses about language. The tertiary response is the reaction that flares at any attempt to question the rightness of a secondary response. Bloomfield tells of visiting the house of a doctor who propounded the theory that a language such as Chippewa could contain only a few hundred words, citing as authority a Chippewa Indian guide. When Bloomfield tried to explain that the situation was not quite that simple, the doctor turned his back.[1] The record does not show that Bloomfield retaliated by offering the medical man a good prescription for scarlet fever.

The tertiary response is like an angry defense of religion or politics. Since language is the property of everyone, everyone claims the privilege of holding opinions about it and defending the true faith. The rules of language are rules of behaving in public; and like other forms of public behavior, the rights tend to be sharply culled from the wrongs. They may be justified by history or good taste or effective communication, sanctioned (like pornography) according to local or

---

[1] Bloomfield 1944.

national standards, taught wisely or pedantically, enforced by persuasion or compulsion. What they always represent is some form of interference in ways of speaking and writing, with rewards for compliance and penalties for defiance. Effective interference expresses the will of some group or groups.

As there is scarcely any group in a society that is not affected to some degree by the way it uses language or the way language is used about it, the forces that would regulate usage are a tangle of sorties, truces, clashes, temporary alliances, gains, losses, advances, and retreats. Every "ought" in language promotes an interest of some kind—the culture-imparting of education, the image-making of commerce and politics, the conflict-easing (or suppressing) of government, the fact-defining and truth-conveying of science, law, and political reform.

Each such interest develops a program of sorts, even sometimes a code of explicit rules, with which it confronts the rest of the world. But within its confines, which may be as narrow as a street gang or as wide as a whole society, it regulates its members covertly. A language or dialect is imprinted on an individual by the speakers with whom he identifies himself. Its authority is informal. It needs no formulated rules but serves as a model to follow and acts immediately—through the surprise, incomprehension, or amusement of its users—to drive offenders back into line. The mistakes are not identified. Nobody takes the trouble to catalog them and give them names. They are fumbles, without status.

Informal-internal authority is inseparable from the speech level or geographical or occupational dialect that enforces it. It may be oriented in any direction: a literary speaker may be ridiculed into being colloquial or a colloquial one into being literary. Until he learns the parlance every newcomer feels out of place, and whether it is high or low, nautical or rural, Northeastern or Midwestern, makes no difference.

Formal-external authority, on the other hand, is self-conscious. Rules are its stock in trade. It comes into existence where informal authority cannot be exercised in the normal way. Informal authority depends on the overpowering effect of the many on the few. One newcomer in a community does not need a school to teach him how to speak; nor does the youngest child in a family where everyone else is more versed in the language than he is require more than their presence to keep him straight. But where large groups of aspirants are isolated from their models, the latter must assume artificial forms—codified rules and the means to transmit them, by schooling if the learning problem is complex, by mere publicity if it is simple. The situation is much the same as that of one who tries to learn a foreign language while staying in his native land: ways must be devised to bring the norms and models before him.

THE IMPOSITION OF LANGUAGE

Imposing a dialect

Hell is for those who are offered the light but spurn it. The heathen is blameless if he ignores a gospel that he has never heard, but damnation awaits our neighbor who has been shown the way and refuses to take it. Speakers of a foreign language are like the heathen; they are forgivable because their only fault has been the lack of opportunity to learn to talk as we do. The speaker of some unfamiliar dialect of our own language we resent because he has had the opportunity—he proves this by the fact that we can usually understand him—but has obviously misapplied it. The foreigner is so unlike us that we can make no invidious comparisons; he challenges our magnanimity. The native speaker betrays himself by being intelligible and nevertheless not getting things quite right—something about his intonation or the way he drawls his vowels or gestures a shade too slowly or a shade too fast fails to measure up. And the yardstick, naturally, is the way we ourselves talk and the way we look and act when we talk.

So we do what we can to bring him into line, as we may once have been brought into line ourselves (if we were not lucky enough to be born to a family that already spoke Parisian French or Tuscan Italian or Received Southern British). The method is not necessarily crude or heartless and its human targets are not necessarily victims: there are always learners—outsiders moving in, younger generations moving up—and they may be as eager to take as we are to give. Especially when the gift is advertised as part of the "cultural heritage": if our learner can be convinced of that he may go for it as he goes for basket-weaving or music appreciation. The art object in question is an establishment dialect, the "standard," which nearly every society sees fit to impose in the schools and to promote through the great army of language wholesalers: the reporters of news, writers of stories, preachers of sermons, and pleaders of cases and causes. (The advertisers, in this linguistic intrigue, are double agents. They have no long-range goals and will serve whichever side pays them best.) In most modern societies the teaching of the standard language—including writing—probably absorbs more educational resources than any other single effort.

To the extent that it is codified, the substance of what is taught is known as normative or prescriptive grammar. Textbooks embodying it—which are a mixture of description along traditional lines and comparisons of good and bad usage—make up the great bulk of writing on language, and go back—as we saw in Chapter 15—to its very beginnings. In the ancient world they were mostly individual products, but with the Renaissance there came a change. An epidemic of learned societies swept

Italy and spread across Europe—"academies," they were called, each
with special interests ranging from meteorology to the study of Petrarch.
Two of the later Italian academies were devoted largely to matters of
language: the Florentine Academy, founded in 1540, and the Accademia
della Crusca, founded in 1582 and still in existence. These two were
influential in establishing Tuscan as the standard dialect of Italy, and
served as models for similar bodies in other countries: the ones still
active include the French Academy, founded in 1630 largely at the
instance of Cardinal Richelieu; the Spanish Academy, founded in 1713;
and the Swedish Academy, founded in 1786. The academies were a
reaction to the collapse of Latin, and had as their aim the "defense"
and "purification" of the new vernaculars—these languages were heirs
to the throne, well and good; but they must now be protected all the
more vigorously against corrupting influences from below. Attempts to
establish similar bodies in Germany (1617), England (around 1712),
and the United States (1821) were failures.

With their official charters, the academies represented the earliest
intervention of governments in matters of language. The existing
academy with the widest reach today is the Spanish Academy, with
thirteen affiliated bodies in Latin America besides Puerto Rico and the
Philippines, a permanent commission recognized by the governments of
nine countries, and interests that include establishing leagues for the
defense of the language even in certain cities of the United States that
have a large Hispanic population.[2]

For all the excessively pedantic tone of pronouncements by official
bodies, the academies, through the dictionaries and grammars they have
published, have supported a great deal of useful linguistic work. In recent years the tide they set in motion is flowing back, as they come
more and more under the influence of scientific linguistics.

In America it has been up to the schools not only to implement the
standard but up to a point to set it, for lack of any official body to make
the decisions. For teachers secure in their knowledge of correct usage
it was enough to say, "Do as I do." But for others it was a case of "Do
as I say," and this demanded a code, which could be embodied either
as *lists* of things to say or not to say, or as *rules* to figure them out. The
lists were easy to draw up. The rules called for an analytical understanding that too few teachers and textbook writers were capable of.
Many misconceptions found their way into the code. Here are some
examples (not, of course, subscribed to by those who knew better):

1. "A *preposition* is something that is put *before*. Therefore a
   preposition cannot be used to end a sentence." Here the name

---

[2] Guitarte and Torres Quintero 1968.

supersedes the fact. If a man is called Paddleford, by definition he paddles a ford.

2. "The possessive must be used with the gerund when the subject of the latter is expressed: *John's saying that annoyed me,* not *°John saying that annoyed me.*" If obeyed to the letter and applied to pronouns (the other-than-personal kind) this would yield *°I don't approve of this's being done so carelessly, °More's voting that way would be a disaster.*

3. "A preposition cannot be compared. Therefore *nearer* and *nearest* in such expressions as *°nearer the front* and *°nearest home* should carry a *to: nearer to the front, nearest to home.*" Besides the fact that these forms have been used for over two centuries, the formulators of the rule seem to have forgotten that *-er* and *-est* are only one kind of comparison. The rule would also exclude *He was so near death,* in view of what happens with other prepositions when we attempt to combine them with *so: °so of, °so to, °so from,* and *°so under* are as bad as *°of-er, °to-est, °from-er, °under-est.*

The difficulty of trying to teach usage by rule is that rules incompletely formulated and ineptly explained often create as many mistakes as they help to avoid: "Grammar mattered even more to Miss Mapes than to most teachers. She jumped Lloyd Furman so effectively for saying **He don't** and **It don't** that she drove him one day into a **They doesn't.**"[3] For a student who only half understands what a grammatical object is, it does no good to say, "Use **whom,** not **who,** when there is a verb or preposition that takes the form in question as its object." Hypergenteelisms such as the almost-standard secretarial **Whom shall I say is calling?** are the result.

Since rules are hard to teach, good conduct in language is most often upheld by explicit prohibitions. If the teacher cannot serve his students as a model of what to do, he can at least memorize a list of things that they are not to do and crack the whip if they do them. In place of an affirmative day-to-day practice in what the community does or approves on various levels of usage from literary to colloquial, the student is triggered to react whenever he has an impulse to do some particular thing that the code of misdemeanors forbids.

A list can be effective when it absolutely forbids a particular expression under all circumstances. The school campaign against *ain't* has been a resounding success. But if the prohibition is qualified the learner is in the same quandary as before, because he has to figure out the rule

---

[3] *The New Yorker* (24 May 1947), p. 61.

for himself and is given few if any clues to it. He is told to avoid *at* in *°Where is he at?* because it is redundant, and he thereafter avoids all terminal *at*'s, even in **Which places do they stop at?** which parallels **Which house does he live in?**—not avoided by anyone except sticklers about prepositions at the end of sentences. He is goaded into saying *were* for *was* in **If I were John** and then goes on to replace every *was* after *if* with a *were: If John were here last night, why didn't he call me?*

Not all itemized prohibitions are futile. Most guidebooks such as Fowler's *Dictionary of Modern English Usage*[4] or Bernstein's *The Careful Writer*[5] are useful to the language wholesaler, the speaker or writer whose messages must not jar the sensibilities of readers and audiences far and near: that one person's limited experience with the language is pitted against the others' collective experience, and he is required to know more than he can easily synthesize on his own. He may need to be told that readers are less apt to be distracted if he distinguishes between **substitute** and **replace, infer** and **imply, to comprise** and **to be composed of.** It may be useful for him to know, not necessarily because he is a fastidious person himself but because he would like to oblige, or perhaps exploit the distinction sometime, that some fastidious people insist on using *each other* with only two and *one another* with more than two.

But it happens all too often that by the time an interloper makes the blacklist, the cause has already been lost. The "error" cannot be listed until somebody takes note of it, and that will not be until enough people are accepting it to attract attention. Once it wins a beachhead all the unconscious processes of adaptation get under way: it crowds into a bit of semantic territory and backs its rivals into their mountain fastnesses. From then on, when the special meaning comes to mind, it is hard to resist using the special expression. Take the phrase *the balance of,* which is condemned as a substitute for *the rest of* or *the remainder of,* as in **He was told to give up smoking for the balance of his life.** If we try to substitute *the remainder of* it sounds as if his days were numbered, and if we try *the rest of* we make the rule against smoking—or anything else in such a context—despairingly absolute: **He abstained from strong drink for the rest of his life, For the rest of his life he was borne down with woes. Balance** has edged its way in as the neutral term: it is *what* is left, whereas *rest* is *all* that is left, and *remainder* is *what little* is left. Or take the phrase *part and parcel,* frowned upon as redundant: *part* alone is supposedly enough. Yet **Alaska is part of the United States** is a colorless geopolitical fact while **Alaska is part and**

---

[4] Fowler 1926 and 1965.
[5] Bernstein 1965.

parcel of the United States is an assertion of sovereignty: the Alaskans had better not try to secede, and the Russians had better stay home.

Some additional examples, culled from high-school and college handbooks:

1. *"He claims that he was cheated.* Use *says, declares, maintains,* etc."* But *claim* connotes skepticism on the part of the speaker. The other verbs cannot substitute for it.

2. *"Don't blame the accident on me.* Say *Don't blame me for the accident."* The value of *blame on* is that it enables the speaker to maneuver *me* to the end of the sentence, a more effective position for emphasis.

3. *"Only* must go directly before the word it modifies." This ignores several things. First, phrasal stereotypes: *If I only could* and *If only I could* mean slightly different things; the first suggests a stronger will to have a try at it; *if only* has become a stereotype of hopelessness. Also *I only got there yesterday* may be a way of avoiding a possible second reading of *I got there only yesterday:* 'not until' versus 'as recently as.' As a rule, any problem of what *only* goes with is cleared up by accent. If *only* modifies a single element and not an entire phrase or clause, the two words are similarly accented: *He ónly found thése* is unambiguous. A worse ambiguity may actually result from putting *only* in the "correct" position: in "Sir Isaac Newton . . . usually got the result before he could prove it; indeed one discovery of his . . . was only proved two hundred years later"[6] the intended 'not until' would become 'not more than' if shifted. *Only* is the victim of an unfair attention that never falls on its companion terms *even, also,* and *just,* which are allowed to go where they please: *It éven terrified mé* (for *It terrified even me*), *I also tried these* (preferred to *?I tried also these*), *It will just take a minute* (for *It will take just a minute,* which is more precise about the time but lacks the overtone of reassurance).

4. "Avoid *the reason is because;* say *the reason is that."* It is odd that, of all adverb clauses, this one should be singled out for reprobation. No one objects to *the time is when, the place is where,* or *the question is why. Is* has the same linking function in all of them.

Concentration on errors is like the concentration on sin in an old-time religion. The list of thou-shalt-nots is somewhat longer than the Ten

[6] *Harper's Magazine* (July 1951), p. 87.

Commandments but still brief enough so that one can substitute learning them by heart for the more arduous task of acquiring a command of a second dialect of English.

If drawing up a grammatical Baedeker of places to avoid as a way of not having to teach when to visit them and when to stay away is not a sound educational practice, why is it tolerated? Perhaps the reason, or one reason, is the same as why students study for exams instead of studying a course—and sometimes purloin the exam questions if they get the chance. When the men of Gilead took the passes of Jordan after defeating the Ephraimites they tested those who tried to filter back by asking each one to pronounce the word *shibboleth.* Whoever said *sibboleth* was killed—betrayed by his dialect. The penalties in modern societies are not that severe, but a simple language test with answers that can be marked by rote suffices to tell whether one comes from a proper background and has been to the right schools. For some social purposes, knowing the correct answers is as good as knowing what the course is about.

This is distressing to the linguist with a social conscience. He complains that language should not be downgraded "to the level of table manners," and points out that children often bring to school a richer conception of language than that of many of their teachers. For children it is instrumental (a way of getting things done), regulative (a vehicle for rules of behavior), interactional (a means of keeping in touch with others), personal (an expression of the self), heuristic (a key to learning about the environment), and representational (a channel for imparting information). The teacher's insistence on the ritual function is unfamiliar and disaffecting.[7] Here is where linguistics can help teachers play their authoritarian role more effectively by giving them a breadth of appreciation to match the child's and the understanding necessary to intellectualize it. The teacher needs to be thoroughly familiar with the regional standard in addition to the universal written standard and to be aware of other dialects and their scales of acceptability, especially the ones that are native to his students. Beyond that, the chief requirement is an ability to make his students see their language objectively. This means overcoming the defensiveness of those who regard their way of talking as an extension of their personalities and any criticism of it as a criticism of themselves. It also means disarming the notions of superiority cherished by other students who already command the regional standard. It is ethically correct and linguistically sound to instill an equal respect for all dialects as forms of language that one puts on and takes off at the behest of the community. One device is the enlightened bidialectalism suggested in an earlier chapter (pages 368–69).

---

[7] Halliday 1973, pp. 9–21.

Another is the capsule lecture that justifies a fault—on all grounds except those of convention—before proceeding to correct it, thus wiping out any stigma that it may carry. For example, if the teacher is working with a newly arrived group that habitually uses *workin'*, *sellin'*, and *playin'*, he might explain the situation like this:

> Of course everyone around here says *working*, *selling*, and *playing*, and that is the way we must do it except at home and on the playground, but if you slip up and someone smiles at you just remember—and keep it to yourself—that the joke is really on him, because *workin'* is historically correct. Some members of the upper classes in England still use it. What happened is that there were two rival forms of pronunciation, just one of which was favored by the schools and became the standard about two hundred years ago. But they never could drive out the other form and I'd bet that if you listened closely to the people here you'd notice that they use it sometimes. They would probably never say **Whatcha composin'?** to a composer, but it wouldn't surprise me at all to hear them say **Whatcha cookin'?** to a cook.

An example or two like this is enough to break the ice—the teacher does not need to be an expert in the history of English. Since false notions of logic are also intertwined with notions of correctness, it is not out of place to point out how much more sensible some of the supposedly incorrect forms are, forms which nevertheless must sometimes be avoided. A constructive approach takes imagination, sympathy, and a little more knowledge than the ordinary, but it achieves a justifiable educational objective, which no fanatical hunting of grammatical scapegoats can do.

But what of the linguists from whom this new wisdom will come? Do they have it to impart? Many teachers of the prestige standard are still smarting from the blows they took a few years back when linguistics became a kind of rallying point for permissiveness—at least that was how they saw it. The linguists, for their part, tended to look upon pronouncements about language from authorities with mainly literary backgrounds as a kind of quackery: those who engaged in it were practicing linguistics without a license. Fortunately today's sociolinguist is not quite so scornful as yesterday's structuralist of the teacher's conception of language as a precision instrument and an art form, ideally the cultural heritage of every member of the society and not the exclusionary password of a power elite. He is a bit less eager to do what a scientist in another field would look upon with horror: interpose himself between his observations and his data. He still feels that he has the right to passionate convictions about the uses to which his knowledge is put; but he does not impute wickedness to the snake that swallows the mouse.

Imposing a language

Formal attempts to impose one dialect as standard on all the speakers of a language are usually superfluous, because the conditions that make it desirable—closer communication and greater economic and political interdependence—are already at work in informal ways to bring about a kind of standardization. As speakers of different dialects are thrown together, they absorb more and more from one another where doing so enriches their communication and discard more and more of their idiosyncrasies where doing the opposite would interfere with it.

Yet for various reasons and in numerous places people have felt that attaining a standard by unpremeditated accommodation would be too slow a process, and reformers and would-be reformers, official and unofficial, have stepped in. The impulse may come from a burgeoning nationalism that seeks identity in a common language, or from a centralization of government with the rising need to communicate with all citizens quickly and efficiently, or from a technological or commercial interdependence that must no longer be hobbled by a division of tongues.

During the nineteenth and early part of the twentieth centuries the typical kind of interference was that which promoted the spread of literacy, a consequence of the democratization that followed the American and French revolutions. Its mechanical genius was the printing press, which demands standardization: a single dialect and a uniform spelling. Its scope was usually confined to the limits of a single language; the speakers all more or less understood one another already and reforms were relatively painless—making them so was one of the aims of the reformers.

Take the standardization undertaken in Norway by Ivar Aasen a century ago. Norway was emerging from domination by Denmark, and the Norwegian peasantry had become a political force. Aasen sought an authentic Norwegian language with which to replace the Danish that was still used by the ruling classes, and he found it by synthesizing Norwegian dialects in a language that all patriotic Norwegians would feel was natural and right. The result was the New Norse, or *Landsmål,* which is still extensively used.[8]

Another example is the re-Latinization of Rumanian at about the same time.[9] Though Rumanian was originally a Latin language, over the centuries it absorbed a great deal from Turks, Greeks, and neighboring Slavs, especially by word borrowing. As in Norway, the upsurge of nationalistic feeling brought with it a desire for an authentic Rumanian, free of non-Latin elements. The other Latin languages, especially French,

---

[8] See Haugen 1972, pp. 191–214.
[9] Pointed out by Professor Dumitru Chitoran of the University of Bucharest.

were imitated, and not only was much taken over in the way of vocabulary, but even the syntax was modified to some extent—with such changes as the simplification of the verb system, the dropping of the neuter gender, and the strengthening of the infinitive at the expense of the subjunctive.

An example from this century is provided by Turkey, among the sweeping reforms carried out by the dictator Kemal Atatürk. In 1932, after he had abolished the traditional Persian script and replaced it with Roman, he created a Turkish Linguistic Society, to which he appointed party members and school teachers, and gave it the job of revamping Turkish.[10]

More typical of the problems faced by language planners now is the rise not of submerged classes but of submerged peoples. It is no longer dialect against dialect but language against language, and easy adjustments are impossible. Parts can be interchanged on the same make of automobile, but where the engineering design is different a composite would refuse to run. This is the situation that confronts most of the new nations that have emerged and consolidated themselves since the Second World War—about forty in Africa alone, besides Indonesia, Israel, Pakistan, Malaysia, the Philippines, and many more. It also confronts some political entities of long standing, such as India and China, whose loosely federated parts the new nationalism has pulled more closely together. In all these countries important segments of the population speak mutually unintelligible languages, so that it is difficult to make any one of them official. At the same time, nationalistic fervor demands that the language of the colonial power—which paradoxically had fed nationalism during the colonial period by supplying a unity that had not existed before—be thrown off.

The upshot is that these nations have had to decide what language to adopt and then seek ways to have it accepted by persons who do not speak it natively.[11] There is a parallel to the consolidation and mergers that one observes on the American business scene, where small enterprises, like languages with but a few speakers, cannot survive in a world of competitive giants.

Conditions around the world are so diverse that no two countries face identical problems and no one typical case can be cited. Two examples will show how wide the range of solutions can be.

First, Israel. In less than thirty years this small country accomplished the most remarkable feat of linguistic engineering in history. No one vernacular language existed among the Jewish people scattered about the world who were migrating to the new homeland, but Hebrew, which

---

[10] Haugen 1972, p. 170.
[11] See Ramos 1961.

died out as a spoken language more than two thousand years ago, had been kept alive in the Jewish liturgy—as Latin was in the Roman Catholic Church—and was enough of a unifying force to be the best candidate for adoption. The schools took on the job, and immigrants from all over Europe and the Near East, as well as the older generations of settlers, were taught what could almost as easily have been an artificial language. One thing that eased the transition somewhat was that the former languages of the immigrants were nearly all of a pan-European type, so that the remodeled language was essentially European in its lexical representation of the world, though Hebrew in its sounds and grammatical structure.[12]

Second, the Philippines. More than three hundred years of Spanish rule and forty years of American rule failed to establish either Spanish or English as more than rather widely accepted trade languages. Just after independence was achieved in 1946, the census showed six languages spoken by at least half a million people each, the chief one being Tagalog with about seven million speakers. The question of which one should be adopted had been officially posed a decade earlier with the creation of an Institute of National Language, after several years of agitation that saw even the Philippine Medical Association appointing its own committee on a national language. With its preponderance in numbers and its strategic position in central Luzon, Tagalog was favored from the first and in 1937 was proclaimed the basis of the new National Language and appointed to be taught in all primary and secondary schools beginning in 1940.[13]

Of the other countries formerly under colonial rule, some have elected, officially or unofficially, to stay with the language of the colonial power, either as the dominant language or as an equal partner with the native language or languages. Malay was legally established in 1967 in Malaysia, but English continues to be recognized in the courts and in Parliament; the ties with England are close, and anyway only 15 percent of the population is Malay, the rest being mostly Indians and Chinese who would rather stay with English.[14] The constitution of India decreed that in 1965 Hindi was to become the official language, with other languages, including English, accorded a special status; but opposition from non-Hindi-speaking Indians was so strong

---

[12] For example, the Hebrew word *taḥana* 'station' in the sense of a stopping place was still semantically close to the root meaning of stopped movement. But when terms were needed for 'radio station,' 'police station,' 'gas station,' 'service station,' and 'first aid station,' the newly formed compounds used *taḥana* in this extended sense just as in most European languages, along with the equivalents for 'police,' 'gas,' 'service,' and other 'stations.' See Rosén 1969, especially pp. 95–96.

[13] See Frei 1959, and Villa Panganiban 1957.

[14] New York *Times* (16 April 1967), p. 10.

that English has kept its dominant position. Indonesia, like Malaysia, adopted Malay as its official language, and has enjoyed much more success in promoting its use; competition from the colonial language (Dutch) was lighter, and Malay was already in extensive use as a lingua franca. In Algeria, which became independent of France in 1962, French continued to be the language of the law courts till 1971. Algeria brings us to Africa, where south of the Sahara the linguistic situation in many areas is chaotic. Niger, formerly under French rule, was still groping for a single national language in 1973. The exclusive official status still enjoyed by European languages in countries such as Guinea (French), Senegal (French), Ghana (English), and Sierra Leone (English) testifies to the difficulty of getting agreement on which of the many native languages to adopt. The Sudan found it necessary to close the mission schools run by Christians because these schools were making it more difficult to nationalize Arabic in a country one part of which was already split among more than a hundred different languages.[15] The psychological problems are acute and painful; language loyalty competes with efficiency, and tribal conflicts are inflamed by the lack of a common medium of communication.

In firmly established societies the imposition of a language generally takes a more tranquil course. The Soviet Union has allowed its constituent republics to keep their own languages and encouraged them to develop regional literatures,[16] while promoting Russian as the national language. In Canada an accommodation has finally been reached between English and French whereby both languages are official and both are required in schools. The situation in China is somewhat like the one described in Norway, on a vastly greater scale. Though numerous mutually unintelligible dialects are tolerated, the schools teach all subjects from the first grade on in a conventionalized variety of the Peking dialect and use a Latinized alphabet to help children with the pronunciation. Here the great advantage of the regular Chinese writing has proved itself: not being tied to any one of the dialects, it is used throughout the country and is understood in other areas as well, such as Japan, which have adapted it as their own system.[17] Nevertheless the goal is eventually—when the standard language is in general use everywhere—to shift to the Latinized alphabet. In the United States, minority languages have had a somewhat harder time owing to racial attitudes. The Indian languages were submerged along with their speakers. Immigrant groups have managed to maintain their languages for a time, but the communities where French or German or Swedish

---

[15] Knappert 1968, p. 66.

[16] Fodor 1966, p. 22.

[17] See Wang 1973 and 1974.

was formerly spoken have gradually given them up, with church services in the old language usually the last vestige to go. English has imposed itself not so much through official policy as by simply swamping the competition. But in twenty-one of the fifty states there were laws sitting quietly in the background to make sure that the swamping was done. In seven states a teacher was subject to legal punishment if he tried to teach bilingually. And some teachers went the law one better. "In a South Texas school, children are forced to kneel in the playground and beg forgiveness if they are caught talking to each other in Spanish; some teachers require students using the forbidden language to kneel before the entire class."[18] In the past few years, with the rise of conscious ethnicity, minority languages have been getting more consideration from federal, state, and local governments. In 1972 New York City invested heavily in a new bilingual education program to help its quarter of a million Puerto Rican children, and Massachusetts enacted a law requiring instruction in any foreign language wherever a certain minimum of its native speakers were enrolled in a given school; this was mainly designed to help the Portuguese- and Spanish-speaking minorities. With the Bilingual Education Act of 1968, federal funds became available for bilingual projects, to the tune of $35 million in the 1975 budget request. The Supreme Court in 1974 interpreted the 1964 Civil Rights Act to require bilingual instruction.

Even in countries with fairly stable governments, attempts to impose a single language can be both a cause and an effect of social unrest. China seems to be the exception; the shoulder-to-the-wheel philosophy of that amazing country has extended even to language, and teams of students are to be found visiting workers and other segments of the society to encourage them in learning and using the standard—there is very little resentment of the fact that those who already speak the standard have an advantage, and the eventual disappearance of the local languages is faced without apparent concern.[19] But in other countries any such program is likely to have explosive consequences. In Spain the Basques and Catalans were the backbone of resistance to Franco during the Civil War of 1936–39, and in Belgium the resentment toward the compulsory extension of French is high though it has not led to any armed insurrection:

> In the complex structure of a European state there are thousands of opportunities to make use of language in order to increase or preserve

---

[18] Charles E. Silberman, *Crisis in the Classroom* (New York: Random House, 1970), p. 94, quoted by Montgomery 1974, p. 3.

[19] Charles A. Ferguson, "Language and Linguistics in China." Lecture at Linguistic Colloquium, Stanford University, 21 November 1974.

the power of the ruling group. In a nation which is 63% Flemish-speaking only 30% of higher education is in Flemish, only 30% of the judges are Flemish-speaking, none of the [military] officers with a rank higher than major is, and none of the bank officials with a rank higher than account-ant is, except in one new bank chain which is exclusively Flemish.[20]

The division of tongues and its enforced liquidation are two of the greatest problems facing the human race.

Constructed languages

What governments have tried to do with the whip, a few intellectuals have tried from time to time to do with the carrot: achieve a common tongue by inventing one so easy to learn that all would be eager to adopt it. Some of the proposals have been sheer romanticism; one of the most recent is Lincos, a "language for cosmic intercourse," brought forth in 1960.[21] The best known is Esperanto, which was invented by a Russian physician, Ludwig Zamenhof; it first appeared in print in 1887. Zamenhof made the sensible decision to keep words as European-looking as possible; Esperanto succeeded because it had the appearance of a natural language and a familiar Western feel about it, in striking contrast with its unlikely-looking and in some cases highly abstract predecessors. Among the latter was Volapük, which had appeared a few years earlier and was the first interlanguage to gain widespread attention, but which faded with the advent of its rival. Some of the erstwhile followers of Volapük then set out to devise a system that would be free of the artificialities that plagued even Esperanto. They took their cue from Mundo Lingue, itself an unsuccessful attempt that died aborning in 1889 but was survived by its master concept, which was that a pan-European language already lay hidden in the common features of the languages of Western Europe, in their shared Latin heritage and cultural interchange through two millennia, and needed only to be coaxed out. The result was a succession of undertakings all along similar lines: Idiom Neutral in 1902, Occidental in 1925, Novial in 1928, Mondial in 1943, and Interlingua in 1951. Idiom Neutral was the most serious rival of Esperanto in its day, and Interlingua, the product of the International Auxiliary Language Association, has in-herited the mantle. An advocate of Interlingua describes it as follows:

> [The interlanguage] is the international vocabulary of the contempo-rary European languages, largely technical terminology of latinate origin,

---

[20] Knappert 1968, p. 66.
[21] Freudenthal 1960.

reduced to the most neutral forms and using a grammar which recognizes features that are shared by all the source languages, but rejects those which are idiosyncratic. It is not surprising then that the interlanguage is . . . readable at sight to any educated individual who knows one or two of the languages of Western Europe.[22]

Interlingua is perhaps the fulfillment of the prediction made by the inventor of Novial, Otto Jespersen, who pointed out the "unmistakable family likeness" in all recent attempts and went on to say that

just as bicycles and typewriters are now clearly all of the same type, which was not the same with the early makes, we are now in the matter of interlanguage approaching the time when one standard type can be fixed authoritatively in such a way that the general structure will remain stable, though new words will, of course, be added when need requires.[23]

Neither Esperanto nor Interlingua is a *universal* language on logical principles as conceived in the first attempts that were made in the seventeenth century. They are European, and what makes them possible and useful as standby languages in the Western world is a quality that sets them apart from the world at large—the same one that imbues Israeli Hebrew, of which an Israeli linguist writes: "Its notional structure, that is, what expression stands for, what makes it worthwhile for me to express myself at all, is shared by it with the principal languages of 'Europe.' "[24] The gulf between this world and other worlds is portrayed by an eminent Sinologist:

No student of Chinese civilization, having crossed the wide gulf of language to examine it from within, can fail to admire Chinese achievements in learning and literature and art, in the sophistication of its political and social institutions, and the essential humanity of its philosophy. But with his initiation into the language, the student enters a world of unfamiliarity. He early finds that, in almost every field of intellectual endeavour, the assumptions he thought were universal prove to be Western, idiosyncratic and confined in space and time to his own heritage. Every basic assumption he has been accustomed to make needs re-examination and reformulation in the Chinese mould before it becomes applicable or useful. In my own special field almost every 'universal' of linguistic behaviour must be set temporarily aside and new hypotheses formulated before the Chinese language yields to useful analysis.[25]

---

[22] Esterhill 1974.

[23] Jespersen 1928, p. 52.

[24] Rosén 1969, pp. 94–95.

[25] Dobson 1973, p. 8.

This is preceded by a homely example: At Panmunjom in the peace talks that eventually led to the end of the Korean War, Western observers were incensed that the Chinese referred to their troops as "volunteers." The Chinese term, *yi-chün,* really means 'troops fighting in a just cause,' but somehow got itself defined as 'volunteers' and led to allegations of Chinese deviousness and double-dealing.

The problem is the broadly Whorfian one of conceptual structures and their embodiment not so much in the superficialities of grammar and morphology as in the lexicon. Instead of Chinese, any native language of Australia, South America, or Central Africa would have served for comparison. There is no basis yet for a world-wide auxiliary language that would not be almost as hard to learn as a totally unfamiliar language. By the time the basis is laid, the need may have passed—a prediction that can be taken in either a hopeful or an ominous sense.

Not all constructed languages are intended for practical use. Some are put together by professors of linguistics to test their students. At least one, called Paku, was invented by a linguist to lend realism to a television series, "Land of the Lost."

The dictionary

The aim of a descriptive grammar is to be consistent and complete, not to serve as a guide to usage. It records what it finds and leaves to the school handbook the selection and elevation of one dialect or set of forms over another. The handbook aims to be authoritative but seldom is very comprehensive; since it is intended for native speakers, the bulk of the patterns in the language can be taken for granted—we do more things "right," without prompting, than we do "wrong."

It is not the same with dictionaries. Until the appearance of *Webster's Third New International Dictionary* in 1961, the fondest hope of the commercial dictionary publisher was that his book would not only be comprehensive ("It contains over 600,000 entries") but would be considered—as the *New International* once dubbed itself—the "supreme authority." With the appearance of the *Third* a new criterion was adopted forthrightly for the first time in a large unabridged dictionary. But the controversy that raged for several years after the appearance of the *Third*—including what amounted to a vote of censure by the editorial board of one magazine—testified to the deep-seated attitudes of the public toward what a dictionary is supposed to represent. That traditional role deserves examination.

Lists of words are both easier to make and easier to understand than grammars. The first overt linguistic interest that the average person acquires is in words; he has learned the framework of his speech and forgotten how he did it, but all his life he is confronted with new terms.

So he finds a dictionary not only more within his grasp but a prime necessity in trade, profession, and pastime (word games are almost the only point where linguistics and entertainment meet—crossword puzzles rival schools as promoters of dictionary sales). Few people need a grammar, but involve a man in a lawsuit over the meaning of a word in a contract and he craves authority fast. What importance the publishers of dictionaries have attached to this may be seen in a blurb for *Webster's Second* that appeared in 1940, citing testimonials from the supreme courts of six states.

But the real key to the authoritative position of the dictionary in American life lies in our history as a colony of England. Cut off from English-speaking cultural centers during the first decades of our national existence and insecure in our own ways of speech, we looked for written standards, like people who lack confidence in their social graces and turn to Elizabeth Post and her sister columnists. "We gradually sloughed off our colonialisms . . . in manufacturing, in producing an American literature, in directing foreign affairs," wrote Allen Walker Read, "but linguistic colonialism was the last to go. . . . The old habit of running to the diction-ary remained, whereas an Englishman simply followed the usage of the people around him." Read's study appeared in the publication of a con-sumers' organization that tests products destined for everyone's medicine cabinet, laundry, and garage[26]—eloquent proof of the importance of the dictionary as a commodity in American life.

With such a background, it is not surprising that word lists were com-piled earlier and have attained wider circulation than any other books about language. The following concerns the influence wielded on pro-nunciation by the dictionary of John Walker, published in 1791:

> Not only does Walker's pronunciation prevail today in many individual words (. . . his recommended pronunciations of *soot, wreath, slabber, coffer, gold, veneer, cognizance, boatswain, construe, lieutenant, nepotism,* although all admittedly not general usage in his time, are now standard American pronunciation); but also Walker's efforts to secure an exact pronunciation of unstressed vowels have had a tremendous effect on modern American pronunciation.[27]

The content of a dictionary is determined not only by what words and idioms are extant in the language (and of course the resources of the publishers) but also by the need the dictionary is intended to serve and the amount of information available to satisfy it. Dictionary-makers rely heavily on other published studies of words; if no comprehensive dialect atlas exists, certain information about pronunciation or meaning may have

---

[26] Read 1963–64.
[27] Sheldon 1947, p. 145.

to be left out even if it falls within the intended scope. But the real shapers are the people who use the book and the kinds of information they want. Here is where the craving for authority has left its mark.

The standard dictionary gives five items of information: spelling, pronunciation, part of speech, derivation, and meaning, usually in that order except that the last two are about as often reversed. Leaving out the part of speech for the moment, we can say that the remaining four are where the average user looks for final pronouncements. If he needs to write a word but has forgotten how to spell it, or sees a word and is unsure of its pronunciation, the dictionary fills his wants. If he is curious about the word as a word, he will probably look for its origin; etymology is the branch of linguistics that has been with us long enough to arouse a bit of popular interest. And if the word is new to him, he will want it defined or illustrated.

The order in which the four items are given has had certain consequences. Putting the spelling first has abetted the tendency of the average person to take the written word as primary and basic and the spoken form as an unstable sort of nuance attached to it. Some linguists might argue for a kind of normalized pronunciation first, using a phonetic respelling. This would have advantages for the child and for the non-scholarly foreign learner of English, who would not need to know whether a word begins with *sk, sch, sc,* or *squ* in order to find it. But to most users the gains would be doubtful, because too many words are encountered for the first time in writing and also because spelling has been standardized more than pronunciation. A second effect of the spelling-first order is that it fastens a left-right letter sequence on every word so that groupings are easy by beginnings but impossible by endings; if one wants to know all the words beginning with a particular prefix they can be spotted immediately, but suffixes are another matter, and English is a language in which suffixes are more important than prefixes. To remedy this, especially in computer programs, reverse lists have been made; the following illustrates how such a list would help to spot the words that contain the suffix *-dom:*[28]

MODEERF	MODLES [29]
MODEKUD	MODLRAE
MODEROB	MODNESTSIRHC
MODEVALS	MODRYTRAM
MODGNIK	MODSIW

---

[28] See Makkai 1974, p. 5.

[29] *Seldom* does not contain the *-dom* suffix. A different kind of dictionary would be required to avoid such accidents of spelling: it would be organized by morphemes rather than by letters.

The limitations that are reflected in the four-way order can be summarized in this way: they emphasize externals. Spelling is the written trace of a word. Pronunciation is its linguistic form, like the shape that a die puts on a coin, but has little or nothing to do with value. Derivation is a snatch of history, sometimes without relevance. The value system, or meaning, comes last, and in reality includes so much that what the dictionary offers is hardly more than a sample, a small reminder that generally suffices only because the average user already knows the language and can guess at what is left out.

Webster's Third did not escape these shortcomings, but it did break with the authoritarian tradition and follow undeviatingly a trail dear to the heart of linguists that was blazed in 1947 by the *American College Dictionary*—still one of the best of the desk-size volumes—with the announcement that "no dictionary founded on the methods of modern scholarship can prescribe as to usage; it can only inform on the basis of the facts of usage."[30] In pronunciations and definitions, and above all in the words it included, the *Third* abandoned the pretense of standing as a lexical canon, an exclusive club to which words may apply but are not admitted until they have been decontaminated in the charity hospitals run by the socially daring among The Good Writers. If a term was pronounced in a certain way by a substantial portion of the population, the *Third* recorded it, and it did the same with meaning. Of course, *any* up-to-date dictionary is bound to give this impression when it first appears—even of the *Second* it was said that it "went to the street" for its new words and meanings. But in the two areas of pronunciation and meaning the *Third* discarded all the trappings of purism. One criticism fairly leveled at it was that, having decided to cover the spectrum, it ought to have labeled the colors more carefully, as the *American College Dictionary* did; it became harder than before to tell when a term was regarded as respectable and when it was not, or what level of speech it belonged to: extreme vulgarity was marked, as for *piss* or *fart,* but most other degrees of formality and informality were not, as for *jerk* or *gripe.*

In one area the *Third* remained almost as authoritarian as ever: spelling. To be consistent, if everyone's pronunciation everywhere was to be used in striking statistical averages, everyone's spelling everywhere—in informal notes and personal correspondence as well as in things intended for print—ought to have been collected and digested before deciding what spellings were to be recorded. Many people "carelessly" write *principle* for *principal,* *lead* for *led,* and *kinda* for *kind of,* just as they "carelessly" say /pʌlpət/ for /pʊlpət/ or /kanstəbəl/ for /kʌnstəbəl/, but the careless pronunciations are recorded and the careless

---

[30] *American College Dictionary,* p. ix.

spellings are not. In spelling the dictionary is not a dictionary in the modern sense but a style manual, one of those authoritative guides put out by learned bodies, publishers, and the government to control the appearance of the printed page: typefaces, spelling, punctuation and hyphenation, syllabication, and paragraphing. (See pages 482–83).

And unfortunately, regardless of reforms, all dictionaries lag as much as their predecessors did when *they* were young, for just as they begin to move forward toward better rapport with linguistics, linguistics moves further ahead and widens the gap again. How would a dictionary look if it tried to satisfy the new demands of linguistic science? It would have to be what it is only in a halfhearted way now: a companion to a grammar. To a transformational-generative grammarian the relationship is that of brother and sister: "The sub-component of syntactic rules which enumerates underlying phrase markers is . . . divided into two elements, one containing phrase structure rules and the other containing a *lexicon* or *dictionary* of highly structured morpheme entries which are inserted into the structures enumerated by the phrase structure rules."[31] To a generative semanticist the relationship is more like that of a pair of Siamese twins—hard to swear where one leaves off and the other begins. If syntactic rules are just the combinatory potentials among words, and those potentials sweep downward from the broadly inclusive "parts of speech" classes to the lowliest grammatical restrictions on individual words,[32] then it is going to be hard to decide what to put in the grammar and what to put in the dictionary. One lexicologist advises "conceiving of both grammar and lexicon as mutually presupposing rather than simply complementary. . . . Grammars determine classes by grouping members, whereas lexicons determine members by specifying class memberships. . . . A smaller dictionary presupposes a larger grammar, and a smaller grammar a larger dictionary."[33] Suppose it had to be decided whether to include a class of "temporal indefinites" in the grammar. Indefinites in general would undoubtedly have to figure there, because they have properties that affect other classes (for example, negation: *something* is matched to *nothing, somebody* to *nobody, somewhere* to *nowhere,* and so on). But if it turned out that the only need for recognizing a subclass of *temporal* indefinites was to be able to talk about the word *else* (it goes freely with indefinites other than temporal ones: *someone else, no one else, no place else, who else?* but not *°sometime else*), then the most economical place to state the fact

---

[31] Postal 1964, p. 253.

[32] For example, *to regard* can be used in the literal sense of 'look at' only when accompanied by a manner adverb: *He regarded me strangely* but not *°He regarded me for five minutes.* See page 103.

[33] Juilland 1972, p. 269.

would be under the entry for *else* in the dictionary. The same would be true, even more obviously, of word-to-word restrictions such as the fact that whereas **mutual** may go with either *friends* or *enemies,* its synonym *common* cannot go with *friends (common enemies, °common friends).* (See page 104 for these examples.)

At present there is a vast unrecorded zone lying between what actual grammars talk about and what actual dictionaries talk about. The facts are not on either record, mostly because too many of them are still unexplored, but also because the dictionaries prefer to ignore much that is quite well known. The grammatical classes that they recognize are merely the traditional parts of speech: nouns, verbs, adjectives, adverbs, prepositions, conjunctions, and exclamations. The label "verb" attached to *eat* gives a crude sort of cross-reference to a grammar, which in turn will explain that *eats* and *eating* are correct forms and that *People eat* is a correct sequence while *°The eat* is not. Correspondingly, the label "noun" on *food* tells us that *the food* is normal but *°fooding* is not. In fact, we are given a trifle more than the undivided categories of verb and noun: with verbs, we are told when they may take an object and when not, by the labels *v.t.* and *v.i.;* and from the capital letters attached to nouns we can deduce sometimes (as with **Taranto** and **Bizet,** though not with *Moor* or *Savior*) that the noun is grammatically proper—that is, used without an article.

But suppose a person who does not already know English wants to compose a sentence using the word **whim.** He looks it up in *Webster's Third,* where he finds it marked as a noun and grouped with the synonyms *caprice* and *fancy,* and also, under *folly,* grouped with **indulgence, vanity,** and *foolery;* but there is nothing to tell him that *a little whim* refers to something small, while *a little indulgence* or *vanity* or *foolery* probably refers to an amount. In short, the dictionary fails to label the subcategories of mass noun and count noun. (This is essential information to any foreign learner of English, and at least one of the smaller special dictionaries provides it—the *Advanced Learner's Dictionary of Current English.*[34]) The definition as often as not throws out some hint from which one may guess the category—for instance, *sugar* is defined as a "substance," and presumably one would know that a substance is a mass (though here the word *substance* itself is not a mass noun!). But this is hit-or-miss lexicography.

Labels for mass and count are only one of many possibilities. In Chapter 6 (pages 147–52) we noted one other major pair—intensifiable and unintensifiable—and several minor ones including sensoriness, negative bias, and animateness. Information about these is often included

---

[34] Third edition, by A. S. Hornby, E. V. Gatenby, and H. Wakefield (New York: Oxford University Press, 1974).

unsystematically as part of a definition; for example, *murder* is defined as 'to kill (a human being) unlawfully,' which is the same as to label the verb [+ Human Object], recognizing a category of human nouns within the larger category of animate nouns.

A dictionary that is supposed to return a profit for its publisher can carry this kind of analysis only so far. There is probably something to be gained, even though the list is small, in labeling the adjectives that normally come after the noun rather than before it. The user of the *Third* cannot tell, if he looks up *afire,* that he is not permitted to say **an afire house,* and he will find a similar warning under *alive* for only one of the senses, when it should apply to all. But must one recognize opposing categories of temporal–spatial on the strength of *gradual, slow, abrupt,* or *sudden* inspiration (something that *happens* in *time*), but only *gradual* or *abrupt* hill, or on the strength of *long, lengthy, short,* or *brief* visit, but only *long* or *short* pencil? Or a dim category of sex in the fact that a man can have *children* but only a woman can have *babies,* or a sub-subcategory of count nouns on the strength of *all that day, all my family* (entities having "homogeneous parts") but not **all that shoe, *all the typewriter* ("indivisible")? What a linguist would find desirable is beyond the reach of any volume likely to be in print for a long time.

The same goes for definitions. A substantial part of them fail to define carefully enough to exclude gross errors. Take the verb *to wage. Webster's Third* defines it as 'to carry on actions that constitute or promote,' and this is followed by a series of typical objects: war, campaign, battle, filibuster. *The American Heritage Dictionary* says 'to engage in (a war or campaign).' The question is, can one wage an election, a seance, a conversation, or a seduction? Or even a fight? The *Third* does include *farmers still waging a losing fight with poor, stony land* among its examples, but while that is normal enough, there is a difference in acceptability between the following:

?Hogan waged a fight against his political adversaries.

Hogan waged a continuous fight against his political adversaries.

It needs to be stated that whatever is waged has to be aggressive and sustained. *Battle* and *fight* are aggressive but too brief (though one might wage a series of battles); an investigation is sustained enough but is not inherently aggressive. On the other hand, *to wage a conversation* might be an effective figure of speech to describe what goes on between two very uninhibited talkers. The examples in dictionaries suggest the semantic range but fail to close it in. Or take the verb *to sag.* The *American Heritage* says 'to sink, curve downward, or settle from pressure, weight, or slackness.' Suppose you live in a house on one of those California hills that dissolve whenever there is a heavy rain, and your house settles ten feet all around. You would not say that it sagged, because the sinking was uniform. If the hill had melted away on one side, the bedroom over there could sag, because it moved down with respect to the rest of the house. The definition needs to incorporate this relativity. Or take the nouns *mistrust* and *distrust.* The *Third* gives no clue to any distinction between them, yet whereas *distrust* is relatively focused, *mistrust* is not. One is distrustful of particular persons or acts, but mistrustful at heart.

It does not take a perfectionist to see how much room there is for improvement in our dictionaries, even if the linguist's ideal is unattainable.

Limited intervention

A government that decrees a single tongue for a whole nation is in the language business wholesale. So is a school system that overlays a single dialect. Besides these grand attempts to turn the rank growth of language into a French garden, there are small efforts aimed at this or that, by agencies here or there, from government to moral uplift societies. Invariably a pressure group is at work.

In business the owners of trademarks would restrain us, if they could, from the "generic usage" of the words they have so carefully coined and copyrighted. Every time a customer enters a store and asks for Band-Aids (instead of Band-Aid adhesive bandages) or goes to a copying service to have his tax return Xeroxed (instead of photocopied by a Xerox copier), he pushes a trademark one step closer to the dictionary of ordinary words, which anyone, including competitors, is free to use. The list of former trademarks that are now common property includes *aspirin, cellophane, linoleum, shredded wheat,* and *zipper.*[35] Unfortunately business does its best to defeat itself by spending millions to make customers forget the true generic term and identify a commodity with a particular brand. The makers of soap are in no great danger because it is unlikely that those who hear and obey the secret wish of the advertisers of *Dove* will forget the word *soap.* But when a name is so well chosen that it comes trippingly on the tongue, and the generic term is awkward, and the product itself has or appears to have something unique about it, then the more it is advertised the more it is in danger of becoming plebeianized. This is the dreadful fate that stalks such terms as *Polaroid, Formica,* and *Levi's.*

---

[35] *Changing Times* (July 1974), inside front cover.

Consumers for their part seem to have no objections to copyrighted names so long as they are not used to obfuscate. When they are, as has happened in the brand-naming of drugs, the government may be prodded into action. Recent legislation, proposed or in the works, would compel the labeling of all medicines by their generic names and prohibit any deceptive advertising of cosmetics and foods.

What government officials have not yet begun to do is to police their own deceptive use of language. This problem came to a head in the United States in the years immediately following the nominal end of the war in Vietnam, with the exposure of some of the means that were being used to conceal activities that many people felt the public had a right to know about, and then to divert attention from the concealment by other forms of verbal magic. The education editor of the New York *Times* declared that of all the assaults on language through sloganeering, incivility, and intellectual slumming, none was "as devastatingly serious as the abuse of language by government itself."[36] We saw earlier some of the examples of the studied misapplication of words that has led to such complaints and to the expression of concern and anger on the part of language teachers (pages 258–59).

While no government has an avowed policy of verbal manipulation, a number of groups, especially among minorities that have become keenly aware of the verbal put-down, have an avowed policy against it. The most noteworthy has been the women's liberation movement (page 249), which has campaigned against sexist preconceptions in language, including things as intimately grammatical as the pronoun system. Thanks to this attention and to the criticism of abuses by government and business, the general public is aware as never before of the need to pay explicit attention to how language affects our lives. It is as much a part of the ecology as our air and our rivers.

LANGUAGE AND EMPATHY

The uses of money have their robber barons and philanthropists, capitalists and day laborers, conservatives and socialists, bearers of the gold standard and coiners of free silver, all concerned in one way or another with how the prime medium of exchange in society is to be managed and distributed. The economy is a material fact with an ethical side, for it concerns who shall have comfort and who shall not, who is to wield power and who is to submit.

---

[36] Hechinger 1971.

Language also has its ethic, though for some reason we seldom pose it to ourselves in the ordinary terms of power and prestige or of good conduct and bad. We feel that we have a right to regulate the use of money in ways that will spread its benefits, for it is a creature of society and must respond to society's needs. But language is no less a medium of exchange, and like money was created by and for society. And like money it is subject to abuse.

The exchange of language is the sharing of experience. If we regard as the highest mark of civilization an ability to project ourselves into the mental and physical world of others, to share their thoughts, feelings, and visions, to sense their angers and encounter the same walls that shut them in and the same escapes to freedom, we must ask how language is to be used if we are to be civilized.

Though laws forbid the undue concentration of economic power, the only laws against the misuse of language have to do with the content of messages: obscenity, perjury, sedition, defamation in its various forms of libel and slander, and, recently, truth in advertising and lending. There are no laws against the unfair exploitation of language as language, in its essence. The individual may carry as many concealed verbal weapons as he likes and strike with them as he pleases—far from being censured for it, he will be admired and applauded as a clever fellow. Perhaps because we feel that language is everyone's birthright and that being born with it means that all have equal access to its storehouse, we have never seen fit to limit even by custom the ways it is used. Custom frowns on the liar, sometimes, but lies again are content, not essence. The only part of the essence that suffers from the slightest disfavor is that small segment of the vocabulary that is affected by taboo, and even that is partly content.

In a small, unstratified society the rule of equal access perhaps applies. No one is excessively rich in either material or verbal goods. In more complex societies it does not apply, because language, like wealth and color, is a weapon of *de facto* segregation. With the disappearance of the less visible tokens of birth and breeding, language has in some areas taken over their function of opening or closing the doors to membership in a ruling caste. There is no question that the Received Pronunciation of Southern British has been just such a badge of admission—this was the theme of Bernard Shaw's *Pygmalion* and its musical version, *My Fair Lady*. The lines are not so clearly drawn in America, but a rustic accent is enough to preclude employment in certain jobs, and even a person with a markedly foreign accent may have an easier time renting an apartment by telephone than someone who exhibits a particular variety of Southern speech.

Society recognizes the problem of equal access only through the unequal efforts of the schools. They are unequal because alongside of schools striving for an ethic of equality there are others striving for an ethic of charity that, for all its good intentions, only deepens class lines. The *public* effort for equal access must be toward the elimination of every sort of verbal snobbery. There is nothing intrinsically bad about words as such, and to exclude a form of speech is to exclude the person who uses it. The task of democratizing a society includes far more than speech forms, of course, but headway will be that much more difficult if we overlook the intricate ties of speech with everything else that spells privilege.

Public cures may be long in coming, but meanwhile some of the ills of unequal access can be avoided if we recognize our personal responsibility toward the sharing of experience through language. We can discharge it by trying as hard to meet our neighbor on his dialectal terms as we would try to meet a foreigner on the terms of his language. This means never using our superior verbal skill, if we have it, or our inheritance of a prestige dialect for which we never worked a day, to browbeat or establish a difference in status between our neighbor and us. It means remembering that language is the most public of all public domains, to be kept free at all costs of claims that would turn any part of it into the property of some exclusive club, whether of scientists, artisans, or the socially elect. The virtue of language is in being ordinary.

ADDITIONAL REMARKS
AND APPLICATIONS

1. Discuss laughter as a weapon of conformity. It is no longer considered proper to laugh at racial jokes, and it long since ceased to be proper to laugh at the behavior of the crippled and feebleminded. Consider to what extent we still laugh at linguistic nonconformity—for instance, as the basis for stage humor.

2. A scientific publication asserted the following: "The linguist, like the microbiologist, has a social responsibility to develop his subject in directions which will produce practical results."[37] Do you agree? If so, discuss ways in which the obligation might be carried out.

3. Discuss the following summary of an article:

   Makers of tests devise tests of auditory discrimination to conform to the dialect that they themselves speak. When speakers of other dialects, particularly children who have not been exposed to a variety of dialects and so far have heard very little except the speech of their family and playmates, take these tests, they naturally do not score very well. Instead of trying to find out what is "wrong" with such children, test-makers would do better to devise their tests so as to find out about the dialect that the children use, to enable teachers to communicate better with them.[38]

4. Discuss the following:

   Power demands compliance, and often gets it even if it means rejection of the mother tongue; but this says nothing about . . . what cultural losses it may entail. . . . The problem for the educator and social planner is to make the process preserve human dignity rather than destroy it.[39]

5. How do you react to a person who says *He don't, I won't go there no more, Who did they see? Me, I wouldn't do it?* If you react unfavorably, what is the basis for your disapproval? How does one strike a balance between two opposing demands: the need for uniformity in language and the equal right of each dialect to consideration and respect?

---

[37] Bross, Shapiro, and Anderson 1972, p. 1307.
[38] Politzer 1971.
[39] Haugen 1972, p. 311.

6. The text says that *so to, *so from, *so of are not normal in English. What about *so under the weather, so out of sorts, so on her toes?* What makes these special?

7. A study of *shall* and *will*[40] showed that *will* has always predominated in sentences of the *I will go* type, with *shall* only in recent times gaining a special favor in England. The effort to impose *shall* when the subject is *I* or *we* is now seen as a classic instance of pedantry. See if you can describe the ways in which you use *shall* and *will,* and compare them with the recommendations of any reference grammar or handbook that you can readily consult.

8. One scapegoat achieved fame in the slogan for a brand of cigarette: *Winston tastes good like a cigarette should.* This way of using *like* has long been common among English writers, including Shakespeare, but nowadays stirs feelings of guilt in many speakers. For those who would also feel uncomfortably formal if they replaced *Do it like I do it* with *Do it as I do it,* what is the two-word substitute for *like?* Can you think of another compromise expression that speakers or writers use in order to avoid both the "incorrect" expression and the uncomfortably formal "correct" one?

9. Would you regard the following as mistakes? *Tell him to kindly leave; a more perfect union; I'll explain whatever you ask about; Whenever Mary or John is at home, they answer the phone.* Decide how you would reword any that you would consider incorrect.

10. When linguists make their sweeping claim about language being "rule-governed behavior," do they refer to the rules that are explicitly stated, as in grammar books? If not, what do they mean by "rule"? Assuming that the two kinds of rules are different, what are the learning problems associated with each one? Do we learn language as efficiently by trying to follow explicit instructions as by using psychological mechanisms (whatever they are—possibly some form of unconscious inference) that enabled us to learn when we were too young to follow instructions? What does this suggest as to the probable success of textbook rules of correct usage?

11. What is the effect of being forced to learn another language? The following was written by a noted linguist. See if you think it is an exaggeration:

    Some time ago I had the opportunity to try, again, to learn to speak a new language. As a professional student of languages, I expected only the

---

[40] Fries 1956–57.

routine—but long and tedious—technical chores of vocabulary, grammar, pronunciation. I was in for a shock.

Once more—as if I had never tackled the job before since the time I grew up as a monolingual speaker of English in a town hostile to anyone found speaking any other language!—once more I felt deep cultural shock, a deep bitter nausea welling up as if to spew out in raging revolt all foreign customs, sounds, words which seemed to be invading to desecrate my very soul.

Language goes deep. It fuses with our personality structure (and our moral structure—is there any other way to say "ought"?). It grows up together. So a man brought up with just one language (the bilingual has far less trouble) is likely to feel pressure to learn a new language as a subtle attack on himself.[41]

12. "Loglan, a logical language," was announced in 1966.[42] It attempted to incorporate Hindi, Chinese, and Japanese along with Western languages. What major handicap do you think it might have?

13. What is the fundamental difference between computer "languages" (which are of course constructed) and a constructed language such as Interlingua? What are some of the linguistic applications of computers?[43]

14. The following is from a prospectus for a book in Interlingua written by a Swedish biochemist. It is on the threat of world famine. See if you can understand it, and comment on the practical utility of this Western interlanguage for scientific purposes.

Le Grande Fame: Un Stato de Guerra

Nos pote jam hodie facer observationes indicante que le etate del grande fame de facto ha comenciate. Nos pote p.ex. in certe paises 'developpante' observar le immigration del regiones rural al grande urbes, le quales se expande enormemente, p.ex. Bombay e Calcutta. Le resultato essera super-population, morte de fame, penuria, demonstrationes e revolutiones.

Adjuta per le paises industrial es necesse e ha jam comenciate in multe paises. Ma le situation es ben remarcabile, e mesmo cynic, pro que le paises povre sovente demanda armas in loco de cereales. Si le paises industrial seriosemente repartira viveres e material in mesura effective pro uso pacific, illos deberea ipse reducer lor proprie standard de vita in grado considerabile.

Le adjuta debe obviemente concentrar se a regiones que, recipiente contribution de materiales e viveres, pote possibilemente ipse meliorar lor situation, de modo que illos essera auto-sustenente.[44]

---

[41] K. L. Pike, in *Translation* (Spring 1966), p. 12.

[42] See the brief review in *Linguistics* 40:9–10 (1968).

[43] See, for example, Winograd 1974.

[44] The book is *Ante-Post,* by Gösta Ehrensvärd.

15. Look up *distrustful* in *Modern Guide to Synonyms and Related Words*[45] and study the discussion of *distrustful* and *mistrustful*. What does it reveal about the inadequacies of the definitions in most dictionaries? Is there any general meaning in the prefixes *dis-* and *mis-* that carries over into the contrast between *distrustful* and *mistrustful*?

16. After the outcry that greeted the "permissiveness" of *Webster's Third New International Dictionary*, another publisher took advantage of the opportunity to bring out a volume that would appeal to "conservative" tastes (and incidentally this dictionary turned out to be a pretty good competitor). But the editors eventually found that they were making many of the same decisions that had got the *Third* in trouble, though they were more successful in disguising them. Did the nature of language make this outcome predictable? Discuss.

17. *Webster's Third* defines the transitive sense of the verb *to hop* as 'to get upon by or as if by hopping: climb aboard.' The following fit the definition, but would you use them?

   a. The bus won't start until you hop it.
   b. I hopped the plane but got right off again because there was a bomb scare.
   c. The engineer hopped the train and we were soon in motion.
   d. The kids used to hop the old locomotive that stood in the park.

How about these?

   e. The best way to get there is to hop a plane.
   f. You can hop a freight without its costing you a nickel.
   g. I hopped a ride to Los Angeles.

Since you can't "climb aboard" a ride, there must be something that the dictionary has missed. See if you can figure it out, then consult the footnote.[46]

18. In July of 1974 the undersecretary of the treasury was on the point of

---

[45] New York: Funk and Wagnalls, 1968, p. 171.

[46] First, only a passenger does the hopping. Second, there has to be a journey with a destination. *Hop* shares some of the characteristics of *by* plus the name of a conveyance: *I hopped a plane = I went by plane;* that is why it is a bit unusual to have *hop* followed by the definite article except to refer to some regularly scheduled line (*I hopped the 9:45 and got there early*).

warning the oil-producing countries that any new cutbacks in production would be regarded by the United States and other oil importers as an "unfriendly act." The State Department objected strongly and the wording was changed to a "counterproductive measure." Is the dictionary of any help in telling what the trouble was? Discuss.

19. Government intervention in the teaching of language to civilians was rare in the United States until 1958, when the National Defense Education Act made funds available for training teachers in foreign languages. It was extended in 1963 to cover teachers of English, and more and more support was given in various forms, especially to the teaching of English in other countries. What economic and political reasons prompted this? Though the government supported the teaching of language it made no rules about what should be taught, as a national academy might do. Was this as it should be?

20. Identify the verbal put-down in the following passage:

During rush-hour traffic one day, my husband suddenly realized he had to make a left turn and crossed over from the right lane without signaling. Behind him, a driver of oriental ancestry slammed on his brakes and swerved to avoid a collision. As he passed my husband's car, he stuck his head out the car window. His eyes still wide with terror, he shouted, "Foul name! Foul name!"[47]

21. Referring to an indefinite antecedent, a writer uses the form *(s)he*. Comment.

References

Bernstein, Theodore M. 1965. *The Careful Writer: A Modern Guide to English Usage* (New York: Atheneum).

Bloomfield, Leonard. 1944. "Secondary and Tertiary Responses to Language," *Language* 20:45–55.

Bross, I. D. J.; P. A. Shapiro; and B. B. Anderson. 1972. "How Information Is Carried in Scientific Sub-languages," *Science* 176:1303–07.

Dixon, R. M. W. 1964. Review of Hans Freudenthal, *Lincos: Design of a Language for Cosmic Intercourse* (Amsterdam: North-Holland Publishing, 1960). In *Linguistics* 5:116–18.

Dobson, W. A. C. H. 1973. "China as a World Power," American Council of Learned Societies *Newsletter* 24:3.1–10.

---

[47] *Reader's Digest* (March 1971), p. 110.

Esterhill, Frank. 1974. "Reversing Babel: The Emergence of an Interlanguage," *The ATA Chronicle, Newspaper of the American Translators Association* 3:3.6–9.

Fodor, István. 1966. "Linguistic Problems and 'Language Planning' in Africa," *Linguistics* 25:18–33.

Fowler, H. W. 1926 and 1965. *Dictionary of Modern English Usage* (Oxford and London: Oxford University Press); 2nd ed., rev. by Sir Ernest Gowers (New York and Oxford, England: Oxford University Press).

Frei, Ernest J. 1959. *The Historical Development of the Philippine National Language* (Manila: Institute of National Language).

Freudenthal, Hans. 1960. *Lincos: Design of a Language for Cosmic Intercourse* (Amsterdam: North-Holland Publishing).

Fries, C. C. 1956–57. "The Periphrastic Uses of *Shall* and *Will* in Modern English," *Language Learning* 7:38–99.

Guitarte, Guillermo L., and Rafael Torres Quintero. 1968. "Linguistic Correctness and the Role of the Academies," in Thomas A. Seboek (ed.), *Current Trends in Linguistics*. Ibero-American and Caribbean Linguistics, vol. 4 (The Hague: Mouton).

Halliday, M. A. K. 1973. *Explorations in the Functions of Language* (London: Edward Arnold).

Haugen, Einar. 1972. *The Ecology of Language* (Stanford, Calif.: Stanford University Press).

Hechinger, Fred M. 1971. "Language and the Intellectual Crisis," *Foreign Language Annals* 4:272–77.

Jespersen, Otto. 1928. *An International Language* (London: Allen and Unwin).

Juilland, Alphonse. 1972. "Entry Words: Grammars and Dictionaries," in Albert Valdman (ed.), *Papers in Linguistics and Phonetics to the Memory of Pierre Delattre* (The Hague: Mouton).

Knappert, Jan. 1968. "The Function of Language in a Political Situation," *Linguistics* 39:59–67.

Makkai, Adam. 1974. " 'Take One' on *Take*: Lexo-Ecology Illustrated," *Language Sciences* 31:1–6.

Montgomery, Katherine. 1974. "Bilingual Education," Library of Congress, Congressional Research Service, 12 March.

Politzer, R. L. 1971. "Auditory Discrimination and the 'Disadvantaged': Deficit or Difference?" *English Record* 21:4.174–79.

Postal, Paul M. 1964. "Underlying and Superficial Linguistic Structure," *Harvard Educational Review* 34:246–66.

Ramos, Maximo. 1961. *Language Policy in Certain Newly Independent States* (Manila: Philippine Center for Language Study).

Read, Allen Walker. 1963–64. Series on dictionaries, in *Consumer Reports*, October 1963, pp. 488–92; November 1963, pp. 547–52; February 1964, pp. 96–97; March 1964, pp. 145–47.

Rosén, Haiim B. 1969. "Israel Language Policy, Language Teaching and Linguistics," *Ariel, a Review of the Arts and Sciences in Israel*, 25:92–111.

Sheldon, Esther K. 1947. "Walker's Influence on the Pronunciation of English," *Publications of the Modern Language Association of America* 62:130–46.

Valdman, Albert (ed.). 1972. *Papers in Linguistics and Phonetics to the Memory of Pierre Delattre* (The Hague: Mouton).

Villa Panganiban, José. 1957. "The Family of Philippine Languages and Dialects" and "A Filipino National Language Is Not Impossible," *Unitas* 30:823–33 and 855–62.

Wang, William S.-Y. 1973. "The Chinese Language," *Scientific American* 228:2.51–60.

———. 1974. "Notes on a Trip to China," *Linguistic Reporter* 16:1.3–4.

Winograd, Terry. 1974. "Artificial Intelligence—When Will Computers Understand People?" *Psychology Today* 7:12.73–79.

STYLE[1] 17

This chapter brings together some of the principles of linguistics that can be applied toward effective communication, especially effective writing. Of course no formal knowledge of linguistics probably ever inspired a readable paragraph or pleasing stanza;[2] if it were a prerequisite, Homer and Shakespeare and Mark Twain would have been carpenters or farmers or explorers. All the same, the fact that a craftsman is self-taught does not put a low value on formal teaching: a medical degree may not create a medical expert but it assures that the supply of ordinary practitioners will meet the demand and is a comfort to their patients. At a time when everyone must write at some level of proficiency, a lift up the hill may be all one can hope for; the mountains can be left to genius.

But first, what do we mean by style? Common to all definitions is the notion that "Y is used in place of X, where both X and Y are practically the same." Style involves a choice of form without a change of message. It involves that, but of course it is more than that. It includes the motives for the choice and its effects. Often these are impossible to distinguish from the content. If a writer wants to convey a supernatural presence and chooses words with phonesthematic supernatural

---

[1] The first portion of this discussion partly follows Ellis 1970, and Gray 1973.

[2] Least of all is linguistic prose the most shining example to emulate—but how many good piano teachers have been good concert pianists?

600

overtones rather than synonyms without them, has he made a stylistic choice or a semantic one? If all differences in form are correlated with differences in meaning, then the style of a piece of writing is simply its meaning. The work may stand out because of its meaning, or the author may be exceptionally skilled in finding the right words for his meaning and we take pleasure in his art, but the wrong choices would have meant something less—they would not have conveyed the meaning. Style and meaning are inseparable.

Still, the matter of choice remains, and as we look at it historically we see that from the beginning it has been a question of *translation*. From the time of the earliest literacy till the nineteenth century, reading and writing were taught through models that used a language differing in important ways from the vernacular of the learners. Homer was already antiquated at the time he was taught to Greek schoolboys. Understanding him meant translating his idiom to theirs—only, since it was "the same language," the differences were put down to style. The use of archaic models was unavoidable in cultures where written documents were few and the only assuredly respectable ones were those that had stood the test of time.

Universal literacy has partially closed the gap between the language of the models and the language of the learners; the more *they* have been able to write, the more up-to-date the writings have become. But the gap has not been closed completely and may never be, for two reasons: first, writing necessarily reaches toward the past; second, writing is writing. The first has to do with who our readers are, the second with the fact that writing is not speech.

Obviously we need not concern ourselves with one class of readers, the relatives and intimates to whom we write informal letters. They forgive us our misspellings and read our meanings between the lines because they know us. It is the unknown reader or the half-stranger who is the problem. He owes us nothing, probably speaks a different dialect from ours, and carries in his head some definite attitudes about any kind of performance that goes public. He feels contempt or pity or annoyance toward a dancer who cannot execute a dance; he is equally impatient with a writer who cannot execute a meaning in the form that he has come to expect.

That form is usually nothing other than our friend the Standard, which roughly embodies the forms that underlie all dialects and accordingly is best able to speak to all of them. The correspondence is not perfect. There is much that is preserved for the sake of preservation. But the core is the "panlectal grammar" that we saw in Chapter 11 (pages 331–32). It tends to correspond to an older phase of the language, from which the current ones have evolved. When we seek a compromise among current modes of expression, we often find it in a set of earlier forms.

So when writing preserves older forms it does so partly out of necessity. This does not guarantee that it will be understood; a given person's experience with various lects may be too limited to embrace it, and anyway there is also the unrepresentative part—the sheer tradition—kept through inertia.

The second reason for the persistence of the gap is the nature of writing as a medium for language. In Chapter 14 we described the literate person as "an expert *translator* from one mode to the other" (page 477); or, as one linguist puts it, "In being required constantly to pass from sounds to letters, and from letters to sounds, we are in the situation of a truly bilingual interpreter."[3] But though bilingual in this sense, the writer is not *natively* so. He learns the basics of his language before he can read a single word, and the learning process itself is partly one of translating what he already knows into a new medium. Furthermore, as best we can tell he is not programmed genetically for reading and writing as he is for hearing and speaking; that may come some day, but meanwhile writing is more truly an overlaid function than speaking is. And being learned comparatively late, it depends more on precepts and less on examples. This is not to say that there is not an abundance of things for an alert mind simply to absorb by being exposed to them, but only that the value of explicit rules is somewhat higher in writing than in speaking.

These things have partly made writing what it is, and have determined that meanings cannot be conveyed in exactly the same ways as through speech. A number of the devices that separate the two were outlined in Chapter 14 (pages 471–78); there we saw that the advantage sometimes lies with speech, sometimes with writing. But whereas we need no practice in adjusting speech to make up for its deficiencies (anyone who can say **my sister's investments** will automatically paraphrase it as **the investments of my sister** if it is liable to be misunderstood as 'the investments of my sisters'), we do need at least to be reminded of the occasions when a paraphrase is needed in the other direction. The reason is that we monitor our writing sub-vocally, reading in an intonation, and the fact that the intonation is not actually shown and our reader is going to have to guess at it is as likely as not to escape our attention. "Intonation" is to be understood in the broadest sense, to include variations not only in pitch but in timing and loudness—that is, the whole of speech *prosody*. As that is the most important adjustment in translating our vocalized thoughts to letters and spaces, we will look at it first.

---

[3] Haas 1970, p. 1.

SUBSTITUTING FOR THE PROSODIC MARKERS OF SPEECH

With two persons communicating face to face, the speaker usually gets immediate feedback when his meaning is unclear. If what he said was too faint he can repeat it; if it was ambiguous he can paraphrase; if something was lacking he can supply it. In writing, such emergencies have to be met in advance. The strategy is to ask ourselves, at every step, "What will our reader infer from this?" Far more than the meaning of individual words is involved, though the right word (and even more, the apt comparison, which no thesaurus can give us) is a critical question too. The worst trouble is our unconsciously expecting our reader to infer the same intonation that is ringing in our ears when we write.

Taking advantage of the unmarked accent pattern

Give a person any such string as the following to read aloud, and he is almost certain to assign it two major accents, one at the beginning (except for function words) and the other at the end, symbolized by ` and ´ (there are also intermediate prominences at rhythmic intervals, but they are less important):

Mònday, Tuesday, Wednesday, Thúrsday

À, B, C, D, É

Òne, two, three, four, five, síx

Àugust the twenty-sécond

Hènry the Fírst

The first Hénry

This habit tells us what our reader is going to do when he scans our sentences: unless we provide him with some other indication (such as italics), which we rarely do unless we want to signal something as *really* prominent, he will tend to put the major accent as close as possible to the end, which is normally the stressed syllable of the last content word before a major syntactic break.[4] Since we also depend on accent

---

[4] This is the same habit we noted earlier (pages 175–76, question 6), which leads speakers, when they are excited, to alter the stress of words, moving it farther to the right—saying, for example, as a radio newscaster did referring to the state of former President Truman's health, *because of lack of appetíte* (instead of *áppetite*).

to highlight the most important and informative *idea* in the sentence, the trick is to arrange our words so that the one signifying that idea will come at that point. The figure of speech termed *chiasmus* is an instance of this kind of maneuvering for effect; the example in *Webster's Third New International Dictionary* is **A sùperman in physique but in intellect a fóol.** Here the writer has taken advantage of both of the usual points of prominence to highlight **superman** and **fool.** If we were speaking the sentence instead of writing it, the prominence could be got by using a marked accent pattern:

But in writing there is no way to indicate this. So a sentence such as **She wasn't responsible** is a problem. It can be interpreted two ways: 'It wasn't her fault' or 'She was an irresponsible person.' The first meaning can be conveyed almost unambiguously in speech by accenting **she** and de-accenting **responsible;** if **responsible** is accented, the sentence is more open to the other interpretation. To avoid the latter, we can choose a different construction which will get the meaning of 'she' into the unmarked position for the accent: **It wasn't because of her.** It is often necessary to change the construction in order to accommodate the accent, and that is part of the survival value of such alternating constructions as active and passive. Sometimes all we have to do is rearrange: **Mary's OK but I hate John** requires accents on both **hate** and **John** (the major one on **hate**) and an inconclusive final intonation:

By changing it to **Mary's OK but John I hate** we get **hate** in the unmarked position and can use a terminal fall, which a reader almost automatically chooses when he comes to the end of a declarative sentence punctuated with a period.

A badly arranged sentence can lead to nonsense as easily as to ambiguity. The following appeared in a medical journal: **Instead of measles, vaccination will be considered essential.**[5] The concept that contrasts

---

[5] *Journal of the American Medical Association,* quoted in *Reader's Digest* (January 1962), p. 72.

with 'measles' is 'vaccination'; the word should move to the end: *Instead of measles, we must have vaccination.*

Highlighting with extra words

When the unmarked pattern is already being used for other purposes, how is one to highlight additional elements in a sentence? In speech, more accents are thrown in. In writing it may be necessary to add a word that will focus the accent. The following appeared in the *New York Times: The tone of the Spanish press in recent weeks has been so openly anti-British and anti-French that neutral observers are wondering whether Spain desires to associate herself more closely with Western Europe.*[6] The key word here is *desires,* but the reader is almost certain to miss it on first reading. Making it *really desires* solves the problem. The sentence occurring on page 469, line 20, was originally written *Some key their primary symbols to distinctive sounds.* In speech there is no problem because *some* can be accented and given a rise–fall–rise intonation. But the reader at first glance sees *key* as a noun and *some* modifying it; the remedy is to add *of them* after *some.* The sentence on page 527, line 31, was originally written *The fact that making a choice in one system constitutes the entry condition into a lower system, and that in turn the entry condition to a still lower system. . . .* The second *that,* without the extra accent available in speaking, appeared to correlate with *the fact,* just like the first *that;* by adding *one* after it, the demonstrative interpretation was clinched. As these examples make clear, there is no way to formulate any general rule for remedying the lack of interior accents. All the writer can do is stay alert and use whatever trick comes to mind. The sentence on page 535, line 12, was originally written *and now that knowledge had to be made explicit. . . .* With an accent and a rise–fall–rise intonation on *now* the meaning 'at the time in question' would have been clear; but as it stood, the *now* next to *that* suggested the adverbial conjunction *now that.* Here the trick was to eliminate *that* and make other adjustments: *such knowledge would now be made explicit. . . .*

Making punctuation marks do their bit

In its miserly regard for intonation, print allows us only nine marks,[7] and even then mixes logical considerations with intonational ones. The

---

[6] (25 February 1957).

[7] They are . , ; : ? ! — ( ) " " (counting parentheses and quotation marks as one each). There are also single quotes and brackets, which are less apt to be intonationally distinctive.

colon is defined more logically than intonationally, though it tends to correlate with a fall to medium pitch. Aside from parentheses (treated later), the period is the only fairly consistent sign intonationally: it marks a fall to a low pitch. Since the reader expects that, it is well not to fool him by constructing the sentence in such a way that the period stands where there has to be a terminal rise or an incomplete fall. We have already seen one example of this: *Mary's OK but I hate John.*—the arrangement *Mary's OK but John I hate.* avoids the problem. All too often there is no way out, and we simply have to hope that our reader will be imaginative enough to add the proper intonation. *He didn't mean to hurt you* would almost always be said with a terminal rise in spite of the conventional period:

He   He
  didn't mean to   didn't mean to   hurt
          hurt you·   OR   you·

As for commas, aside from avoiding them when they slow things down too much (*After that we had no trouble* is racy by comparison with *After that, we had no trouble*—but the choice depends on the intention), the main thing is to put them wherever an intonational break is needed to avoid ambiguity. In one instance this is amenable to rule: always put a comma before the conjunctions *and* and *or* when they are at the end of a series of equal items. Newspapers and a few other publications that imitate newspapers have the habit of omitting the comma on the theory that when it is used it replaces the conjunction, and if the conjunction is there, the comma is useless. So we get sentences like this one, which must be read twice to be understood: *After this dialog, the dialog repetition and the directed dialog are thoroughly mastered, the instructors should explain the whole German verb system.*[8] Another place where mass publications frequently leave out an intonational comma is before a *not* that introduces some contrasting parallel construction, as in this citation: *The veteran's advice to the young MP is the best prescription for success: "Make your name in committees not in the country."*[9] Without comma intonation the *not* phrase is restrictive: 'Make your name in committees that are not in the country.'

The question mark is a problem because more than with any other sign of punctuation, the grammatical meaning often conflicts with the

---

[8] From a German textbook.
[9] *Harper's Magazine* (May 1963), p. 22.

intonational one. We can test the interpretation that readers are tempted to put on it by having them read aloud: their tendency is to use a rising pitch at that point whether it is appropriate or not. Grammatically, the conventions of punctuation require that questions of all types be punctuated with the question mark (except, occasionally, exclamatory questions: *How did he do it!*). But interrogative-word questions more often than not have a terminal fall:

<pre>
          time   go
  What   Where are you
        is   ing?
          it?
</pre>

To complicate matters further, there are rhetorical questions, questions that do not really ask, which are also conventionally given the question mark. Note the difference in the following:

<pre>
                    do   what was I
      what was I to   to d
  But   But
                       o?   o?
</pre>

The second usually implies either 'There was nothing I could do' or 'There was nothing for me to do other than what I did'; it then calls for no answer. In the first intonation there is at least an overall rise before the terminal fall, which gives some justification for the question mark. Writers nowadays often use the period in the second type. The conventions should yield at this point, because interrogative-word questions are always recognizable as questions in their structure, and the punctuation should be free to indicate whether they really ask.

The only other mark with a fairly clear intonational correlation is the parenthesis. It signifies an overall drop in pitch, with the normal internal pitch contrasts still maintained at the lower level (page 138):

<pre>
  (What ever   you   say
                           this
                    about   (and I'm sure you're going to say
</pre>

<pre>
            just don't make me out to be re spon
                                                      sible
  some   for it.
       thing)
</pre>

In speech it is even possible to have three levels going at once. The most striking example is the old-time spelling bee in which the contestants were required to syllabify as well as spell and give the accumulated word as far as they had gone. The result was a high-pitched naming of letters, a mid-pitched pronunciation of the newly spelled syllable, and a low-pitched repetition of previous syllables up to that point:

Spell *Constantinople.*

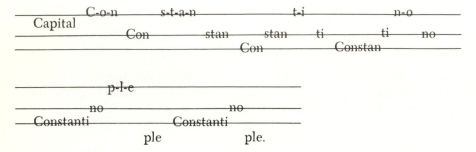

The levels here are a virtual chant, but their significance is apparent: the more known, expected, and therefore incidental the element is, the more it can be thrust into the background.

The dash serves logically the same purpose of an "aside," but it tends to be used where there is no drop in pitch—if dashes replace the parentheses in the foregoing example, the whole interpolation *and I'm sure you're going to say something* may be interpreted as staying at the same high level as the parts that surround it; the information is foregrounded, felt to be just as vital as that of the main sentence. (The *single* dash, such as the one in the first sentence in this paragraph, has a different purpose, similar to that of a colon or a semicolon but suggesting a closer tie.)

As the intonational correspondence is fairly clear-cut, the writer does not run much danger of misapplying these marks; but there is danger of abusing them, especially the parenthesis. The overly meticulous writer, who wants to make sure that he does justice to all the side issues as well as the main ones, is apt to stud his lines with so many parentheses that the reader feels as if he were pushing through an obstacle course. To understand a sentence we have to organize it in our heads, and we can tolerate only so much extraneous stuff. The best advice is either to write another paragraph in which all the *ifs* and *buts* are given their due, or trust your reader to know that there is nothing absolutely positive in this world and that when you make a flat statement you mean to allow for exceptions.

Supplying formulaic guideposts

Many instances of supposedly free arrangements of elements in a sentence are actually designed with some illocutionary purpose—to separate topic from comment, mark what is important, show where the connections lie, signal a transition, and so on. The bulk of this burden in spoken communication is carried by intonation and gesture, so that little attention needs to be paid to it *verbally*. When a speaker wants to change the topic he can shift his position in his chair or stand up, or look in a different direction, or pause and take a deep breath, or make an abrupt change in pitch or rhythm. A writer has to use more subtle means. Take a sentence such as ***It helps to explain the many striking ways in which transformational derivation resembles historical derivation.*** When we say it aloud we can adjust the accents on ***transformational derivation*** and ***historical derivation*** so that they are on the same footing—each can be made to sound as much like a "new idea" as the other. But in writing, given the fact that grammatical arrangements tend to coincide with psychological ones (page 149), it may appear that ***transformational derivation*** is "known" (the topic already under discussion) and ***historical derivation*** is "new" (the comment). To avoid this, the construction can be changed to a coordination, which is more democratic: . . . ***the many striking ways in which transformational derivation and historical derivation resemble each other.*** (This sentence is from pages 331–32.) It might seem that when items are not in this kind of coordinative balance, the reader can be trusted to infer an intended imbalance, but that too has to be guaranteed in writing. Take the following sentence, which appeared at the beginning of a paragraph (page 506) and was supposed to signal a transition to a new idea, something to do with Greeks: ***The Greek tradition was philosophical as well as grammatical.*** In speaking, a strong accent on ***Greek*** is enough to announce the change, and it might seem that italicizing the word would be the proper written substitute; but italics here are too forceful—they would suggest a fact in some respect *dissimilar* to what precedes, rather than merely a different item in an enumeration. (In speech the distinction is gradient: a strong accent for change of topic, a stronger one plus a head gesture for contrast.) The transition has to be marked verbally; one way is to add ***as for: As for the Greeks, their tradition was philosophical as well as grammatical.*** This tells the reader to highlight ***Greeks*** intonationally. Again, it is just as important to make sure of the opposite reading if the wording suggests an accent where one does not belong. The sentence ***There is good psychological evidence for the primacy of meaning over syntax—in comprehension, for example, which is a "sloppy process in which syntactic rules are used as a crutch . . ."*** (from page 541) causes no trouble when said aloud because the speaker can lower the pitch on *in comprehension* and put a deep fall after *example,* to show that *comprehension* is not to be highlighted as a supplementary topic which is about to be elaborated on, but only carries on with the syntax of what precedes. Without this to aid him, the reader is apt to interpret the initial position of a locative phrase (*in comprehension*) as introducing a new sentence, and he will not know that he is wrong till he plays the record through and finds no verb anywhere. By inverting *in comprehension* and *for example* the trouble is avoided. There are probably hundreds of similar "false cognates" that the skilled translator from speech to writing learns to watch out for— far too many at least for us to do more than sample them.

MAINTAINING CONTRAST

The most constantly recurring theme in linguistics is contrast. It defines the phoneme as a distinctive unit; it sets the limits of morphemes as the distinctive stuff in words and the limits of words as the distinctive carriers of meaning. It is the expression of *value* in language, of one sign for one signification and one signification for one sign. It is what drives the wedge between one form and another the moment that speakers perceive a difference, as when *arrant* and *errant* come to assume different meanings because they look different, though to begin with they were only variant spellings of a single word. Its lack is the death knell of words that we feel ought to be different in form because they are different in meaning or function, but fail the test: *succor* could not survive the backstage laugh of *sucker.*

Contrast lurks in every cranny of language and mostly was there when we came on the scene, waiting to be learned—we did not have to make one phoneme or one syntactic rule different from another. There are few demands to maintain it when we speak, because the resources are there and we use them automatically; if one message fails, we deliver another. For the writer the test is harder. He cannot sit at his reader's elbow and deal another card from his deck of synonyms when the one he has written plays him false. He has to make sure in advance not only that the numbers and faces are distinct but that diamonds will not be confused with hearts.

Mostly his task involves the choice of words. We saw earlier how certain of them are restricted in their contexts: *her too happy children* sounds the same as *her two happy children,* and here the difficulty is so predictable that it leads to a virtual rule in English: no *too* with an adjective that precedes a plural noun (page 439). Ordinarily the writer does not have his decisions made for him like this and he has to go through what he has written and carefully spring each of the traps he has unwittingly laid for his reader.

One warning sign for the self-editor is his repetition of a word. We saw earlier (pages 214–15) that it is false to regard the avoidance of repetition as a *rule*—we must be ready not only to "call a spade a spade but to double spades and redouble." But that is only when the spade truly *is* a spade. Except when an object is being given a name (and must thereafter be referred to by the same name whenever a pronoun cannot replace it), most repetitions of the "same" word turn out to have slightly different senses, and then if we can find a suitable synonym we had better use it, trusting to the context and the something-like principle to establish a semantic difference to suit our purpose. The problem is a psychological one. When the reader encounters the same word on one line that he has just met two lines up, he tends to assume that it has the same meaning. The two different uses to which the writer has put it may be perfectly legitimate as far as the normal definitions of the word go, but the result is a kind of pun—not usually funny, just misleading. The passage on page 512, line 11, was originally worded as follows: *Though Hjelmslev was first by right of discovery, it was not till the publication of . . . Syntactic Structures . . . that theory came into its own. Several of Chomsky's contemporaries were elaborating systems of their own. . . .* The repetition of *own*, again with a possessive and under a main accent, suggested an unintended relationship between *its own* and *their own;* the solution was to change *systems of their own* to *other systems,* substituting another expression of uniqueness. It is well to lean over backwards. On page 524, line 36, there occurs the expression *what passes for communication;* a few lines later (page 525, line 3) the wording at first was *when no information passes through.* It was hardly likely that there would be any confusion, but nothing was lost by changing *passes* to *travels.*

Of course one must be on guard lest the new expression turn out to be as bad as the old one, or worse. The word *only* has quite different meanings in *an only child* and *only a child.* In the singular the position of the article helps out, but in the plural the homophony is perfect: *only children.* Apparently sensing this and hoping to avoid it, one pair of authors wrote *Adam and Eve were single children when we began the study.*[10] Now we seem to be talking about *unmarried* children. A better solution would have been to say *Adam was an only child, and so was Eve, when we began the study.*

---

[10] In the *Harvard Educational Review* 34 (1964), p. 134.

AVOIDING OUTRIGHT AMBIGUITY

Not all unwanted meanings come with intonational tags. Many are as apt to plague us in speech as in writing, but the writer must use extra caution because of the gap in space and time between him and his audience.

The accidental pun is the more subtle offender: *There was a sprinkling of children among those who were baptized.*[11] It does not so much create a misunderstanding as beguile the reader onto a bypath. The ordinary ambiguity can do either or both. A word may undergo a change that degrades it (see page 256) and the writer or speaker who is accustomed to the older sense neglects to update himself. On page 418 there was a phrase reading *like gay dirges or circular squares.* Most readers would probably accept this, but there is a special breed that delights in such opportunities; so to remove it, *gay* was changed to *joyous.* A word may be defined in a special sense in the writer's field, and this puts it off limits for him in some everyday sense; for example, in a chapter dealing with linguistic theory it would be ill-advised to use the term *model* to mean 'something to be imitated.'

Grammatical ambiguity is more treacherous because writers tend to pay less attention to constructions than to words. The novelist who wrote *Peter nodded. Sir Douglas Froude had commanded the army before he was born and had retired soon after that event*[12] was obviously nodding alongside of Peter. The writer who criticized the New York *Times* because it *skirts the question of whether all verdicts in civil actions designed to punish rather than to recompense the plaintiff are invalid*[13] failed to see that using *punish* intransitively and following it by *recompense the plaintiff* was bound to make *plaintiff* seem to be the object of both verbs; the solution would have been to write *punish the defendant.* The sentence *He* [Nehru] *wants their* [the Russians'] *planes and he wants to limit Russian assistance to his enemies, the Chinese*[14] can be taken to mean that Nehru wanted only the Chinese to have the planes; the ambiguity lies in what *to his enemies* is a constituent of: does it go with *limit* or with *assistance?* By using *set a limit on* instead of *limit,* or by inserting *offered* after *assistance,* the undesired grammatical construction is avoided.

---

[11] Example from Bernstein 1965, p. 10.

[12] Nevil Shute, *On the Beach* (New York: Signet Books, 1960), p. 76.

[13] *The Nation* (27 January 1964), p. 95.

[14] *The Saturday Evening Post* (19 January 1963), p. 65.

AVOIDING OTHER DISTRACTIONS

Ambiguity distracts because of some clearly statable form-to-meaning duplicity in the language. But the reader comes with many other expectations that are much harder to formulate and yet may bait him into traps equally dangerous if the writer does not lay out a clear path.

Denotations that detonate

The thesaurus addict who writes ***They impetrated the concessions*** for 'They obtained the concessions by entreaty' may impress us with his learning but not with much else. This is really just a special case of choosing the wrong register, but is a virulent form that attacks writers especially. Not that they are not entitled to sympathy, for all too often the logically best word is the very one that cannot be used. English badly needs a one-word verb to avoid the phrase ***make possible,*** with its usual requirement of end position for ***possible: Hybridization makes possible such new crops*** is awkward and ***Hybridization makes such new crops possible*** deprives ***new crops*** of the sentence accent; yet ***possibilitate,*** despite its dictionary entry, is out of the question. English is in the same predicament with many such causative expressions—***to make possible, to make feasible, to render useless.*** We simply have to bear with the infirmities of our language.

Wrong register

We saw earlier that most writing tends to be upgraded to the deliberative level (page 359). A writer who slips down to the casual is apt to call attention to the shift and distract his reader. A sentence such as ***Secretary Kissinger was worried about the agreement*** may cast an overly personal light on an affair of state; if we say that he was ***apprehensive*** we make him a diplomat again. Nothing needs to be said about the introduction of folk speech or slang in high company—calling a violinist a ***fiddler*** or a dancer a ***hoofer*** is excusable only if it is intentional.

Misuse of demonstratives

The demonstratives most often misused are ***this*** and its plural, ***these.*** Three uses are involved, two of which need little discussion. One is the "impertinent" ***this,*** used by speakers and writers who are too lazy or too chummy to bother with introductions and assume that their hearers or readers already know what or whom they are talking about. It came on the scene at least as early as the 1930s: *Only a year ago, in Brooklyn, there was this . . .* begins Edward Everett Horton in a 1935 movie, *In Caliente.* The other is the "organization man" *this,* dating from around 1950, which has brought about what appears to be a switch in markedness between *this* and *that: This is true,* referring to what the *other* person has said.[15] The result is that whereas formerly *that* was the usual demonstrative for cross-reference and *this* was chosen only to emphasize closeness, now *this* is becoming the unmarked term with *that* relegated to emphasis on distance. The third *this* is normal by all existing standards but is a greater menace to the reader. It is a verbal taking-by-the-shoulders and pointing-in-a-direction that has to be used sparingly if it is not to shake the reader too rudely. In a passage like *Holding the registration down to twenty was the only way to keep the class manageable. We saw this the first time we set this limit in this school,* the reader is being compelled to focus three ways almost at once. It is better for the writer to avoid the arm signals by arranging for the referents to be inferred from the context. One instance of a *this* or *these* should be the maximum up to the point where there is a change of subject. The passage could read: *Holding our registration down to twenty was the only way to keep the class manageable. We saw this the first time that limit was set here.* The phrase *that limit* removes one *this,* and *our* and *here* take care of *this school.*[16]

AVOIDING OVERSTATEMENT

"As a rule," complained Somerset Maugham, "the amateur is rhetorical. He has an inordinate liking for picturesque words and highflown phrases. At the back of his mind are all manner of literary tags and he brings them in under the impression that they look workmanlike."[17]

---

[15] Bernstein 1965 theorizes that the start may have been from Yiddish, which lacks the distinction between far and near demonstratives. But something else is needed to explain the preference for *this* over *that*—perhaps the increasing compactness of society and nearness of everything and everybody to everything and everybody else.

[16] Puzzle: Why should *this* be so much easier to overuse than *that?* Perhaps because the field of *that* is wider and the focus it demands less sharp.

[17] *Don Fernando, or, Variations on Some Spanish Themes* (New York: Doubleday, Doran, 1943), p. 94.

This is again a problem of translation. That amateur at writing may be accounted a brilliant conversationalist. It is only when his tricks are set in type that they stand exposed as exaggerations, banalities, or plagiarisms.

Any resource has a sporting chance in the heat of speaking. There is no time to edit; the speaker's memory serves up whatever gets caught in the drift and seldom labels it new or secondhand. And the audience is usually not a captive one—words must not only carry a message but hold the attention (see pages 18–19).

For writing, the fires must not be stoked in this fashion. Unless a reader is attracted by what you have to say, your way of saying it is not likely to win him over (though it can easily drive him off). No rival speaker is waiting his chance to interrupt you, and there is no surrounding din to pit your loudness against. Much of the work of translation is therefore the simple act of pruning.

What is pruned is the twofold redundancy of speech—overemphasis and repetition—needed to tone things up and overcome the noise in the channel. Overemphasis is a kind of loudness that makes our words and meanings intelligible against background hiss; repetition makes certain that if our hearer misses what we say the first time he will get a second chance. Writing must tone things down. Neither kind of redundancy is necessary. There is no background noise, and if the reader misses, the passage is still there and can be re-read.

Overemphasis is most glaring in the surplus of intensifiers, above all with adjectives that are absolutes in their own right. We saw earlier how calling something *very unique* saps the adjective (page 417); the same goes for *so perfect, so unparalleled, very devastating.* Unless the adjective is stronger than the noun it can only subtract from it—*a serious crisis* is less than *a crisis,* though *a grave crisis* may be a little more; as for *a serious catastrophe,* it might not do for Susie's fall off her tricycle, but it is hardly apt for the destruction of Herculaneum either. So far the mixers of dynamite and water have not got around to *a bad cataclysm,* but give them time.

The writer is in a position to restore some of the vitality of these debilitated nouns, adjectives, and verbs. In fact, it has come to the point that omitting the intensifier (especially *very*) makes words stronger than using it; this is as true of the ordinary words as of the powerful ones. So if someone congratulates you and you express your appreciation by writing that you are *gratified,* you compliment him more than if you say you are *very gratified.* (The difficulty is again partly prosodic. The reader is apt to infer the tongue-in-cheek, damn-with-faint-praise intonation and gesture that so often accompany *very* in speech. Omitting it leaves nothing to hang such an interpretation on.)

Some overstatement comes from trying too hard—a different kind of mistranslation. The writer is aware that he must compensate for the loss of all those rich harmonies in speech, but he overdoes it. He is determined to make sure that no question any reader might want to ask is left unanswered, so he answers them all, including the obvious ones. There is something basic to human perception in the problem this creates. When we recognize an object we do not fix on every detail but only on the high points—it is as if some aspects of reality were categorized in a roughly "emic" way, with "etic" details left aside. A greater realism may be achieved with less detail rather than more. The artist senses the distinctive trait and trusts his viewers to fill in according to *their* perceptions; some irrelevant particular may actually be a distraction if it happens to be one that a viewer customarily ignores or views in a different way. It is the same with readers. They expect to be given just the particulars they need, and they approach the writer on these terms; whatever he says they assume is necessary, and if a lot of it is merely incidental they are confused. An unnecessary word is not merely a dead weight, it is a stumbling block. It is not the obvious tautology that causes the most trouble, like the remark of the United States senator who wrote that **while the people are numerically more numerous, they are collectively weak;**[18] rather it is the broadside that blankets the target instead of making a clean hit. The following passage is not really bad by comparison with some of the worst writing in the social sciences, but it will do for an illustration:

> To cite a definite example of how deeply seated this inner need for suffering is, we may mention the following well-known clinical fact: many neurotic patients begin to feel subjectively worse as soon as they sense a slight improvement in their symptoms or even at the very beginning of the analytical treatment; they then develop severe anxiety states and at times even a weird drive for self-destruction; one could observe clearly in such patients how they cling with at least the same persistency to the suffering as they clung to the gratification which the symptoms usually provided.[19]

First a pruning, then a commentary:

> The inner need for suffering runs deep. It is well known, for example, that many patients will begin to imagine they feel worse the moment they

---

[18] Senator Paul Douglas, in *The American Scholar* (Winter 1967–68), p. 40.

[19] Franz Alexander, M.D., and Hugo Staub, *The Criminal, the Judge and the Public* (New York: Collier Books, 1962), p. 74.

feel the least bit better—or even at the very beginning of treatment. They develop severe anxiety and at times even a drive toward self-destruction. They cling at least as hard to the suffering as they clung to the gratification that they usually got from their symptoms.

The original abounds in explications of the obvious. It not only cites an example but announces that it is going to *(to cite a definite example)*; not only mentions a fact but specifically assumes the *may* of permission to do so *(we may mention)*; not only makes an observation but takes care that there will be no mistake about it *(one could observe clearly)*. The account from which the passage is taken is already known to concern *neurotic* patients and *analytical* treatment, but that is not good enough: the labels have to be supplied. No context is needed to see that if an example is to be given it will naturally *follow,* and as for *weird,* the authors plainly intend the weirdness to consist in the very fact of there being such a drive, since they say no more about it, and the reader might as well form his own impression. The word *states* adds nothing to anxiety; either it is pure makeweight or it can be inferred from the authors' general position. Even if all the traffic signaling in these expressions is retained, the cited example will still surely be a *definite* one and the observing will be done *clearly.* And would it be possible for a patient to feel *objectively* worse? Yet the real failure of this sentence is that it tries to conceal a paradox instead of exploiting it—feeling worse at the same time as feeling better: *feel* is transformed into *sense,* and the opposite of *worse,* which should be *better,* is disguised as *a slight improvement.* These are only the obvious turns in the whole circumlocutory journey. The long-winded predicative construction with *be (how deeply seated . . . is)* says no more than the two words *runs deep.* The only clinical improvement possible is the one *in their symptoms* (would we assume the authors are talking about an improvement in the weather or the national economy?). *Such patients* have been the dramatis personae of the whole paragraph; the phrase gives no more information than the pronoun *they. With persistency* is a self-important way of saying *hard.*

What anxiety state do the clinical symptoms of such neurotic writing point to? A weird, severe, and persistent *insecurity* in the powers of expression and a *mistrust* of all readers. The two add up to verbiage: on the one hand, words that will identify the writers as professionals in their field; on the other, words to answer questions that no one needs to ask.

AVOIDING JARGON[20]

Something over two hundred years ago the Secretary to the Commissioners of Excise sent a warning to the Supervisor of Pontefract, the Yorkshire town that gave its name to Pomfret cakes:

> The Commissioners on perusal of your Diary observe that you make use of many affected phrases and incongruous words, such as "illegal procedure," "harmony," etc., all of which you use in a sense that the words do not bear. I am ordered to acquaint you that if you hereafter continue that affected and schoolboy way of writing, and to murder the language in such a manner, you will be discharged for a fool.[21]

If the Commissioners were upset with *illegal procedure* and *harmony*, what would they have made of the following?

> For the purposes of subparagraph (1) of this paragraph, if a farmer-producer has a maximum price for a given class of sales or deliveries of a given variety and kind of vegetable seed, but not for another class of sales or deliveries thereof, he shall determine his maximum price for such latter class of sales or deliveries by adding to or subtracting from his maximum price for the class of sales and deliveries for which he has an established maximum price hereunder the premium or discount, as the case may be, in dollars and cents normal to the trade during said base period, for the class of sales or deliveries to be priced in relation to said class of sales or deliveries for which he has an established maximum price hereunder; and the resultant figure shall be his maximum price for the class of sales and deliveries in question.[22]

This was from the collection of former Congressman Maury Maverick, the coiner of the term *gobbledygook,* who sees the motive for it as "just an attempt to impress the reader or the boss with the writer's learning."

---

[20] The "jargon of anatomy" mentioned on page 342 uses *jargon* in another sense, that of technical vocabulary, which of course is essential in every specialized field. Language becomes jargon in the reprehensible sense only when the technically informed person uses it to browbeat his audience—or, even within the field, when plain language serves equally well. When persons in set theory refer to a *set-theoretical approach* instead of a *set-theory approach* they gain nothing technically and create confusion because of extraneous connotations of the adjective *theoretical.* The scientist who dotes on the trappings of his science is like a Ph.D. who wears his robes to bed.

[21] Gowers 1962, pp. 46–47, quoting from John Aye, *Humour in the Civil Service* (London: C. Palmer, 1928).

[22] Quoted by Maury Maverick, "The Curse of Gobbledygook," *Reader's Digest* (August 1944), pp. 109–10.

But in addition to the more or less innocently self-seeking motive there is often a sinister one: to say, or to be able to say that one has said, the literal truth without being caught in it. L. E. Sissman puts his finger on both motives in his definition of "Plastic English":

> All of those debased and isolable forms of the mother tongue that attempt to paper over an unpalatable truth and/or to advance the career of the speaker (or the issue, cause or product he is agent for) by a kind of verbal sleight of hand, a one-upmanship of which the reader or listener is victim.[23]

If we want separate terms we can use Maverick's *gobbledygook* for plain jargon and *doublespeak* for jargon that is a sophisticated form of lying.

For a writer who *has* the ulterior motive, the admonitions here and in Chapter 8 will only be so many temptations, and all we can hope to do is to expose him when he tries to fool us. But if there is a chance to save the soul of a still uncorrupted beginner who listens to the sound of jargon and is mesmerized by it, then we must repeat that the only good writing is honest writing and the only readers who will be captivated by a windy fool are other windy fools. More than the uncorrupted beginner there are all those who are now and then betrayed into windiness by the gusty prose blowing around them. Jargon is like the common cold. It can probably never be abolished, but it can be avoided by living a clean life and keeping out of drafts.

The regimen has already been laid out and need not be repeated here—such matters as question-begging (page 251), grammatical ambiguity (page 262), hidden sentences (page 166), explicitness (pages 261–62), and truth in general (pages 257–64). Jargon unfortunately is not as "isolable" as Sissman thinks; its effectiveness, for those who use it deliberately, is precisely a labyrinthine quality that defies isolation. There is no limit to nor immunization against the sowing of confusion. The best treatment is by example. So here is another, made to order by Mark Twain, to show that the song goes to the tune of fine writing as well as government reports:

> It was a crisp and spicy morning in early October. The lilacs and laburnums, lit with the glory-fires of autumn, hung burning and flashing in the upper air, a fairy bridge provided by kind Nature for the wingless wild things that have their homes in the tree-tops and would visit together; the larch and the pomegranate flung their purple and yellow flames in brilliant broad splashes along the slanting sweep of the wood-

---

[23] "Plastic English," *Atlantic Monthly* (October 1972), p. 32.

land; the sensuous fragrance of innumerable deciduous flowers rose upon the swooning atmosphere; far in the empty sky a solitary esophagus slept upon motionless wing; everywhere brooded stillness, serenity, and the peace of God.[24]

BEING LITERATE

When Archie Bunker complains of being prostate from the heat, everybody in the audience except the other Archie Bunkers gets a good laugh.

Malapropisms are the tip of an iceberg. They are the misuses of words that all but the most ignorant are aware of. Yet the general reaction to them is the same emotion as the more selective one felt by those who are more or less in the know toward countless other misuses or near-misuses of language. Since the writer's audience will usually include a few who catch such dissonances and are distracted by them, it behooves him not to flout their sensibilities. This is just as important as not fueling a locomotive with diesel oil for an 1860 movie set. Six-year-olds will enjoy the picture, but anachronisms and other incongruities will spoil it for others.

Avoiding such trouble in language calls for more than an acquaintance with the most obvious meanings of words. It demands a vast and deep familiarity with the inferences as well as the references, with the hovering meanings as well as the central ones, with what the words were as well as with what they are, with what they might be for others as well as what they are for us—and with their potential for evocation in the context in which we use them. On pages 302–03 John Ciardi told us how the poet, with the words he summons in his effort to be accurate, "will have leaked a ghost that was nowhere in his mind at starting." All words leak ghosts, which are the shadows in a hall of mirrors that glance in ever dimming regression to infinity, the reflections of every sense and association that was ever set up in our minds between a word and its universe. We can only hope to form enough of those associations ourselves so that our minds will resonate with others', and we can evoke compatible ghosts.

A trivial example will be found in the second paragraph of this section, in the use of the word *audience.* For the person who *is word sensitive,* as Ciardi says in italics, this noun may possibly seem out of place, for it comes from the Latin *audīre* and refers to an assembly of

---

[24] From Twain's "Double-Barrelled Detective Story," quoted in *Word Study* 16:2 (1940), p. 5.

hearers, not of readers. So the writer, if he is not merely careless, will use it with discretion. He might, instead, say *readers, readership,* or *public.* But these evoke their own ghosts, which perhaps are even more disquieting. *Writer's readers* summons a raucous alliterative ghost (it would be about as happy a choice as *jeepers creepers* in this context), and *writer's readership* summons a two-headed ghost, half alliterative and half techno-editorial. As for *public,* it has the swagger of the actress who l-o-o-v-e-s all the lovely people out there who love her. Of course if the word *writer's* is omitted, then the first alternative is acceptable: *the readers will usually include . . . ;* but this weakens the sentence by leaving its most important actor to be inferred and *behooves him* must be changed to *behooves the writer.* If the choice is *audience* it is at least an informed choice, and wagers the hope that most readers will construe the word to include all receivers of the message, and that the few others will accept the slight metaphor of readers who listen as they read.

No practiced writer trudges through all his decisions in the way this description suggests; as in most other uses of language, the proper choice offers itself in an intuitive flash. But some decisions are pored over by even the most skilled, and the best advice to the apprentice is to be as thoughtful as possible.

Also to be as attentive as possible. No recipe in this book or elsewhere will substitute for the observant absorption of one's own culture. Linguistics, rhetoric, and stylistics have not codified a tenth of the verbal instruments that make for intelligible and pleasing written communication. It may be that the highest goal of writing is out of their reach. "The caverns of the imagination and the hall of memory," says the Scots linguist Angus McIntosh, "have very little in common with the world which users of language come to terms with and interpret in the normal everyday way."[25] But the average writer does not have to aim at the stars in order to write better than he does. There is much that he can observe and much that he can learn, and linguistic knowledge is part of it.

The first and last rule is that communication is a joint effort, shared between a sender and a receiver, with the sender, to the extent that he monitors his transmission, playing both roles, and the writer, in the sense that he must monitor more severely than any speaker, playing both roles almost equally. Not only must he inspect each word and phrase as it emerges, but he has, by comparison with the speaker, almost unlimited leisure to come back and revise. If he puts aside for a time what he has written until the body heat radiates out of it, he can return to it and play the reader, noticing its infelicities with almost

---

[25] "The Myth of Stylistic Analysis." Lecture at the University of Aberdeen, 24 November 1973, p. 10 of manuscript.

the same objectivity as if it had been written by someone else. He will
know that the least difficulty he has interpreting his own words will
be multiplied tenfold with a stranger. Perfect clarity for him will be
at best average intelligibility for the other. Good writing, after all, comes
down to the width of the gap between what a passage is meant to say
and what it seems to say. The ambiguity gap is a credibility gap—truth
is part of it; but it is more, for many things contribute: a wrong
emphasis as easily as a wrong word, a mannerism as easily as a violation of grammar. The writer's task is first to say what he has to say,
and then to address himself to narrowing the gap to the vanishing
point.

ADDITIONAL REMARKS AND APPLICATIONS

1. How have many linguists tended to view *style?* (Re-read page 552.) Given the notion of transformational equivalence or paraphrase (see page 160), what would *style* seem to mean in transformational grammar? How does this square with the general definition of style on pages 600–01?

2. If the style of a poem is what distinguishes it from a roughly equivalent piece of prose, does *style* then coincide with the *meaning* of the poem as a poem, in which the literal message is overshadowed by persuasions, word magic, and phonetic echoes? Discuss the following statement: "We should not speak of the stylistic function of a linguistic item but, instead, of its precise function; not of the style of a piece of language, but instead of its precise meaning and effect."[26]

3. Review the listener's strategies in interpreting a sentence (pages 200–05) and apply them to the writer's strategies in writing for easy interpretation.

4. Is it only writing that is edited, or do speakers sometimes edit their speech? Where is the better editing done? Comment on the following, by Victor Lasky in a radio interview on the subject of Robert Kennedy: *He cut corners when it was—they were necessary.*

5. Which has the advantage in the following, writing or speech? *Is lunch served in all-day schools?*

6. On page 610 a rule is stated for the non-use of *too* with plural nouns. Is the singular affected as well? Use the following to help with your answer:

   a. a too easy lesson

   b. too easy a lesson

   c. a too impertinent remark

---

[26] Ellis 1970, p. 75.

    d. a too rude remark

    e. a much too rude remark

    f. too harsh punishment

    g. too severe punishment

    h. too inflexible punishment

(Compare phrase a with *a very easy lesson.*) Does your answer suggest something about a tendency to generalize a rule somewhat beyond the practical need for it, if the result is a simpler rule?

7. Re-read pages 478–79. Then select three or four sentences from a piece of expository prose and note as many ways as you can find in which the passage differs from consultative speech (or from casual speech, if the writing is relatively informal).

8. Is professional jargon at times a kind of shibboleth? Re-read pages 344 and 573.

9. Senator Thomas McIntyre quoted the following from a government regulation. See if you can interpret it.

> Exit is that portion of a means of egress which is separated from all other spaces of the building or structure by construction or equipment as required in this subpart to provide a protected way of travel to the exit discharge.[27]

10. Comment on the following: " 'Enough of this sloppy nonsense. Are you hinting at *foul play?*' That, added Perry, was an expression he'd always hankered to use."[28]

11. On pages 588–89 occurred the following: *Suppose you live in a house on one of those California hills that dissolve whenever there is a heavy rain. . . .* The word *dissolve* is inexact. Would it be better to replace it with something like *that get soft and tend to slide,* for greater precision? Give reasons for your answer.

12. Re-read pages 171–72, and then take a piece of expository writing and study the devices used to mark transitions at the beginning of a dozen or so paragraphs. Judge the paragraph organization for its effectiveness; does it help you comprehend the text?

---

[27] *Reader's Digest* (April 1974), p. 158.

[28] Robert George Dean, *A Murder by Marriage* (New York: Bantam Books, 1945), p. 70.

13. Imagine that you are writing the following. Decide which arrangement would be better and explain why.

  a. How did they manage to trap the thieves there?—(1) They placed cops around the building. (2) They surrounded the building with cops.

  b. "Thirty?"—"More," Robert said. (1) "And there'll be even more." (2) "And there'll be more still (yet)."

  c. (1) There is no radioactive fallout because the reaction is caused by the fusion of hydrogen atoms. (2) There is no radioactive fallout because the reaction is caused by the fusion of hydrogen.

  d. (1) They plan to discard the others but this one they intend to keep. (2) They plan to discard the others but they intend to keep this one.

14. A radio announcer was heard to say **We can do it without his guidance,** accenting only the last word (de-accenting **his**). Would you say that he was coding his meaning as he spoke, or reading from notes? What is the evidence?

15. English has a carrier for accent, the auxiliary **do,** which can be used to make any verb emphatically affirmative except **be** and the auxiliaries. In speech, if we want to emphasize a form of **be** we accent it without adding **do: He's crazy, but he is nice.** Suppose you have been told to avoid italics, but want to show this kind of emphasis in writing. Justify your use of the devices in the following:

  a. He's crazy, but he's not unattractive.

  b. He's crazy, but he does have something nice about him.

16. A syndicated column contains the following:

  What the nation needs now is not visible government so much as working government. Poor leadership does not regain public confidence by absenteeism, instead it just passes from lethargy to the comatose state.[29]

  Comment on the word **state** and its effectiveness or ineffectiveness in that position.

---

[29] Tom Tiede, NEA Syndicate, San Francisco *Chronicle Sunday Punch* (28 July 1974), p. 1.

17. In a sentence that appears on page 608 we find the following: *the more known, expected, and therefore incidental the element is, the more it can be thrust into the background.* Three elements are correlated at the beginning. Why must the one with *therefore* come last? Re-read pages 135–36. Comment on the sentence beginning *The regimen* on page 619.

18. An unrevised sentence in an earlier chapter read as follows: "The fairly new verb *to fit* with its past *fitted* resembles the verbs *put* (past *put*), *set* (past *set*), *bite* (past *bit*), and other one-syllable verbs so closely that. . . ." It was revised to "The fairly new verb *to fit* with its past *fitted* bears such a close resemblance to. . . ." Why the change? Why not say *resembles so closely the verbs?* Does this suggest that some rules in a language can be a nuisance?

19. On pages 571–72 there occurs the following sentence: "Yet *Alaska is part of the United States* is a colorless geopolitical fact while *Alaska is part and parcel of the United States* is an assertion of sovereignty: the Alaskans had better not try to secede, and the Russians had better stay home." Would it be just as effective to reverse that final coordination and say *the Russians had better stay home, and the Alaskans had better not try to secede?* If not, why not? Do such instances of *climax* have anything to do with the unmarked accent pattern discussed at the beginning of this chapter?

20. A professor who was arranging a public meeting wrote the following to one of his participants: *Now that I have you two, I shall have to get two more competent speakers.* He rewrote the line before mailing the letter. What was wrong? How would you change it?

21. Discuss the following two passages from the standpoint of what the writers have taken for granted where intonation is concerned:

    a. Very little has issued from Hollywood that has any claim on the most transient memory.[30]

    b. To my anxious American eye it looks even worse: it looks as if America's "fight against communism" is really a struggle to save face, not to lose prestige.[31]

22. In writing, if the reader is not to be misled, a sentence such as

---

[30] *The Nation* (25 August 1962), p. 72.
[31] *The American Scholar* (Autumn 1964), p. 518.

He's ^{going} $_{to}$ ^{fa}$_{ll!}$

would require something like *if he doesn't look out.* Why?[32]

23. Suppose with the sentence *We don't have to worry if he doesn't,* you sense the danger that the reader will interpret it as

We $^{don't}$ have to ^{wor} ry if he ^{does}$_{n't.}$

rather than your intended

We don't ^{have} $_{to}$ ^{worry} ^{if} ^{he} ^{does} $_{n't.}$

Would adding *even* help? Suppose that the last verb is affirmative rather than negative. Can *even* still be used for the same effect? But with the affirmative verb is there another solution involving just the verb forms? Check your answer with the footnote.[33]

24. It is impossible for a writer to do justice to the sentence *I didn't believe him for a minute,* unless the context makes the intention very clear. Why? What can be done—say by adding a word—to salvage one of the senses?

25. On page 315 there is a sentence that originally read as follows: *Here is how Morris Swadesh describes the possible origin of one vocalized meaning that must have overlapped most of the period when gesture was the prevailing mode of communication.* When it was edited, the word *long* was added before *period,* not primarily to stress the length (though adding it may have made the sentence a little more colorful), but to accomplish something else. Study the sentence in its context with and without *long* and see if you can

---

[32] Example from McIntosh 1966.

[33] In the affirmative we can use *if he does do it,* which suggests the desired accent because it contrasts with *if he does* or *if he does it.* This is less clear in the negative, in which the auxiliary *does* is required in any case.

decide what is gained by its use. Then consult the footnote.[34] See if you can find other instances in which words are added mainly for their side effects.

26. See if you find the following sentence troublesome, and if so, decide what to do about it: *The humanists and the reformers believed that usage not a grammar should give the rule.*

27. The following is about clear writing, but it is hardly clear itself: *The best reminder is one that is concise, clearly written, and put in a place where it is likely to be found in time.*[35] What is the problem? (Suggestion: look up the meanings of *in time.*)

28. A linguist writes *The distinction between a word and its designation proves necessary for learning the difference between word identity and synonymity.*[36] What is the grammatical ambiguity that underlies *its designation?* How would you remedy the confusion?

29. The cross-referencing or anaphoric elements in language are among the things that a writer must watch most closely. Look at page 571 and count the number of times the words *he, his,* and *him* appear in lines 13–18 referring to "the language wholesaler" in line 10. Then look at the first six lines of the next paragraph and see what the effect would have been if instead of using *The "error"* and *it* or *its* to refer to the term, the word *interloper* had been fully personified and a *he, his,* or *him* had replaced both *The "error"* and *it, its.* (That was how the paragraph was originally written.)

30. On successive days, the following were heard on radio newscasts, both in description of fires:

    a. It destroyed three classrooms severely.

    b. The place was pretty well engulfed in flames.[37]
Comment.

---

[34] *Long* supports *when* to clinch a temporal meaning for the otherwise slightly ambiguous *period.* It also makes *period* unambiguous in another way: the preceding pages have been about the millennia during which gesture was the prevailing mode, and *long,* by repeating that concept, shows that *period* refers back, and not forward to some new period.

[35] *Harper's Magazine* (March 1959), p. 39.

[36] *International Journal of Slavic Linguistics and Poetics* 1,2:279 (1959).

[37] Stations KCBS and KGO, San Francisco, 6 and 7 January 1975, respectively.

31. On page 617 the expression *dramatis personae* appears. It replaced the word *actors.* Does the change strike you as advantageous? (Recall what was said about *model* on page 612.)

32. To what extent are some of the criticisms made in this chapter of certain practices in writing just a matter of adjusting one's mental focus? If we *expect* to have to make a guess on the basis of context, are we less apt to be bothered by having to do so than if we are deprived of some conventional aid that we have become accustomed to?

References

Bernstein, Theodore M. 1965. *The Careful Writer: A Modern Guide to English Usage* (New York: Atheneum).

Ellis, J. M. 1970. "Linguistics, Literature, and the Concept of Style," *Word* 26:65–78.

Gowers, Sir Ernest. 1962. *Plain Words: Their ABC* (New York: Alfred A. Knopf).

Gray, Bennison. 1973. "Stylistics: The End of a Tradition," *The Journal of Aesthetics and Art Criticism* 31:501–12.

Haas, William. 1970. *Phono-graphic Translation* (Manchester, England: Manchester University Press).

McIntosh, Angus. 1966. "Predictive Statements," in C. E. Bazell et al. (eds.), *In Memory of J. R. Firth* (London: Longmans).

SUGGESTED
SUPPLEMENTARY READINGS

I. FOR CURRENT READING

To keep abreast of developments in linguistics, you will want to watch the periodicals that deal with language. The following are classified roughly in terms of difficulty. Journals devoted to languages other than English are not included.

General and semi-popular

American Speech
College Composition and Communication
College English
English Studies
ETC.
Names
Verbatim

Less technical

Canadian Journal of Linguistics
Journal of Child Language

Journal of English Linguistics
Kivung
Language in Society
Language Learning
Language Sciences
Lingua
Linguistic Reporter
Linguistics
La Linguistique
Studies in Linguistics
Visible Language
Word

More technical

Folia Linguistica
Foundations of Language
Glossa
International Journal of American Linguistics
Journal of Linguistics
Language
Language and Speech
Linguistic Analysis
Linguistic Inquiry

II. FOR TOPIC-RELATED READING

Chapter 1

Britton, James. 1972. *Language and Learning* (Harmondsworth, England: Penguins). See especially Ch. 2.

Harrison, Helene W. 1970. "A Case Study of a Baby's Language Acquisition," *Word* 26:344–61. Re-read after Chapter 9.

Jakobson, Roman. 1971. "Why 'Mama' and 'Papa'?" in Aaron Bar-Adon and Werner Leopold (eds.), *Child Language: A Book of Readings* (Englewood Cliffs, N.J.: Prentice-Hall).

Oller, D. K. 1974. "Simplification as the Goal of Phonological Processes in Child Speech," *Language Learning* 24:299–303.

Chapter 2

Fromkin, Victoria, and Robert Rodman. 1974. "What Is Language?" Ch. 1 of *An Introduction to Language* (New York: Holt, Rinehart and Winston).

Ruesch, Jurgen, and Weldon Kees. 1956. *Non-verbal Communication: Notes on the Visual Perception of Human Relations* (Berkeley and Los Angeles: University of California Press).

Schlauch, Margaret. 1955. "Family Relationships Among Languages," Ch. 3 of *The Gift of Languages* (New York: Dover).

Whatmough, Joshua. 1957. *Language* (New York: New American Library), pp. 13–55.

Chapter 3

Abercrombie, David. 1967. *Elements of General Phonetics* (Chicago: Aldine Publishing).

Gimson, A. C. 1962. *An Introduction to the Pronunciation of English* (London: Edward Arnold).

Householder, Fred W., Jr. 1971. "Sounds," Ch. 4 of *Linguistic Speculations* (Cambridge, England: Cambridge University Press).

Ladefoged, Peter. 1971. *Preliminaries to Linguistic Phonetics* (Chicago and London: University of Chicago Press).

Lehmann, W. P. 1971. "Articulatory Phonetics" and "Acoustic Phonetics," Chs. 2 and 4 of *Descriptive Linguistics: An Introduction* (New York: Random House).

Malmberg, Bertil. 1963. *Phonetics* (New York: Dover).

Pierce, Joe E. 1971. "On the Interpretation of Formant Three on Spectrograms," *Linguistics* 74:62–65.

Resnick, Melvyn C. 1972. "The Redundant English Phonemes /č ǰ š ž/," *Linguistics* 86:83–86.

Chapter 4

Falk, Julia S. 1973. "Phonetic Features" and "Phonemics," Chs. 8 and 9 of *Linguistics and Language* (Lexington, Mass., and Toronto: Xerox).

Lehmann, W. P. 1971. "Autonomous Phonemics" and "Distinctive Feature Analysis of Sounds," Chs. 3 and 5 of *Descriptive Linguistics: An Introduction* (New York: Random House).

Wang, William S.-Y. 1973. "Approaches to Phonology," in Thomas A. Sebeok (ed.), *Current Trends in Linguistics*. Linguistics in North America, vol. 10, part 2 (The Hague: Mouton). See pp. 101–21, especially p. 115.

Chapter 5

Adams, Valerie. 1973. *An Introduction to Modern English Word Formation* (London: Longman).

Bolinger, Dwight. 1971. *The Phrasal Verb in English* (Cambridge, Mass.: Harvard University Press).

Juilland, Alphonse, and Alexandra Rocerik. 1972. *The Linguistic Concept of Word* (The Hague: Mouton).

Lipka, Leonhard. 1972. *Semantic Structure and Word-Formation* (Munich: Wilhelm Fink).

Makkai, Adam. 1972. *Idiom Structure in English* (The Hague: Mouton).

Marchand, Hans. 1969. *The Categories and Types of Present-day English Word-Formation*, 2nd ed. (Munich: C. H. Beck).

Soudek, Lev. 1971. "The Development and Use of the Morpheme *-burger* in American English," *Linguistics* 68:61–89.

Chapter 6

Daneš, František (ed.). 1974. *Papers on Functional Sentence Perspective* (Prague: Academia).

Davies, Eirian C. 1967. "Some Notes on English Clause Types," *Transactions of the Philological Society*, pp. 1–31.

Fairclough, Norman. 1973. "Relative Clauses and Performative Verbs," *Linguistic Inquiry* 4:526–31.

Fraser, Bruce. 1973. "On Accounting for Illocutionary Forces," in Stephen Anderson and Paul Kiparsky (eds.), *A Festschrift for Morris Halle* (New York: Holt, Rinehart and Winston).

Friedrich, Paul. 1970. "Shape in Grammar," *Language* 46:379–407.

Palmer, Frank. 1971. *Grammar* (Harmondsworth, England: Penguins).

Chapter 7

François, Frédéric. 1971. "Du sens énoncés contradictoires," *La Linguistique* 7:2.21–33.

Lawson, E. D. 1974. "Women's First Names: A Semantic Differential Analysis," *Names* 22:52–58.

Leech, Geoffrey. 1974. *Semantics* (Harmondsworth, England: Penguins).

McNeill, N. B. 1972. "Colour and Colour Terminology," *Journal of Linguistics* 8:21–33.

Wescott, Roger W. 1971. "Labio-velarity and Derogation in English: A Study in Phonosemic Correlation," *American Speech* 46:123–37.

Chapter 8

Bross, Irwin D. J. 1964. "Prisoners of Jargon," *American Journal of Public Health* 54:918–27.

Burr, Elizabeth; Susan Dunn; and Norma Farquhar. 1972. "The Language of Inequality," *ETC.* 29:414–16.

Dieterich, Daniel J. 1974. "Public Doublespeak: Teaching About Language in the Marketplace," *College English* 36:477–81.

Hechinger, Fred M. 1974. "In the End Was the Euphemism," *Saturday Review/World* (9 March), pp. 50–52.

Lakoff, Robin. *Language and Woman's Place* (New York: A Torch Book, Harper & Row). To appear in 1975.

Mey, Jacob. 1971. "Computational Linguistics in the 'Seventies," *Linguistics* 74:36–61.

Moran, Terence P. 1974–75. Series in *College English.*

Newman, Edwin H. 1974. *Strictly Speaking: Will America Be the Death of English?* (Indianapolis and New York: Bobbs Merrill).

Rank, Hugh (ed.). 1974. *Language and Public Policy* (Urbana, Ill.: National Council of Teachers of English).

Chapter 9

Arbib, Michael A. 1970. "Cognition—a Cybernetic Approach," in Paul L. Garvin (ed.), *Cognition: A Multiple View* (New York and Washington: Spartan Books).

Blount, Ben G. 1972. "Parental Speech and Language Acquisition: Some Luo and Samoan Examples," *Anthropological Linguistics* 14:119–30.

Bolinger, Dwight. "Meaning and Memory," in George Haydu (ed.), *Experience Forms* (The Hague: Mouton). To appear, probably in 1975.

Brain and Language. Journal.

Child Language Newsletter. Issued as part of *Linguistic Reporter,* November 1974 and thereafter.

Condon, William S., and Louis W. Sander. 1974. "Neonate Movement Is Synchronized with Adult Speech: Interactional Participation and Language Acquisition," *Science* 184:99–101.

Dale, Philip S. 1972. *Language Development: Structure and Function* (Hinsdale, Ill.: Dryden Press).

Engel, Walburga von Raffler. 1972. "The Relationship of Intonation to the First Vowel Articulation in Infants," *Acta Universitatis Carolinae—Philologica 1, Phonetica Pragensia III,* pp. 197–202.

Ferguson, Charles A., and Dan I. Slobin. 1973. *Studies in Child Language Development* (New York: Holt, Rinehart and Winston).

Greenberg, Joseph H. 1971. *Language, Culture, and Communication,* ed. by Anwar S. Dil (Stanford, Calif.: Stanford University Press). See especially Chs. 10 and 20.

Lewis, Michael, and Roy Freedle. 1973. "Mother–Infant Dyad: The Cradle of Meaning," in Patricia Pliner, Lester Krames, and Thomas Alloway (eds.), *Communication and Affect: Language and Thought* (New York: Academic Press).

Patel, P. G. 1973. "Perceptual Chunking, Processing Time and Semantic Information," *Folia Linguistica* 6:152–66.

Piaget, Jean. 1973. *The Child and Reality* (New York: Grossman Publishers). See especially Ch. 6.

Rosemont, Henry, Jr. 1974. "Some Implications of the Innateness Hypothesis," *Modern Language Journal* 58:403–11.

Van Lancker, Diana. 1973. "Language Lateralization and Grammars," in John P. Kimball (ed.), *Syntax and Semantics,* vol. 2 (New York: Academic Press).

Chapter 10

Green, Jerald R. 1968. *A Gesture Inventory for the Teaching of Spanish* (Philadelphia: Chilton Books).

Herder, J. G. 1969. "Essay on the Origin of Language," in Peter H. Salus (ed.), *On Language* (New York: Holt, Rinehart and Winston).

Hewes, Gordon W. 1957. "The Anthropology of Posture," *Scientific American* 196:123–32.

————; William C. Stokoe; and Roger W. Wescott (eds.). 1975. *Language Origins* (Silver Springs, Md.: Linstok Press).

Jakobson, Roman. 1972. "Motor Signs for 'Yes' and 'No,' " *Language in Society* 1:91–96.

Key, Mary R. 1970. "Preliminary Remarks on Paralanguage and Kinesics in Human Communication," *La Linguistique* 6:2.17–26.

Kolata, Gina Bari. 1974. "The Demise of the Neanderthals: Was Language a Factor?" *Science* 186:618–19.

Lieberman, Philip. 1975. *On the Origins of Language: An Introduction to the Evolution of Human Speech* (New York: Macmillan).

Linden, Eugene. 1975. *Apes, Men, and Language* (New York: Saturday Review Press).

Stokoe, William C. 1972. *Semiotics and Human Sign Language* (The Hague: Mouton).

Chapter 11

Allen, Harold B. (ed.). 1971. *Readings in American Dialectology* (New York: Appleton-Century-Crofts).

American Speech 46:1, 2 (1971). Papers from the International Conference on Methods in Dialectology.

Burling, Robbins. 1970. *Man's Many Voices* (New York: Holt, Rinehart and Winston).

English Record. Issue of April 1971.

Fishman, Joshua A. 1972. *The Sociology of Language* (Rowley, Mass.: Newbury House).

Gage, William W. 1974. *Language in Its Social Setting* (Washington, D.C.: The Anthropological Society of Washington).

Garvey, Catherine, and Ellen Dickstein. 1972. "Levels of Analysis and Social Class Difference in Language," *Language and Speech* 15:375–84.

Haugen, Einar. 1971. "The Ecology of Language," *Linguistic Reporter* 31:1.19–26.

Hymes, Dell. 1973. "Speech and Language: On the Origins and Foundations of Inequality Among Speakers," *Daedalus* 102:3.59–85.

————. 1974. *Foundations in Sociolinguistics: An Ethnographic Approach* (Philadelphia: University of Pennsylvania Press).

———— (ed.). 1964. *Language in Culture and Society: A Reader in Linguistics and Anthropology* (New York: Harper & Row).

Key, Mary R. 1975. *Male/Female Language* (Metuchen, N.J.: Scarecrow Press).

Kramer, Cheris. 1974. "Folk Linguistics: Wishy-Washy Mommy Talk," *Psychology Today* 8:1.82–85.

Labov, William. 1973. *Sociolinguistic Patterns* (Philadelphia: University of Pennsylvania Press).

Laver, John, and Sandy Hutcheson (eds.). 1972. *Communication in Face-to-Face Interaction* (Harmondsworth, England: Penguins).

Moulton, William G. 1968. "Structural Dialectology," *Language* 44:451–66.

Peng, Fred C. C., assisted by Junko Kagiyama. 1973. "*La Parole* of Japanese Pronouns," *Language Sciences* (April), pp. 36–39.

Pride, J. B., and J. Holmes. 1972. *Sociolinguistics* (Harmondsworth, England: Penguins).

Shuy, Roger W. 1973. *Some New Directions in Linguistics* (Washington, D.C.: Georgetown University Press).

Sledd, James. 1971–72. "Doublespeak: Dialectology in the Service of Big Brother," *College English* 33:439–56.

Wolfram, Walt, and Ralph W. Fasold. 1974. *The Study of Social Dialects in the United States* (Englewood Cliffs, N.J.: Prentice-Hall).

Chapter 12

Fries, C. C. 1969. "On the Development of the Structural Use of Word Order in Modern English," in Roger Lass (ed.), *Approaches to English Historical Linguistics* (New York: Holt, Rinehart and Winston). Also in *Language* 16:199–208 (1940).

Gougenheim, Georges. 1971. "L'Action de l'homonomie sur le lexique," *Bulletin de la Société de Linguistique de Paris* 66:1.299–302.

Hymes, Dell (ed.). 1971. *Pidginization and Creolization of Languages* (Cambridge, England: Cambridge University Press).

Kiparsky, Paul. 1970. "Historical Linguistics," in John Lyons (ed.), *New Horizons in Linguistics* (Harmondsworth, England: Penguins).

Lithgow, David. 1973. "Language Change on Woodlark Island," *Oceania* 44:101–08.

Seymour, Richard K. 1970. "Linguistic Change: Examples from the Westfalian Dialect of Nienberge," *Word* 26:32–46.

Chapter 13

Gage, William W. 1971. "The African Language Picture," *Linguistic Reporter* 13:3.15–27.

Hooley, Bruce A. 1971. "Austronesian Languages of the Morobe District, Papua New Guinea," *Oceanic Linguistics* 10:2.79–151.

Lehmann, W. P. 1973. *Historical Linguistics: An Introduction*, 2nd ed. (New York: Holt, Rinehart and Winston).

Palmer, Leonard R. 1972. *Descriptive and Historical Linguistics* (London: Faber and Faber). Part 2 only.

Penzl, Herbert. 1969. "The Evidence for Phonemic Changes," in Roger Lass (ed.), *Approaches to English Historical Linguistics* (New York: Holt, Rinehart and Winston).

Ryan, William M. 1968. "Affixes and the Making of Homographs and Homonyms," *American Speech* 43:138–41.

Traugott, Elizabeth Closs. 1972. *A History of English Syntax: A Transformational Approach to the History of English Sentence Structure* (New York: Holt, Rinehart and Winston).

Chapter 14

Chatterji, S. K. 1974. "A World Roman Script on the Basis of the International Phonetic Association Writing," in *World Papers in Phonetics: Festschrift for Dr. Onishi's Kiju* (Tokyo: Phonetic Society of Japan).

Dewey, Godfrey. 1971. *English Spelling: Roadblock to Reading* (New York: Teachers College Press, Columbia University).

Downing, John. 1973. "Is Literacy Acquisition Easier in Some Languages Than in Others?" *Visible Language* 7:145–54.

Francis, W. Nelson. 1974. "Language, Speech, and Writing," *Spelling Progress Bulletin* 14.

Gough, Philip B. 1972. "One Second of Reading," *Visible Language* 6:291–319. Also in Kavanagh and Mattingly (see below).

Kavanagh, James F., and Ignatius G. Mattingly (eds.). 1972. *Language by Ear and by Eye* (Cambridge, Mass.: M.I.T. Press).

McClure, J. D. 1975. "Modern Scots Prose Writing," in *The Scots Language in Education*. Association for Scottish Literary Studies Occasional Papers No. 3.

Vachek, Josef. 1973. "The Present State of Research in Written Language," *Folia Linguistica* 6:47–61.

Venezky, Richard L. 1970. *The Structure of English Orthography* (The Hague: Mouton).

Walpole, Jane Raymond. 1974. "Eye Dialect in Fictional Dialogue," *College Composition and Communication* 25:191–96.

Chapter 15

Algeo, John. 1970. "Tagmemics: A Brief Overview," *Journal of English Linguistics* 4:1–6.

Bobrow, Daniel, and Allan Collins (eds.). 1975. *Representation and Understanding* (New York: Academic Press).

Botha, Rudolf P. 1973. *The Justification of Linguistic Hypotheses* (The Hague: Mouton).

Griffin, Peg. 1974. "Linguistic Terminology," *Linguistic Reporter* 16:9.2.

Hetzron, Robert. 1973. "Surfacing," *Studi Italiani di Linguistica Teorica ed Applicata* 2:1, 2.3–71.

Hockett, Charles F. 1968. *The State of the Art* (The Hague: Mouton).

Koerner, E. F. K. 1972. "Towards a Historiography of Linguistics: 19th and 20th Century Paradigms," *Anthropological Linguistics* 14:255–80.

Lockwood, David G. 1972. *Introduction to Stratificational Linguistics* (New York: Harcourt Brace Jovanovich).

Makkai, Adam. "Acronymy in English: A Stratificational Reexamination," in Luigi Heilmann (ed.), *Proceedings of the 11th International Congress of Linguists* (Bologna: Società Editrice il Mulino). To appear, probably in 1975.

Robins, R. H. 1970. "General Linguistics in Great Britain, 1930–1960," in *Diversions of Bloomsbury: Selected Writings on Linguistics* (Amsterdam: North-Holland Publishing).

Schank, Roger, and Kenneth Colby (eds.). 1973. *Computer Models of Thought and Language* (San Francisco: Freeman).

Chapter 16

Dilworth, Donald W., and Louisa R. Stark. 1975. "Bilingual Education in the Highlands of Ecuador," *Linguistic Reporter* 17:2.3, 5.

Encyclopaedia Britannica, 11th ed. 1910–11. "Universal Languages" (Henry Sweet).

Fishman, Joshua A. (ed.). 1973. *Advances in Language Planning* (The Hague: Mouton).

Haugen, Einar. 1966. "Linguistics and Language Planning," in William Bright (ed.), *Sociolinguistics: Proceedings of the UCLA Sociolinguistics Conference* (The Hague: Mouton).

Jernudd, Björn H. 1972. Review of Jyotirindra Das Gupta, *Language Conflict and National Development: Group Politics and National Language Policy in India* (Berkeley, Los Angeles, and London: University of California Press, 1970). In *Kivung* 5:62–67.

Landau, Sidney I. 1970. "*Little Boy* and *Little Girl,*" American Speech 45: 195–204.

Lehnert, Martin (compiler). 1971. *Rückläufiges Wörterbuch der englischen Gegenwartssprache* ('Reverse Dictionary of Present-day English') (Leipzig: Verlag Enzyklopädie).

McDavid, Raven I. (ed.). 1973. *Lexicography in English.* Annals of the New York Academy of Sciences, vol. 211.

Pyles, Thomas. 1970. "Sweet Art the Usages of Diversity," *American Speech* 45:252–60.

Rubin, Joan. 1974. "Selected Bibliographies: 3, 4," *Linguistic Reporter* 16:4, 5. On language planning.

———— and Roger W. Shuy (eds.). 1973. *Language Planning: Current Issues and Research* (Washington, D.C.: Georgetown University Press).

White, Ralph G. 1972. "Toward the Construction of a Lingua Humana," *Current Anthropology* 13:113–23.

Chapter 17

Crystal, David, and Derek Davy. 1969. *Investigating English Style* (London: Longman).

Halliday, M. A. K. 1967. "The Linguistic Study of Literary Texts," in Seymour Chatman and Samuel R. Levin (eds.), *Essays on the Language of Literature* (Boston: Houghton Mifflin).

Householder, Fred W., Jr. 1971. "Corrections, Revisions, and Centos," Ch. 15 of *Linguistic Speculations* (Cambridge, England: Cambridge University Press).

Moerk, Ernst L. 1970. "Quantitative Analysis of Writing Styles," *Journal of Linguistics* 6:223–30.

Osselton, N. E. 1963. "Anaphoric *This* Expressing Shared Experience," *English Studies* 44:38–41.

Smith, Carlota S. 1971. "Sentences in Discourse: An Analysis of an Essay by Bertrand Russell," *Journal of Linguistics* 7:213–35.

WORD AND SYMBOL INDEX

NAME AND SUBJECT INDEX

A   5
B   6
C   7
D   8
E   9
F   0
G   1
H   2
I   3
J   4